2-

AMERICA'S
CAMPING BOOK

Revised Edition

AMERICA'S
Camping Book

PAUL CARDWELL, Jr.

CHARLES SCRIBNER'S SONS · New York

Library of Congress Cataloging in Publication Data

Cardwell, Paul.
  America's camping book.

  Bibliography: p.
  Includes index.
  1. Camping. I. Title.
GV191.7.C37 1976   796.54   75-29405
ISBN 0-684-14388-7

Frontispiece photograph of the Muir Woods by George A. Grant for the National Park Service.

Photographs on pages 41, 62, 64, 96 (upper left) by Gerry; on pages 48, 54, 57, 85, 86, 87, 96 (lower right), 191, 194, 299, 314, 316, 317 (upper and lower), 318, 319 by Recreational Equipment; on page 495 by Travel Equipment Corp.; on page 496 by Honorbuilt Division, Ward Manufacturing, Inc.; on page 514 by Hugh Nash for the Sierra Club; all others by the author

Drawings on pages 45, 49, 52, 57, 67 (upper right), 77, 78 (upper and lower left), 79 (upper and lower), 153, 157 (upper), 192, 326, 327, 329, 330, 356, 357, 359, 366 (right), 372, 373, 375, 383, 394, 430 (upper), 442, 473 (right), 478 by Nancy Lou Gahan; on page 476 by Ken Fitzgerald; all others by the author

1 3 5 7 9 11 13 15 17 19   MD/C   20 18 16 14 12 10 8 6 4 2

Printed in the United States of America

This book is dedicated to the countless groups
and individuals who have worked to preserve our
areas of natural beauty. Without their work,
this book would be rather pointless.

CONTENTS

FOREWORD

This book is written for the person, beginner or expert, who really wants to camp but doesn't have the money to go farther into the wilderness than some of the wilderness areas in our national park and forest systems.

A single book can't adequately cover all aspects of camping, and I have left out whole topics for various reasons. For instance, there is no collection of camp recipes. Not only would it require a book to do justice to the subject, but most recipes can be adapted quite easily for use over a campfire. The techniques for this adaptation are discussed in Chapter 20.

Also, there is little on camping in snow. Being a native Texan, I have not had that experience—the lower twenties, with a high wind blowing from the north, is cold enough for me. However, I understand that snow camping is far more comfortable than a Texas Norther. The special techniques for snow camping are covered in books you will find listed in Chapter 54, but the essentials are included in this volume.

I have tried to keep up with the new developments in camping, and to evaluate them in terms of their value in the field—not just their novelty value. This includes some of the new inventions which are still in the laboratory stage but should hold promise in the future.

I have personally tested everything I have discussed in the book with a few exceptions, which include the more serious treatments in the first-aid section and some of the survival techniques which are illegal except under survival conditions. For the exceptions, I have had to depend on the literature available, including technical papers in some cases, and interviews with people who have had the experience.

Writing such a book as this is not the best way to make friends. My evaluation of some of the equipment and techniques will displease some novices and some experts—the novice because he has his heart set on a latest gadget, and the expert because conflicting experiences have given him a different opinion.

Horace Kephart, in his classic *Camping and Woodcraft,* quotes Richard Harding Davis as saying, "A man's outfit is a matter which seems to touch his private honor. . . . You may attack a man's courage, the flag he serves, his intelligence, or his camp manners, and he will ignore you; but if you criticize his patent water-bottle he will fall on you with both fists." This applies also to his favorite camping techniques.

This book is not intended as a textbook to tell you the best way to camp. There is no such thing as a best way to camp. What is "best" changes with the climate, terrain, travel method, number of persons in the group, and their personalities. Camping includes a vast range of techniques from plush camping machines in a state park to backpacking the length of Grand Canyon. This entire spectrum will be discussed in this book.

Most of you who are reading this have done some form of camping at some stage of your life. It may have been while in the Scouts or as a part of a hunting or fishing trip or during a vacation, or it may have been only partly camping, such as a mule ride down Grand Canyon, a skiing trip, an afternoon's hike, or even a picnic. All of these use skills which are also used in camping. Indeed, the boundaries which define camping are quite fuzzy.

One of the problems which has arisen from these fuzzy boundaries is that camping, as a popular concept, has polarized in two extremes, neither really representing much of what camping has to offer.

One extreme is that of the big game hunter in the farther reaches of the wilderness. While he is obviously camping in the course of this activity, it is still a distorted view of camping since it is beyond the financial resources of most of the public. Books on this form of camping spend much of the time discussing butchering and skinning trophies in the wilderness, selection of guns and rods, survival techniques, etc. They are well written, and are of value to even the casual camper, but the techniques used in the tundra of Canada, the hills of Mexico, or the bush of East Africa are hardly what the average person needs to know even in the National Wilderness Areas of this country.

The other extreme is harder to pin down. It is not really camping, although it calls itself that. It is a sort of overnight picnicking. Just as a day picnic requires ten to twenty pounds of stuff for one meal, overnight picnicking requires a carload of equipment. Most experienced campers can recall seeing a family of four or six arrive at a public campground in two station wagons, both loaded to the ceilings, take two to four hours setting up "camp," and then pull out the next day for another spot.

Camping must have the challenge of pitting one's ability against the environment, and when no more effort or skill in this regard is required than at home, then you are simply traveling. Except for the scenery, which you are experiencing with less intensity than you would if you were camping, you might as well be at home.

Camping, as the term will be defined in this book, lies somewhere between overnight picnicking and the near-survival conditions of the self-sufficient expedition, although it will include these extremes to some extent.

I write like I talk, and so my writing sometimes ends up with a Texas accent. I tend to use such spellings as "varmit" (I never have heard the "n" pronounced in the word, so I have concluded it really isn't there, despite the dictionaries) and "tromping" instead of "tramping."

My philosophy of spelling is that the word should be spelled as phonetically as possible without radically changing things. While I won't use "nite," I find "ax" far superior to "axe." The latter, logically, should be pronounced the same as "aches," which is what you get when you don't use an ax correctly.

I also have a preference for the original spellings when they are still phonetic. Therefore I like "tipi," which is how the Sioux spell it, and "ded reckoning," since it avoids the ominous connotations which don't belong to this fine old navigational system.

I would like to thank the publisher for letting me indulge in these idiosyncrasies.

Since writing such a book as this is the result of a lifetime of camping, giving proper credit is difficult. I have been doing some form of camping since my parents took me on fossil-hunting trips with them when I was less than a year old. I have used so many techniques for years that I don't remember where I first encountered them. I know of a few I thought I was the first to use, only to find that it had been in use by others for quite a long time. While I did my own typing, much of my own art work, and, except where otherwise noted, my own photography, there are still a lot of people who deserve a statement of thanks:

Neyland Hester for wading through the rough manuscript in its early days with suggestions and comments.

Wally Chappell for his numerous hints and mutual "brain-picking" sessions on the subject of camping, and for furnishing the design for the pack frame.

Johnny Hassler for ideas on improving the tipi.

Dr. Maryhelen Vanier, whose card-file assignment in the Camp Leadership class at S.M.U. started the reservoir of data which grew into this book.

The staffs of the various state, provincial, and national parks, forests, recreation areas, etc., of the U.S.A., Canada, and Mexico, for their help in compiling the Campground Directory.

Bill Noll for his artistry with the oxy-acetylene torch in connection with my camping machine.

The anonymous reader at Scribners who had the idea of putting the do-it-yourself parts in one convenient section instead of scattered throughout the book.

My two Scribner editors, Donald Hutter, for making it possible for me to get into print at all, and Eleanor Sullivan, for infinite patience past the deadline.

Scott Stella of *Field and Stream* for giving Scribners an advisory reading of the manuscript. Like all campers, we disagreed on many points but the book is better because I had to answer his objections.

My parents, especially my father, an amateur paleontologist of modest note (three discoveries) and proofreader extraordinary, for giving me an appreciation of nature in my formative years.

My wife, Gladys, for help with the photographs of me and for running the sewing machine on some of the projects.

My children, Paul and Diana, for their help in indexing.

My whole family for going along on numerous "vacations" as test runs for various parts of this book.

So, with apologies to the countless other people who should be mentioned here but whose names my tired mind can't recall, here is a part of my experience in camping.

Paul Cardwell, Jr.

PART I

The Philosophy of Camping

For someone who has never camped, campers seem a strange sort. They give up air-conditioned houses to go off thousands of miles to live in tents. They brave mosquitoes, rain, and assorted other ills. To make matters worse, they keep coming up with the most unreasonable things to do in camp—climbing mountains, canoeing down a stream turbulently white with spray, sitting in a cramped blind all day to get a couple of photographs of a bird, and all sorts of equally unreasonable things.

Yet these "unreasonable" things are perfectly reasonable from the camper's viewpoint. It is that viewpoint and what makes it that this part is about.

CHAPTER ONE

For the Beginner

Camping, as a means of relaxation instead of simply a way of staying alive in the wilderness, is practically a twentieth-century sport. There were, of course, earlier forms which had many of the features of camping, yet they are not quite what we call camping. Thoreau, at Walden Pond, built a small shack out of lumber. The hunting lodges of the aristocracy (hereditary or financial) were more opulent than most people's houses and were equipped with a retinue of servants besides. With others, camping was a sideline to exploring, prospecting, fighting, trapping, ranching, or whatever it was that pulled them from civilization into the wilderness.

The National Park Service, which supplies much of the camping facilities of the United States, celebrated its fiftieth anniversary during the final revisions of the first edition of this book in 1967, Canada's National Parks date from 1885, and Mexico's first was in 1898, although most of theirs are fairly recent. Before the twentieth century, large areas of the nation were in the public domain, with no restrictions at all on their use. Many millions of acres of additional land belonged to large timber companies. Game laws were just coming on the scene and were liberal with the bag limit and season. The first conservation laws were still fairly new. In those days and in those areas, the camper could do almost as he wished. The only problem was that only the rich could take time off from making a living to go into the wilderness and relax. The rest had to keep to the twelve-hour day, six days a week!

Today, most camping is done in the developed campsites of state and national parks and forests, although backpacking and canoeing in wilderness areas is growing fast, in part due to the over-development and over-use of these established campsites. Open wood fires are restricted—usually to prepared fireplaces, and practically always to established areas. Even the few exceptions to this usually require the camper to get a fire permit from the authorities, and often to give a good reason why the established areas are not suitable. In these back areas, backpacker's stoves are required more and more as the use-load and fire hazard often precludes the use of more traditional campfires.

At the turn of the century, the mark of a skilled camper was the ability to make a log shelter in half a day. Today, the cutting of trees is prohibited, and it is often the mark of a good camper to be able to find any squaw wood. The beginner is left chopping up poor-grade firewood he has had to buy, or using a gasoline stove—and the stove is definitely preferable. While it lacks some of the challenge that camping should offer, it at least preserves the trees which the suppliers of the concessionaire wood often cut down with no regard to conservation in their great urge to make another dollar.

Hunting your own food supply is restricted by open seasons and bag limits—when it is permitted at all. Usually, fishing is the only form of food gathering permitted in camp—and even this, too, only in season. Even wild berries must sometimes be protected or the supply will be permanently depleted by campers.

Despite all these restrictions, the number of

campers is rising. With shorter working hours, and even three- and four-day work weeks, weekend camping trips are common (and longer). Prepared campsites are more numerous and more accessible to population centers. More families are taking their vacation in station wagons and tents. Backpacking is growing to the point where it is quite common now, even though only a few years ago the backpacker was looked upon with an awe more logically befitting a creature from beyond the solar system. The new "leisure class" is not the rich, but the working man. Camping has become a leisure activity that can be fitted into any budget.

However, time and money are not the only requirements for the would-be camper. Camping is a skill. You have to learn it. No one automatically becomes a good camper. Much of the beginner's dissatisfaction with camping comes from trying to do more than his skills enable him to do. Yet camping is not a difficult sport to master. There is no deep, hidden, inborn talent required.

Of course, some forms of camping, such as month-long backpacking trips, require exceptional skill. But this skill is developed over a long period of time. A *Cordon Bleu* chef also requires exceptional skill, but this does not mean that anyone can't learn to cook an adequate meal—or, if given the incentive, even to become a *Cordon Bleu* chef. Likewise, anyone with a little instruction can take a weekend camping trip—and, given the incentive, ultimately be able to take the month-long backpacking trip (or canoeing trip, or whatever else his interests dictate). With practice comes the additional skills. And with the additional skills comes the ability to engage in the more difficult types of camping without danger or discomfort.

The primary rule in learning to camp is: never try too much at once. Of course, this doesn't mean that you should not accept the challenges that camping has to offer, it means that you should not knowingly exceed your limitations. The Reverend Wallace Chappell, a pioneer in the use of backpacking trips in church camping, gave me this advice on introducing my wife to camping: "Never let her have an unpleasant experience." This is a good rule for any camper, beginner or experienced. And if a little rain produces this "unpleasant experience,"

you are not cut out for camping anyway.

If you have never camped before, borrow or rent a tent, air mattress, sleeping bag, cooking gear, and gasoline stove and go to a state park for the weekend; it is a good way to find out if you are interested. If you are not, you have only lost twenty dollars at the most—probably much less.

If you find that you want more challenge, you are ready to progress to true camping. The main distinction between this beginning session and overnight picnicking is not the equipment nor the lack of skills needed, but that it is considered merely a stage in learning to camp rather than the ultimate in camping.

Actually, the only badge of the overnight picnicker in this list of equipment is the stove (meaning the large two- or three-burner "camp" stoves rather than the little one-burner backpacking kind). There is a good and proper reason for this. The beginner usually has trouble with two areas of camping skills at this stage: setting up the tent, and cooking over an open fire. But to recommend that the beginner use something other than a tent for his shelter would be to cheat him of any shred of camping from the start.

Nothing is more pathetic than the novice trying to pitch a tent for the first time in a state park. The campers are tired out from the trip, darkness is approaching, and with every failure they get more discouraged. They start blaming each other for everything, from the tent to the current international situation. If you want to like camping, learn the major techniques such as tent erection and fire building in your own back yard where there is no rush. In fact, it wouldn't hurt to give a quick run-through on how to inflate an air mattress or how to start a gasoline stove too.

If you should ever have trouble in a public campsite with a contrary tent, ask for help. Campers are a friendly and helpful group, but they will rarely intrude—even if it is obvious that you need help. Too many beginners are offended by such unsolicited offers, apparently thinking it insults their ability.

First of all, admit that you are a beginner. After all, you can't hide the fact from experienced campers anyway, so why try? Experienced campers are glad to help any beginner (or an experienced camper who is inexperienced in a new piece of equipment), but they are a lot happier if the one they are helping is under no illusions as to his own ability.

After your first camping trip, evaluate where you went wrong (because you will, unless you were just plain lucky, in which case watch out and don't get over-confident). Don't take the lazy way out and say, "We went wrong when we thought about going camping in the first place," but take a careful, objective look. They will be minor if you have made a few dry runs in the back yard first, but there will be problems nonetheless. In most cases, you can see where you made the error and simply correct it on the next trip—say in a couple of weeks. Make the second weekend trip close enough to the first one so that you don't forget what you learned, but unless things went exceptionally smoothly, don't make it the following weekend or you may wrongly decide that you have had enough.

If you have had some trouble and can't figure out what went wrong, see an expert. The place where you bought or rented the equipment is the logical place. (Renting is better than buying at first—aside from the possibility that you might not like camping at all, it is an inexpensive way to try out several types of equipment before deciding which one to buy.)

After the second trip is over and has gone at least well enough to correct, it is time to start thinking about further aspects of camping—especially the way to cook. An outdoor fire is a mystery to the novice, but it is just as flexible as the kitchen stove once you learn how to use it. Practice in your back yard or in a local park. The back yard is better, even if you have to get an old chunk of plywood and fireproof it with dirt to protect your lawn. City parks practically always have large, three-wall-and-a-grate fireplaces, which are hard even for an expert to cook on easily, though almost any picnicker can roast hot dogs on them.

Camp food should be more varied than picnic food, it should store in less space, and it should keep largely without refrigeration. If you look the next time you visit a park's picnic grounds, you will see very few cooks using any kind of utensil other than a spit, usually improvised out of a coat hanger. In camping, you use the same kind of utensils (with slight modifications) that you do at home. And you prepare the same kind of food that you do at home, in the same way.

For the beginner, this takes practice—in building a fire as well as in cooking the food. Once again, as with the tent, camp is not the place to learn. If you make a total mess of things when practicing at home, you can simply go in and fix something in a more conventional manner. If you make a total mess in camp, you have three choices. You can do without. You can start over with something intended for the next meal. You can leave camp and go to the nearest restaurant. The first is rather uncomfortable, the second has the problem of what to do for the next meal—as well as often being psychologically unwise—and the third is just plain chicken (although usually the best alternative at this stage of learning).

After about a year of these weekend camps, you will have learned the basic skills. You probably know what you want in the way of equipment, and even may have bought it, or at least some of it. You are now ready to take a longer camping trip. However, it should not be for more than one week and you should go to one campground and stay there instead of changing camps every day or so.

In time, the skills will develop, and you not only will travel all over the country like a seasoned camper, you will begin to get away from the car as well. You might try an overnight backpack trip from the main camp, or some canoe camping, renting or borrowing the canoe. You might even splurge on a pack-horse trip (with a wrangler). You are now a camper.

However, one final word to the beginner. Cultivate a good sense of humor. It is of immense value when things go wrong, because no matter how good a camper you become, from time to time something will go wrong. With a sense of humor, you can shrug off these few times and go on to enjoy the great experiences camping holds in store.

CHAPTER TWO

Why Camp?

Camping is basically a way of living. The camper voluntarily cuts himself off from much of the interdependence of society. Other than for the gear and provisions he carries with him, he is dependent entirely on himself and the others in his small group. In this miniature culture, he lives life as he wants to, not as the "organization" requires him to. This is the main reason many church camps are moving from the institute-in-a-camp-setting to real camping and a growing number of commercial camps are changing from a resort to a camp format. The camping situation requires cooperation from all in the group without the artificial class system of our present "organization man" culture. This built-in requirement of cooperation is an excellent aid in the child's process of maturing.

Yet, this need for cooperation should not force conformity. The individual camper in a small group should still retain his individuality. Camping with a small group is a welcome relief from the restrictions of the "organization man" society while retaining the certain amount of self-discipline we all need. This is one of the reasons why camping is becoming so popular today with adults as well as with children.

Many writers in recent years have pointed out the very low number of delinquents who have had a background of camping. "Increase camping," they say, "and wipe out juvenile delinquency." Of course, these days the claim of fighting juvenile delinquency is used to gain support for almost anything, including highly competitive athletics for grade schools, so that the first impulse is to dismiss the statement as baseless propaganda.

But, assuming that these people are sincere, they still have cause and effect reversed. It is not that campers don't become delinquents, but that delinquents aren't campers. Anyone interested in camping in the first place is someone who can "stand on his own feet." Delinquent behavior is the result of inability to stand on one's own feet and the need to cover up this inadequacy.

The potential delinquent is afraid of (rationalized as "not interested in") camping. Many inner-city-gang workers have reported absolute terror on the part of gang leaders when they took them to a state park to camp overnight. The delinquent is afraid of not being able to meet the challenge that camping has to offer, just as his anti-social behavior is a symptom of his fear to meet the challenge that life has to offer. Without including both social and psychological guidance, camping is neither a preventative nor a cure for delinquency. However, with this help included, camps have had some measure of success in this area.

The claim of the Boy Scouts and similar groups that their members or former members have a higher rate of "success" than others in society is the other side of the same coin. The ability to face challenge, to discipline oneself to meet challenge, and to have the creative imagination needed to find the answer to a camping problem, are the same qualities which make for success in society—for camping is life in miniature.

What good is camping then? If you insist on a product that can be measured in statistics, camping is worthless. The advantages of camping are made up entirely of intangibles.

First, there is the matter of the various outdoor activities. Here camping is basically a sideline. The hunter, fisherman, wildlife photographer, or biologist needs to camp in the course of his other activities. It is not his purpose, it is simply a way to stay alive and comfortable while doing something else.

The second is relaxation. People need to relax by doing something different from what they do in their daily jobs. Those whose job is essentially mental will go in for the more strenuous forms of camping, such as backpacking trips or white-water canoeing. Those whose job is physical tend to loaf, to motorboat, or to go float fishing. Thus camping is recreation in its true sense— re-creation.

There is a third advantage which often underlies the others, and this is aesthetic. This was Thoreau's motivation at Walden Pond. He did not go there to fish; nor did he go to relax from work. He did much of his best work there.

This aesthetic motivation is the prime reason for camping, yet it is practically impossible to communicate it to someone who does not understand it in the first place—although there is some hope one may get to understand it through experience.

The sights and sounds, even the feel, the smells and the tastes must be experienced. This is not the sentimental "beauty of nature" attitude toward a world unspoiled by man which is held by so many whose main experience of nature is through the photographs in *National Geographic* and *Arizona Highways*. Nature is beautiful, but this beauty is not expressed solely in the pleasing combinations of patterns and colors that bring sighs from your guests when you show a color slide of a sunset.

To the outdoorsman, the true beauty of nature is in what nature does to the person. George Leigh-Mallory gave the classic reason for climbing a mountain—"Because it's there." Campers are sometimes tempted to say the same thing when people ask them why they go off into the wilds, yet there is more to it than that. People had campgrounds at their disposal three decades ago—they were there then too, as were the money and the time—yet there were comparatively few campers. Today campgrounds are overcrowded, despite the fact that they have three times the capacity, and phoney energy shortages too.

Part of the reason for this is our need to get away from the artificial concerns which permeate our lives; to go into the quiet areas and be alone. Yet these places are becoming more and more rare as they are crowded by more campers, flooded by the Corps of Engineers and Bureau of Reclamation, or turned over to private developers or mineral and timber exploiters for their private gain.

The wilderness provides value to the individual not by permitting him to escape from reality, but by letting him face another reality—one which demands more of him as a thinking, reacting, working individual, not simply as a cog in a human machine. The wilderness gives him the quiet in which to find himself. Vast plains, thick woods, or towering mountains give us rest by softening the details we constantly encounter. It has been estimated that the average city worker is bombarded with over twenty-five-thousand separate stimuli per day—most of them trying to change his mind about his attitudes and the products he uses or directly instructing him to do this or that. In the wilderness, looking into the distance, the details of the landscape are softened by perspective and become part of a whole. This not only gives us rest from the "rat race," it also gives us a challenge. The country is open to us to the degree we have the ability to meet its challenge. There are no inter-office throat slittings here, no caste structure due to financial status. It makes no difference whom we know, we are on our own. As a result, we learn more about ourselves.

We don't just learn our limitations. As we are forced to press on in the face of difficulties in order to make camp before dark or to get down from a mountain before a storm hits, we discover resources we did not know we had.

Dag Hammarskjold once wrote, "Only by our

own efforts can we get a complete experience of the mountains." It is only by our own efforts that we can get a complete experience of any wilderness area. To fly over it or to drive through it is not the same as to hike or canoe or horsepack through it. This is not entirely because of the speed—you can circle or drive slowly—it is because from a plane or a car you do not really participate in the wilderness, you are just a spectator.

On the other hand, if you use the more muscular means of transportation, your very presence requires effort; you blend into the wilderness; you are truly a part of it. A mountain is not simply a stretch of ground sloping upward, it is a thrust against gravity. You know, because you are personally fighting gravity to scale it. A stream is not just a gurgling ribbon of water, it is a living thing, full of eddies, haystacks, and other currents, both vertical and horizontal. You know because you are trying to put your canoe into the proper part of it so you can work with it instead of against it to reach your goal.

We get to know the forces of nature. We cannot fight the storm, but we can foresee its approach and be prepared for it. We see the work of the water flowing to the sea, and constantly cutting its channel as it goes. We see evidence of forces strong enough to bend the layers of rock as they thrust up the mountains.

We can compare these forces with those of man.

He can take the workings of the sun and make a device which can destroy all living creatures on the earth he was given. He can dam mighty rivers until it becomes an obsession, but the lakes he creates are mud flats in two or three centuries because the river still carries the silt it used to carve the canyons with. By getting to know nature, man gets to know himself.

The Sierra Club titled one of its books with a quote from Thoreau, "In wildness is the preservation of the world." They admitted that at first they thought the title was a bit extreme, even for a group which has done as much as they have to preserve nature, but on reflection they thought not. We now know that the vast Sahara Desert is man-made—the result of grazing land past its capacity. We also know that the area of the United States now under paving is equal to the area of the largest state east of the Mississippi.

It is only through the experiences of camping and the related wilderness activities that an individual can truly appreciate the value of the wilderness, since, in the final analysis, it is only what affects us personally that we really fight for. By gaining a personal appreciation of wilderness, perhaps people can finally work to preserve it, and prevent this nation from becoming a mass of pavement, of silting, polluted river-lakes, and of growing desert.

The Ethical Camper

The camper's ethic is based on two things. The first is his love for nature and his enjoyment of being in a world unencumbered with what is commonly called "civilization." The second is a love for one's fellow man. A person can love nature in an exploitive way (although it is a decidedly second-rate form of love of nature), but a person who loves his neighbor as well will always be a good camper, even if he is the worst tenderfoot alive. The feet can always be hardened, but the conscience cannot always be softened.

The camper operating from these two bases will leave an area as undisturbed as possible for those coming after him. Extra care will be taken in areas of borderline environment, such as high-altitude meadows or desert vegetation.

Fires will not only be kept under control at all times and properly extinguished when not in use, the firesites will be carefully selected so as to damage the least amount of vegetation. Stoves will be used whenever there is a problem of adequate firewood or wildfire danger.

Disposal systems will not pollute watercourses in the vicinity, and trails made for use in the camp will not be used to the extent that the vegetation can no longer prevent erosion along them.

When horsepacking, the ethical camper carries feed for his livestock and lets the animals roam at night, possibly hobbled, but not picketed or tethered wherever the meadow is delicate because of soil or altitude.

The matter of conservation ethics extends beyond the condition of the campsite and into other areas. It means checking on all laws and regulations beforehand and not just assuming. This is particularly true in regard to game laws, but also applies to campground rules.

It means getting permission whenever you enter private land, even if it is just to cross. Most landowners are understanding, but they may have routes they would prefer you to take. Be sure and close all gates you find closed and leave open all those you find open, otherwise livestock may be where it is not wanted as a result. And take care not to disturb the livestock or trample crops.

The camper's ethic includes respect for other campers. Campgrounds today are usually quite crowded throughout the entire summer-vacation period. Because of the problems of light, campers are more diurnal than most people. Real campers will go to bed shortly after it gets completely dark, and wake up around daybreak. Modern gasoline and propane lanterns shed a fantastic amount of light. Turn them down to their lowest setting when you go to bed, if small children's toilet needs make turning them completely off inadvisable.

With tents close together, noise is a problem. The ethical camper will keep down the volume level of any late-night talking and will use earphones on radios. He will drive in and out at night or early in the morning only if absolutely necessary, and load and unload his vehicle with the least noise possible.

This problem of noise level is especially acute with snowmobiles and motor scooters built for back trails. They are desirable in their place, but part of the attraction of the wilderness areas is the quiet solitude which permits contemplation along with the camping activities. The trail scooters (or any other form of motorcycle) are just too noisy for the true wilderness. Because of the low level of background sounds, these rigs can be heard over a mile in the daytime and several miles on a still night. Besides that, they erode the trails with their tires and they are a definite hazard to pack trains, which could spook when confronted by one of these vehicles appearing suddenly around a bend in the trail. Because of their poorer muffling, they are almost as bad in developed camping areas.

They should be restricted in privately controlled areas where those who wish to be with nature will not be cheated of their rights. This is the basis for restricting aircraft and motorboats in the Quetico-Superior Wilderness Area, and the restriction of snowmobiles in many areas. Usually, anyone who can afford a trail scooter already has a hunting lease or a friend with a large ranch. These areas are its natural habitat, so such restrictions do not infringe on the scooter owner's rights either. Snowmobiles are useful in the far arctic but can be considered the same as the trail scooters anywhere else. If you want to go into the back reaches of the wilderness, hike, horsepack, canoe, or ski, but don't go in with a roar!

Second only to noise in a crowded campsite is the problem of privacy. Traditionally, the area within the guy ropes of a tent is private property. While this is often hard to follow strictly in campgrounds so crowded that the guy ropes interlock, the spirit of this tradition should be followed. The ethical camper respects this privacy to the utmost. This means, for instance, that borrowing equipment (unless it is offered) is out. Part of the challenge of camping is developing a kit for all needs with the minimum of weight and bulk, and this would be cheating.

Finally, this aspect of the camper's ethic means that the clean-up situation is helped, not hindered, by the camper. Make sure all lids are on garbage cans. This not only keeps out most animals, it keeps the flies down. (Raccoons can usually open a garbage can, and bears can open a locked ice chest or car trunk!) In the less-crowded, wilderness campsites, burn and bury your garbage and use a grease trap, and in extensively used wilderness areas, carry it out—you were able to carry it in.

The ethical camper not only obeys these rules himself, but notifies the proper authorities when others are flagrantly violating them. To do otherwise can destroy an entire campground.

The ethical camper is interested in helping new campers get started in camping. One of the great features of camping is the way that veteran campers are always willing to lend a hand with the novice. With the increasing popularity of camping, there is the possibility that this esprit de corps may be lost. If it is, the current trend toward camping will be just another fad—quick to die out from overcommercialization. If the custom of helpfulness continues, more and more people will discover the joys of camping, and, in turn, help to get better camping facilities for all of us.

Yet this help of the veteran for the novice must not be done in a condescending manner or with an "I am a better camper than you" attitude. It should be offered only if there is a sign that it is needed. A beginning camper often feels honorbound to do everything himself and therefore he will not ask for help nor will he accept it unless it is clear to him that he needs it.

As stated in Chapter 1, the primary rule in learning to camp is: never try too much at once. This rule applies even more to experienced campers trying to teach beginners. With skilled campers, camping is easy and natural. But with the beginner it is confusing and often difficult the first time through. Patience is required. Try to remember—you were once as unskilled yourself; if not on one particular problem, then on another. (If you can't recall ever being confused or awkward, you probably learned camping as a child and camping skills, like all other living skills, were just another thing you were uniformly bad at until you learned.) Just as you should never knowingly exceed your own limitations, you should never push another person to exceed his. In the case of a stranger you are helping at a camp, you don't know what his limitations are, so it is best to stick strictly to the problem at hand. If conversation flows easily, however, you might be able to work a few helpful hints into the conversation.

The ethic of camping binds all campers to an unceasing warfare against those who would take public land and despoil it for their own benefit and wealth. This includes those who commit acts of vandalism in parks, those who put high-speed roads through the national parks and scenic areas, and those who put pressure on lawmakers to give them public land to flood for hydroelectric power, to make an overdeveloped ski resort "to have the olympics," or to turn into a Pentagon hunting preserve in the name of "national security."

It means that the camper will work positively too. The camper must work for better campsites as well as to keep existing ones from being destroyed. He must work for adequate appropriations to maintain existing ones as well as simply fighting cuts in existing budgets for state and national parks.

This ethical responsibility binds all campers, for, without it, camping will surely cease to exist.

PART II

Selecting the Equipment

The beginner often gets gadget-happy in selecting his equipment. New camping devices are put on the market every day. Some of these are good; others are bought anyway. The overnight picnic their manufacturers advocate is not only a poor substitute for camping, it is expensive too.

The real problem is not that there are people who like this sort of thing—after all, they have a right to their pleasures. The real problem in overnight picnicking is that it has been played up to the point where the public is beginning to think that this is really camping.

The beginner, often with no close camping friends to borrow gear and instructions from, is a natural prey to the Madison Avenue boys and others who have a monetary interest in selling expensive and useless junk. Aside from the fact that what they are doing is morally a fraud, even if not legally defined as such, the real tragedy is that most of the blame the beginner should place on the junk gadgets he has been sold usually gets placed on the entire concept of camping. He instinctively knows that he is missing out on something because what he is getting simply isn't as good as it is made out to be; yet he doesn't quite know it is the fault of the gadget because he *is* a beginner. As a result, he is soured on camping before he has really experienced it at all.

This in turn brings about a series of tragedies. There is one less camper among us, one less person interested in seeing camping developed, which means that when the land grabbers try to take good camping land for their benefit, there is one less voice trying to protect the property of all of us. So not only do the manufacturers of expensive but useless camping gear make their money on the transaction, the land grabbers also get their legalized theft of public land for private power, mining, logging, or real-estate developments.

I once read an article on equipment required by beginning campers. Toward the end of a fairly reasonable discussion of tents, sleeping bags, air mattresses, cooking and eating equipment, camp stoves (which are still predominately optional for the type of camping done by the beginner although becoming more required), lanterns (still optional), axes, and first-aid kits was a list of "miscellaneous equipment" which included, without discussion, a medium-size screwdriver, pliers, and a roll of tape. What kind of tape? Adhesive? That would be included in the first-aid kit. Friction? Possibly, I can conceive of uses, but not enough to lug the weight for since the adhesive tape would substitute in an emergency. Pliers? Again, occasionally useful, but not worth the weight (except for the little compound-action ones with wire cutters, which the average reader wouldn't think of—even if that is what was meant). A screwdriver? What for? What item of camping gear even uses a medium-size screw?

This is the problem. The old hands at camping try to get new campers to put their money on quality camping gear (and a reasonable amount), and then along comes an article like this, in a normally reliable publication. The money spent on tools for which there is no logical use could be better put on a match safe and a good compass (which the article never mentions, preferring to discuss "extras," such as tables, chairs, and heating stoves, a hundred feet [30 m] of "thin nylon rope"—parachute cord?—and quarter-inch [5 mm] hemp rope). Nowhere in the entire list is there such an essential item as a knife. There is nothing to indicate that something is needed to store food and water. Even that old standby of auto campers, the ice chest, is missing.

The real problem is in getting publishers of popular magazines to realize that camping is not overnight picnicking. The only magazines in which you will find good camping information are the hunting and fishing magazines. Because of their purpose, the space devoted to camping, although the quality is usually good, is quite limited. Many will give considerably more space to the side issue so important to all campers—conservation—especially at the legislative end of it, where the average person can do the most good by prompt action.

The camper's equipment has only one real purpose—to make the trip as enjoyable as possible. Just as the overnight picnicker considers the amount of gear required for comfort to be so great that transportation becomes a major factor, many veteran campers make their list of gear far too short. Because of their skill, they can be comfortable without many items that the beginner will feel positively tortured to omit. Some seem to think that "roughing it" means that comfort is not quite cricket; that if you want comfort you should stay at home. The degree of roughing will depend a lot on the individual. Some simply can't sleep unless they are off the ground. Others, like the great naturalist John Muir, considered even a tent unnecessary. Most of the difference is mental; very little is really physical.

As the skills develop, more comfort can be derived from less equipment.

This becomes essential as the developing skills take the camper farther from motorized transportation until, when he works up to extended backpacking trips, twenty pounds (9 kg) plus food will be positively plush accommodations.

The farther removed from the internal-combustion engine the camper progresses, the better designed, better built, and better used his equipment must be. The equipment must be chosen with care, considering not only its capacity but also its weight, bulk, appearance, and durability. The ironic thing about the usual line of camping gear from the big mail-order houses, and similar suppliers for auto camping, is that a four-person eighty-pound (36 kg) tent costs the same as two two-man twelve-pound ($5\frac{1}{2}$ kg) tents from a mountain climber's outfitter! While the cost in money is about the same, and the capacity identical, the tents from the "expensive" mountain-climbing company costs almost half as much as the "inexpensive" mass-market tent in weight, bulk, and durability.

The next few chapters will discuss the various items of camping gear and the total amount of gear you will need to carry on different types of camping trips.

• CHAPTER FOUR •

Tents

In spite of the frequent use of the station wagon and camping machines for camping, a tent is still the standard camp shelter, and is growing in popularity with the growth of backpacking. It is even used with some of the most elaborate camping machines. The tent is probably the most expensive single item of your camping equipment, with the exception of the means of transportation. Therefore, it must be chosen with care.

There was once a fad, fortunately died out now, of having large tents in all sorts of wild colors and patterns. This was to appeal to the tenderfoot who subconsciously thinks that camping will be dull.

Despite this misuse of color, it can be used to great advantage in tents. European colored tents are quite aesthetic. The fad involved yellow and rust stripes and blue and green awning patterns rather than the blues and russets of the European tents. The Indian tipi was often colored on the outside and the lining was always decorated. An authentic tipi is very beautiful. But the color must be used tastefully. The more traditional extreme is equally bad. Dark-khaki, olive-drab, and dark-green are as bad thermally as they are aesthetically. Neither wild colors in gaudy patterns nor drab solids fit into the natural beauty a campsite should have. The bright reds and yellows of the small tents are for visibility when used for mountain climbing. They are also helpful in finding the tent site in thick wilderness.

A tent should be color-fast—a factor not always present in oil-base waterproofing tents. To test, rub the tent fabric briskly against a piece of white cloth.

While it costs more, the "dry" (silicon or fluorocarbon compounds) waterproofing is far superior to the paraffin "oil-treated" waterproofings. It not only avoids the waxy feel and makes the tent much lighter but is a more nearly complete waterproofing as well.

Seams should be the French-fell variety, both for strength and water-tightness, and they should be sewed with a double row of stitching.

For mosquito netting, a nylon marquisette is the best. A sixteen mesh is the largest that will still stop bugs—an eighteen or twenty mesh is far better. (The mesh number refers to the number of threads to the inch in the net. Bobbinet will stretch a considerable amount. As a baffle in a down sleeping bag, it is adequate, although even there it may damage the down some; as mosquito netting, it may stretch out of shape so that a mosquito can crawl through. Here Murphy's law definitely applies—if it is possible for them to crawl through, they will crawl through! Marquisette employs a different weave so that the individual hexagons of the weave cannot pull out of shape.

Make sure that the ropes on a tent you buy are either manilla or nylon. Also, get a hundred feet (30 m) of quarter-inch (5 mm) manilla rope or one-eighth-inch (3 mm) parachute cord for replacement and other camp uses. The staking loops should be made of nylon twill-tape instead of pieces of tent fabric, or be rope beckets through grommets. And they should be large enough to fit over a large wooden stake. Nylon is needed since it is rotproof and abrasion-resistant. The ground is usually damp at least some part of the day or night and there is quite a strain on ropes from stakes and rocks. Grommets should be aluminum or brass rings sewed on with grommet stitching; the two-piece, stamped brass grommets are inadequate even for light use. All areas of strain—stake and rope loops, pull-outs, ridges, and similar points—should be reënforced with double layers of fabric or twill-tape reënforcements.

Pull-outs or side guys help keep the sides from sagging in and robbing you of room. They work best tied to a pole or tree rather than staked to the ground, so the pull will be upward instead of downward. For explorer tents, another method is to run a rope from the rear of the ridge to a stake some distance from the tent and tie the pull-out to this rope at an upward angle. On other tent designs, use the suspension, shear pole, or just as long a rope as possible on the pull-out to reduce the downward pull. These techniques get the effect of an upward and outward pull without going to the trouble of setting up a pole or finding a suitably placed tree.

There is no such thing as an ideal tent for all purposes. The type you should get depends on several factors. However, all tents should have these qualities: should be easy to pitch and strike; should open as fully as possible for drying out after a rain; should be dry inside even in a blowing rain; should have adequate ventilation, even when closed up in bad weather; should open on at least one side

enough to view the country without a normal rain getting inside; should be as lightweight as possible for the features and the usage it will receive; should have effective insect protection, especially in mosquito country; should be proofed against ground moisture; should pack into a compact bundle for transportation. A sod cloth and ground cloth, or sewn-in floor, is preferable to no flooring, and a ground cloth, even if under each bed individually, is absolutely required, even when going ultralight.

The type of transportation limits the weight and complexity. You need a very lightweight tent for backpacking. A medium-weight one can be used for horsepacking, canoe camping, and auto camping, although with a car even a tipi can be used if you don't mind the weight. Complicated poles are ruled out unless you have the means of carrying them.

The climate governs the tent design that can be used. A tent for hot weather must have good ventilation. A cold-weather tent must have either a front that opens completely for the heat from a reflector fire, or a venting arrangement that will make a stove inside the tent safe to use. A long tent won't heat well. In dusty weather, the tent should close completely. If there is no blowing rain, in mild or hot weather you don't need sides except for privacy. In wilderness areas, where remoteness contributes to the privacy, you can use tents that are more open, and thus save on weight.

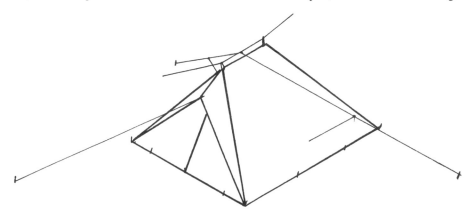

PULL-OUTS

You will need different stakes for rocky ground, for loose sand, and for regular soil. You will need a tent that goes up and comes down quickly if you change your campsite daily, but a more complicated tent may be more comfortable if you are to stay in one spot for a while.

A tent for a semi-permanent camp needs twenty-seven square feet ($2\frac{1}{2}$ m²) of floor area per person; a backpacking tent requires eighteen square feet ($1\frac{1}{2}$ m²).

Obviously, no tent can meet all these requirements. If you are the average camper, you won't be camping under all of these conditions anyway, so don't worry about how you will be able to afford all these expensive tents. You will probably need only one, or, at most, two. Which one or two will depend on where and how you camp.

You can use a tent for slightly different conditions than it was designed for, with some degree of comfort and convenience, but, generally speaking, this practice is not recommended. The following list is a breakdown of the best types of tents for various camping conditions, although tents from adjacent transportation methods can be used without too much trouble. However, moving over more than one category is asking for trouble.

BACKPACKING	Warm weather: tarp tents
	Cold weather: mountain tents
BICYCLING	Warm weather: tarp tents
	Cold weather: mountain and lightweight baker tents
	Mild weather: lightweight explorer and miner tents
TRAIL SCOOTERS	Same as Bicycling
CANOEING	Warm weather: tarp tents
	Cold weather: mountain and baker tents
	Mild weather: explorer and miner tents, double-tab tents, parachutes
HORSEPACKING	Same as Canoeing
AUTO CAMPING	Same as Canoeing, plus umbrella, parabolic, and French tents; tipis may

be used, especially in cold weather; tarp tents are generally inadequate since larger tent types can be carried

CAMPING MACHINES	Same as Auto Camping; canvas "living rooms" extending from the side of the vehicle are most popular with the "breadbox" type of machines, although they do not have enough roof slope to make them really adequate in rainy weather
TRAILERS	Same as Camping Machines

FLOORS

You can usually start an argument among campers by bringing up the subject of tent floors. Some will tell you it's the only way to keep out bugs and snakes. Others will say a floor gets dirty too fast and stays that way too long; the ground will pack enough to keep clean. Of course, all arctic and mountain tents have floors, but that is a special case since they help insulate the tent against the cold wind.

You could take your tent down and turn it inside out to clean a dirty floor, but this is really too much trouble—especially if you are still having the sloppy weather that dirtied up the floor in the first place. Also, there are no floored tents on the market with a reënforced spot for the tent poles to rest on, and thus here is a likely spot for serious wear. On the other hand, a floor makes the tent quite easy to set up, since you can stake out the bottom by merely smoothing out the floor and you will get it exactly the right size and shape the first time—something you are unlikely to do on the first attempt with a floorless tent.

As you will notice on the tent plans in Chapter 12, all of them, except for the tarp tents, mountain and bivouac tents, and parachutes, have sod cloths. (The tipi lining serves this function, so it is hardly a modern invention.) When first used on standard tents about a century ago, they were covered with dirt to keep out the weather and varmits. Since this rotted the cloth, they now rest on top of the ground. You can weight them down with gear in case of a strong wind. This will keep out the elements and most of the wildlife.

You can have the advantages of a floor without its disadvantages by making a tarp the size and shape of the tent floor. Lay it over the sod cloths. This arrangement is almost bugproof. (Snakes really have too much sense to come in an occupied tent anyway, so the other argument in favor of floors is not really valid. The sod cloth and tarp arrangement would keep them out of an unoccupied tent.) It is easier to clean the tarp than the whole tent. Since tarps are usually mildewproof, they are not damaged by contact with the ground as easily as tent canvas. For long tarp life, you should air them daily with your bedding. With either the tarp or the floor, keep hobnail boots out and be careful with edged tools.

The parachute and tarp tents are usually used with a sleeping bag. If you use a mosquito-netting curtain over your bag (with or without the basically useless canvas hood), you won't be bothered much by bugs. Except for mosquitoes and kindred flying insects, bugs getting in the tent won't be much of a problem if you keep the food supply cached outside.

If you don't use any form of tent floor, you should use a ground cloth under each bed. This cuts the dampness of the ground and makes the insulation of your bed easier. In backpacking, you can use a polyethylene sheet. Although it won't last over one week, at least it is light in weight. Your poncho can double for the job quite well, although you will have to unmake your bed if you go out in the rain.

FLIES

Some types of tents can be kept cooler in the summer with a fly. A fly is a piece of cloth over the tent. Its placement on a tent gives a four-to-six-inch (10 to 15 cm) air space between the hot fly and the shady tent. The fly can be used alone as a shade over the cooking or eating area as well.

Another advantage of the fly is that you can strike the camp under it and later leave with only one wet item—the fly itself.

Except for the rare exceptions of tents made of ultra-light fabrics, such as the mountain tent, the weight of the fly restricts it to auto camping since it weighs as much as a light tent. Carrying two tents for the usage of one is ridiculous when weight counts.

POLES AND STAKES

Ideally, you should be able to find your poles and stakes at the campsite. However, in most camping areas you aren't permitted to cut green wood. Most dead wood has been cut up for firewood if it was straight enough to use for a pole in the first place. If you go by car, you can carry the poles easily. By canoe, you can use paddles or suspend your tent. On foot, the tent pole can double as a hiking staff.

I have found some who think that the staff is strictly a psychological aid, and to some extent it is. But try this experiment. Walk, using the staff (an old broomstick will do for the experiment). On one step, let the staff bear down on a bathroom scale. It will register up to twenty pounds (9 kg). This is how much weight is taken off your feet. The staff is also useful for "bush-whacking" through underbrush or as an aid in climbing. Braced between two rock piles, it makes a serviceable seat for an improvised latrine.

Probably the most ingenious use of tent poles while hiking appeared in *Fieldbook* (see Chapter 54). There they had plans for a pack frame which used tent poles (jointed metal ones) for the uprights of the frame. At the campsite, the frame was dismantled and the poles were used on the tent, while the crosspieces formed coat hangers.

However, strictly for tent poles, I don't recommend jointed poles on large (over two person) tents because they won't hold tight after a couple of seasons' use. The metal telescopic poles are even worse. They hold up a little better, but bend out of shape rather easily and create a dangerous lightning hazard if you camp near tall trees.

(The main hazard of metal tent frames is not from being actually struck. If you are in an open area, you will probably be struck with wooden poles

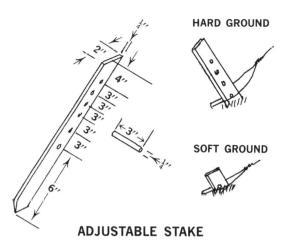

HARD GROUND

SOFT GROUND

ADJUSTABLE STAKE

just as likely as with metal ones. However, if you are under a tall or isolated tree, or any other potential lightning target, you may get a side discharge from the struck object to your metal frame. While this is only occasionally fatal, it is still most uncomfortable and dangerous.)

Wood for stakes can always be found at the site if you hunt long enough. But, unless you are backpacking, it is better to carry it with you. The saving in time is worth the additional weight. Ash is the best wood, although any hard, light wood is suitable. Tubular or angle aluminum stakes are somewhat lighter than wooden ones. They are available in a wide variety of sizes. A wooden stake should be about a quarter-inch (5 mm) thick, two inches (5 cm) wide, and about a foot and a quarter (35 cm) long. All types of stakes should be kept in a canvas bag to keep the rest of the gear clean.

To save your toes in poor light, paint the tops of the stakes white or bright-yellow. The guy ropes should also be bright. Granted, you could probably remember where they are and avoid them, but by letting the others in the campground know, you not only make them feel happier about avoiding a nasty fall, but you may keep them from tripping your tent down.

The tent stake will have to be driven deeper in soft ground than in hard in order to hold well. You can make an adjustable stake by drilling a series of holes in the side of the stake. Fit a dowel in one of the holes to hold the guy rope. This way, you will not have to drive the stake any deeper

than is necessary for it to hold, and the guy rope will still be fitted near the ground where it will set the tent properly. If you camp much on sand, this is the stake you need since its length lets you drive it deeply into loose sand, yet it is adaptable for hard ground too. Otherwise, it is too much trouble.

Metal stakes, whether the pointed length of aluminum angle, the tube, or the rod shape, have several advantages and a few disadvantages. In the "pro" column, there is the light weight—a most valuable feature when backpacking. Their holding power is good in most soil types. They clean easily for storing in the pack. And they are compact and don't take up any more space than a quarter of their wooden counterparts.

On the "con" side is their lack of holding power in sand—a particular fault of the rods. The rod is also hard to drive in rocky soil and the aluminum angle or tube can get quite beat up. A wooden stake, on the other hand, simply refuses to go any deeper when it strikes a rock. The point may be frayed, but it doesn't bend into a useless (and often hard-to-straighten) form with little advance warning.

If you are car camping (and therefore can afford the weight), several types of stakes may be necessary—light stakes for turf or heavy sand, long broad ones for loose sand, and large steel rods for the new "cobblestone" campsites some state parks are building. If you are going to be traveling light, find out before time what type of soil is in the actual tentsite so you can take the lightest one which will do the job properly.

If you can avoid it, never have the pole(s) on the inside of the tent. If it comes down in the middle of the tent, it robs you of valuable floor space. If it comes down the side, it wears the fabric and may start a capillary leak in rainy weather. Suspension or shears outside the tent are both preferable.

WALL TENT

A wall tent seems to be popular because it is shaped like a house. It seems logical that if a house is comfortable a tent shaped like a house must be too. As a result, some wall tents on the market look

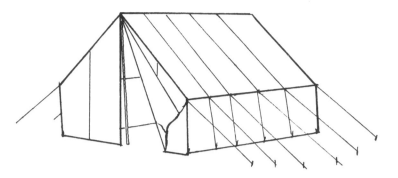

WALL TENT

exactly like a small cottage, windows, porch, and all.

Actually, this theory doesn't work out. The wall tent has only two advantages: it has a large, useable floor area, and good headroom. Against these advantages, there are several disadvantages. It has very high wind-resistance and, unless you set the poles absolutely perpendicular to the ground, it will blow over easily. There is a large pole in the doorway, which gets in your way. It is quite heavy for its floor area and can be used only in permanent camps or carried by motor vehicles. The ventilation is usually poor in rainy weather when the windows (if present at all) must be closed.

The stability problem can be reduced somewhat by using a ridgepole, but there is the added problem of getting and transporting the extra pole. In the case of a large tent, this pole must be jointed, with all of the problems that brings.

The wall tent is about to disappear from the camping scene as the umbrella tent sprouts more rooms and gets larger.

PUP TENT

The pup tent is too small despite its use by the Army and the Boy Scouts. Tarp tents have the lightweight features without the cramping shape. There should be at least one spot in a tent where you can stand (or at least sit) upright.

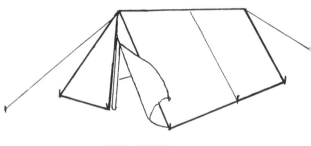

PUP TENT

POP-UP TENT

The pop-up tent is one of those new gadgets that just doesn't do all it is supposed to do. It looks like a canvas igloo or the roof of a yurt. Its only good feature is that it is quick and almost foolproof to set up once you learn how—and learning how isn't as easy as the directions imply.

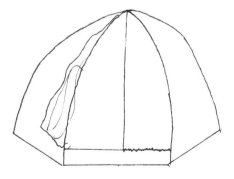

POP-UP TENT

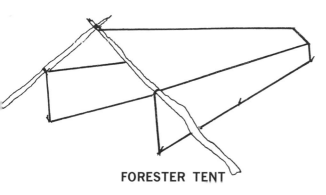

FORESTER TENT

Among its disadvantages are: it is generally too small for more than one or two campers; it has a sewed-in floor; the telescopic poles can get bent and make it ridiculously heavy; and, despite what they say about it not needing to be staked down, unless you or your gear is inside it can act like a tumbleweed if the wind gets high enough. A parabolic or umbrella tent is almost as easy to set up and a lot cheaper as well as being generally better for auto camping.

FORESTER TENT

The old forester tent is something of a half-cone lying on its side. It was once quite popular as a backpacking tent in the days when the necessary ridge poles could be cut at the camp. Its main advantage was that it could be heated by a fire at the entrance and it didn't weight much. Its disadvantage is much the same as a pup tent, although the size is not quite as confining.

TIPI

If you want a large tent for a permanent camp, you may be interested in a tipi. (The spelling is the one used by the Sioux.) There is no true tipi on the mass market today. There are tents available called tipis. These are pyramids and cones. Some even have smoke-flaps like true tipis (but considerably smaller). But all fall short of the values of the true tipi—and most other good tents as well.

The tipi is a tilted cone. This seemingly unimportant feature is the key to the tipi's value. The fire can be in the center of the tipi and the hole for the smoke to leave is right above it—and not at the junction of the poles, as on the imitations. The aerodynamics are perfect for controlling the smoke with the smoke-flaps.

Also, the tipi is not cut from a flat sheet but has gores at the base of the smoke-flaps. This permits it to fit tightly against the bunched poles, making a weathertight seal for rainy weather, when the smoke-flaps are closed. This feature is lacking on the commercial imitations.

The tipi has an inner wall five feet ($1\frac{1}{2}$ m) high called a dew cloth or liner. This provides insulation in the winter. This feature also is lacking on all imitations.

For comfort, the tipi is the best tent of all. It is the only tent in which you can safely build an open wood fire. (This is both from the standpoint of fire hazard and the more likely hazard of carbon-monoxide poisoning.) This is an advantage in wet weather as well as cold.

The floor is an oval, eighteen by twenty-one feet ($5\frac{1}{2}$ x $6\frac{1}{4}$ m). You can stand erect within two feet (60 cm) of the back wall and three feet (1 m) of the front. In spite of its large wall area, it doesn't have the tendency to blow over that the wall tent does. In fact, the pegs and anchor rope are rarely needed at all.

TIPI

I have known of one of these to sleep fifteen people (five on cots around the walls and the other ten on the ground with their feet under the five cots, radiating from the center of the tipi), but the owner says "never again!"

Spoiling this impressive list of features are several bad ones. First, it is heavy. The total weight of the cover, lining, poles, and pegs comes to almost 300 pounds (135 kg). Most of this is in the poles, as the cover alone weighs only fifty pounds ($22\frac{1}{2}$ kg)—about the same as a large wall tent. Since cutting wood for poles is prohibited in most camping areas, and good pole trees are hard to find anyway, the entire tipi must be carried in. This restricts it to areas that can be reached by car or truck.

Second, it takes time to erect and strike. With only the cover, it takes fifteen minutes for either. With the lining, the time is doubled or tripled. A good tent of another design takes only five to ten minutes. When the camp is moved every day, an hour is wasted just handling the tent.

Third, it costs about $100.00 for the material for the cover and lining. But this isn't the total cost. While the poles and pegs are cut instead of bought, there will be some expense in travel to get them as well as in the cost of the preservative. And you still have to make it yourself or hire someone to do it (a very expensive proposition). But while this is expensive for a do-it-yourself project, it is no higher than the cost of buying a comparable-size wall tent which is decidedly inferior.

Fourth, it is hard to find the heavy-duty, double-needle sewing machine that is required for sewing the heavy canvas.

Despite all this, while the poles will need replacing from time to time, the tipi itself will last almost indefinitely. For a stationary camp, it can't be beat.

TENTS FOR SEMI-PERMANENT CAMPS

In this situation, the tents are moved fairly frequently, but are used for more than just overnight shelter. Here you find the greatest variety of design.

The ideal tent for this purpose should be easy to erect and strike, provide good protection against blowing rain, have sufficient headroom and floor area, give privacy, and be fairly light in weight (under ten or twelve pounds).

EXPLORER TENT

Basically, the explorer tent is a large pup tent. It has low wind-resistance but good headroom at

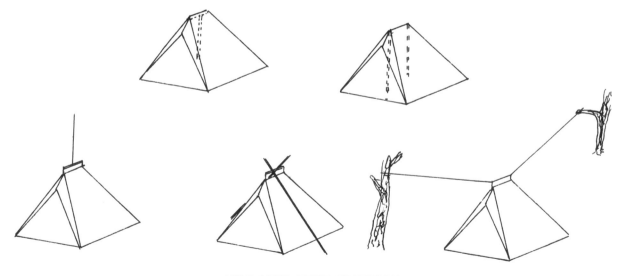

EXPLORER TENT ERECTION

the entrance where it counts. It is not a "wasteful" design that uses too much cloth—which is more than can be said about most highly modified designs.

The explorer tent can be set up in wide variety of ways. You can erect it with two poles or a T-shaped pole inside. Or you can use a shear of two poles outside the tent with a short pole along the ridge to hold it straight. Or you can suspend it from trees or poles by a rope.

There are plans for an explorer tent in Chapter 12.

MINER TENT

The miner tent is a four-sided pyramid. It is one of the oldest designs in the semi-permanent-camp category, dating at least back to the Gold Rush days. It is falling out of favor somewhat now, which is unfortunate considering its features.

It is one of the quickest to set up and the protection from wind and rain is excellent. It can be set up several ways. You can use a center pole, but it usually gets in the way. Shears or suspension is the best method. Simply stake it down around the sides and pull up the top.

You can set the doors in an open position for ventilation on hot days or to get heat from a reflector fire on cold ones. Be sure, however, to get a zippered door rather than the tie tapes since the old tape models do leak a bit at the door.

There are plans for a miner tent in Chapter 12.

BAKER TENT

The baker tent is designed for cold-weather use with a reflector fire. It is quite roomy and easily set up. However, it has two very bad disadvantages. First, you have to reset it if there is a driving rain from the direction of the door. Second, it gives practically no privacy whatsoever. Both disadvantages can be reduced to some extent by dropping the porch roof, but then there will be a ventilation problem. You could rig a curtain that can be pulled over the door from one side, but that adds considerable weight and bulk to the pack. A fire-retardant porch roof is a good idea.

Despite its disadvantages, for camping far from others and in cold weather, it is an excellent tent. There are plans for one in Chapter 12.

UMBRELLA TENT

The umbrella tent (sometimes called a marquis tent) is a cross between the miner and wall tents. It has the low wind-resistance of the miner tent with the floor-saving vertical walls of the wall tent. Some models have an opening in the back wall to fit around the back of a station wagon and give even more space. Others are as large as a large wall tent, but, although having the same problems of

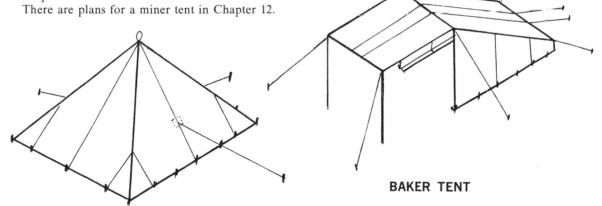

MINER TENT

BAKER TENT

weight and bulk, are considerably easier to set up. The umbrella tent and the parabolic tent are the best standard commercial tents.

The umbrella tent's big disadvantage is its pole arrangement. If it has a single pole (now practically extinct), it has to have a little umbrella frame to hold out the cloth. You could use guy ropes outside for this purpose, but it takes up too much space around the tent since they would have to be about fifty feet (15 m) long. Besides, it is hard to set up that way as well. In any case, the center pole takes up too much space inside. Its only advantages are, in case of rain all you have to do is reach up and slack the umbrella frame a bit instead of having to go out in the rain and loosen up the stakes outside, and there are hooks and shelves which can be attached to the center pole which are rather useful.

If the tent is the more common four-pole variety, the poles can't be made in camp. They are too bulky for anything except auto camping. The poles are usually aluminum and subject to bends and loose fittings after several seasons' time. The metal poles are also a lightning hazard if you camp near a potential lightning target.

Because internal poles rub against the canvas and create wear and capillary leaks, stay with the external-pole models. These are by far the most common

on the market today. This design is quite simple to erect—stake down the floor, erect the frame over it, and tie the roof and walls to the frame—it takes about five minutes when you know how.

However, the commercial world has not been content to leave this fine design alone. Since an eight-by-eight-foot ($2\frac{1}{2}$ x $2\frac{1}{2}$ m) umbrella tent is excellent for two people and a ten-by-ten (3 x 3 m) for four, they are trying to convince the public that a twelve-by-twelve ($3\frac{1}{2}$ x $3\frac{1}{2}$ m) will be even better and a ten-by-twenty (3 x 6 m) absolutely the best (until they come up with another size, of course). Do not believe it. Any umbrella tent larger than the ten-by-ten (3 x 3 m) is too large and takes far too long to set up. If you have more than four in your family get two tents. Two umbrella tents, face to face with the porches overlapping, are far better than one oversize tent. Many times I have completely set up camp with a paratipi by myself in the same amount of time it took a whole family to erect one of these monsters which bears only the faintest resemblance to the umbrella tent from which it descended.

However, regardless of how the design has been mutilated, the external-frame umbrella tent is quite rigid in a high wind, and when there is any degree of gear at all inside, it will not blow over. A simple staking will assure an empty one remaining

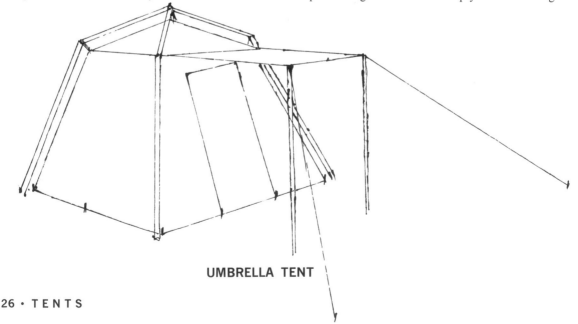

UMBRELLA TENT

in place. Unlike most tents, a well-designed umbrella will keep its shape.

Since the poles for umbrella tents are hard to make, and since there are many good ones on the market, there are no plans for an umbrella tent included in this book. You can buy one cheaper.

PARABOLIC TENT

The parabolic tent is a development of the wing tent, that sway-backed version of a tarp tent that usually gets marketed in the most atrociously loud colors. The parabolic tent simply added vertical walls and, in most instances, tamed the color scheme.

The problem with the umbrella tent is in keeping the walls extended at the roof. The parabolic tent avoids the problem altogether by setting the poles at two diagonally opposite corners, tying the other two corners to stakes, and letting the ridge sag in a prescribed parabola. While this sounds like a wall

tent erected by a Cub Scout, it is really a very efficient tent and, if the colors are tasteful, quite pleasing aesthetically. It has almost the headroom of a wall tent and can be erected almost as easily as the umbrella tent.

Because of the difficulty of engineering the proper parabola and the difficulty in working with the large amount of netting required for proper ventilation, there are no plans for this tent in the book. However, this fine tent is becoming scarce commercially. But some are being made and they will still be available for a while longer, although some effort will be needed to find them. It and the umbrella tent are good examples of those few instances where mass-produced camping equipment is economically better than that you could make yourself.

FRENCH TENTS

This is a broad category of several fairly large pup-tent variations, so called because they were originally developed in France. They are currently made in France, England, and Germany; I have not found any being manufactured on this continent.

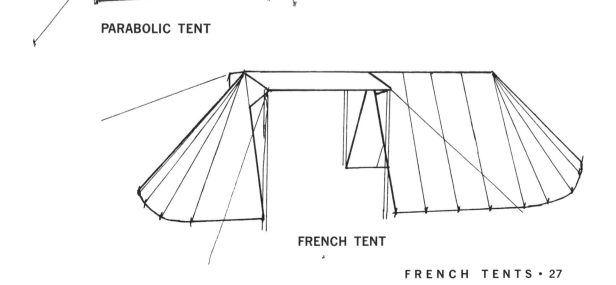

PARABOLIC TENT

FRENCH TENT

These tents are roughly the equivalent of our larger umbrella and parabolic tents in usage, but have several advantages over them. The first advantage is space. Only the side-room umbrella tents (which are considerably heavier) compare with the floor area. Second, the tent logically divides into a sleeping area, living area, and gear-storage area, which makes for an orderly camp. And third, the weight is not out of proportion to the size of the tent.

Like every other tent, these have disadvantages too. First, the sloping walls take up floor space which the umbrella and parabolic tents avoid with their high vertical walls. Second, they are a bit harder to set up than the traditional car tents because they have no floor. Third, like the other two car tents, they are too heavy for backpacking or canoeing. Finally, because they are imported, the price is a bit higher because duty payments are included in the cost.

PARACHUTES

You can have a tent that sleeps three, has twelve feet ($3\frac{1}{2}$ m) of headroom in the center, is waterproof (even after you touch it in the rain), can be put up or taken down by only one person, will permit cooking fires inside with complete safety, weighs only nine pounds (4 kg) including stakes, costs less than $25.00, and has over 300 feet (90 m) of one-eighth-inch (3 mm) nylon rope thrown in with the bargain.

This is no camper's idle dream, but a real possibility for anyone who likes to do his camping in comfort but without a lot of heavy and bulky gear, and without spending a year's salary on camping equipment.

After seven years, the government declares their parachutes overage and sells them. You can buy them for very little (my first one cost $6.00 and I got another for $1.98, but the standard price is around $20.00). This includes at least the main canopy, and often the pack, over 300 feet (90 m) of parachute cord, the little pilot chute (the one which pulls the main chute out of the pack in a jump), and a useful little pamphlet, "Emergency Uses of the Parachute." The chutes are in excellent condition. The main canopy is twenty-eight feet ($8\frac{1}{4}$ m) in diameter and weighs a little under nine pounds (4 kg).

You can sometimes buy parachutes at surplus stores, but be careful. Most of them are only selling the canopy. Some have even taken out the parachute cords inside the canopy seams. These cords are needed for extra strength. Also, the pamphlet, the pack, and about ten dollars' worth of parachute cord will be missing. If you possibly can, get parachutes directly from Air Force or Airborne bases. Not only will they be cheaper, you will get more material.

This bargain does have several disadvantages as a tent—the greatest being that they are so good you can't always find one to buy. Then, the chutes are nylon and this makes them air-tight. However, for open tents (as is the usual parachute-tent setting) this is not too bad. They are usually made of alternate panels of white and bright orange, which can be offensive aesthetically. (Some in white or other colors, or even camouflage, are available if you hunt hard enough, but they are quite rare.) The weight of the tent prevents its use in backpacking.

If you set it with two layers of cloth together, it will be waterproof. Many Boy Scout troops have bought parachutes for camping, but used them wrongly, so naturally don't like them, and have them stuffed in a box, going to waste in some corner of the meeting place. You might try talking such a troop out of one if you can't buy a fresh one. The error they have made in using a parachute was to erect it as they would a dining fly, seven or eight feet ($2\frac{1}{4}$ to $2\frac{1}{2}$ m) above the ground and spread out in a flat circle. While this makes a fairly good sunshade, it is useless for rain protection.

The secret in making a parachute waterproof is quite simple. There are no chemical waterproofings to worry about. All you have to do is fold the canopy in half, and make sure that the water can run off and not collect at a low spot on the tent. When the cloth is doubled, a thin layer of water is trapped between the two layers of cloth. This absorbs the force of the raindrops hitting the tent. The layers are so close together that capillary action and the slope of the tent wall prevents that pesky leak that occurs on most tents if you touch the inside in the rain.

The first time I used a parachute, we got caught in a cloudburst. By counting the interval between the lightning and the thunder, I know there were at least three thunderheads which passed directly overhead. There may have been more, but I went back to sleep when I was satisfied that the tent was holding off the water. Except for one capillary leak where my wife's air mattress was touching the cloth, there were no leaks. After we moved the bedding away from contact with the tent, even that leak stopped—something that never happens with the single-layer tent canvas. All this is in spite of the fact that it is only closely woven cloth and not treated to be waterproof.

Paratipi

The best tent design for a parachute is the paratipi. This is the standard pattern used by the armed forces in survival training and was the setting I used in the gully-washer described above. It makes a most comfortable tent that will sleep two adults and one child in addition to their gear. Yet it weighs only two-thirds as much as the standard Boy Scout explorer tent.

An adult can set this tent alone with no difficulty at all unless there is a very high wind. First, tie two or three lengths of parachute cord together. Tie three or four stakes to one end of this cord for weight and, holding onto the other end, throw them over a limb at least fifteen feet ($4\frac{1}{2}$ m) above the ground and eight feet ($2\frac{1}{2}$ m) from the tree trunk. Lower the stakes, by snaking the rope to slack it, until you can reach them.

When you can reach the stakes, take them off and tie that end of the rope to the doubled length of cord at the top of the canopy (the one that held it to the pilot chute) with a bowline. Pull the canopy up toward the limb until only about a foot of it is still on the ground. Tie your hoisting rope to the tree trunk and untie the extra length of cord.

Stake out the edge of the canopy in a twelve-foot ($3\frac{1}{2}$ m) circle. Remember, there are two loops to each stake since the canopy is doubled, and the panels at the folded edge overlap to form a door, making three loops on the two door stakes when

the door is closed. It will be pure luck if you can stake out the circle right the first time around, no matter how experienced you become at setting up a paratipi. I have had mine for fourteen years and have only lucked out six times. Two, even three tries are usually needed. Just keep at it, resetting one stake at a time around the tent until all stakes are as far out as they can go and still form a circle.

Finally, take up any slack in the tent walls by pulling the hoisting rope tight. While this whole procedure sounds complicated, it is really easy once you get used to it. With practice, you can set up one of these tents in ten minutes alone, or about seven minutes with some help from your tentmate.

The paratipi is wind-tight, yet there is enough air coming in at the bottom edge of the tent to provide adequate ventilation. Except in winter or during a rainstorm, you will probably prefer to keep the door open. In windy weather, the door should point down-wind when it is closed. This keeps the tent from filling with wind and going back to a parachute again!

You can build a small fire inside a paratipi, but it may smoke up the top of the tent. In rainy weather, however, this feature is a most welcome change from cooking in the rain.

The tent will dry out much faster after a rain or heavy dew if the two layers are separated. Leave the outside layer staked out and take the inner layer loose from the stakes and let it fall inward. You don't have much of a tent in this position, but sunshine will dry it out in less than a half-hour.

You may want to improve the paratipi. A parachute is not a flat circle—it wouldn't trap air efficiently if it were. Because it is a hemisphere, the sides sag inward when it is set as a paratipi. At the bottom, this sag will take up over a foot (30 cm) of floor area all around the tent. You can regain much of this lost floor area by guying out the sides a bit. Either sew loops in the side or use Visklamps. With this arrangement, three adults can sleep in a chest model parachute's paratipi and still have space for their gear.

Striking the paratipi is easy. A kid can do it if there is no wind. However, if there is a wind, an adult will have his hands more than full when the

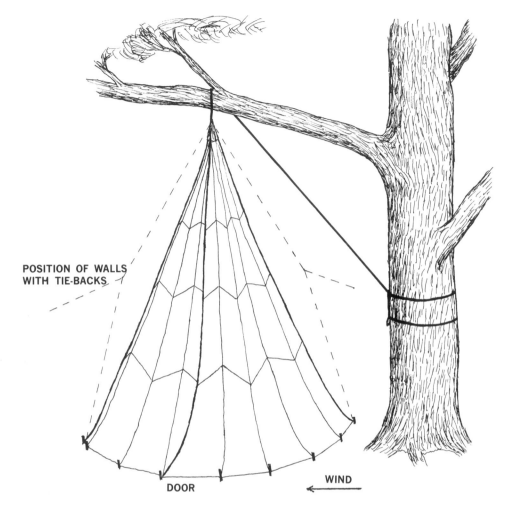

POSITION OF WALLS
WITH TIE-BACKS

DOOR WIND ←

PARATIPI

canopy makes a small spinnaker. The procedure is just the reverse of putting it up.

If you used side guys, take them off first. Next, tie the extra length of cord onto the hoisting rope. Then go around the bottom of the tent removing the loops from the stakes with one hand while holding the ones you have already removed in the other. Lower the hoisting rope until you can reach the top of the tent, and tie the rope back on the tree.

Stretch the canopy out level and off the ground.

Make sure that the fabric falls in folds between the cords rather than being over some of them or otherwise tangled. Be sure there are no twigs, leaves, or dirt on the canopy. Carefully and tightly, roll the tent up, from the bottom to the top, and untie it from the hoisting rope. Roll the doubled length of cord around the canopy and tuck it under itself to keep the tent from unrolling. You can leave the hoisting rope attached and use it to tighten the bundle. Pack it in its bag.

Pull up the stakes, scrape off any dirt that sticks

to them, and put them in another bag. Put this bag and the coiled parachute cord you used in setting the tent into the tent bag.

Other Settings

Although a permanent loop for guy ropes sewed through both layers of the cloth for the paratipi improves the tent setting, it doesn't interfere with

BACKPACKING TENTS

The mountain tent and tarp tents are generally too confining for general use. However, they are very light and compact when folded. Any time you have to carry your whole outfit—either on a backpacking trip or a canoe portage—for more than a short distance one of these tents will be required.

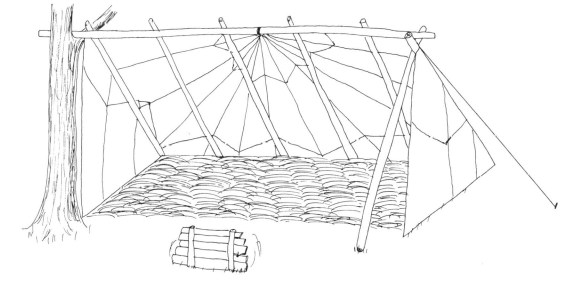

PARACHUTE AS A LEAN-TO

other methods of setting a parachute tent (but does make the drying time after a rain or heavy dew considerably longer). The "Emergency Uses of the Parachute" pamphlet shows you several other methods of setting a parachute tent, including a lean-to and a jungle hammock.

A parachute is made to stand rugged treatment, but it cannot be mistreated. It will snag far more easily than other tent fabrics. Keep it clean, out of briers, and otherwise take good care of it and it will last longer than a canvas tent—a good investment for $20.00!

Details of modifying a parachute for camping are given in Chapter 12.

The mountain tent is for winter camping (or high altitudes where the temperatures are rather like winter) and the tarp tents are for summer. The bivouac tent is strictly for emergency shelter when mountain climbing or in similar ultra-light conditions.

When the doors are fully opened, the mountain tent can be used for all except very hot weather; and, with a reflector fire, a tarp tent can be comfortable in the wintertime; but this is not the ideal use for either of them.

A poncho can double as a tarp tent by using Visklamps or tying around the snaps. However, it has the very strong disadvantage that you will have

PARACHUTE AS A JUNGLE HAMMOCK

to take down your entire camp if you need to go anywhere in the rain.

MOUNTAIN TENT

The mountain tent is a fairly cramped design, but it has many features in its favor. It is commonly used for backpacking in areas where it is too cold to use tarp tents comfortably.

The front of the tent may be used for cooking (with a stove, not an open wood fire), but be sure the vent at the top of the tent is open before you light the fire. The fumes can be deadly.

One or two (depending on the tent) telescopic poles should be carried for the tent if you will be going above the timberline. There wood is unavailable and rocks are not suitable anchors for a suspension mounting since the tent requires an anchor point at least five feet off the ground. The pole can be a nuisance and even a lightning hazard on the high baldies. A hiking staff will do the job if you carry one. The fiberglass-wand tent poles are best, if your tent will accept them.

There are plans for a single-pole mountain tent in Chapter 12.

ATC TENT

Once I had some district-level jobs in the Boy Scouts of America. There was a horrible fad of trailers and scout leaders (not the boys) were literally whining about having to pack a hundred yards from the parking lot to the tent sites! I kept claiming that any boy of Scout age can backpack conveniently and cheaply. Finally I was given an assistant scoutmastership of a new troop with the implication of "we call your bluff." After trying to list a proper kit that the boys could both afford and carry, I had all but the tent. Everything kept coming up either twelve pounds ($5\frac{1}{2}$ kg) or

$125.00—neither feasible for the boys. Therefore I did what this book still claims you shouldn't try—I designed a tent from scratch.

Because the camper who is equipped for backpacking can camp with any type of transportation (put the backpack in the canoe, on the horse, in the car, on the bicycle, etc.), the total concept was called "All Transportation Camping," thus the ATC of the name. *Boy's Life,* fearing loss of sales of Scout-approved equipment, refused to print the article, but *Wilderness Camping* magazine did; the kit in the July/August 1971 issue and the tent in the September/October one.

The ATC tent is sort of a cross between a floorless mountain tent and a tab tent. It is possible to close it up completely against a blowing rain, or open it flat for a fly. It is waterproof fabric so there is no capillary drip, but a vent system prevents moisture from collecting on the inside. (I have never had "rain" inside my tent, but once on a clear night with the temperature under 20°F (−7°C), the breath moisture did condense on the tent and break loose as snow!) It weighs, including stakes, poles, ropes, and bags, four pounds, ten ounces ($2\frac{1}{8}$ kg) and costs just over $30.00 to make. Plans are in Chapter 12.

BIVOUAC TENT

Bivouac tents are good for nothing except an emergency shelter in mountain climbing when a night must be spent on the slopes in order to conquer the peak the next day. They are even more cramping than the pup tent.

To use one, you put your sleeping bag inside the tent and slide into both at once. They are the absolute bare minimum in shelter. They keep the wind out and the rain off, and that is all. Yet where

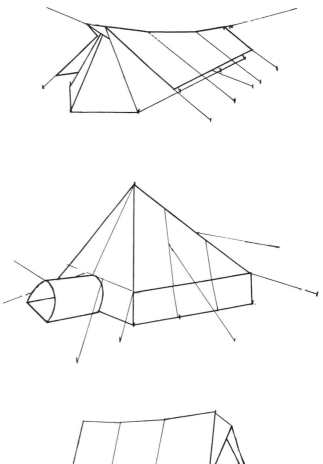

MOUNTAIN TENTS

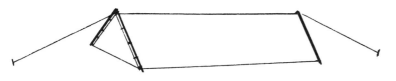

BIVOUAC TENT

any weight is too much and the cold wind blows all night, they are essential.

There are plans for a bivouac tent in Chapter 12.

TARP TENTS

Tarp tents are simply pieces of treated sheeting which can be improvised into shelters.

The tab tent is a tarp tent with short lengths of twill-tape. These tabs permit the tent to be tied into a great variety of shapes to fit the needs of the camper in any given circumstance. A Visklamp permits setting a tab at any point on a tarp, thus permitting the use of a poncho or vinyl tarp in the same way as a tab tent when going ultra-light.

The tab tent is not large enough for prolonged use by more than one person, but as a shelter for a couple of campers and their equipment during the night, it can't be beat. Its light weight makes it perfect for backpacking.

The double-tab tent is really in the category of tents for semi-permanent camps. It is a bit too heavy for the move-every-day type of packing;

however, it makes a wide variety of good, lightweight tent designs. Made of lightweight cloth, it will provide shelter for four and still weigh no more than a more standard two-man tent. Its best use is with groups, such as a Boy Scout troop, or church camping, using a small trailer.

There are plans for both single- and double-tab tents in Chapter 12.

The plastic tarp has the same advantages and disadvantages as the tab tent, plus the advantage of even lighter weight and the disadvantage of tearing easily. The plastic tarp, with Visklamps, can be made into the same variety of patterns as can the tab tent—possibly more because of the flexibility of placing the tabs.

CARE OF THE TENT

Your tent is probably the most expensive item of your camping equipment, yet it is often the most mistreated. The tent should be dry before you pack it. If you have to pack it during a rain, set it up and dry it when the weather clears. This will do more than chemical mildewproofing to save the fabric. Even the mildewproofing can't help a wet tent in an air-tight, hot pack. If your pack has D-rings on the outside, lash the tent onto that, piled up loosely, to let it dry. Change the position of the tent periodically to give all the dampness a chance to dry out. This way, you don't have to stop to dry out your tent, but can do it on the trail.

Mildew is not the only enemy of tent fabric. Trees shed all manner of things on tents. This is especially bad in the late spring when trees start dropping their blossoms. All small twigs, leaves, and such contain a little sap when green, and this can damage the tent fabric, especially the waterproofing and possibly the dyes. Wash off any such sap as soon as you notice it.

Birds also damage the tent. Wash droppings off before they dry, if possible—at any rate, as soon as you can.

Open the tent daily so that air can circulate through it. If possible, do this even in rainy weather if it will not get rain on the gear inside. The inside of a tent can get damp even in dry weather, from the condensation of moisture. Airing the tent gives

Visklamps. On right is view from the inside.

KEY

EDGE OVER GROUND	EDGE ON GROUND	FLAT ON GROUND	SUSPENSION POINT	STAKED OR TIED TOGETHER

SINGLE-TAB TENTS ONLY

SINGLE- OR DOUBLE-TAB TENTS

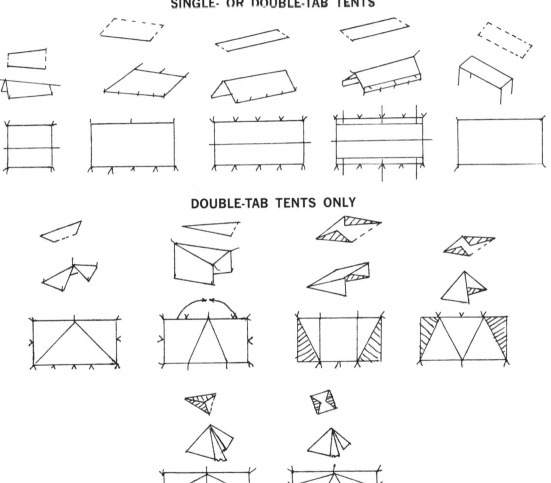

DOUBLE-TAB TENTS ONLY

TAB-TENT SETTING PATTERNS

this moisture a chance to dry out. Weather permitting, the bedding and ground cloth (if not a sewed-in floor) should be taken out and aired.

Whenever possible, a tent should be rolled instead of folded. Folding it along the same line every time breaks the fibers in the cloth. After you get home from a trip, the tent should be pitched, hosed down thoroughly, dried overnight, and packed loosely.

These simple precautions will add years to the life of your tent.

SETTING THE TENT

With the exception of the basically shapeless tents, such as the parachute and tarp tents, all tents erect essentially the same way. The quickest way to set one up is to stake it down around the bottom, erect the poles or suspend the top, and adjust the ropes to the proper tension. In striking, the order is simply reversed: remove the ropes, lower the top, remove the stakes, and fold up the tent and pack it.

However, erecting and striking is not all that must be done with the tent when camping. Changing weather conditions, soil types, and other factors require additional skills.

You should have some means of adjusting the loop around a stake. One method is to use a tent runner. This is a piece of wood or metal with two holes. The guy rope goes through one hole, around the stake, through the other hole, and there it is tied. Friction between the runner and the rope holds the loop fixed while there is a strain on it. To change the size of the loop, you pull the guy rope slack and slide the runner to a new position.

Another method is by the taut-line hitch (see page 429). Like the tent runner, it holds under strain, but you can change it by slacking the rope and sliding the knot to a new position.

A third method is to use a length of shock cord (such as is used on trampolines) for part of the guy rope. A cheaper, but less durable, method is to make large rubber bands by slicing an old inner tube. Both cord and rubber band have the advantage of holding the tent tight regardless of how the rope stretches or slacks due to the weather.

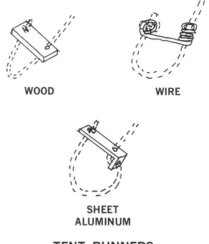

WOOD   **WIRE**

SHEET ALUMINUM

TENT RUNNERS

When one of the first two methods is used, all ropes should be loosened during a rain. The ropes shrink slightly, as does the fabric, and can put excessive strain on the tent and stretch it out of shape or even tear it. If the strain is removed, the tent will expand again when dried. Suspended tents can be lowered slightly to slack all the guy ropes by moving only the rope actually suspending the tent.

The same effect can be achieved with a tent having an inside pole. Dig a two- or three-inch-deep hole and put the pole in it. This slacks the tent without having to go outside in the rain. With a tent with shear poles, spread the shears a bit farther apart at the base. However, make sure they are not so far apart that they continue to spread on their own, collapsing the tent.

When there is a chance of heavy rain, the tent should be ditched. However, this is an emergency procedure and should not be done unless necessary. Be sure and fill in the ditches after breaking camp. The ditch should be at least three inches wide and deep enough to allow run-off. It should be around the entire tent, with a carry-off ditch at the lowest spot. The side of the ditch next to the tent should be at the edge of the tent and vertical. Don't ditch a tent pitched on turf unless you are on or at the base of a slope—and then at the up-slope side only

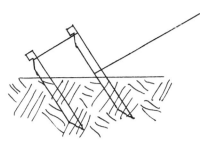

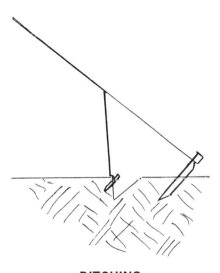

DITCHING

(diversion ditches rather than the usual tent ditches). Keep the sod intact so when the ditch is filled, there will be no evidence of the ditch having been there and thus no erosion danger. Selecting the tentsite for easily drained soil and gentle slope away from the tent in all directions will render this extreme measure unnecessary most of the time.

In case of a high wind, when using a wall or wedge type of tent, diagonal staking is recommended. This is simply the running of a rope from the forward pole to the rear stakes and from the rear pole to the forward stakes with the ropes lying against the tent. Especially where a ridge pole is used, this greatly strengthens the set of the tent against high winds—and these tents are rather sensitive to high winds.

The tent should never be set where you can pull branches over to touch it. In a high wind, they could rub against the tent and wear out the fabric. A tent pitched under a tree will be dripped on for hours after the rain stops. If the tree is considerably taller than the surrounding area, there is a lightning hazard.

When set up on sand or other soft ground, stakes don't hold and poles settle into the ground. There are several ways to increase the holding power of these.

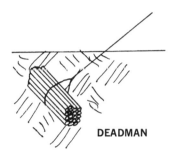

DEADMAN

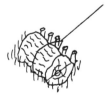

SOFT GROUND TECHNIQUES

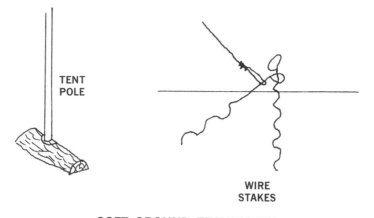

TENT POLE

WIRE STAKES

SOFT GROUND TECHNIQUES

Likewise, sometimes camp must be made on bare rock or on ground so rocky that it presents the same problems. Once again special techniques are required—sometimes special adaptations of the tent are helpful. One of these adaptations is to make the sod cloths double width, fold them, and stitch them into pockets; put rocks in the pockets and place the sod cloths on the outside of the tent instead of the inside. That way, no ground stakes are needed. A tree or boulder can anchor the guys. Lacking these special sod cloths, put a stick through the loop for the stake and place a rock on top of that to anchor it. The stick is to increase the friction with the rock to prevent the loop from slipping out from under the rock.

CHAPTER FIVE

Sleeping Equipment

You spend one-third of your life in bed. This is true in camp as well as at home. Since you will generally exert more energy while camping, you will need all the rest you can get in this third. Otherwise, when you get back you may have to rest up from the effects of your vacation. Proper pacing of your activities and rest during the day is, of course, required, especially if your normal daily work is on the sedentary side; but a comfortable bed and a good night's sleep is essential. Camping is no fun if your nights are spent on the hard ground with a rock trying to make a spinal tap—and you are cold besides.

The challenge of selecting your camp sleeping gear is in finding the compromise between the lightest bedroll possible and the least sacrifice of comfort, all with a view to avoid depleting the month's budget.

SLEEPING BAGS

The sleeping bag is traditional in camping. Like most traditions, it has earned its position. In an extreme, a good sleeping bag can be used alone—if there is no precipitation. Still, this is far from an ideal arrangement. A sudden rain puts you in a sloppy mess unless you have a tent. In fact, the lightweight tarp tents or ponchos are used so much now that the hood is omitted entirely from sleeping bags except those made for the overnight-picnick-ing crowd. (Actually, the hood is of practically no use anyway. A rain will generally blow under it; it makes the bag hard to get into; it is hard to rig, requiring a frame of some sort; and any sleeping-bag cover waterproof enough to provide shelter in a rain will soak you anyway—from the one or two pints of moisture sweated out in the average night.)

One of the most limiting factors in the use of a sleeping bag is its insulation. The average bag has a fixed insulation. This prevents it from finding year-round use since it will either be too hot for summer or too cold for winter camping. The expense of having separate bags for winter and summer is usually beyond the budget of the casual camper. On the other hand, the casual camper usually camps only during his summer vacation, so this is not critical.

You can make a bag without insulation, but having space inside for a couple of blankets. This way, the insulation can be varied to suit a wide range of temperatures. However, this arrangement is fairly heavy and is not worthwhile for backpacking. It is also too heavy for canoe camping, if there are any major portages. Its best use is with kids who are still a bit too rough on equipment to have a proper bag, or for the occasional camper who does not camp enough to warrant the expense of a good sleeping bag.

As for fixed insulation in a sleeping bag, waterfowl down is by far the best, with Dacron-fluff batts second. Dacron has the disadvantages of slight moisture-retention (although seldom enough to really be a problem) and poor compression for packing, but, unlike down, it can be machine-washed rather than only dry-cleaned. Polyurethane foam has been used quite successfully in insulated clothing, but not in any commercial sleeping bags except for the bottom of shells for snow camping. It is comparable to Dacron fluff, with a bit more compressibility. It should be used more for camping. Relatively new sleeping-bag materials are the closed-cell vinyls. These combine the characteristics of warmth, lightness, and waterproofing.

Most of the other materials either compress too little (making it hard to roll into a small enough bundle to pack conveniently) or are not resilient enough (matting down more and more, reducing their effectiveness). Actually, any porous material with high resilience and compressibility would make a good sleeping-bag insulation since the insulation quality is proportional to the thickness of the dead air trapped in it. Gerry Cunningham, of Gerry's outfitters, is fond of pointing out that, except for resilience, steel wool is just as good an insulator as Grade AA goose down.

In buying a down-insulated bag, make sure that it has baffles inside to prevent the down from shifting. Some are simply stitched through. No matter how thick these bags may look, they are, as far as effective insulation is concerned, only as thick as they are at the stitching—about one-eighth inch—because all your heat will leave at these spots. The box baffling is slightly superior to the overlapping tube construction, but so slightly that it is of little real concern.

If your bag has synthetic batts (Dacron, etc.) for insulation, make sure that the batting goes to the edges and is quilted in small sections to prevent shifting. Make sure that the quilting goes all the way through and is not just decorative, as some companies still working under *caveat emptor* ethics make them. The stitching should be loose so that the batting is not compressed too thinly, losing insulative qualities, but not so loose that the thread will tend to catch on things and pull loose. If your fingernail catches and pulls the thread, it is too loose; if the thickness is obviously different at the stitching (without really looking for it), it is too tight.

For shell fabric, cotton is best because it is moisture-absorbent and "breathes" well. Wool has insulation advantages, but gets dirty rather quickly. Nylon is too air-tight for the best comfort, but is a must in the backpacking bags because of its light weight, downproofness (the down can't work out between the weave), and great strength in the rip-stop (parachute cloth) form. Where weight is not a problem, a windproof, lightweight tent fabric is best for the outer shell with a flannel inside.

Most sleeping bags on the market have two pairs of twill-tape at the foot so you can tie the bag into a bundle to keep it from unrolling when not in use. Those of better quality (i.e., the better down bags) have a stuff bag, usually of rip-stop nylon or similar strong, light fabric, in which the sleeping bag is stuffed when not in use. This makes a smaller bundle than with the tapes and gives the fabric of the sleeping bag more protection from abrasion and dirt. It also avoids the wear on the sleeping-bag fabric from the twill-tapes being in the same spot each time. The stuff bag weighs only slightly more than the tapes and is definitely worth it. Because of the reduced compressibility of the batting insulation, stuff bags are less useful for them, although they do very well for foam-insulated sleeping bags.

You can save on cleaning bills on your sleeping bag by making a liner from an old sheet. It should fit the inside exactly. With the liner, all you have to do is wash it in a washing machine and the bag itself stays clean, assuming you take the proper precautions about keeping the outer shell clean. When you have to have your bag dry-cleaned, make sure the cleaner knows how to clean sleeping bags. The solvents used, especially by the coin-operated machines, are deadly and the fumes stay in the bag for quite some time. This is especially critical in the mummy bags when only the sleeper's nose protrudes from the bag on cold nights.

Basically there are two types of sleeping bags. The sack is the most common. It is easy to make and thus is low in cost—especially with the synthetic batts for insulation. It is roomy inside and also comes in double models for two people. The mummy bag follows your body shape and turns over when you do. It is harder to manufacture—almost entirely insulated with down or a down-and-feather mixture—and priced accordingly. You have to get one to fit your individual size and weight, and it may seem cramping to some. However, it is quite comfortable since it retains the body heat because of the smaller amount of wasted space inside. It only takes a couple of nights to learn how to turn over with the bag following you, without rolling off the air mattress in the process. (As with riding a bicycle and other kinesthetic skills, you don't have to relearn it each time out, so it is not nearly as bad as it sounds at first. Basically it is humping up slightly to take your weight off the mattress, flexing your arms and knees to apply pressure on the inside of the bag, then turning as you fall back to the mattress. It sounds frightfully complicated and far more exaggerated than it really is, but soon you can do it without even waking.) In addition, the mummy bag is much lighter in weight than the sack type—even with the same type of insulation—a fact of importance to backpackers. Plans for both types appear in Chapter 13.

For those living in what is euphemistically called "temperate climes," a single sleeping bag is either too hot for summer camping or too cold for winter. Since few campers can afford two or three sleeping bags, especially of the quality required for backpacking, the usual answer to the problem is to restrict the camping to only one season and get a sleeping bag for that temperature range.

The obvious drawback to this solution is that one misses the camping enjoyment that comes with the other season. A less obvious drawback is typical of areas of the United States where winter temperatures may be as high as the 80's or well below freezing with a high north wind.

So a better answer is to vary the insulation in the bag. While this method doesn't permit the compressibility of a good down bag, it is not too bulky using polyurethane-foam sheets, and it is a lot lower in cost, although about the same weight as Dacron. Since the insulation can be removed, the shell can be washed in a washing machine. If the shell is made from rip-stop nylon, the weight will be brought to a point midway between down and Dacron bags. However, there is no such bag on the market and you will have to make it yourself. To help you do this, there are plans in Chapter 13.

AIR MATTRESSES

The very mention of an air mattress may lose some of you who think they are just for the tenderfoot. As I mentioned earlier, enjoyment is the prime reason for camping. If you get real enjoyment out

Windproof shell over mummy bag lowers bag's temperature range at least 10°F(−12°C).

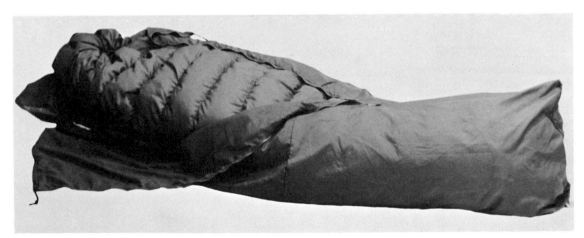

Variable-insulation sleeping bag with quarter-inch foam inside bag with hood closed.
Three-quarter-inch foam lies alongside with hood in open position.

of out-suffering everyone else, that's your privilege. Of course, where every pound counts, their one and three-quarters to six pounds will probably be in the way; and you can get used to sleeping on the bare ground. But if you can conveniently carry one with you, it is well worth its weight along about three or four in the morning when soreness often awakens someone accustomed only to a bed.

If you are going to buy an air mattress, don't get a plastic one unless it will never touch the ground. Even then it is an inferior product. The plastic is quite delicate in campgrounds covered with sharp rocks. Sunlight breaks down its chemical

compound so that it gets thinner each year. Even when treated with care, it gets pinpoint holes which are hard to find and even harder to repair. Rubberized fabric is the best. It holds up for several seasons of hard use and can usually be patched easily.

There are patching kits on the market, but you can make a cheaper and probably better one yourself. Get some canvas scraps and coat both sides with rubber cement or a fabric-rubberizing compound and let it dry. To use, coat the punctured area with the cement and press on the patch. Keep it weighted down until it is dry. (The mattress, of course, should be completely deflated first.)

The best kind of rubber cement is Flex-o-Fix or Plastic Rubber, or some of the new silicon-rubber compounds. When dry, they look and act like natural rubber. They stretch, bend, and even bounce. They are far better than the old type, clear rubber cement which will peel off and is practically useless for patching rubberized goods. The self-vulcanizing compounds are also good for sealing those "unpatchable" places like corners, creases, and around inflating valves. Just spread it on the surface and let it dry; you don't even need a patch. It's available in black, white, or brown.

When you use an air mattress, don't inflate it too much. This will give you a hard bed. You should just clear the ground when lying on your side.

The ridges caused by the tubular construction of the air mattress are a bother to some. You can get

Standard and shorty air mattresses.

an air mattress which uses posts instead of walls to keep the top and bottom the proper distance apart. However, they are really too expensive for the slight advantage unless the ridges actually keep you awake. If weight and bulk are no problem, cot pads are a fine addition to an air mattress. They not only smooth out the bumps, they also provide insulation on the bottom so that you will only need cover on top.

If you are really going light and still want an air mattress, get the short ones that support only the body from the shoulders to the hips and not the legs or head. They are fairly comfortable and weigh only a couple of pounds. With them, you rest your head on a bundle of clothes from your pack or use an air pillow. Your feet rest on the ground. Since this type of camping always means a sleeping bag, the insulation of the bag will make an adequate mattress for your feet. The only real problem with the shorties is that there is a very close balance between over- and under-inflation.

One of these short models is excellent when camping with a child. If your child is small enough to still be in the toss-and-tumble stage and might wake up somewhere on the ground, you might try to make a wall around the air mattress with a badminton or fishing net. It could be supported by one-and-a-half-foot-long poles at the corners and will roll up into a compact, lightweight bundle for carrying. The wall should be at least a foot high to keep him from rolling over the top.

Children like camping in general, and air mattresses in particular. We had a custom, when one child was sick, of letting the other use an air mattress in another room. The only problem we experienced was in getting the well one off the air mattress and back in bed after the period of contagion was over. This use of camping techniques in a home setting prevents the sudden newness of situation which is often so disturbing to small children. Back-yard campouts are also a good training ground for children. The parents can keep a watch on them and there is always the security of knowing the house is near.

Pumps are useful for inflating air mattresses, especially if you have several air mattresses to in-flate each night. However, their weight and bulk are most bothersome on backpacking trips. Their real advantage is that they keep the moisture from the breath out of the mattress where it could do some damage. The occasional addition of a little talcum or cornstarch will help prevent deterioration of the rubberized insides from the effect of condensed breath.

The easy way to lung-inflate an air mattress is to lie on your stomach and hold the inflating tube in your mouth. Breathe in through your nose and out through your mouth in even, deep breaths. Use your tongue over the tube as a valve to prevent the air from coming out again. Take one full breathing cycle for yourself after nine or ten for the mattress. Twenty to twenty-five cycles will inflate a large air mattress; six will fill a shorty mattress.

When not using an air mattress, many campers use a ground blanket to help insulate the more compressed bottom of the sleeping bag as well as cut the thermal loss to the ground. The usual ground cloth protects it from ground moisture. The ground blanket is a British device, but American mountain climbers have adapted it for snow camping by using a sheet of Ensolite foam between the ground and the sleeping bag. Some outfitters even have shells for mummy bags with the Ensolite built into the shell. These shells have even been used on open snow with a good mummy bag with fairly comfortable results.

CAMP BEDS

There are many kinds of camp beds and the worst of all is the cot. It weighs twelve to fifteen pounds. It takes up to twenty-five cubic feet of tent space. It is so high off the ground that it wastes too much floor space in most sloping-walled tents. It takes a short wrestling match for one person to set up and it is slightly dangerous to the fingers to take one down. What's more, it is too firm to be worth the effort.

If you think you can't sleep on anything except a bed (or something that looks like a bed), borrow a cot and an air mattress and test the two. The air mattress on the ground feels more like a bed in comfort than a cot does.

The lightweight, low aluminum cots now on the market represent a vain attempt to ease the problem of the cot. But even the aluminum ones are too bulky and heavy to transport easily. Their metal frame is not sturdy enough for rough use and soon resembles a very sagging hammock.

On the other hand, the surplus jungle hammocks are quite good for camping—if you like sleeping in a hammock. They have a top which keeps off the rain and insect netting all around to keep out the wee beasties. Its greatest advantage is in swampy or just-rained-on campsites where the more you can keep off of the ground (or ooze), the better. You can usually find two trees the proper distance apart at any wooded campsite. Its greatest disadvantage (outside of deserts, prairies, and above the timberline) is that you have to get out to undress—and you will be vulnerable to the mosquitoes and the weather.

The trapper bed is a kind of cot without the waste of vertical space or the wrestling match. Since you carry only the canvas part, it is lighter. However, finding the proper wood will probably pose some-

thing of a problem outside of wilderness areas, even where there are no restrictions on wood-cutting.

Camp beds made from straw, boughs, or other springy plant matter tend to mat down after a couple of nights. For this reason, they are usually too much trouble to make, and there is the chance that one bough will get dislodged from its place in the pile and turn over and start boring into your backbone instead of the ground. When you are going too light for even a shorty air mattress and sleeping only one night at each spot, they might be worth it. Otherwise, get something better. They are illegal in national parks and the Forestry Service discourages their use in national forests, which eliminates most of the camping areas in this country since state and provincial park authorities usually follow the lead of these two federal agencies in campsite policy. Those who contend that nothing has the fragrance of a balsam-bough bed can always take one small twig and crush it and put that by their head and get the very same results—at the same time practicing conservation a lot better.

The willow bed, however, does not mat down but remains springy. It is the original bed for the tipi. It rolls into a somewhat compact bundle for transportation or storage. Its main disadvantage is that it is too large for any but a permanent camp. Another disadvantage is in finding the willow shoots. You will need 300 for one bed with its two backrests (which double as chairs during the

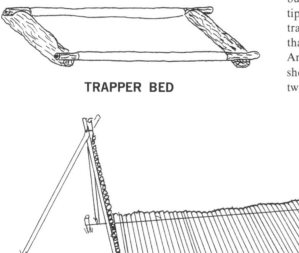

TRAPPER BED

WILLOW BED

day). However, the willow bed lasts for quite a long time, and in the tipi improves the appearance considerably.

BEDDING

To keep warm, you must have as much insulation under you as above. At home, the mattress more than does the job. In camp, an air mattress does as much as a very light quilt and a cot as much as a sheet. Too many tenderfoot campers have set up a cot, crawled under a blanket and quietly frozen most of the night. They go away, never to camp again, because it is too uncomfortable.

While the sleeping bag is definitely the standard in camp bedding now and the prices of the cheaper Dacron-batt bags are low enough so that anyone can afford them, the beginner, not knowing whether he will like camping or not, not knowing anyone who will lend him a sleeping bag, and not living

in an area where it is easy to rent one, can still try out camping in reasonable comfort using blankets—after all, campers used them for years before the sleeping bag became common.

The central item in this low-cost camping equipment is a wool blanket. The insulating qualities of wool, wet or dry, have not been matched by any synthetic yet developed. However, I have a problem with wool: it gives me the same sensation as rolling in freshly mowed grass—it itches! Dacron blankets may help in such a case, but they are too expensive for camping. Sheets help, but only in the uninsulated sack sleeping bags, since a wool blanket crawls on a sheet. A sheet also will get dirty more easily than a blanket and the dirt can't be brushed off as it can from a blanket. A very lightweight cotton blanket would be a better substitute for the sheet in camping.

You can improvise a sleeping bag that solves this problem nicely. Pin the cotton blanket to the wool

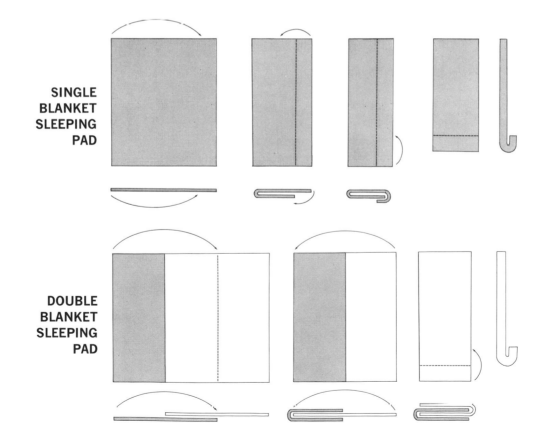

SINGLE BLANKET SLEEPING PAD

DOUBLE BLANKET SLEEPING PAD

one at the foot and a couple of feet up the side. The blankets will stick together and not slip, and, unlike the regular sleeping bag, you can turn down the top one if it gets too hot and still be covered by the inner one.

Your body is a fairly efficient radiator. Turn the cover down just enough to be comfortable. Your bloodstream will keep your whole body the same temperature whether you are out or under the cover. Of course, a wind will reduce its efficiency if you don't have a tent or some other windbreak.

For those who can use a wool blanket, get a double blanket for each person. Roll it up into a flattened cylinder with a little more than one-third on the bottom. A little less than half goes on top. The rest goes under the whole thing to keep out the cold air at the side. The foot is tucked under.

For colder weather, you can do the same thing with two blankets. Fix one blanket as usual, but without tucking the foot under. Then fix the other blanket in a similar way, but going around the other direction. Then tuck under the foot.

Don't use an old, worn-out blanket for camping, reasoning that "if it gets ruined, it won't be much loss." You need the finest-quality blanket possible if it is to do the job at all. Don't mistreat it and it won't get ruined. These blanket bags are suitable only for motor-vehicle transportation because of their weight, so there is no excuse for damage to them.

However, if you are going to do any extensive camping, a sleeping bag is vastly preferable.

PILLOWS

Pillows are a matter of personal choice. If you use them, the inflatable ones sold to go with air mattresses are the best. They not only make good pillows, you can use them for cushions too. This feature is especially welcome in wet weather when there is no dry spot to sit on anywhere in camp outside your tent.

Clothes, neatly folded and packed in a bag, make a serviceable pillow for going really light. But you can feel every wrinkle in the bag if they are simply stuffed in.

Probably the easiest pillow to improvise is simply to wedge almost anything under the end of the air mattress, tilting it upward. The only requirement of the wedge is that it must be even, otherwise the bumps will force the air somewhere else and you may get poked in the face. This method is very good with the shorty mattresses where the normal head position is barely on the rounded edge of the mattress.

CARE OF THE BEDDING

Bedding should be aired every day. Lunchtime is best since it takes the least time from the day's activities. A tent guy rope is a perfect clothesline. Open the sleeping bags flat and expose the insides to the sunlight. Mummy bags rarely open flat. With them, open the bag as much as possible and turn the foot inside-out for airing. With the polyurethane-foam, variable-insulation bags, pull the inner shell wrong-side-out out to air.

Proper airing in camp will double the time between cleanings. Keeping them out of the dirt by use of a good ground cloth will also add to their life. Especially when you get the down-filled mummy bags, you have quite an investment in these things. They deserve good treatment.

CHAPTER SIX

Cooking Equipment

Since good food is an important part of camp life, the selection of the cooking equipment must be done with care. As usual, lightness is an important consideration. The whole load—pots, pans, utensils, etc.—should weigh no more than two or three pounds for four people, with an extra pound allowed if a stove or oven is carried.

Extreme lightness will cost you in durability. While the equipment should be light, it must not be so thin that it is easily bent out of shape. Also, the equipment must be compact. Everything should fit into two or three compact groups, not exceeding a cubic foot in volume. Since, especially in the utensil kit, there are many small items, this clustering is needed to prevent loss. Generally, you will have a cooking kit (the pots, pans, skillets, and their lids, and sometimes plates and drinking cups as well), a utensil kit (with the tools used in preparing the food for cooking), and a stove and/or oven, if you carry them. The clean-up kit may be separate, or carried in the utensil kit or a spare space in the cooking kit.

CHUCK BOX

A chuck box, while often disparaged by true campers, does have some good points in car camping.

First, it keeps things together. The average camping kit will have five or six containers for the items

covered by the chuck box: a cooking kit, a utensil kit, possibly a clean-up kit, possibly a stove, possibly an oven, and from two to five food bags. While these are all fairly small, and are generally together with the rest of the camping gear, they can get separated. In a camping machine, the chuck box has a stove on top, an ice box under, and the utensils and food around the sides. The chuck box is, however, limited to motorized transportation. It is too bulky and heavy for even horsepacking or canoeing without portages. The chuck-box mania has infiltrated the Scouting movement along with the elaborate status-symbol trailers, so that what used to be carried in on the back of four boys is now towed to the site and unloaded by the adults because it is too heavy for the boys to lift.

The chuck-box mania with overnight picnickers has gotten so out of control that one home-mechanics magazine once had a cover story with plans for a chuck box that was so "complete" that it took up a complete trailer all to itself.

COOKING KIT

A camp cooking kit must be a nesting set. It takes up less room, is generally lighter, and the pieces don't get separated and lost as easily.

You can buy sets made for one, two, four, six, or eight persons, but, unless you have a tent-load of kids, or are organizing for a group camping trip, the two- or four-person models are best. The one-person Boy Scout model doesn't have enough pieces for much variety in meals, even for only one person.

There are many helpful items lacking in these commercial sets and some items are included that are far from ideal. The standard four-person kit has a couple of pots, a skillet, a coffee pot, four metal plates, and four aluminum cups. An aluminum cup couldn't be worse. It gets hot too quickly and stays hot too long. Stainless steel is slightly better and porcelain a bit better than that. Melamine plastic is the best, but it is usually too heavy. A polyvinyl cup, of the type which will stand the heat of boiling, is probably the best compromise. Although it does tear rather easily, it is light and doesn't break when dropped.

If you don't like coffee (or will use instant or boiled coffee) the coffee pot is an unnecessary weight.

For two to four people you will need these items:

a ten-inch (25 cm) skillet
two or four metal plates
saucepans with lids (five-quart and three-quart [5 and 3 liter] sizes for four people, three-quart and one-and-a-half-quart [3 and 1½ liter] for two people)
a coffee pot or tea kettle (optional)
two or four plastic cups
a set of condiment shakers (may be in the utensil kit)

Each item, or set of items, should fit into the one listed before it, although the plates may be larger and carried outside the skillet.

As you probably know, if you have studied any camping catalogs, you can't buy a set like this. However, you can buy a good skeleton to build it on. The pans, skillet, and coffee pot may be found in many of the sets on the market. The tea kettle may be a bit more trouble, but a coffee pot without its insides or even a small pot will work as well. The rest will have to be bought separately, but will not be hard to find.

Usually the largest pan is the container for the nest, with the skillet forming the lid. You will need

Some nesting sets even come with a built-in stove for backpacking.

some means of holding the skillet to the large saucepan if the kit doesn't furnish one. Cloth bags for each pot can help in several ways. First, the big bag for the whole set solves the problem of how to clamp the nest together. Second, the small bags reduce the amount of rattling in the nest. And third, it allows the bottom of a pan to get blackened without endangering the inside of the one below it. A blackened pot heats faster and more evenly. Just wipe off the excess from time to time or always cook over coals or on stoves instead of open wood flames.

To save space, the skillet should have a folding handle or a socket for a wooden handle. The pans should not have side-handles since you can't lift such a pan with only one hand. Bails are preferable, but be sure the bails don't have wooden or plastic handles as they will be in the heat of the open fire frequently.

Some kits have a single handle that fits into a socket on all of the pots. These are good too, although they have a tendency to get hot rather quickly. The only requirement on handle design is that it must not interfere with the nesting and will let you lift the full pan with only one hand. Handles for the lids should meet the same requirements.

Bags prevent rattling, hold the nest together, and reduce clean-up time.

A rigid bail on the bottom of the coffee pot, on the side opposite the spout, makes pouring much easier. Just hook a stick through it.

Some nesting-set skillets and pots are now available with Teflon coating to prevent the food from sticking. While this seems like a great advance in saving clean-up time, the durability of Teflon must be considered. Not only do you have to carry special tools in the utensil kit (adding to the bulk and weight), the nest itself poses a danger of scratching the Teflon. Even with the use of bags, this danger remains. Teflon utensils are great in the kitchen, but don't stand up as well to the conditions in camp.

The problem of cups is never completely solved. The melamine plastic will stand hot temperatures and is scratch-resistant and practically breakproof. The polyvinyl plastics may or may not be boilable

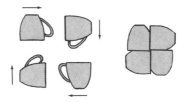

CUP NESTING

and certainly scratch easily, but because of their light weight they are probably the best as long as you get the boilable kind. The polyvinyl cups made for camping usually have handles with the bottoms out, so that they can nest easily. However, you can nest cups with regular handles by putting them on their sides in a circle, the handles pointing the same way around. Reduce the size of the circle by fitting the handles of one into the bowl of the next. A better way, however, is to hacksaw and file the handles off the cups. You don't need them. Or buy bouillon cups which have no handles.

A condiment set is well worth its weight in good food. Save little pill bottles. Fit a piece of aluminum window-screen in the top to regulate the flow of the seasoning. A screen is better than a perforated lid since it will break up the hardened chunks that inevitably develop. The regular lid of the container prevents spillage in the kit.

A top with a small hole (about one-sixteenth inch [1 to $1\frac{1}{2}$ mm] in diameter) should be used in place of the screen for liquids such as vanilla extract or garlic juice. Just make sure the lid will not, under any circumstance, allow leakage. These two can smell up a pack as badly as kerosene. Garlic

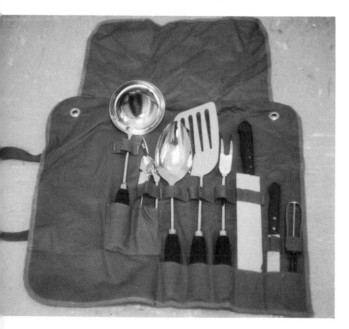

powder is vastly superior to garlic juice; just make sure that it is powdered garlic and not garlic salt, which is mostly plain sodium chloride at a higher price.

You should have a shaker for each seasoning you use in cooking at home. A cloth roll with pockets for each one prevents both scattering and breakage. An embroidered label on each pocket (nothing fancy, just the lettering) will help get things back where they belong after use. This label can't rub off, but you can remove it with scissors if you need to change it. The total roll should not weigh over a half-pound (250 g), even for a prolonged trip. It should weigh much less for the usual weekend camp.

Using pill bottles in which the lid fits into the bottle as a stopper, you can saw off the top to make a smaller container. You can also do a trim job on flip-top bottles, but here you will have to keep at least a quarter-inch (5 mm) of both the top and bottom and glue them together after removing a sufficient amount of the middle. Be sure to use polystyrene glue for best results.

Cutting the bottles down like this will give you a container only a half-inch (1 cm) tall. Several will fit into the odd spaces of the nesting or utensil kits and permit you to take the condiment set, even when going light. Label the lids with plastic paint (available from model supply stores).

UTENSIL KIT

It is more convenient to carry most of the other cooking tools in a utensil kit rather than loose or in the nesting set. The equipment is most easily carried in a cloth roll. It should include the following:

forks
spoons
table knives (optional)
a butcher knife

Utensil kit. This particular model is the one used by the Boy Scouts. Stock cardboard sheaths for knives should be replaced by leather ones. Ladle and potato peeler will find limited use by most campers.

two paring knives (or, optionally, one for each person instead of the table knives)

a can opener (if canned food is carried)

a few large aluminum nails (optional)

an egg flip (optional)

a perforated serving spoon (optional)

a ladle (optional, for large groups only)

In another bag, you may wish to carry some of the optional items, some or all of which may be omitted when going light:

a plastic sheet two feet (60 cm) square

a roll of aluminum foil

heavy cotton or asbestos gloves

scouring pads with soap

detergent and sponge

a collapsible canvas water pail

a water-tight, unbreakable container

The forks and spoons should be aluminum to save weight, but the table knives should be stainless steel. Extra paring knives or steak knives are an even better substitute for table knives since they can also be used in preparing the food for cooking. Get the government-surplus soup spoons. They are about two-teaspoon in size—large enough for cooking and small enough for eating. A knife, fork, and spoon per person and a couple of extra forks and spoons for cooking and serving should take care of the matter in all but backpacking, where cooking and eating is done with the same utensil.

To really save weight, you can omit the plates from the nesting set and use the cooking utensils for eating. Or you can even leave out the nesting set and use the aluminum pans from frozen-food containers for both cooking and eating and throw them away after using (using proper disposal procedures, of course).

Keep paring and butcher knives sharp. You should carry a whetstone in the repair kit. Use it frequently. A small riveted sheath for each knife will keep them from cutting the cloth roll or other gear in the pack. Also, be careful when you are cutting your food that you don't cut too hard—aluminum will cut easily with a sharp knife. This leaves gashes in the bottom where food will stick and it is quite difficult to clean without extreme

pressure from the scouring pads, which, in turn, scar the utensil some more.

Carry a can opener if you have any canned foods. Using a can-opener "blade" on a pocket knife is not only inefficient, it is a quick way to gum up the knife. A small twist-type can opener is the easiest to use and takes up very little space in the pack.

An egg flip is not only good for cooking, it is also a good scraper for cleaning stuck food off pots and pans, as well as a knife for cutting dough for pies and cobblers.

You can use aluminum nails to conduct heat to the center of meat or potatoes and make them cook quicker and more evenly. This is a good trick in the kitchen oven as well as in camp.

Aluminum foil is now practically required equipment on camping trips. It can be used to make a griddle by stretching it between the sides of a trapper fire. You can make a small pressure cooker by tightly sealing the food in the foil. It is the best way to bake food as it retains all the nutritional values in the food. It is also a good heat reflector for an oven or a reflector fire. Its only real drawback is that it punctures easily and therefore care must be taken to avoid this.

A sheet of plastic about two feet (60 cm) square is a good material for mixing dough. A one- or two-mil thickness is what you need as the plastic wrap is too thin and delicate, and the four-mil tent plastic is not flexible enough. Its main advantage is that you don't have to touch the dough, but can wrap it up in the sheet and knead it. Not only do you avoid having it stick all over your hands, you can get a better mixture. The sheet can be reused simply by opening it fully after removing the dough and letting any that stuck to the sheet dry out; then flake it off and wash the sheet.

Gloves such as are used for home barbecuing are good protection against the radiant heat of the fire and the conductive heat of hot utensils.

You should have adequate cleaning equipment, but what and how much depends on where you find the balance between convenience of operation and the weight and bulk to carry. The scouring pads with soap in them are the most convenient for cleaning utensils, but when going light you can use fine sand for scouring. A couple of ounces of powdered cleanser will do a week of camp-stained pots and pans. All types of detergents should be kept in waterproof containers.

The canvas pail is a nice convenience, but hardly a required item.

Now, that water-tight container on the list? Beans. Dried beans are a great saving in weight, but need to be soaked before cooking. When you move camp every day, this is difficult. Usually it is solved by using the heavier canned beans. However, a leak-proof container can be used to soak them while you are on the trail. This way, you neither have to carry the heavy weight of water-filled cans nor waste time in one spot waiting for them to soak. (Yes, you could soak them overnight, but you will still need something to hold them until dinnertime.) A wide-mouthed polyethylene bottle or an aluminum-and-plastic can (made for carrying margarine) is best for either soaking or carrying them after soaking. These are also good for mixing powdered foods such as powdered milk or eggs, since they are easily held for the proper agitation.

The handles of the various utensils should not be varnished or painted. With wear, this starts flaking off and, at best, it looks bad; at worst, it flakes into the cooking. Plastic handles may or may not take boiling water. Find out before you buy. Rosewood handles, oiled and rubbed, are best, although any close-grained hardwood, similarly treated, will do almost as well. The handle should be riveted on the blade.

CAMP STOVES

The camp stove has a long history. The early ones burned wood, as did the kitchen stoves of that time. They were first cast iron and later heavy-gauge sheet steel. Both materials were quite heavy, but they were for wagon transportation—anyone camping was expected to be able to build a fire, even in a downpour.

Shepherd's Stove

The shepherd's stove is the last remaining example of this old type. It has the unique problem of doing its job too well. Given half a chance, it will put out enough heat not only to drive everyone

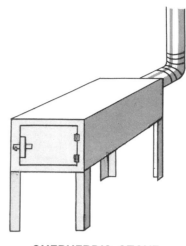

SHEPHERD'S STOVE

from the tent, but burn the tent down as well. Even when controlled, it is a potential source of burns—from accidentally brushing against it. It has the further problems of weight and bulk, and of requiring a hole in the end of the tent, lined with asbestos, for the chimney. It is generally practical only in a large wall tent, which, itself, is of extremely limited practicality.

Petroleum Stoves

Just before World War II, the pressurized gasoline and alcohol stoves came on the scene. These weighed only a few pounds. You can even buy some of them weighing only a few ounces, but because of their special applications these will be discussed in the section on backpacking stoves. The gasoline stove liberated the camper from his dependence on wood, an item quickly becoming extinct in many campsites.

However, they do have several drawbacks. Denatured alcohol or white gasoline is not always available. The fuel is hard to store to prevent leakage. It goes right through polyethylene bottles and can seep out of all but the tightest-fitting lids. Even the fumes from the petroleum products can taint food. The stove itself is bulky (except for the backpacking stoves). However, since they are used mostly with motor transportation, the size is not really much of a problem.

After World War II, stoves were developed using liquified petroleum (LP) gases—butane and propane. The small versions of the big tanks which supplied rural homes were convenient for carrying fuel for lanterns and stoves. Still, they are not perfect. The fuel bottles are quite heavy. You have to carry two of them since there is no convenient way to tell if you are running out of fuel. The size and weight of the stoves give them the same disadvantages as the gasoline stoves in that department.

Regardless of the type fuel your stove uses, be sure of these features. 1. The top should be large enough to hold as many large skillets as there are burners. Several burners do no good if only one can be used at a time. This is especially a fault of many three-burner stoves which can hold only two pans at a time. 2. If it is a gasoline stove, will it take all types of fuel? The stoves which will take leaded gasoline without clogging up the generator are much better if you are far from white-gas pumps. 3. The stove which only needs depressurizing, filling, pumping, and relighting is far superior to one which needs to cool down a bit. 4. If it is an LP stove, is there a cut-off at the bottle? This is an added safety feature in case something makes a leak in the supply line, and it makes refueling easier. Is it easy to change the fuel bottles, or do you need a small tool chest to do the job?

Always carry a jet-cleaning wire for either type. With the gasoline stoves, also carry a funnel with a wire strainer in it for ease in filling and a spare generator (the most likely part to break down). With the LP stoves, carry an extra bottle and any tools needed to change them.

Backpacking Stoves

The best camp stove is one (or two) of the lightweight backpacking models which burn alcohol or white gasoline. Two stoves and enough fuel for a week's cooking will weigh less than one of the two-burner gasoline stoves without any fuel.

Many of these small stoves have a wind-screen which surrounds the stove, concentrating the heat upward and supporting the pan. Some of the smaller models, in fact, require the screen to give adequate heat. With the screen, however, they are excellent. Regardless of stove size, the screen represents a saving of fuel and a convenient carrying container for the stove—and you should make one if it doesn't come with the stove.

Fuel containers should be metal with fully sealed caps to avoid any leakage and prevent breakage if dropped. They should be red in color to conform with the law in several states regarding the storage of inflammable liquids. As added insurance, carry the fuel bottle in one of the outside pockets of the pack.

Since there is not as much demand for the backpacking stoves as for the larger models, there are fewer companies making them (none domestic) and the quality has not been sacrificed for large-volume production. Most outfitters will furnish a list of features: size, weight, capacity, time it takes to boil water, fuel, etc. The roarers do a better job that the silent ones, especially in a wind. The pump-pressure ones are easier to start, especially on a cold morning when the hand-warmed ones give you frostbite while you try to expand the fuel up the tube to prime them, but the pump is just another thing to go wrong. A jet-cleaning wire is essential for trouble-free service from both types.

While food tastes better when cooked over a wood fire, in rainy weather, or when wood is unavailable, the camp stove may be quite welcome.

Solar Stoves

The cheapest stove to operate doesn't even use fuel in the usual sense of the word. Sunlight is free and is just beginning to be tapped for cooking purposes. There are two basic types of solar stove. The first uses a fresnel lens to concentrate the light (and heat) from the sun. It has the disadvantages of heavy weight and the breakability of the lens.

The second type uses a parabolic reflector. This type is currently being used in many parts of the world which are desert or semi-desert and have a permanent fuel shortage. Although no heavier than the petroleum stoves, they are quite bulky and only one-burner size.

You can make your own from a surplus thirty-inch radar reflector and a lot of chrome tape,

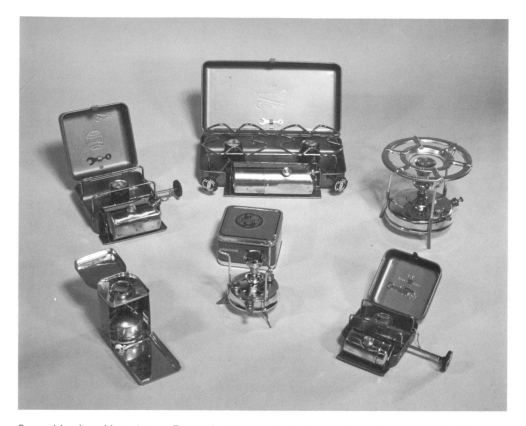

Several backpacking stoves. For scale, the one in the lower left is three-and-a-half inches (9 cm) square on top.

mounting the reflector on a tripod with a swivel head and putting a grill at the focal point.

The main disadvantage of the solar stove, in addition to its bulk, is that a non-wood fire is usually needed only during a rain. This is also true when the fuel for the solar stove is unavailable. However, for campsites which don't permit open fires, or for desert areas where there is plenty of sunshine and little wood, the solar stove is ideal.

Catalytic Heaters

While these are space heaters rather than cooking stoves, this is about as logical a time as any to discuss them.

Catalytic heaters are fairly new as camping equipment, although the principle has been in use for some time in the little hand warmers. Because of the use of a catalyst, the fuel is burned almost completely, leaving practically no fumes. The advertising claims that they are perfectly safe in enclosed tents. I wouldn't quite trust them that far, but since all my tents have vents anyway, it is a moot point with me personally.

They generally run on the special stove fuel, but can take benzene and similar unfortunately unavailable petroleum products.

They come in just a few sizes, so you may have the problem of the shepherd's stove—too much

heat for the space. This would especially be true with some of the backpacking tents and may well be the case with the semi-permanent camp tents.

Their main problem is that they are bulky and far too heavy for their usefulness. I have often heated my rather large paratipi to dressing temperature with nothing more than a Primus 71L, one of the smallest of the backpacking stoves.

REFLECTOR OVEN

One of the easiest ways to bake food in camp is with a reflector oven. You can keep a watch on your food as it cooks and it doesn't get sooty from the fire. Made of sheet aluminum, it is light in weight and folds into a compact unit.

The heating is more even if the shelf is stainless steel, but an aluminum shelf will make the whole thing a couple of ounces lighter.

A reflector oven that stays in one piece when folded is far better than one which disassembles. For one thing, you can fold them up as soon as you finish with them instead of having to wait for them to cool down. Sides are a waste of weight and materials as they add little to the heating.

A bag will protect the oven while in the pack. The shinier it is, the better it will cook, so take care not to scratch it.

The metal should be as thin as possible without being flimsy. Thicker walls add nothing but weight.

Erected, the shelf should hold at least ten pounds without a severe distortion of the shelf or reflectors.

If you wish to make your own reflector oven, there are plans for one in Chapter 15.

Reflector oven.

DUTCH OVEN

The dutch oven is a heavy cast-iron pot with a sunken lid. It has stubby legs to keep the bottom from direct contact with the coals which would burn the food. The lid is filled with coals.

You can improvise a lighter version out of any saucepan and lid, but there is a greater chance of small burned spots on your food and ashes dropping down from the lid when you remove it. Rest the bottom on a rock tripod with the live coals under, but never more than barely touching, the pan.

Size permitting, any food baked in a kitchen oven can be baked in one of these dutch ovens.

Use a small amount of water with meat or vegetables. Rig a grillwork arrangement (green sticks will do) when baking pastries or breadstuffs

The dutch oven is a versatile cooking device if you have the transportation to carry its weight— they are made of cast iron.

This box oven, shown ready for use and collapsed, can be modified for use on wood fires.

so the dough doesn't directly touch the bottom of the oven. The exception is cobbler, which has only the liquid filling touching the bottom.

Too heavy for all but auto or horsepack transportation, the dutch oven is still a top-quality utensil when you can carry it conveniently.

BOX OVEN

A standard, kitchen-type oven is on the market for gasoline stoves. It is collapsible and fitted with a thermometer. While it is a little small for an oven, it has about the same capacity as the average dutch oven.

It can be modified for use on wood fires, but use the oven only over coals, never over a flame, or your food will get smoked. To modify it, cut off the indented part from the bottom. Weld, braze, or rivet a sheet of stainless steel flat over the hole. That's all.

In use, watch the thermometer closely and regulate the amount of coals accordingly.

PRESSURE COOKER

A pressure cooker is practically required for high-altitude camping since the boiling point of water drops with the increase in altitude. Many mountain-climbing outfitters carry an aluminum pressure cooker which is designed for campers— light in weight, ruggedly built, and not too high in price.

Get a two-quart (2 liter) size for four people.

The pressure cooker is also useful in lower-altitude camps, especially on the road in car camping. A good lunch can be cooked in ten minutes with the aid of one of these cookers.

Dividers, available as an extra, permit you to cook up to three different foods at one time in a single cooker. These are well worth the nominal

Camp pressure cookers are lighter, but otherwise the same as the kitchen variety. Dividers permit more than one food to be cooked at a time.

extra price in increasing the versatility of the pressure cooker.

GRATES AND GRILLS

While fairly light in weight if made from heavy wire, a grate is hard to clean and a trapper fire does just as well. The cast ones, even in magnesium, are far too heavy for any use. Don't use an old refrigerator shelf for a campfire grate as there are still too many of the old cadmium-plated ones around. Cadmium, in the heat of a campfire, is poisonous.

Grills are the same as grates, only more so. Even the magnesium ones are too heavy for all except motorized transportation and horsepacking. There are far too many substitutes to bother with them.

Still, there are some who like them in spite of their drawbacks, so here are a few variations.

GRILLS

REFRIGERATION

There are two types of camp refrigeration: the ice box and the mechanical refrigerator. The ice box is the most common, and very low in initial cost, but requires a constant supply of ice. The mechanical refrigerator is available in gas, electric, or both in the same machine. It is expensive to purchase and moderately expensive to keep operating, but will keep even frozen foods ready for the camp table. Because it requires access to LP gas tanks or 12- or 115-volt current, it is restricted to the camping machine—too bulky even for cars.

Some of the new thermoelectric devices are now available, so you could build yourself one from plywood and Styrofoam. All you need is a box and one of these units operating off of the car battery. At the time of this writing, they are not available for six or twelve volts, but a little work with a transformer should cure that. While a bit expensive, this method would bring the price down to a range more in line with the average camper's budget. The commercial electric refrigerator (which uses a motor and compressor rather than a thermoelectric cooler) costs almost as much as a full-size one for the home—definitely more per cubic foot of capacity.

As with any camping equipment where the inside temperature must be quite different from the outside, insulation is of prime importance. Styrofoam is one of the best insulation materials for ice boxes. Fairly cheap ones are now being made entirely from the stuff. However, they are quite susceptible to chipping. Don't carry heavy loads in them, set them down on rocks, or drop food or ice into them —they will tear apart—or get them near gasoline which will dissolve the plastic.

The metal-walled, fiberglass-insulated boxes are stronger, but impossibly heavy and slightly less insulating because of the conducted heat through the metal walls. The best ones—and you will have to do quite a bit of hunting to find them—will have Styrofoam insulation in fiberglass walls. However, they are so expensive that if you can do fiberglass work at all you probably would be better off making your own.

The same insulation standards apply to the mechanical refrigerators, although there is less of a choice of materials—high-impact styrene walls over glass fiber or Styrofoam insulation being most popular (and quite susceptible to cracking under too much strain).

With either the ice box or the refrigerator, precool it before you put in the food. Turn the refrigerator on the night before packing, put ice in the ice box several hours before packing the food.

Melting ice can be a problem in the ice boxes. The boxes made from Styrofoam beads (without hard walls) seldom have a drain for the water, which makes emptying quite a problem. Bailing them out with a sponge is a hand-chilling chore and keeps the box open longer than is preferred; yet it is often the only way to keep your food from getting flooded and damaged by the melting ice.

There are two ways around this. One is by enclosing the refrigerant. There are several commercial concoctions on the market which are chemicals in tin cans or plastic bags. These are frozen in the home refrigerator and absorb the heat of the food in the ice box. They can be reused indefinitely. The only real problem is on extended trips. You can practically always buy more ice, but almost never find a place to refreeze your artificial ice. Also, they are often low-freezing-point chemicals such as anti-freeze, methyl alcohol, and such. These are typically poisonous. The cans are safe enough, and the plastic bags are fairly thick, but care must be taken that they do not get punctured or develop leaks, as this can endanger your whole food supply.

You can make a poor substitute for these yourself with milk cartons and water. When the ice melts, you can simply pour out the water. However, take care that they remain upright in the box, or they may pour out too early. They are much lower in cost (being scrap) than the commercial ones, are slightly less efficient, and have the same problem of refreezing.

A second method is to use dry ice. The solid carbon-dioxide is fairly accessible in larger towns (although rarely at the campsites themselves). Yet many foods must be packaged in air-tight containers to prevent the taste from changing because of the CO_2 atmosphere in the box. Also, you must take care when handling dry ice to prevent frostbite.

When using dry ice, it is advisable to have a vent. A hose running from a drain at the bottom of the box to the outside is a good method. There are two reasons for this. First, dry ice subliming in a sealed ice box will build up pressure which, if it has a sturdy lid locked on it, will explode the entire box. Second, if you are going to sleep on the floor of a camping machine which has one of these in it, the heavier-than-air carbon-dioxide will settle all over the floor during the night and possibly suffocate you. A flutter valve fitted over the vent to the outside lets the gas out as it builds up pressure and keeps out any hot air from the outside.

While ice boxes with drains are both heavier and more expensive, they are the most logical solution to the problems of melted ice water and venting carbon-dioxide. An old drain and a bit of epoxy cement will enable one of the plastic bead-type boxes to have this feature. However, you must then take care not to knock the drain off (with the resulting disintegration of the box around the drain) by hitting or scraping it against some unyielding object.

EQUIPMENT MADE IN CAMP

Personally, I find the lug pole with its pot hooks and the dingle cranes so prized by many campers generally to be a waste of time for most cooking jobs. A good trapper fire is easier to make and control. However, many excellent campers can't do without them, and they are useful for some forms of cooking. This is what they look like.

The spit is used so much in back-yard barbecueing today that little needs to be said about it here. A wooden spit won't conduct the heat to the center as does a metal one, but it is still useful for holding the food in place over the fire.

The tennis-racket broiler is woven out of a forked stick about two feet long, not counting the handle. The meat goes between the "strings" of the tennis racket. This makes it quite easy to handle. Use green wood!

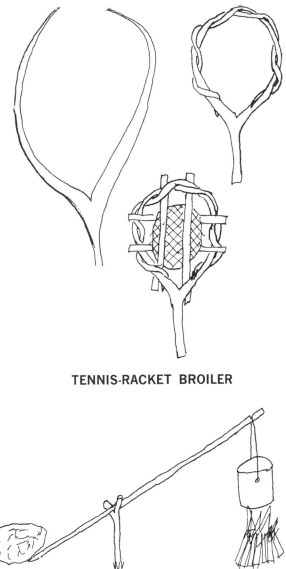

TENNIS-RACKET BROILER

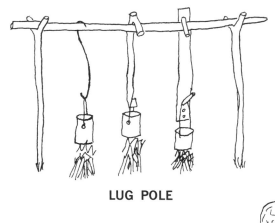

LUG POLE

DINGLE CRANE

The stirring stick is nothing unusual except that it has a built-in fly whisk. It should be made of cedar. Peel one end of the piece for the stirrer. Use the "leaves" on the other end to scare away the flies.

In the use of sticks, planks, or other wood for cooking utensils, peel the bark off a piece and taste the wood. If it has an unpleasant taste, it will make the food taste bad also. Green wood should be used to prevent the utensil from igniting.

STIRRING STICK

CHAPTER SEVEN

Packs

Whenever you need to carry your gear any distance on foot, you will need some sort of pack. For auto camping, just any old container will do, although even there a proper one is vastly better. For backpacking or canoeing with portages, a well-designed pack is absolutely necessary.

A pack must meet two requirements: it should hold all of your share of the gear you have on the trip, and it should be comfortable. Extra features, such as ease of packing and unpacking or good appearance, are nice, but these two are absolutely necessary—even with improvised packs.

BELT PACK

The belt pack is still fairly new. It was developed by skiers to carry ski wax, lunches, extra jackets, and other such accoutrements of skiing, without the inconvenience of a backpack with shoulder straps. It is also good for carrying photographic supplies. It is fairly small, good only for day-long hikes; but because it rides low and has no shoulder straps, it is a comfortable way to carry lunches and rain gear without bother. Ten pounds is its maximum capacity.

If you want to make a belt pack, there are plans in Chapter 14.

The belt pack, plus a water supply, contains all that is needed for an all-day hike. Note poncho lashed under the pack.

KNAPSACK

The knapsack is about as plain as a pack can be. It is just a canvas bag fitted with shoulder straps. It is light in weight and fairly cheap and easy to make. For short trips with a light load, it is adequate; for anything else, get another type.

Plans are in Chapter 14, if you wish to make your own.

DULUTH PACK

The Duluth pack, of canoeing fame, is simply a very large knapsack without sides and fitted with a tumpline. However, it is too large (300-pound capacity) for normal backpacking, although it is

good for the short portages between canoeing lakes and streams.

It comes in three sizes (logically called #1, #2, and #3), weighing about $2\frac{1}{4}$, $2\frac{1}{2}$, and $2\frac{3}{4}$ pounds empty.

There are plans in Chapter 14 for the do-it-yourself fans.

RUCKSACK

The rucksack is a knapsack with two outside pockets added. The advantages and limitations are about the same as the knapsack's, although there is less "going to the bottom of the pack" with the rucksack.

There are plans in Chapter 14, if you want to make yours.

BASKET PACK

The basket pack is woven from splints—thin strips peeled from ash or willow logs. The basket pack has three advantages: 1., it is light in weight, 2., it is rigid and can be packed and unpacked more easily while resting on the ground, 3., it protects breakables from knocks from the outside quite well.

On the other hand, it has four bad limitations. First, it gets hot against your back (a fault shared by the knapsack variations). Second, it is difficult to repair when broken, although it is far stronger than it looks and seldom gets damaged if it is not mistreated. Third, it has to be unpacked to get to the bottom. And fourth, suitable materials are hard to find to make one.

However, many camping outfitters sell such a pack for much less than it would cost you to make it yourself unless you can peel the splints rather than buy them. Plans for a cheap (and not too durable) form, made out of plastic wastepaper basket, are included in Chapter 14.

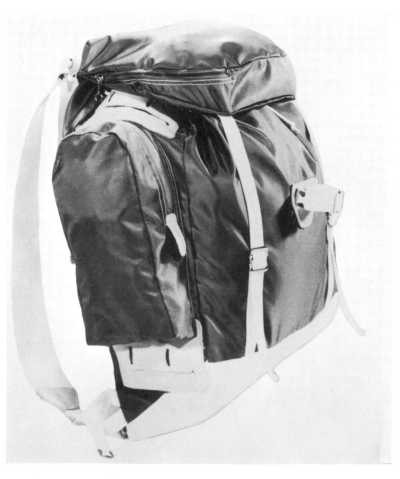

Ski pack with slots above and below side pockets for skis and loop on back for ice ax. Used in ski mountaineering.

SKI PACK

The ski pack, a variation on the Bergans Meis design, is an excellent pack design. It has a stainless-steel or aluminum frame which holds the pack rigid. The hip strap keeps it off your back, permitting the ventilation that is so welcome on a hot hike. The three outside pockets help reduce the need to "go to the bottom of the pack."

Because the space inside of the main bag is not very large for prolonged trips, the bedroll is usually carried on the outside, the old bedroll in a horseshoe shape, the modern sleeping bag in a more compact cylinder under the top flap. The ax is often carried through a loop on the outside of the pack.

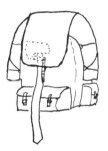

AX PLACEMENT

More recent designs of the ski pack are almost as large as the pack-frame packs. Because of the low center of gravity, the ski pack is often preferred to the pack frame in climbing and many models are available, especially modified for snow camping. These have slots for carrying skis, loops for ice axes, and leather pads to keep crampon points from sticking the pack.

The chief disadvantage of the ski pack over the pack frame is its smaller capacity in many models, and the ease with which the frame gets out of shape.

Chapter 14 has the plans, if you want to make your own.

PACK FRAME

The pack frame is one of the most versatile packing methods. It is more than just a method for carrying your camping gear—you can use it to haul game, firewood, mineral samples, or even a toddler.

As well as being the most versatile method, it is also one of the most comfortable to use. The frame keeps the load off your back. This permits air to circulate between the pack and your back, and your back not only feels cooler, the load feels lighter because of it. With the pack frame, you can carry hard, lumpy items without having them bore into your spine.

In camp, you can remove the pack from the frame. You will be able to move the pack around without the shoulder straps tangling on everything as other packs often do, and you will have the frame available for other hauling jobs.

Instead of one big pack, you can pack several small bags directly on the frame. This avoids the need of going to the bottom of the pack to get something when packing a lot of gear; or having

 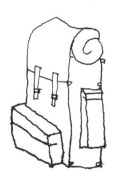 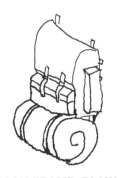 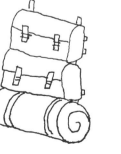 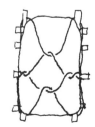

PACK-FRAME PACKING

Packaged design: mountain tent, foam mattress (shown rolled and open), and sleeping bag are all designed to fit into their own section of this pack. Fourth section is for other camping gear and food. Package is for 12 lbs. with space for 8 lbs. more gear.

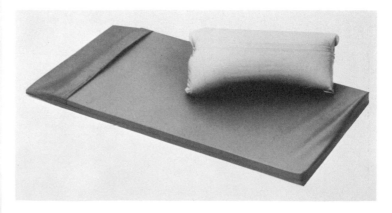

a large, flopping, half-empty pack when taking an overnight hike. I use this method with a sleeping bag, a polyethylene bag one foot square, and a poncho, when going ultra-light. The plastic bag holds my food supply and accessory kits (first aid, etc.) and thus I can go for several days on less than twenty pounds total weight.

Here are some packing variations. The cylindrical item is an externally carried sleeping bag.

Gerry has a four-part unit of pack, mattress, sleeping bag, and tent which uses the "several bags" principle in a single pack. The whole unit is only twelve pounds in weight for the men's version and ten pounds for the women's (the same, but without the tent), with space to carry other camping gear, food, etc.

Plans for a pack frame and its pack are both included in Chapter 14, although excellent low cost packs are now available on the market which are even cheaper than making it yourself unless you have a lower-cost supply of fabric.

IMPROVED PACKS

In an emergency, you can make a pack from many things. All that is really needed is something to hold the gear. Comfort is a necessity, especially if you will need it for any considerable distance, but in an emergency you may not have much. You might as well forget about ease in packing and unpacking, and aesthetic appearance.

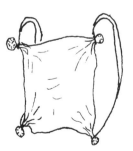

SACK PACK

When using a sack, tie a small rock in each corner to keep the rope from slipping off. Join both corners on the same side with enough rope to make the proper-size shoulder straps. Wrap these ropes with cloth to keep them from cutting into your shoulders.

With a pair of pants, tie the legs to the belt. The legs make the shoulder straps.

PANTS PACK

TRAVOIS

The travois is an Indian invention for moving heavy or bulky loads. While it is not a replacement for the usual packing methods, you may find it valuable for moving rocks or firewood in camp, moving game or an injured camper out, or some other emergency use.

Historically, it was first used with dogs, and later, after the European invasion, the horse. The man version will probably be the most useful, although you may find the others of some use under unusual conditions—assuming you have a well-broken horse or a strong dog.

Incidentally, the word "travois" is of French Canadian origin (from *travail,* meaning "work"). The Sioux picked it up from their enemies, the Algonquins, who were allied with the French. It came into the English language from the Sioux. The correct pronunciation is trav-vwah'.

PAPOOSE PACK

As mentioned in Chapter 1, camping is changing. So are the attitudes toward camping. It is no longer

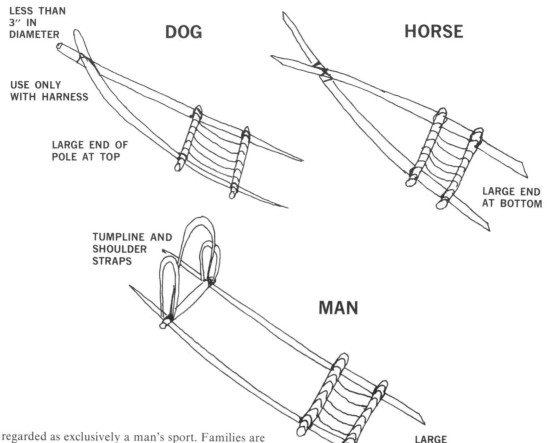

DOG

LESS THAN 3″ IN DIAMETER

USE ONLY WITH HARNESS

LARGE END OF POLE AT TOP

HORSE

LARGE END AT BOTTOM

TUMPLINE AND SHOULDER STRAPS

MAN

LARGE END AT BOTTOM

TRAVOIX

regarded as exclusively a man's sport. Families are camping together, and this includes toddlers. My own son took his first camping trip when he was six months old. In many ways, this is an easier age to camp with than the toddler. With the toddler, there is the problem of transportation, even on short hikes from base camp. The little ones simply can't walk very well over rough ground—or very smooth ground either, for that matter.

They can still go along if you use an adaptation of the Indian method. The easiest way is to build a seat and back from half-inch waterproof plywood. Brace it with strap iron and fit it with D-rings so it can be attached to a pack frame. A T-shaped adjustable safety belt keeps the child in. A canvas awning will be welcome in the direct sunlight.

A small load can be packed under the seat, but this will probably be limited to the diaper bag.

Another way is to take a worn-out knapsack. Cut holes in the corners nearest you for the child's legs. He rides facing you with legs around your waist. This is easier to carry, if the child is over two years old, than the papoose pack. This is the basic design of the multitude of commercial kid-carriers on the market today.

With the pre-toddler, the authentic cradle board is more practical. These are still used by many Navajos, Hopis, and Apaches and can be bought in their lands in Arizona and New Mexico. However, a cradle board is not sturdy enough for a

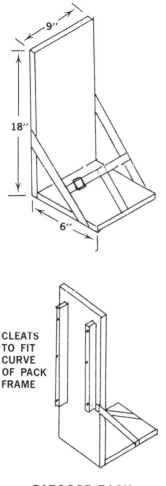

CLEATS
TO FIT
CURVE
OF PACK
FRAME

PAPOOSE PACK

toddler—nor will the toddler tolerate the restriction of leg movement it imposes.

TUMPLINE

The tumpline is a pack strap that goes over the front of the head rather than over the shoulders. It is designed to take some of the weight of the pack off of your shoulders. The Duluth pack uses a tumpline instead of shoulder straps since the shoulders cannot hold the heavy weights often

TUMPLINE

carried in the Duluth pack. However, you have to get used to the tumpline since it adds considerable strain to the neck muscles. For short distances with extremely heavy loads, however, the tumpline is far superior to the shoulder straps.

EQUIPMENT BAGS

An old definition of a well-equipped pack is "a bag of bags." Each item of equipment should be in its own space in a small bag or container. This way, any item may be reached with a minimum of unpacking. The bags also protect the equipment from damage by other items of equipment in the pack. The bags are made out of canvas, twill, or denim in one of three designs.

The first is a miniature duffle bag. It is just a cloth sack with a drawstring. Some types, such as the stuff bag, have no drawstring.

DUFFLE BAG

SMALL PACK

The second is like a miniature knapsack, much the same size and shape as the outside bags on the large packs. These may be fitted with snaps, straps, or just a loose flap for closing.

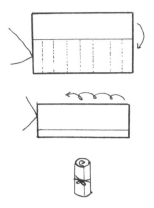

TOOL ROLL

The third type is like the tool rolls for auto tools. It has pockets sewed into the sheet of fabric which holds the equipment in individual compartments. The flap is folded over the top of the pockets to keep them from sliding out, and the whole thing is rolled up and tied with a cord or twill-tapes.

On all equipment bags, waterproofing is optional since they will usually be carried in the protection of the pack.

Thirty-five-millimeter-film containers are good for small items. You can still find some in various colors. They have the added advantage of a gasket in the lid which makes them water-tight. Baking powder or shortening cans make good storage containers, especially for food.

Some method of coding should be used to identify the contents of the bags without unpacking them. Position in the pack, shape, and/or a system of color codes help to identify the various bags.

PACKING

All of your gear should be in (or on) the pack when traveling, regardless of the transportation method employed. Of course, in automobile camping or camping machines, the term "pack" will refer to the boxes and built-in cabinets, but by function they are nonetheless packs. In backpacking, canoe camping, bicycle and horse packing, packs, as the term is usually understood, are essential. In the case of the first two, these mean backpacks, in the latter two, panniers.

The concept of all gear going in the pack also includes items which the Boy Scouts used to, but fortunately no longer, think should go on the belt—such as hatchets, first-aid kits, rope, pocket knives, etc. The only possible exception is a sheath knife, which may be carried on the belt, projecting into the right hip pocket. Of course, a sheathed hatchet or ax may be carried on the belt when making camp—it is much handier that way—but not for walking any distance. You will get a sore leg from the handle hitting it.

Aside from the rules given in this section, the arrangement inside the pack is purely a matter of individual preference. Experiment with several arrangements to find which is the most comfortable for you.

Unlike most packing procedures, the backpack must have the heavy items high and close to the camper for greatest comfort in carrying. When you carry a load on your back, you have to lean forward somewhat to keep from falling backward. The heavier the load, the more you will have to lean forward in order to balance. If the load itself is close to you and high in the pack, you will not have to lean forward as much as with the same weight farther back or closer to the ground. The more erect you can walk, the more comfortable you will be after several hours on the trail.

Protect your back from hard, heavy equipment with blankets or clothing if you use a pack which doesn't have a frame to keep the load off your back. With that exception, always pack heavy gear close and high.

Of course, this must be tempered with moderation. Strike a balance between a load so high you are top-heavy and your balance is hard to maintain, and a load so low that you have to bend too far forward to carry it.

Personally, I prefer to carry my pack low, so it will sit in the small of my back, held by a waistband, but loaded high to make balancing easier. This way most of the load is transmitted directly through my pelvis to my legs and feet, instead of having to go through my shoulders and down my spine, etc., and this way the shoulder straps are used partly for carrying and partly for keeping the pack balanced—about sixty per cent of the weight

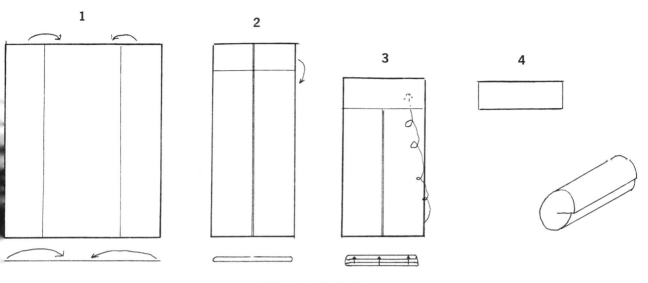

BEDROLL FOLDING

on the waistband and forty per cent on the shoulder straps. A tumpline (which I haven't used enough to become so proficient that it really carries its share) will change the load distribution to thirty per cent on the tumpline, ten per cent on the shoulder straps, and the waistband the same. If I carried loads heavy enough to use the tumpline more often, it would carry almost all the weight.

The only real objection I have to the waistband is that if you are wearing a belt, it tends to get on top of your belt and presses it relentlessly into the top of your pelvis—resulting in rubbed hips and a sore back. Leave off the belt, and everything is fine—as long as your pants fit.

BEDROLL

You can carry a sleeping bag almost anywhere it is comfortable. On top, under the flap, or underneath the whole pack, all in a water-resistant stuff bag, are the most common locations. Inside the pack is usually not possible since it takes up too much of the space needed for carrying other items of gear.

A blanket bedroll is another matter. The bedroll should include a waterproof ground cloth. This should be on the outside of the roll. (It is a good idea to carry one on the outside of an externally carried sleeping bag too, just to give it added protection.) With most packs, it is easier to carry the bedroll in a horseshoe shape, attached to the outside of the pack (as shown in the sketch with the ski-pack description). This will also give you more space inside your pack. When it is properly made, the bedroll holds its shape without being tied.

CHAPTER EIGHT

Tools

Part of the challenge of camping is in trying to reduce the amount of equipment used on the trip as far as is consistent with comfort. In backpacking, this means getting down to essentials or near-essentials. Some form of camping tool is one of these essentials—a vital one.

Camping tools are as old as man himself. Non-humans may, on occasion, use some basic form of tool, improvised from a rock or limb, but only man makes and keeps the tools. Man's progress in pre-history is represented by the material of the tools he used: Old Stone Age, New Stone Age, Bronze Age, etc. Man had tools before he had clothing (since tools are needed to get the materials and to fabricate the clothes from it), and probably even before any form of shelter was developed with more complexity than a simple windbreak or un-improved cave.

Which camping tool you select must depend on the use for which it is intended, the quality of the design, the steel and other materials in it, its comfort in use, and its portability. With one or two types of well-selected tools, camping is easy and rewarding. With poor tools, a carload is inadequate for the job. Many of the camping tools on the market today are of fantastically inferior quality, depending on the average person's unfamiliarity with the marks of quality in order to sell at all.

KNIFE

The most useful tool in any camp is a knife. A two-bladed pocket knife is the usual arrangement. One blade should be two and a half to three inches (65 to 75 mm) long and a half-inch (1 cm) wide, the other two inches (5 cm) long and three-eighths inch (8 mm) wide. The larger one is for rough work and the smaller one should be reserved for fine work. If the knife has three blades, the extra one should be another fine blade. All blades should be kept razor sharp.

It should have a good-quality steel which will hold an edge well, and a bit on the hard side. The handle should be a hard plastic or real antler—bone, ivory, or any of the other fancy materials chip too easily. The frame should be of brass, both because of its strength and because it will not corrode beyond a light-green coating if moisture gets in the blade groove. The springs should be of sufficient strength to hold the blades in both open and closed positions but not too strong to make opening difficult or closing dangerous.

While extra blades, such as a can opener or screwdriver, do work, they have very little value. You will probably never need the average knife-blade screwdriver in camp—it is far too large for any screws or bolts on camping gear. The syrupy mess from a can of beans opened with a knife's can opener will gum up the insides of the knife and will be impossible to remove entirely. The can opener should be in the utensil kit, not on a knife; and if you have equipment which may develop loose screws, a small screwdriver which fits the screws should be carried in the repair kit.

Some campers prefer a sheath knife to a pocket knife. It has the advantage of always being open; you can get it out and use it with only one hand free. It will do heavier work than a pocket knife (including, if necessary, the nearly impossible job of field butchering a deer without a hatchet). However, it can't do fine work like a pocket knife, and even if you do prefer a sheath knife (as I do), you will still end up carrying a pocket knife as well.

No camper's sheath knife should have a blade over five inches (12$\frac{1}{2}$ cm) long. The Bowie pattern, with its double edge at the tip, is more of a hazard than a useful camping tool. The Bowie knife is not even a skinning knife. The tenderfoot seems to think that since the frontiersman was a good camper and carried a Bowie knife, such a knife is an indispensable tool of good campers. Actually, the Bowie knife was a fighting knife. The frontiersman carried it as a reserve weapon to use when he didn't have time to reload his single-shot Kentucky rifle. As a result, the true Bowie knife was more of a short, heavy sword, often having a sixteen-inch (40 cm) long blade and weighing a couple of pounds (about 1 kg). His pack horse carried a full-size ax while he possibly carried a tomahawk (used for fighting by the frontiersman as well as the Indian); a small knife on the strap of his gun pouch was used for skinning game, cutting rifle-ball patches, and the more normal camping activities.

While fewer manufacturers are making Bowie knives these days, the sheath knives they are making leave much to be desired. They are still too long. Even when they are short enough, they are too thick, often still retaining the fighting knife's blood groove along the back. They are typically too hard a steel, so that breaking is a distinct possibility (which is probably the real reason they are so thick). They usually have leather washer-handles which, while they look nice, are easily damaged by the heat and moisture of cooking—and a sheath knife should be prepared to do double duty in this regard when going light.

The ideal camper's sheath knife can cost under a dollar. One of the best on the mass market is a utility knife from a leathercraft store. It is a fairly soft steel as knives go (although not soft by other standards), and it is made to be resharpened often. Leather is rougher on knife edges than any other material, paper included, so the knife designed for leather will be good for any other purpose. Also important, it has a thin blade. You have to take care of it, as it will snap if you are careless, but with proper precautions it will last indefinitely. It has a wooden handle which will hold up under any condition, and the handle is riveted on with large brass rivets.

In fact, while you are in the store, you might as well pick up a bit of eight-ounce tooling cow, a dozen snap rivets, and be prepared to make a proper sheath for your knife. If you don't have leatherworking tools and business is slack when you are there, you can probably borrow the tools and put it together on the spot. The only important thing to remember about a knife sheath (or an ax sheath) is that it must be fastened with rivets. A fancy lacing will look very nice, but if there is not a row of rivets, spaced close enough so that the knife cannot go between them, the knife will cut its way out in a remarkably short period of time. When this happens, it is as dangerous as if it had no sheath at all—perhaps a little more so, since you wouldn't be prepared.

The sheath should have two thicknesses of leather on the back—even the rather square-tipped leathercraft knives can cut through a sheath in use, but the knife will usually hang up in the space between the layers and let you know that you need a new sheath. This is a far better reminder for you than being stabbed.

With the more conventional pointed knife, a metal lining is advisable. If you are buying the sheath, make sure it has such a lining. If you are making your own (or can't buy such a sheath), make a lining from a proper-sized copper or soft brass tube. Get as thin a wall as possible and still have a rigid tube. Flatten it very carefully. The knife should slide in and out easily, but still not have too thick a sheath.

Even without the lining, the sheath should be stiff. Don't use neat's-foot oil or other leather softeners on the sheath. The best finish is one of the compounds used to fix the tooled design in leather. It waterproofs the leather and stiffens it slightly.

USING THE KNIFE

The first rule is to keep the blade(s) sharp. A sharp knife cuts better and with less effort. It is safer because it is more easily controlled. A dull knife will require excessive force to move it and, should it slip, it cannot be stopped quickly. As a result, it is more likely to cut you. Even if you should cut yourself with a sharp knife, it is not likely to be as deep and it will certainly heal quicker than the half-torn cut from a dull blade.

The best way to sharpen a knife is to use diagonal strokes on the whetstone to get the edge. Then use a few rotary strokes to remove the burrs. This is faster than just the rotary strokes and doesn't produce as large a burr as straight strokes do. A leather whetstone case can double as a hone to finish the sharpening. Rub a little jeweler's rouge into the leather on one side.

The proper way to sharpen a knife. Note that the fingers are below the surface of the whetstone to avoid any possibility of getting cut.

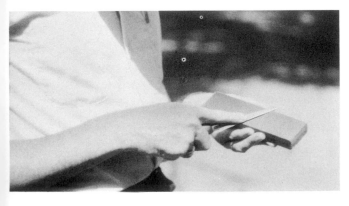

On rough work, always cut away from you. This is not only safer, it gives you more leverage. Only on fine cutting with a pocket knife is it ever permissible to cut toward you. Even then, it should be restricted to short, smoothing cuts which can't be made from any other angle.

When you carry a knife, it should always be closed or in its sheath. A sheath should be worn on the belt with the point sticking in the hip pocket. Carrying the sheath in front is dangerous as a fall could ram the point into the femoral artery in the pit of the groin. Even if the sheath is sturdy enough to protect you from the point, it will produce a painful bruise.

When passing a pocket knife, fold it first. When passing a sheath knife, place the knife flat on the extended hand, the handle toward the receiver—who takes it carefully by the handle, being careful to turn the edge upward to avoid scratching the hand. A snap on the belt loop of the sheath is a useful modification of the standard pattern. This will permit the sheath to be removed without taking off the belt. With such a rig, the sheath knife can be passed in its sheath in total safety. It is quite simple to reach back and flip the snap open to remove the sheath with the knife in it. When sheathing, make sure the knife is going into the sheath and not your pocket.

AX AND HATCHET

There was a time when every true woodsman carried a full-length ax. The hatchet was looked down upon as a sign of a tenderfoot. Wood was plentiful then and a good woodsman could build a shelter in half a day to use as a base of operations. Today, anyone wanting that type of shelter should stick to the cabins. Wood is too precious to waste on shelters that are used only for a short time and then allowed to fall into ruins. Almost all public camping areas prohibit such cutting anyway.

Since there is no longer any need for extensive heavy cutting, the hatchet is now the most common camp wood-chopping tool. However, this does not mean that the ax is no longer of any use. The hatchet is really too small to be efficient. The three-quarter ax is used much more than the full ax in camping now. It is both light in weight and an efficient wood cutter. The full ax is generally left to the lumbermen who need its size. However, if you have the means of transportation, the full ax is more comfortable in a prolonged chopping session.

What is the best camping-ax design depends on the type of camping done. With a large group in a wilderness area, a full-size lumberman's ax is still needed, even when backpacking. In less demanding conditions, a three-and-a-half-pound ($1\frac{1}{2}$ kg) ax is enough and a two-and-three-quarter-pound ($1\frac{1}{4}$ kg) single-bit ax is adequate. If you are going light and will still need an ax, the Hudson Bay pattern is probably best. It has a lighter head than the regular styles, but cuts almost as efficiently.

The double-bitted ax is excellent in full length, but seems to lose some of its wonderful balance with the shorter handle. The double-bitted hatchets are absolutely dangerous in all but the most skilled hands. The straight-handled, double-bitted axes have the advantage of an excellent balance and two edges so that you can cut for the day without having to stop to resharpen. The single-bitted ax has the advantage of having a tent-stake-driving maul, which is useful for pounding wooden stakes (but not metal ones). Also, it is a bit safer in the hands of beginners at chopping.

The steel in an ax head should be rather mild, as it will nick very easily if too hard. This not only makes sharpening easier, but required much more often. The width of the head at the handle should be at least two inches (5 cm) in the Hudson Bay pattern and three or more inches (75 mm or more) in the more standard shapes.

The handle should be straight-grained and free from any defects in the wood, such as knots, checks, etc. A double-bitted ax has a straight handle, gently tapered to a slightly flaring tip. A single-bitted ax has a curved handle. Test the feel to make sure that they are comfortable. Practically all single-bitted ax handles come with the "fawn's foot" tip which comes to a point at the end. This is not only useless, it is a detriment to secure ax heads. Cut it off about halfway along the straight slope and seal the scar with linseed oil or shellac to prevent moisture from entering.

The handle should not be painted, as that makes it hard on the hands and liable to slip as well.

The same qualities should be used in selecting a hatchet as for an ax, although a smaller head-size is permitted. As stated earlier, avoid double-bitted hatchets. There are some excellent one-piece models which avoid the problem of loose heads by making them a part of the handle. There is no eye to spring or handle to come loose or break. However, stay clear of those with heads which are thin as a piece of heavy sheet steel; get a head that is practically as thick as a wooden-handled model. The thin ones simply don't hold up and are too light-headed to do the job. A machete is better, and slightly lighter. (A one-piece ax is on the market now, and it is terrible. There is practically no weight at the head, where it is needed.)

Unfortunately, most of the one-piece hatchets use rubber, neoprene, or vinyl-nylon handles. Estwing used to make hatchets and half-hatchets with a leather washer-handle (similar to the leather-handle knives, but much more reasonable, since it is not subject to the adverse conditions that a knife is). They are still available if you look hard enough.

The main advantage of the wooden and leather handles over the cushions found on the one-piece models is that they transmit the shock of impact instead of cushioning it. While at first glance, this seems to be more of a disadvantage than an advantage, the opposite is true. While the cushions may feel more comfortable at the time of the impact, it is no way to learn to chop effectively. If you make a bad or ineffective stroke with a wood or leather handle, you feel it. This type of handle will make you automatically improve your chopping in self-defense. After a few hard stings, you will find that you have learned to use the hatchet much more efficiently. (Actually, these shocks are not really painful, just uncomfortable. In the long run, they are less painful than the sore arm you would get from ineffective chopping.)

A variant on the hatchet has more advantages than the standard model. Since an ax or hatchet may be damaged by using it to hammer metal (because of the softness of the steel), the half-hatchet is sometimes used as a substitute. The half-hatchet has a regular hatchet blade on one end

A wide variety of axes. Reading from the top, they are: a double-bitted ax, a three-quarters ax, a full ax, a half-hatchet, and a hatchet with sheath.

of its head and a hammer on the other. Because the hammer is tempered for the job, it can be used to hammer metal stakes or nails without damage. It is also available in the one-piece version. In addition, it is slightly lighter in weight than the standard hatchet.

USING THE AX AND HATCHET

Sharpening

The standard rule for edged tools applies here— keep the edge sharp. A surprising number of campers have more of a rounded wedge than an edge on their axes or hatchets. This has apparently been the situation for some time, for Thoreau remarked, "Near the end of March, 1845, I borrowed an axe and went down to the woods by Walden Pond. . . . The owner of the axe, as he released his hold on it, said that it was the apple of his eye; but I returned it sharper than I received it."

Sharpening an ax or hatchet requires two tools: a mill file and a double-grit whetstone. For safety

and efficiency, you must anchor the ax firmly. At home use a vise. In the field, wedge the head and handle between two pairs of stakes with the edge of the ax upward. With the file, use downward strokes, first on one side of the head and then on the other. Remove burrs and increase the sharpness with the whetstone. Use straight strokes, as you did with the file, with the coarse side of the stone; use rotary strokes with the fine side. You won't need to take the file on the camping trip if you use the whetstone after every cutting session with the ax or hatchet. A small pocket on the ax sheath makes a good storage place for the whetstone in the field. A double-bitted ax is held for sharpening by masking one edge into a log while sharpening the other edge.

Safety

While the first rule of ax and hatchet safety is to keep it sharp so it will cut into the wood rather than bounce around all over the place, the second is to keep your head—not just your own, but the ax's as well. The idea of soaking the head to tighten

First use a mill file, . . .

. . . then a whetstone. The whetstone is held the same as when sharpening a knife since a properly sharpened ax can cut the fingers just as easily.

Sharpening a double-bitt ax is done the same way, but mask the other bitt rather than resting it on the ground. With a small log, stakes will keep it from rolling.

it is no good. You might tighten it for a few minutes (after several hours of soaking) but it will dry out in use and be even more of a danger than before.

There is only one proper way to tighten an ax head, and that is with the correct combination of wedges. First make a saw cut in the handle along the long dimension of the head and a little over half as deep as the head is wide. Bed the head on the handle by hitting the foot of the handle (which is why the foot must be cut off flat). This is more efficient than if you hammered the head onto the handle, since the head has more inertia.

After the head is as tight as it will go onto the handle, place a wooden wedge in the saw cut and pound it down as far as it will go, flaring the part of the handle sticking out of the eye over the head as well. Then saw off all but about one-eighth inch of the handle over the head. Finally, put in one or two small metal wedges, crossways to the wooden wedge to flare the handle along the long dimension of the eye. Paint the end with linseed oil or clear shellac to keep out moisture, which will loosen the head.

Both the ax and the hatchet should be equipped with a sheath. Keep it in the sheath when you aren't using it. If you just stop for a short while (to build up a fire, check the cooking, pull up another log to cut to length, or just to rest), mask it. Chop it into a large piece of wood and leave it imbedded there. You could mask a double-bitted ax by masking one edge in a small piece of log, then masking the other edge as usual, being careful to leave the small piece still attached; but putting it back in its sheath is easier. Never mask an ax or hatchet in the ground. Such treatment will dull it and may even nick the edge.

There is a slight danger in handing the ax or hatchet from one person to another. The best way is for the person having the ax to hold it by the head, the edge pointing away from both persons. A firm grip over the eye is what is needed. The ax is handed and the person receiving it takes it by the handle, just under the head. This is better than the inverted, end-of-the-handle method which may allow the ax head to swing and holds the greater danger that one person's grip may slip and drop the ax. The receiver should say "thank you" when he gets a proper hold on it. This is more than just politeness, it is a signal to the person handing it that he can let go.

Care

In order to take care of the ax and hatchet properly, there are several do's and don't's. As mentioned before, don't hammer metal unless your tool has a hammer head, the poll isn't tempered for it; and don't use it as a sledge hammer on rocks under any circumstances. It isn't a wedge either.

Keep it out of the sun and away from the fire as the heat can hurt the temper. Use a chopping block so you don't even accidentally chop it into the ground. In cold weather, warm the head to a

The safe way to pass an ax. The person receiving it will slide his hand up the handle to the head before taking hold of it. The edge is pointing slightly away from the person holding it.

An ax should not be used to hammer metal or as a wedge. This one was.

temperature which is comfortable in the hand. A cold edge may break on impact if it isn't warmed up first. If it should become wet, dry and oil it. A small pill bottle of penetrating oil is good for this purpose and doesn't take up much space in the pack.

Make sure of your target so you don't nick the handle on the log or otherwise strain it. Keep the handle smooth and the head on tight. Keep the edge sharp with a few strokes of the whetstone after each chopping session.

Chopping

In camping today, you will seldom, if ever, have the opportunity to fell a tree. Still, the occasion may arise and you should know the procedure, just in case.

You should have a clear area equal to twice the reach of the tool with your arm extended. You will not need that much space normally, but blown branches and slipped strokes can take up much of it. If a branch so much as touches your ax while you are swinging it, it may be deflected just enough to be dangerous. Regardless of what you are cutting, make sure that no matter how the ax or hatchet may slip, it can't possibly cut you. Both tools are dangerous when handled carelessly.

Also make sure that there is room for you to move out of the way when the tree starts to fall. This not only includes the obvious direction the tree is falling, but also the opposite direction (trees often jump back as they fall), and a couple of yards to either side (they will roll if they land on a particularly stout branch). This means that the footing along your route of escape must be firm—this is no place to trip. Attention to this sure footing includes clearing away the chips from time to time if they build up too thickly, as well as making sure there are no obstructions in the way.

The first step in felling (after the chopping area is cleared) is to choose the direction the tree will fall. If there is no absolute requirement of one particular direction, the logical choice is in the direction the tree is leaning. The ax itself is an excellent tool to measure this lean. Hold the ax by the end of the handle so that the head hangs down. Sight along the length of the head and

USING AX AS PLUMB

compare the vertical line of the handle with the lean of the tree. Your first cut will be on the side of the lean.

Whether you are felling the tree down-lean or not, the first cut will be on the side of the fall. Make the initial notch as low as is comfortable. This is a conservation rule. There is no need to leave high stumps around a cleared area. The stumps are no good as trees and no good as field—they just get in the way. Often they will sprout again, and if the tree wasn't cut to clear space or because it was dead or diseased, it should have been left standing in the first place.

The bottom of the notch should be level and the upper edge should be at a forty-five-degree angle to it. This initial cut should be a little more than halfway through the tree; therefore, the greatest opening of the notch should be a little more than half the diameter of the tree at that point.

The felling notch should be directly on the opposite side of the tree and slightly higher than the initial notch. This part can be sawed horizontally or chopped with a similarly proportioned notch.

When you start hearing the fibers breaking, stop chopping and see if they continue to break. If not,

CORRECT NOTCH

start chopping again. If they keep breaking, start moving back. When the tree actually starts to fall, yell "timber" if anyone is around, and keep out of its way.

While felling is a rare camp job these days, cutting up deadfalls which block a trail or stream is still fairly common in the wilderness areas. When traveling in these areas, a full-size ax is a requirement. Typically, these jobs require the removal of at least some branches to get at the log itself to cut.

When lopping branches from a limb or trunk, cut up-branch to avoid jamming the ax in the wood

LOPPING

at the crotch. The wood is so hard and the grain so twisted at this point, you can easily break an ax head this way. Stay on the opposite side of the trunk from the limbs—they may deflect the ax up-limb if the ax doesn't bite well. Roll the trunk off the branches it is resting on before trying to cut them. They are far easier and safer to lop off if there is no pressure on them. Otherwise, the trunk might start rolling on you.

When chopping heavy wood, make a V-notch as broad as the diameter of the log. Make the cut on the side, not the top of the log. You not only get better leverage that way, you reduce the chance of cutting into the ground and ruining the edge.

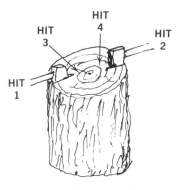

SPLITTING SEQUENCE

In splitting a large piece of wood, there is no substitute for a wedge; so don't try to use an ax or hatchet as one. Don't use the ax or hatchet on metal of any kind. However, either may be used on wooden stakes or wedges, and the big advantage of the standard ax-head shape is the use of the poll as a maul in driving such items. Two axes, one attacking the log at a time and the other left in place, make good wedges. Hit the log at the edge and leave the ax in it (as in masking, only deeper), then hit the opposite side of the same end with the other ax; remove the first ax and repeat the whole procedure until the log is split completely.

Gluts are wooden wedges used in splitting logs. The best wood to use for making them is dogwood or hornbeam. The easiest way to drive them is with

CUTTING A LOG

a maul. The maul can be as simple as a short length of three-inch (75 mm) diameter log. Make the initial split with the ax. Place a glut in the split and remove the ax. By alternately driving the gluts and extending the split with the ax, split the length of the log.

Unless you are in the far wilderness with a fairly large group, establishing a permanent campsite, or in an overcrowded public campground in which the only wood furnished is log-size, the most chopping you will ever do in camping will be sticks. Unfortu-

nately, this does not always make the job any easier. The average tenderfoot tends to use the bang-and-duck method in which the two ends of the severed stick fly off in all directions and to astonishing distances.

Always cut at an angle when cutting a stick to length. This reduces the distance the end will fly. It is also easier since the edge bites deeper into the wood than if it had been hit at a right angle to the grain. Use a chopping block, not the ground, to hold the wood. Any sizeable log will do.

In splitting a small piece of wood, there are two techniques; one works best with an ax, the other with a hatchet. The ax technique works best with a forked log for the chopping block. Place the stick against the chopping block (in the fork, if there is one). Wedge the end in the ground so it won't tend to fly up when hit. Chop into the end of the stick. If it is not split the full length, leave it on the ax and bring it down, stick and ax together, on the chopping block. Bend saplings when cutting them down.

With a hatchet, the easiest way looks dangerous. Hold the stick upright with one hand and let go of it just as you start your swing down with the

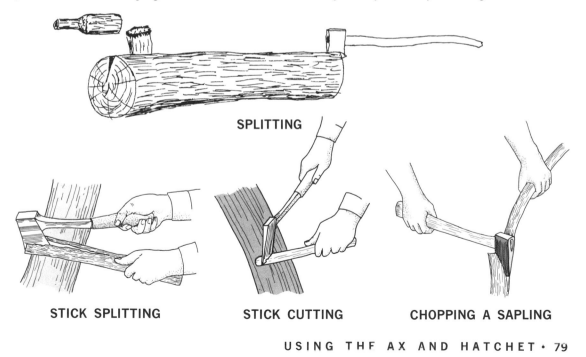

SPLITTING

STICK SPLITTING   **STICK CUTTING**   **CHOPPING A SAPLING**

hatchet. Inertia will hold it in place until the hatchet hits it. Treat one not completely split the same as with the ax: leave it on the hatchet and bring them down together onto the chopping block.

The hatchet has neither the weight nor the leverage that the ax has. The temptation is to "lean into it" more to compensate for this deficiency, but it is easier to go slow and make each stroke count. This "go easy" rule applies equally well to the ax, although it is more natural with the larger tool.

A good practice routine with the ax or hatchet is to wedge a kitchen match upright in a block of wood and try to split the match and ignite it. Naturally, do this in your back yard since the camp is no place to be playing with matches. Since being able to hit the exact spot is the most important skill with these edged tools, this is one of the best ways to improve axmanship ever devised. When you become proficient at it, start angling the matches to correspond with the line of strokes for cutting logs. Chopping is done by alternating two angles: a right angle to the bite in the wood, then one at about 45° to clear out the chip. After you are able to hit a vertical match stuck into the bark, the next stage is to set up two matches, one in the position of the initial right-angle cut, the second in the position of the 45°-angle cut. Then, using the same rhythm you use when chopping, light the two matches in sequence, one stroke per match. When you can do this, you can do anything that needs to be done with an ax in the field. The same techniques are usable with the hatchet and machete also.

MACHETE

The machete is a long, heavy knife designed for cutting cane and jungle vines. Its principal use in camping is as a lightweight substitute for the hatchet. It is definitely too light for heavy wood-cutting, but will do fairly well on light firewood. Since this is practically the only chopping to be done in most camping situations these days, this is not a major objection. Its light weight is a decided advantage over the heavier hatchet when going light.

Besides its advantage of lightness, it is the only camp tool that can cut grass (except, of course, the knife, and that takes too much work). This feature is handy in clearing the campsite and paths, or getting grass for bedding or grease traps. It is a survival tool of the best quality, doing quickly what a sheath knife does slowly, leaving more time for other activities.

The surplus machetes are no good. There is almost always a groove in the handle where the metal doesn't quite come up to the level of the wood or plastic. This is most uncomfortable to use. Also, they are of a quite poor grade of steel and won't hold an edge. Machetes made for cane cutters and surveyors are top quality and very comfortable to swing. They cost a lot more (but no more than a good hatchet), and are worth it. Incongruously enough, you can buy them at many large drafting-supply stores because they cater to the surveyor and cartographer trade, but you will rarely find them stocked in sporting-goods stores. The forester's version, with a brush hook, is also good—especially with saplings.

USING THE MACHETE

The machete is a knife and should be sharpened the same way. It must be sharp; a dull machete is practically useless. For chopping wood, the technique is similar to that used on heavy wood with a hatchet—take it easy and make every stroke count. It doesn't have much weight, but good aim will help make up for it.

For painless chopping, think of a baseball bat. There is a spot, the center of percussion to the physicists, which will not set up the vibrations which create the sting of a bad stroke. Find that point on the machete and make that the point of impact when chopping. Pull it toward you just as you hit, so that the blade will slice into the wood rather than bite into it as an ax does. This increases the efficiency of the tool.

Keep it in its sheath when you are not using it. It can't be masked. Be sure of your swinging area—it is a most deadly weapon otherwise.

Carrying a machete hanging from your belt may make you look like the intrepid explorer, but it is a poor way to carry it. It will keep banging your leg as you walk and will get in the way as you bend and crouch when setting up camp. Rather carry it either between your pack and frame or on the side of the pack. This way, it won't get in your way, but you can get to it easily by reaching over your shoulder.

If you carry it between your pack and pack frame, the edge should be toward the hand you draw it with. This prevents the machete from swinging up, edge forward. You may get a most unusual haircut if you neglect this simple precaution. The machete will be backward in your hand and you will have to turn it around when it is out.

If you carry a machete on the side of your pack, the edge should face away from you since it may come in contact with your shoulder while being drawn. Be sure no one is close behind you when you draw it. The handle is in the correct position when you draw it this way.

Aside from that, the machete is treated either as a knife or a hatchet, as the situation requires.

SHOVEL

A small shovel is handy around camp. The entrenching shovel folds into a small package and is fairly light in weight. You can pick one up for a reasonable price at a surplus store. You can make an even lighter version by removing the handle that comes with it and using a heavy stick cut in camp for the handle. There are times when it is too light for fast work, but keep at it. Remember, it has made fox-holes in some mighty hard ground.

For large groups backpacking together, a garden trowel will be most useful, provided it is sturdy. In this situation, excavation is a fairly light job— latrines and an occasional fire hole being the total job required. In well-grassed areas, the trowel is far more efficient than bare hands.

SAW

There are basically two types of saws for camping, although even the standard carpenter's rip saw will work. The first is the bow saw or Swedish saw. This is a tubular steel U- or L-shaped frame with a miniature version of the big lumberman's crosscut

saw for a blade. It cuts wood better than any saw except the big crosscut or powered chain saws. Its only disadvantage is its bulk and its one and a third pounds of weight.

The U-shaped frame is vastly superior to the slightly more compact L, since the acute angle where the long part of the L and the blade meet prevents the full length of the blade from being used. The important quality point to watch for is the blade. It should be quite sharp and have a definite musical tone when plucked. There should be sufficient depth between the teeth to keep them from filling with sawdust when working. The blade holders should not be able to come apart or out from the frame, as this invites loss. Extra blades should be obtainable and you should get one extra when you buy the saw. Treated well, they will last a lifetime, but accidents do, unfortunately, happen.

The second type of saw is the wire-saw blade. It has a spirally cut tooth running the length of the wire. At each end of the wire is a ring. Two people can hold the rings and use it like a big crosscut saw, but it is more comfortable to put sticks through the rings and hold to these handles. It can also be strung in a bowed stick and used as a bow

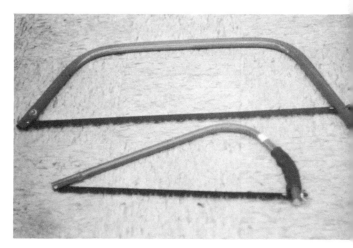

Two types of bow saw. The lower one has a twenty-inch blade, the upper one a twenty-eight-inch.

saw by one person. It is tiring to use and cuts rather slowly; but it cuts, nonetheless. Since it weighs only a half-ounce (15 g), its best use is as a hatchet substitute while backpacking.

Other saws have been crowded out of the camping picture by these two, but they have some points of value and should not be overlooked just because they aren't best sellers.

The old-fashioned buck saw has been almost replaced by the bow saw, but has several advantages over it. First of all, it is easy to make, using a bow-saw blade. In fact, there are plans for one in Chapter 15. Secondly, it is fairly light in weight, only consisting of three pieces of wood, four bolts, and some parachute cord in addition to the blade. The wood can protect the blade from snagging on anything and the parachute cord keeps the pieces together. A stick, found in camp, is used to operate the tourniquet tie that provides the tension on the blade.

Pruning saws are also used in camping, especially the folding versions. They are sort of a cross between a keyhole saw and a crosscut saw with a bit of jackknife occasionally thrown in. They are made for cutting tree limbs, so they are ideally suited for the job in camp. They are a bit slow-cutting for their size and the groove in the handle of the folding models is uncomfortable; still, they are fairly light in weight. The rigid model poses a problem of sheathing the blade since the teeth cut a bit sideways and this wears out the sheath.

Other saws are either too bulky, heavy, or inefficient to bother taking to camp.

GEOLOGIST'S PICK

The geologist's pick is included in this chapter because it is the greatest aid to camping since the invention of the waterproof match. Also called a prospector's pick, rock-hound pick, etc., it weighs one and three-quarters pounds (800 g). It has a square hammer head opposite a pick.

If you get a pick, be sure to get one that is one piece, head and handle. A wooden handle will wear in two just below the head from striking rocks. The handle itself has a few uses. The leather-handle

Two potential camping tools. The mason's hammer is on the left and the geologist's pick on the right.

Estwing is best and is still available, generally from rock-hound outfitters, if you look hard enough.

The first cousin to the geologist's pick is the mason's hammer. Instead of the pick point, it has a chisel edge an inch or so (about 25 mm) wide. This difference has both an advantage and a disadvantage. The broad edge is better for digging out a hole and for chopping wood. The edge is a passable adz. However, you can't keep an edge sharp enough for chopping if you dig with it. The geologist's pick splits rather than cuts because of the small area of pressure, therefore it does not need an absolutely sharp point as an edged tool does.

USING THE GEOLOGIST'S PICK

For once, sharpness is unimportant as long as there is a point.

While it is a poor substitute for the hatchet, a geologist's pick can be used for one. For splitting, use whittled hardwood wedges; or if it is a small diameter, hit it hard with the narrow edge of the handle (another advantage of the one-piece model). Squaw wood (dead wood still on the tree) can easily be broken with the handle or by chipping with the

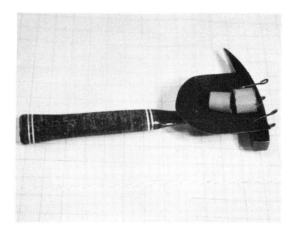

The modified geologist's pick, folded for carry-ing . . .

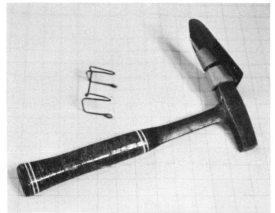

. . . and as a shovel.

point until the piece is small enough in diameter to break off.

The pick's real advantage comes in the things that you can't do at all with a hatchet. The pick is perfect for digging holes, especially in rocky soil. Cooking-fire holes, hip and shoulder holes for sleeping, tent ditching, and latrines are all a cinch for this tool. And it will do it in most any type of soil, rocky or not. Loosen up the soil with the pick and scrape it out with the side of the head or with your hands.

The pick is also useful for lifting pots off the fire or removing lids to check cooking. However, don't use it for a fire poker—there's a limit even for this tool. The temper is needed on rocks.

With a small application of do-it-yourself skills, you can fix up a geologist's pick into a multiple-use camping tool which needs only the accompaniment of a good knife to handle all your camp problems in less than two pounds' total weight. Plans for this modification are given in Chapter 15.

CHAPTER NINE

Miscellaneous Equipment

Much of the equipment you need in camp does not fit into the categories covered by the first five chapters on equipment. These accessories are necessary for a well-run camp, yet few people take sufficient care in their selection. Few of these items cost over a couple of dollars, yet most buyers look only at the price tag rather than the performance data. Like most camping equipment, a little more expenditure at the time of purchase will save itself many times over in trouble-free operation, light weight, and small bulk, when used in the field.

MATCH SAFE

An adequate supply of matches is a necessity in any camp. All of them should be the large, wooden, kitchen-type matches which have been waterproofed. Melted paraffin or shellac makes a good coating to keep out moisture. Both are inflammable and increase the temperature of the flame. Coat the entire match to prevent the water from reaching the waterproofed head from inside the wood.

Safety matches are worthless for camping. Not only does a little moisture ruin them, they don't even burn hot enough to ignite wood easily. Moisture will also ruin the special striking surfaces they require. Because of their paper packaging, sweat in the pocket will supply the moisture just as readily as a downpour or an accident at a stream crossing.

Even waterproofed matches won't hold out in

a prolonged soaking, so store them in a waterproof container. The little plastic pill bottles are adequate as well as cheap. A small bottle will hold a week's supply. Glue a strip of medium-grit sandpaper to the side to provide a sure striking surface for wet weather.

The best commercial match safe is made by Marble. Since it is drawn aluminum, it cannot crack, break, or come apart at the seams if you should fall or drop something on it. A rubber gasket seals it completely watertight.

COMPASS

Anytime you get away from the well-marked trails, out of sight or sound of the main tourist areas, you will need a compass and a map. Even within the more populated areas of these regions, the compass is useful if there are several forks in the trail system. In the wilderness, it is of primary importance.

You can make a compass by floating a magnetized needle on the surface of an overfilled glass of water (the water kept in the glass only by its surface tension). However, such a compass is plainly limited to grade-school science labs. A proper compass for camping is going to cost money—there is no way around it. In fact, it is by far the most expensive item in this whole chapter.

All good compasses have several features in

common. They have either a liquid-filled housing or a magnetic induction system so the needle stops swinging quickly. A jeweled needle-bearing allows free movement of the needle. Often a lock on the needle protects the bearing from damage from jarring when not in use, but this is not necessary in liquid-damped compasses.

Some means of declination correction is provided, making it unnecessary for you to compute the declination every time you read your compass. Some form of illumination—either a luminous dial or a mirror or both—is provided for reading it in poor light. A map-making card (usually a plastic or aluminum rectangle holding the compass) marked in inches and centimeters is for making maps as you go. An unbreakable (in normal use) housing, including a cover, is a must in the wilderness. And finally, it is marked accurately to the nearest one or two degrees.

The old surplus Army lensatic compass lacks the map card, but it is good for following straight-line compass bearings since the prism in the sight lets you read the compass dial and look at your line of travel at the same time, in order to find a target landmark more accurately. It is tops in the sport of orienteering.

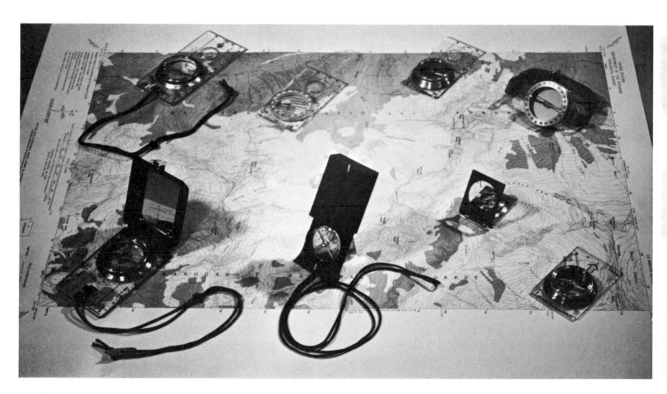

Campers' compasses. Clockwise from the upper left: three map-making compasses, a wrist compass, another map-making compass, a trail compass that pins on your shirt so the dial is always facing upward, a sighting compass which slides into the box for protection, and a combination sighting and map-making compass with the sighting mirror built into the protective lid.

A couple of the more expensive Silva compasses have all of the map-making features, plus a sighting arrangement that gives the lensatic compass's advantage as well. They cost close to fifteen dollars, but they are the best on the market, short of getting into the extremely expensive alidades and other pocket-sized surveyor's gear.

The compass should be safeguarded against loss either by pinning it to your shirt pocket (many models come equipped with a safety pin attached to the housing) or on a lanyard around your neck or belt loop. The shirt pocket is the best place to carry it since you are less likely to land on it hard in case of a fall.

Instructions for using a compass begin on page 349.

LIGHTS

There are many types of lights used in camping. Each type has its advantages and disadvantages. Which is the best one for you will depend on the type of camping you are doing, and how much you are willing to work to get the light. Generally speaking, the faster the lighting or the brighter the light, the heavier it is and therefore the more difficult to carry with the rest of the gear.

Candle

A steric-acid plumber's candle is good for going light. With it you can start a fire with damp wood or give light to your tent. It burns slowly, hotly, and with a bright flame, and, most important, it won't melt in the heat of your pack as a paraffin candle will.

A lantern improves its light. You can make a stonebridge lantern but it is quite bulky for just a candle. You can buy a compact candle lantern for less than you would spend to make the much larger stonebridge.

The Ski Hut's 1966 catalog supplement had a tongue-in-cheek ad for one of these which, despite the schmaltzy words, does sum up the advantages of the candle lantern. "Forget not the homely virtue

Campers' lights come in a wide variety of types—large lanterns for car camping, headlamps for spelunking, regular flashlights, carbide lamps . . .

. . . candle lanterns in the small collapsible type and the larger folding stonebridge, and mantle-type lanterns using butane or gasoline.

of the candle: no moving parts, 100% reliability, soft and steadfast glow. Our one-candlepower model lantern weighs less than a flashlight, operates modestly on our seven-cent stearine candles. Its warm, suffusing light quiets the anxious heart and draws wisdom from the mouths of philosophers."

Electricity

A flashlight is the handiest type of light since you only have to switch it on or off. However, you should carry an extra set of batteries and an extra bulb, and this makes it fairly heavy. Be sure and tape the switch in the off-position or reverse one

battery to prevent the batteries being drained by the flashlight accidentally turning on in the pack.

Dry-cell batteries lose power in cold weather, so when the temperature is below freezing, you will have to take the flashlight into your sleeping bag with you.

Flashlights are usually spotlights and won't light up a very large area. Those which have the floodlight lens tend to spread the light too much and are, as a result, generally too dim.

The little pencell flashlights are excellent for backpacking. They are generally made as key rings and hold one battery and use a magnified tip bulb.

They weigh only a couple of ounces and are great for lighting up the trail or tending to the tent at night.

The rechargeable batteries (nickel-cadmium, etc.) stand the cold better (down to about zero F.) but don't have as much power in relation to their weight. The pencell size, however, will be just as serviceable as the dry cell. You can get them from model-airplane supply stores where they are used in radio-controlled models. You will have to buy a separate charger for the smaller sizes, but you can get the larger ones with built-in rechargers.

Liquid Fuel

Lanterns (kerosene, gasoline, or bottled gas) are brighter than either candles or flashlights. However, they are too bulky and heavy for anything but auto camping. The fuel of the kerosene and gasoline lanterns is hard to store since even the fumes will taint food. You will have to carry two bottles of the LP gas, since there is no way to tell when the bottle is getting empty, except by weighing—and you will have to work out your own charts on burning time remaining in a bottle since each has a different weight and burning speed is not evenly proportional to the weight remaining. The bug-drawing power of these lanterns is amazing. Yet they are fairly trouble-free and provide the most light for the trouble.

While gasoline lanterns today are far less bother than the temperamental ones of the first half of the century, there are still a few things that can go wrong. The mantles are still rather delicate things and you had best carry one or two spares. They weigh only a little and the lantern is not much good without them.

A spare generator is also welcome in case anything goes wrong with the one in the lantern. The rest, pumps and such, are usually quite dependable, but you should check them over carefully before starting on your trip.

Kerosene lanterns are not as bright as gasoline lanterns, and they smell a bit worse, but they have a softer light and don't draw as many bugs. They also have fewer things to go wrong with them. The only care they need is a periodic cleaning of the glass and trimming of the wick. This can be kept to a minimum by keeping the flame low and clear.

LP-gas lanterns have no problem other than the mantle, but they do have a weight problem with the spare tank. While they are the cleanest and brightest, and relatively trouble-free, that extra tank brings them back alongside the gasoline lantern in over-all practicality.

Carbide Lamp

The carbide lamp is probably the best general-purpose camp light. Its qualities are exceeded only by the light weight of the candle and the speed of lighting of the flashlight. It burns brightly, but you can control its brightness from that of a single candle to an automobile headlight on "bright." It not only draws less bugs than a flashlight (at a more normal light intensity), it exterminates the ones it does draw with the flame. Yet the flame is not hot enough to be a fire hazard and it is quite difficult to ignite anything with it—it usually just soots it up. The lamp, with one week's supply of fuel, weighs about the same as a comparable flashlight without the spare batteries.

The carbide lamp works by dripping water over small chunks of calcium carbide. This liberates acetylene gas (the same as in a welding torch), which is burned with the oxygen in the air to produce the light. A sparking flint on the reflector is used to light it and so saves your matches. In below-freezing weather, you will have to keep the water from freezing, but you can use your drinking water for the purpose.

Like matches, the carbide should be kept in a waterproof container. This means completely waterproof. Not only will water reduce the amount of acetylene that can be liberated in your lamp, the gas is highly inflammable and a leaking container could be a fire hazard. Under certain conditions (in cave streams) these containers have even exploded. (Of course, the same thing can be said about the fuel for gasoline lanterns, but people more readily recognize the danger and avoid the problem.) Besides, leaking acetylene stinks. An ideal way to carry carbide is to seal several small packages, each containing enough carbide for one loading of the lamp. These can be kept completely sealed until needed. It is also an easy way to

A carbide lamp with normal and large reflectors and a can of fuel.

measure the needed amount of carbide in the dark.

The carbide lamp, like the gasoline lantern, should be checked to make sure it is in perfect operating condition. But because it gives far less trouble than the gasoline lantern, this can easily be overlooked—especially the condition of the gasket or felt, until you get a pesky flame around the carbide container from a leaking gasket, or the lamp keeps dying out in a slight wind from a hard felt. Then it is usually too late because it is dark and the parts are at home. However, you will need a new felt in a carbide lamp only about as often as you would need a new mantle in a gasoline lantern, and you will never need a new gasket if you keep it clean.

The only other precaution is to keep the carbide, especially the dust in the bottom of the can, away from the eyes, as it can be extremely irritating. Irrigate for at least ten minutes if any does get in the eyes, and go to a doctor.

This lengthy bit on the carbide lamp is not meant to imply that it is a dangerous or unreliable piece of equipment; quite the contrary, it is so reliable that the manufacturers rarely include an adequate set of instructions with the lamp. The stranger to carbide fouls up a few times, through no fault of his own, and naturally blames the lamp. He shouldn't. It is a great device. I use it anytime I am not going light. (I use a candle lantern when traveling light, and a pencell flashlight when traveling ultra-light.)

WATER CONTAINER

You must have an adequate supply of water in camp. In the developed campsites, this is no harder than at home—just go to the nearest hydrant and get it. In campgrounds with more wilderness, however, this will often present more of a problem. If there is a stream nearby, you still have to have a container to hold the water while it is being purified, and afterward. If there is no stream or other useable water source, you will have to carry it in with you.

Insulated jugs are too heavy for anything but car camping and there you usually have a good water supply, so they are practically worthless. The five-gallon jerry cans are good for hauling water, but they will not cool it nor keep it cool. Also, they are too heavy for anything except car or horse transportation.

Rubberized fabric water bags are lighter in weight when empty and hold a gallon of water. They can be rolled up when empty and take up little space. However, like the metal containers, they don't cool the contents. Except in the summertime, though, this is not really too critical.

Polyethylene water bags are even lighter than the rubberized ones. However, only the neck has any degree of rigidity and the body is quite thin. This must be protected from puncturing. A cloth jacket not only reduces this prospect, but can be dampened to cool the bag by evaporation.

The flax canvas water bags made for desert travel by car are excellent for storing water in camp. The water is cooled by the evaporation of the seepage through the bag itself. But since the outside is damp, these can be quite sloppy if you carry them up against something—your back, for instance.

The camp drinking-water supply should be kept in a shady convenient spot, and each camper should have his own cup.

Canteens are useful when individuals go from base camp for long periods of time on hikes. Their biggest disadvantages are that they are rather heavy and they bang against the hip while hiking. One way to avoid these problems is with a bota. These Basque wineskins (now available with a plastic lining) are both light in weight and reasonably soft

Water containers should be light and as unbreakable as possible. From the left: a half-gallon bleach bottle, an army canteen, a bota, a quart bleach bottle.

on the hip. In addition, they squirt the water out so slowly that by the time you get a tablespoon or so of water, your throat is rinsed out as much as if you have had a cupful. One squirt, whenever your throat feels dry, will maintain your body's water level and still not waste the water. However, a problem has arisen since the first edition: the quality control on these things has gone to pot and they just don't last. Anyone who starts manufacturing a quality liner for them will have the gratitude of campers and a modest income as well.

WATCH

While the most important use of camping in modern society is to get away from the rushing routine, a timepiece other than the sun is still quite useful. You can tell how fast a thunderstorm is approaching by timing the interval between the lightning and the thunder on the fairly accurate basis of four and a half seconds per mile. Most freeze-dried dinners give you full directions on how the food should be cooked, and the camp cook who has not used this wonderful method of food preservation cannot tell by looking when the time has

come to yell "come and get it." A watch is also useful for telling how long until dark, for checking pulse rates, and even for an emergency compass (see page 359).

There are two basic types of camping watches, pocket and wrist. The old pocket watches with the flip-up cover are good, rugged timepieces, but the watch pocket has just about disappeared from pants. This leaves two alternatives to the pocket-watch user: sew in a watch pocket (which can be done, although it is harder than it first seems) or carry it somewhere less protected and accessible.

Waterproof pocket watches are fairly rare; however, you can make any pocket watch waterproof by encasing it in a rubber balloon. You can still wind it through the balloon, and by stretching the rubber over the face you can read the watch through the rubber. Keep out as much air as possible to reduce the bulk, and tie the end securely.

Wrist watches are now just about as durable as the old pocket watches and a lot more convenient. A low-cost, waterproof wrist watch is probably the best camping watch. Split-second accuracy is not really needed since you are not that dependent on an accurate schedule. However, it should be consistently off and not gain one day and lose the next so that you can't estimate how far off it is.

INSECTICIDE

A spray bomb of a good insecticide is a good investment in camp. Spray the tent about fifteen to twenty minutes before turning in for the night. Go easy on the trigger as the odor will last for hours if you get too much. A little spray will do the job just as well. Be careful that you don't spray the tent itself as the spray will destroy the waterproofing.

Mosquitoes will often group at the top of a large tent in the daytime. This is a good time to get rid of a sizeable number at once by swatting. Also look kindly on your insectivorous friends the bats, dragonflies, mantids, and spiders.

PERSONAL EQUIPMENT

You should carry a certain amount of equipment other than pure camping gear. You should have a kit for personal cleanliness. A small, rubberized kit, canvas bag, or metal or plastic box is best for this. It should include the following:

soap in a waterproof box
a washcloth
a small but absorbent towel
a toothbrush
toothpaste or powder (salt is as good as any)
a comb
a small package of tissues
a small metal mirror
toilet paper (flat sheets)

A hotel-size bar of soap is adequate. The washcloth is useful, but should be omitted if going light, because of the bulk more than the weight. The towel should be the size of a guest towel, but unlike that impervious material it should be able to absorb water and actually dry. There are folding toothbrushes which weigh little and take up a minimum of space. They even have space in the box for the toothpaste. The rest of the list is fairly obvious.

If you wear glasses, take along a spare pair. It is a good practice to have two frames. When you need new glasses, have the old lenses put into the other frames. They won't be as good as your present pair, but they are a good spare and cost nothing. Also take along lens tissues if you use them.

Men will need some kind of shaving device unless they prefer to grow a beard (as is still somewhat traditional in wilderness camping). The safety-razor user has no problem at all, especially with the aerosol shaving-cream cans available. Electric-shaver users might have a problem away from a car and its electrical system. You can buy several types of shavers that operate off rechargeable batteries (all referred to as "cordless"), but they cost as much or more than regular shavers. They are also rather heavy.

Around a car, you can use a shaver that works from a lighter socket. Some shavers (unfortunately no longer being manufactured) have built-in transformers for this purpose; others will need a separate transformer. Several models of inverters are available, including a do-it-yourself version from Heathkit, which permit the operation of a wide range of electrical appliances from a 12-volt car battery. A few wind-up shavers can still be found with considerable searching.

Women may prefer to take some make-up, but, again, don't use hair spray near a tent or it will ruin the waterproofing. Women will also have to provide for their monthly problem. The added exertion and change in routine will sometimes make the period come earlier than usual. Tampons are vastly superior to napkins in camping because of their bulk and weight. Check with your doctor if you are leery of trying them.

FIRE STARTER

Into each camp, some rain must fall. How, then, do you start a fire? First, keep your wood supply under shelter. A small tarp is enough. Make your fireplace on high ground. This not only prevents it from becoming the center of a mud puddle, it will also help the smoke dissipate better in the still of the morning.

When you arrive at a campsite in the rain, you will have to make a fire with wet wood. You can split dry wood out of the center of wet logs. Yet this requires a full ax, a let-up in the rain, and sizeable logs to do any more than exchange wet wood for damp wood. However, unless it has been raining for some time, the lower limbs of evergreens are often still dry. If you carry your tinder with you, you will have a dry supply.

Usually you will need some sort of fire starter to dry out a wood supply in order to ignite it. Half-inch (1 cm) slices of plumber's candles will work for small wood, but three or four of them are needed at once. Newspapers, rolled up and soaked in paraffin, will burn hot enough to dry out a sizeable amount of wood, but they are rather heavy. The old paraffin-coated milk cartons were great, but the plastic-coated ones now are practically fireproof.

There are several commercial fire starters. The oldest is Sterno, which is an alcohol mixture in a can. You just open it and light it. It works well but is expensive and relatively heavy. But, in an emergency, you could cook your whole meal over it.

A buddy-burner is a do-it-yourself version, given unwarranted popularity by a girl's organization. It is made by cutting against the corrugations in corrugated cardboard to get a strip one and a

Fire starters. A buddy burner, a plumber's candle (should be cut into half-inch [1 cm] sections), a highway flare, a roll of paper soaked in paraffin.

quarter inch (3 cm) wide. Roll this into a tight spiral and fit it into a tunafish can. Pour melted paraffin into the can, up to the top of the cardboard. It is more efficient if you heat the can and cardboard slightly before adding the paraffin. This allows the paraffin to soak into the cardboard before it hardens. When needed, simply light the paraffin by dropping a burning match on it. The cardboard acts as a wick. To extinguish, cover and allow the paraffin to harden before turning it over and pouring out the melted paraffin. The buddy-burner is very sooty, produces a very low heat (barely enough to simmer water), and is hardly worth the effort; but it does burn, which is more than can be said for wet wood.

If the only wood available is slightly punky (it will light, but soon goes to a glowing spark), a fire starter is a necessity. With this type of wood, coals are impossible and quite a bit of firewood is needed for even a small amount of cooking.

Another good fire helper is a blowpipe. It is a rubber tube, one and a half to two feet (45 to 60 cm) long, with a flattened copper tube at the end. A length of plastic clothesline with the cords and wire removed will do as well. Using the blowpipe is more efficient than fanning to get a small spark into a good fire. It is also useful in lighting a new fire from yesterday's coals. It takes up little room in the pack when coiled and weighs less than one ounce (30 g). The inside of a pill-bottle match safe is a good place for it.

Never use inflammable liquids for fire starting. They are a bother to carry and dangerous to use. They also tend to burn too much wood while lighting it.

A small alcohol or white-gasoline stove will weigh as little as six ounces (175 g) plus fuel and will provide the best insurance for rainy weather.

When the wood is really soaked, a flare will light it since it burns well even in wet weather. It is used by forest fire fighters for lighting backfires. Move the flare as needed rather than building the fire over it. This is an expensive way to light a fire, really being in the emergency category, but when the wood is really soaked, there is often no other way unless you have an ax.

REPAIR EQUIPMENT

There are two items of equipment which you should carry, but ideally never use. They are the first-aid kit and the repair kit. (In wilderness areas, you should include a survival kit as well.) A good repair kit includes materials and tools to repair the essential items of your camping equipment which can't be repaired using improvised equipment and materials.

For general tent camping, it should include the following:

a pair of compound-action pliers with wire cutters
three feet (1 m) of picture-hanging wire
twenty-five feet ($6\frac{1}{2}$ m) of fishing line
a one foot (30 cm) square piece of tent cloth (waterproof and pre-shrunk)
cloth for clothing repair
needles and thread on a notched stick (thimble optional)
blanket pins
spare buttons and shoelaces
twenty-five feet ($6\frac{1}{2}$ m) of parachute cord
a whetstone with two grits

The repair kit should provide materials to repair camping equipment, yet still be light in weight.

Optional equipment may include any of the following:

a saw (either a keyhole saw with a regular and hacksaw blades, or a wire saw)

gun and/or fishing-equipment repair tools and parts

a patching kit for air mattresses

equipment and tools to repair camp equipment such as a canoe

a grapnel

The list is fairly self-explanatory. The pliers are the little six-inch (15 cm) kind which weigh little but are fantastically useful. The wire is both for lashing and for raw material in fashioning replacement parts. The parachute cord is for any use that may come up—it contains many useful parts as well as being useful whole. It is discussed at greater length in Chapter 36.

The grapnel can be invaluable if any of the trip is taken over water. It is made from as large a triple fishhook as you can find, and a four-ounce (100 g)

sinker. This will snag and recover all manner of gear from the bottom of water that is too deep, swift, or cold for diving. You can substitute a large plastic pill bottle for the sinker to reduce weight, and fill it with sand to use. In the bag, the rig should be protected with small corks on the points or the hook fitted into the plastic pill bottle. The barbs should be filed off.

It is easy to make the list of repair equipment too large and too heavy for its usefulness. As with all equipment, keep the weight down. A repair kit should never weigh over a pound and a half (750 g). When you don't have a canoe, gun, or fishing tackle to take care of, half of that is the maximum.

HOBBY GEAR

Hunting, fishing, photography, and nature study are the usual reasons for camping. It is very easy to overload on this type of gear. We would like to take enough of this stuff to kill any type of game, catch any type of fish in any type of water, or photograph anything under any condition. Yet a small-bore rifle, large-bore rifle, shotgun, and plinking pistol would make a full load even without the ammunition. So would a fly, spinning, and plug-casting rod and all that goes with it. Ditto a mass of cameras and accessories.

There is quite a bit of good equipment on the market that is lightweight, made especially for camping. This type should be preferred if you plan to use it mainly in camping. The selection of this equipment is discussed in greater detail in Part VI.

EQUIPMENT FOR IN-CAMP ACTIVITIES

What do you do on a rainy day in camp? If you had planned fishing or photography, you probably won't do anything. You should invest a few ounces (less than 250 g) of your pack's weight in such things as a pack of cards, a pocket chess set, dominoes, or paperback books. These will help pass the time when you get tired of watching the rain fall.

Unless it is a downpour, a short hike in the rain can show you a whole new world in nature.

CHAPTER TEN

Clothing

The selection of clothing for camping should be so obvious that nothing need be written about it. Yet many beginners have some odd ideas of what should be worn. Clothes should be selected for comfort in the outdoors. In our central-heated, air-conditioned society, we dress about the same all year 'round except for overwear. Fashion, not comfort, dictates what changes we make between winter and summer clothing. As a result, we are raising a generation which literally does not know how to dress for the weather.

In camping, your clothes furnish the insulation; your body is its own heater and air-conditioner. It is well designed for this, but you have to help it with your choice of clothing.

In warm weather, it should allow a free flow of air through the cloth to carry off the excess body heat. You need clothes only to protect you from sunburn and underbrush.

In cold weather, clothing should retain body heat, but still permit the evaporation of sweat. Several layers of lightweight clothes are better insulation than one heavy layer. It is not only warmer per ounce because of the greater amount of trapped air, but you can remove a layer or two, if necessary, to prevent overheating.

Regardless of the weather, camp clothing should always allow free body movement. The fabric should be strong so that it will not tear on underbrush. Outer garments should be water-resistant.

The fabric should be porous for summer use, since that lets the wind blow through, removing sweat and cooling the body by evaporation. Porosity should be low in the winter so that the wind doesn't take away body heat and make you cold.

Heavy-duty zippers and snaps are preferable to lighter ones, which wear out, and preferable, too, to buttons, which come loose.

Although there are some rather serious exceptions, a good rule of thumb is to follow the lead of those who work in camping situations—trappers, guides, loggers, wildlife biologists, etc. Military equipment, on the contrary, in practically all nations is generally of poor design—having superfluous features or lacking needed features, or both. This is especially true of footwear, packs, and tents.

SHOES

Since extensive walking is practically unknown in this country, shoes are the biggest problem with beginners. Even when some experienced camper takes them in tow and insists they get the proper kind, they have a habit of using them the wrong way. On one trail hike through the Rocky Mountains, one girl got the right kind of shoes—the pre-hike literature had got that point across—but she waited until she started the five-day hike to put them on. Her feet were broken down before the shoes were broken in.

There are shoes designed for every camping purpose. All types should give good protection to your feet. This includes a good arch support, since you will often wear them when carrying a load for quite a distance. They should give you good arch and ankle support and a good grip on the ground, especially on rocks, both for ease in walking and to protect you from falls, which can be quite dangerous on rocks or with the weight of a pack.

The shoes should "breathe"; that is, let the sweat evaporate. Wet feet always get blisters. The shoes should be snug at the top to keep out those "half-millimeter boulders" but still not bind. There should be room to wiggle your toes too, as this does wonders in preventing sore feet.

Tops over eight inches (20 cm) high are a waste of weight. Tops that extend up the calf are a positive detriment since they will constrict the leg muscles and restrict free circulation.

In climbing, scree and snow both present problems to low tops. Half-millimeter boulders and cold slush can both be kept out with the use of gaiters. These are little sleeves of waterproof fabric which lace or hold with elastic over the ankle. They reach high enough to be above the scree or wet snow and so keep those unwanted materials from coming down your boot tops. The ones with elastic generally fasten with zippers, the laced ones are sufficiently large cylinders to fit over the boots when putting them on.

Crampons are used strictly in hard mountain climbing. They should fit your individual boot sole. The little instep crampons are often useful in hiking, especially on slick grassy slopes or loose humus soil.

Backpacking

Leather, high-top hiking shoes are essential for backpacking. They should be as flexible as possible and give good arch and ankle support. The soles should be neoprene rubber or corded composition to give good traction. A cleat-like tread on the rubber soles is practically required if you will use them on rocks.

The best possible hiking shoe is a lightweight mountain-climbing shoe. They come in both six- and eight-inch (15 and 20 cm)-high tops. They are rather broad as shoes go, especially at the heel, but this helps increase the area of friction with the rock. They should fit snugly at the ankle and heel, and have plenty of wiggling room at the toes, even when wearing two pairs of socks.

The toe should be hard, to give protection, especially when having to kick steps in a mountainside or having the pressure of crampon straps over your toe. The tongue should be attached the whole length of the laced instep so that water does not enter too easily. The top should open wide so you can get them on even when the weather has been so unkind as to get them wet.

The soles of climbing boots are no larger than the uppers. Since there is no extra rim of sole around the shoe, you can turn a half-inch (1 cm) "ledge" into a secure foothold. The soles themselves come in two varieties: with lugs or nails. The lug sole is a cleat pattern built into the sole itself. These force against the roughness of the ground or rock and give excellent traction on those surfaces. However, they have poor traction on wet grass, hard wet dirt, or worn logs such as are often used for footbridges in climbing country. In these cases, nails are far better. In this country, the hard tricouni nail is preferred over the better-gripping but shorter-wearing soft Swiss nail. The main disadvantage of the nails is that they are rough on the trails and conduct the heat from your feet faster on snow. Also, they are poor on rock slabs. In snow, double boots are used in climbing.

While climbing shoes are the best all-around hiking boots, there are conditions in which others may be better. In extremely wet areas (mud as well as the standing water of swamps), rubber shoes are helpful. However, an all-rubber boot won't let any water out either, so you will have to change your socks frequently.

Bean developed a compromise which is excellent in the canoe country of woods and small lakes. The lower part is rubber and the top is leather. While it is not as comfortable in a prolonged hike on dry ground as the more typical hiking boot, where the moisture content of the ground is high it will be far more comfortable than wet socks.

Climbing boots, with their lug soles, insure footing while hiking as well. This boot has a padded lining for comfort and hooks on the tops for fast lacing.

The so-called hunting boots are fairly good for all but long hikes with a heavy load, but they are too often sold with very high tops. Eight inches (20 cm) should be the limit.

Second only to the tent, boots are the backpacker's biggest purchase. Therefore, the choice should be made with care. Examine the leather. It should be soft on the uppers for comfort, yet fairly rigid at the sole, with a hard toe and heel. It should have double layers over the toe and around the heel to protect against the abrasion of rocks. The "suede-leather" (more properly "rough outside") boots are easier to keep looking good because abrasions don't show on them as readily as they do on smooth leather. However, they absorb water more readily than smooth leather ones, and are therefore not as good in areas with extensive rainfall. Regardless of the type of leather, make sure the stitching is smooth and regular. Check to see that the soles are not only glued to the boot but are screwed with brass screws as well.

Next, try them on, remembering to wear two pairs of bulky socks (they are the best insulation and shock absorbers). Take a few deep knee bends. If they bind anywhere when you are down, they may be hard or even impossible to break in comfortably.

Proper care extends the life of any hiking shoe. When you get back from a hike with your boots all muddy, wash off the mud, stuff them full of wadded-up newspaper, and put them in a dry, moderately warm place (not over 100°F [38°C]). After they dry, rub them with shoe grease to waterproof them and keep the leather soft. However, don't overdo the grease or your boots will be *too* soft. Take particular care to treat the stitching, the wrinkles, and the cracks between the uppers and the sole and between two layers of leather, such as around the heel and toe.

Horsepacking

For pack-horse trips, hiking boots are the best because, even though you are riding a horse into the camping area, you will still be doing most of your activities on the ground. Horsepacking country is rough terrain, so you will need the protection of hiking boots just as much as if you got there on your own power.

Cowboy boots may or may not be uncomfortable in the camping routine on the ground. Mounted, they are definitely comfortable—if they fit. The fit in cowboy boots comes in two types: perfect and painful. None are merely uncomfortable.

A good cowboy boot, once it is broken in and you are accustomed to the heel, is one of the most comfortable forms of footwear. While it does not seem so at first glance, it is completely functional.

Double climbing boots are used in extremely cold conditions.

The long pointed toe is admirably suited for spearing a stirrup. The high, tapering heel is a cleat for digging into the soft ground of the corral when on the opposite end of a very light lasso to some fighting critter. The high top gives the ankle protection against the thorns and stobs of mesquite thickets and other chaparral. Even the fancy applique and stitching on the top helps reënforce it so it doesn't get floppy. The sole is quite thick in the instep so it won't break down from the strain of holding the weight in the stirrups (since standing in the stirrups is the best way to avoid saddle sores).

While cowboy boots are completely suited for life on horseback, you should get used to walking around in them long before you go on a horse-packing trip, or you may look as graceful as an adolescent girl in her first high heels.

Canoeing

For canoe trips, there are two types of shoe to choose from, both light enough to swim in, in case of a canoe upset. The first type is the canoe moccasin. These are basically made of two pieces—the part over the toes, and the rest of it. There is no separate sole. As a result, they are quite flexible and comfortable in the canoe. They still have enough protection on the bottom for short portages over rocky ground.

The second type is the crepe-soled, canvas-top sneaker. They are sufficiently flexible for use in the canoe and excellent for general, around-camp wear. They are not very good for hiking since they don't give you any ankle support. Worse than that, they can soak up a lot of moisture from the grass after a rain or heavy dew. When you get soaked through these shoes and your socks, you will get blisters fast. As long as the tops are dry, they are quite good. The thick rubber sole gives a good spring to your step. They are cool and light in weight. And they have sure footing on rocks.

For regular camping shoes, they are of very little value outside the highly developed campsites of the car camper. The same goes for the high-top canvas shoes that kids like to wear. They do have the advantage of being inexpensive—a vital factor with those fast-growing feet—but they suffer the same disadvantages of the low-cut shoes. For kids, though, they may be all right since children can't

take too long a hike without exhaustion anyway. Their seemingly boundless energy is really good only in short spurts.

When you have a long portage, especially on rough ground, it will probably be better to change to regular backpacking shoes than to try it with canoeing shoes which lack the ankle support and strength needed on long distances and rough ground.

SOCKS

Thick wool socks are best unless you are an unfortunate who can't stand wool. Athletic socks in a cotton-nylon blend tend to get gaping holes in them during the second season of use, but they are heavy enough to cushion your step. They are also available in wool, which wears slightly better. Either type is reasonably priced, even considering their rather short life span.

When hiking, you should wear two pairs of socks to prevent blisters and to get better cushioning. On an all-day hike, take two extra pairs and change at midday. Your feet will feel better. I wear a stretch pair under the two pair of ribbed, cushioned athletic socks. The stretch pair keep the ribs of the other two pair from becoming embossed on my skin. When I change, I change the stretch pair (which is usually rather damp) and switch the athletic socks so that the former middle pair can dry on the outside.

However you switch them on an overnight hike, wash out your socks after each day's wearing. That way, you don't have to carry a load of socks (which, while they are not too heavy, are quite bulky for going light). If it is necessary, you can endure dirty clothes, but your socks must be clean to protect your feet.

When you are not doing much hiking, it really doesn't make much difference what kind of socks you wear. For convenience in the camp "laundry," the wash-and-wear stretch type is probably best.

In snow, plastic bags over each of the two layers of heavy socks will keep them dry and thus preserve their insulating bulk. There will be some dampening from sweat, but not as much as from the melting snow. Any suitably-sized food bag will do. Rubber bands at the tops will keep them from creeping down into the boot. While not as good as double boots, this method is a lot cheaper.

UNDERWEAR

Except for cold weather, the normal kind and amount of underwear can be worn in camping—and since of the wash-and-wear variety, only one extra set need be carried when going light.

For cold weather, the traditional long-handles in a waffle weave is best. Wool, naturally. For those who can't tolerate wool against their skin, there are two-layer ones with cotton on the inside for comfort and wool on the outside for insulation. For colder weather, wear two, or use one of the string suits under the long-handles. Clothing insulates by dead air spaces—between the fibers in the cloth, between cloth layer and cloth layer, or between cloth and skin. This latter method is supplemented with the waffle weave or the string suit.

Thermal underwear is a quilted suit of a fluffy fiber between two close-woven fabrics. It is quite comfortable in cold weather, even in a wind, but it is fairly heavy and doesn't permit too much movement, especially when worn under clothes designed for less bulk under them. Whatever the style of underwear you use, it should permit free movement and not bind, no matter how you bend and twist.

PANTS

Despite their popularity, shorts have only a limited use in camping. They are useless in any kind of underbrush because they don't protect your legs from scratches. On horseback, they are a sure way to get saddle sores. In a canoe, you can get a bad sunburn on your upper legs. In grass, bare legs are a banquet for chiggers and in open country mosquitoes will have a feed, since it is hard to slap down at them when wearing a pack.

On the other hand, they are useful when camping on beaches, in the desert, or in the cleared camp areas of parks. They also have use in base camp. However, even in these circumstances, you need to have a good tan on your legs; otherwise get something which will give you better protection.

Blue jeans are good only if you get them to fit a bit looser than is usual, and don't put anything in the pockets. A full blue-jean pocket will rub your skin raw just under the hip bone after the full day of crouching, kneeling, and sitting required to operate a good camp, If you can force yourself not to regard the pockets as miniature packs, blue jeans are quite good. In horsepacking, the tighter fit is better protection against saddle sores and bounced innards.

Surplus fatigues have some usefulness—and some serious limitations. The bellows pockets really are miniature packs and can be used as such as long as you keep the weight down. It takes three times as much energy to carry something there instead of on your back. The fatigues are baggy and hardly an aesthetic color, but the principal problem is that they don't come in a wide enough range of sizes and they don't fit women properly.

A good compromise in the matter of pants is the twill or denim work pants. Their rugged construction, comfort, roominess without being baggy, and low cost make them ideal in camp.

Women have a wide selection of sportswear to choose from. However, just as in the matter of shorts, they must not be so short that they give inadequate leg protection. Also, they must not be tight. Neither skirts nor culottes give adequate protection against underbrush or insects. However, either is well worth carrying along in all but the most distant wilderness as they can be put on quickly when civilization requires an appearance other than that of a wilderness camper.

For either sex, pants should fit loose at the knees and permit squatting without binding. Pants legs that tuck into shoes restrict the leg almost as much as a high-top boot. Elastic cuffs are good over shoe tops to keep out scree, but, except when climbing, this is generally unnecessary.

Knickers still have some popularity in mountain climbing, although they have lost it in most other sports. Mountain climbing is a special case, though, since there is a very real danger of hooking a heel in the pants cuff—especially when using crampons. Most mountain-climbing pants, even the long variety, have the leg a couple of inches (about 5 cm) shorter than is usual for other pants, and they have no cuff.

Many campers, even those who normally wear belts, will wear only suspenders to keep up their pants when camping. They say it gives them more freedom of movement (and they generally wear a size larger waist in their camping pants too). I can't really see their point, but they are welcome to it. The only real matter to consider in this regard is to have the waist loose enough to be able to breathe deeply without feeling it constrict you, and tight enough to keep your pants in place.

A woman is more likely to cinch the waist too tightly. But in camping, her ability to be a full part of the camping situation is valued far above the thinness of her waistline, and this can be done more successfully when her clothes are comfortable.

SHIRTS

Except in deep underbrush, shirts serve part of the function of overwear—the regulation of body heat. In the winter, they should be soft, almost fluffy wool flannel. In a milder weather, gabardine is good because it wears well, although it contributes only a slight amount to the insulation. In warm weather, a light, porous, long-sleeved shirt is best. Short sleeves should be worn only if you have an excellent tan. The heat of a lightweight long-sleeved shirt is nothing compared to the heat of a sunburn.

Shirts should be fairly loose-fitting to permit the full use of your arms in chopping wood, and should allow perspiration to evaporate. They should have long tails to keep them from working out at the waist and roomy pockets, equipped with flaps, to keep the contents from spilling when you bend over.

T-shirts are adequate only for in-camp wear or to reduce the chance of sunburn when swimming. They don't give good protection against underbrush and they tear rather easily. They are good as underwear, however.

SLEEPING WEAR

Regular pajamas are really as good as any in most camping situations, but don't seem to be considered "outdoorsy" enough for many. T-shirts and shorts are good for hot weather, and an athletic sweatsuit is good for a chilly night—especially when you are trying to take a sleeping bag down ten more degrees than it is rated.

For very cold weather, you will often need something to keep your head warm—especially your ears. A stocking cap and/or a mummy sleeping bag will be needed in such cases.

Especially in the winter, but to a lesser extent at other times, you need to sleep dry. Heat escapes rapidly from a sweat-filled sleeping bag. You will normally lose up to a pint ($\frac{1}{2}$ liter) of water by sweating in the eight or so hours you spend in the bag. Many campers will try to dry rain-dampened clothes by wearing them inside the bag, but generally they just manage to sleep with a chill instead. The clothes will either dry outside the bag during the night, dry the next day on the trail, or get wet again the next day anyhow. It is hardly worth risking illness simply to dry them out, especially with a method which is none too efficient in the first place.

OVERWEAR

Because you lose body heat faster in a wind than in still air, both wind velocity and temperature are factors in determining how cold you will get. This has been developed into what is known as the wind-chill factor (see page 100). The factor number is approximately equivalent to the degree of temperature with no wind.

At winds over 40 m.p.h. (60 km/h), there is less than one factor number decrease per 5 m.p.h. (10 km/h), wind increase in the safe zone.

The wrong interpretation of this chart can make it appear far worse than it is. The wind-chill factor does not consider the effect of insulation, wind protection (either clothing or shelter), or activity. Windproof clothing will decrease the wind velocity at the skin practically to zero over most of the body. Insulation will increase the skin temperature well above the air temperature. Strenuous activity will generate more heat, which can be retained by proper clothing. If properly clothed, there is little or no danger above a wind-chill factor of −25°F (−32°C). The danger of dying from exposure, however, is severe at any number below −75°F (−65°C) and special arctic clothing, a structure,

Temperature (Fahrenheit)

	70	60	50	40	30	20	10	0	−10	−20	−30	−40
0	70	60	50	40	30	20	10	0	−10	−20	−30	−40
5	69	58	48	37	27	16	6	−5	−15	−26	−36	−47
10	63	51	40	28	16	4	−9	−21	−33	−46	−58	−70
15	61	48	36	21	10	−4	−18	−32	−45	−59	−72	−85
20	59	45	32	19	5	−10	−25	−39	−53	−68	−82	−96
25	58	44	30	16	3	−14	−30	−44	−59	−74	−89	−104
30	57	43	28	14	−1	−17	−34	−48	−63	−79	−95	−110
35	56	42	27	12	−3	−19	−36	−51	−66	−82	−99	−114
40	55	41	26	11	−4	−21	−38	−53	−69	−85	−102	−117

Wind Velocity (m.p.h.)

Temperature (Celsius)

	20	15	10	5	0	−5	−10	−15	−20	−25	−30	−35	−40
0	20	15	10	5	0	−5	−10	−15	−20	−25	−30	−35	−40
10	19	14	9	3	−2	−8	−12	−16	−21	−29	−37	−39	−45
20	17	9	3	−3	−9	−17	−20	−28	−34	−43	−50	−54	−60
30	16	8	0	−7	−14	−22	−25	−34	−41	−51	−56	−63	−65
40	15	7	−1	−9	−16	−25	−30	−38	−46	−55	−65	−72	−75
50	13	6	−2	−10	−18	−27	−32	−41	−49	−58	−70	−76	−79
60	12	5	−3	−11	−20	−29	−34	−45	−51	−60	−74	−79	−83

Wind Velocity (km/h)

and/or artificial heat is required for survival.

In the summer, only a light sweater will ever be needed outside the mountains, and that only on those cool nights which often follow a squall-line rainstorm. My own is a long-sleeved sweatshirt I bought once when I discovered I hadn't packed a jacket for a major backpacking trip. It is far lighter and warmer than a jacket and easily slips into a corner of the pack.

At high altitudes and other near-polar conditions, the layer theory of insulation breaks down with too much thickness for easy movement. The only answer is the expensive, but very warm and light, down-filled parkas and pants. They weigh only about a pound and a half each, but are proof against the lowest of temperatures encountered outside the polar ice caps themselves.

It is, however, with that wide range of temperature in between these extremes that the camper must be most concerned. Here, the layer theory is most valid. As the temperature climbs in the day, you can remove one layer at a time, and as it drops in the afternoon, you can put them back on again—keeping up with the changes all the time.

The temperature changes during the day are not the only ones you must contend with. When you do heavy exercise, such as chopping wood, you will need less insulation because you are generating more heat yourself. On the other hand, you will need more insulation at night in bed than you would ever need when up and doing even the lightest of tasks.

On the outside of this layered arrangement of sweaters, shirts, and such, is an anorak or similar-type jacket. The term "anorak" (a Greenland Eskimo word for "parka") had not had much use in North America at the time of the first edition, although it was quite common in Britain. However, since then they have become quite common, particularly in the thin nylon form which gives wind protection but little against rain. It is useful to distinguish between this uninsulated garment and the insulated Eskimo fur parka which comes to mind most readily with the word "parka" (which is an Aleut word).

The anorak is made of tightly woven, water-repellent cloth (such as element cloth, ventile, Alpine or Cascade nylon). It has a large pocket (usually a kangaroo-pouch arrangement since the anorak usually slips over the head), a hood, and a drawstring at the waist to keep the wind from billowing it out. Some even snap between the legs like a toddler's pants to further reduce the flopping about in a wind. The top half is of doubled fabric both to provide even greater wind-resistance and to keep the shoulders from getting wet in a rain. It is roomy inside to permit extra clothing underneath. Since the fabric is practically wind-tight without being air-tight, the insulation of the clothes under it has unimpaired efficiency.

Do-it-yourself fans will be interested in the fine plans for an anorak in *Light Weight Camping Equipment* (see Chapter 54).

The overwear under the anorak is largely a matter of personal choice. In any case, it should be as fluffy as possible, since dead air is the actual insulation. A sweater will roll up into a tight bundle when not being worn, for putting into a belt pack or the pocket of the anorak while on a hike.

On days when the weather problem is more a matter of wind than of cold, an anorak by itself is adequate overwear. Even a poncho will serve in this capacity, although it tends to act more like a sail.

HEADGEAR

The best camp hat is the twill sports cap and its insulated, ear-flapped, skiing counterpart in the winter. Its main disadvantages are that the visor restricts upward visibility when climbing, and that it lets the rain run down the back of your neck. However, a poncho or anorak hood will cure that problem. A puggaree (the French Foreign Legion-style neck cloth) will protect the back of your neck

from too much sun. This can be worn tucked inside the cap or even attached to the cap by means of snaps or a zipper so it can be removed when not needed.

In cold weather, there are many other types of headgear in addition to the skiing cap. A beret is good in cool weather but gives no protection to the ears in really cold weather. The knitted wool stocking cap is quite warm and will easily fit under most hoods. The balaclava helmet pulls down farther, covering the face except for a large opening for the eyes and nose. Peruvian versions cover the entire head except for small holes for the eyes, the nose, and sometimes the mouth. Embroidered with fanciful features, they are popular in skiing areas.

The pork-pie style is a favorite with fishermen, largely because it makes a nice fly-holder. The pith sun helmet is too noisy from wind whistling under the brim and is hard to keep on even in a moderate breeze. A straw cowboy-style hat is good if there is no high wind or rain.

Mountain climbers and spelunkers will find a fiberglass hard hat valuable when the leader dislodges some rocks or when the ceiling lowers rapidly.

Then there are the girls, who tie a scarf over their heads for protection against heat, cold, rain, sun, sand, dust, etc.

An anorak in normal and cold-weather styles. The hood covers all but the eyes and nose.

RAIN PROTECTION

Unless you are in the middle of the Sahara or the Gobi, you will need a good cloth raincoat or poncho. The plastic raincoats may do for the city, but just won't hold up in the woods. Besides, they are so air-tight that perspiration can't evaporate. When hiking, this can build up to a very uncomfortable level.

Even the city-style cloth raincoats are not the best design by any means. They fit too closely, and while the sweat can evaporate through the cloth to some extent, there is too little air circulation inside the coat for comfort in warm weather.

The main problem with rain protection is that not all of the water is on the outside. Your rain gear must keep the rain out, that much is obvious. However, it must also let the sweat out. Otherwise, you will be as wet from perspiration inside your rain gear as you would be from a light drizzle without any protection.

The problem isn't quite as difficult as it first seems. All you really need is more than one point for air circulation—an entrance and an exit. The air currents set up merely by walking will take care of the rest. The only exception will be along the shoulders where the rain gear rests, because the air currents can't reach there, especially if you are wearing a pack.

The most striking example of this circulation is when the rain lets up and you push back the hood of a poncho. You can actually feel the clammy air rising through the head hole. Even as slight a deflection as the hood causes the air to build up inside the poncho. With the sleeves of a raincoat, this is even more of a problem.

A poncho allows more freedom than a raincoat in many activities. About the only exceptions are in shooting and chopping. A poncho can be worn over the pack to protect your gear as well as yourself (and, in this position, lifts the poncho off your shoulders so they don't get wet with perspiration). Of course, the poncho tends to flap a bit in the wind, but for protecting both you and your gear while moving it is the best form of rain protection. It can be used just as well in a canoe and keeps you dry even in the kneeling position. In a kayak,

it will almost make a spray cover and will certainly keep out a lot of the rain water that you would have to bail out otherwise.

In horsepacking, the traditional slicker is still the best. It has a long skirt, deeply divided in the back so that it will fit comfortably around the horse and still help protect your legs from the rain. The wise horsepacker will dismount and have someone hold his horse while he carefully gets it on. Many otherwise excellent mounts spook easily at the sudden sight of one flapping around.

The poncho can also be used mounted. (In fact, the original ponchos were heavy wool rain sheds worn by Latin American horsemen.)

The poncho can be used for a shelter too, although it is not a very good one. You can set it up like an undersized tarp tent. Visklamps prevent undue wear on the fabric in tying the ropes to it for a tent. Some even have grommets at the corners to make the job even easier.

In areas where heavy rain is rare, the poncho is quite adequate if you have a sleeping bag. However, it gives poor protection in a driving rain. Two or more can be snapped together to make a more functional tent, if they are all the same kind.

The plastic poncho, like the plastic raincoat, just won't stand up in the wilderness. The rubberized or plastic-coated nylon is best. It is light in weight, and keeps the water out.

If you are going to be using a pack, get a poncho that is longer in back than in front. Most outfitters stock them. Get one that will reach just below your knees in front. Some modification may be necessary for the pack versions. Although the extra length in the back will usually be taken up by the pack, you will have it dragging in the underbrush when you are not carrying a pack. Add three extra snaps, one on each side and one in the middle, to snap the extension up so that both the front and back are the same length. These modifications are included in the plans for a poncho in Chapter 15.

Even with the poncho, you may get soaked below the knees in a prolonged, driving rain. There are two alternatives to this soggy state. First, you can buy waterproof pants. These are the same rubberized or plastic-coated nylon as the poncho. For this reason, sweat evaporation may be a considerable

Poncho and rain chaps.

problem, although not nearly the problem you would have with the usual improvised method—wrapping the legs with polyethylene sheets held in place with rubber bands.

The second possibility is loose chaps over the pants legs. These are also made from the same material as the poncho, but since they extend only from the ankle to mid-thigh, there is better air circulation than with the waterproof pants. The chaps fasten to the belt with snaps or tie tapes, and sometimes at the bottom with a strap under the shoe. Rain suits are good except in very hot weather. (Be sure to choose one made of lightweight nylon rather than the hotter, less expensive rubberized canvas or duck.)

Shoes should be able to "breathe" so you don't get wet feet; but high tops and a fully attached tongue on the shoes will keep out standing water very well. A change of socks every three or four hours will take care of what little does get in (or doesn't get out). A wax waterproofing designed for

ski boots will keep the water from soaking through the leather without affecting its ability to breathe.

INSECT PROTECTION

Bug dope will help protect you from insects, but it is not foolproof. You still have to rub it on. Spray cans are quite heavy and, as a rule, must be left behind when going light.

In heavy mosquito country, cover up everything except your face, and hide that behind a net. Wear heavy, loose clothing or they will bite right through it.

This is a hot rig, but fortunately there are few localities or seasons when this extreme measure is needed; but when it is, there is no substitute.

SNAKE PROTECTION

Caution is the best preventative for snake bite. In known areas of poisonous snakes, you can buckle on heavy canvas or canvas-and-wire-mesh leggings. While not foolproof, they are generally effective against all but the largest snakes. You can buy high boots which contain a fine mesh in the uppers which cannot be penetrated by snake fangs. However, they are naturally expensive and generally unnecessary.

Actually, unless you are in swampy areas, there is little danger of being bitten by a snake if you use proper caution. Anywhere else, you will either see the snake ahead of time and be able to avoid it, or it will hear and see you and be able to avoid you. Unless you surprise snakes while they are sunning or asleep, they will get out of your way.

See pages 379 and 387 for more about snakes.

When you are climbing on rocky hillsides, watch where you put your hands. A snake may have the spot already occupied and it will make a fight for it if it is rudely awakened from a comfortable afternoon nap by someone trying to use it for a hand-hold. Sun-warmed rocks are snakes' favorites on all but the hottest days.

Keep alert and you won't need expensive, snakeproof clothing—or to use your snake-bite kit either.

CHAPTER ELEVEN

Outfitting

The type of trip you want to take will dictate the equipment you bring with you. A trip made on foot limits the weight and bulk more than one taken by car. In every form of transportation, however, you should keep down the weight and bulk as much as possible. Not only will the outfit cost less, it will be easier to handle.

If you select the equipment with care, a small amount will do the work of a big load of poorly selected stuff. When choosing between two items that are otherwise equal, take the one that weighs less. If it is useful, the more equipment you have the more comfortable you will be at the campsite; but, on the other hand, the weight of the gear reduces the comfort in carrying it—and this includes auto camping. If you backpack, light equipment is a must. The maximum of comfort from the minimum of equipment is the mark of the expert camper. As Kephart said, "The less a man carries in his pack, the more he must carry in his head."

Multi-purpose equipment is good within limits. The geologist's pick is good because it can be used as a pick, shovel, hammer, pot-lifter, pint-sized alpenstock, and even a hatchet. On the other hand, a pocket knife with ten blades, including a miniature monkey wrench, scissors, and tack hammer, will probably find use only as a pocket knife. The additional weight and bulk just gets in the way.

You should keep your camping equipment completely separate from your household equipment. This presents no conflict with the larger items such as tents and cooking kits, but the smaller items, such as first-aid equipment and repair gear, which are used both in the home and camp, get scattered. When you are ready to go on a camping trip, most of them will be all over the place. Some will be used up and others will be forgotten until you need them in camp. Therefore, keep your camping gear in one spot and don't use it for anything else. These are inexpensive items and it will cost no more than $5.00 to duplicate them—well worth not having to do without them in camp.

Unless you are unusual, you don't have unlimited funds for buying equipment, so choose your gear carefully. Don't buy on impulse. Save a certain small amount regularly for your camping equipment. (I used to save all the half-dollars I got until they almost disappeared from circulation.) It adds up fairly fast, but slowly enough so that you can be shopping while you are waiting to save enough, and thus avoid impulse-buying.

If you have the necessary skills, you can make much of your equipment. Usually you can save money by doing so, but check the market first. Plans for several items of equipment are given in Part III to start you out. The greatest advantage in doing it yourself is custom design. This will permit you to try out some new invention for camping with little loss if it doesn't work, and a tremendous gain if it does.

In the case of equipment bags, you will practically have to make them yourself. I am a great believer in having every piece of equipment protected by its own bag. It is good insurance against getting them scratched, bent, or dented, as well as against the loss of small items from the set. I endured a lot of kidding from my wife when I came home one time with several yards of denim, had her teach me to use the sewing machine, and converted most of it into bags. The sewing machine, incidentally, is a device which all campers should know how to use. More camping equipment can be made with it than with any other tool.

With all of your gear, buy carefully. Keep the weight down. Buy for quality, even at a higher price. A high-quality piece of equipment, well cared for, will last a lifetime. The equipment available from the sources listed in Chapter 56 is of this quality.

EQUIPMENT FOR VARIOUS CAMPS

Since the equipment used in camping varies with the type of camp, outfitting can easily become a confusing problem. The less experience one has in camping, the more confusing it will be. Too many camping books present an elaborate set of charts showing what you should take, with weights down to the last fraction of an ounce, in a hard-and-fast "this is your proper camping gear" manner. Outfitting is far too individualistic a matter for such rigid lists.

The gear you will want to take will depend on your individual preferences, your transportation, the season of the year, the number in your group, and the type and amount of gear you have available. You will probably want to make a list of your own and check off items with a pencil as you pack your gear.

If there are more than eight in your group, divide the party into a group of groups, in which each group (of four to eight) is essentially self-supporting. Even though the entire group may camp at the same campsite during the night, the hiking, canoeing, or riding will be done separately. In some of the more delicate wilderness areas (marginal land of desert or high altitudes), even in the night's camping, the groups should be separate so that the landscape isn't damaged by too heavy usage.

In the following series of charts, items will be referred to in the terms used in this book. This will save the space of listing all the things in, say, a "First-aid kit, hiker's" or a "Repair kit" since they are listed in the discussion of the item. The Index will help you find them.

The weight given in the charts is that of a typical item. Where there is a wide range of weights between two makes of the same item, both extremes will be given. There is no attempt to total the weights in each category since there are so many optional items a total would be meaningless. Permissible total weights are given in the introductory portions of each chart.

Weather is rather broadly broken down into: all year 'round, (a); hot, (h); cold, (c); and mild, (m). Rain is an unpredictable item at best and some rain protection should be carried regardless, so temperature (which influences the type of gear) is the only weather information mentioned.

How many of an item to carry is almost as much of a problem as what to carry. Most items of camping gear need only be carried by one or two members of the group. The following code will be used for this information: each member of the party carries one (or more), (1); every other member, or one item per two persons, ($\frac{1}{2}$); every fourth member, or one item per four persons, ($\frac{1}{4}$); only one member in an entire party of eight, ($\frac{1}{8}$). The number of individual items to be carried will be discussed in the Notes column since this is, to a great extent, dependent on the length of the trip. If no mention is made, only one is needed. Duration, also mentioned in the Notes column, will be broken down into "overnight," "short" (one to five days), "week" (six to ten days), and "long" (over ten days).

Backpacking

Backpacking weight should be kept to a minimum. For any trip longer than an overnight hike, forty pounds (18 kg) is the maximum for a man in good condition on level terrain; twenty-five pounds (11 kg) for a woman. In mountainous terrain, this should be cut drastically, even as much as one-half. Durable equipment is also needed since the pack is usually the only protection that the gear will have other than a poncho in case of a rain. Food will be practically restricted to the dehydrated and freeze-dried varieties in order to keep the weight down.

	WEIGHT	WEATHER	NUMBER	NOTES
Tent				
Plastic tarp	10 oz. (300 g)	h, m	1, $\frac{1}{2}$	8' x 8' (2$\frac{1}{2}$ x 2$\frac{1}{2}$ m), with Visklamps, parachute cord, no stakes
Single tab	3 lbs., 4 oz. (1$\frac{1}{2}$ kg)	h, m	1, $\frac{1}{2}$	9' x 9' (2$\frac{3}{4}$ x 2$\frac{3}{4}$ m), with parachute cord, no stakes
Double tab	6 lbs., 8 oz. (3 kg)	h, m	$\frac{1}{2}$, $\frac{1}{4}$	9' x 18' (2$\frac{3}{4}$ x 5$\frac{1}{2}$ m), with parachute cord, no stakes; longer than overnight
Explorer	6 lbs. (2.7 kg)	m, c	$\frac{1}{2}$, $\frac{1}{4}$	with aluminum poles and stakes; longer than overnight
Miner	same as Explorer			
Mountain	4 lbs, 8 oz. (2.1 kg)	c	$\frac{1}{2}$	with aluminum pole and stakes; fly 3 lbs., 6 oz. (1$\frac{1}{2}$ kg) extra
ATC	4 lbs., 10 oz. (2$\frac{1}{4}$ kg)	a	$\frac{1}{2}$	with aluminum poles and stakes, parachute cord, bags
Bivouac	2 lbs., 8 oz. (1.1 kg)	m, c	1	with aluminum pole, stakes not necessary but useful if you can carry them
Pack	3 lbs., 8 oz. (1.6 kg)	a	1	type depends on individual
Sleeping Equipment				
Sleeping bag	3 to 6 lbs. (1$\frac{1}{3}$ to 2$\frac{2}{3}$ kg)		1	type depends on temperature, weight on temperature and type of insulation
Air mattress (short)	1 lb., 12 oz. (800 g)	a	1	optional, but very comfortable
Cooking Equipment				
Nesting set	2 lbs., 8 oz. (1.1 kg)	a	$\frac{1}{2}$	
Utensil set	1 lb. (450 g)	a	$\frac{1}{2}$	carried by same persons who are carrying nesting set
Foil utensils	10 oz. (300 g)	a	$\frac{1}{8}$	for going ultra-light (cook and throw away); 10 oz. (300 g) per week
Reflector oven	1 lb., 14 oz. (850 g)	a	$\frac{1}{8}$	luxury
Pressure cooker	2 lbs., 12 oz. to 3 lbs., 6 oz. (1$\frac{1}{4}$ to 1$\frac{1}{2}$ kg)	a	$\frac{1}{4}$	high altitudes only

	WEIGHT	WEATHER	NUMBER	NOTES
Stove	8 oz. to 2 lbs., 6 oz. (225 g to 1.1 kg)	a	$\frac{1}{2}$, $\frac{1}{4}$	plus 1 lb. fuel plus container per 4 man-days

Tools

Knife, pocket	2 oz. (60 g)	a	1	
Knife, sheath	4 oz. (115 g)	a	1	optional
Ax, $\frac{3}{4}$ size	2 lbs., 6 oz. (1.1 kg)	a	$\frac{1}{8}$	only when extensive wood-cutting will be required
Whetstone	1 oz. (30 g)	a	$\frac{1}{8}$	for ax (see above)
Shovel	1 lb., 12 oz. (800 g)	a	$\frac{1}{8}$	optional; needed only with a large group
Saw	2 oz. to 2 lbs. (55 g to 1 kg)	a	$\frac{1}{8}$	optional; alternative to ax

Miscellaneous Equipment

Match safe	3 oz. (85 g)	a	1	filled with waterproof matches
Compass	6 oz. (170 g)	a	1, $\frac{1}{8}$	any who leave base camp should have one
Light	3 oz. (85 g)	a	1	candle or pencell flashlight
Canteen	2 oz. to 2 lbs. (55 g to 1 kg)	a	1	bota is lightest, military type quite heavy
Personal equipment	1 lb. ($\frac{1}{2}$ kg)	a	1	
Repair kit	1 oz. (30 g)	a	$\frac{1}{8}$	
Hobby gear	8 oz. (225 g)	a	1	up to the individual; keep weight down

Emergency Equipment

First-aid kit, hiker's	2 oz. (60 g)	a	1	any who leave base camp should have one
First-aid kit, main	1 lb. ($\frac{1}{2}$ kg)	a	$\frac{1}{8}$	
Survival kit, hiker's	1 oz. (30 g)	a	1	any who leave base camp should have one
Survival kit, main	8 oz. (225 g)	a	$\frac{1}{8}$	if trip is into remote areas

Clothes

up to the individual; must consider weather, prepare for rain (poncho best because it protects pack also, rain chaps also useful) and for cold if it is winter or camping will be in high altitudes or there is the possibility of a sudden cold front; number of each article depends on weight limitations and laundry facilities on hike; good hiking boots and change of socks twice a day a must

Food

well-balanced menu of lightweight (preferably dehydrated or freeze-dried) food

Bicycling

Bicycle camping is, as far as equipment is concerned, a rapid-movement hiking. Except for the heavy hiking boots and the supply of clean, dry socks required in backpacking, and the bicycle and its equipment required for bicycle camping, the equipment is identical for the two.

The weight limits are a bit higher in bicycle camping. A man's load can be as high as eighty pounds (36 kg), although if the way is hilly or unpaved sixty (27 kg) is more realistic. The woman's load can be around forty pounds (18 kg) for ideal conditions, thirty (13½ kg) for rough terrain.

Backpacks should generally be avoided as they raise the center of gravity to a dangerous degree.

	WEIGHT	WEATHER	NUMBER	NOTES
Bicycle, 3 to 10 speed	20 to 30 lbs. (9 to 13½ kg)	a	1	in good repair
Repair kit	1 lb.	a	1	for bicycle
Tent, paratipi	10 lbs.	a	½	with aluminum stakes, Visklamps, and parachute cord
Pack, pannier	3 lbs.	a	1	keep the weight low in the panniers to keep center of gravity low and avoid spills

Horsepacking

One of the advantages of horsepacking is that the usual problems of weight limitations are, to a certain extent, removed. Any amount of weight can, theoretically, be carried. However, as a practical matter, the fewer pack horses required, the more flexible the trip, the less trouble with stock, and the lower the cost. All trips are assumed to be "short" or longer—overnight trips with pack horses are ridiculous.

For horses or mules, 150 pounds (70 kg) should be the limit; for burros, the limit is 100 (45 kg)—less for a small animal. One of the advantages of the burro is that it is a good carrier of the packs on what is otherwise a backpacking trip. However, few burros are large or strong enough to carry the weight of a male camper. The people of cultures which depend on the donkey for riding are typically smaller and lighter than the average American. Also, their animals are slightly larger than the average burro—and are often overworked.

Tent

Same as backpacking plus:

	WEIGHT	WEATHER	NUMBER	NOTES
Paratipi	10 lbs. (4½ kg)	a	½	with aluminum stakes, Visklamps, and parachute cord
Parabolic	43 lbs. (30 kg)	h, m	½, ¼	with aluminum poles and stakes
Baker	20 lbs. (9 kg)	c	½, ¼	with aluminum poles and stakes
French	45 lbs. (21 kg)	a	¼	with aluminum poles and stakes
Umbrella	45 lbs. (21 kg)	a	¼	with aluminum frame
Pack, panniers and pack-saddle rigging	15 lbs. (6.7 kg)	a		one set per pack animal

	WEIGHT	WEATHER	NUMBER	NOTES

Sleeping Equipment

	WEIGHT	WEATHER	NUMBER	NOTES
Sleeping bag	3 to 6 lbs. ($1\frac{1}{3}$ to $2\frac{2}{3}$ kg)		1	type depends on temperature, weight on temperature and type of insulation
Air mattress	4 lbs. (1.8 kg)	a	1	

Cooking Equipment

	WEIGHT	WEATHER	NUMBER	NOTES
Nesting set	2 lbs., 8 oz. (1.2 kg)	a	$\frac{1}{2}$	
Utensil set	1 lb. (450 g)	a	$\frac{1}{2}$	carried by same persons who are carrying nesting set
Reflector oven	1 lb., 14 oz. (850 g)	a	$\frac{1}{8}$	normally a luxury, but the transportation allows it
Pressure cooker	2 lbs., 12 oz. to 3 lbs., 6 oz. ($1\frac{1}{4}$ to $1\frac{1}{2}$ kg)	a	$\frac{1}{4}$	a high-altitude necessity, speeds cooking at any level
Dutch oven	6 lbs., 8 oz. (3 kg)	a	$\frac{1}{8}$	normally an impractical luxury because of weight, a traditional utensil on horse-packing trips
Stove	1 lb., 3 oz. to 25 lbs. (440 g to $11\frac{1}{3}$ kg)	a	$\frac{1}{2}$, $\frac{1}{8}$	plus 1 lb. ($\frac{1}{2}$ kg) fuel per 4 man-days; use only when wood will be hard to get

Tools

	WEIGHT	WEATHER	NUMBER	NOTES
Knife, pocket	2 oz. (60 g)	a	1	
Ax	2 lbs., 6 oz. to 5 lbs. (1.1 to 2.3 kg)	a	$\frac{1}{8}$	only when wood-cutting will be required
Whetstone	1 oz. (30 g)	a	$\frac{1}{8}$	
Shovel	1 lb., 12 oz. (800 g)	a	$\frac{1}{8}$	
Saw	2 oz. to 2 lbs. (60 g to 1 kg)	a	$\frac{1}{8}$	optional; alternative to ax

Miscellaneous Equipment

	WEIGHT	WEATHER	NUMBER	NOTES
Match safe	3 oz. (85 g)	a	1	filled with waterproof matches
Compass	6 oz. (170 g)	a	$\frac{1}{8}$	any who leave base camp should have one
Light	9 oz. to 4 lbs., 12 oz. (255 g to 2 kg)	a	$\frac{1}{2}$, $\frac{1}{8}$	plus 1 lb. ($\frac{1}{2}$ kg) if carbide, or 2 lbs. (1 kg) if gasoline, per week
Canteen	2 oz. to 2 lbs. (55 g to 1 kg)	a	1	
Personal equip-ment	1 lb. ($\frac{1}{2}$ kg)	a	1	

	WEIGHT	WEATHER	NUMBER	NOTES
Repair kit	8 oz. (225 g)	a	$\frac{1}{8}$	
Hobby gear		a	1	up to the individual
Emergency Equipment				
First-aid kit	1 lb. ($\frac{1}{2}$ kg)	a	$\frac{1}{8}$	plus hiker's model for any leaving the base camp
Survival kit	8 oz. (225 g)	a	$\frac{1}{8}$	plus hiker's model for any leaving the base camp
Smith's kit	3 lbs. ($1\frac{1}{3}$ kg)	a	$\frac{1}{8}$	for shoeing and treating injuries to stock
Clothes				up to the individual; must consider weather, prepare for rain (horseman's slicker best because it fits over the horse, rain chaps also useful), number of each item depends on weight limitations (and on the number of pack animals) and laundry facilities in route; any type of shoe acceptable, cowboy boots helpful if route goes through scrub brush (chaparral)
Food				a well-balanced menu of lightweight food, although some canned goods can be carried if there is enough pack stock to carry it; if pasturage is lacking or delicate, hay and grain (oats, etc.) should be carried for the animals

Canoeing

Weight limits in canoe camping follow a wide range, depending on the route (and thus the amount of portages you will encounter). Many or long portages will restrict the weight limit so that your list should look like that for backpacking, plus the items required by the canoes themselves. On the other hand, a trip made almost entirely by water will permit equipment more like that for horsepacking (except for items directly relating to the means of transportation). Even when heavy loads can be carried, the heavier tent designs are still too heavy. Supplies should be scattered between all canoes in a party in case of upset and loss.

	WEIGHT	WEATHER	NUMBER	NOTES
Pack				
Duluth	2 lbs., 3 oz. to 2 lbs., 12 oz. (1 to $1\frac{1}{4}$ kg)	a	$\frac{1}{2}$	the traditional pack for canoeing; basket packs sometimes used; pack frames good for carrying but difficult to stow in a canoe (and all but impossible to stow in a kayak)

	WEIGHT	WEATHER	NUMBER	NOTES
Emergency Equipment				
First-aid kit	1 lb. ($\frac{1}{2}$ kg)	a	$\frac{1}{8}$	plus hiker's model for each canoe
Survival kit	8 oz. (250 g)	a	$\frac{1}{2}$	plus hiker's model for each canoe
Canoe-repair kit	1 lb., 12 oz. (800 g)	a	$\frac{1}{2}$	one per canoe
Canoe and Equipment				
Canoe	65 lbs. (30 kg)	a	$\frac{1}{2}$	
Paddles	1 lb. ($\frac{1}{2}$ kg)	a	1	plus at least one spare per canoe
Yoke	2 lbs. (1 kg)	a	$\frac{1}{2}, \frac{1}{8}$	one per canoe makes portages quicker but one for the entire party will suffice for short portages; optional, since canoe paddles can be rigged for the purpose
Clothes				up to the individual; must consider weather (poncho good for rain since it makes a tent-like fitting over the canoeist and permits the paddling to be done under it, a spray cover, which does double duty in high waves, is welcome if there is much rain); a bathing suit should be included as water sports are a natural with this transportation; the number of each article depends on the duration of the trip, since laundry facilities are at hand (unless the water is too muddy); light-weight shoes (canoe moccasins or light-weight tennis shoes) should be worn in the canoe, although hiking boots will be welcome if there are long or difficult portages
Food				a well-balanced menu of lightweight food eases the job of packing; available water supply makes dehydrated and freeze-dried food most logical

Automobile Camping

It would seem, at first glance, that in car camping, especially with a station wagon, weight limits are not a factor. Many beginners attempt to camp from this basis and as a result they generally manage to fill two station wagons in the process. It is not unusual in state parks to find "campers" with regular, home-type beds in their "camps."

To really camp from a car, the same sport of trying to get the most comfort out of the least weight and bulk should apply, the only difference being that the maximum limit is raised because of the transportation device. Bulk is generally more of a problem in car camping than weight.

	WEIGHT	WEATHER	NUMBER	NOTES
Tent				same as for horsepacking; plastic tarp and single-tab tents are used as shelters to protect gear or as sun shades or dining flies
Pack				wooden or heavy cardboard boxes make the best packing containers; a belt pack for hikes or a lightweight pack for an overnight hike will be useful for such activities, but otherwise unnecessary
Sleeping Equipment				same as for horsepacking
Cooking Equipment				same as for horsepacking
Tools				same as for horsepacking
Miscellaneous Equipment				same as for horsepacking; if any hiking is done, water fountains are available at most public campsites within reasonable distance of any tentsite; water container is helpful for transporting it to the tentsite although a pot from the nesting set will do for the cooking supply
Emergency Equipment				
First-aid kit	1 lb. ($\frac{1}{2}$ kg)	a	$\frac{1}{8}$	plus hiker's model for any leaving the base camp
Survival kit	8 oz. (250 g)	a	$\frac{1}{8}$	plus hiker's model for any leaving the developed area of the campground
Car-repair kit	5 lbs. ($2\frac{1}{4}$ kg)	a	$\frac{1}{8}$	all parts and tools needed for minor repairs
Clothes				up to the individual; normal sports clothing for the season is generally adequate; poncho and rain chaps are usually most comfortable for rainy weather although many prefer a rain suit because woodchopping, etc., is easier; prepare for cold if camping at high altitudes or in winter (desert or high altitudes can be quite cold at night even though mild or even hot during the day); the number of each article—more dependent on space available than on weight factors—is not strictly limited because of the extreme mobility of the transportation system, and access to coin-operated laundry facilities will reduce the number, especially if a large amount of wash-and-wear clothes are used; hiking boots are helpful if an extensive amount of hiking is done; tennis shoes limit activities before the dew has a chance to evaporate

Food

a well-balanced menu is easy since the weight and bulk requirements of other transportation forms is not a factor; canned goods can be carried, but to save on space these should be limited as much as possible and the more typical light-weight foods used more; an ice box can be carried which practically solves the problem of milk, butter, and eggs; sand-wich fillings are good for lunch-making since they are quick to fix and take up little time from the day's activities

REDUCING THE WEIGHT OF THE GEAR

The more you depend on your own muscles for your transportation, the less weight you will be able to take. On the other hand, the natural tendency is to take as much as you possibly can. This usually results in a ten- or fifteen-pound overload ($4\frac{1}{2}$ or $4\frac{3}{4}$ kg).

There are two methods of avoiding this. The first is in the selection of the equipment in the first place. Pick light, compact items of gear and cut down on the weight by careful selection of the kit.

The second is an old traditional one. After you get home from a trip, put all of your gear in three stacks: the first for those items you used every day, the emergency kits (first-aid, repair, and survival), and rain gear; the second for the things you used only once or twice the whole time; the third for the things you didn't use at all. Then, the next time you go camping, take the first stack, leave the third, and take a good hard look at the second.

PART III

Make It Yourself

The term "do-it-yourself" is fairly recent, not because the activity is new, but because it is now sufficiently out of the ordinary. People have been making things for themselves since the beginning of civilization, but it is only within the last half-century or so that the techniques of mass production have taken over so completely that an item a person makes from raw material, all by himself, is so unusual that a special term is needed to describe it.

I mention this not to wax philosophical on the Industrial Revolution but to reassure the reader who has never done any handicrafts that, far from being a secret art known only to a few, it is a quite normal way of going about things. This is especially true in the field of camp equipment, for few of the truly mass-produced camping products are really good. Most commercially available camping gear, especially for such camping needs as backpacking, is largely handmade. This is the primary reason they are priced so high—but it is also the reason that they last so long.

Most American families today, in the socio-economic strata which go in for camping in the first place, have sewing machines and garage workshops with a few modest-to-elaborate tools.

Because it is strong, light, and capable of being formed into something that will hold something else, fabric is a prime material for camping equipment. Tents, packs, sleeping bags, clothing, and storage bags all are primarily fabric, and all are practically required if any extensive camping is done.

Since I learned to use the sewing machine on small equipment bags, my wife contends that all I know how to sew are bags. Yet my "bags" have not only included a pack-frame pack (which is sort of an elaborate bag), but also a tent, a sleeping bag, and an anorak. Every man should know how to sew—if only to avoid the feeling of dependence on his wife and the department store. It really isn't all that hard. Any man who can read a simple blueprint and run a buzz saw can sew.

For too long women have staked out certain activities for themselves and men have meekly obeyed these prohibitions as reflecting on their masculinity or something. Of course these activities, such as cooking, sewing, etc., are often boring and tedious on a day-in, day-out basis, and so provide a built-in excuse for men to obey the "keep out" signs—but they are also the essential skills for maintaining life, and thus the woman can become indispensable for reasons other than those which nature has provided.

When a man is forced into these jobs which tradition has not encouraged him to learn, it can be quite embarrassing. Bachelor cooking has long been a source of poor jokes, especially when the bachelorhood is temporary, a wife being sick or out elsewhere. (When Kit Carson signed on with Frémont's expedition as a scout, he insisted on being provided with a tipi—no uncomfortable Army tents for him. The only trouble was that tipi erection was a woman's job and though he had lived in one for years, his wife had always set it up. A passing Indian woman was persuaded to give him lessons, so he finally learned the very simple skills. Under the circumstances, it is easy to understand why the Plains Indian cultures were some of the strongest matriarchies known to anthropology.) Every man should know how to cook and sew, if only to retain his self-sufficiency.

Most of the equipment which doesn't require sewing involves basic wood and metal work which most men learn sometime in life. Some of the more minor projects included in this book involve work in fiberglass, but they are rather special items of less general interest, included because they are not available anywhere else.

As important as the skills involved are the materials. The specific qualities of the materials will be discussed with each type of project, but a few general statements are needed here. Materials, especially for tents and packs, but to some degree for other equipment too, should be purchased from camping outfitters. At first glance, the prices seem a bit higher than those in the mail-order catalogs and department stores, but they are designed for the camper who really camps and not the one who simply unpacks an overloaded station wagon and calls it camping. As a result, they are especially made for combining the maximum of strength with the minimum of weight.

Camping, especially the rougher forms such as backpacking and canoeing, puts a far different set of stresses on your gear than carrying it in the back of the car, or even in the panniers of a good pack mule. Materials which may be quite good for such easy treatment will simply not hold up under all conditions in the wilderness.

Also, the more remote you get, the more you will have to depend on each item of equipment, because it will be all you have, there will be no corner store to go to. As a result, you will need a built-in margin of strength. This is generally failing in the more mass-produced materials.

Finally, your tent is not just a shelter from the rain, it also has to keep out cold wind howling down from the mountains in late-spring cold spells. Your pack is not just something to hold all of your gear, it also must protect the gear from being banged around or ripped by a passing thorn. Rugged conditions require special material, and the established camping outfitters will have it. If you can't get it from at least one of the outfitters listed in Chapter 56, you don't really need it anyway.

I would especially like to recommend *Light Weight Camping Equipment* (see Chapter 54) to anyone making his own equipment. This is not so much for the plans offered, although they are excellent, but the vast amount of information on materials. This is an absolute must to any serious do-it-yourself maker of camp equipment.

The plans included in this book are not really hard, although all of them may seem impossible at first glance. Take your time. Read the directions, following along with the sketches and working the whole project out in your mind before you start.

Nylon fabrics, especially the lightweight tent fabrics, are easier to work if you seal the edges. Otherwise very fine threads ravel out and get in the way. Use a candle flame, and be careful that you keep the fabric the proper distance from the flame and move it at the proper speed. Too little heat will do no good, and too much will burn the cloth. You should see the frayed edge smoothly disappear but not have any noticeable balling of melted nylon. The proper result will be a small bead of melted nylon on the edge, which you can feel as a slight stiffness but not see without some effort. Practice on a scrap until you get the feel of the process.

Go slowly when you are making an item. Be sure you know what you are doing before you do it. Be sure that no part of the material other than what you want to sew gets near the needle when using the sewing machine. When you are sewing a long seam on a tent and have to crowd most of the tent into that narrow space under the arm of the machine, you will be convinced there is some attachment pushing the cloth under the needle. Keep it clear and you won't have to cut the seam out and start over. Pockets present the same problem in making packs.

Above all, make sure of all dimensions before you cut the fabric—it costs over $2.00 a yard, so don't waste it. In the case of clothing, a pattern made out of newspapers works almost as well as the traditional muslin and is a lot cheaper. This pattern can be tried on (using pins instead of stitches at the seams) and any adjustments made in the paper before the real fabric is cut. The paper then will smooth out to a true flat shape (muslin can be pulled out of shape) and provide the pattern for cutting the fabric.

Always be sure to allow enough for seams, joints, and all other parts of material which are seemingly wasted in joining two pieces together—regardless of the kind of material.

Start on simple projects. After you gain experience and confidence, you can

Newspapers can be glued into panels of almost any size to use for patterns in cutting cloth for camping gear. A living-room floor is an adequate lofting floor. The item here is an anorak.

tackle complex ones, knowing that you are producing as fine a product as the professional outfitters, at a lot lower price as well.

The secret of a good tent is good design and good materials. As mentioned in the introduction to Chapter 4, design changes with the purpose of the tent. To a certain extent, so does the material.

Choose your fabric with care. Especially if you are ordering by mail (as is usually necessary with lightweight fabrics), get as much information as you can before you choose. You will need to know the weight of the fabric. This may vary ten per cent either side of the stated weight, and the weight will usually be per square yard. (If it goes by the running yard, it will say so.)

You will also need to know the width since you may have to re-do your pattern if it is a different size than your plans. Tear-strength and porosity (how wind-resistant it is) are both important, although the figures will probably have meaning only in comparison to the figures of other fabrics, rather than as absolute statistics.

The best tent fabric for the tents for semi-permanent camps is what, in the old days, was called balloon silk. Despite its name, it is cotton—a very long staple, tightly woven fabric that weighs only four to six ounces per square yard.

While it is hard to find, it is still available under a variety of trade names. It is fairly expensive (as are all lightweight tent fabrics), but makes an excellent tent for semi-permanent camps. An even lighter material, such as a nylon or nylon-and-cotton mountain-tent fabric, is absolutely required for backpacking.

Both of these categories of fabrics (which really overlap a bit) are of the finest quality. They come in a wide variety of colors and are all dry-treated to be water-resistant. They have some close relatives which are coated with rubber or plastic and make excellent tent floors (essential on high-altitude or winter tents to keep out drafts) and ponchos.

The best inexpensive cloth is eight-to-ten-ounce, double-filled canvas. It is so heavy it practically requires a motor transportation, but it does make an inexpensive tent which will take a lot of wear. It also requires a lot to be done to it which is already done on the lighter fabrics, such as waterproofing, and often dyeing.

You can buy it either bleached or unbleached, but it should not be dyed. It is almost impossible to find dyed tent canvas that is not dark-khaki, olive-drab, or dark-green. (The backpacking tent fabrics, fortunately, come in a wide choice of reasonable colors—and some which are so bright that they are reasonable only in mountain climbing, where their visibility is an asset.) Dye bleached fabric a heat-reflecting color—light, but not bright—or leave it the natural off-white of the unbleached fabric. The pure-white tent will have a horrible glare from the sun (and even from a full moon and from lightning), and will form a projection screen for your undressing which may prove embarrassing in a public campsite.

If possible, buy the canvas already waterproofed. It is usually cheaper, and always more convenient. Get a dry waterproofing. It is not only lighter, but it does not have the slightly greasy or waxy feel of the oil-base treatment, nor will the fabric be as stiff.

If you have to waterproof it yourself, get a chemical waterproofing agent, typically a silicon or fluorocarbon base. The old paraffin-and-gasoline or turpentine method makes the fabric heavy and too stiff to handle easily, and the tent fabric tends to rot in too much sunlight. The chemical waterproofing, on the other hand, is stable in sunlight and adds practically no weight to the canvas. Although it will cost almost one-fourth of the total cost of the tent, it is a good investment toward a long life for your tent.

Before making the tent, regardless of the type of material you use, soak the fabric in water and let it dry overnight. This will shrink the fabric. If you don't shrink it beforehand, the tent may shrink out of shape. On some tents, even the one per cent shrinkage will pull it so out of shape that you can't erect it with a smooth surface.

Tent seams must be both strong and waterproof. Therefore, a French fell is required. It is not only impossible for water to run under this seam, it is quite rugged as well—a vital factor with the thinner backpacking fabrics. It has both edges turned under to prevent fraying, and a double row of stitching though all four layers.

The easiest way to sew this seam is as follows: place the cloth together with a half-inch (1 cm) overlap, pin it in place, and sew it down the center of the overlap, removing the pins as they get near the needle. Slide the two pieces together to give some slack, and then turn the overlap without turning the rest of the cloth. This forms the correct fold. Then stitch one-eighth of an inch ($2\frac{1}{2}$ mm) from each edge, making two rows, one quarter-inch (5 mm) apart. The tucked edges interlock.

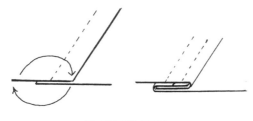

FRENCH FELL

Tent doors were formerly closed by tying short lengths of twill-tape which were attached to the edges of the doorway. A more elementproof method is by a full-length zipper. The zipper should have pulls on both the inside and the outside of the tent so it can be opened from either side, and should open from the bottom up. The zipper costs about a dollar more than the tapes, but is much more convenient. Also, no rain will run in nor will high winds open the door.

If you are using tent plans from an old book which calls for tapes, it is very easy to change it over. If the tapes fit on the edges of the fabric at the door, sew the zipper to this point. If one column of the tapes is over from the edge (to provide an overlap when the door is closed), cut the fabric so that this line is the edge and sew on the zipper as with the first method, providing, of course, for an adequate amount of hem so that there are no raw edges of fabric to fray and catch in the zipper.

CHAPTER TWELVE

Making Your Tent

Making your own tent has two advantages over buying it. First, you can usually save money. Second, you can add features not found in the commercial tents.

With the exception of the very heavy tents, such as tipis, the only equipment you will need is a sewing machine with a heavy needle, scissors, a steel tape measure, a chalk line, and carpenter's chalk. In place of the chalk line and chalk, you could use a large number of adequate straight edges. If the seams are such that the marked part will be hidden, the nylon-tipped pens are easier to use than chalk. The ink doesn't rub off and it comes in enough colors to be visible on any color fabric.

The only skills you need are those involving the use of these few items of equipment, plus the ability to read and follow fairly simple plans. While not absolutely necessary, a fairly large floor area and an assistant to help with the chalk line make the job easier.

DESIGNING YOUR OWN TENT

Tent design is not generally something for the amateur draftsman. Even if you make your own tent, it is usually best to copy a commercial tent design or update plans from an old camping book. This generally involves little change in the over-all configuration, but does nonetheless require designing ability. The most obvious change needed with the old plans is that they generally call for thirty-six-inch (91 cm) fabric (which was standard then) and the best modern fabrics are more in the neighborhood of forty-four inches (110 cm) wide.

This difference in width will involve several changes. Not only are the panels themselves going to be wider, the lengths of the pieces, especially along angles, will be different. This will involve extensive paper work with T-square and triangle, and probably require mock-ups as well. Remember the seam width in these computations, as they might not be the same as the seam width on the original. (In fact, this is really the hardest part of tent designing, because the seam width can never really be accurately figured. About the best you can do is come close, keep the right-angle ends even, and hide the differences in the diagonal ends in the seam they make with the other piece of fabric.)

There are, however, good and proper reasons for making a radical change in the dimensions of a tent. Few commercial tents, except for the extremely large wall tents, will adequately accommodate anyone over six feet (182 cm) tall with any degree of comfort (and a fairly large portion of the camping population is in this group). These tents are those seven feet (215 cm) long, since you need at least six inches (15 cm) at each end to prevent your bedding from rubbing the walls and creating capillary leaks in a rain. If you are over six feet (182 cm) tall, you will simply have to enlarge the plans, using procedures similar to those when using a wider fabric. The plans included in this book are adequate for taller campers. I am six-two (187 cm) and I designed them for me.

As for some entirely new design that you might

have in mind, you are hereby warned. Most possible designs have already been tried and, with the exception of some extreme modifications of wall and pup tents (such as the explorer tent or umbrella tent), few were worthwhile and all required a tremendous amount of fabric and were fairly heavy as a result. However, there is always the possibility that you may come up with some practical new concept in tent design—but take a good, unemotional look at it first.

The easiest way to design a tent (unless you are a competent draftsman) and the most nearly foolproof is to make a sketch showing all the dimensions you need to know. This means length and width of the floor, height of the whole tent, walls, etc. Using this sketch and an assortment of poles, stakes, chalk line or seine cord, make a full-size model of your tent. Put a cord at each seam, including those just joining two pieces of cloth in the same surface. Be doubly sure you allow for the seam in figuring the width of your cloth. A half-inch (1 cm) French fell takes a little over three-quarters of an inch (15 mm) from each piece.

When your mock-up is finished, get in it. Is it roomy enough? Sloping walls can remove much of the room that the floor plan shows. Will it shed rain? A flat or gentle slope in the roof may collect water. Flat roofs are permissible only for awnings over doorways. There, a capillary leak won't get your gear wet and you can push up the sag and empty the water after a rain. Otherwise, have at least a thirty-degree slope—a forty-five-degree one is much better. Gentle slopes also waste floor space if you don't have at least short walls around the sides. On the other hand, pull-outs will save some floor area otherwise wasted by sagging roofs when the roof goes all the way to the floor.

Be sure the width of the fabric you are planning to use is readily available. Twenty-eight-, thirty-, and thirty-six-inch (70, 75, 90 cm) widths are common for duck, although you can sometimes get seventy-two-inch (180 cm) widths as well. Thirty-six-, forty-, forty-two-, forty-four-, forty-seven-, and fifty-inch (90, 100, 105, 110, 117½, and 125 cm) widths are most common for the lightweight materials, with an inch variation below those figures fairly common. These fabrics are likely to crop up in all sorts of odd widths, mainly because some are based on inches, some on meters, and some only on the width of that particular loom. Regardless of the material, allow for shrinkage and seam width in making your model.

Don't be afraid to make adjustments in your model—that is what it is for. Two inches more headroom at this point and an inch less width at that will make the difference between a hard-to-make, hard-to-set, uncomfortable tent and a prize that you wouldn't go without on your camping trips.

Measure the string accurately while it is still set up and stretched tightly. Allow for seam width at the ridges and dew cloths (if separate from the panels) on floors as well as between panels on the sides—and record them on a revised sketch of the tent. Next, drawing to scale, lay out your pattern (similar to the tent plans in this chapter) so that you make the most use of your fabric. Order a little extra for errors and patches.

When you get your fabric, shrink it, lay it out on the floor, and with a metal tape measure mark the dimensions on the cloth. Stretch a chalk line from these points and mark your cutting lines. Then cut it out, sew it up, and take it out in the back yard to give it a try. You can usually correct any mistakes you have made then (assuming your plans were accurate) and not when you are—or should be—camping.

MAKING THE TIPI

I have not included a tipi plan for two reasons. First, I would have to simplify the construction in order not to give too much space to it. The tipi is too complicated to permit simplification without suffering from it. Second, anyone interested in making a tipi will be interested in the definitive source, *The Indian Tipi* (see Chapter 54). It has plans for a nineteen-foot (5.7 m) Sioux tipi, plus other information of interest to a tipi owner.

The consensus of those who have made tipis following this plan is that a few modifications are needed: Put parachute cord in all hems for reënforcement. This is especially needed around the opening of the pockets on the smoke-flaps. It is difficult to spear these with the smoke-flap poles under the best of conditions. The added cord helps hold them open.

Double the canvas in a semi-circle from the points of the smoke-flaps. This is where the greatest strain is on the cover.

The best material is a twenty-two-ounce, waterproof and fire-retardant, double-filled white duck, similar to that used for canvas mailbags. You can get it from Webb Manufacturing Company, Fourth at Cambria, Philadelphia, Pennsylvania. Otherwise follow the directions in the book.

MAKING THE EXPLORER TENT

Practically all of the construction features of the tents included in this chapter are found in the explorer tent. Therefore, most of the other tent-making descriptions will refer to the explorer-tent plan for details on many construction features.

The explorer tent has many features to make camp life more comfortable—good headroom, low wind-resistance, moderately large floor area, no inside poles (with most setting arrangements)—and although a fairly highly modified tent design (from its pup-tent ancestor), it is not a difficult one to make.

First, the panels of each side, the rear, and the doors should be sewed to each other. The two halves of the front should be sewed together at the top and the rest should be joined by a zipper extending from this point to the ground. The zipper must have pulls on both sides of the slide so it can be operated from both the inside and the outside of the tent, and it opens from the bottom upward.

Twill-tapes, eight inches (20 cm) long, coupled back to form a four-inch (10 cm) bight, are sewed at each seam, halfway between seams on the full-width panels, and at the corner of each door (all at the bottom after it is hemmed and while the sod cloths are being attached). One inch (25 mm) of the end of each is used in the sewing, making the finished bight three inches (75 mm) long.

Next, sew the rear to the sides, and the sides together at the ridge, putting a length of twill-tape inside the seam for the whole distance. Sew twill-tape bights at each end of the ridge, perpendicularly to the ridge line.

Sew the two halves of the hood together at the top and include a twill-tape bight at the lower end of this seam also. Then sew the front to the sides (this is easier with the door zipper fastened), including the hood folded with the side. The top nine inches (23 cm) of the front is sewed to two small zippers rather than directly to the side (the hood still folded with the side so that the door peak drops down, but the hood and side remain fixed when the vent is opened).

The vent zippers have the pulls on the inside of the tent and open from the top. Since these zippers have locks, the vent can be opened in any amount less than fully opened, as well as all the way. In any tent zipper, get heavy-duty brass zippers from camping outfitters. Dress zippers won't hold up under the strain and upholstery zippers will rust. A triangle of netting may be sewed over the outside of the vent opening to make it insectproof when open.

A nine-inch (23 cm) square of fabric should be used on the inside of the tent to spread the strain at the pull-out. Tuck the edges under and sew around it. Sew the tapes to the center of these squares and then stitch the squares with diagonal stitching.

For better ventilation, it is often necessary to keep the doors open, and this is an invitation to mosquitoes. An inner door of mosquito netting, about nine inches (25 cm) longer than the opening (to fold at the bottom like the sod cloths), with a zipper opening is helpful. Tie-back tapes, sewed to the inside, help keep the netting out of the way when not needed.

MAKING THE MINER TENT

There are no plans included for a miner tent because it is somewhat outmoded by more modern designs and there might not be many people interested in making one, and the explorer-tent pattern can be used to make a miner tent.

The miner tent takes twenty-three yards (21 m) of tent fabric, twenty-two feet ($6\frac{2}{3}$ m) of tape, and a four-foot (120 cm) zipper. In place of the rectangular side panels, the door, front, and hood patterns, make a duplicate of the rear and diagonal

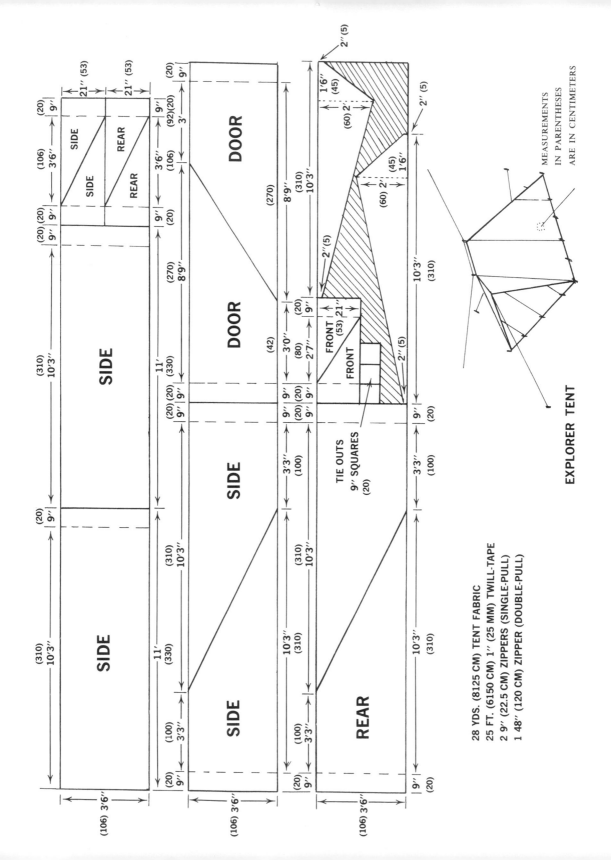

EXPLORER TENT

MEASUREMENTS
IN PARENTHESES
ARE IN CENTIMETERS

28 YDS. (8125 CM) TENT FABRIC
25 FT. (6150 CM) 1″ (25 MM) TWILL-TAPE
2 9″ (22.5 CM) ZIPPERS (SINGLE-PULL)
1 48″ (120 CM) ZIPPER (DOUBLE-PULL)

side panels and the little corners of side and rear (the forward corners of the sides are now triangular instead of square).

Stitch all sides identically except the front, which has a zipper in place of most of the center seam. All other construction techniques are the same as with the explorer tent except for the hood and vent. An explorer tent is basically a cross between a miner tent and a pup tent.

The zippered front door is absolutely required despite the fact that those of the Gold Rush (which gave the tent its name) were tied. The doorway is a potential source of leaks otherwise.

The miner tent is less practical in wet weather than most other modern tents because of its sloping door. On the other hand, with the exception of the tarp tents, it is the easiest of all tents to make, and quite easy to erect, even when you are alone.

MAKING THE BAKER TENT

This is the smallest of the semi-permanent camp tents discussed in this chapter in terms of floor area—a tall person lying down may stick out a bit. But because the tent is used in cold weather with a reflector fire, this makes no difference.

There are very few seams, but the pieces marked "top" are, in reality, the porch, the roof, and the rear wall with its sod cloth (as indicated by the dashed "fold" lines).

To make the baker tent, sew the two panels of each side and the two panels of the top to each other. Sew a length of one-inch (25 mm) twill-tape along the fold line between the roof and the rear wall on the top piece, letting a foot (30 cm) hang out on each side. Sew the sides to the top, this tape going through all of the fold—it will be doubled all over the place, but will preserve its strength.

Sew loops in the twill-tape hanging out at the top of the back wall and sew a similar tape across the porch/roof fold line, ending in loops. Sew similar-sized loops at each seam at the bottom and at the mid-point of the side and back panels and at the corner of the porch.

For privacy, you can either drop the porch or hang a curtain the same size as the porch across a rope stretched across the fold line. This latter method adds a bit of weight, but gives privacy while still permitting the advantages of the porch.

MODIFYING A PARACHUTE FOR CAMPING

The main problem with this tent is in finding the parachute. They are increasingly hard to obtain. As a result, you will often have to take less than the whole rig. Sometimes the parachute cord is cut off military-surplus chutes so they won't be used by sky divers and such. (The only reason they are available at all is that they are overage and therefore considered dangerous to use.)

If the only ones you can get are military-surplus chutes, try to get the cords with them. If not, you will have to buy a couple of hundred feet. If they are cut off at the canopy, you will have to put short lengths back again. Seal the ends of eight-inch (20 cm) lengths by burning. Holding one end flat against the edge of the canopy, sew it on with a zig-zag stitching. There are enough examples of this technique on the chute so you can easily see how to do it.

From there on, the procedure is much the same as when you are able to get an entire parachute.

If you are so fortunate, the modification of it into a tent is a very easy job, requiring all of thirty minutes to do. First, remove the little pilot chute from the main canopy. Do not remove the length of doubled parachute cord that connects the pilot chute to the main canopy or cut the loop at either end. It is most useful in hanging a paratipi.

Remove the main canopy from the pack, stretching it out on the floor. Cut the cords off six inches (15 cm) below the edge of the canopy. Burn the ends to keep them from fraying. Tie each one in a bowline knot at the edge of the canopy.

Remove the lengths of parachute cord from the pack. Burn both ends of each length. You can do what you like with the remainder of the pack material. You may find a use for it. Don't forget to remove the pamphlet "Emergency Uses of the Parachute" before you throw away any of the pack. It is in a small pocket on the pack and it may give you some ideas on how you can use the remainder of the parachute.

Keep the salvaged cords in individual coils.

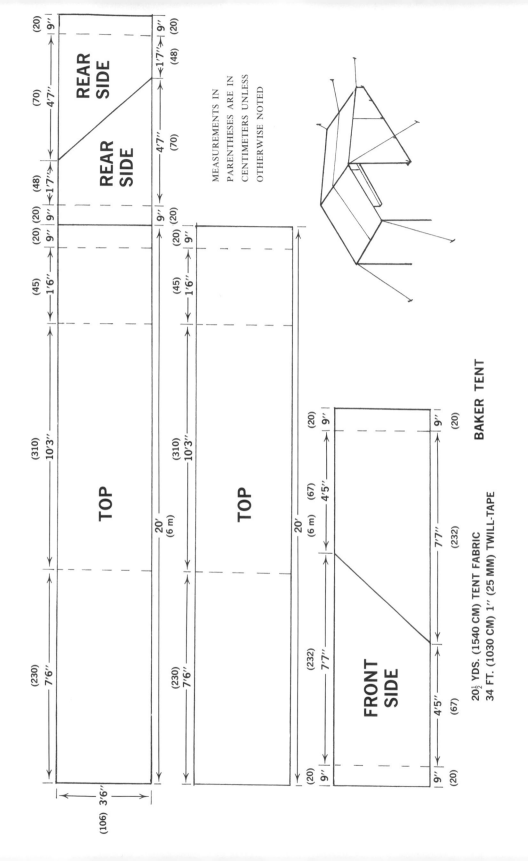

REAR SIDE

REAR SIDE

(20) 9"
(70) 4'7"
(48) 1'7"
(48) 1'7"
(70) 4'7"
(20) 9"

(20) 9"
(20) 9"
(45) 1'6"
(310) 10'3"
20' (6 m)
(230) 7'6"
3'6" (106)

TOP

(20) 9"
(20) 9"
(45) 1'6"
(310) 10'3"
20' (6 m)
(230) 7'6"

TOP

MEASUREMENTS IN PARENTHESES ARE IN CENTIMETERS UNLESS OTHERWISE NOTED

(20) 9"
(20) 9"
(67) 4'5"
7'7" (232)
(232) 7'7"
4'5" (67)
(20) 9"

FRONT SIDE

BAKER TENT

20½ YDS. (1540 CM) TENT FABRIC
34 FT. (1030 CM) 1" (25 MM) TWILL-TAPE

Three or four should be kept with the canopy for use in setting up the tent.

A problem with the paratipi is that a parachute is a hemisphere rather than a flat circle. As a result, the sides sag in, robbing you of almost two feet (60 cm) of space. You will note that the panels have three diagonal seams across them. At the valley of the second of these zig-zags around the canopy, sew a short loop of parachute cord through both thicknesses of the semi-circle of the modified tent. When the paratipi is erected, these loops enable you to guy the tent out, giving a considerable increase in the floor area over the more standard setting pattern. Since the other parachute-tent settings use the semi-circle too, none of the parachute's features are lost in the change. The only disadvantage is that the tent takes longer to dry out after a rain.

An easier way is with a patented rig called a Visklamp. This is a rubber ball and a heavy wire dumbell. The ball is pushed from the inside of the tent into the larger end of the dumbell. The dumbell is lowered so that the ball is inside the smaller end and the guy rope is tied to the larger end. The Visklamp was designed to make a plastic-tarp into a tab tent, so it won't slip down the sides of the paratipi, regardless of the wind. Six or seven of these ten-cent gadgets will do the job adequately and can be removed for drying the wet tent faster. Add one coil of parachute cord and an extra stake for each. Two or three more Visklamps without the cords or stakes make a good device for keeping the door closed during a high wind.

MAKING THE MOUNTAIN TENT

For its capacity, this is the most expensive tent to buy or make. It costs almost as much as a four-man tent to buy and it is one of the most complex tents to make. Yet when the cold wind blows, this is the best portable shelter. For this reason, it is necessary to get a fabric with as little air penetration as possible. It is expensive—from two to four dollars per yard—but the tent is worthless without it.

Note that two different types of cloth are required. The first is any mountain-tent fabric such as ventile, element cloth, Shirley cloth, etc. The other is Horcolite, Nylport, or any similar vinyl-coated nylon of extremely light weight. The latter is completely air- and moisture-tight and is used for the floor.

Since the tent is made of such lightweight material (five pounds [$2\frac{1}{4}$ kg] for the complete two-man tent, three and a half pounds [$1\frac{1}{2}$ kg] without the optional fly), twill-tape is used to reënforce the ridge seam from the anchor loop at the end of the vent hood to the anchor loop at the rear of the tent. This is the point of greatest strain on the erected tent. The tape is sewed into the French-fell seam.

The first step after cutting out the pieces is to sew together the two halves of each side and floor so there is one full-length piece of each. Next sew the ridge seam. On this, sew a flat seam with the tape on the bottom; then fold it over to form the French fell so that the tape is completely enclosed from the top and visible only at the edge from the inside. The tape should be formed into a two-inch (5 cm)-long loop at the rear, but the front should extend out flat since the hood is added later.

The next step is to sew the floor to the sides, taking care that the sides are over the floor. At this point, the middle stake-loops, four inches (10 cm) long, are inserted into the seam at the point where the seam is folded over. You now have a long, tapering tube.

Sew the rear triangle into the small opening of the tube, using the French fell and inserting the stake-loops at the rear of the tent. The ridge tape loop will be folded with the seam.

Turning to the other end, sew the sod cloths to the door triangles, inserting the stake-loops at the door. Sew the zipper to the doors, folding the raw edge under so that it will be held with the same stitches that hold the zipper. The zipper should open upward. Toward the end of the zipper (about one inch from the end), pull the two doors toward each other so that they overlap when the zipper teeth run out, and finish sewing the rest of the way with a folded fell (a French fell without the interlocking of the cloth). The selvage edge of the door should be at the seam with the side walls.

Sew the short vent zippers to the door, letting one zipper overlap the other at the apex of the triangle so there isn't a large gap where the two

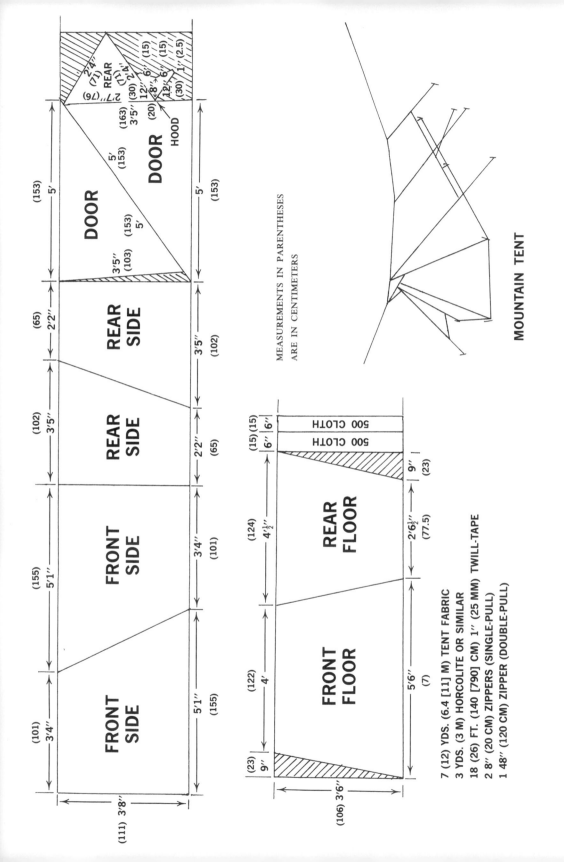

REAR

DOOR

DOOR

HOOD

24" (71)

27'1" (76)

12" (30)

8" (20)

12" (30)

6" (15)

2'4" (1')

12" (30)

6" (15)

6" (15)

1" (2.5)

3'5" (163)

5' (153)

5' (153)

5' (153)

3'5" (103)

5' (153)

5' (153)

2'2" (65)

3'5" (102)

3'5" (102)

2'2" (65)

5'1" (155)

3'4" (101)

5'1" (155)

3'4" (101)

3'8" (111)

FRONT SIDE

FRONT SIDE

REAR SIDE

REAR SIDE

500 CLOTH

500 CLOTH

REAR FLOOR

FRONT FLOOR

6" (15)

6" (15)

4½" (124)

4' (122)

9" (23)

9" (23)

2'6½" (77.5)

5'6" (7)

3'6" (106)

MEASUREMENTS IN PARENTHESES
ARE IN CENTIMETERS

MOUNTAIN TENT

7 (12) YDS. (6.4 [11] M) TENT FABRIC
3 YDS. (3 M) HORCOLITE OR SIMILAR
18 (26) FT. (140 [790] CM) 1" (25 MM) TWILL-TAPE
2 8" (20 CM) ZIPPERS (SINGLE-PULL)
1 48" (120 CM) ZIPPER (DOUBLE-PULL)

zippers meet, short of the peak of the vent. Remember, the slide pulls go on the inside of the tent. Sew the doors to the side, with a double row of stitches over a flat seam (both the side and the doors have a selvage edge here), inserting the hood at the top and the stake-loops at the bottom. Sew the ridge tape to the hood, ending in a loop two inches (5 cm) long. Finally, sew the pull-out loops halfway up the seam between the two side halves on each side. A stuff bag, made from a light fabric, completes the job.

Because this sway-backed tent is so small, bedding is reduced to individual sleeping bags and short air mattresses for its two residents. Even then there is some danger of brushing against the inside of the tent in wet weather and this usually starts a dripping, although it isn't as bad as with most tents because of the angle of the slope and the short distance to the ground. Also, there is the problem, when it is used in the mountains, that the cold wind can't be kept out completely by the tight weave of the fabric because of the high velocity (and therefore force) of the wind. Because of these two factors, a fly is a decided advantage in this tent. The fly acts as a windbreak and the tent itself can be more efficient in keeping the heat inside the tent. Also, since the fly gets wet and not the tent proper, accidentally brushing against the inside of the tent will not start the endless dripping or trickle that is a problem with most tents.

The fly should be a separate piece, resting on the ridge line. In construction, a fly is just the sides, including the ridge tape, of the regular tent. The bottom of the sides should be hemmed so that no raw edge shows and the stake-loops are sewn in place. The loops may be the two-inch (5 cm) size instead of the four-inch (10 cm) size required for stakes, since they will be fitted with ropes in use. The bottom of the fly should be spread farther apart than the main tent's so that the angle is not quite as steep, but the ridge line should be on the same catenary so that the fly will fit the tent properly. Generally, the fly will rest directly on the tent and be supported by its ridge. However, if you have the rope, it is better to set it separately and a couple of inches (about 5 cm) above the tent itself. For this reason, it should have loops at each end, although no hood will be needed.

The main advantage of the separate fly (as opposed to one sewed onto the main tent) is that it can be left at home if there is no chance of rain or if the weather will be too cold for water to be on the tent in a liquid form to make a capillary leak. The fly alone can be used over the wood supply or suspended higher as a sunshade over the eating area. In the latter case, it can be moved from that to its tent-fly function as the weather requires.

As an option, the rear triangle could be attached with a zipper and two such tents be joined back to back for foul-weather camping. The advantages are very slight in such arrangements since it is hard to heat that far back into a tent, but it does permit movement from one to the other without getting out in bad weather.

MAKING THE ATC TENT

Because it lacks a floor, the ATC tent is easier to make than the mountain tent, taking about half a day to finish. The fabric is fifty-five-inch (140 cm) urethane-coated nylon and is fantastically light, strong, and airtight. Because of this airtightness, the tent is vented at each end to permit moisture to escape. Because it also can be set flat as a tarp or fly, special zippers must be used, and there is a small problem of finding zippers with slides at each end and pulls on each side of the slides. A little work on the phone will find your closest source. You may have to assemble your own from parts.

Construction is easy. Lay the fabric down, plastic side up, and mark the cuts according to the plans. After cutting, join the two halves of each side with a flat seam (it is on the selvage, eliminating the need for the French fell) with the rear half on the outside.

Next sew the two sides together at the ridge, sewing an eleven-foot (330 cm) length of twill-tape under this seam, keeping it centered along the length of the seam and extending a foot (30 cm) beyond each end of the seam. Use a French fell seam with the tape completely inside the finished seam.

Sew the rear to the left side. Sew the right side and rear to the three-foot (90 cm) zipper. Extend the ends of the zipper about two inches (5 cm) at the peak of the rear triangle not sewed to the sides.

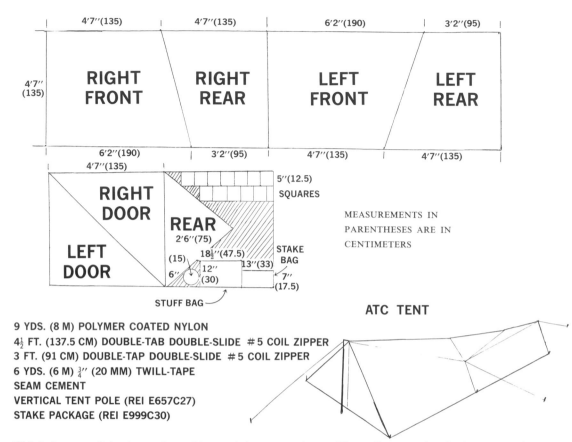

MEASUREMENTS IN PARENTHESES ARE IN CENTIMETERS

ATC TENT

9 YDS. (8 M) POLYMER COATED NYLON
4½ FT. (137.5 CM) DOUBLE-TAB DOUBLE-SLIDE #5 COIL ZIPPER
3 FT. (91 CM) DOUBLE-TAP DOUBLE-SLIDE #5 COIL ZIPPER
6 YDS. (6 M) ¾″ (20 MM) TWILL-TAPE
SEAM CEMENT
VERTICAL TENT POLE (REI E657C27)
STAKE PACKAGE (REI E999C30)

This is for ease of zipping and provides a minimum vent with the zipper completely closed. (Both zippers should have their teeth pointing downward.) Push this part of the zipper inside the tent to get it out of the way and take the end of the ridge tape and place it one inch (25 mm) inside the tent. Sew it to form the rear guying loop with a square stitching followed by an X inside the square.

Sew the two doors together with the 4½-foot (135 cm) zipper, leaving a two-inch (5 cm) gap at the top like the foot triangle. Sew the door triangle to the sides and make the front guying loop the same as with the foot.

Cut the remainder of the tape into eleven six-inch (15 cm) lengths and two two-inch (5 cm) lengths. These form the loops for the stakes and pull-outs and the two ridge-rope loops on the ridge. These are sewn with a one-inch (25 mm) overlap and the square and X pattern as with the ridge

loops. The pull-out and stake loops may be reënforced with a five-inch (125 mm) square of fabric to ease the strain on the tent cover itself.

Waterproof all seams with seam compound, using as light a coat as possible to seal the holes in the plastic coating made by the sewing needle. Coat from the outside only, since the tape inside the ridge will not dry easily if moisture gets into it.

The stuff bag is made by sewing the rectangular piece into a tube along the twelve-inch (30 cm) side with a quarter-inch (5 mm) French fell seam. The round piece is pinned to the tube and sewn, in the wrong-side-out position, at the point where the pieces fit together. Two small grommets are stitched in the top of the tube so they will be on the outside when the edge is folded under to form a half-inch (1 cm) hem on the inside of the finished bag. Small buttonholes make good grommets on a stuff bag. A shoestring or parachute cord sheath is run through this hem to form a drawstring and is tack-stitched opposite the grommets so it won't come out of the hem.

The stake bag is made in the same manner except there is no round bottom and the side is sewed flat across. The poles can be carried loose (or in their original plastic bag until it wears out) in a pack, but the bicycle case may be helpful for backpacking too. This is a golf bag divider tube cut down to twenty-one and a quarter inches (435 mm) long. A $1\frac{3}{8}$-inch (33 mm) diameter flip-top pill bottle is cemented to the bottom with epoxy or cynoacrylate cement (the bottle can be cut down to a half-inch [1 cm] length first), and the lid exactly fits the flared top of the tube. This fits in the frame behind the seat of most bicycles, making this normally cumbersome item of equipment almost custom-fitted to the bike.

Finally, in Recreational Equipment's stake package comes forty feet (12 m) of parachute cord. This should be cut into three pieces, two short ones nine and a half feet (285 cm) long. Fuse the ends by burning so the rope doesn't fray. The short lengths are for the pull-outs and the long one for the ridge. The ridge rope is threaded through the two ridge loops and attaches the ridge guys to the poles with two full turns of the ridge rope before staking out.

The tent is set foot-to-the-wind for aerodynamics and to keep rain off the doors. A little experimentation will show how much vent opening is needed for the wind conditions—the more wind, the less the opening.

MAKING THE BIVOUAC TENT

While comparatively easy to make, the bivouac tent does have some tricky parts. Most of these come from the rather odd location of seams. The polyurethane or vinyl-coated nylon floor extends up the wall six and a half inches (16 cm)—seven inches (175 mm) of the fabric, the rest in a French-fell seam with the top. The top has no seams other than at its edges, but it has a twill-tape down the center to help support the strain on the fabric when pitched. Twill-tape is also used at the foot of the triangle where it joins the top and floor, but not on the seam joining the two halves of the

foot. As with the mountain tent, these tapes are inserted with the final double row of stitches.

The construction procedure starts by sewing the two halves of the end—the only such piece in this tent. Next, sew the tape down the center of the top with a double row of stitches. Then sew the top and floor together.

The end is sewed onto this tube, and finally the door is attached with two 28″ (71 cm) zippers, opening from the top, and with pulls on both sides.

The poles are fairly easy to make. A five-foot (150 cm) length of one-quarter- or three-eighths-inch (5 or 8 mm) diameter aluminum will do the job. Make them in an inverted V with the top dipping in a one-inch radius to keep the top loop of the tent from slipping down. The poles are threaded through the loops before the tent is erected.

Fore-and-aft guys are all that are essential, but in a wind the tent will stay better if it is staked out on the bottom also. Twill-tape loops, sewed to the floor, take care of this problem.

MAKING TARP TENTS

The easiest tarp tent to make is to take an 8′ x 12′ (240 x 360 cm) piece of four-mil polyethylene sheeting, six or eight Visklamps, and several lengths of parachute cord. However, if you want something a little more durable, a tab tent will be what you need.

Again, lightweight fabric with low air penetration is required. Since the tent is set in basically open designs, the featherweight plastic-coated nylon is quite good. This will give you a tent weighing under three pounds (1.35 kg)—your empty pack could easily weigh more than your tent.

The only tricky part about making a tab tent is in keeping the center panel outside the other two. Since some of the settings will have an outer panel higher than the center one, the seams must be French fells to prevent leakage under the seam.

Both the regular and double-tab tents have the same construction techniques: sew the panels together the same as the panels on any other tent, and sew the tabs on the same way as the pull-out loops on the other designs.

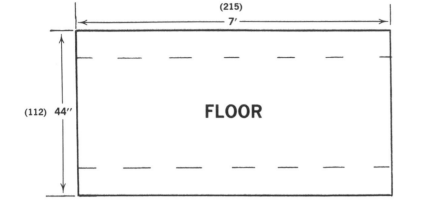

FLOOR

(215)
7'

(112) 44''

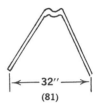

32''
(81)

(215)
7'

(40)
16''

TOP

END

DOOR

END

(112) 44''

17'' (43)

17'' (43)

BIVOUAC TENT

7 FT. (215 CM) 44'' (112 CM) NYLSURF NYLON
8½ FT. (255 CM) 44'' (112 CM) TENT FABRIC
2 ¼'' OR ⅜'' (5 OR 7 MM) DIA x 60'' (152 CM)
  ALUMINUM RODS
25 FT. (7.5 M) 1'' (25 MM) TWILL-TAPE
2 28'' (70 CM) ZIPPERS (DOUBLE-PULL)
2 TO 8 STAKES

MEASUREMENTS IN
PARENTHESES ARE IN
CENTIMETERS

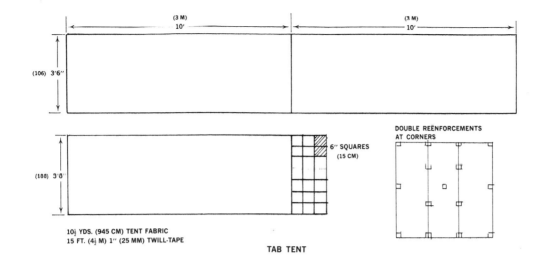

(3 M)
10'

(3 M)
10'

(106) 3'6''

(100) 3'0''

6'' SQUARES
(15 CM)

DOUBLE REËNFORCEMENTS
AT CORNERS

10½ YDS. (945 CM) TENT FABRIC
15 FT. (4½ M) 1'' (25 MM) TWILL-TAPE

TAB TENT

(106) 3'6''

(6 M)
20'

(15)
6'' SQUARES

(106) 3'6''

(106) 3'6''

21 YDS. (1865 CM) TENT FABRIC
35 FT. (4.5 M) 1'' (25 MM) TWILL-TAPE

DOUBLE-TAB TENT

MEASUREMENTS IN
PARENTHESES ARE IN
CENTIMETERS UNLESS
OTHERWISE NOTED

CHAPTER THIRTEEN

Making Your Sleeping Bag

Making a sleeping bag can be very easy (for an uninsulated bag with blankets) or very hard (for the down-filled mummy bag).

In general, sleeping bags are slightly harder to make than tents. The fabric is thinner (generally rip-stop nylon or thin rayon for the shell, with mosquito netting for the baffles). Down is difficult to handle as it needs a totally draft-free room to keep it from floating away. Batts of Dacron fluff are far easier to handle, but make a bag of inferior quality. The commercial price is probably too close to make it worthwhile to make your own.

The design of sleeping bags, especially the mummy style, is quite complicated, requiring considerable sewing. The seams must never go completely through the insulation or it will reduce the effective insulation thickness to that at the seams—the rest of the insulation will be wasted. Also, zippers or other fastenings must be covered with insulation in a manner which neither interferes with the operation of the zipper nor permits the insulation to be too thin at that point.

Despite this, a down-insulated bag is not beyond the skill of anyone experienced in the use of a sewing machine. The variable-insulation bag, while not as compact when folded, is just as serviceable, and can be made by anyone who knows the basic operation of a sewing machine.

One stage between regular sleeping bags and improvised bags using blankets (Chapter 5) is simply a sack, with snaps or a zipper down one side and filled with blankets. It is easy to make, being the size of the improvised blanket bag, and it keeps your blankets clean when camping. Because of its weight, it is impractical in all but auto camping. Because of its simplicity, there are no plans for it included in this chapter.

MAKING A SACK SLEEPING BAG

If you need a sleeping bag with down insulation, it is not very difficult to make one in a sack shape. Essentially it is a bag inside another bag, with the insulation in between.

Obviously, you can't just fill the space between the two bags with insulation since it would become very uneven in thickness as the insulation shifted in the space between the two bags. Also, you can't just sew a quilt-work of stitches to hold the down in place as you can with wool or synthetic batts, since that would just compress the down and have the effective insulation thickness from one-eighth to one-quarter inch (3 to 5 mm).

Of the two methods of enclosing down, the box construction, with its vertical walls, is the most difficult since it requires a separate piece for each baffle and great care in keeping the two bags properly lined up when sewing them in place. It also requires more baffles.

The overlapping tube is easier to handle and

practically as good. You make the tubes by sewing a piece of cloth (usually mosquito netting because of its lightness and elasticity) in a zig-zag between the two walls of the bag. In cross-section this should look like a series of triangles (the box looks like a series of squares). The base of the triangles should be equal to about six times the thickness of the insulation (as opposed to the box construction which can be no greater than twice).

The thickness of the insulation you should have in a particular bag is determined by the temperature range you expect to encounter on your trip. One inch (25 mm) of insulation is good for temperatures down to about freezing. From there, add a quarter inch for each ten degrees F (1 mm per degree C) lower you expect. Remember, the insulation on the bottom tends to compress with your body weight, making it thinner and less effective. Also, these temperature/thickness ratios are only approximate. Some people sleep comfortably in cold which would keep another awake and shivering. Warm sleeping wear, such as athletic sweatsuits, will extend the range downward or will permit a "hot sleeper" to be comfortable in the rated temperature of that particular bag.

To make a sack sleeping bag, sew the top and bottom halves of each bag (inside and outside) to each other. Then sew them together along one side, making sure they are even at the foot. You now have two panels, one on top of the other, the narrower one on top, sewed along one edge.

Nylon mosquito netting is best for the baffling. Sew the baffles in place between the inner and outer bags in the order shown in the plans. When you reach the other side, sew the two halves together along that side. Sew the two halves together at the pillow and at the top. You now have a flat, double-walled, baffled sheet in the shape of an opened sleeping bag, but with no insulation and the foot of the tubes still open.

Fill the tubes with insulation material from the foot. Shake the bag to settle the insulation. It should be well settled, but not packed, in order to get the maximum insulative qualities from the down. Try to keep each tube about equal in bulk to the next one. Close each one with a clothespin when you finish, to keep the down from coming out and floating off. After the tubes are filled, adjust them for equal insulation, and sew them closed at the foot. You now have an open sleeping bag laid flat.

Fold the bag into its final shape, but wrong-side-out. Pin it shut at the foot with straight pins. Turn the bag right-side-out, but leave a couple of inches (about 5 cm) at the foot still tucked under in the wrong-side-out position. Now sew up the foot, with a zipper forming the seam, through the outside walls only. Continue the zipper and the seam around the corner and up the side, about two inches (5 cm) up the outside bag (so that some of the outside bag is inside the zipper) and sew the zipper on up to the top. At the side as well as at the foot, the zipper is sewed only through the outside bag.

As long as the bag is sufficiently long, and your feet aren't pressing tightly against the zipper, this method will give the foot and side seams at the zipper adequate insulation, and still permit the bag to be opened at the side and foot to unfold flat for airing.

MAKING A MUMMY BAG

While definitely not for the beginner at sewing, the mummy bag is not difficult for those skilled at the sewing machine. The construction techniques are almost the same as with the down-insulated sack bag. The obvious exceptions are: the zipper is down the center rather than on the side, there is a hood that fits around the head, and the foot seam is vertical while the bag itself lies flat.

Note that the long dimension of the bag is cross-wise to the fabric. This makes two seams —one at the end of the taper, the other across the hood—on both the inside and outside bags. Sew the three pieces of each half together, using a French fell. (This is needed to make it downproof, most of the edge is on selvage and there is not the usual danger of ravelling.)

Next, sew the inside and outside together at the foot so that the seam will be on the inside of the finished bag. You now have the flat panels of the shell, fastened with a seam hidden inside the fold at the foot.

Next, start the mosquito netting on the inside

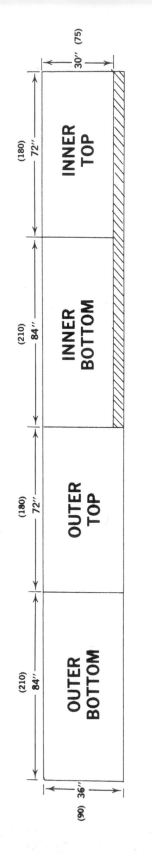

INNER
TOP

INNER
BOTTOM

OUTER
TOP

OUTER
BOTTOM

(75)
30"

(180)
72"

(210)
84"

(180)
72"

(210)
84"

(90)
36"

9 YDS. (7.8 M) SLEEPING-BAG FABRIC
2 YDS. (2 M) MOSQUITO NETTING
100" (250 CM) ZIPPER (DOUBLE-PULL)
1 LB. (½ KG) DOWN

MEASUREMENTS IN
PARENTHESES ARE IN
CENTIMETERS

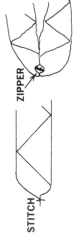

ZIPPER

STITCH

STITCHING AND ZIPPER DETAILS

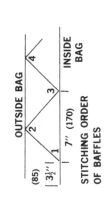

OUTSIDE BAG

2   3   4

1

INSIDE
BAG

(85)
3½"

7" (170)

STITCHING ORDER
OF BAFFLES

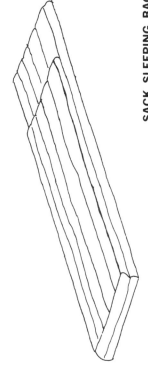

SACK SLEEPING BAG

bag, three and a half inches (9 cm) from the seam across the foot. Then zig-zag it up the two bags in the same manner described on the insulated sack bag.

You will discover that you can't get mosquito netting in a sixty-three-inch (160 cm) width (the width of the outer bag) and at first glance it would seem impossible to fit it on from seam to seam. However, this is not cloth but netting, and the forty-four-inch width will easily stretch to the sixty-three-inch width. Stretch it for the outer-shell seam and let it slack up a bit for the inner-shell seam. Make sure at all times that you keep the center lines of both bags and the netting baffle lined up. After you sew the edges closed, you can cut the baffle off even so that it is even with the shell material along the edges. The tension of the netting will automatically make this adjustment on the straight part. However, this trimming is done later. You now have the two bags connected at the foot and by the baffle, much like corrugated cardboard, except that one bag is considerably wider than the other, making it difficult for them to lie flat.

Tucking the edges under so that there are no raw edges showing, and getting the baffle into the seam, sew along one edge from the foot past the center of the hood so that there is about a three- or four-inch (75 to 100 mm) opening to the inside of the last tube in the hood. Start with the hood and fill the tubes with the insulation. Pin the openings with clothes pins as you finish each one. Shake the bag to settle the insulation, but do not pack it.

After you fill all the tubes and the insulation is even, pin it shut with straight pins. Sew up the tubes, tucking the edges under and including the baffle as you did with the first side. Remember to keep the center lines lined up. The outer bag is considerably larger than the inner, to compensate for its larger circumference in the completed bag. At this stage, you have an insulated, more or less flat bag, one side larger than the other.

Folding the bag around in its final shape, pin it down the center. Turn it wrong-side-out, then right-side-out leaving a couple of inches (about 5 cm) inside, and sew the foot through the outside bag only, the same as the sack bag, to give full insulation at that seam (but without the zipper, of course). Sew the two twill-tapes (if you will be using them instead of a stuff bag) in this seam at their centers, so that they will be on the outside of the completed bag. Make sure that the foot seam is vertical as the bag lies flat. Then turn the bag back wrong-side-out.

The sack is only sewed up through the outside shell. Sew the mummy bag through both shells on the inside (at the edge) as well, since it doesn't open at the foot. This also keeps your feet from pushing to the seam where there is no insulation to keep them warm. Now turn it back again right-side-out. The foot is now sewed at two points: at the extreme edge of the bags, which is now permanently inside the completed bag, and two inches (5 cm) away, through only the outside bag, which is the apparent foot of the bag as viewed from the outside.

Sew the zipper down the front, sewing each side of the zipper to only one bag from each side (the inside of one half to the outside of the other). There should be a three-inch (75 mm) overlap here. Sew the part from the end of the zipper to the foot seam in the same way as the zipper, sewing through only one bag. However, use a double row of stitches for added strength. At no place in the entire bag should there be a stitch through the entire thickness of the bag. You now have the completed bag except for the hood.

Sew a one-inch (25 mm)-wide strip of scrap fabric around the edge of the head opening (from zipper to zipper) to hold a drawstring. Take the sheath from a length of parachute cord. (Remove the small cords from inside, and seal the ends by burning.) Lace it in the hem and sew it at the center of the hood to keep it from coming out accidentally. It will emerge at each side of the zipper through grommets sewed in the hem.

If you need a longer bag than the one shown in the plans, add the difference equally in the straight and tapered sections, keeping the head and foot widths constant as well as the distance between zig-zags. (Increase the size of the foot tube, adding another if necessary.) The bag is designed for one inch (25 mm) of insulation (one pound [$\frac{1}{2}$ kg] of down) and will be effective to just above

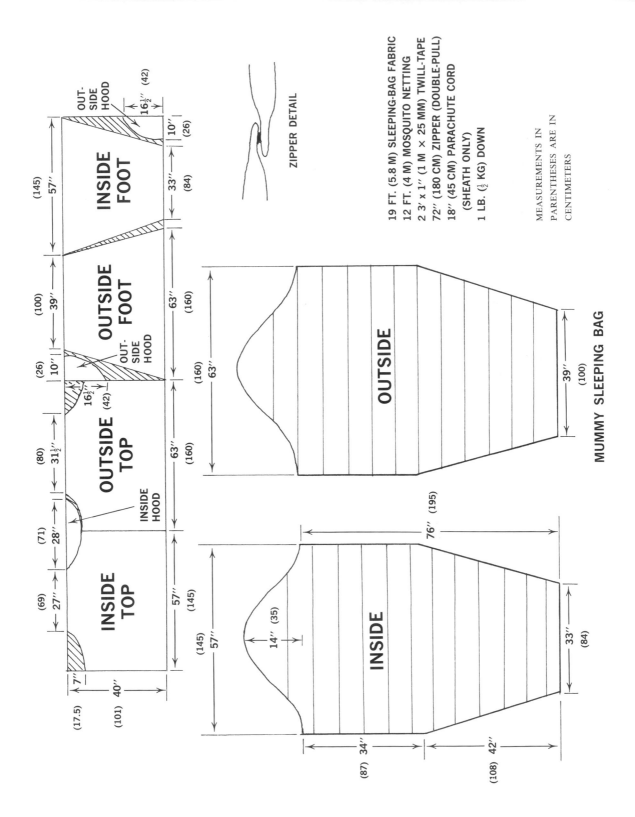

OUTSIDE HOOD

16½" (42)

INSIDE FOOT

(145) 57"

10" (26)

33" (84)

ZIPPER DETAIL

19 FT. (5.8 M) SLEEPING-BAG FABRIC
12 FT. (4 M) MOSQUITO NETTING
2 3' x 1" (1 M × 25 MM) TWILL-TAPE
72" (180 CM) ZIPPER (DOUBLE-PULL)
18" (45 CM) PARACHUTE CORD
(SHEATH ONLY)
1 LB. (½ KG) DOWN

MEASUREMENTS IN
PARENTHESES ARE IN
CENTIMETERS

(100) 39"

OUTSIDE FOOT

OUT-SIDE HOOD

(26) 10"

16½" (42)

63" (160)

(80) 31½"

OUTSIDE TOP

INSIDE HOOD

63" (160)

63" (160)

OUTSIDE

MUMMY SLEEPING BAG

39" (100)

(71) 28"

(69) 27"

INSIDE TOP

57" (145)

76" (195)

7" (17.5)

40" (101)

(145) 57"

14" (35)

INSIDE

33" (84)

34" (87)

42" (108)

freezing. If you need a bag for colder weather, the width of the outer bag must be increased about three inches (around 75 mm) for each half-inch (1 cm) increase in insulation thickness.

The twill-tapes may be omitted and a stuff bag used instead for packing the bag. Take the measurements of the smallest bundle you can roll the mummy bag into, then make a cloth sack slightly smaller. When made of rip-stop nylon, the stuff bag weighs a little more than the tapes, but helps to protect the sleeping bag, produces less wear on the fabric, and permits a smaller bundle. The stuff bag can be used for the sack type of sleeping bag equally as well.

MAKING A VARIABLE-INSULATION SLEEPING BAG

Not only the most versatile sleeping bag to use, this fairly new concept in sleeping-bag design is one of the easiest to make since there are no bothersome baffles to sew in. The foot of the inside bag is sewed and the outside bag is fitted with a zipper at the foot to permit access to the insulation. These are standard seams and zipper installations, there is no need to have overlaps to maintain full insulation.

The fabric of the bags should be cut differentially—that is, the inside bag should be smaller than the outside one. The easiest way is to cut the inside bag the same size as the foam (and two inches [5 cm] shorter), and make it smaller by the amount lost in the seams. The outside bag should be two inches (5 cm) longer than the foam, in both length and width. The dimensions on the plans are for the foam. Standard seams can be used, since the rip-stop nylon can be fused to prevent ravelling and therefore treated as selvage since all seams are on the inside of the insulation space.

The inside and outside bags are joined at the head in the same manner as the sack sleeping bag and each is separately sewed down the side to form a tube which is closed at the foot by sewing (inside) or with a zipper (outside). What you have now, except for the protruding "pillow" portion of the head, is quite similar to the glass in a vacuum bottle.

The side edge of the pillow portion and the top edge of the upper half of the shell are fitted with zippers so that the pillow can be bent around to form a hood in cold weather. A drawstring of parachute-cord sheath, fitted into the top edge of the pillow in the same manner as the mummy bag's drawstring, will permit the hood to be closed tighter.

There are four insulations for this bag. The first is nothing. This gives two layers of rip-stop-nylon covering for summer camping. This is enough to discourage, if not completely frustrate, mosquitoes biting through the bag, as well as insulate against the evening chill.

The second insulation is one-quarter-inch (7 mm) polyurethane foam, cemented in the shape of the insulation cavity (including the pillow). It is first joined along the side to form a cylinder and then along the bottom to close the foot. This is for fall or spring camping, and is adequate for temperatures down to around fifty degrees F (10°C).

The third insulation is three-quarter-inch (2 cm) polyurethane foam prepared in the same manner as the one-quarter-inch (7 mm) foam. This is for winter camping, and will handle temperatures down to twenty degrees F (−7°C).

If you should camp in even colder temperatures, another fifteen or twenty degrees F (8 to 10°C) can be gained by using both the three-quarter- and the quarter-inch (20 and 7 mm) at the same time. Thermal clothing worn in the bag will lower it another ten degrees F (5°C). These temperatures will vary, of course, with the preferences of the camper, the degree of warming which the tent will permit, and the weight of the camper (since a heavier person compresses the insulation underneath more and reduces its effectiveness). A mummy-bag version will take it down about five degrees F (2 or 3°C) further than a sack version.

If you camp below these temperatures, you could keep adding more foam, although too much of this would require considerable modification to the bag sizes and be ridiculously bulky to transport.

The foot of the bag may be finished either flat and broad, like the sack, or vertical and tapered, like the mummy bag, depending on your prefer-

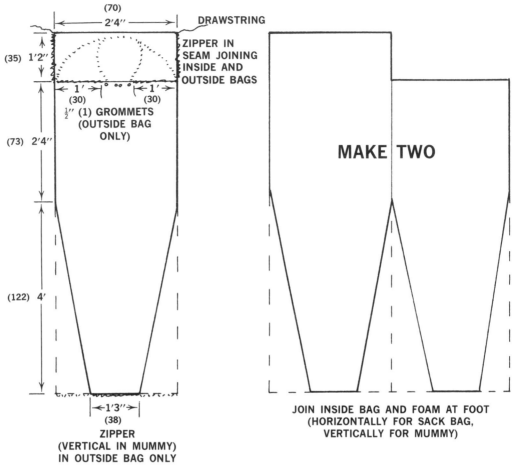

(70)
2'4"
DRAWSTRING

(35) 1'2"

ZIPPER IN
SEAM JOINING
INSIDE AND
OUTSIDE BAGS

←1'→   ←1'→
(30)   (30)
½" (1) GROMMETS
(OUTSIDE BAG
ONLY)

(73) 2'4"

(122) 4'

MAKE TWO

←1'3"→
(38)
ZIPPER
(VERTICAL IN MUMMY)
IN OUTSIDE BAG ONLY

JOIN INSIDE BAG AND FOAM AT FOOT
(HORIZONTALLY FOR SACK BAG,
VERTICALLY FOR MUMMY)

28 FT. (850 CM) 30" (75 CM) RIP-STOP NYLON
4'8" x 7'6" (140 × 230 CM) POLYURETHANE FOAM ($\frac{1}{4}$" x $\frac{3}{4}$" [7 x 20 MM] THICK)
2 12" (30 CM) ZIPPERS
1 12" (30 CM) ZIPPER (MUMMY)
OR
1 24" (60 CM) ZIPPER (SACK)
36" (1 M) PARACHUTE-CORD SHEATH (DRAWSTRING)
$\frac{1}{2}$ PT. ($\frac{1}{4}$ L) FOAM CEMENT

VARIABLE-INSULATION SLEEPING BAG

MEASUREMENTS
IN PARENTHESES
ARE IN CENTIMETERS

ence. Be sure to shape your insulation accordingly.

The foam is easy to handle. Get, if possible, a single sheet, the size shown on the plans. Fold along the thin line. With the sack type, the cutting is only at the head to form a pillow/hood; with the mummy style, the cutting also includes the taper at the foot. With foam cement, cement the edges together to form a tube. (With the mummy style, cement the taper on the folded side first, then the taper on the opposite side, then the untapered part of the side. With the sack, cement the side in two stages to keep the cement from drying before you are ready.) After this dries overnight, cement the foot—flat for the sack, vertical for the mummy. On some parts, especially along the side seam with thick foam, you will need assistance to keep the foam from unrolling and accidentally making contact, but otherwise it is quite easily a one-person job.

Stuffing the insulation is relatively easy. Pull the inside bag out and roll the foot of the outside bag up to the head. Insert the foam, pushing it into the corners of the pillow portion. Hold the bag (and the foam) by the corners of the pillow, and shake the outside bag down over the foam. Zip the outside bag shut and push the inside bag back in, being careful that you get it into the cavity of the foam insulation. The easiest way to get the inside bag back in is to get in the bag, carefully pushing it down with your feet. The fantastic amount of static electricity generated by handling the foam will alarm you at first, but it slowly diminishes as the bag is used.

Make two stuff bags, one for each size insulation. A third one will be needed only if you camp in climates sufficiently cold for both sizes of foam at the same time.

CHAPTER FOURTEEN

Making Your Pack

As with tents, making your own pack has two advantages: saving money and offering custom design. With the packs, however, the saving of money (except with the large ski packs and pack-frame packs) is only a slight advantage over the commercial packs, and being able to add features, to enable you to pack your own individual equipment better, is the primary advantage of doing it yourself.

The tools and techniques of making packs are quite similar to tent construction, since both use canvas and twill-tape a lot. Straps, however, will often have to be hand-sewn, and a sewing palm and sail-making needles will be useful.

MATERIALS AND TECHNIQUES

A pack is not hard to make if you know how to use a sewing machine. Most of the "hardware" is available from camping outfitters. The only specialized item of equipment is a sewing palm and sail needles, which will be required for hand-sewing heavy webbing straps on packs. However, the operation can be done on the average sewing machine by using a heavy needle, wide-stitch spacing, and turning the machine by hand rather than using the motor. This latter technique is also useful in sewing on the closing straps as the webbing is too thick to run the motor without the risk of having the machine run away with it (from requiring too much power to start the action and not

being able to get your foot off the rheostat in time to run it at any but full speed).

As for materials, the first requirement is to use strong fabric. The pack carries a considerable strain. Heavy-duty nylon is by far the best and is available from several camping outfitters. It is not waterproof (except for the plastic-coated varieties), but a hiker's poncho, made to go over such a pack and still not be too short in back, will give this protection.

Reënforce all seams with twill-tape, as this eases the strain on the fabric. Many of the packs are designed in a cross shape, the arms of the cross being folded over to form the box. Since the seams do take up some of the cloth (a quarter inch [5 mm] at least), you will have a problem at the corner—your stitching will be "inboard" of the edge. Simply stitch diagonally, about a quarter inch (5 mm) from the edge, to form a rounded, or at least mitered, corner. Since the stitching is done with the pack wrong-side-out, this will not be unsightly and it will help strengthen the pack at a weak point.

Three or four pairs of D-rings on each side of the pack are valuable in making the half-filled pack more comfortable to carry, since you can lace a length of parachute cord between the D-rings to tighten the bag around the contents. D-rings were originally used to lash on an outside bedroll. Now that the sleeping bag has almost replaced the blanket bedroll in camping, you can use the same provision to lash a wet tent on the pack until it can be dried out.

The D-ring goes in a loop of twill-tape which is inserted in the seam of the pack before sewing it. Where you have to attach D-rings to a folded edge (no seam), use the twill-tape flat against the fabric, an inch or two (25 to 50 mm) on either side of the D-ring. Sew around the tape to anchor it securely to the pack and to keep the D-ring from sliding. For appearance, you may wish to cover the tape with a scrap of the pack fabric before sewing it in place.

DESIGNING YOUR PACK

For all practical purposes, designing a pack is simply redesigning a pack to a certain size and/or adding or removing certain attachment features from an already existing design. Aside from some experiments in form-fitting pack boards being conducted as a part of research in equipment for para-military operations, all possible pack designs are on the market now. Packs are older than houses by several hundred thousand years, and, except for new materials, the weeding-out process has already happened. While the form-fitting pack boards are more comfortable, they are custom-fitted and therefore can only be used by one person comfortably. The average camping family needs more leeway to interchange equipment than that.

In designing a pack, make sure that the bag is larger than you need, so you won't have to stuff it full of the gear. When the proper size, it lies flat against your back instead of rounding into a barrel shape and moving the center of gravity back farther. It is also easier to pack and unpack. D-rings are helpful to lace a partly filled pack tight so that the contents don't settle to the bottom of the pack. These features enable the pack to have the correct balance—an essential feature for a comfortable pack.

Basically, any container which will hold the stuff will serve if it is comfortable. Thus straps become almost as important as the bag in pack design. The angle between the pack or frame and the place where the straps go over the shoulders should be approximately forty-five degrees. The straps should come together at the top of the pack to provide a yoke effect over the back; otherwise you may be carrying your load on the outer edges of your shoulders, where the leverage forces are definitely against you.

Padding is definitely an advantage. However, it must be soft. I have seen some post-office pouch-strap "pads" which were about as soft as a piece of armor plate.

A waistband is a great aid, but it can only be used on packs which have some kind of frame (ski pack or pack frame). Some sort of quick-release buckle is useful so you can jettison the pack if you start to fall on a hillside or in a stream. Mine is a miniature car-seatbelt which a service station once had their employees wear on their pants as an advertising gimmick to sell seatbelts. I managed to get two, and one is now the waistband for my pack frame and the other forms the belt of my belt pack. Scuba-type quick-release buckles are just as useful with packs as with divers' weight-belts.

A pack with a frame is more comfortable than one without. A frame keeps the pack rigid so that the contents don't settle to the bottom and it is off your back—it is both softer and cooler.

A pack-frame pack can be made of either wood or metal rod or tubing—one outfitter even offered one of cast aluminum—but the ski-pack frame is restricted by its shape to either rod or tube.

If you use tubing, you have the problem of finding a competent welder with heli-arc equipment (assuming you can't do it yourself). Tubing is quite

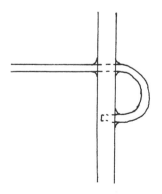

PACK-FRAME WELD

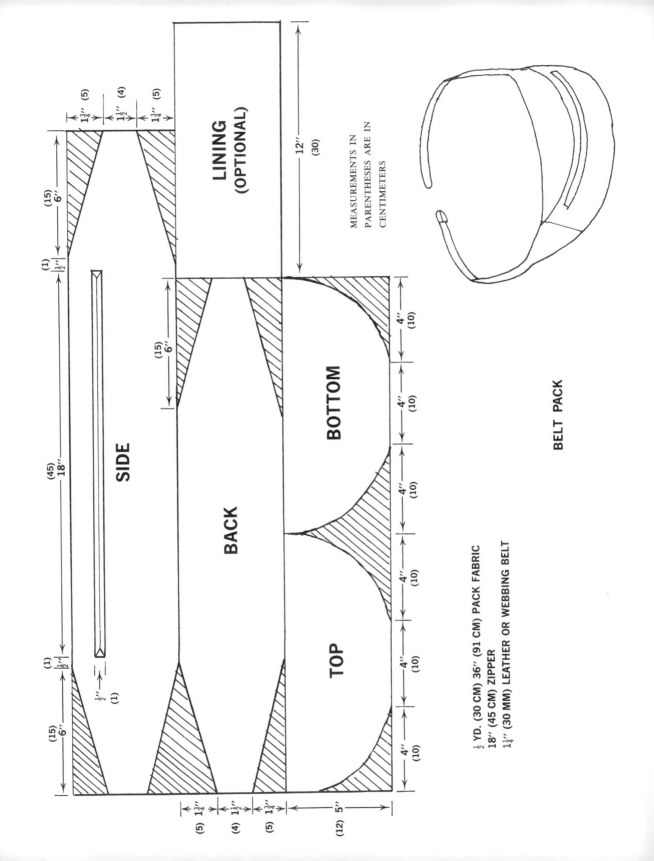

LINING
(OPTIONAL)

MEASUREMENTS IN
PARENTHESES ARE IN
CENTIMETERS

SIDE

BACK

BOTTOM

TOP

BELT PACK

½ YD. (30 CM) 36″ (91 CM) PACK FABRIC
18″ (45 CM) ZIPPER
1¼″ (30 MM) LEATHER OR WEBBING BELT

resistant to bending under normal conditions; however, accidents such as falls will damage it. Tubing will collapse it if it is bent sharply and will break it if straightened back again.

If you use solid rods, a stainless steel (18-8 cold drawn) is best with a spring temper. It weighs a little more than aluminum and is much more serviceable (as well as permitting the use of regular welding equipment). Welding does, however, anneal the metal, so welds should not be in the middle of cross-pieces, braces, or shelves, since these have the greatest strain on them. Extend the cross-pieces past (or through) the uprights, around in a half-circle, and back to the upright. This will not only keep the end from catching on underbrush, it makes a good lashing eye for the pack, or, if larger, for the shoulder and waist straps.

A pack designed around your equipment is the ultimate in pack design. It is nowhere better illustrated than in Gerry's "CWD (Controlled Weight Distribution)" system, in which the tent, sleeping bag, air mattress, and pack are all designed around one another, with space still left in the pack for food, cooking equipment, and other camping necessities. This was shown in Chapter 7.

MAKING A BELT PACK

First, sew the zipper to the opening on the side piece. Then sew the belt to the back piece, keeping it centered. Assemble the complete pack, wrong-side-out. Turn it right-side-out through the zipper opening. Sew the triangular piece of the side to the corresponding pieces of the back, and to the belt throughout the length of the triangular area, tucking under the edges of both pieces so that no raw edges will show.

You can have an even more comfortable belt pack if you wear the leather belt awhile before making the pack. This will enable it to take the proper "set"—high at the hip bones, low in the small of the back. Or you could cut the whole belt to this shape from a larger piece of leather, using an old belt for a pattern.

While a fabric belt is generally too weak, a length of light webbing, an inch and a half wide (35 mm), will make an excellent belt. It is not stiff like leather, but is strong enough for the job. You can get a buckle for it at leathercraft supply stores. The webbing, of course, is available from a camping outfitter and there is often some choice of color.

If you have a smaller waist than twenty-four inches (61 cm), take out the required amount from the pack itself. Be sure to deduct the same length from the side, top, bottom, zipper, and optional lining.

The lining is formed by a twelve-by-fifteen-inch (14 x 30 cm) piece of the cloth being placed over the belt when it is sewed to the back piece. It isn't necessary but it hides the belt inside the pack—if you care about how the inside of a pack looks in the first place.

A more useful detail for the sake of appearance is to dye the belt to match the color of the fabric. Or you can even cover the whole belt with fabric (more feasible with a webbing belt than with leather).

MAKING A KNAPSACK

Sew the bag wrong-side-out. Turn it right-side-out and attach the closing straps. Attach the shoulder straps with at least one inch (25 mm) of stitching on each side of the strap.

MAKING A DULUTH PACK

This is probably the only pack sewed right-side-out. Turn the edges an inch (25 mm) under to hide the raw edge and sew a double row of stitches one quarter-inch (5 mm) apart, the first row three-eighths of an inch (1 cm) from the edge.

Attach the closing straps, as with the knapsack, and the tumpline with at least three inches (75 mm) of stitching on the webbing. Shoulder straps may be attached the same as with the knapsack, but, strictly speaking, the Duluth pack has only the tumpline. Since most campers are not accustomed to the tumpline (and it does require some getting used to), the shoulder straps are advisable. Note that the tumpline fastens to the front of the pack instead of the back. It is designed for heavy loads and the back balances better that way. The tumpline should be long enough to let the top of the pack be even with the top of your shoulders.

A waterproof liner of polyethylene sheet should

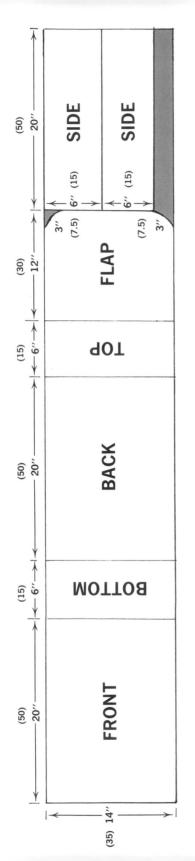

SIDE

SIDE

(50) 20″

6″ (15)

6″ (15)

3″ (7.5)

3″ (7.5)

(30) 12″

FLAP

(15) 6″

TOP

(50) 20″

BACK

(15) 6″

BOTTOM

(50) 20″

FRONT

(35) 14″

2 YDS. (160 CM) PACK FABRIC
5 FT. (150 CM) 2″ (50 MM) WEBBING
2 2″ (50 MM) D-RINGS
2 2″ (50 MM) SNAP SPRINGS

} SHOULDER STRAPS

1½ FT. (45 CM) 1″ (25 MM) WEBBING
1 1″ (25 MM) WEBBING TIP
1 1″ (25 MM) BUCKLE
12 1″ (25 MM) D-RINGS

} CLOSING STRAP

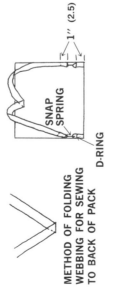

KNAPSACK

1″ (2.5)

SNAP SPRING

D-RING

METHOD OF FOLDING
WEBBING FOR SEWING
TO BACK OF PACK

MEASUREMENTS IN PARENTHESES
ARE IN CENTIMETERS

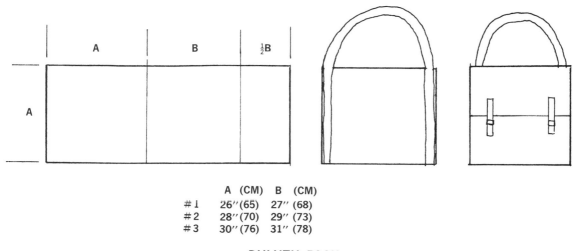

	A (CM)	B (CM)
#1	26″(65)	27″(68)
#2	28″(70)	29″(73)
#3	30″(76)	31″(78)

DULUTH PACK

be made to fit inside the pack and seal up completely. Since the Duluth pack is a canoeing pack, you must protect your gear from more water than just rain. Even in a stable canoe, there is usually a little water in the bilge—just enough to get the pack wet even when it is put on a platform made of a couple of sticks.

The Duluth pack is made in three standard sizes, so the plans give the dimensions for all three.

MAKING A RUCKSACK

The basic bag is the same as the knapsack and uses the knapsack plans in the previous section. Attach the pockets by stitching around the edges and diagonally across in both directions.

In order to save cloth, you can omit the area marked "back" and sew the four pieces directly to the pack. This is a bit harder and not quite as strong as the other method. A second alternative is to use a pattern similar to the side pockets on the pack-frame pack (the dimensions will be different, but the construction technique is the same). This method uses a zipper closing rather than the strap and buckle.

MAKING A SKI PACK

The hardest part is in finding the tubing for the frame. It should be one half-inch (12 mm) in diameter if hard aluminum, three-eighths inch (8 mm) if stainless steel. When working with the tubing, use one of the spring-like tube benders to keep the tube from collapsing when bent. Ideally, weld the joints. If you can't get aluminum welding equipment, use expansion bolts. Use wooden plugs to keep the bolt from collapsing the tube it crosses through.

After you build the frame, the rest is just a matter of sewing the pack, which is much like the other packs. The side pockets are identical in size to the rucksack pockets, as are the sewing techniques, so they are not duplicated in the ski-pack plans.

As an option for skiers, don't sew the side bags on at the top and bottom, but only along the sides. Sew reënforcing pieces of scrap cloth or light leather around the top and bottom and stitch with a grommet stitching, if cloth. Then you can slide a ski through each slot, tie them together at the top, and have a relatively convenient way to carry them. The poles can fit into the pack with the baskets sticking out over your head. Needless to say, do not use the backless form of the side bags shown in the pack-frame pack plans.

These bags often omit the horizontal bag and provide loops for attaching an ice ax, with the ax head where the outside bag would otherwise be. They also have a large leather wear-patch on the side to keep crampons from cutting into the pack.

Part of the scrap cloth may be doubled over and used for an ax loop, centered under the flap. A

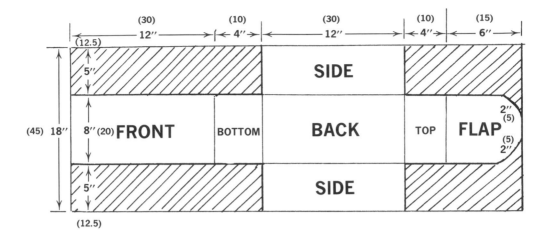

| (30) | (10) | (30) | (10) | (15) |
| 12″ | 4″ | 12″ | 4″ | 6″ |

(12.5)

5″

(45) 18″ 8″ (20) **FRONT** BOTTOM **BACK** TOP **FLAP**

SIDE

SIDE

2″ (5)

(5) 2″

5″

(12.5)

MEASUREMENTS IN
PARENTHESES ARE
IN CENTIMETERS

IN ADDITION TO
KNAPSACK LIST

1 YD. (90 CM) PACK FABRIC
2 6″ (15 CM) STRIPS 1″ (25 MM) WEBBING
2 1″ (25 MM) WEBBING TIPS
2 1″ (25 MM) BUCKLES

RUCKSACK POCKET

second one, lower down, helps keep the ax handle from flopping against the pack when you are hiking. Small D-rings along the side seams help hold an old horseshoe bedroll or a wet tent on the outside by lashing to them. The top edge of the pack should be provided with grommets so that the top can be closed with a drawstring. This prevents water from entering at the edge of the flap in the rain and reduces the rattling around of gear in a partly filled pack. The technique is useful on all fabric packs—but almost essential on the ski pack.

The hip and shoulder straps attach to the frame, not to the pack itself. A leather pocket, made to fit the top curve of the frame, is sewed to the pack. Snaps on the pocket keep it from coming off the top of the frame. Use at least ten-ounce leather. Short lengths of twill-tape at the bottom of the pack hold it to the bottom of the frame.

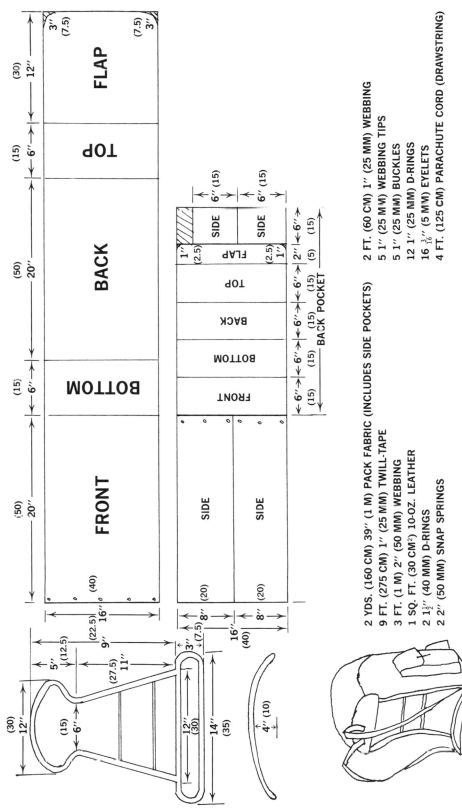

SKI PACK

3'' (7.5) | (7.5) 3''
(30) 12''

FLAP

(15) 6''

TOP

(50) 20''

BACK

(15) 6''

BOTTOM

(50) 20''

FRONT

(40)

16''

(22.5) 9''

5'' (12.5)

(27.5) 11''

(30) 12''

(15) 6''

(7.5) 3''

16'' (40)

(30) 12''

14'' (35)

4'' (10)

6'' (15) | 6'' (15)

SIDE | **SIDE**

1'' (2.5) | **FLAP** | (2.5) 1''

TOP

BACK

BOTTOM

FRONT

6'' (15) | 6'' (15) | 6'' (15) | 6'' (15) | 2'' (5) | 6'' (15)

BACK POCKET

SIDE

SIDE

(20)

8''

(20)

8''

2 YDS. (160 CM) 39'' (1 M) PACK FABRIC (INCLUDES SIDE POCKETS)
9 FT. (275 CM) 1'' (25 MM) TWILL-TAPE
3 FT. (1 M) 2'' (50 MM) WEBBING
1 SQ. FT. (30 CM²) 10-OZ. LEATHER
2 1½'' (40 MM) D-RINGS
2 2'' (50 MM) SNAP SPRINGS

2 FT. (60 CM) 1'' (25 MM) WEBBING
5 1'' (25 MM) WEBBING TIPS
5 1'' (25 MM) BUCKLES
12 1'' (25 MM) D-RINGS
2 1'' (25 MM) D-RINGS
16 $\frac{3}{16}$'' (5 MM) EYELETS
4 FT. (125 CM) PARACHUTE CORD (DRAWSTRING)

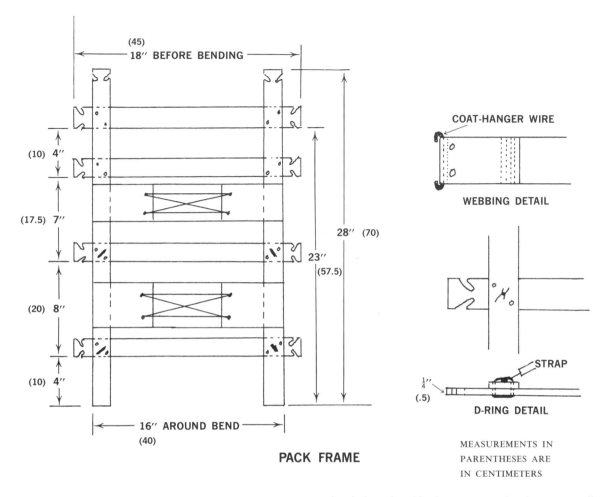

(45)
18″ BEFORE BENDING

(10) 4″

(17.5) 7″

(20) 8″

(10) 4″

16″ AROUND BEND
(40)

28″ (70)

23″
(57.5)

PACK FRAME

COAT-HANGER WIRE

WEBBING DETAIL

STRAP

$\frac{1}{4}″$
(.5)

D-RING DETAIL

MEASUREMENTS IN
PARENTHESES ARE
IN CENTIMETERS

MAKING A PACK FRAME

Frame

There are two types of pack frames. One is made from wood, the other from metal. The metal one will be a little lighter and will last longer. However, cost is a factor here. You can make a wooden frame for under three dollars. With the metal ones, unless you have either heli-arc welding equipment or free access to scrap aluminum tubing, you can probably buy one cheaper than you can make it.

The best wood for a pack frame is ash or hickory. The wood must be softened before bending. Steam-ing is best for this, but you can do almost as well by soaking it in hot water for an hour. If you soak it, you must keep it under water, not just floating on top.

The best jig for bending the wood is a wooden soft-drink case: wedge the ends of the wood between the dividers, arching up. There should be about a four-inch (10 cm) bow in the wood. There is always one of the pieces that takes a better "set" than the others. This should be the one at the bottom of the frame.

With the woman's pack, omit the top cross-piece and shorten the uprights to twenty-three inches (575 mm). Otherwise, the design follows the plans.

The back bands may be of heavy canvas, but the best material is parachute-harness straps or webbing. The coat-hanger wire is to prevent the lacing from tearing out of the band. The ubiquitous parachute cord is the best lacing material. Some outfitters now stock a new nylon-mesh back, which can be laced on the pack frame described here. This mesh fits much like the canvas back of the old Trapper-Nelson pack frame, but it is cooler and more yielding than the close-weave canvas.

Attach the pieces of the frame with two copper rivets or bolts and nuts at each joint. With either method, reënforce with half-inch (12 mm) washers. The holes may be drilled but it is better if they are burned with a heated rod, as this seals the grain. Finish by sanding and waxing. Then attach coat-hanger-wire D-rings and lace on the back bands and attach the straps.

Pack

The pack proper is a matter of choice. The most common form is a big bag with small bags on the outside like the ski pack. It is usually the same size as the frame and ten inches (25 cm) thick, with small pockets on the sides and back. It is made the same way as the other packs described in this chapter.

A woman's pack is identical, but reduce the thickness of the main pack by two inches (5 cm) (leaving the side packs the same width) and reduce the height of the main pack five inches (12½ cm) and the side packs four inches (10 cm). This is to bring it into proper proportion for the smaller pack frame.

Ten or twelve inches (25 or 30 cm) may be omitted from the bottom of the main pack and the small bags reduced in size and raised on the main bag. This permits a rolled sleeping bag to be lashed on the bottom of the pack sack. If you do this, don't forget to add four D-rings to the bottom—on the edge and one inch (25 mm) in from the corners—to have something to lash the sleeping bag to.

Note on the plans that the cloth is thirty-nine inches (100 cm) wide instead of the usual thirty-six (91 cm). I happened to use this width of cloth in making mine and it is far more economical than

the thirty-six-inch (91 cm) because of the small bags.

Note also the different construction technique used on the small bags. There is no back to them—a half-inch (1 cm) of cloth along the top, bottom, and sides is turned under to form the seam with the large bag. The heavy lines are for the zipper openings, another option to the webbing straps for closing the small bags. The zippers are fitted the same as with the belt pack. (Incidentally, there is enough scrap from this pack to make a belt pack.)

The hook, which supports most of the pack's weight on the frame, is made from coat-hanger wire. The hook band is folded double and the hook is run through grommets in the band. The band is then folded again, over the hook, and sewed to the back of the main bag, two or three inches (50 or 75 mm) under the top. This stitched line goes through four thicknesses of the hook band and one of the bag. Use at least three rows of stitches, one eighth-inch (3 mm) apart.

The pack hooks over the top bar of the pack frame and the sides of the pack lash on the frame by parachute cord between the notches of the frame and the D-rings on the pack.

This particular pack will carry quite a load. I made mine from Trailwise's heavy-duty nylon (hence the thirty-nine-inch [1 m] width) and reënforced all of the main bag's seams with twill-tape for greater strength. Its first big test was taking a forty-five-pound (20 kg) load down into Havasu Canyon in Grand Canyon National Park—and that's no super highway.

As mentioned in Chapter 7, almost any system of packing the gear can be used. If you design another type of pack for the frame, it should be adequately provided with D-rings for lashing to the frame, and the hook should be used if it is to carry any extensive load.

IMPROVISING A WASTEPAPER-BASKET PACK

This item could just as easily have gone in the Improvised Packs section of Chapter 7, but since it can't be improvised in camp, it appears here. It is definitely an inferior product, included for only

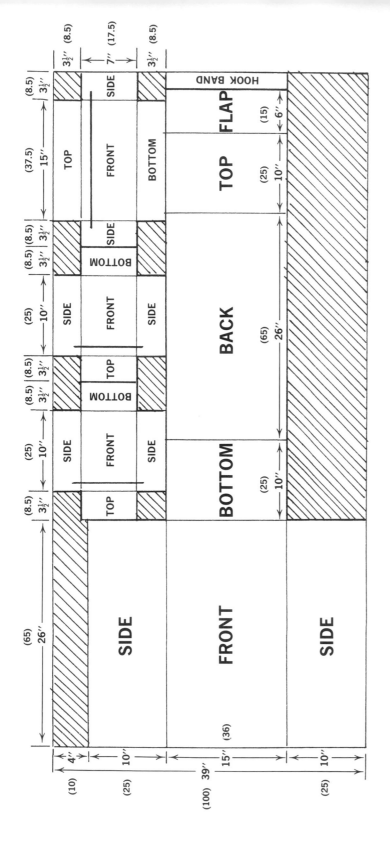

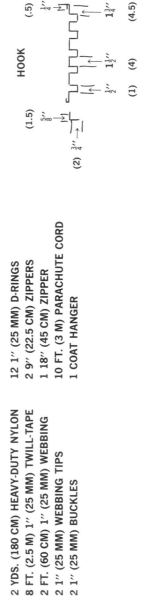

2 YDS. (180 CM) HEAVY-DUTY NYLON
8 FT. (2.5 M) 1" (25 MM) TWILL-TAPE
2 FT. (60 CM) 1" (25 MM) WEBBING
2 1" (25 MM) WEBBING TIPS
2 1" (25 MM) BUCKLES

12 1" (25 MM) D-RINGS
2 9" (22.5 CM) ZIPPERS
1 18" (45 CM) ZIPPER
10 FT. (3 M) PARACHUTE CORD
1 COAT HANGER

PACK-FRAME PACK

MEASUREMENTS IN
PARENTHESES ARE IN
CENTIMETERS

one reason—it is cheap and quick to put together.

There are occasions when an accident has befallen your prized pack and repairs or (horrors!) replacement is not yet made, and you want to go camping. Or your growing young camper is now getting big enough to start carrying his share of the load, but is hardly ready to have an expensive pack of his own. In either case, the wastepaper-basket pack will fill in until something better comes along.

Start out with a plastic wastebasket, a fairly rectangular one about 8″ x 12″ (20 x 30 cm) at the top and twelve to fourteen inches (30 to 35 cm) deep. Make sure it has a thick rim molded into it, otherwise it won't work. A reënforced rim at the bottom helps, but isn't as necessary as at the top.

Seven or eight feet ($2\frac{1}{4}$ to $2\frac{1}{2}$ m) of one-and-a-half-inch (35 mm) webbing is all else that is required to make the pack. The webbing is attached to the basket by sets of slots, one and a half inches (35 mm) long, one quarter-inch (5 mm) high, and one and a half inches (35 mm) apart. (The last figure is not too critical.) It will help if you drill out the end of each slot and then cut along the long dimension. If you simply cut out the slot, the knife will go slightly past the intersecting cut and the basket will tend to tear.

A trio of these slots is cut into one side (which will be the back) about one inch (25 mm) down from the rim and about one inch (25 mm) out from the center, another pair is cut about a half-inch (1 cm) from the bottom (about one inch [25 mm] from the edge), and a final pair is cut in the front in a position identical to the bottom slots on the back. Similar slots are made on the other side of the vertical centerline.

One end of each three-and-a-half-foot (105 cm)-long piece of webbing is threaded into the top slot of the front pair and back out the bottom one, extending about four inches under the basket. The longer end is taken under the basket (lying on the shorter end), then in the lower slot on the back

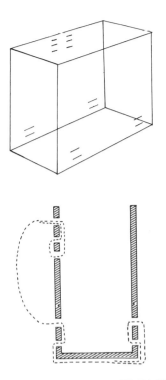

WASTEPAPER BASKET PACK

and out the upper one of that pair. From here, the webbing forms the shoulder straps of the pack. After going over the shoulders, they go through the triple slots in the following manner: first, through the top one from the outside in; second, through the bottom one from the inside out; third, through the middle one from the outside in; finally, through the top one from the inside out, lying parallel to the strap where it entered the series of slots.

By slacking the strap and pulling or pushing the short end at the top, the strap may be adjusted.

This method can be used on larger plastic baskets, but there is a definite limit to the amount of weight the plastic can hold.

CHAPTER FIFTEEN

Making Other Camping Gear

This chapter is a catch-all of do-it-yourself plans. Making these items of equipment requires a wide variety of skills—working in wood, metal, leather, and plastics, as well as sewing with a requirement of waterproofness instead of the usual water-resistance. Most are fairly simple projects, as camping-gear construction goes. They are generally one-day projects. However, some are quite complicated and are more in terms of how to make a similar device for your own equipment rather than an out-and-out construction project. As a result, the plans as well as the descriptions will often give several variants of the same article.

MAKING A REFLECTOR OVEN

There are two basic ways to make a reflector oven from these plans. The first one uses .025-inch (0.75 mm) sheet aluminum (with a further option of stainless steel of the same thickness for the shelf). In this version, the half-inch (12 mm) tabs are folded under to make the sheets more rigid. The three-eighths-inch (1 cm) tabs are bent around the rods to make hinges.

In the second version, .048-inch (1.25 mm) sheet aluminum (and stainless steel, if desired) is used. In this version, the stiffening tabs are not needed as the metal is sufficiently rigid by itself, but the hinge tabs must be made a half-inch (12 cm) wide because of their greater circumference when bent around the rods.

In both versions, the dimensions of the basic shelf and reflectors and the width of the hinge tabs remain unchanged, as do the rest of the construction techniques.

It is easiest to bend the hinge tabs around a piece of rod so that they fit snugly, but not tightly, bending each sheet's tabs and removing the rod after each sheet is bent. The sheets can then be fitted together and filed where needed to make a good fit with the other sheets in the back hinge. When this is fitted, round the end of one of the rods and drive it into the back hinge, bending the tabs as needed to come into proper alignment. When it is driven through and centered, bend the ends to form the back legs.

The front hinges are made by bending the tabs over in the same manner as the back one, although it is considerably easier to fit the rod in place. When fitted, they are likewise bent to form legs.

While dimpling the shelf will usually hold the front legs in place, it is more rigid to drill two small ($\frac{1}{16}''$ or so [2 mm]) holes in each corner of the shelf. The ends of the front legs are filed to a point with at least a five-to-one taper, so that they go through the holes.

Standard welding rod makes the best rods. The tabs on the sheet stock are most easily sawed out using a jeweler's saw, although it can be done with a sharp chisel if you drill a small hole at each corner to keep the cut from tearing into the tabs and weakening them.

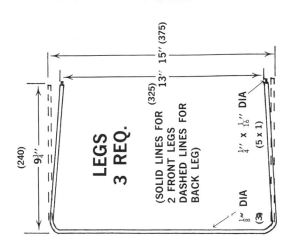

LEGS
3 REQ.

(SOLID LINES FOR
2 FRONT LEGS
DASHED LINES FOR
BACK LEG)

$\frac{1}{4}'' \times \frac{1}{16}''$ DIA

(5 x 1)

$\frac{1}{8}''$ DIA

(3)

(240)

$9\frac{3}{4}''$

15'' (375)

13'' (325)

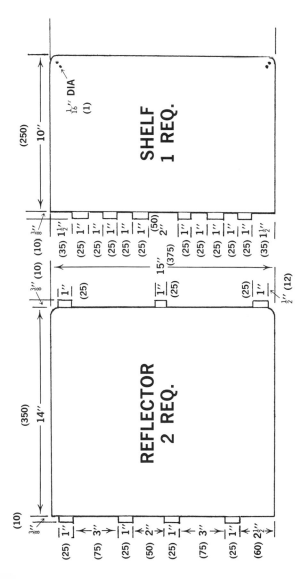

SHELF
1 REQ.

$\frac{1}{16}''$ DIA

(1)

(250)

10''

$1\frac{1}{2}''$ (35)

$1''$ (25)

$1''$ (25)

$1''$ (25)

$1''$ (25)

$1''$ (25)

$2''$ (50)

$1''$ (25)

$1''$ (25)

$1''$ (25)

$1''$ (25)

$1''$ (25)

$1\frac{1}{2}''$ (35)

$\frac{3}{8}''$ (10)

$\frac{3}{8}''$ (10)

15'' (375)

$1''$ (25)

$1''$ (25)

$1''$ (25)

$\frac{3}{8}''$ (10)

$\frac{1}{2}''$ (12)

REFLECTOR
2 REQ.

(350)

14''

(10)

$\frac{3}{8}''$

$1''$ (25)

3'' (75)

$1''$ (25)

2'' (50)

$1''$ (25)

3'' (75)

$1''$ (25)

$2\frac{1}{2}''$ (60)

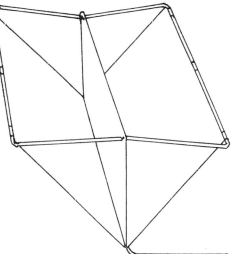

REFLECTOR OVEN

MEASUREMENTS IN
PARENTHESES ARE
IN MILLIMETERS

Care should be taken to keep the metal as shiny as possible since it greatly improves the oven's performance. A stainless-steel shelf spreads the heat better. If you are going to have adequate transportation, the thicker version is far sturdier. If you will be backpacking, the lighter one will probably be better. In either case, protect the oven from scratches by making a cloth bag for it to fit into snugly.

MODIFYING THE GEOLOGIST'S PICK FOR CAMPING

The geologist's pick can be modified to make an all-purpose tool that weighs only two pounds (well under 1 kg)—less than a three-quarter-length ax. To make this item, you must have a solid metal-handled pick. The wooden or tubular-steel handles just won't work.

The first modification is to file the edge of the handle to a dull edge. This makes it into a hatchet which cuts rather than just breaks the wood. Don't put a sharp edge on it as this will then require a piece of leather to wrap around the handle to act as a sheath, and the edge will be dangerous if it is exposed. The purpose of the edge is for splitting firewood, not for chopping down a tree. Make sure that this is on the edge on the pick side, otherwise you may be hammering in a wooden tent-stake and split the stake in two if you should miss with the hammer head and the splitting edge comes down on it.

Second, make a shovel blade out of sheet steel, just a little smaller than the blade of an entrenching shovel. Drill two holes one eighth inch (3 mm) in diameter along the centerline, the first an inch (25 mm) from the top, the second two inches (5 cm) below it. Make two loops of heavy leather or sheet steel and rivet them to the holes. The pick point fits into these loops. Don't try to break ground with this shovel—use the pick for that. The leather isn't strong enough and the metal loops are on the borderline. The shovel attachment is a fast implement for removing dirt or rocks loosened by the pick or digging in sand or loose clay.

Two holes near the top of the shovel blade, the proper distance apart, will permit the shovel to be

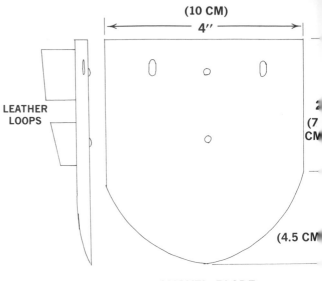

SHOVEL BLADE

hooked onto a clip for carrying on the belt. The pick point can be further protected with an ax-type sheath.

Since the geologist's pick already has a pick and a hammer, these modifications, plus a good knife and possibly a folding saw, will handle any job all of the tools described in Chapter 8 can. Some jobs, such as tree-felling, are so infinitely slow this way that you could call them impossible, but these jobs don't come up much in camping nowadays. For slightly over two pounds (1 kg), you can have the equivalent of over five pounds (2½ kg) of separate tools.

MAKING A BUCK SAW

Probably the best camp saw is the old buck saw. They are fairly scarce nowadays, but it doesn't really matter because it is so easy to make one. All that is needed is three pieces of wood, four bolts with wing nuts, a bow-saw blade, and a length of parachute cord or rawhide lacing.

Note that on the plans the wood has a shoulder cut into it. That is to form a groove for the blade when the saw is folded. It is one of those details which improves the looks more than actually being needed. The set of the teeth of the blade will, in time, wear enough of a groove to do the job.

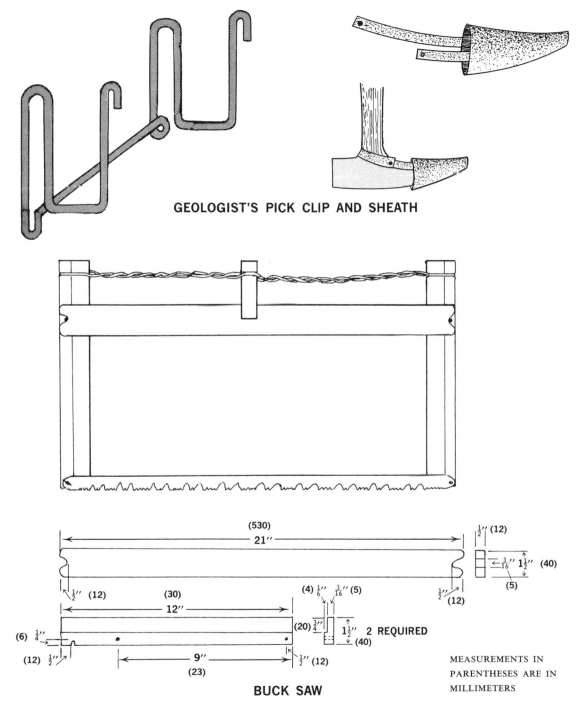

GEOLOGIST'S PICK CLIP AND SHEATH

(530)
21″

½″ (12)

¾₁₆″ 1½″ (40)

(5)

½″ (12)

(4) ⅙″ ¾₁₆″ (5)

½″ (12)

(30)

12″

(20) ¾″ 1½″ **2 REQUIRED**

(40)

(6) ¼″

(12) ½″

9″

½″ (12)

(23)

BUCK SAW

MEASUREMENTS IN
PARENTHESES ARE IN
MILLIMETERS

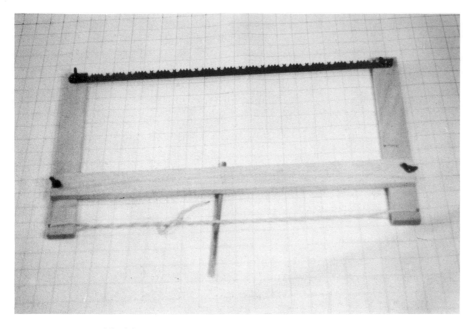

Buck saw assembled for use . . .

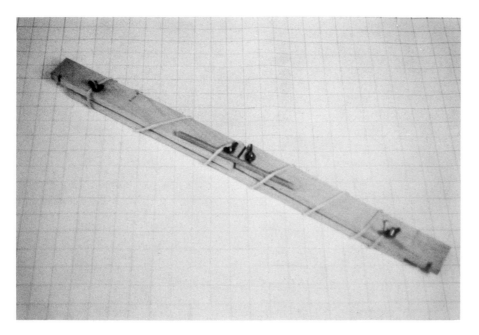

. . . and folded for transportation (the blade is between the pieces of wood).

The bolts on the uprights are piened over so that the nuts won't come off and get lost. The notched end of the back simply fits in place and the wing nuts are tightened. Use countersunk heads so that the uprights will fit tightly against the back when the saw is folded.

In its erected position, the blade bolts fit through the blade and the notches in the back hold the uprights in place. Any old stick found on the site will serve to twist the cord and provide the needed tension on the blade. Finding this piece at the site eliminates another piece which would enlarge the bundle.

The wood should be three-eighths to one-half inch (10 to 12 cm) thick and an inch and a half or so (about 35 mm) wide. The back should be as long, notch to notch, as the saw blade is between holes, plus a half-inch (12 mm) at each end. The shoulder notch (if used) should be deep enough to hold the blade with its back even with the edge of the groove. These dimensions depend on the size of the blade you get, but the drawing is for a twenty-inch (51 cm) blade as measured between the centers of the holes. The uprights should be over half as long as the back, with the pivot about one-quarter of its length. A notch in the side provides an anchor for the tension cord. This notch should be rounded as it circles the upright, in order to reduce the strain on the cord. A screen-door turn-buckle can be substituted for the cord, but you would then need something to hold the bundle together as well as two more bolts to attach the rods to the uprights.

MAKING A PONCHO

The camper's poncho has evolved considerably from the Latino's heavy, wool, general-purpose protection from everything. Today, it is made from a lightweight coated fabric weighing less than three ounces per square yard. Two of these fabrics, Horcolite and Nylsurf, are available in the forty-four-inch (112 cm) width which these plans use. Reevair is an inch (25 mm) wider, a fact you can ignore on these plans as long as you measure from the center, but it is unique in that it breathes.

The important factor in making a poncho is to get total waterproofing. A poncho, being open at the bottom, will have enough air currents stirred up when walking to prevent the usual problem caused by body moisture condensing in totally watertight clothing. There are as few seams as possible in the plans, and all should be the French-fell variety. The seams must be coated with a waterproofing compound such as Flex-o-Fix, Gaco, or Reevair seam compound to keep them from leaking at the threads. Since the color of the compound won't match the fabric, coat only the inside, but make it complete without being heavy.

This poncho has two seams—one where the two halves of the hood join, and the other where the hood joins the neck. Unlike most commercial ponchos, this has no seam at the shoulder (a typical spot for the first leak to develop) or at the extension. The extension permits the poncho to fit over a backpack and still come down far enough in the back to keep a blowing rain off when you are wearing rain chaps.

First, cut out the pieces. The hood will look too large, but will be a fairly close fit when you finish. Sew the back of the hood, turning the top as needed to make a French fell.

Attaching the hood is the only really difficult part of the project. Cut out a hole nine inches (225 mm) in diameter. Sew the hood to this hole, the raw edge of the hood flaring outward, with a half-inch (1 cm) overlap and a single row of stitches. Roll it one half-turn so that the raw edges are tucked under. Stretch the fabric where needed to keep it from puckering, and sew the double row of stitches to finish the seam. Stitch a couple of inches (about 5 cm) up the front of the hood (with a flat fell) to keep water from running in at the neck seam.

Turn all exposed edges under three-eighths of an inch (1 cm) and stitch. Attach snaps at the bottom corners of the front and back and two up the sides. Put four snaps along the edge of the extension and at the corresponding points where it folds up. It folds up under the poncho, of course, rather than on the outside where it would become a rain barrel. It should be folded up except when carrying a large pack or it will get underfoot.

Waterproof all seams, being sure to seal the

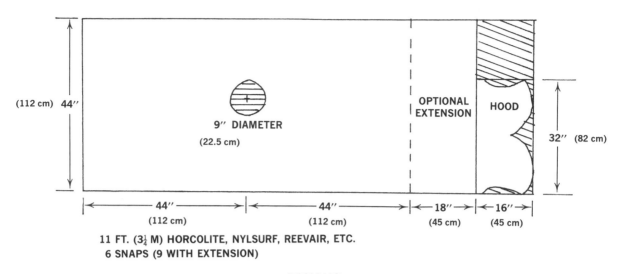

(112 cm) 44"

9" DIAMETER
(22.5 cm)

OPTIONAL
EXTENSION

HOOD

32" (82 cm)

44"
(112 cm)

44"
(112 cm)

18"
(45 cm)

16"
(45 cm)

11 FT. (3¼ M) HORCOLITE, NYLSURF, REEVAIR, ETC.
6 SNAPS (9 WITH EXTENSION)

PONCHO

stitching and the punctures made by the snaps. Be careful not to get it inside the snaps themselves as this will keep them from working. A little knife work, after the compound dries, however, will remove any that accidentally gets into them.

Using the largest size in the plans, the poncho will weigh under eighteen ounces (625 g). The hem of the poncho should be down past the knees—six inches (15 cm) below is about the maximum length—so add to the measurements if you are over six feet (180 cm) tall, and subtract if you are under five feet six (155 cm).

MAKING A WATER STILL

A distilling apparatus is a requirement for the coastal camper who doesn't have a readily accessible fresh-water supply.

For the safety of the soldered joints, never let the boiler get completely empty while you are heating it. To avoid all chances of lead poisoning, silver solder or copper braze all joints.

Use a gallon (4 liter) paint-can with a friction lid for the boiler. The large opening at the top gives you easy access to the inside of the boiler. Salt water will build up scale rather quickly and it is easier to scrape the walls when you have that big

an opening. Just be sure that all the dried paint is removed from the inside of the can before you build the still. Better yet, try to get an unused can from a paint manufacturer.

Drill a quarter-inch (5 mm)-diameter hole in the top. It should be over to one side rather than in the center, as it puts the condenser farther from the fire. Solder a male connection for evaporative cooler water tubing to the hole.

Make the condenser from evaporative cooler water tubing. Attach a female connection to one end of a piece about a foot and a half (45 cm) long, and a male connection to the other end. Take another piece about six feet (2 m) long and attach

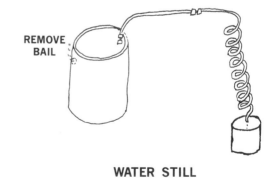

REMOVE
BAIL

WATER STILL

a female connection to one end, leaving the other end plain. Bend this piece in a loose coil with a two-inch (5 cm) diameter and a one-inch (25 mm) pitch. Be careful that you don't collapse the tubes when bending or handling them. In use, put a wet towel inside the coil to speed the condensation and keep the towel wet.

The condenser, when taken apart, will fit inside the boiler for carrying. A cloth bag for the whole unit will keep the black from the bottom of the boiler from rubbing off on your gear.

One of these little stills is quite useful at home too, for making a supply of distilled water for spray irons and car batteries. Use it strictly for water and you won't have any trouble with the Treasury Department.

MAKING A FREEZE-DRYING CHAMBER

A freeze-drying unit might seem the least likely item for the home outfitter, yet it is quite possible to make your own. A fairly competent scrounger should be able to get all the needed materials for less than a hundred dollars.

The specific idea comes from the Museum of Northern Arizona in Flagstaff, which had such a machine as their "Exhibit of the Month." They used it for freeze-drying displays of one of the most fragile of all plants—fungus. Freeze-drying is the only way it can be preserved, otherwise it will turn black. Similar rigs are used by many museums today as a form of taxidermy.

The basis of the unit is a three-foot (1 m) length of two-foot (60 cm)-diameter high-pressure gas main with shelves inside. The back is welded tight with a piece of boiler plate. The door is a similar piece with a rubber gasket making a seal at the joint. A standard vacuum pump, capable of .02 to .015 Torr vacuum, draws out the air and water vapor. To avoid a problem of water vapor condensing inside the pump cylinder, a water trap, consisting of a double-walled cup filled with dry ice, condenses the water out as it is pulled through the space between the walls. A pressure-tight tap will permit the water to be drained after the operation is finished.

The water trap can be eliminated if you use a vacuum pump made specifically for the purpose, since it can carry the water vapor through the pump without damage. These are often available from the more complete chemical and scientific supply houses and will state this feature on the specifications. The evacuation volume should always exceed the volume of your chamber (in other words, the chamber should reach operational vacuum in a maximum of one minute).

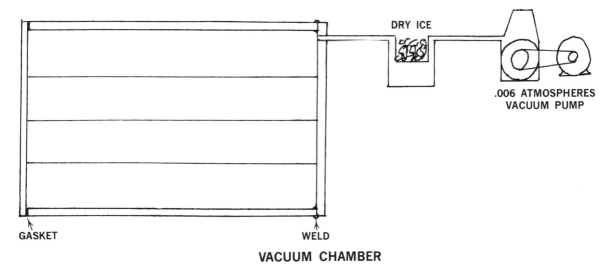

DRY ICE

.006 ATMOSPHERES
VACUUM PUMP

GASKET

WELD

VACUUM CHAMBER

Finally, a heating coil should be placed in the top of the chamber which is capable of raising the inside temperature to about 150°F (65°C). The vacuum should be turned on for five to ten minutes, then the heat turned on. A thermostat control will be valuable. This heat reduces the vacuum time from one week per centimeter of food thickness to only eight hours.

To use, freeze the food in the usual way, the faster the freezing, the better. Place it in the chamber and turn on the pump. Check the pressure dial (or better, although more expensive, have an automatic switch activated by the pressure rise) and keep the pressure low enough (never over .01 atmospheres). The whole procedure will take about one week per centimeter of thickness (approximately $2\frac{1}{2}$ centimeters per inch). It is possible to stop the action any time after the first day to add more items to the chamber as long as it does not take long enough for the food to start thawing.

The freeze-drying equipment can also be used for vacuum-drying. The procedure is the same except that the food does not have to be frozen first.

MAKING CAMERA STOCKS

A camera stock is a useful item for the serious nature photographer and can be made fairly easily. The design is up to you—in fact, since you can make it to fit your own body proportions, it can be even better than a commercial one. Fit in camera stocks is just as important as fit in guns.

Most camera tripod mounts take a $\frac{1}{4}$-20 bolt; also, most cameras can be fitted with a cable release for the shutter. This means that for about five dollars, you can have a fifteen- or twenty-dollar stock.

Most home-built stocks are made out of wood, since it is light in weight and easy to work. It is essentially like a gun stock except for a couple of important items. First, it is not going to have to absorb or comfortably transmit any recoil. As a result, it can be lighter than a gun stock. It can be made out of thinner stock, even one inch (25 mm) thick, and be cut out so that it has a fairly odd shape for a stock but still is strong enough to hold the camera steady.

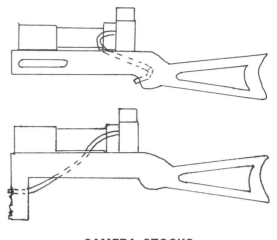

CAMERA STOCKS

Second, the top of the stock (where the camera fits) is lower than that for a rifle, since the distance from the bottom of the camera to the center of the viewer is longer than the equivalent distance on a rifle.

Some camera stocks will have the cable release (trigger) operated by the forward hand. This is a bit awkward to get used to, but once that is accomplished it is just as effective as the more conventional way. The fewer bends you put into the cable release, the freer it will work. If you have one long enough, by all means have it go to the close hand—just be sure it will still work smoothly in that position.

The camera attaches to the stock with its tripod mount. A $\frac{1}{4}$-20 bolt, its head cut off, and epoxied into a hole in the proper place in the stock, will hold the camera in place. If you will be using an extremely high-powered lens, enough of the stock should extend forward so that it can support the telephoto lens as well as the camera proper. This part of the stock should be made to fit the lens, or a system of blocks should be carried in the accessory bag to shim it up. Use a webbing band to hold the lens firmly against the stock, yet let it turn, if necessary, for focusing.

The stock can be rested on some firm object for an even greater degree of steadiness.

KAYAK MODIFICATIONS

While it won't quite carry the load of the Canadian canoe, the kayak is far steadier, more maneuverable, and gives better protection to the camper's gear. Still, there are several ways to improve a stock kayak to make it a better camping vehicle.

Seat

The average kayak seat is a piece of plywood, usually bent or carved into a more comfortable shape than a flat piece, but that is all except for a swiveling piece of bent plywood which forms the backrest.

As austere as it sounds, this is usually quite comfortable for an afternoon on a lake. But for white-water, surf, or canoe competition, it just won't do the job. What is needed there is a seat more like those which come with the single-seat slalom models (and cannot be had on the tandem cruising versions used for camping).

The object of this modification is to give the canoeist greater control over the kayak, by greater sensitivity to the movement of the kayak—by feeling one unit with it. The stock seats permit you to slide around a bit. This can be dangerous in white water, where you sometimes need to do a bit of swivel-hipping like a broken field runner to dodge the rocks. The modified seat makes the kayak more comfortable even in calm water—like the bucket seat in a sports car.

The place to start is with a footrest. Usually your feet just sort of rest on one of the rungs of the keel ladder, out of the way, contributing little. If the rung happens to be in the right place, this is as good as any (provided the ladder is wide enough at the point for you to get both feet on the rung), but it rarely is where you need it. Resist all urges to use a rib to rest your feet on—especially if it is a folding model.

The footrest does not have to be elaborate. A piece of plywood at about a 60° angle and firmly braced against a block base can be attached to the keel ladder in the same manner as the seats. The "back-seat driver," when a rudder is used, has a footrest already since the kayak's rudder is usually operated by foot pedals there.

An essential feature of the footrest is a set of knee-rests. These are small pieces of plywood (three by six inches [75 by 150 mm] with semi-circular ends), padded with foam, and fitted under the cockpit-coaming rail. Sometimes, if there is nothing else to fit them to, you will have to build a small stringer from one rib to the next and fit the knee-rest to this piece. Regardless of the method you use to attach it, the upward force against the knee-rest should bear against the underside of the cockpit coaming.

The final item in the unit is the seat itself. There

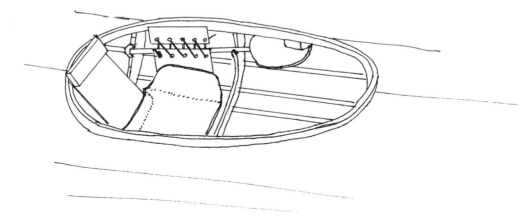

SLALOM KAYAK COCKPIT SHOWING BUCKET SEAT AND KNEEBOARDS

should be support against movement backward and to either side. The footrest prevents forward movement and the knee-rest prevents upward movement. The stock backrest will not prevent backward movement since it is not used in heavy paddling nor in rough water, but the body is leaned forward to get more leverage against the water. Besides, it is too high and you can slide under it.

There are two ways of attacking the problem of kayak seats. The first is to find an old fiberglass chair with enough of a bucket in it that it will shift when you do. Most plastics of the vinyl or styrene varieties won't hold up, so make sure it is fiberglass. Garage sales, junk furniture stores, etc., are the best places to find one—it doesn't even need to have legs. When you find one, cut it horizontally so that it comes to about the level of your belt. Round the corners at the sides and round the edges all around. This will take a bit of work with a coarse-mill file, finished with successively finer grades of garnet paper and emery cloth. When you have rounded it to shape, attach it to the stock seat in some way which does not run hardware through the plastic seat. Epoxy to the plywood, run screws through the plywood into wooden plugs epoxied into leg sockets of the plastic, or some similar method is best. Also, while cutting the seat down, make sure that the leg-attachment points don't raise the new seat over an inch (25 mm) higher than the stock seat. If it does, cut that much off the leg sockets or attach the seat directly to the keel ladder rather than to the stock seat.

The second method is to use nylon canvas to build up from the stock plywood seat in a T. The intersection of the T fastens to the underside of the stock seat. The upright of the T ends in a sleeve which fits over the backrest. If there is any tendency for the backrest to swivel, you may have to attach a dowel at right angles to the backrest bar and anchor it to the coaming.

The side pieces (the cross-pieces of the T) are slack when no one is in the kayak, hanging from the cockpit coaming, where they clamp between the cockpit stiffener and the cockpit coaming. These must be custom-designed for the individual since they must be tight when the paddler is in place.

The canvas is the same type as is used for packs.

Some commercial versions use leather, but this is rather expensive and hard to form.

Spray Cover

In wet weather or white water, a spray cover makes the trip far more comfortable. It is fairly easy to make, but must be custom-fitted to your particular kayak.

The fabric (I used Reevair in the one I made because it breathes and doesn't get as stuffy inside the cockpit) is fitted around the entire cockpit, over the backrests when they are in their upright position, and down to the base of the cockpit coaming. A half-inch (1 cm) hem is sewed all around and a length of one-eighth- or three-sixteenth-inch (3 to 5 mm) shock cord, about three feet (90 cm) shorter than the circumference of the cockpit on a tandem kayak or one foot (30 cm) on a single, is threaded twice through this hem and the ends joined together. You should barely be able to get the spray cover over the cockpit coaming because of the tension of the shock cord.

The result is a solid piece of fabric over the cockpit with an oversize rubber band holding it tightly in the groove of the coaming rail. The shock cord goes over the cockpit-coaming clamps to hold it in place in spite of waves, but you can still pull it loose if you are unable to slide out of the cockpit opening in case of upset.

Next, cut openings at both paddling positions about one inch (25 mm) forward of the backrests and one or two inches (25 to 50 mm) larger than your largest clothed circumference (depending on how much you anticipate spreading in the next few years). Leave about one foot (30 cm) of this opening uncut at the back. Sew the three-quarters circle back up with a zipper and attach a six-inch (15 cm)-wide sleeve to the outside of the zipper and underside of the "hatch" so that it can be pulled up when the hatch is open or will be hidden inside the kayak when it is closed. Finally, fit a piece of half-inch (1 cm) elastic, stretched to its limit, into the top of the sleeve.

On a single kayak, the closing feature is not needed, so you can omit the zipper and hatch and simply cut out the hole and fit the sleeve around it.

Any folding or rigid kayak can be converted to surfing with only a few modifications.

A spray cover which can be completely closed at either cockpit position greatly increases the versatility of the tandem kayak.

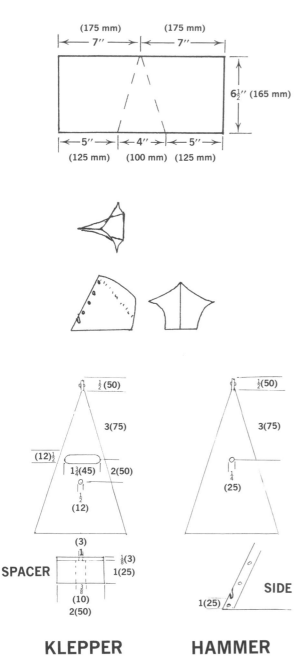

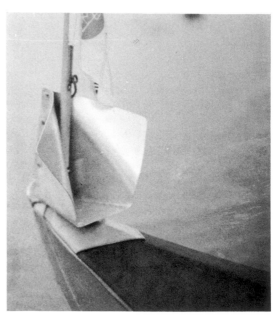

Kayak wave breaker in mounted position.

SPACER

KLEPPER   **HAMMER**

inches x millimeters

SIDE

WAVE BREAKER

Wave Breaker

The kayak makes an excellent surfing vehicle, easily riding waves too small for the surfboard rider to get enough speed to ride. The main problem with the kayak in surfing is that the bow is well in the water and a wave breaking unexpectedly can flip the boat end over end (called "pearling" by surfers).

There are two solutions to this problem. The first is to stick to small waves which are weak—and not much fun. The second is to make a wave breaker. The wave breaker is an odd-shaped piece of metal or fiberglass attached to the bow of the kayak. It keeps water from pouring over the bow on small waves, and acts as a submarine's diving planes in an up position on waves large enough to cover the bow.

It can be permanently attached to the kayak, but severely interferes with the folding features of a faltboot unless it is removable. My kayak is a Hammer and so the wave breaker hooks under the bow ring and over the flagpole bolt and is held in place by screwing the flagpole back on. For the

Klepper, the Z-bent bight (which forms the bow ring and forestay anchorage) slips through the slot in the bottom of the wave breaker and the vertical part (flag pole base) fits through the hole. A spacer is placed over the hole and the flag pole anchors the whole thing down. This renders the bow ring fairly inaccessible, so the painter should be attached before the wave breaker is anchored.

I made mine from aluminum sheet, but fiberglass is better because of corrosion.

The wave breaker is also useful in white-water streams with many haystacks, but it gets in the way under other conditions.

MAKING A CAMPING MACHINE

The particular camping machine included in this section is for a Volkswagen station wagon with a split front seat—but it is adaptable, with some modification, to any other "breadbox" vehicle. The bench front-seat type would have a wider seat over the toilet and no need of a small seat to fill the front-seat gap when using it for a bed.

Because of its lower engine, the Corvair would not require the seat elevation when converting from seat to bed in the rear. Because of its front engine, the Ford may work better if it uses the back door for the main entrance rather than the side door. However, these are adaptations which any user of these vehicles can readily discover, and present no real difficulties to the skilled do-it-yourself artist.

The camping machine has fallen into disrepute because the vast majority have either reduced their load to backpacking levels or have gone up in weight to the gas-guzzling motor homes and house trailers. Still, as a fuel conservation measure, those who went to the larger size had better come down or go the way of the dinosaur. The one included in this section is based on the old Volkswagen "breadbox" bus. Front-engined imitations would be better designed to use the rear door for the primary access rather than the side. Travel Equipment Corp., Sportswagon Conversions Division, Box 68, Elkhart, Indiana 46514, offers a wide selection of components for the do-it-yourselfer in the camping machine line.

Vehicle Modification

Obviously, with an eye to resale value, you can't modify the vehicle too much unless you are willing to sell the interior unit at the same time. Yet some holes here and there are needed to have the unit work.

In using a toilet with a holding tank, some means of draining the tank is needed. The easiest way is to cut a four-inch (10 cm) hole through the floor of the vehicle, directly below the tank drain. A short length of trailer sewer line is attached to the tank, through the hole, for draining into a trailer sump. This hose only needs to be two or three feet (60 to 100 cm) long and fold back under the car, where it is held by a strap. Weatherstripping around the hose at the hole keeps dust and road spray out of the car. In very dusty and rough conditions, it might be better to remove the hose (the engine compartment is an adequate storage space) and seal the hole with a plate of sheet metal.

Another almost-required modification is a spare-tire mounting on the front of the car. This is not necessary in the bench front-seat models, but in the split front-seat ones you will have a tire in bed with you if you don't. It is not a stock item (although often available at automotive supply houses). The front mounting is far better than putting it on a roof rack since a tire and wheel is far heavier than it looks when you try to raise it over your head. It is helpful to have a cover over the tire to protect it from the elements, and a lock to protect from loss when in "civilization."

A roof rack will help keep the junk out of the inside. The storage space inside will just about take care of clothing, cooking equipment, and about a week's supply of staples and two or three days' supply of perishables. Anything else should go on top or in a small trailer. If the amount of gear is kept down to camping standards instead of portable-house standards, the only thing that needs to go on top is something on the order of boats (folding or otherwise), packing equipment for horsepacking, or some other transportation device you will use to camp from this base.

If you use the car's electrical system much, a second battery, with a switch to use either it or the original as desired, will help keep from running it down too far to start the car in the morning. By using one to drive and the other for camping, you can always start in the mornings, then switch to the camping battery while under way to charge it. An ammeter to replace the idiot light is a necessity if you go in for such modifications, since the idiot light cannot tell when the battery is fully charged or getting low—it can only tell if it is too low already.

A telescopic roof over the kitchen is useful for headroom, but hardly necessary. It requires a considerable amount of work to install, and is difficult to waterproof. Under most conditions, cooking will be done with the door open and the cook standing on the ground outside. It is far too dangerous to cook while under way—especially if there is someone in the front passenger seat. The small seat used to bridge the front aisle is also useful for the cook, when inside, as it avoids that bent-over position required by the low ceiling.

Seat Bed

The only part of this which will give trouble is the hardware—the hinge for the backrest and the frame which elevates the seat when in the bed position. This can be obtained from Travel Equipment and in the front engine vehicles, the bed will generally be parallel to the length of the vehicle and present no problem.

The seat itself is two pieces of five-eighths- to three-fourths-inch (15 to 20 mm) plywood. The width should be about four inches (10 cm) less than the width of the car at that point; the seat is twenty-four inches (60 cm) deep and the backrest eighteen inches (45 cm) high.

Upholstering is basically simple. Polyurethane-foam sheeting is used, with the seat and backrest two inches (5 cm) thicker than the deck pad. The commercial models use six- and four-inch (15 and 10 cm) thicknesses, but I have found five and three inches (125 and 75 mm) to be perfectly adequate. Vinyl upholstery material, backed with fabric, is the cheapest, and quite durable. Make the pieces the same size as the foam, sew an upholstery zipper in the end of the edge, and stitch it together, wrong-side-out, a quarter of an inch (5 mm) from the edge. This makes the cover smaller than the foam, which means the foam will be under a slight compression and make the cover fit smoothly.

On the seat and backrest, straps of upholstery material, or twill-tape, should be installed in the seam when sewing the covering together. This permits the cushion to be strapped on the plywood so that it won't slide around, yet can be removed when carrying cargo in the vehicle.

Cabinets

Two cabinets bolt to the back wall of the front seats. One of these is the kitchen. It is a cabinet about two feet (60 cm) high and large enough at the base to hold an ice chest. A door is cut into the front (preferably swinging into the car rather than to the car door) and a hole is cut in the top for a plastic dish pan which serves as the sink. There should be space on one side of the sink to install a pump faucet and a water supply under the cabinet top (and at the side of the sink). A drain can be installed in the sink by using a bit of epoxy cement. Towel racks, fold-out tables, and other accessories can be added, but watch clearances on doors, aisles, etc.

The other cabinet is on the driver's side of the car and encloses a flush toilet with built-in holding tank. There will usually be space for a reserve fuel supply in small cans. Also leave room for a roll of toilet paper. (Because of space, the roll is simply put over the flush lever in mine.) The particular toilet will have to be selected with care since, on the Volkswagen, one of the frame cross-pieces is directly under this area. (Actually, this can be a help with the hole immediately back of it, since it forms a serviceable gravel shield to protect the sewer line from damage.)

The easiest construction technique is to use one-fourth- or three-eighths-inch (5 to 10 mm) plywood over a 2 x 2 (4 x 4) frame. The kitchen needs only two side walls, a front (with door), and a top. The toilet needs only one side wall, a front, and a top (with lid), since the car furnishes the other walls. The toilet will often have to have the lid removed to fit into the cabinet, as otherwise the cabinet would be too high for a seat. The toilet cabinet has a cushion over it (three-inch [75 mm] foam is adequate) to form a seat while not in use.

The cushion is removed when the lid is opened. It doesn't have a tendency to slide around (stopping is the strongest force, and there is a wall there) so no arrangement of straps is needed on the cushion.

Other Items

A table is almost required, although a card table will do. A table can be made of three pieces of five-eighths- to three-fourths-inch (15 to 20 mm) plywood. Two pieces, one 33 x 18 (80 x 45 cm) the other 3 x 18 (7½ x 45 cm) form the table. These pieces are hinged together on the bottom with a piano hinge, and are attached to the car, at the top of the liner panel, by sheet-metal screws and another piano hinge. The short piece folds upward while the large piece folds downward and wedges against the floor mat. The remaining piece is thirty-two inches (80 cm) long and four to six inches (10 to 15 cm) wide. It attaches to the end of the table with a T-hinge and forms the leg. It folds up against the underside of the table as the table is folded. A top of plastic laminate protects it against stains from spilled food. You may have to remove a small amount from the edge of the seat so it will clear the folded table when it extends for the bed.

A small seat (actually more of a stool) is made from scrap plywood to fit into the space between the front seats. This is topped with a thin layer of upholstered foam to duplicate the "give" of the front seats. In this way, the split front seat can be used for a child's bed just as the bench type is.

Curtains are easy to make. Denim is best because it is inexpensive and heavy enough to be opaque. Two curtains, 12 x 18 (30 x 45 cm) when finished, cover each of the side windows. Sew a half-inch (12 mm) hem in the top and bottom, to fit over a curtain spring. The springs are attached to the wall, an inch (25 mm) above and below the window, with sheet-metal screws. The back window is curtained in the same way, but with 18 x 24 (45 x 60 cm) pieces and two springs linked together. Tie-backs made of scrap curtain material keep the curtains open except when privacy is needed. They have snaps to fasten them around the curtains and are also fastened to the wall with sheet-metal screws. The center curtains share one tie-back each.

The windshield can be hidden by a curtain simply hanging from the sun visors. Pockets in the upper edge of the curtain fit over the sun visors when they are swung over to the sides. Small snaps or hooks and eyes attach the ends of this curtain to the forwardmost of the side-window curtains to cover the rest of the space.

A shower-curtain rod, of the type designed for making a small shower-stall in a tub, can be fitted to the side of the car, around the toilet. A six-foot (2 m) length of three-eighths-inch (8 mm) aluminum rod can be bent between the side wall and the driver's seat back wall to hold the curtain. A shower curtain is adequate, although a 4' x 5' (125 x 150 cm) piece of curtain material looks better. This curtain can share the tie-back with the side window.

As with any other vehicle used for camping, an adequate set of repair tools and materials should be carried. All seats should be equipped with seatbelts, and a fire extinguisher should be mounted within easy access of the kitchen.

The camping machine, of course, can be designed to be as simple or as elaborate as your individual taste desires. As stated at the beginning of Part III, the main advantage of building your own equipment is that you can have features not offered anywhere else.

Outside showing spare tire mounting

Looking forward, curtains closed for the night

Rear seat fold-out to make queen-size bed

Dining table unfolded

Bathroom "wall" in position,
dining table folded

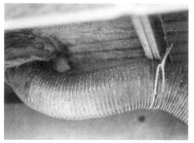
Holding tank toilet under middle seat

Sanitary dump hose under vehicle

Ice chest under sink and stove

PART IV

Cooking

Probably the greatest psychological factor in determining the success of a camping trip is the quality of the food. Therefore it should be carefully planned. The menus should be prepared both with a thought to the supplies and cooking equipment on hand, and to the likes and dislikes of the members of the group. You should have an adequate set of cooking utensils within the weight and bulk limits set by your means of transportation. Cooking gear for camping is quite low in cost compared to its use, so buy good equipment which will give good service. The slight difference in cost will be more than repaid in better camp meals.

To someone who is accustomed only to the modern kitchen with its knobs, dials, and switches, camp cooking seems impossible. Yet only a few years ago, the wood-burning kitchen stove was quite common. There is not much difference between using a wood-burning kitchen stove and using a campfire. In fact, the campfire can actually be a little more flexible. There is even less difference between the modern range and the campfire than between the campfire and the wood stove. Too often, the beginning camper sees only the differences. If he (or more likely, she) would look at the similarities, the transition would be easier.

In both methods, regulation of the heat is by adjusting the amount of fuel fed to the fire or by the distance between the heat source and the cooking utensil. For the experienced camper, an open fire can be regulated with all the fine adjustments of a modern range. Automation of the modern range is the only significant difference.

While the beginner is often confused with a new cooking medium, the expert falls into the opposite trap. Because of his familiarity with the campfire, its use is automatic with him. Unfortunately, the menu often gets the same way. As a result, he often gets into a rut with the same foods or techniques of preparing it. I still can't fully appreciate baked beans because in my Boy Scout

171

days baked beans were absolutely required on each day's menu while camping.

We have survived a fad of a real ptomaine producer called "s'mores," made of toasted (more often burned) marshmallows, milk-chocolate bars (not the camper's tropical kind), and graham crackers. The problem is, these are often perfectly valuable parts of the camp menu which are ruined for succeeding generations, since those who had them too often now hate them and don't teach the beginners to use them. Fortunately the fad now is experimentation—freeze-dry, wild food, trail snacks, etc. Let's hope it stays that way.

There are, of course, some limitations to the variety of foods practical in camp; but these are due to the problems of refrigeration, size of possible ovens, and the bulk and weight of special equipment that would be used for preparing only one or two dishes. Even these limitations are being slowly removed by technological advance. Freeze-drying makes almost any refrigerator-inhabitant of the past readily available in camp. About the only item that is still unavailable by this means is ice cream—and where there is an adequate supply of clean snow, even it is a possibility.

A knowledge of indoor cooking is certainly an advantage in learning camp cooking. Recipes can be adapted, with a little ingenuity, to the campfire. The main problem, as Kephart pointed out years ago in *Camp Cookery,* is that the cookbook is always calling for things we don't have, and it doesn't tell us what to do with the things we do have.

Adapting cookbook recipes does require some effort and occasional strokes of sheer inspiration. This is especially true when going light, when the utensils have been reduced to the bare minimum, often to the point of eliminating all utensils or simply carrying a roll of aluminum foil.

Yet, even under these rather rigorous conditions, the imaginative cook will never lack appetizing and nutritious meals. A knowledge of simple Second Class Boy Scout cooking techniques (the old no-utensils requirement) will make this entirely possible, and without spending half the day on K.P.

The camp cook not only has to know cooking and nutrition, he must also know fire building, wood selection, and, quite often, fireplace construction. Yet these are basic skills, easily learned, and they quickly become merely another interesting part of the challenge camping offers to those who are willing to try something for themselves.

CHAPTER SIXTEEN

Fireplaces

With the final awakening to the problems of ecology and the need to conserve our wilderness resources, the open fire has fallen on times of disrepute. True, if one extreme or the other must be practiced, then I am willing to sacrifice the wood-burning campfire to the Primus, Svea, Optimus, and even Coleman. However, I don't think that the times call for extremism but for careful thought. There are still times when an open campfire is the more responsible alternative—particularly where the demand on the environment is relatively low, the wood supply abundant, and the use of nonrenewable petroleum resources questionable. Many areas, within reach of even the camper just beginning to backpack or canoe camp, have abundant wood, all quite dead but still standing on the trees, quite suitable for campfire use. However, unfortunately a small camp stove must now be carried, just in case. Where the wood fire is still a viable alternative, the safe use of this facility requires a proper fireplace.

In camp cooking, a fireplace is a device to make cooking easier than simply with an open fire. It does this by making the fire easier to control, by making the heat more even, by making a hotter flame, or by making the utensils handier. Fireplaces may also be made for other purposes, such as heating a tent or smoking meat. Each purpose requires a different type of fireplace and sometimes a different type of fire.

There are several factors which go into design of the fireplace. Frying will require a different type than will baking with a reflector oven (although you can build the two side-by-side to accommodate both cooking methods at once). The number in the group will be a factor since, obviously, you will need a larger set-up for a large party than with just your family.

The fuel supply is another factor. If you have no hardwood, you will have to cook over open flames and so you need a design which will let you feed the fire easier than if your cooking could be over coals which are set in place and can be ignored (if you put the right amount in the fireplace in the first place). If everything is soaking wet, or you are above the timberline, it is time to get out the little backpacking stove, which is its own fireplace, and use it to cook.

Time is another factor. Building a fire to "boil the kettle" (the northwoods' term for a noonday tea break) will be quite simple, just enough preparation to make the fire safe, while the more leisurely and elaborate evening meal will require an equally elaborate fireplace to prepare it. Altar fireplaces are great if you have the time to build them.

Similarly, the materials at hand will determine, to a certain extent, the type of fireplace. Obviously a clay bank oven is out of the question in the black gumbo soil of the South, while stone fireplaces are impractical where all of the rocks are moist shale.

Regardless of the type, you should have someplace to keep an adequate supply of firewood and a container of water to put the fire out. The shade of a tent fly is welcome in hot or rainy weather.

FIRESITES

The location of a campfire is determined by its use. A heating fire should be close enough to the tent so that it radiates the heat inside with little loss, yet it should not be so close that blowing sparks will create a fire hazard if the wind changes during the night. A heating fire (except in a tipi, or the generally impractical shepherd's stove) should be a reflector fire, downwind from the tent.

A cooking fire should be far enough away from the tent to keep the smoke out of the tent on calm, foggy mornings, but still close enough for convenience.

The big, fellowship-type bonfires, so prized by organizational camps which have a big "campfire program" with everyone there at the end of the day, have only one use in real camping: they make good signals for help when you are lost or otherwise need assistance. The organizational camps should use small fires, with each cabin having its own fire. You can get close enough to enjoy it, and get to know each other as well.

Regardless of the type fire or fireplace, the fire should be built on a completely fireproof surface. Under certain conditions, humus soil can retain a smoldering fire for days before it breaks out in a blaze. There are several ways to avoid this problem, as well as the more common one of the fire spreading on top of the ground.

For a cooking fire, the altar fire is perfect. Otherwise dig down to mineral soil and line the hole with rocks, or build the fire on a solid layer of rocks. In snow, a log or bark platform, fireproofed with dirt, will prevent the fire from melting its way into the snow. A thinner version will help in wet weather when the ground is soaked.

There should not be any overhanging branches at least ten feet (3 m) above the highest flame. This is as much a conservation practice to avoid killing the branch as it is a matter of fire safety. The greater the distance, the better. You should clear the area of any dead vegetation for at least a six-foot (2 m) radius. Firewood and water for extinguishing the fire should be within easy reach of the cook.

The fire should be downwind from the tent to avoid getting the smoke inside. A tarp spread over the fire gives good protection from sun or rain. However, it should be treated with a fireproofing compound and kept high enough so that it does not feel warm on top when the fire is going. The fire should be controlled so that no sparks rise up to reach it, even when you are stirring the fire. At least one day's supply of wood should be kept dry at all times—more if you expect rain.

In putting out the fire, water is almost a necessity since a fire can smolder for days in a log covered with dry dirt. Pour the water on lightly rather than dumping it or barely sprinkling it. Make sure all the wood gets drenched. Stir the coals with a stick while pouring the water to make sure that no sparks remain. When the fire is absolutely out, cover the firesite with a mound of wet mineral soil and place crossed sticks on top of the mound to let those who follow you at the site know not to dig there.

TRAPPER FIRE

The trapper fire is one of those old traditions in camping that has so earned its place that the only improvements have been in combining it with other accessories, such as the keyhole or altar fireplaces. The trapper fire is a fire built between two rows of stones or logs, about four inches (10 cm) farther apart on one end than the other. The wider end should be into the wind, and as wide as possible and still securely support your largest pot.

The superiority of the trapper fire is readily seen when you consider the purposes of a camp fireplace. The logs or rocks confine the heat to the cooking utensils only, rather than allowing the heat to radiate out and be wasted (or make cooking harder in the summer). While not as efficient as a reflector fire (nor should it be, considering its purpose), the sides have a reflective function in concentrating the heat. Because of these two features, you don't need as much wood as you would otherwise.

Because the large end is facing the wind, the

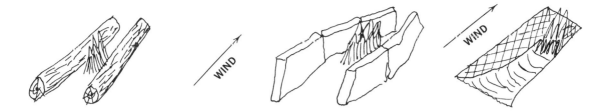

TRAPPER FIRE

TRENCH FIRE

trapper fire has good draft. If the wind is too high, burning the wood too rapidly and with too much heat, a rock or small log placed across this entrance will reduce it in an easily regulated manner.

Finally, the trapper fire has the added feature of providing a built-in rack for supporting the cooking utensils. When a pot is too small to bridge the gap, even at the small end, you can use the same principle working in the other direction. Take two green sticks, about an inch (25 mm) in diameter, and lay them across the sides of the fireplace. This will hold the small items.

In a similar manner, a stone slab, a half-inch or less (1 cm) in thickness, may be laid across the fire to make a griddle. Build a fire on top of the slab as well as under it. Let the fire on top burn down to coals, but keep the one beneath it going. It should be hot enough to move a drop of water.

In building a fireplace, never use shale, slate, or similar layered rocks; nor the "glasses," such as flint, chert, and obsidian; nor rocks taken from stream beds. All of these have moisture deep inside which will crack open the rock when turned to steam by the heat of the fire. In the case of shale, this cracking is as loud as a cap pistol and has considerable force. Very fine-grain sandstone (too fine to see the individual grains), if dry, limestone, and metamorphic rocks such as granite and marble make suitable griddles. Grainy rocks with shiny pieces in them (gneiss, schist, etc.) are unsuitable because they tend to come apart.

A sheet of aluminum foil, doubled over and weighted down at the ends, will make a fair griddle. You have to keep coals under it while you are using it, but it needs no starter fire on top to pre-heat it. The main problem in using a foil griddle is in

keeping from breaking a hole in it while turning the food.

Both wood and stone have their advantages and disadvantages as a material for making the fireplace. The cracks between the rocks help the draft, especially on days with little or no wind. On the other hand, you have the same problems of selecting rocks as you do in making a rock griddle, although you don't have to be quite as choosy as to thickness. You also have to dig a bit of a hole at times to plant some of the rocks in order to keep the tops level. This means that it takes time to build such a fireplace.

Wood is a quicker medium, as all you have to do is lay two logs the proper distance apart and start building your fire. But logs do have some disadvantages. Besides difficulty in finding, you need green ones that won't burn up, and green logs four to six inches (10 to 15 cm) in diameter are hard to find in campgrounds these days. You can avoid this problem to a certain extent by wetting the logs thoroughly before using, and rotating them each time you use them so the fire does not have a charred area to start on when a new fire is built.

TRENCH FIRE

The trench fire is the reverse of the trapper fire. With the trapper fire, the fire rests on the ground and the utensil support is built up. With the trench fire, the utensils rest on the ground and the fire is down in a trench. The windward end should be sloping, but the other sides must be vertical to avoid wasting heat or weakening the support of the pots. The lee end should be narrower than the windward end for the same reason as with the trapper fire.

The technique of using green sticks to bridge a gap too wide for a pot applies to the trench fire as well as to the trapper fire. In fact, the techniques for using the two are practically interchangeable.

In forests, be sure to dig down to mineral soil before you start digging your trench. The trench fire is a potential fire hazard (fire traveling through dead roots) if this precaution is not maintained.

TRIPOD

The tripod, as a camp fireplace, consists of three metal tent pegs, rocks, or thick green sticks stuck into the ground around a small fire or bed of coals. The utensil rests on top of this tripod.

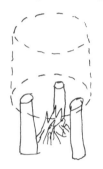

TRIPOD

This is a good technique for a trail lunch as it is easy to heat up some soup or boil water for coffee or tea. It will only hold one pot but, since it is open on all sides, it is very easy to feed the fire and therefore regulate it quite closely. Principally, it is a simple replacement for the complex dingle crane since it usually takes too long to find suitable material to build one.

Again, the wood should be green or the rock immune from popping, or your fireplace may disappear in the middle of your cooking.

IN HOLE

This method—with the fire built in a small hole—is the standard method for emu, clambake, bean pot, and many other traditional camping banquets. For long baking sessions, this is an excellent fireplace since it can be safely left unattended

(provided it is built correctly to begin with), leaving time for an elaborate meal and other activities as well.

In the beach sand of a clambake, just an adequately large hole will do the job. In more humus soil, however, rocks are needed both for fireproofing and for heat retention. For the average small group, dig a hole about a foot and a half (45 cm) in diameter and a foot (30 cm) deep. Line it with small stones, about golfball size. As with all uses of heated rocks, never use shale, slate, or rocks from water. After the rocks are firmly in place, cover them with sticks about one inch (25 mm) in diameter and a foot (30 cm) long. Build a small tipi fire in the bottom to light the larger sticks.

After they have burned to coals, scrape them in between the rocks. Add the food, wrapped in aluminum foil, wet paper or cloth, or green leaves (such as grape leaves, corn shucks, or seaweed), and cover the whole thing with a piece of wet cloth or the green leaves, and then a layer of dry dirt. Check the taste of the leaves before using them to avoid bitter or peppery ones which will affect the taste of the food.

A totally different "in hole" fireplace is the Dakota fire. This is valuable in grassland when there is a high enough wind blowing to make a severe fire hazard. It will handle only one pot.

Dig the hole with about one inch (25 mm) less radius than the pot, and about a foot (30 cm) deep. Dig a smaller hole, about three inches (75 mm) in diameter, angling from about six inches (15 cm) upwind from the main hole to the base of it. A spoon is a good tool to use for this digging. The fire is built in the large hole and lit. When it is burning well, but the flames are not as high as the top, place the pot over the hole. The small hole provides air.

It is possible to make several of these around a similar-sized hole, with the small air holes connecting all the cooking holes to this central air shaft. In this way, the technique can be used for several dishes at once.

Wood can be added, if needed, by removing the pot, putting in the wood, and replacing the pot before the fire gets too big.

KEYHOLE FIRE

It is more efficient to cook over coals than flames; however, an ample supply of coals is often a problem. The keyhole fireplace is a solution which puts the production of the coals outside the stove itself, and thus avoids the ups and downs of temperature which result from the flames when new wood is added or additional coals must be built because of the length of the cooking process.

The keyhole fire can be built in conjunction with any open fire. Because of the popularity of trapper and trench fires, the shape of the total operation is usually that of a keyhole—a circle adjacent to the small side of a rectangle. With round fireplaces, the shape would be more of an hourglass composed of two overlapping circles.

While originally only one fire was used, two are more efficient if an extensive amount of cooking is needed. These should be built side by side, an equal distance from the cooking part of the fireplace. This way, there is a continuous production of coals and there is always a clear trail for the coals to be moved from the fire to the cooking area.

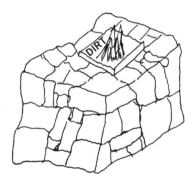

ALTAR FIRE

KEYHOLE FIRE

One fire is built up and lighted. When it dies to coals, light the second fire and scrape the coals from the first one into the cooking area. Rebuild the first fire, but don't light it. Then start your cooking. When you need more coals, scrape them from the second fire into the cooking area and relight the other fire. Keep one fire burning and one built for lighting at all times until you clearly have no further need for the fires. Keep the fires quite small (about the size you would use to cook one pot on) to save wood and not over-produce coals, and to keep the general area cooler.

Hardwood is a necessity for this technique.

ALTAR FIRE

The altar fire is the ultimate in camp fireplaces. It is a table, made of stone or wood, about a foot (30 cm) lower than the height of the cook's waist. Another type of fireplace is built on top of this table. This makes it far more comfortable because the cook can stand while working—just like at home, on the range. The discomfort of squatting and duck-walking around while cooking is avoided. Unfortunately, with one exception, it takes too long to build for use in any except a permanent camp.

With the exception, the altar is built on a boulder, requiring no construction at all. However, the boulder should be flat enough on top that the burning wood doesn't roll down the sides to burn the vegetation (or the cook's ankle). Also, the sides should be steep enough, at least on the cook's side, to enable him to get close enough to cook without having to lean forward.

If the altar is made of wood, there are two ways of building it. The first is to pile up the wood in the same manner as a log-cabin fire (see page 187). This requires no more materials than the wood itself, but it takes quite a bit of wood and, unless made very carefully, it will fall down easily if there is any side pressure on it.

The second way is to make a table—four legs and bracing—by lashing the wood together. It takes longer and requires an ample supply of lashing rope, but it is considerably stronger.

Regardless of the medium, and especially with wood altars, a layer of dirt—about one to two inches (25 to 50 mm) thick and tightly packed—should be put on the platform of the altar. Applying it as a thick mud keeps it from moving about under the fire. This will prevent the wood from burning or the stones from cracking in the heat. Leave part of the top uncovered by the dirt to provide table space for the utensils and ingredients so you can be fixing them while the longer-cooking foods are on the fire. Sprinkle water on the dirt after cooking to keep it packed and to prevent it from blowing off the top or into the food at the table end.

The altar fireplace can hold any type of fire or fireplace on its top. This makes it versatile as well as comfortable. A keyhole-trapper fire combination on top of an altar fireplace is even superior to the bulky petroleum stove in good weather. For practical purposes, however, excavated fireplaces and most uses of the reflector fire are not really suitable on top of an altar platform.

REFLECTOR FIRE

As its name suggests, the reflector fire uses some means of reflecting the heat of the fire to someplace where it is needed. The reflector may be made from logs, planks, rocks, dirt, aluminum foil, or any solid material. Naturally, the smoother the reflector and the shinier its surface, the better it will reflect.

The fire in front of the reflector is usually a tipi fire (see page 186), since its heat can be controlled most accurately. While this is important for using a reflector fire for cooking, a half-tipi, built against the reflector itself of fairly large wood (around one-inch [25 mm] diameter and a foot [30 cm] long), is used for heating purposes, since in this case long-term heat output is more important than producing the heat within a few degrees of an exact figure.

The reflector fire is typically used to heat a baker tent, but can be used to heat almost any other kind which opens wide in the front. Under survival conditions (or simply clear, cold nights), you can sleep comfortably in the open with no more aid than a reflector fire on either side of you and possibly a windbreak. A rock cliffside can substitute for the second reflector fire.

In cooking, the reflector fire is primarily used to heat an oven. While the reflector oven is the most efficient form of this oven, the reflector fire can

LOGS

ROCKS OR SOD

ALUMINUM FOIL

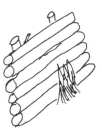

REFLECTORS

make several other utensils into ovens. A skillet full of biscuit dough placed before a reflector fire makes bannock, a traditional breadstuff of the north-woods, and an excellent one anywhere.

Regardless of the purpose of the reflector fire, it should be kept going, with flames, for as long as it is needed. Coals radiate in all directions and, because they are lower than the reflector, they bounce upward off of it. Flames, on the other hand, are on the same level as the reflector and can be reflected straight into the area needing the heat. The problem of the coals could be cured with an aluminum-foil reflector tilted forward, over the coals, to reflect more heat horizontally, but few natural reflectors can be made to do this. You would still need a mound of coals to produce the heat anyway.

CLAY OVEN

Where there is suitable clay, you can make a clay oven like the Pueblo Indians use. This is a hollow mound, two to three feet ($\frac{1}{2}$ to 1 m) high, with an opening in the side big enough to get food in and out, but no larger. The opening should be into the prevailing wind.

It is easier to build it over a framework of brick or stone the size of the inside, or over a large can (a potato-chip can or a small fuel drum). After the clay hardens, remove the brick or stone through the opening, being careful not to damage the inside wall of the oven and crack it. If you use a can, it is left in. When you don't use the can, build a roaring fire in the mound to fire the clay and prevent a cave-in before you attempt to cook in it.

The best fire to use in such an oven is a bed of live coals with a very low blue flame dancing on the surface. A wooden paddle, fireproofed with dirt, is the traditional means of getting both the fire and the food in and out of the oven. Use the clean side of the paddle, or another one, for the food.

To use the clay oven, put the fire in the mound. When the oven is properly heated, remove the fire. Very quickly, put the food in and seal the opening with a rock to retain the heat. The oven should be about a hundred degrees F (55°C) too hot when you remove the fire to compensate for the heat loss when the door is open.

Size permitting, the clay oven will handle anything a kitchen oven will. As with most complicated camping techniques, it is worthwhile only in a permanent camp.

CLAY BANK OVEN

Where both the terrain and the soil is suitable, the clay oven can be hollowed out instead of built up. You can dig it out with only your bare hands, if necessary. Fire it the same as the Pueblo-type clay oven. Block the chimney to retain the heat just before you remove the fire.

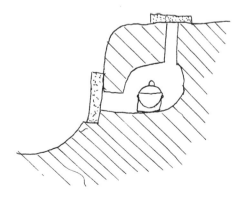

CLAY BANK OVEN

CROSS-SECTION

CLAY OVEN

CHAPTER SEVENTEEN

Firewoods

The ideal wood for a campfire should give a hot, even flame, die into long-lasting coals, and never smoke or pop. Since cooking is easier over coals than open flame, the quality of the coals is the most important of the three. Coals radiate the heat more evenly, are usually hotter than open flames from the same wood, are more easily controlled than flames, and don't soot the bottom of the utensils. Generally speaking, the harder the wood, the better the coals.

Firewood should be dry. This is in the sense of "not green" as well as "not wet." However, it should not be the opposite extreme—punky wood will not make coals and is hard to ignite in all except an already roaring fire. You can use it for smoking meat, and sometimes for holding a spark overnight when you are low on matches, but for little else.

The best source of firewood is squaw wood. This is dead wood still standing. It can be broken off without the use of an ax or hatchet. After pulling off, thick limbs can be broken by banging them on a sharp rock outcropping. Since squaw wood is standing off the ground, it is rarely punky. If wood under a half-inch (1 cm) diameter bends very much without breaking, it is still too green for firewood. On the other hand, if it breaks without much effort, it is too punky. It should break with a resounding snap.

Often limbs of otherwise healthy trees will be dead. These can be gathered easily by throwing a rock-weighted rope over the limb and pulling it down. If the limb doesn't break easily, it is still too green and the rope can be retrieved with no harm done. This applies to limbs under an inch or so (1 cm) at the base. Heavier limbs rarely break this way, and when they do they are dangerous as they fall.

Birch bark and the lower parts of pine limbs are a couple of squaw-wood items which will burn even when wet from a rain.

The best wood for cooking is either white ash or the white oaks, or, in the semi-desert of the West, mesquite. Close behind comes hickory, the red oaks, birch, and, if seasoned, poplar. These woods burn slowly, but with intense heat, and leave excellent coals. After them come maple, the other ashes, the nut and berry trees, and so on down to the firs, pines, cedars, and other softwoods.

On the seacoast, driftwood is a usable wood if it has had a chance to dry out thoroughly. However, it usually requires the use of an ax to get firewood size and is often quite hard. Any shrub will work in an emergency—even moss and lichens will burn if dead. In areas of little wood, however, it is usually better to pick it up as you see it, and carry it with you. It makes your load heavier, but at least you will have some. One of the backpacking stoves and some fuel is good insurance in case you can't find any wood.

As a rule of thumb (and there are exceptions), trees near water will be poorer burners than those far from surface moisture. The dry-ground trees have less sap as a water-saving device; also, they grow more slowly because of less water, and the wood is denser as a result.

WHITE ASH

The white ash is a versatile wood which can serve the camper in many ways. Not only is it one of the best of the firewoods, burning with a hot, even flame and dying to even hotter coals, but it is also an excellent wood for ax handles and canoe paddles, and can be used for this purpose in an emergency.

The white ash has fairly small leaves, two or three inches (50 to 75 mm) long and less than one inch (about 1 cm) wide. They are arranged in pairs on a stem with a single leaf at the end. The underside is lighter in color, which gives the tree its name.

The seeds are in thin seed pods, drooping in small clusters along leafless twigs.

The tree is fifty to one hundred feet (17 to 33 m) high at maturity and grows throughout the entire eastern half of the nation except for Florida.

WHITE OAK

The term "white oak" has two separate, and only partially overlapping, meanings. One is a specific tree, *Quercus alba;* the other is the lumberman's term for a whole variety of trees, in the genus *Quercus,* which have a certain type of wood and whose acorns mature in one year. (The red oak's take two years.) With one exception—the live oak—they have rounded points on typical oak leaves. The live oak has small, simple leaves, although still rounded at the tip. The live oak gets its name from its evergreen condition, which often makes it the only green tree in the winter in much of its range.

The *Quercus alba*'s leaves consist of seven deep and well-rounded lobes. They are about eight inches (20 cm) long and five inches (12½ cm) wide. The acorns are about an inch (25 mm) long with the caps covering about one-third of the length. The tree grows from fifty to a hundred and fifty feet (17 to 50 m) high and gets its name from the light-grey, scaley bark.

The live oak (*Q. virginiana,* plus some similar evergreen species) has leaves rarely over an inch and a half to two inches (4 to 5 cm) long and about a half-inch (12 mm) wide. They are rounded (or

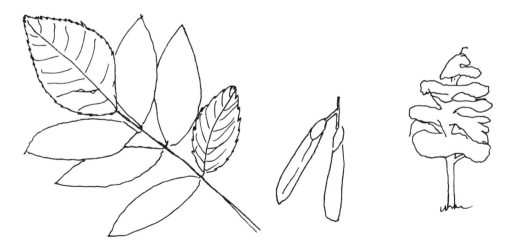

WHITE-ASH LEAVES, SEEDS, AND TREE

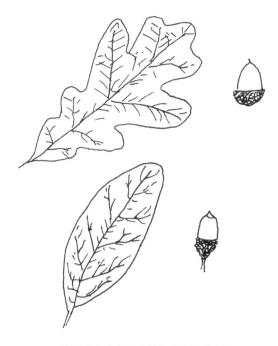

WHITE-OAK AND LIVE-OAK
LEAF AND ACORN

occasionally flattened) at the tip and pointed at the base. The tree is usually scrub brush to fifteen feet ($4\frac{1}{2}$ m) tall, although under ideal conditions they will grow over thirty feet (9 m) tall.

Most of the others have leaves more or less like *Q. alba,* with the more typical firm bark of most oaks. In the winter, an oak with no leaves but many acorns is probably a red oak, still a very good source of firewood, although not quite as good as the white oak.

MESQUITE AND THE DESERT WOODS

Throughout much of the Southwest, the mesquite is the predominant tree. Outside the stream banks and washes where cottonwood, willow, pecan, and other broader-leafed trees (which are also good firewoods) appear, the little live oak or pin oak will be the only other trees. In these areas, it is safe to assume that if it is a tree, it can make a good fire.

The mesquite is usually a scrub brush, but will occasionally get as high as thirty feet (9 m)—probably twice that if the slanting and twisted trunks could grow straight up. The leaves are very small, an inch to an inch and a half (25 to 40 mm) long and less than a quarter-inch (5 mm) wide. They are arranged in pairs on the stems with as many as twenty pair on each with a paired tip. The flowers are long yellow catkins in the late spring and the bean-like pods are often on all year. The beans can be dried and ground into flour or made into penole.

Mesquite wood is prized for fence posts because of its rot resistance. Even wood that has been lying about for several years will still burn with a hot flame. The coals are the best of any wood and were the principal branding-iron fire before the propane torch took over.

In the Sonoran Desert, there are a couple of woody shrubs which are tempting to use. Palo verde stinks when burned, so leave it alone. Creosote

MESQUITE LEAF AND PODS

bush is too smoky and hard to use. Most other desert bushes burn like grass—a big flame but little heat, and absolutely no coals. Cow chips are actually much better. They have no coals, but they do produce an adequate amount of heat.

SOFTWOODS

The division of wood into softwoods has little to do with hardness—the toughest wood, *lignum vitae,* is a softwood, while the model builder's balsa is a hardwood. Nor is the evergreen characteristic completely valid since not only is the live oak an evergreen hardwood, but the tamarack loses its needles in the winter. The hardwoods have leaves, while the softwoods have needles or scales. While these distinctions become blurred in smaller plants, they are accurate enough for the camper seeking the best wood for a campfire. Hardwoods are vastly superior to softwoods as a fuel for campfires.

Pines and other evergreens burn too quickly to make coals, but they are usually hot enough, especially if they have large amounts of resin or pitch in them. Standing dead pines, especially lightning victims, have heavy amounts of pitch in the base of the branches or in the base of the trunk. If the remains of a softwood tree is old enough to be bleached to a light-grey, with most of its bark flaked off and gone, and still is firm, giving a resounding thud when hit with an ax or solid stick, it has a sufficient amount of pitch in it to make a good fire.

The dead twigs on a living tree are also high in pitch and make excellent tinder or kindling, depending on their size. The only real problem of a pitch-filled pine is that it throws sparks quite badly. Outside of the fact that they burn too fast to make coals, and so all cooking must be done over flames, they are as good as many hardwoods.

Softwoods have several more uses in fire building besides as fuel itself. Pine cones, if thoroughly dry, make excellent kindling if you have enough of them. They should break easily, although not cleanly, with the fibers still holding the cone to-gether. You will need a hot flame from your tinder to ignite them, but once they catch they will provide enough heat to light even wet wood.

Cedar bark is unsurpassed as tinder. It takes a lot of blowing to get it into a flame, but it is easily lighted and the blowing is not all that hard. Break the fibers apart in your hands before using, so you have a loose mass of a wool-like material.

THE POPPERS

Two woods have a bad feature that overbalances all the good features they have. These are the poppers, which may even knock over a coffee pot with their explosions. The only way to prevent this is to use another wood, unless you can get a piece which has been drying for several years.

The worst one is bois d'arc (usually pronounced bo'-dark), or osage orange. You can recognize it easily by its hard, rough bark, its many thorns on younger shoots, and its large, green "horse apple" fruit. The wood is yellowish in the sapwood and almost orange in the heartwood. The name "bois d'arc" was given it by the early French explorers and means "wood for bows." It makes excellent bows, but terrible campfires.

The other (and slightly less violent) popper is the sweetest-smelling wood of all—red cedar (which really isn't a cedar at all, but a juniper). Cedar bark and "leaves," however, are quite useful for tinder.

Other wood, especially box elder, hackberry, and chinaberry, may pop occasionally due to a pocket of sap that is turned into steam rapidly, but these cases are not common and are rarely violent. Several others, notably the pitch-filled softwoods, spark like fireworks, but no real violence accompanies this display unless you get hit by the sparks. Both bois d'arc and cedar can upset utensils on a trapper fire. Popping by the other woods can be reduced by using small pieces or only coals. Cedar makes very poor coals, and bois d'arc will pop even when reduced to coals.

CHAPTER EIGHTEEN

Fire Building

The secret of outdoor cooking is in using the proper fire. A kitchen stove has a knob to adjust the heat. The type and size of fire, as well as the distance between it and the utensil, controls the heat of a campfire. With a wise combination of fire and fireplace, you can have a cooking fire for any purpose.

REQUIREMENTS OF A FIRE

Fire requires three things to exist: a fuel, oxygen, and a kindling temperature. Furthermore, the only fuel which will burn is a gas which chemically unites easily with oxygen. Solids or liquids must first be vaporized by heat before they can burn.

The reason for this postage-stamp course in the physics of combustion is that the skilled camper must improvise, and if he knows the "why," he can often figure out the "how." Several useful lessons can be drawn from the first paragraph. First of all, oxygen, normally carried to the fire in the air, must be able to get to the fire. A large pile of wood simply blocks the easy access of air to the fire, and the fire dies quickly, if it can be lit at all.

Secondly, we need to note the relationship between fuel and kindling temperature. With fuel of the same type (firewood, in this case), the larger the piece, the more heat is required to light it because the greater volume simply absorbs the heat as fast as it is applied. The obvious demonstration

of this is to light a match; with it you can light a toothpick easily, but you won't be able to do much more than smoke a six-inch (15 cm) log. The main mistake the tenderfoot makes is to use wood which is too large for the fire. If they avoid trying to build the fire with tree trunks, they still try to add the larger pieces too soon. These large pieces either block the oxygen, or they absorb too much heat and cool the smaller wood. In either case, the fire goes out.

Some people get around this problem of wood size by using kerosene, lantern fuel, or even gasoline as a primer, so that even a large log will light with one match. In the first place, this simply wastes wood (as well as the inflammable liquid). In the second, it is often an invitation to a burned hand or arm as the fire flames up with intense heat before the tenderfoot can get out of the way. It is not only wasteful, it isn't even sporting. Anyone with any camping skill should be able to pass the basic Boy Scout requirement of building a fire with no more than two matches. Anyone who can't do this should practice until he can.

Tinder

The key to a quick fire is good tinder. An old Boy Scout fire-building requirement was that all materials must grow wild at the site. My father kids about looking for "wild paper" (trash left lying about by litterbugs). While paper is excellent tinder, it is too bulky to carry for that purpose, although many auto campers carry a small stack of old newspapers for tinder, as well as for wiping off after changing a flat, for traction on loose sand, and for other emergencies. "Wild paper" is not always available, although it is all too plentiful at most sites. And paper, like the wood it is made from, can become punky if it stays on the ground for a prolonged period of time.

Some people think that because paper is good, leaves must be good also, since they slightly resemble paper. Like many other common beliefs about nature, it is wrong. Leaves, even when completely dead, have a very low burning temperature and generally just smoke without getting much of a flame at all. There are a few people with the magical ability to light a fire this way—but they require the considerable use of a hat or a breeze to do it.

On the other hand, dry pine needles do fairly well (with a lot of blowing). Cedar "leaves" are good, green or dry. Cedar bark will do if you rub it between your hands to break up the fibers. Even then, it requires quite a bit of blowing. Shredded birch bark is very good and often can be made from the inner bark when the outer bark is wet.

Dry moss, lichens, and some grasses will work as tinder with the aid of a small breeze. Old birds' nests, mouse nests, cattail fuzz, pussywillow fuzz, and similar dry, fuzzy vegetation make excellent tinder.

If there is any dead wood around at all, the best tinder is a double handful of small twigs, the size of match sticks and four or five inches (10 to $12\frac{1}{2}$ cm) long. Build these in a small tipi fire.

Sometimes there won't be any such twigs available except green or punky ones. Large sticks can be split into small ones. An even better way, if the wood isn't extremely hard, is to make a few fuzz sticks. These are large sticks whittled into chips with the chips still attached. They act as both tinder and kindling.

Fuel

The ideal fire goes from very small pieces at the bottom of the fire, upward through larger pieces to the large ones at the top. For this reason, a tipi fire, built in layers, is the best and easiest to build. The fire, as it moves upward, increases its heat through each layer so that each layer is met with the proper kindling temperature to ignite it.

Because the disturbed fibers admit oxygen, split wood burns better than round wood of the same size. Have an adequate supply of wood of all sizes, especially the larger ones, within reach before you light your fire. This way, you won't have to leave your cooking to get more wood.

Unless you want the fire to last all night, or are making coals, no piece should be over one inch (25 mm) in diameter. Except for the star or log-cabin fires, none should be over one foot (30 cm) in length. The chief mistake beginning campers make in fire building is in using pieces that are too large. You have to have several pieces in a fire to maintain kindling temperature; a single piece, by itself, won't burn for long unless it has an extremely large amount of pitch in it. As a result, several large pieces will make the fire too hot to serve any useful purpose.

Branch Method

A single dead branch with a base diameter of about one inch (25 mm) will furnish all the wood you will need for a meal. Start with the twig ends in a tipi fire and work your way up the branch until you get to wood about a quarter-inch (5 mm) in diameter. Now light the fire. As it starts burning, keep adding wood until you reach the half-inch-diameter wood. Now start cooking. As you add wood, keep using larger and larger pieces from your limb.

Never use pieces over four or five inches (10 or $12\frac{1}{2}$ cm) long for one pot, or eight inches (20 cm) for any number. Don't put too much on at a time; this just wastes fuel. Before you start the fire, you

FUZZ STICK

should break up several pieces more than you will need of each size, and arrange them by size within reach. Sometimes, especially if you are working with softwoods or low-grade hardwoods, the fire will quickly go to coals and you will need some of the smaller pieces to build it back up again before the food starts cooling.

While this method is for cooking over flames, it is a very quick way to build a fire and cook a meal. If you have time to build up a bed of coals, the same method will work, although you may need more of the larger-size wood.

TIPI FIRE

The tipi fire is the basis of all camping fires. It is made by stacking sticks in a cone over the tinder. When building it, leave a gap on the windward side. Light the tinder through this opening after first blocking any high winds with your body. Move around so as to allow the right amount of wind to strike it to aid combustion, or simply blow on it as needed. After it catches, close the gap.

It is more efficient to leave off the heavier wood until the fire has caught and there is no danger of it going out.

TIPI FIRE

After the cone collapses, simply lay additional sticks over the mound of ashes or coals, being careful that you don't pile them in the same direction or too thickly and air cannot get into the fire.

STAR FIRE

The star fire is basically a tipi fire that has collapsed. To keep it going, you push the sticks toward the center, letting them burn off each time. As noted before, a stick will go out when burning alone, away from the kindling temperature of the main fire, so there is little likelihood of a stick burning too far down before the end burns off to permit you to move the stick up again.

The more sticks there are in the center, the hotter the flame will be. Since only one or two sticks are likely to burn through at any one time, the star fire requires very little time tending it. Because the addition or subtraction of one stick has only a slight effect on the total output of the fire, it is very easily regulated for cooking.

The sticks should be one-half to one inch (1 to 2½ cm) in diameter. Wood this thick will burn if over a bed of coals hot enough to maintain the kindling temperature, but they don't ignite easily. When a piece burns through, push up more wood quickly. It should be just past the center of the fire so that it will burn along a large length yet not have a loose piece of solid, unburned wood drop off the end when it burns through. Don't let the coals start to die out. If you do, you will have to build up another tipi fire to rekindle it.

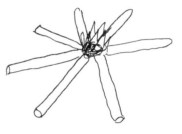

STAR FIRE

Start with a normal tipi fire and add the longer pieces just before the tipi collapses. Add two or three and wait for them to start burning well before adding any additional long pieces.

The star fire is sometimes called a squaw fire because it was a favorite of Indian women who had more jobs to do than to sit and watch a fire. Its main use is for cooking with a dingle crane, or for a watchin'-an'-thinkin' fire for the cool of the evening before turning in for the night. Because of the space it takes up, it just about excludes the use of a fireplace such as is described in Chapter 16.

LOG-CABIN FIRE

The log-cabin fire is the biggest and hottest of all. This is rarely a good feature, however. It will not permit you to make close adjustments and it generally wastes wood. When the tenderfoot builds it, you usually can't get close enough to use it.

It is built over a small unlit tipi fire by interlocking four walls of sticks like a miniature log cabin with a flat roof. Its best feature is that it is a quick way to get a good bed of coals, especially for a fairly large group.

The log-cabin fire is the standard campfire in organizational camps where the fire is used more as an aid to fellowship than for a utilitarian purpose such as cooking. Fortunately, the current trend in organizational camps is the decentralized camp where groups of eight or ten spend the day in small group activities and use the main camp only for eating and sleeping. In these small groups, a reasonable-sized tipi or star fire is just as good. Besides,

LOG-CABIN FIRE

it doesn't waste wood and you can get close enough to enjoy it.

The log-cabin fire does have one other use—that of a beacon fire in survival conditions. It will produce a bright flame and, with the addition of a sufficient amount of greenery, will make a column of smoke that can be seen for miles.

Other than these few uses, it is pretty much the badge of the tenderfoot.

CHAPTER NINETEEN

Camp Food

A camp, like Napoleon's army, travels on its stomach. Food is one of the main factors in camp morale. It can rain, the fish can stop biting, or there can even be mosquitoes, but if the cooking is good the camper can still enjoy the trip. On the other hand, the weather can be fine, the wildlife right in the camp but not in the gear, no varmits, and everyone in good health, but if the cooking is bad even the seasoned camper will wish he were back home. Poor camp cooking practices have turned more potential campers against camping than all the mosquitoes that ever bit.

The problem can be divided into two parts: selection and preparation. While preparation seems hard compared to the home stove, it is really quite easy. Selection problems range all the way from easy to extremely difficult—a range that parallels the difficulty of the other aspects of camping. Selection is fairly easy in car camping where there is adequate space and power to carry canned foods and at least the refrigeration of an ice chest. In backpacking, this problem reaches more difficult stages with the distance the load must be carried. It is probably the most difficult in extended mountain-climbing trips where the food must be measured in ounces (or now, grams).

Regardless of the difficulties, the problem again divides into two aspects: menu-planning and food-preservation. You need a balanced menu regardless of your transportation; foods not requiring refrigera-tion can be used farther from motorized transporta-tion than those which do, and those with the water removed can be used with still weaker transporta-tion methods (assuming there is a supply of water to reconstitute them when you get to the camp).

Broken down in this manner, the problems of camp food are of getting the necessary information and acting accordingly.

MENU-PLANNING

Menu-planning is usually one of two extremes. The first camper, and unfortunately the most com-mon, simply dumps whatever is on hand or easily obtained into some sort of container and pulls out. This is hardly worth the term "menu-planning" since so little planning is actually done before mealtime arrives. The second camper plans the whole operation with the aid of nutrition charts, weight tables, and every other resource at hand and ends up with a menu for an overnight camp which would do credit to the quartermaster of a major expedition.

The problem is, the first ends up with a heavy load and poor nutrition, the second provides for absolutely no flexibility. The first makes monotony of the meals, the second leaves no place in the menu for a fine fish caught or a patch of wild blackberries found in camp.

Menu-planning isn't as easy as the first camper

makes it, but neither is it as hard as the second would make it. All you really need is a bit of basic information. First, the number of meals you will have of each type (breakfast, lunch, dinner, trail snacks, etc.); second, where they will be prepared (in camp, on the trail, in a blind, or on the mountainside); third, the method of transportation used to get the grub where it will be consumed; finally, the number in the group and the size of their appetites.

Now you know the amount and type of food needed, the weight permitted by the transportation system, and the simplicity or complexity of utensils needed or permitted for preparing it. From this base, you consider the likes and dislikes of the individuals in the group and a basic knowledge of how to plan a well-balanced meal, and start working it out.

Basically, food is divided into three main groups: proteins, carbohydrates, and fats, with vitamins and trace minerals forming two equally important minor groups. Proteins predominate in lean meat, fish, and eggs; carbohydrates are in two forms, starches (flour, cereals, beans, potatoes, etc.) and sugars (both the granulated white and brown sugars and the fruit sugars found in fresh and dried fruit); and fats are, of course, found in fat meat, butter, grease, cream, etc.

Proteins build (and repair) the body tissues while carbohydrates and fats provide fuel for running it. Carbohydrates are broken down into the amino acids, which are actually used by the tissues more rapidly than are the fats (which are usually stored in the form of body fat for future use). In emergencies, body fat, and even muscle, will be broken down to form fuel to keep the body functioning.

In winter or in cold regions, you would have more fat in your diet. This is because it is high in calories per pound and you would require more calories in your diet to keep warm, and because it builds body fat, which would insulate you from the cold better. In arctic environments (which can be found at high altitudes as well as in high latitudes), the failure to take this precaution in the diet results in a deficiency disease called rabbit starvation (typically the result of eating no meats other than rabbit, which is very low in fat).

Vitamins and minerals also must be present to prevent deficiency diseases such as beri-beri, scurvy, pelagra, anemia, and similar problems. However, it takes quite a while for these serious problems to show up in a healthy person. In established campsites with groceries available, this is no problem at all since you can prepare menus like the ones you have at home. On the trail, for a prolonged trip with dehydrated food, this balance of proper nutrition must be considered.

Proteins and carbohydrates provide just over 1,800 calories per pound (4,000 per kg), fat slightly over 4,000 calories per pound (8,800 per kg). Other than car camping (which uses little more energy than your normal home activities), camping activities require about 3,000 calories per day. Canoeing, cycling, or backpacking campers burn around 4,000 calories. In addition to this, remember that calorie figures are the absolute totals of what is theoretically available in that particular food. The body cannot digest every bit of food value fed it. Therefore, easily digested foods have higher value as far as usable food value is concerned than hard-to-digest foods of the same caloric readings. In addition, some hard-to-digest food (roughage) must be included to prevent either constipation or diarrhea, which may be caused by a high content of easily digested food in the diet.

Condiments are an important, although not really necessary, part of an appetizing camp menu. Proper containers are discussed in Chapter 6. Regardless of your taste preference, two items are absolute musts in this category: salt, which is a necessary mineral as well as a condiment, and monosodium glutamate, which brings out the natural flavor of food without adding any of its own and thus improves the flavor of all food.

In addition to these, your own preferences should guide you. Pepper is high on most lists, but chili powder, oregano, and cumin also help most meats. Worcestershire sauce, catsup, and mustard are welcome condiments when you can carry them. Mayonnaise and tartar sauce would be excellent, but unfortunately must be left behind unless you can find them in the little plastic one-serving containers, as they spoil very quickly outside of refrigeration.

Paprika is good with eggs, especially boiled ones. A powdered barbecue seasoning lends zest to many foods in addition to meats. Garlic is another versatile seasoning, the powder (no salt) being far easier to handle in the pack than the juice. Clove is not only a good seasoning, but also a mild anesthetic in case of a toothache. Cinnamon is tasty on toast, especially bannock, as is maple syrup, which can be made in camp from sugar and water if a little maple extract is taken. (However, like garlic juice, keep the lid on tight to keep its aroma from permeating the pack.)

Bouillon is really a seasoning since it has little food value, but it makes a great soup base and a flavoring for cooking meat. While technically a vegetable, dehydrated onions are often used strictly as a flavoring. Lemon juice has a value as condiment, and can be obtained as dehydrated crystals as well as concentrated or from a fresh lemon.

These condiments should be considered when you are making up your camp menu. Naturally, you wouldn't take the whole load. Five or six would be the most you would need on even a two-week camp. However, make sure the ones you do take are the ones you will need with the food you are cooking. That way, there won't be that missing ingredient in your camp cooking, nor will you carry that unnecessary gram which the expert camper avoids.

When you come out with what is needed in the way of ingredients, add them all up and maybe do a little condensing (substituting lighter-weight items and carrying a little more quantity of a little less variety). But variety is essential to good camp meals, and in this day of good dehydrated and freeze-dried foods a wide variety of foods can be carried without too much total weight.

Generally speaking, breakfast and dinner will be in camp and lunch on the trail or a similar spot which restricts, or even prohibits, cooking. Because of this, trail food is a type to itself—with special requirements. It is usually prepared in base camp or before starting rather than on the trail itself.

FOODS NOT REQUIRING REFRIGERATION

Camping is usually done away from refrigeration. Therefore, the food must be selected and prepared with this in mind. Generally, food needing refrigeration can be frozen and eaten the first day—it will thaw on the way to camp.

Where the transportation method permits, ice boxes can be used, but they are always starved for ice. The newer gas/electric refrigerators are restricted to camping machines, but are quite adequate for moving camps. Natural refrigeration should not be overlooked. One of the advantages of winter camping is that this problem is greatly reduced. Even in the summer, in certain areas, glaciers, ice caves, and similar unmelted patches can be used for refrigeration. Where they occur, cold springs can be used by simply sinking a box in the spring and putting the food in there. In the absence of a box, rocks can be stacked to form a box which keeps the food from drifting off. Food with paper labels should be marked with a grease pencil so you will know what its contents are in case the label should leave. Even then you still have the problem of refrigeration while on the way to the campground.

In most camping situations, any form of refrigeration is impractical. In these cases, all food must be able to stand exposure to air temperature without ill effects. As a result, this food must be selected with care. While it limits the menu somewhat, the skilled camper will not be troubled by this restriction, for, even excluding the foods preserved by dehydration, freeze-drying, vacuum-drying, irradiation, etc., there is a wide variety of foodstuffs which require no preservation of any kind.

Some of these are dry foods which have little weight—dried beans and peas, pasta foods such as spaghetti and macaroni, breakfast cereals, bread and cake mixes, etc. In another group are raisins, nuts, peanut butter, hard candy, cheese, etc. While they are not particularly light in weight, they need no refrigeration.

You can also buy many kinds of food in very small quantities. These include items like jellies and pickles which require refrigeration after opening, but not before. With small amounts, you can eat it all at one meal and not worry about left-overs. You can also buy peanut butter, jelly, mustard, etc., in tubes like toothpaste or in little plastic containers (often they are served in restaurants this way, so take them home).

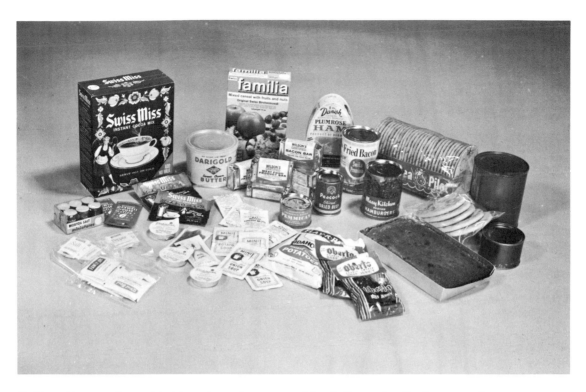

Refrigeration can be avoided by using mixes, canned foods (in moderation), one-serving packages (such as the preserves in the round containers with the tab), special breads (such as the round pilot bread or the Logan bread in the pan), and special meats such as jerky and bacon bar.

You can buy the empty tubes and package your own. Polyethylene tubes can be used over and over. Since very little air comes in contact with the food in the tube, there is very little chance of spoilage. Like the old gag about getting the toothpaste back in the tube, it is easy if you know how.

After filling, fold the end over one time, then slide the clip over the fold. A stick of oleomargarine fits easily into a six-ounce (170 g) tube. Other foods to put into tubes are: peanut butter (including the crunchy kind), honey, most jellies and preserves, and any other more or less pasty food.

A raw egg broken into a tube will usually have the yolk intact for frying in the morning. For obvious reasons, don't try it for too long a period without refrigeration.

When using the tubes, squeeze them from the bottom. The pressure of the contents may force the clip off the end if you are a middle-squeezer—especially if the contents are as thick as peanut butter.

Since whole milk requires refrigeration and powdered non-fat milk tastes horrible (as well as being only slightly more nutritious than water), milk is a problem. Evaporated milk can be mixed with an equal amount of water for cooking. For drinking, add a little vanilla extract and you have a fair substitute for fresh milk (not good, just fair).

Powdered whole milk is available, but not in less than one-pound ($\frac{1}{2}$ kg) (one-gallon [4 liter]) amounts. It is of excellent quality and taste. One company marketed a skim milk with powdered cream added, but ran afoul of the Federal Trade

Commission by advertising it as powdered whole milk instead of a "milk product" which, under the law, it was. Although the price and quality were acceptable, it was withdrawn from the market. It should come back sometime with a more accurate label. It was a good approximation of milk in taste, but you needed an extreme amount of agitation to mix it properly.

Canned food keeps indefinitely before opening. However, most canned foods are mostly water. Water weighs more than sixty pounds per cubic foot (1 kg per liter). That's a lot of unnecessary weight to carry around. You should leave out as much water as you can in all of your food supplies. However, in the case of meats and some other foods, it is about the only way you will get it without resorting to refrigeration or to the more expensive freeze-dried foods.

DEHYDRATION

The easiest way to cut down on the weight of camp food is to leave out as much water as possible. Dehydration is the most extreme method. Beef, venison, non-citric fruits, and vegetables are the best foods for dehydration. (For the purposes of this section, the term "dehydration" will be restricted to air-dried processes using only heat, as distinct from vacuum- or freeze-dried foods, which are treated differently in preservation and in preparation.)

Many writers on camping have mentioned how much dehydrated food has improved in the years since World War II. I have to file a minority report which agrees in part and disagrees in part. The mass-produced dehydrated food, marketed for campers under brands used exclusively for that type of product, are still bad. They are generally devoid of all seasoning except a few bell peppers, and you have to be very hungry to enjoy it.

The dehydrated food you buy from top-quality outfitters (except for those brands just mentioned, which some otherwise good outfitters sell) and in the supermarkets is of high quality and edibility. The outfitter's stuff is often a bit high in price, especially when you figure in the postage, but there is often no other way to get it.

The supermarket ad writers seem a little embarrassed to call their food "dehydrated"—so they call it "instant" or "dried." Unfortunately, all "instant" and "dried" food in the grocery store is not dehydrated. For instance, the dried beef you buy in a grocery store is flexible and salted; true dehydrated meat (jerky) is as stiff as sole leather and no salt has been added.

Fruit, onions, soup mixes, and potatoes are the best dehydrated foods from the supermarket. However, this field is rapidly expanding and they may carry more such foods by the time you read this. The dehydrated soups are good, but often you can make your own cheaper, with bouillon cubes for the stock and dehydrated "fixin's."

Some foods are unavailable at the supermarket in a dehydrated form, but you can make your own. You can fix a dehydration oven quite easily if your kitchen oven will maintain an accurate temperature between 110° and 130°F (43° and 55°C). Otherwise, all you need is a heavy cardboard box, a couple of 100- or 150-watt light bulbs, sockets, wiring for each, and a thermometer.

Food for dehydration should be sliced thin and all inedible parts removed. When dehydrated, the

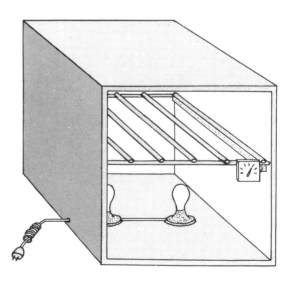

DEHYDRATION OVEN

food should feel dry but flexible. You should not be able to squeeze any water out. Pack the dried food in polyethylene bags and seal them tightly with a warm iron. Squeeze out as much air as possible before sealing and make sure the seal is completely air-tight.

The temperature of the oven should be kept between 110° and 145°F (43° and 63°C). The time will vary with the temperature and the humidity. Most vegetables will take about three hours and fruit will need about five. Boil apricots and plums twenty minutes before dehydrating. Test by feel, not the clock.

Vegetables for soup mix are best grated into short strips before dehydrating. That way, they reconstitute easily when added to the stock. Bouillon grains or a crumpled cube can be added to the package before sealing to make the soup mix.

Dehydrated food should be cooked before eating to get the water back in it. Dried fruit is better than fresh fruit in pies.

Dehydrated meat—jerky—is not available in your supermarket. Some is occasionally available from camping outfitters, but it is usually easier and cheaper to make your own. To jerk meat, take fresh, lean meat (other than pork) and slice it into thin strips, "with the grain" of the muscles, up to three inches (75 mm) wide and less than a quarter-inch (5 mm) thick. Dry these strips in your dehydration oven until they look like stiff leather. They will be leathery to the feel and keep as long as leather if no moisture is added (including from the atmosphere).

Fish can be jerked much the same way, although it should be done outside over a very smoky fire. Keep the temperature range the same as for the dehydration oven. The process should take about three days. Smoked fish has a taste which may or may not be agreeable to you.

Jerky (regardless of its source) can be eaten raw or mixed into a soup. Raw beef jerky tastes like good barbecue, although a slight bit salty. The salty taste is due to the salt naturally in the meat—no salt should ever be added. In soup, it tastes the same as soup made from fresh meat. Jerking removes only the moisture, not the food value, and (except for smoked fish, where the smoke is a

factor) has little effect on the taste. For soup, powder it—e.g., with a hammer—before adding the water.

Beef or venison jerky is also the basic ingredient for that other survival meat dish, pemmican. Pemmican is made by powdering the jerky and adding an equal amount of rendered fat. This must be equal by weight, not volume, or you will have a greasy mess. (By volume, the correct measurement is around five of jerky to one of fat, although the exact amount will vary with the meat.)

You may want to add berries or raisins, or just leave it plain. It makes a sausage that will keep without refrigeration and provides fat that is necessary in the diet—especially in cold weather. Package it in plastic as you do the other dehydrated food, but while the fat is still hot (to preserve sterility), and you won't have to worry about any other means of preserving it.

One-pot meals of dehydrated "fixin's" can be assembled from commercial or homemade dehydrated products cheaper than the commercial one-pot meals. Since there are few commercial one-pot meals of good quality available in dehydrated form, you will practically have to make your own if you care about the taste. Since you can season it (before packaging rather than in camp) to suit your own taste, you also avoid that horrible bland, starchy taste of most commercial one-pot dehydrated meals.

There are a lot of two-pot meals which can easily be packaged: spaghetti in one, a jerky-based meat sauce in the other; chili con carne in one, tortillas in the other; and similar items which go together, but must be prepared separately.

In fixing your pre-packaged meals, be adventurous and experiment. You will be surprised at what you can do in the way of high-quality camping food—and the money you save will more than pay for the few inevitable failures along the way.

FREEZE-DRYING

Although a form of dehydration, in the sense that it removes water from the food, freeze-drying is completely different in its results, as well as its techniques. Normal dehydration equipment can be

Freeze-dried and vacuum-dried foods are essential when going light, and quite useful at other times as well.

built from the contents of the average well-equipped home workshop in about thirty minutes' time; freeze-drying equipment will run around a hundred dollars if you can do high-pressure welding. (And, for the camper who wants to do everything himself, there are directions for making a vacuum chamber in Chapter 15.)

Freeze-drying finds a very practical use for what was once a laboratory curiosity. The boiling point of water varies with the air pressure; therefore, it is possible, by means of a vacuum pump, to lower the boiling point to below the freezing point. At that point, any water (ice) will not melt (turn liquid), but will sublimate (go directly from solid to gaseous form).

In freeze-drying, the food is quick-frozen and placed in the vacuum chamber. The pressure is reduced to around .003 atmospheres and heat is usually applied to speed the sublimation. The process normally takes from eight to thirty hours depending on the thickness of the food and the amount of the heat.

The food comes out looking slightly unreal. It is still the same size, a slight bit paler, but considerably lighter in weight. Most important, unlike other forms of moisture removal the cells of the food are undamaged. As a result, all you have to do is soak the food for ten to thirty minutes and it looks, feels, and tastes just like fresh food. You can (and commercial freeze-dried foods do) add seasoning and meat tenderizer directly to the soaking water so that they work their way all through the food.

Freeze-dried food seems a bit high-priced at first; yet the convenience on the trail and the generous servings make it less out of line than it seems at first. The initial limited selection is rapidly expanding, along with the further development of other forms of dehydration, so that the camper can have variety, even when going ultra-light. Also, freeze-dried food has another advantage—it is odor-free, and therefore doesn't attract pests.

VACUUM-DRYING

Vacuum-drying is something like freeze-drying without the freezing. The same process is used except that the water in the food is already liquid. It still "boils" off with no damage to the cells. It

is normally done to foods which do not require refrigeration to prevent spoilage. The vacuum-dried foods currently on the market are all fruits which are also available in the supermarkets in the air-dried form. Air-drying does not remove all of the moisture, and they are soft and flexible. About twenty to thirty per cent of their total weight is still water.

Vacuum-drying apples, plums, peaches, apricots, and such takes about ninety-eight or ninety-nine per cent of the water out. My first experience with vacuum-dried fruit was not what I had expected. I was prepared to get a rock-hard version of the supermarket product. Instead, I got a very small plastic bag with something that looked like the fine gravel used in mosaic kits—and it claimed to be peaches. Never one to let money go down the drain, I prepared the two ounces of gravel according to directions and got the best peach butter I have ever tasted.

You can do your own vacuum-drying if you are brave enough to make a vacuum chamber for freeze-drying (see page 161). Stick to the non-citrus fruits, at least until the commercial processors market something else. Cut them into small pieces (a quarter-inch [5 cm] cube is the maximum practical, although there is no logical reason why slices wouldn't work too, if kept to that maximum thickness, though reconstituting may be a little harder). Place them in the chamber and turn on the pump.

As with all dehydrated food, place it in a polyethylene bag when it comes from the chamber, squeeze out as much air as possible, and seal with a warm iron. If you live in a particularly humid region, you might buy a tank of helium and blow the air out with a short squirt (being careful not to blow the food out with it) to make sure that there is no chance of spoilage. Under normal atmospheric conditions and reasonable care in preparation, there is no reason why the food won't keep at least a year. The commercial versions of both freeze-dried and vacuum-dried foods will keep indefinitely if the bag is undamaged.

PACKING

Care in packing is the best safeguard against spoilage.

For foods which do not require special preparation for packing, the best package is a plastic wrap inside a cloth bag or a can with a screw-on lid. Flour and sausage sacks and baking-powder cans are a good, cheap source of packaging for small amounts. Plastic packaging, such as polyethylene, cellophane, or saran, is an excellent protection against damage by air, moisture, or spilling as it is flexible, strong, and easily resealed. But it, in turn, needs protection against punctures and tears. Glass should be avoided both because of weight and breakability.

Baking-powder cans make excellent food containers for small amounts, and, although the weight may be a factor, shortening cans do the same job with larger items. They help protect the food, especially those with plastic packages, from the hard knocks of moving camp whenever weight is not of prime importance. They can even be worth the extra weight in backpacking if your trail leads through any underbrush which may rupture a plastic or foil food package without actually tearing your pack.

If you use cans, coat the insides with wax (paraffin or beeswax) by sloshing the melted wax inside the warmed can so that only a thin coat adheres, but the can is completely coated. This not

Food packing containers are a varied lot—shortening, baking-powder, and nut cans with plastic or screw-on lids; large pill bottles; plastic bags; sausage sacks; and commercial containers such as polyethylene squeeze tubes or aluminum provision boxes.

only cuts down on the tendency of the can to rust, it also prevents the transference of a metallic taste to some kinds of food. A thin, inner-tube-type rubber gasket in the lid or the plastic snap-on lids will make it waterproof as well.

Plastic bags are good for carrying pre-measured amounts of biscuit mix, cornmeal, cracker crumbs for frying fish, or any other item which you buy in bulk but need only a small amount of at a time. This avoids the need to carry too much of the food for your needs and measuring cups and mixing bowls as well. Coordinate them to a reasonably accurate measure in your camping gear. For instance, package the exact amount of mix to add to one drinking cup of water, then you will only need the cup, the package, and a mixing pan, with no other measuring devices needed.

Cheese can be kept for months without refrigeration if it is properly prepared. This means real cheese, and not processed cheese or cheese spread, which are just flavored milk solids and highly susceptible to spoilage. A little mold may form around the edges, but scrape it off and eat the cheese anyway. The mold is a harmless form of penicillin. Some people even like it—note the popularity of Roquefort cheese.

To pack cheese, wrap it in two or three layers of cheese cloth. Press the cloth tightly against the cheese. Dip this quickly into melted paraffin. This combination will keep out mold as long as the shell is intact. You will probably prefer to fix your cheese in one-meal chunks to prevent spoilage between meals. Pack it in rigid containers to keep the shell from being broken. In addition to the paraffin-and-cheese-cloth shell, the cheese will develop a thin layer of very dry cheese which protects it from further drying. Normally, this layer can be grated and used in cooking, but the paraffin shell makes this a little waxy-tasting in camp.

Without a refrigerator, eggs can be carried two ways (three, if you include powdered). The first is in aluminum or plastic egg boxes which immobilize the egg so that it doesn't break. The second is to pack it in a bag of flour, biscuit mix, or some other powder which will have a cushioning effect. While this method works well against jarring, I still don't trust it without putting the bag inside a can to protect it from squeezing. Coating the egg with hot wax will help preserve it longer without refrigeration. The rotten-egg smell of hydrogen sulfide is ample warning that an egg is not fresh. In the absence of that smell, you can trust the freshness of any egg.

When packing your pack, the food should go in the area least likely to be damaged by underbrush, in a fall, or a similar accident. The food should be divided into types and put into separate, waterproof bags. Oily and greasy items like shortening should be in one bag, dry items in another, seasonings in another, and so on. Different-colored bags are a good way to identify the contents of each bag without opening it.

With a little care in packing, all the food you carry into camp will be usable.

TRAIL FOOD

There is probably more do-it-yourself experimentation in this area than in any other aspect of camping. Mountain climbers spend almost as much time working out a new trail food as they do studying a new route up their favorite mountain.

Aside from items which the most fanatical regard as mere ingredients (such as raisins, nuts, dates, and chocolate) all trail food is a do-it-yourself combination of raisins, peanut butter, bacon bar, and cashews (to quote one actual example), or some other impossible-sounding mixture. Have fun, if you are so inclined. I have managed to avoid this camping sport totally (being a raisin and a Tropical Hershey, alternately, man myself) and have never regretted it.

One reasonable idea for trail food is to use fruit cake. It has high food value, keeps well in most climates, and is very high in calories-per-pound. All of these are characteristics of a good trail food. Besides, it is rather good-tasting too.

The object of trail food is to furnish quick energy on the trail while the meals furnish the longer-lasting fuel. The simple sugars (fruit sugar) are best for this because of their quick digestability. Protein in the form of nuts or a bacon bar (pre-cooked bacon dried to one-quarter its original weight) are good for the long haul. Hard candy not only furnishes energy, but also keeps saliva coming so that your mouth doesn't dry out so quickly. However,

it often leaves a sickly sweet after-taste which must be washed down with some of your water supply.

There is one warning in regard to concentrated trail rations, however. These foods are very high in carbohydrates and fats, but have practically no indigestible bulk. If the total food supply is principally this type of food, the roughage your body needs will be missing and serious digestive complications will result.

This is where that traditional trail food of the frontier—penole comes into its own. Penole is seed corn toasted golden-brown and ground coarsely. It is eaten/drunk by adding a tablespoonful to a cup of water and swallowing it before it thickens. It has excellent bulk and roughage qualities as well as an agreeable taste. It and jerky, together with any wild berries you might find, provide a balanced (and terribly monotonous) diet for months at a time. Both penole and jerky are excellent trail foods if you have the water to reconstitute the corn and meat.

A quick snack during one of the trail breaks is often a better way of eating trail food than constantly nibbling on the trail.

FOOD FOUND IN CAMP

While it should not be depended upon for a significant portion of the camp menu, food you find in camp is a most welcome addition, lending variety to the food and adventure to the camp routine.

Almost any of the foods mentioned in the chapter on survival (Chapter 34) are suitable for camp menus for two reasons. First, there is the change from routine just mentioned. Second, it is good training for survival conditions in that you will know both how to recognize the plants or catch the animals, and how to prepare them should the need arise.

In most "civilized" campgrounds, this whole subject is out of the question, with the possible exception of fishing. If such activities were permitted, there would be no nature left after the first year. In the wilderness, or on your own property, both survival and the more normal hunting and fishing techniques can be used. However, in all cases of using natural food, obey all laws—both statutory and conservation.

CHAPTER TWENTY

Cooking Techniques

While space doesn't permit an adequate collection of recipes (and most kitchen recipes can be adapted easily), something should be said about camp cooking in addition to how to build a fire. Although, as Kephart noted, a good fire is half the job of camp cooking, the remaining half is just as important.

Cooking over an open wood fire is new to most beginning campers. Many avoid it entirely by using the heavy gasoline stoves that restrict their camping to automobiles and developed campsites, or they use the more familiar, though bulkier and less flexible, charcoal—missing the real wilderness living that camping offers.

Most techniques used in the kitchen can also be used in camp with wood fires. However, there are certain techniques that are better than others.

HOW TO COOK

In the kitchen, you have a wide choice of cooking methods; in camp, because of the special utensils required and the problem of carrying them, many home methods, such as those requiring special-shaped dishes or refrigeration, must be ruled out as impractical. In compensation, however, there are ways of preparing food in camp which cannot be done in the kitchen.

Frying

True frying is deep-fat frying—the fat completely covers the food being cooked. Its advantage is that the food cooks evenly and rapidly. Its disadvantages are that the weight and bulk of the fat is difficult to transport; the food will be greasy and a siesta afterward is recommended for best digestion; and, because it is easy, many campers cook this way exclusively and wonder why they lose interest in food after the third or fourth day.

Normal frying uses a half-inch (1 cm) or so of fat—the food is not completely covered. The advantages and disadvantages are the same as with deep-fat frying, but to a greatly reduced degree. You will have to watch and turn the food to keep it from burning whereas in deep-fat frying, you don't have this worry.

Sautéing is the best frying method for campers for several reasons. It requires only enough grease to prevent sticking. As a result, the food absorbs less and is light and easily digestable. It is a fairly rapid cooking technique. In the case of vegetables, there is far less vitamin loss. Do not puncture meat with a fork to turn it when sautéing as it breaks the crust which holds in the flavor and juices.

Left-over fat from frying can be saved to use again. Sometimes you will have to strain out food particles which broke off and were over-cooked, but otherwise there is no preparation needed. Be sure to keep the fat from fried fish separate from the other. If you fry chicken with it, the taste will ruin your reputation as a camp cook.

Broiling

Pan-broiling is almost the same as sautéing, but no grease is used. The advantages of sautéing are increased but there are some disadvantages. You have to keep a constant watch or the food will burn, especially in the early stages before the crust has developed. Also, a mess is left in the pan which is harder to clean than the residue from most cooking methods. A little scouring, however, will remove this fairly easily if it is done before it cools. Teflon cooking utensils ease this problem considerably, but the delicate nature of that plastic makes it difficult to go camping—especially banging and scraping around against each other in a nesting set.

Regular broiling gets rid of the pan and either uses a grill or some substitute such as a tennis-racket broiler or a skewer. Broiling uses a higher heat than most cooking techniques.

Baking and Roasting

These are the same—the term "roasting" applies only to meat or corn-on-the-cob. Baking is probably the most versatile of the cooking methods. Meat, vegetables, desserts, and breadstuffs can all be prepared by baking.

It differs from all the other methods in that the direct heat of the fire is not used, only the radiant heat. The various camping ovens described in Chapter 16 show the wide variety of equipment used for this method.

There are three ways of determining the temperature in a camp oven. The first is with a small oven thermometer. It is about three inches (75 mm) square and weighs a couple of ounces (about 50 g). It is the dial type and fairly easy to read. However, it is another item to carry, and hardly worth it when going light. In the absence of a thermometer, a teaspoon of flour will turn light-tan in five minutes at 250°F (125°C), light-brown in five minutes at 350°F (175°C), dark-brown in five minutes at 450°F (235°C), and dark-brown in three minutes at 550°F (285°C). A faster method is to stick your hand in the oven. At 200°F (100°C) you can keep it in ten seconds, at 300°F (155°C) seven seconds, at 350°F (175°C) four seconds, at 400°F (200°C) three seconds, at 450°F (235°C) two and a half seconds, at 500°F (255°C) two seconds—above that, any length of time hurts.

Boiling

Boiling uses water as frying uses fat. However, it does have two advantages over frying: there is little or no clean-up problem with the pan, and the water can often be used for soup so that the vitamin loss is minimized.

Two sub-divisions of boiling are useful in camp cooking. The first is steaming, in which only a little water is used and a lid retains the heat and moisture as well as slightly increasing the pressure inside the pan. Steaming avoids the digestive problems of frying. Steamed shoestring potatoes are quite good and a quick way to prepare whole, fresh potatoes.

Stewing is a cross between steaming and boiling, in which the water barely covers the food, to prevent sticking and burning, and it does not boil but just simmers. The process takes quite a long time, but requires practically no tending if done over coals. Stew is obviously the result of this process when meat and vegetables are prepared together. Many vegetables and even fruit can be stewed also.

Pressure-Cooking

Pressure-cooking doesn't quite fit in either of the previous two categories because the added factor of pressure fogs the boundary between roasting and steaming. There are two basic means of pressure-cooking in camp: the pressure-cooker and aluminum foil.

The camp pressure-cooker is a lightweight version of the home pressure-cooker and produces the same pressures. It is an absolute necessity at high altitudes where the boiling point of water is in the mid-to-upper 100's F (60° to 70°C) rather than the sea-level 212°F (100°C). In lower-altitude camps, it has the same advantages it has at home: it speeds up cooking considerably, as well as enhancing flavor and retaining vitamins. Since pressure-cookers are so common in the home, most cooks know how to use them and little needs to be said about them other than to keep the valve clean at all times and carry an extra fuse.

Aluminum foil is common in camping, but few people take advantage of it as a pressure-cooker. The pressure is only around five pounds ($\frac{1}{3}$ atmosphere) (the lowest on a home cooker), but it does speed up the cooking and seal in the vitamins. Care must be taken to fold the edges over at least three times, each fold smoothly creased and flat. Otherwise, it will unfold and let the nutrient-laden steam escape. Also, take care that you don't puncture it—a special problem when you don't use the heavy-duty foil. Dry foods will require the addition of a little water before sealing.

Of course, aluminum foil has the other advantages of being a lightweight substitute for a nesting set when backpacking and a good way to avoid cleaning up after cooking.

WHAT TO COOK

In this day of freeze-dried foods, lightweight cooking equipment, lighter gear, and easy transportation there is no excuse for camp menus which are all fried fish and canned beans. Camp cooking can and should be varied both in the ingredients and in their means of preparation.

Meat

This means red meat, mammal muscle, to distinguish it from fowl and fish, which, while definitely meat, are treated quite differently in the cooking process.

With pork, the meat must be well done; you can cook other meat to your own taste, or, with extensive seasoning, eat it raw as tartar steak.

The cooking method you use on the meat should depend on its cut. A big chunk of meat must be cooked one of two ways. It can be hung from a dingle crane between two reflector fires. In this case, it should not be over any flame, but cooked only by the radiant heat from the fires. A small pan should be placed under it to catch the drippings. Baste the meat with these drippings and/or bouillon to keep it from drying. An alternate method is to sear the meat all over in the flames for one minute before roasting. This forms a shell of hardened meat which seals in the juices and reduces both the dripping and the drying out.

The second way is to cook it in a clay or dutch oven (or wrap it in a wet cloth, cover it with a one-inch [25 mm] layer of clay, and put it in live coals). With the oven, a small amount of water should be added before cooking to prevent drying.

Of course, one of the easiest things to do with a large piece of meat is to cut it up into a bunch of smaller pieces. This gives you a large number of alternate cooking methods.

If you slice the meat, you can use a skillet for frying or pan-broiling. Or you can soak the slices in a sauce for several hours and broil them over coals on a grill, basting them with the sauce for real barbecue. (Most "barbecue" these days is simply a sliced or chopped roast with a sauce added later.)

If you cut the meat into chunks, you can soak them in a marinade and put them on a skewer, alternating with vegetables, for a shish kabob. Bacon wrapped around the chunks helps keep them from drying. Chunks can also be boiled with vegetables to make stew.

Jerking (described on page 193) is another method of preparing meat. It is often a way to preserve meat in camp without refrigeration, especially if the weather is too warm to provide natural refrigeration as sometimes happens when a warm spell hits during deer season.

Jerking will also work with fish but it must be smoked first.

Many types of game meat are too tough to prepare straight. Parboiling is often needed to tenderize it enough to do anything with it. Some meats, such as jackrabbit, absolutely require it, but it helps on other game as well, especially if the animal is old (as many deer are when bagged by a hunter more in search of a hat rack than a banquet).

Fowl

Frying is the usual way to prepare birds, with the less-greasy pan-frying a close second. With small game fowl, such as dove or quail, pluck and gut them and fry them whole. With larger birds, cut them into serving-size pieces. Dip them alternately in milk and/or eggs and then into flour to make a juice-sealing batter.

While many purists are horrified at the idea, you can avoid the problems of plucking by skinning the birds.

Baking is an alternate method, which, although not used as often as frying, is in many ways better because of the ease of digestability, the fewer utensils requiring cleaning, and the change in taste from fried food.

Baking can be done much the same as for roasting red meat. It can be done in a dutch oven or hanging from a dingle crane between two reflector fires. Because of the size of most game fowls, they can also be baked in a reflector oven.

The clay-envelope method, briefly mentioned in reference to red meat, is an ideal way to prepare fowl. Mix the clay to the consistency of putty. Work the clay well into the feathers so it is firmly against the skin, leaving no part of the skin untouched by the clay. Build this coating of clay up to about an inch (25 mm) thick. Then bury it in live coals. It will be cooked in a couple of hours. Crack the shell and the feathers will come off with it—including the pin feathers, which are almost impossible to pluck.

Clay envelopes can be used as well for cooking fish, red meat, and many vegetables (such as corn-on-the-cob or potatoes). It is, in essence, an aluminum foil-less aluminum foil, since the principle is the same. However, the clay-envelope method takes much longer but is much cheaper and never, as too often happens with aluminum foil, burns when the meat and a particularly hot coal are both touching the same part of the envelope.

Fish

A fish can be filleted quickly at the same time it is cleaned. Scale as usual (by rubbing against the lay of the scales with a dull edge, such as the back of a knife). Next, remove the fins by cutting deeply on each side of them and pulling them out (omit the tail; the pectoral fins—those under the gills—are optional). Slit the belly from the throat to the vent, being careful not to cut any internal organs.

Cut the spine just above the gills, from above. Take the head in one hand and the back in the other and peel the head downward to the tail—the internal organs will come with it.

You now have the meat ready for baking or, if the fish is small, frying whole. Wash the body cavity with water and dry to reduce grease spatter when frying.

You can finish the job of filleting by cutting next to the spine, taking care to go outside the ribs, dissecting the meat from the bone with a quick, tailward stroke on each side. You need a thin, sharp knife for this.

Like the fowl, you can speed the job by skinning rather than scaling, and again the purists will howl. Skinning is required with catfish and scaling is optional with small salmon or trout.

Fish are usually fried in camp. While this is a good method, many campers never try any other. Frying should be done much like fowl. The batter helps seal in the flavor.

Fish can be baked in a wide variety of ways. These are often welcome in hot weather when fish are biting and fried foods are tiring. The most obvious way is to simply put the fish in a reflector oven, possibly with a strip of bacon over the top to keep it from drying or with a basting in butter before putting it in.

A simple way to cook a small fish, such as a blue gill, is to clean it as usual (both gutting and scaling), push a green spit about the diameter of a pencil along and just under the spine, and roast it over live coals.

The tastiest way to cook a large fish is to plank it. After cleaning the fish, open it, using the backbone as a hinge. Peg it with wooden pegs, skin down, on a plank or flat part of a split log. (Taste the wood first to be sure it has no unpleasant taste.) Put strips of bacon over the fish to keep it from drying out. Season with salt, pepper, and lemon juice (which may be reconstituted from lemon crystals) and cook it in front of a reflector fire.

Regardless of the baking method, the easiest way to tell if it is done is to poke a straw in it. If it goes in easily and comes out clean, the fish is done. Frying fish can be tested by observing the color of the batter—golden-brown is done.

Fish may be preserved by smoking and jerking. The smoke fire should be of punky wood over coals. You should have very little heat and no flame. Support the filleted fish on a framework over the fire. Smoke for several hours—until the fish are a dark-brown. Continue to dry them without the smoke until they are hard. They may be eaten as is or used in a base stock for chowder.

Crustaceans

While you probably won't be able to catch any shrimp, the coastal camper who goes in for skin diving may get lobsters, and almost anyone with the proper net can catch crabs. In most inland streams, you can catch crayfish with your bare hands, a baited hook (with or without barbs), or a trap.

There are two ways to fix these little critters for eating—boil or fry. To boil, put them live (or at least very recently dead) into cold water and bring it to a boil. Continue boiling until they are red. (This isn't particularly cruel, they have very poor nervous systems.)

To fry, kill them by putting them in cold water and bringing it to a boil for a few minutes. Remove and drain. Throw away all but the jointed tails and skin those, possibly leaving the flippers at the end, as with commercial frozen breaded shrimp. Remove the dark "vein" down the tail also. Dip them alternately in a batter of egg and/or milk, and flour. Fry until golden-brown.

All crustaceans can be boiled. Shrimp and crayfish may also be fried. Crabmeat may be deviled after boiling. Lobster, shrimp, or crayfish may be barbecued or used in a shish kabob—after boiling a short time.

Vegetables

Many vegetables can be eaten raw. When this is possible, do it. While most fresh meat contains at least a trace of vitamin C (barely enough to prevent scurvy), vegetables and fruit alone have a nutritionally significant amount. Just be sure to wash them well in drinking water first.

While little needs to be said about how to cook vegetables (you can use almost any method), you should try to retain as much food value as possible. Never let food boil violently. It cooks better if it simmers slowly and it tastes better too. Sealing it in aluminum foil or using a dutch oven or pressure-cooker before cooking it helps preserve the valuable nutrients. Whenever steam rises from cooking vegetables, vitamins and some minerals are being lost.

Fruit

Almost all fruit can be eaten raw. In this form, they have their greatest food value. The non-citrus fruits are good whole, sliced, or as a salad. The citrus fruits can be used for their juice; and the oil from their rinds as a flavoring in puddings, cakes, and cookies.

Since both berries and nuts are classified as fruits, this is one of the best wild sources to supplement your camp menus.

Breadstuffs

To the average camper, this category includes only pancakes, biscuits, and bakery bread. Actually, it includes anything made with dough or batter. Aside from cakes and cookies, which are usually too much trouble to make in camp (but still possible), there is a wide range of interesting and easily made foods you can prepare with a little imagination.

Bread baked in camp is fresher and better-tasting than commercial bread. You can carry mixes (either commercial or your own) and add the water. This way, you can bake small quantities and always have fresh bread or biscuits available.

Sourdough is the original "mix" for camp breadstuffs. Sourdough starter is kept in an air-tight package. To use, break off a tablespoon-size piece and mix it with flour and water with a small amount of sugar and salt. After a couple of hours, the yeast in the starter has taken effect and the dough is ready. A little flour and water should be added to the starter supply to keep about one cup on hand for future use.

We are a wheat-based culture and tend to forget cornmeal. Not only is it a good breading for fried foods, cornbread is easy to make and a welcome change in the camp menu.

Pies are surprisingly easy to make in a reflector or dutch oven if you use a crust of quickly mixed cooking oil, water, and flour or use a piecrust mix. Wild berries found in camp, or mincemeat or dehydrated fruit brought from home, make this luxury possible even when backpacking.

In camp, you have a wide variety of ways to bake breadstuffs: in clay ovens, in reflector ovens, in dutch ovens, twisted around a green stick, etc. You can use mixes, sourdough and flour, ingredients mixed in camp, etc. There are bread dough, pastry dough, cornmeal, pancake batter, etc.

Many items are not even baked at all. Dumplings are boiled, doughnuts and hushpuppies are fried, pancakes are grilled. For a change, try tortillas. They keep without refrigeration, or, if you are brave enough to try to pat out your own, you can buy the *masa* mix and make your own. (Be warned, it is harder than it looks. I have given up trying, but found the *masa* makes a flavorful substitute for regular cornmeal when frying.)

Unleavened bread will keep over a month if you keep it dry, and Logan bread is not as flat-tasting, but keeps as well.

Beverages

The main camp beverage, naturally, is water. You seldom have to carry it in, if your campsite is well provided. It is versatile—useful as a drink, mixed in cooking, for cleaning both your gear and yourself, and, if you have enough of it, as a good recreational medium for fishing, boating, and swimming.

However, as a beverage to go with the food, it lacks flavor (or has the wrong kind, depending on your source). Four substitutes—coffee, tea, milk, and cocoa—should be considered. Each pack easily and have good psychological benefits, and two of them have a good nutritional value by themselves. The other two can be improvised from wild materials, if you know how and you are not too particular about quality.

Coffee and tea can be considered together. Both need heat, both come in regular and instant varieties, and both are valued because of the stimulant, caffeine, which they contain. If you drink the instant form, any old pot will do to prepare it; if not, you will need additional gear—a coffee pot or either tea bags or perforated tea balls.

As mentioned earlier, powdered milk (low-fat and whole) is developed and simply waiting for someone to market it in small amounts for campers. It doesn't taste quite as good as your neighbor-hood dairy's product, but it is considerably better than nothing. A plastic bottle for agitating the mix is the only additional item of equipment needed for this drink.

Cocoa is under-rated as a camp beverage. It is an excellent evening drink since it makes a person sleepy (unlike coffee or tea), yet it has the same warm-inside effect as the other two. Also unlike coffee and tea, it has food value, which, despite this diet-conscious age, is needed wherever you can get it when camping.

Some of the powdered "instant breakfast" mix-with-milk type of drinks are also good in camping if you have the milk. They add very little to what you would get from straight milk, but are better-tasting to some people (especially compared to reconstituted milk), and do represent a change of pace.

Fruit juice can be reconstituted from dehydrated crystals and makes a good drink for a midday break.

One- and Two-Pot Meals

One- and two-pot meals present more of a prob-lem in preserving and transportation than they do in cooking. Because of the low quality of these dishes in the mass-produced dehydrated packages, it is practically a do-it-yourself project.

Beyond that, the problem is that the average camper thinks immediately of stew and then is stuck for other dishes in this category—especially others which can be prepared far from refrigera-tors.

Actually, this is not as much of a problem as it first seems. Freeze-dried meat can be bought in cans—hamburger, steak, pork chops, ham, and meat balls. With this as a start, adding dehydrated vegetables, adequate seasoning, and possibly tomato-soup mix instead of tomato sauce or paste, a whole range of dishes become quite possible. Spaghetti and meat balls, chili con carne (with or without the beans), beef and noodles, macaroni and cheese, and even such odd-ball items as meat tacos or chicken chow mein can replace endless bouts with stew.

The key ingredient in these dishes is a large amount of imagination.

PART V

The Camp

To read some camping catalogs, one would think that all one needs to be a great camper is to buy the products. In the first place, the outfitters who give this impression seldom have the best equipment; in the second place, it neglects factors other than equipment which are very important to the success of a camping trip—such as the campsite and the way the equipment and site are used together in the act of camping.

While a certain amount of information can be given in the printed word, a very large amount of it can only be gained over a period of years. For this reason, if for no other, it is a good idea to get with experienced campers for your learning periods. To be sure, you can learn without them, and you may even develop some valuable new techniques as a result of not being exposed to the traditional approach, but you will be more comfortable learning from others. If you are not sure whether you will even like camping or not, it could mean the difference between finding a lifetime source of pleasure and getting "soured" on the sport at the beginning, before you've really tried it.

CHAPTER TWENTY-ONE

The Campsite

The perfect campsite is hard to find. Even good ones are becoming scarce. Usually if you do find one, it is either on private land and unavailable or so many people try to use it that it does not remain perfect for long. Although all campers keep looking for this perfection, in bitter reality you will have to be satisfied with just finding as many good features as you can in one place.

Most of the features which make a campsite "perfect" are factors of scenery, weather, companionship, and other variables which have no direct bearing on the site itself yet are nonetheless thought of as features of "that wonderful campsite we used year before last."

There are nine major features a site should have, and even an overnight campsite should have the first three. These features are: 1. pure water; 2. a level, open spot with good drainage; 3. an adequate supply of firewood (unless stoves are carried); 4. privacy; 5. breeze in the summer and a windbreak in the winter; 6. exposure to direct sunlight in the mornings, but shade in the early afternoon; 7. security against fire; 8. grass or browse if pack or riding horses are used; 9. a suitable supply of poles and stakes for tents. As you can see, they are in descending order of importance, with the last two being rather specialized requirements and the seventh being something that can be provided regardless of the condition of the site as found.

Except for developed campsites with piped water, the ideal camp should be near running water but well above the flood level. Mosquitoes don't breed in swift water and the run-off is faster after a rain. While all drinking water not from pure-water-system pipes or a spring flowing from living rock should be boiled for at least five minutes, running water is usually clearer and better-tasting. The site should be far from any standing water smaller than a small lake, unless there are fish in it. The fish will eat mosquito larvae. If there are no fish, there will probably be mosquitoes, although frogs, bats, swifts and swallows, and other natural enemies will keep the number down to a tolerable limit. With rare exceptions, swampy areas will have mosquitoes in objectionable quantities.

Alkali water can be made a little more potable if vinegar, lemon or lime juice, or even a small bottle of hydrochloric acid is carried to help neutralize excesses on the pH scale.

Check for signs of the flood level of streams when camping near running water (grass in tree branches, a thin coating of mud on trunks, etc.). Never pitch camp in a narrow canyon or arroya, the danger of flash flooding from a thunderstorm fifty miles away in the mountains is far too great.

The ground should be reasonably level or you will have difficulty in pitching your tent satisfactorily and your uphill tent ditches will have to be quite large to keep the run-off from washing over it in a sizeable rain. Still, it must slope enough for good drainage.

Soil type is important. Special techniques are needed for pitching a tent in loose sand and the sand gets into everything. Black gumbo makes a sticky mess after a rain. Clay gives a fast run-off in a rain—often right through the tent—and the puddles take longer to dry since there is very little ground absorption. Thick, high grass almost requires bushwhacking techniques everywhere you go, and it shelters an amazing number of mosquitoes and other biting insects. A marsh also has a large mosquito population as well as the problem of camping in ooze. A tight, well-grassed, sandy loam is the best since it provides good tent-stake anchorage and will absorb a tremendous amount of water without a run-off.

You should not have your tent in the middle of an open field, since this invites lightning. On the other hand, it shouldn't be under a large, broad-leafed tree which will drip for hours after a rain. The site should be free of poisonous plants, and there should be a suitable spot for a latrine (see Chapter 22) if the campsite isn't in a public park furnishing one.

The campground should have an adequate supply of firewood, either already cut for use or in the form of squaw wood. Test any wood for sale in a public campground before buying. I once thought I had lucked onto a great find when I picked up almost a week's supply (by my standards—I build small fires) of concessionaire's wood left by the party before us. It turned out to be completely green billets of very hard red oak. These not only were practically fireproof, they defied cutting into a decent size.

Privacy depends on personal likes, the extent the campsite is used by others, and the natural layout of the site (trees, terrain, etc.). The average public campground is goldfish-bowl living, even with a fully enclosing tent, while in most wilderness areas a tent's only use is as a protection from the elements.

A breeze is cooling in the summer, and desirable; in the winter, the same velocity is a wind which is cold and undesirable! The ideal year-round campsite would have a tall tree and a thick underbrush windbreak on the north side and a large expanse of reasonably level terrain, perhaps even a cool lake, on the south.

Unless modified by temporary conditions such as large air-pressure areas (highs and lows on the weather map), or front movements, or nearby hills, the wind is generally from the northwest in winter and southwest in summer. It blows up narrow valleys in the daytime and down them at night (hot air rises, etc.). It blows inshore by day and off-shore at night. (Large bodies of water tend to keep a more constant temperature than surrounding land, and the wind flows toward the warmer area where the air is rising.)

The relative locations of the fire to the tent, the latrine to the main camp, and the camp to natural windbreaks such as trees or hills require a knowledge of prevailing winds.

The Indian tradition of pitching the tipi or building the hogan facing east not only had religious significance (the sun, the giver of life), but was immanently sensible. Storms rarely come from the east, and when they do they are rather weak. The sunlight helps wake you in the morning, warms up the camp, and evaporates the dew. Shade in the afternoon helps keep the area cool.

The discussion of firesites in Chapter 16 gives most of the rules for keeping a campsite safe from fire. In addition, don't build the fire near a punky log, it can retain the fire for days. Make backlogs green, if possible, and extinguish the fire with water before you leave. Don't bury a smoldering log to put it out. This process is often used to conserve a fire when out of matches—it won't extinguish it unless the dirt is so moist as to almost be mud.

Overuse is becoming a problem even in wilderness areas. The alpine meadow is a delicate ecological type—overgrazing will destroy it. Therefore, it is now practically required that campers on horsepacking trips take along enough feed for their mounts in order not to destroy these meadows.

Camping is a lot easier if an adequate supply of tent-poles and stakes can be found on the site rather than having to be carried in. In the case of backpacking and bicycling trips, or canoe trips with lots of portage, this is a deciding factor between two otherwise similar sites. With other transportation, it is a nice feature, but hardly essential. Unfortunately, it is a feature rapidly becoming extinct.

Public Campsites

Public campsites are of two basic types—those publicly owned and those privately owned. The publicly owned campsites are more heavily used and consist of campgrounds in the state, provincial, and national parks and forests, as well as Corps of Engineers' facilities on many of our larger lakes. These campgrounds offer facilities which include tent space, fireplaces of some type, rest rooms of various types (often flush), water, usually flowing in pipes but at least a tested well with a pump, and a good view of the surrounding scenery. Camping is either free or costs a small permit fee.

A few privately owned, public campsites have been started to take advantage of the demand for tent space. The permit fee is about twice as much as for park campsites, while the same facilities are offered—usually minus the scenery and plus a coin-operated laundry facility, which most publically owned campgrounds do not have. Their greatest value is in providing a tent space while traveling to your chosen campground. However, they are designed primarily for tent trailers and camping machines and seldom have suitable ground for staking.

Halfway between the publicly and privately owned campgrounds is a new form of park—the tribal park. These are operated by tribal cooperatives on Indian reservation land. The facilities are comparable to a good state park and the scenery is matched by only a very few of our major national parks. Apache, Navaho, and Havasupi tribes were pioneers in this field, but other tribes are now in the planning stages or have opened these fine facilities. Many tribes are discovering that tourism is a good means of providing employment and tribal income on land not very well suited for agriculture and difficult even for the traditional sheep and cattle grazing.

Regardless of the ownership, most public campsites have running water (but rarely hot water) and flush toilets. The vented-pit chemical toilet (recognizable by a large turbine vent on the roof, spinning in the breeze) is just as odor-free as the flush type, since air is constantly being pulled into the pit and the odor cannot escape inside the building, although it is sometimes unpleasant downwind from them on a muggy day with little wind.

Practically all of these parks have electricity, although oddly enough it isn't always turned on, particularly at times other than the summer rush. (This has, so far in my somewhat restricted experience, been the case only in some state parks.) More parks have wall outlets for such things as electric shavers than a few years ago, but I still carry an adapter in my shaver to permit me to plug into a light socket. Some parks have electricity going right to the tent site, with outlets, lights, and all, but they charge for the dubious privilege.

Most public campsites restrict fires to prepared fireplaces. These are usually the three-walls-and-a-grate type which are not the best for ease of cooking. Some have a cast-metal fireplace on a stand which is the right height for standing while cooking. Unfortunately, the draft qualities are miserable and temperature-regulation is difficult. Camp stoves, of course, are usable anywhere, and the picnic tables provided in most sites make excellent stands for them. Lacking the tables, the stoves will rest on the ground.

Some campsites prohibit gathering wood for fires (because of the scarcity of wood) and require you to bring your own charcoal or camp stoves. On the other hand, one tribal park said no wood was available and, after backpacking a Primus with an extra pint of fuel, we found a wealth of fairly good wood lying around the ground and dead on the many cottonwoods and mesquites there. It was small, about one quarter-inch (5 mm) in diameter, and cooking had to be done over flames because it made poor coals (the mesquites were young and had few dead branches), but it was good wood and completely adequate for a most enjoyable stay in that fantastically beautiful canyon. The Primus emerged with all its fuel intact.

The problem with charcoal is that it takes awhile to get ready to use, and it is messy besides. Camp stoves are relatively heavy (except for the backpacking models which are strictly one-burner) and the fuel is something of a problem to carry because of its weight and ability to taint food unless kept completely sealed up. Solar stoves, whose fuel is both clean and free, are well adapted for desert areas, if you have the means of transporting their bulk.

Many parks permit wood gathering in theory, but because of intensive use by campers, wood is almost impossible to find. The parachute-cord-and-rock method of pulling down squaw wood high in a tree is about the only way of obtaining good firewood. Gathering green wood is almost universally prohibited.

One of my pet peeves about campground directories (besides the fact that they are about two years out of date when they come out) is that they don't answer enough questions, and the ones they do answer are often not the ones I need to know. I couldn't care less how many trailer spaces there are although I recognize the need for that information by some, but I would like to know the soil type at the tentsites (so I could bring the proper type of stakes—or boycott the area entirely because of cobblestone tentsite paving). Until a campground directory comes out with this information, the old word-of-mouth system will have to fill in. You can always write to the campgrounds, but you probably won't get accurate answers, and with several thousand campgrounds in the nation, you can quickly go broke on postage alone.

If your tendrils on the grapevine are well placed, you might be able to get a lot of the information you want about a given campground. This is easier than it seems at first, since at most campground campfire programs you can find someone who has just been to the campground you are considering visiting next. In a brief conversation you can gather most of the information you need.

If you use the suspension method for your tent, check on two things before going: first, if there are trees big enough to suspend your tent; second, if the campsite is likely to be too crowded to afford you much chance to choose a proper tree to suspend your tent from. As a last resort, you may have to carry a couple of long poles to make a shear pole or use some other erection method. This is, however, primarily a problem with only the paratipi when a car is your transportation.

Many of the larger parks will issue a special permit for camping outside of the prescribed campgrounds. This will be "roughing it" since there will be no electricity or running water, but you will get more privacy and usually better scenery. Generally, however, you will need a good reason to camp outside of the prepared campsite areas.

A recent development in some of the state parks is enough to drive any camper into the wilderness. This is the practice of dumping small rocks (from concrete "coarse aggregate"-size to cobblestone) in the tent area of the campgrounds. The reason may seem sound at first—the drainage problem is greatly reduced and no longer is there a three-day to three-week drying-out period after a long hard rain until the site can again support a tent. The hidden disadvantage is that some of the more packed rock patches practically require a ten-pound ($4\frac{1}{2}$ kg) sledge hammer and one-foot (30 cm) stakes made from old drilling rods to pitch a tent in the "pavement." This is another problem resulting from the trailers and pick-up trucks driving campers out of the campsites.

Some of the national parks use a much more sensible method for drainage. They have a sand (apparently the same size as the sand used in concrete) mixed with just enough soil to prevent it from becoming too gritty. The sand is too coarse to get into everything, like dune sand does. It drains well, even after a soaking rain, but a simple tubular aluminum stake won't end up looking like a pretzel because of a rock blocking its path into the ground and even a seven-inch (175 mm) lightweight stake holds so well that it is difficult to remove it when striking the tent and will therefore anchor even a large tent with ease. It can be put into the ground with no more effort than stepping on it firmly. This is a method which should be encouraged in all heavily used campgrounds. With more moderate use, well-tended grass or clover is best.

The time of year is as important as the condition of the campground in determining how much you will enjoy the trip. You will probably find the off-season more enjoyable. The campers are quieter, friendlier, and more expert than in the overcrowded campsites of the summer. While the weather is a bit colder and often a bit wetter, you don't have the heat of the summer. If you go in the winter, you miss the insects too—which is the worst pest of the warmer seasons, with the possible exception of noisy campers, who also don't go camping in the winter.

Camping techniques in the off-season are, of course, different since keeping warm is now a problem, especially in the morning. The additional expense of special equipment, such as a heavier sleeping bag, will be required for winter camping. On the other hand, there is a change in the scenery—especially in the fall and spring when the leaf colors and blossoms give the countryside a festive air. And there is a little change in the challenge that camping has to offer—it is a slight bit harder since you have to contend with more wet firewood and a greater need for fire. Water sports are usually out, but you have a better chance of finding a patch of wild blackberries or seeing more wildlife because there are fewer campers to scare the animals off and because the concealing vegetation is either being reduced by fall or only just coming out. Also, in the spring and fall, many animals are very active because they have just come out of hibernation or they are getting fat to go into it.

The best way to see a national park is to go first to the Ranger station or museum and get what literature is available. They will have at least a pamphlet with a map and physical, biological, geological, and historical descriptions of the park. Go to the campfire program and the early-morning park naturalist-guided nature walks, and take any self-guiding nature trails as well. Study about the park and the area before you go. Above all, don't hesitate to ask questions. The average Ranger or naturalist gets more pleasure out of answering an intelligent question from an interested camper than from any of his other duties.

More state parks are beginning to follow the lead of the national parks and provide the same educational facilities. However, they have a long way to go in this respect since most state legislatures are not willing to spend the money required to build the facilities and staff them, despite the increased revenue such attractions bring to the state from tourists. Some state governments consider the whole concept of parks and recreation a waste of money, but they are growing fewer and those remaining are almost all in the hands of special-interest groups and are also noted for being at the bottom of the list on other programs for the benefit of the people.

Most state parks have outgrown the stage, but several still have such uncalled-for facilities as dance pavilions, miniature golf courses, baseball diamonds, city-park-type playgrounds, and a large number of other facilities which are available in most small towns and have no place in these natural areas because they are too noisy and visually disturb the environment. A modest number of safe climbing trees will satisfy most children whose parents won't let them explore the natural beauty around them.

Wilderness Areas

The greatest number of scenic attractions is usually found in the wilderness areas. Many of these are in the national parks and forests. As such, they are open to the public, although special permits are usually needed for building fires in the area.

Transportation (see Part IX) is often a problem. Rarely is it possible to enter these areas by car—usually horseback, canoe, or hiking is the only way in. This, of course, creates problems because of the weight restrictions imposed by these methods. Lightweight equipment and provisions are a must.

A large number of campers stay away from wilderness areas because of the lack of the gadgets of civilization, such as plumbing. Yet everything, with the exception of houses, can be had in these areas that was available to the average American a century ago, when few Americans were on what could be considered the frontier. Yet at that time, the typical family had the bathtub in the kitchen (for use on Saturday nights only) and the toilet in the back yard, they chopped their own firewood, pumped their own water (or bought it from a passing wagon), and used kerosene lamps.

In many ways, the wilderness camp is far superior. It is much more sanitary than the cities of a hundred years ago. The meals are better balanced and prepared due to our knowledge of nutrition. And people themselves are more healthy today. Furthermore, the equipment available today is superior to that of a hundred years ago because of advances in chemistry, metallurgy, and design. The few inconveniences should not keep anyone

The Adirondack hut is quite popular on the major hiking trails in the country.

from enjoying the beauty of our wilderness areas.

The major hiking trails bring some wilderness areas conveniently close to civilization. Because the only access is by foot, most of those who are likeliest to damage the wilderness are excluded. As a result, many have well-developed campsites with reasonably clean privies and often even springs or pumps. The underbrush is cleared out and often there are Adirondack huts so that tents are not required in the pack. (However, a light mountain, tab, or ATC tent is well worth the four pounds [1.8 kg] in case the hut is taken or you are unable to make the next campground before dark.)

These trails, such as the Pacific Crest Trail and the Appalachian Trail, and many that are now in the planning or construction stages, are unique in the camping situation. They are usually on private property, maintained by a voluntary association, and receive no help from any level of the government. Yet, somehow, they are able to cover literally thousands of miles with well-marked trails and modest campgrounds.

Organizational Camps

This particular section is written for the owners, operators, and counselors of organizational camps. The campers and their parents have only a limited influence in such matters—the boycott being their only real say-so.

As far as the physical requirements of these camps is concerned, the American Camping Association's Camp Standards are as good as any and better than most. However, since they are designed for all organizational "camps," from the resort type on up, there is little on the type of program each camp should offer.

Organizational camping offers an excellent training ground for the campers of the future. It is beginning to change to a real program of camping, but the summer-resort concept is still very much with it, and this creates some interesting ideas of what camping should be.

What is needed is not a hybrid of resort and camp, but a real camp for children and teenagers.

First of all, an organizational camp (commercial or non-profit) should be labeled honestly. If it is a resort or dude ranch, it should be called that. There is nothing wrong with a resort or dude ranch. But a complicated program of athletics and power-tool crafts, and air-conditioned bunkhouses with built-in TV, should not be called camping.

Church camping programs fall into a similar trap—that of making the camp in reality an institute. Now an institute has values a camp can't offer—it is the only way a large amount of information can be transmitted to a large group in a short time and still provide for effective feedback—but that doesn't make it a camp, nor offer the advantages found only in a camp. In most church camping programs, the grade-school group's "pioneer" or "primitive" camping program and the older youth or young-adult "trail hikes" and canoe trips are the only real camping offered.

The family camps too often are simply the "primitive" camp program with the parents present, instead of some real experimentation with a potentially valuable ministry to families which too often in our culture have been fragmented by too rigid a set of age-group divisions in practically all of their activities. Even the parents are often split up by separate activities, and so the family meets only occasionally for meals. As a result, vacation time finds a group of almost-strangers being thrust together to try to find some activity of common interest. Churches could perform a valuable service in family church camps, but unfortunately there is very little service being done.

In a real camp, as opposed to these pseudo-camps, the campers learn from their dependence on each other. This sort of program requires small groups, ten or twelve at the most, living entirely together, preparing their campsite, cooking their meals, and performing all the activities which make a well-run camp. The central camp functions only for food purchase, health service, and an occasional recreational activity for all the camps together.

In this situation, the camper learns from his interdependence with others. If someone fails to do his part, the whole group suffers. The withdrawn camper discovers his importance as a person. Under the gentle guidance of the counselor, the group makes its decisions (with the counselor preventing anarchy).

The selection of counselors is the key part of a commercial camp that really camps. The football star on vacation, who depends on hero-worship for control, will usually keep the campers from killing each other, but he will rarely teach real camping. Similarly, the specialist who can run a top-quality music, drama, craft, or waterfront program in the resort set-up will be a complete failure in a camp unless he is also a top-notch camper.

Here is the greatest potential problem in organizational camping. The counselor may have the notion (held by many otherwise competent campers) that there is only one way to camp—his way. The unfortunate camper who prefers a different way stands about as much chance as the organization man who bucks the organization. Campers must be permitted to use the techniques they prefer, assuming, of course, that they are safe. If not, the reasons they are not safe should be explained to them. The fact that the counselor has not encountered the technique before is no reason he should automatically reject it. If he knows it won't work, he can explain why he thinks it won't but still let them try it if they insist. If it doesn't work, they will abandon it and the group will learn a little more about camping.

Nature study should be an important part of the camp program. The average camper doesn't care about the scientific names of plants and animals, but he is interested in the use the plant or animal has for people, the folklore about it, and its place in the balance of nature. However, fact and folklore must be clearly distinguished to avoid teaching misconceptions. The camper should be taught the identifying characteristics of the plant or animal—not just have it pointed out and named without being told how the identification was made.

An integral part of the nature program should be an active conservation program. Conservation in camp should apply to plants, wild animals, soil, and water. Working on a needed conservation project, selected by the campers themselves from a list prepared by an expert in the field, is an excellent teaching device. There are fewer problems in camp since the project makes the camp "belong" to the camper. Since organizational camps generally make intensive use of the land, you might not even have a nature program at all after a few years without such a program.

Experienced campers in the group should be allowed to take the lead in the activities. The skilled ones will be eager to show off their knowl-edge and teach the inexperienced ones. With campers skilled in camping as a whole, and not just one or two phases of it, all the jobs will get done and "kaper charts" and other such artificial devices needed with a totally inexperienced group will not only be unnecessary but may cause some resentment on the part of the campers.

CAMPSITE DIRECTORY

One of the best campground guides you can have is one you have made yourself. This supplements rather than replaces the commercial ones. With your own, you can keep a record of the features you want to know and skip items you are not interested in.

I took a looseleaf notebook, added a tooled leather cover, and printed up several forms to be filled out as a record of our camping. You could do the same, being less fancy about the cover or the printing or more elaborate with artwork or in bind-ing after it reaches a certain size, depending on your talents and inclinations.

Another approach, which my father prefers, is to write a several-page narrative of the trip, illustrated with photographs, maps, and drawings. These are kept in a paper binder such as students use for term papers. It not only provides a memory of the trip, but gives valuable information when you or your friends want to take a similar trip in the future. By including as much technical description of the site, weather, wildlife observed, pests encountered, and all other good, bad, and indifferent aspects of the trip, you will have enough information in a few years' time to help you plan future camping trips. And, of course, in gathering this information you are getting the practice needed to become an even better camper.

As mentioned earlier, one of my complaints with commercial campsite directories is that they are generally two to three years out of date when they reach the bookstores. To include such a directory in this book would compound the fault. Yet because of the need for some indication of what facilities can be found in the various state and national campgrounds, a broad survey is offered.

Questionnaires were sent to pertinent adminis-trative offices in the United States, Canada, and Mexico, asking questions about policy for present campground facilities and long-term plans for the development or expansion of new facilities. While it won't replace the annually published directories, the over-all trends indicated here will give you some guidance in up-dating your information in them.

In the survey for the directory, essentially the same questionnaire was sent to all agencies. The cooperation varied widely. Several made no at-tempt to answer the questionnaire and simply sent prepared literature which often did not answer the questions. Some states were in the process of mak-ing similar studies and sent rough copies of these studies which were most valuable. A few were able to answer the questions right down the line.

In order to keep the number of words to a mini-mum in the directory, I am including the defini-tions here. These were largely included in the ques-tionnaires sent to the agencies.

Location

Population centers: Is a park located close to pop-ulation centers in order to make the facilities accessible? Far from them to preserve as much wilderness as possible? Or is it irrelevant as a factor?

Natural features: Are the natural features of the park unique? Are they important, but partly because of some historical significance or the presence of an artificial lake which would attract people anyway? Or is some more artificial cri-terion the prime reason for the park's existence?

Physical Facilities

Acreage range: What is it? (These figures include the two extremes of size; if these are completely away from the norm, the range of the majority will also be included. It is assumed that there is a fairly even spread between these extremes unless otherwise noted. You will note that, except for those including large, artificial lakes, the larger the park, the more wilderness is likely.)

Campsite terrain: Is that part of the park which contains the campground itself wooded, rocky, flat, etc.?

Tentsite ground: Is the space under the tent natural soil (either bare or grassed), or has the agency ruined it with gravel or cobblestones or improved it with coarse sand to help drainage?

Wood availability: Are you permitted to collect your own wood? Can you find wood naturally in the area, if collecting it *is* permitted? Is there a woodlot set aside for gathering? Is it for sale? (It is assumed that you wouldn't be cutting down any trees, so the matter of wood gathering is confined to down-wood [pieces lying about] or squaw wood [dead wood still attached to the tree].)

Fireplaces: What kind can be found on the campsites? (Three-walls-and-a-grate are usually rock or concrete block, but sometimes sheet metal with a metal grate over. They are on the ground. The waist-high are metal three-walls on a post, at a convenient level. Fire rings are metal rings protruding from the ground, in which you can build almost any type of fire, the ring preventing the spread of the fire and the scattering of the charcoal and ashes. Do-it-yourself is about the same thing, except that you have to provide the safety.)

Cabins: Are there any? What kind? (Lodges and resort-type hotels are excluded. Cottage-types have one to four rooms, generally with both a kitchen and a bath. Adirondacks are log and/or stone one-room cottages without windows and with one wall missing. Screen shelters are one-room cottage-types with window screening for walls. Open shelters have only a roof.)

Trailers: Are they permitted? What are the facilities? (These questions are restricted to house trailers since tent trailers are almost always considered as tent camping. Connections will refer to water, sewer, and electricity. Fee will be stated if it is different from tent camper's fee. "Length" will be trailer length unless "combined length" (trailer and car as a unit) is used.

Motor homes: Are they treated any differently than trailers?

Transportation: Does the campground have facilities for private aircraft? Is it served by scheduled rail or bus lines?

Utilities

Toilets: Flush? Vented pit (practically as good)? Chemical (some odor but mostly of the chemical)? Privy (generally the worst because of the odor)? Or do-it-yourself (any restrictions regulating these will be included)?

Sanitary dumps: Are there any?

Water: Piped, pumped, stream, etc.? Hot water? Showers? With hot water? (Sometimes the rest room has hot water in the lavatories but not in the showers.)

Electricity: Is there any? What is the fee?

Grocery, Ice, Restaurant (or snack bar), *Gasoline* (white, regular, kerosene), *Laundry:* Which of these services are included within the parks themselves? (Practically all parks, other than wilderness areas, have such facilities in nearby towns.)

Activities

Museums: Are there any? What kind?

Trails: Naturalist tour? Scheduled or request? Self-guiding? Hiking? Horse, etc.?

Boating: Restrictions on power-size or system? Boat ramp? Fees? Are boats for rent?

Swimming: Pool? Lake? Ocean? Fees? Restricted to certain areas?

Fishing: Fresh or salt? License required? Other restrictions? Ice fishing?

Hunting: Permitted? License required? Restrictions on firearms or archery where prohibited?

Horses: Restricted to certain areas? Rental horses available?

Winter sports: Skiing? Tobogganing? Ice skating? Ice fishing? Ice boating? (Skiing is downhill unless cross-country is noted. Tow ropes are usually present although some have lifts.) Snowmobiling?

Playgrounds: City-park equipment? Athletic fields, etc.?

Other Rules

Camping fee: How much?

Time limit: How long can you stay? What is the camping season (if any)? When is check-out time?

Reservations: Are they permitted? What is the procedure?

Fires outside fireplaces: Prohibited? Permit only? Permitted freely?

Pets: Permitted? Restrictions?

Motorcycles, trail scooters, snowmobiles, etc.: Permitted? Restricted?

Gate locked: If so, what time? Any provisions for campers already set up to come back after closing? Quiet time?

Alcoholic drinks: Permitted? Restrictions?

Minors camping: What are the restrictions, if any, on minors using the campground?

Roadside camping: Permitted? (This refers primarily to roadside parks erected for picnickers and travelers, usually by highway departments but some states answered for highway right-of-way as well.)

Open Beach law: Is there one?

Energy problems: What are the plans of the administrative agency relative to energy shortages: more catering to backpackers, canoeists, and horsepackers and less to recreational vehicles and trailers? Encourage mass transit to come to parks as in the days of the passenger trains? Cut back on parks because tourists are getting scarce? Forget reservations as the demand is down? Lower fees for backpackers and canoeists to discourage gasoline consumption? The "energy crisis" of 1973–74 had no effect, so no changes are contemplated? Usage has changed and campers are coming from a significantly shorter distance than 1971 or 1972?

Winter sports has been eliminated from some because they are sufficiently south and no information was received. However, these can be deceptive (such as downhill skiing in Hawaii and

Arkansas and ice boating in Missouri) and an omission should not be regarded as a flat no. Likewise, *Open Beach law* is omitted for inland states and provinces.

While I intentionally avoided a true campground directory on the grounds that it would become out-of-date too rapidly, I have given some statistics in regard to some of the features. While these will probably be out of date by the time you read this, they can be of help—in cases, for instance, where some camps have one type of facility and others have another. It is reasonable to assume that future campgrounds will either continue the same ratio (if it is due to some factor such as degree of wilderness) or at least the minority will not shrink.

The categories of *Winter sports, Roadside camping* and *Open Beach law* have been eliminated from some lists when there is lack of information or no information for obvious reasons, as with winter sports in Florida.

Sometimes, generally in systems with quite a few campgrounds, giving the precise number would be too cumbersome. In these cases, "very few" indicates less than about one-fifth, "a few" between a quarter and a third, "several" between a third and a half, "over half" between a half and two-thirds, "most" over two-thirds, and "almost all" over eighty-five per cent. Terms like "about half," "a quarter," etc., are approximate, but accurate within five per cent.

Likewise, the total number of parks is given for two reasons. First, the number, in relation to the state's population and area, indicates the agency's interest in providing campgrounds and in preserving a bit of the area as it originally was. Second, the ratio of campgrounds to the total number of parks is more than likely to remain the same, so, as new parks are added, you can generally guess how many new campgrounds are also being added. Parks which are purely historical (an old house, a fort, or a village), without any recreational facilities other than possibly picnicking, were omitted from the total number.

Where the information given by the agencies was too precise (or ambiguous) to fit easily into the categories, I put it in quotes.

While there is a natural tendency to assume that

the absence of a detailed reply is indicative of a basic apathy toward serious campers, there are probably other reasons. The questionnaire, as you can see, is quite long, and I have some evidence (tourist councils not forwarding them to the proper agencies, e.g.) that they didn't always bother to read the whole thing.

I did notice indications of a sensitive area or two. Very few answered the question about tentsite ground. However, the glare of an NI on their entry in the first edition stimulated several to fill in that blank in the revision. With the others, is there still the nagging fear that the gravel and cobblestone paving brought too many complaints and they don't want to admit that it is what they have? There was very little detailed response to the query on campsite terrain, although that may be because it can vary extremely between campgrounds.

There are a few rules which may safely be followed in trying to guess a "NI" (no information) reference.

Location is based on a lot of factors: the availability of land, the size of the budget, "dirty politics," gifts from philanthropic organizations or individuals. Most states really don't have a policy on a campground's relation to population centers, although in several states they are quite close. Most consider natural beauty, yet all too few really make it a major part of their selection policy. This fogginess on the part of park officials makes guessing here almost impossible. The term "artificial lakes" means large hydroelectric, flood-control, or navigation lakes. These are significant because they are usually too new to have a natural setting on the shoreline or the level fluctuates too much for vegetation to grow. As a result, they are seldom spots of great aesthetic beauty.

Under *Fireplaces,* most agencies simply listed "grates." It would seem logical that this would mean the three-wall type, but it doesn't always. Photos in the literature help give a rough idea, but be prepared for the worst.

NI under *Cabins* usually means none. NI on fees means ask ahead of time. NI under *Trailers* means no connections. Whether self-contained trailers are permitted or not depends on the size of the trailer and the availability of empty tentsites. Tent trailers are permitted unless specifically prohibited. NI on *Motor homes* can probably be taken to mean that they are treated the same as trailers—sites, maximum lengths, and connections.

NI under *Transportation* means none.

NI under *Toilets* could mean anything—prepare for the worst. "Pit" is used too often as a euphemism for privy instead of for the vented-pit toilet. NI on *Sanitary dumps* means probably not.

NI under *Water* will usually mean none available, so prepare your own source. NI on hot water practically always means only cold water. NI on showers means no showers, but sometimes they are available in swimming-area bathhouses, and you can usually bathe in the stream which is usually present in such areas.

NI under *Electricity* usually means none, but many agencies will list "electricity" and, unless there are flush toilets, this will mean strictly overhead lights strung through the tent area. Where there are flush toilets, there will be at least an over-the-mirror light which can be screwed out and a socket adapter screwed in for appliances such as shavers.

NI under *Grocery, etc.* usually, but not always, means none. While few parks have restaurants, many have a small concession stand which ranges anywhere from hot dogs and soda pop to a staple grocery market, and yet there is no mention in the survey answer or literature about it. However, these are usually available at nearby towns except in the wilderness, where you will carry everything in anyway.

NI under *Museums* means none. The quality of campground museums is rising rapidly now and many are well worth the hour or so spent before setting out on the nature trails. Interpretation centers, either under a simple roof or totally outdoors, do much of the park museum's function at a considerably lower capital cost. These are becoming quite common.

NI under *Trails* usually means unguided hiking trails. Few state parks have naturalist tours (although more are getting them, at least for the summer), but all national parks and monuments (other than historical) do. Self-guiding trails vary from an occasional sign identifying a tree to elaborate printed booklets giving an excellent one- or two-hour nature walk.

NI under *Boating* usually means none, NI on rentals almost always means the same.

Many areas permit creek, lake, or ocean swimming without mentioning it in their information. Take a bathing suit. It will usually find use somewhere on the trip.

NI under *Fishing* means none. Except in a few federal areas, a state license is needed. These are usually quite exorbitant for non-residents, but most states have a cheaper, short-term license. Unless you just like to fish, it is seldom economically feasible unless they are really biting.

NI under *Hunting* means absolutely prohibited. There are a few public areas permitting hunting and they require state licenses—which are even more expensive than the non-resident fishing licenses.

NI under *Horses* means you'd better leave yours at home. It may or may not have to do with horse rental. This is usually concessionaire and has a rather high turn-over rate, and the administering agency doesn't like to publicize something which might not be there when the camper comes.

The topic of *Winter sports* brought some surprises. Because of the amount of research needed, I Xeroxed my letter, thus this topic was included in all that were sent out. While I knew Hawaii had a ski run (that mountain is high), Arkansas surprised me, even though it is on artificial snow. NI will probably mean that there are no organized facilities. However it does not require more than a couple of inches for sledding or cross-country skiing, and six inches (15 cm) (occasionally happens even in the South) provides some good x-c skiing. even if the natives do think you are nuts.

NI under *Playgrounds* doesn't mean a thing either way. These are usually the same old unimaginative things the kids left behind in the park at home.

NI under *Camping fee* practically always means free camping, but be prepared to pay, in case. Unfortunately, there are not that many free campgrounds left for the car camper, although the backpacker or canoe camper still can get by in many areas paying only with his muscles.

NI under *Time limit* usually means none, but the way campgrounds are overcrowding, this will not be valid long. Soon all campgrounds will have to limit stays, and even start taking reservations, which few do now.

NI under *Reservations* means none accepted. Everywhere the talk among park officials is that reservations will be the pattern in the future. I was surprised at how few have them now. This will probably change in the next ten or twenty years to be the norm rather than the exception. Several states are using a commercial reservation service which has offices in major population centers in the eastern half of the country and uses computers to take care of the load. These have the advantage of being accessible to much of the country (as opposed to the alternative which usually requires a letter to the agency or even campground in question), but has the disadvantage of being higher in price than the government-operated systems. Even at this edition, however, it is a trend that is still talked about more than practiced.

Because of overcrowding, fewer and fewer parks will be permitting open fires anytime and practically none will during the summer crowd and fire hazard. For another decade or two, experienced campers will probably be able to get permits to go off into the wilderness, but beyond that, it looks rather grim.

The only bright spot is the return of backpacking and ski touring in sufficient numbers so that the agencies are being compelled to build trail systems in order to reduce environmental damage and increase the carrying capacity of the wilderness. However, there are still limits on how many hikers the area can absorb without damage, so this is an improvement but not a cure of the problem.

NI under *Pets* probably means permitted under restraint. The trend is toward absolute prohibition though, mainly because of crowding. Leash length is maximum permitted.

NI under *Motorcycles, trail scooters, snowmobiles, etc.* generally means restricted to roads and specially marked areas. In developed areas, automobile standards are generally in force, including adequate mufflers and licenses. Snowmobiles are still a bit too new in some areas to have specific rules, but this will be changing as they range farther south. The trend seems to be to provide special trails and areas for snowmobiles and ban them elsewhere.

NI under *Gate locked* means it isn't. In campgrounds where the gate is locked, NI means ask the superintendent before you are held an overnight prisoner—some have mighty early lock hours.

NI under *Alcoholic drinks* probably means no restrictions (other than under public-nuisance laws), but you had better check first. In some areas, this is assumed.

NI under *Minors camping* generally means that it is all right. This term does not refer, as one respondent assumed, to little children camping by themselves, but upper teenagers who are on their own but still legally under age. The market in camping gear provided by these summer holiday wanderers has been a decisive factor in getting good quality, low cost equipment available to the beginner. So there is a significant number of campers in this category.

NI under *Roadside camping* probably means no camping. At any rate, it is rarely wise to do so. Where *Open Beach law* has NI it means one of three things: (1) there is no Open Beach law, (2) the agency hadn't the foggiest notion what I was talking about, (3) there is an Open Beach law but enough politically powerful people own beach property that the agency won't admit to it for fear the public will use their property instead of giving it, by default, to the bigwigs. An Open Beach law outlaws private beaches—all areas between the water and the vegetation line area accessible to the public. While camping may be restricted for reasons of public health or preservation of the delicate dune *oikos,* and within the strictly-defined area below the vegetation line camping would rarely be feasible in periods of maximum tides, it is certainly within the spirit of the law that there be camping facilities, at least in the "primitive" form at convenient points along the beach. A true Open Beach law would permit camping between the vegetation line and the water.

I have no idea what an NI under *Energy problems* could mean, although considering the overwhelming vote of the agencies for the status quo, I am afraid that is precisely what no answer means. This probably won't change until there is a genuine energy crisis, and then all rules are off.

Since there are literally thousands of campgrounds in North America, it is impossible to personally check each one and still have anything resembling an up-to-date report. With the exception of what I could see in photographs in the literature sent by these agencies, or with fewer cases, what I personally knew, all information in this directory is supplied by the agency. The few exceptions are noted in the text.

BUREAU OF INDIAN AFFAIRS

Department of the Interior, Bureau of Indian Affairs, Washington, D.C. 20242.

There is no over-all policy regarding the development of tribal parks—that is left up to the individual tribes. In fact, the Bureau didn't even have a list of the tribes operating parks except for the 1964 booklet, "Vacationing with Indians," which would be excellent if brought up to date at least every two years.

These tribal parks are in states such as California, Texas, and Wisconsin, as well as states with more famous reservations. Oklahoma has some even though there are no reservations in the state.

There is no one set of features which would typify the average tribal-park campground—they range from the highly developed resort to a table, fireplace, and garbage can beside the road. Some reservations will require a tribal hunting or fishing license in addition to the state license. Indian ceremonials are featured at several tribal parks, many of them still quite authentic. Bear in mind, however, that picture-making is a religious act with many tribes, especially among the older members, and this includes photography. You are literally their guest, so act accordingly.

BUREAU OF RECLAMATION

Department of the Interior, Bureau of Reclamation, Washington, D.C. 20240.

The Bureau of Reclamation has 251 areas under its jurisdiction. These areas range from 1 to 1,758,889 acres ($\frac{1}{2}$ to 110,591 hectares) land area and 1 to 193,477 acres ($\frac{1}{2}$ to 78,165 hectares) water area. (A hectare equals 2.471 acres.) Camping facilities are at almost all, although the type of facilities vary considerably. Boating is at almost all, but only about two-thirds permit water skiing. Swimming is at most, fishing at almost all, and hunting at most.

Off the road vehicles are restricted to designated areas. No other information was received.

It is the policy of the Bureau of Reclamation to turn a flooded area over to some other agency (either federal or state) for administration. However, there are several areas still under the control of the Bureau and in 1965 eighteen of them had 99,012 visitor-days of camping.* While most of these were under 250, one was 44,000—a considerable camping load. There is no policy regarding campground development—that apparently is being left up to the local administrators.

CORPS OF ENGINEERS

District Engineer Office. There are thirty-four of them, so inquire at the nearest Corps of Engineers, Department of the Army, Office of the Chief of Engineers, Washington, D.C., 20314; or nearest District Engineer Office.†

The Corps of Engineers got into the campground business quite unintentionally when roads which dead-ended at the shores of their artificial lakes were being used for boat ramps, picnicking, and other activities. In the interest of sanitation and proper management, a minimum of primitive camping facilities were built. As more of the lakes, originally built for flood control, were used for municipal water supplies, certain changes were required in these facilities.

Here are the existing facilities:

Location

Population centers: Being on artificial lakes, population centers often grow from once small towns nearby.

*One person for two days or two persons for one day would each total two visitor-days.

†Try U.S. Government Offices, Department of Defense, Corps of Engineers, District Office; or write the Corps in Washington; or wait until you get to the lake, find the dam, and ask.

Natural features: Practically all are on coves or peninsulas and most have gently sloping waterfronts for swimming and boat ramps. A few are on fairly high ground and provide a panoramic view of the lake area. The lakes, of course, are all artificial and most are still recent enough to have a barren, artificial-lake look.

Physical Facilities

Acreage range: 1 or 2 to 500 ($\frac{1}{2}$ to 200 hectares).
Campsite terrain: Varies widely in contour, vegetation, and drainage.
Tentsite ground: Varies widely. No indication of artificial treatment of tentsites, but some are naturally rather rocky.
Wood availability: Find-it-yourself, generally available in dead or down wood. NI but probably no cutting.
Fireplaces: Mainly two- and three-wall, some waist-high.
Cabins: Not on sites still under Corps jurisdiction.
Trailers: No connections, but permitted.

Utilities

Toilets: Increasing use of flush, remainder mostly vented pit.
Water: Usually piped. Some pump. No hot water or showers.
Electricity: NI. Probably not.
Grocery: At very few. *Ice:* NI. *Restaurant:* No. *Gasoline:* At some concession marinas. *Laundry:* NI, probably not.

Activities

Museums: Some dam houses have a display on the operation of the dam and a few exhibits on local natural history. NI on other types.
Trails: Most are too small for a trail system.
Boating: Primary reason for most campgrounds. Ramps free. Life preservers required. Some lakes require a permit after three days.
Swimming: Where there is a natural beach.
Fishing: Some from bank and artificial berms (usually built from junked cars). Mostly from boats.
Hunting: At several lakes. State license required.

Horses: NI.
Playgrounds: NI, probably not.

Other Rules

Camping fee: As of 1974 there were 448 camp-grounds which have fees. As this number has risen steadily, it can be assumed that more will be added. Class A facilities have flush toilets, showers, sanitary dumps, tables, fireplaces, garbage cans, paved or dustproof roads, designated tentsites and trailer spaces, and permanent staffing; fees range from $3.00 to $3.50 per day. Class B is the same except that there are no showers or vented pit toilets, and the roads are not paved or dustproofed. Fees are from $2.00 to $2.50. Class C is as Class B except that the toilet may be a privy, and there are no sanitary dumps. Fees are from $1.00 to $2.00. Class D is as C except that toilets may be portable chemical or privy, and there is no picnic table. Fees are $1.00 per day. Class E has designated sites, portable chemical or privy toilets, and access roads only—no fees. All classes where electricity is provided charge 50¢ per day extra for the connection.
Time limit: NI, probably none.
Reservations: None for families; required for groups.
Fires outside fireplaces: A local matter.
Pets: Permitted. NI on restrictions.
Motorcycles, trail scooters, etc.: NI. Since there are no trails, there are probably no restrictions other than standard noise restrictions.
Gate locked: No.
Alcoholic drinks: NI.

At the average Corps lake, there are from one to thirty camping areas under Corps jurisdiction, with about five being average. In addition there will often be almost as many under state park systems, municipal park and recreation departments, and other agencies which also provide camping facilities. Also, there are a large number of private marinas serving the public, some of which permit camping. An inquiry at the local Corps office (usually at or on the dam) will get you this information.

The Corps publishes leaflets on individual lakes.

FISH AND WILDLIFE SERVICE

Department of the Interior, Fish and Wildlife Service, Bureau of Sport Fisheries and Wildlife, Washington, D.C. 20240.

"In general, camping is permitted on refuges only when it is essential for full enjoyment of the wildlife on the area by the visitor. Facilities as such are generally lacking and where camping is permitted the camper must have a self-sufficient outfit."

Out of 351 refuges, 190 are staffed. In these, 26 permit camping. These are divided into 15 wild (no facilities); 11 primitive (water and basic sanitary facilities); 6 improved (facilities in addition to the basics of primitive); and 5 concession (facilities nearby). The total is more than 26 because some refuges have more than one type of camping area. Some of these permit camping only during certain seasons.

NATIONAL FORESTS

Department of Agriculture, Forest Service, Washington, D.C. 20250.

Location

Population centers: Irrelevant. Location is restricted by presence of a national forest.
Natural features: A factor, especially in wilderness areas. However, other factors, such as accessibility (for Development Scale 3 and 4), logging and similar land-use operations are taken into consideration.

Physical Facilities

Acreage range: Campground boundaries are indefinite. Forests from 10,777 to 16,016,140. Most are 100,000 to 2,000,000.
Campsite terrain: Varies widely, but almost all, naturally, are wooded.
Tentsite ground: With the possible exception of a Scale 5 campground (which have not, at this writing, even been planned yet), all have natural ground with varying amounts of grass and rock.
Wood availability: Dead- and down-wood gathering. None furnished.

Fireplaces: Scale 1 and 2 are do-it-yourself (fire permit required). Scale 3 are mostly three-wall. Scale 4 have some waist-high.

Cabins: At some forests.

Trailers: No connections, but permitted.

Utilities

Toilets: Scale 1 almost all do-it-yourself. Scale 2 mostly privy, some do-it-yourself. Scale 3 some privy, some vented pit, a few chemical. Scale 4 some flush, a few privy, some vented pit and chemical. Scale 5 would be all flush.

Water: Scale 1 and 2 natural sources. Scale 3 and 4 some piped, some pump. Scale 5 piped. Hot water and showers, Scale 5 only.

Electricity: Possibly some, for lighting only, in Scale 4. Basically a Scale 5 facility.

Grocery, Ice, Restaurant, Gasoline, Laundry: No. Usually available in fairly close communities.

Activities

Museums: Scale 3 has "informal and incidental" visitor information centers (bulletin-board-type displays). Scale 4 has more elaborate information centers, including indoor ones. Scale 5 would possibly even have full-fledged museums.

Trails: Hiking trails are available in all scales. Formal trails in Scale 3 or higher. Trails in Scale 1 require advanced camping skills. Nature trails not provided.

Boating: At a few campgrounds, ramp fee usually extra. Many forests have streams and rivers suitable for canoeing, but it would be best to check with the local Forest Rangers about access, exit, and difficult passages. NI on boats for rent.

Swimming: At a large number of waterfront campgrounds. However, none have lifeguards or developed swimming areas and caution should be exercised.

Fishing: Practically all have fishing lakes or streams. State laws apply.

Hunting: In almost all areas. State laws apply.

Horses: The only way, other than backpacking, to reach Scale 1 campgrounds. Permitted in all areas. Some guide/wrangler services available in many areas.

Playgrounds: Scale 5, if at all.

Other Rules

Camping fee: $1.00 per vehicle per day or $7.00 per year (Golden Eagle) at over 2,000 out of 7,500 campgrounds in 1966. More will require Golden Eagle fees in the future.

Time limit: None as yet.

Reservations: No.

Fires outside fireplaces: With permit only—this includes gas stoves.

Pets: "Under control by their owners."

Motorcycles, trail scooters, etc.: Prohibited on primitive-area trails (access to Scale 1 campgrounds). Currently permitted on formal trails but the practice is discouraged and may ultimately be abolished.

Gate locked: No. No stated quiet time, although spread of camping facilities is such that noise is not a factor except possibly in Scale 4 (or 5) campgrounds.

Alcoholic drinks: NI.

The divisions of the Development Scale are not rigid, they are merely convenience terms. The most common types are 3 and 4. Scale 5 has not yet been built nor are there plans to do so at this writing. The following are pertinent passages from the scale:

1. Primitive

Site Modifications: "Minimum . . . designed for protection of the site rather than comfort of the users." Natural materials, subtle controls. "Spacing . . . extended to minimize contacts with others. Motorized access not provided or permitted."

Recreation Experiences: "Primitive forest environment is dominant. Rudimentary and isolated development sites beyond the sight or sound of inharmonious influences. Maximum opportunity for experiencing solitude, testing skills, and compensating for the routines of daily living. User senses no regimentation. Feeling of physical achievement in reaching site is important."

2. Secondary Primitive

Site Modifications: Same as 1 except that "motorized access provided or permitted. Primary access over primitive roads."

Recreation Experiences: "Near-primitive forest environment. Outside influences present but minimized. Feeling of accomplishment associated with low-standard access is important but does not necessarily imply physical exertion to reach site. Opportunity for solitude and chance to test outdoor skills is present."

3. Intermediate

Site Modifications: "Moderate. Facilities about equally for protection of site and comfort of users. . . . Improvements . . . usually based on use of native materials. Inconspicuous vehicular-traffic controls usually provided. Roads may be hard surfaced and trails formalized. . . . Density about three family units per acre."

Recreation Experiences: "Forest environment is essentially natural. Important that a degree of solitude is combined with some opportunity to socialize with others. Controls and regimentation provided for safety and well-being of user sufficiently obvious to afford a sense of security but subtle enough to leave the taste of adventure."

4. Secondary Modern

Site Modifications: "Site heavily modified. Some facilities designed strictly for comfort and convenience of users but luxury facilities not provided. Density three-five family units per acre. . . . Visitor Information Services frequently available."

Recreation Experiences: "Forest environment is pleasing and attractive but not necessarily natural. Blending of opportunities for solitude and socializing with others. Testing of outdoor skills on site mostly limited to the camping activity. Many user comforts available. Contrast to daily living routine is moderate. Invites marked sense of security."

5. Modern

Site Modifications: "Facilities mostly designed for comfort and convenience of users include flush toilets; may include showers, bathhouses, laundry facilities, and electrical hook-ups. . . . Formal walks on surfaced trails. Regimentation of users is obvious. Access usually by high-speed highways. Density five or more family units per acre. . . . Designs formalized and architecture may be contemporary. Mowed lawns and clipped shrubs not unusual. (Class 5 site only provided in special situations or close to large cities where other lands are not available.)"

Recreation Experiences: "Pleasing environment attractive to the novice or highly gregarious camper. Opportunity to socialize with others very important. Satisfies urbanites' need for compensating experiences and relative solitude but less intensive than in classes 1–4. Obvious to user that he is in secure situation where ample provision is made for his personal comfort and he will not be called upon to use undeveloped skills."

NATIONAL PARKS, MONUMENTS, SEASHORES, RECREATION AREAS, ETC.

National Park Service, Department of the Interior, Washington, D.C. 20240

Location

Population centers: Irrelevant.

Natural features: Unique—not duplicated at other facilities (and rarely anywhere else in the world).

Physical Facilities

Acreage range: 1 (land area of Assateague Island National Seashore) to 2,213,207 (Yellowstone). Variation fairly consistent between these points.

Campsite terrain: Varies widely.

Tentsite ground: Mostly natural soil. Some have coarse sand mixed with loam. Soil type varies widely.

Wood availability: Collection of dead and down wood generally permitted, but on heavily used campgrounds this is a moot point. Bring your own just in case.

Fireplaces: Mostly three-wall, with some fire rings.

Cabins: Operated by concessionaires. Rates vary.

Trailers: Permitted in all parks. No connections. Dumps for self-contained trailers are available in some parks. A few trailer facilities are operated by concessionaires and additional fees are charged, but connections are provided.

Utilities

Toilets: Flush in Campgrounds. Usually privy in Camping Areas.

Water: Piped in Campgrounds. Various sources including natural in Camping Areas. Hot water, NI. Showers in most Campgrounds.

Electricity: NI.

Grocery, Ice, Restaurant, Gasoline, Laundry: Handled by concessionaires when present.

Activities

Museums: At all parks and most other areas. Both nature and history.

Trails: Naturalist tours at most parks. Self-guiding nature trails at all parks and most other areas. Hiking trails at all areas where practical.

Boating: Coast Guard regulations concerning safety and registration apply. Motorboats may be launched only in designated areas and may require a permit.

Swimming: NI.

Fishing: Permitted at any suitable waters. Only very few require state licenses.

Hunting: Prohibited.

Horses: Rental at most large parks. NI on using your own.

Playgrounds: City-park type at a few.

Other Rules

Camping fee: No camping fee, but entrance fee is charged at most areas—$7.00 per year (Golden Eagle) or short-term charge (usually $1.00 per day).

Time limit: Generally fourteen days. Some areas have a low enough demand to allow for longer, but others are so crowded in the summer that even shorter periods are enforced. Some areas are closed in the winter by snowfall, but none have a scheduled closing time.

Reservations: For group camps only. There is talk of possibly requiring reservations in the future, especially for the more crowded parks, but this will be a last-ditch method to cope with the rapidly increasing usage the parks (and, to a lesser extent, the other areas) are getting.

Fires outside fireplaces: Prohibited except for those both a fire permit and a check of equipment by Park Rangers (to reduce the number to those properly skilled and equipped for wilderness camping).

Pets: On leash or under other physical restraint.

Motorcycles, trail scooters, etc.: Prohibited on trails.

Gate locked: No. Quiet time "late at night and early in the morning."

Alcoholic drinks: NI.

Camping is permitted at thirty out of thirty-two national parks, one out of ten historical parks, thirty out of seventy-seven national monuments, the one memorial park, one out of five national battlefields, three out of six national seashores, two out of three parkways, three units of the national capital park, and eight out of eleven recreation areas. More areas are being designated and developed, including lakeshores and riverways—two new classifications. The Department defines camping categories as follows:

Campground (*Type A*)

A campground is an area with an organized layout, having well-defined roads, parking spaces, and campsites. Drinking water and sanitary facilities, including toilets and refuse cans, are furnished on a community basis on the number of campsites therein.

A campground site, or campsite, is a clearly marked plot or location within a campground which provides accommodations for camping by an individual, family, or party. A typical campsite in a campground would include a parking space, fireplace, table-and-bench combination, and a tent space. However, in a walk-in campground or walk-in section of a campground, the parking space is provided but not as an integral part of each campsite.

Camping Area (*Type B*)

A camping area is an area (other than a campground) designated and regularly used for camping by individuals, families, or parties. Camping areas may be accessible by either road or trail. Facilities provided are minimum, generally being limited to access roads, basic sanitary facilities, and a limited number of fireplaces and tables. Trail camps fall within this category, and shelters of the Adirondack or fully enclosed type may be provided. Each camping area has an assigned, as differentiated from designed, capacity based on the number of camping spaces therein. Superintendents assign to each camping area a capacity figure, in terms of camping spaces, based on a realistic evaluation of acreage involved, topography, and facilities provided.

A camping "space" in a camping area is one which is normally occupied by an individual, family, or party.

Group Camp (Type C)

A group camp is an area designated for use by organized groups, such as Boy Scouts, school groups, or other large parties. It is composed of one or more group spaces, each of which is provided with a large fireplace, several tables, and parking space for buses or a number of cars. Capacity of group camps is rated on the basis of the number of group spaces within the camp and the number of persons each can normally accommodate.

With very few exceptions, all camping accommodations under the jurisdiction of the National Park Service have Campgrounds. Most also have Camping Areas, especially on the more extensive trail systems. A few have Group Camps, most just a few, but some a large number.

The Park Service has guide pamphlets for each park, monument, etc., under its administration, available free at the gates to these places or from the Government Printing Office for ten or fifteen cents each.

LIST OF CAMPSITES

ALABAMA

Department of Conservation, Administrative Building, Montgomery, Alabama 36104

Location

Population centers: Close.
Natural features: A major factor.

Physical Facilities

Acreage range: 40 to 9,940 (16 to 4,016 hectares); the smallest with camping 103 (42 hectares); even spread of sizes.
Campsite terrain: NI. Photo shows flat and wooded.
Tentsite ground: NI. Photo shows natural soil.
Wood availability: NI.
Fireplaces: NI.
Cabins: At eleven; rates vary from $12.00 to $24.00 per day to $72.00 to $130.00 per week.
Trailers: Sewer connections at one park.
Motor homes: Same as trailers.
Transportation: No.

Utilities

Toilets: Present at most. NI on type.
Sanitary dumps: At at least one.
Water: At most, NI on system; showers at at least some.
Electricity: NI.

Grocery, Ice: At most; *Restaurant:* At several, snacks at most; *Gasoline:* NI; *Laundry:* At least two.

Activities

Museums: NI.
Trails: At all parks; trails out from parks being developed.
Boating: At most, marina at a third, some power and speed restrictions.
Swimming: At most, in designated areas only.
Fishing: At most, license required.
Hunting: No; no firearms permitted.
Horses: Designated areas only; stables at three.
Playgrounds: "Play areas" in most.

Other Rules

Camping fee: $4.00 to $1.50 per night, weekly six times the daily rate.
Time limit: Two weeks in season; season April 1 through Labor Day; checkout 2:00 P.M.
Reservations: No.
Fires outside fireplaces: No.
Pets: Six-foot (182 cm) leash; horse-type animals in designated areas only.
Motorcycles, trail scooters, etc.: NI.
Gate locked: NI.
Alcoholic drinks: NI.
Minors camping: Under 18 must be accompanied by an adult accepting responsibility.

Roadside camping: NI.
Open Beach law: NI.
Energy problems: Coming from a shorter distance, no changes anticipated.

Those under twenty-one must be accompanied by responsible adults. Out of ten state parks, camping is permitted at three. Pamphlets are published on individual parks.

ALASKA

Camping is permitted at 16 out of 17 parks; 13 campsites have full facilities and 10 are primitive.

Department of Natural Resources, Division of Parks, 323 E. 4th Ave., Anchorage, Alaska 99501

Location

Population centers: Close (because that is where the state-owned land is, rather than for any other reason).
Natural features: Of minor importance. (Very little of the state doesn't have spectacular scenery.)

Physical Facilities

Acreage range: Waysides 1 to 240 ($\frac{1}{2}$ to 97 hectares); parks and recreation areas 183 to 282,000 (74 to 113,928 hectares).
Campsite terrain: Generally levelled (artificially).
Tentsite ground: NI.
Wood availability: Cut wood available.
Fireplaces: Two- and three-wall.
Cabins: No.
Trailers: No connections.
Motor homes: Same as trailers.
Transportation: No airstrips, but float and amphibians use lakes; future may designate certain lakes and prohibit use of others by aircraft. Rail access to two State Parks on "special unscheduled stops" arrangement. Unscheduled bus stops also possible at units along highway.

Utilities

Toilets: At all campgrounds; NI on type.
Sanitary dumps: At one park, additional dumps are being built at some highway rest areas.
Water: At about half; NI on system, hot water, or showers.
Electricity: NI.
Grocery, Ice, Restaurant, Gasoline, Laundry: NI.

Activities

Museums: NI.
Trails: Hiking trails at ten, one canoe trail.
Boating: Ramps at 23, canoeing at 27; one park can be visited most easily by boat and has only rental.

Swimming: At thirteen.
Fishing: At most.
Hunting: In three parks and one recreation area only; all others discharge of firearms is illegal.
Horses: NI.
Winter sports: One park with downhill skiing, one with cross-country trails, and another in planning stage; snowmobile areas in one park and one recreation area.
Playgrounds: NI.

Other Rules

Camping fee: Presently none, but there has been in the past and probably will again.
Time limit: Fifteen days in most, shorter in special situations.
Reservations: No.
Fires outside fireplaces: Prohibited except with permit.
Pets: Leashed in developed areas, under control everywhere.
Motorcycles, trail scooters, etc.: NI; *Snowmobiles:* In designated areas and at announced times only.
Gate locked: NI.
Alcoholic drinks: NI.
Minors camping: NI.
Roadside camping: Majority of campsites are at wayside parks which are adequately spaced for emergency use in most areas.
Open Beach law: NI.
Energy problems: NI.

Camping is still undeveloped at the three state parks, but will be developed soon. Facilities exist at two of the four recreation areas with the others planned. There is camping at 44 of the 53 waysides.

ARIZONA

State Parks Board, State Capitol, Phoenix, Arizona 85012

At the time of writing, Arizona had only one state park, which was 5,750 acres, had water and rest rooms (NI on type), fishing, and a two-week time limit. NI on fees or on other activities. It is located on an artificial lake.

ARKANSAS

Arkansas Department of Parks and Tourism, 149 State Capitol, Little Rock, Arkansas 72207

Location

Population centers: NI, but most are fairly close to towns.
Natural features: A major factor in most. Some historical.

Physical Facilities

Acreage range: 29,000 (11,716 hectares) total with no breakdown given.
Campsite terrain: Varies widely.
Tentsite ground: "Some tent bases"; much natural ground, sometimes bare or rocky.
Wood availability: Furnished. Collection permitted.
Fireplaces: Waist-high and three-wall.
Cabins: At eight; $12.00 per day or $72.00 per week to $15.00 per day or $90.00 per week.
Trailers: No connections. Two parks have sharply winding access roads which make trailers unfeasible.
Motor homes: NI.
Transportation: No.

Utilities

Toilets: Most flush, few privy and vented pit.
Sanitary dumps: At several.
Water: Spring at one, piped at rest. Hot water being installed. Showers at one-third.
Electricity: At three-quarters. Free, but mainly for light only.
Grocery, Ice: At seven; *Restaurant:* At seven, snacks at seven (all different seven); *Gasoline:* At one. *Laundry:* At one.

Activities

Museums: At two.
Trails: Hiking trails at half; nature trails at two-thirds; horse trails at few.
Boating: At over half. Some are on small lakes, others on rivers. Rentals at almost all lake, NI on rates.
Swimming: At all but three. One pool. Rest are lake or creek pools.
Fishing: At all but three. State license is needed.
Hunting: Prohibited.
Horses: Trails at some parks. Rental increasing.
Winter sports: Downhill skiing at one (snow machines).
Playgrounds: At almost all.

Other Rules

Camping fee: $1.50 per night without electrical outlets, $2.00 with.
Time limit: None.
Reservations: No.
Fires outside fireplaces: Prohibited.
Pets: On leash.
Motorcycles, trail scooters, etc.: Permitted.
Gate locked: No.
Alcoholic drinks: Restricted to tents.
Minors camping: NI.
Roadside camping: Permitted. Facilities are being developed at twenty-seven state parks out of twenty-eight.
Energy problems: NI.
Camping is permitted at eighteen out of twenty-seven state parks.

CALIFORNIA

Department of Parks and Recreation, P.O. Box 2390, Sacramento, California 95811

Location

Population centers: Irrelevant.
Natural features: There are five major divisions of the California Park System: wilderness, parks, preserves, historical units, and recreation units. Natural features are the primary criteria in all except historical, where it is still a present factor. Carrying capacity of the site is a factor both in its development and in the number permitted to visit the site. No permanent improvements are permitted in wildernesses, their value as natural areas is the reason for their classification. Parks combine the wilderness with people and thus some development is necessary to protect the site from those coming for enjoyment and education. Most parks are land, but some are underwater. Preserves are selected for unique natural features, and improvements are limited to those needed to protect the site from day-use public. Historical units are to preserve objects of historical interest. Use is daytime only. Recreation units are heavier use areas for outdoor recreation, beaches, wayside campgrounds, and winter sport areas. Natural preserves are areas within other classifications in which unique specimens require the care of a wilderness but are not geographically large enough for this classification.

Physical Facilities

Acreage range: Twelve to 490,000 (8½ to 198,000 hectares); most between 500 and 5,000 (200 and 2,000 hectares).
Campsite terrain: NI.
Tentsite ground: NI.
Wood availability: For sale. Collection, including down wood, prohibited.
Fireplaces: Various types. Beaches have mostly fire rings.
Cabins: NI.
Trailers Permitted where they will fit.
Motor homes: Same as trailers.
Transportation: One experiment at one lake with amphibious aircraft facilities, use of nearby airstrips encouraged. Two Sky Trails offer pilots a

way of seeing parts of a park that cannot be seen any other way; booklet makes it a self-guiding nature trail. No bus service. Amtrack had a run from Los Angeles to a state beach, but has abandoned it.

Utilities

Some primitive campgrounds are simply designated areas with no facilities.
Toilets: Flush in developed, chemical or "pit" in primitive.
Sanitary dumps: At a few.
Water: Piped in developed, "central water supply" in primitive. Hot showers in some developed.
Electricity: NI.
Grocery: At a few. *Ice:* NI. *Restaurant:* At one. *Gasoline, Laundry:* NI.

Activities

Museums: At historical areas.
Trails: Most areas of sufficient size have extensive trails for both foot and horse travel. Several have naturalist tours (NI on schedule). The state is building an extensive system under the California Riding and Hiking Trail Act which will provide 3,000 miles of connected trails in the state. This will be in addition to the Pacific Crest Trail and will provide one of the best trail systems in the country when finished. A cut-off of funds in 1957 has made this program currently inactive, with about one-third completed.
Boating: Permitted. NI on rental. Five-knot speed limit at night. Must meet Coast Guard safety requirements.
Swimming: Ocean, lake, river, or pool.
Fishing: State fishing license required.
Hunting: Prohibited except in some recreation areas.
Horses: At designated areas only.
Winter sports: Unspecified snow activities at three, "winter camping" at three.
Playgrounds: NI.

Other Rules

Camping fee: Developed $3.00, primitive $1.50.
Time limit: Thirty days, except for certain heavy-demand areas which have a fifteen-, ten-, or seven-day limit. Checkout 2:00 P.M.
Reservations: Ticketron, at department's address.
Fires outside fireplaces: Generally prohibited. Some permits given for trail campers. In times of high fire danger, stoves and smoking may be forbidden.
Pets: Dogs in enclosed vehicle or tent or on six-foot (182 cm) leash, campground and day-use areas only except for some beaches. Dog license and

proof of rabies inoculation is required if over five months old. 50¢ per night fee.
Motorcycles, trail scooters, etc.: Prohibited on trails. NI on other places.
Snowmobiles: on roads only.
Gate locked: No. Quiet time 11:00 P.M. to 6:00 A.M.
Alcoholic drinks: NI.
Minors camping: NI.
Roadside camping: NI.
Open Beach law: NI.
Energy problems: NI.
Non-camping activities such as sports may be carried on only in specifically designated areas. Camping is permitted at over 70 state parks with facilities, under construction at others. There are over 200 units (of all classifications) in the State Park System.

The Department publishes a book of recreation landing strips (26), pamphlets on individual units of the system, and several books. A list of the books can be obtained from the Department.

COLORADO

Colorado Division of Parks and Outdoor Recreation, 1845 Sherman, Denver, Colorado 80203

Location

Population centers: "A factor."
Natural features: "A factor."

Physical Facilities

Acreage range: 40 to 70,708 (16 to 28,566 hectares) land and 0 to 3,308 (1,336 hectares) water; most land below 5,000 (2,000 hectares), water evenly distributed.
Campsite terrain: Varied.
Tentsite ground: Level, natural soil.
Wood availability: Collection permitted at most areas.
Fireplaces: Several have no facilities, rest have "grates."
Cabins: No.
Trailers: In designated areas only.
Motor homes: NI.
Transportation: Airstrips at two, near two more; NI on other systems.

Utilities

Toilets: Chemical at most, flush at one-third.
Sanitary dumps: At almost all.
Water: Three with no drinking water (on lakes, however) and two with wells. Rest bring in. Hot water and hot showers at six recreation areas.
Electricity: No.

Grocery, Ice, Restaurant, Gasoline: No. *Laundry:* Coin-operated at four recreation areas.

Activities

Museums: One.
Trails: Hiking at one-third, nature at one-third, rock climbing at a few.
Boating: At three-quarters. Three more permit only hand-propelled craft, and two more have a 10 m.p.h. speed limit. Rental at half of those with boating.
Swimming: At one-fifth. All except one unsupervised and in lakes.
Fishing: At all, state license require; ice fishing.
Hunting: At all in season; prohibited within 100 yards (91 m) of designated campsites, nature, boating, swimming, or picnicking areas.
Horses: Prohibited at established campgrounds. Concessionaire rental at several.
Winter sports: Cross-country skiing, ice skating at one-third, snowmobiling at eight. Ice fishing at all.
Playgrounds: No.

Other Rules

Camping fee: At seven, $2.00 per night; entrance fee of $1.00 per day or $5.00 per calendar year at all but one (with primitive camping only).
Time limit: Fourteen days in a 45-day period. Check-out time 12:00 noon.
Reservations: No.
Fires outside fireplaces: Prohibited.
Pets: On six-foot (182 cm) leash.
Motorcycles, trail scooters, etc.: On approved roads and trails only.
Gate locked: At one, 10:00 P.M. to 6:00 A.M.
Alcoholic drinks: Permitted.
Minors camping: NI.
Roadside camping: Prohibited.
Energy problems: NI.
Camping is permitted at twenty-eight out of twenty-nine state parks and recreational areas.

CONNECTICUT

Department of Environmental Protection, State Office Building, Hartford, Connecticut 06115

Location

Population centers: Irrelevant. Parks are quite evenly distributed outside main urban areas.
Natural features: Of major importance.

Physical Facilities

Acreage range: 95 to 2,294 (38 to 1,988 hectares). Smaller parks do not permit camping.

Campsite terrain: Open woods.
Tentsite ground: Flat, grassed areas.
Wood availability: "Available," some concessionaire.
Fireplaces: Small masonry, without grates.
Cabins: No.
Trailers: Thirty-five feet (10½ m) limit, no connections.
Motor homes: Permitted.
Transportation: None.
Toilets: Flush at most, pit in rural areas.
Sanitary dumps: At most.
Water: Piped and pumped; coin operated hot water showers at most.
Electricity: Safety lighting only; no connections.
Grocery, Ice, Restaurant: NI, snacks at most. *Gasoline:* NI. *Laundry:* None.

Activities

Museums: No.
Trails: Hiking trails in all, naturalist trails in three.
Boating: At about one-third. Restricted to posted areas. No rentals.
Swimming: At about half. All but two in fresh water ponds or streams.
Fishing: At most. Two salt water; license required for fresh water only; ice fishing at half.
Hunting: Prohibited in state parks, permitted in state forest; license required. Carrying of firearms prohibited under the same conditions.
Horses: Prohibited on foot trails or swimming and picnic areas; rental available.
Winter sports: Cross-country skiing and toboganning at all; ice skating at half; no downhill facilities.
Playgrounds: No city-park-type or athletic areas.

Other Rules

Camping fee: $3.00 for salt water beaches, $2.00 for inland parks.
Time limit: Fourteen days. Season April 15 through September 30. Out of season camping permitted at four areas. Check-out time 12:00 noon.
Reservations: Permitted.
Fires outside fireplaces: Prohibited.
Pets: Not permitted in parks, permitted in forest campgrounds.
Motorcycles, trail scooters, etc.: On authorized vehicular roads only. *Snowmobiles:* No.
Gate locked: No.
Alcoholic drinks: Permitted.
Minors camping: One adult at least 18 years old.
Roadside camping: Prohibited. Emergency camping may be done in any state park between a half-hour after sunset and 8:00 A.M. per vehicle.
Open Beach law: No.
Energy problems: More use by state residents and

reservations are for longer periods. No specific plans have been made.

Fourteen parks out of a system of seventy-seven permit camping.

DELAWARE

Department of Natural Resources and Environmental Control, Division of Parks and Recreation, Dover, Delaware 19901

Location

Population centers: Irrelevant. They are spread fairly evenly throughout the state.
Natural features: Of major importance.

Physical Facilities

Acreage range: 965 to 2,020 (390 to 816 hectares). Smaller parks without camping.
Campsite terrain: Level, cleared, or partially wooded.
Tentsite ground: Natural soil, sandy at half.
Wood availability: NI.
Fireplaces: Fire rings.
Cabins: No.
Trailers: Fifty-foot (15 m) combined length.
Motor homes: Within trailer length.
Transportation: NI.

Utilities

Toilets: Flush.
Sanitary dumps: Yes.
Water: Piped; hot water in showers.
Electricity: At one, $3.50 per night.
Grocery, Ice, Snacks: At concession stands. *Restaurant:* Refreshment stand. *Gasoline, Laundry:* NI.

Activities

Museums: No.
Trails: Naturalist tour and self-guiding.
Boating: "No wake" speed limit at one. Rental at one: rowboats 75¢ per hour, $5.00 for eight hours, paddleboats $1.00 per hour.
Swimming: At all designated areas only when lifeguards are on duty.
Fishing: Half in fresh water, other half in salt. License not required for salt water fishing. Fresh water license required except under fifteen years old or women with a licensed adult.
Hunting: Permitted on some Game and Fish Commission lands. Firearms prohibited in state parks.
Horses: Restricted to bridle paths.
Winter sports: No facilities.
Playgrounds: NI.

Other Rules

Camping fee: $3.00 per night, $3.50 with electricity.
Time limit: Total of fourteen nights. Checkout 5:00 P.M.
Reservations: No.
Fires outside fireplaces: Prohibited.
Pets: On leash. Prohibited on beaches.
Motorcycles, trail scooters, etc.: Crossing sand dunes is prohibited.
Gate locked: NI. Quiet time 10:00 P.M. to 7:00 A.M.
Alcoholic drinks: Must be twenty years old or over.
Minors camping: NI.
Roadside camping: NI.
Open Beach law: No.
Energy problems: No effect.

Camping is permitted at four out of eleven state parks and recreational areas.

FLORIDA

Department of Natural Resources, Larson Building, Tallahassee, Florida 32304

Location

Population centers: Irrelevant in selection; near cities.
Natural features: A factor in most parks. Most of the remainder are primarily historical.

Physical Facilities

Acreage range: 78 to 50,515 (35 to 20,408 hectares). Only three parks over 4,000 (1,600 hectares).
Campsite terrain: NI. Photos show flat and wooded.
Tentsite ground: NI. Photos show natural soil.
Wood availability: At two, charcoal at just under half.
Fireplaces: "Grills" at all.
Cabins: At a few, wide variety of types and rental rates.
Trailers: To fit space, most at least thirty feet (9 m), some less than twenty feet (6 m). Electricity and water hook-ups in all but one. NI on rates.
Motor homes: Same as trailers.
Transportation: None.

Utilities

Toilets: Flush.
Sanitary dumps: At over half.
Water: Piped. Hot water in rest rooms and showers.
Electricity: At most. 25¢ per day per site if used.
Grocery, Ice: At a third; *Restaurants, Gasoline:* NI; *Laundry:* washers and driers at a third, tubs at over half.

Activities

Museums: At a few; interpretive areas at over half.

Trails: Nature trails at all but four; bicycle trails at six; canoe trail system.

Boating: At most; ramps at over half; docks or piers at almost half; rental at several, NI on rates; marine supplies at five.

Swimming: At most; skin and scuba diving at one-quarter.

Fishing: Salt water at half, fresh water at over half. License required for over fifteen years old in fresh water.

Hunting: Prohibited.

Horses: Prohibited.

Playgrounds: At all except four.

Other Rules

Camping fee: $4.00 plus tax per night per campsite (with electricity); $3.50 plus tax for nonelectrical sites; $1.50 plus tax for primitive campground (pump and privy). 50¢ per person per night on backpacking trails with a maximum of twelve people on the trail at any one time (two parks with such trails).

Time limit: Two weeks; checkout 2:00 P.M.

Reservations: Half of tentsites may be reserved. Reservations $1.50 through Ticketron, Hollywood, Florida, no more than ninety days in advance.

Fires outside fireplaces: Required at two parks (no fireplaces). NI on others. Photo shows an open fire at a park which has three-wall.

Pets: Prohibited except at picnic areas (closed at night).

Motorcycles, trail scooters, etc.: NI.

Gate locked: At various times. Gate keys are issued to campers for a refundable deposit.

Alcoholic drinks: NI.

Minors camping: At least one eighteen years old or over in each camping group.

Roadside camping: Prohibited.

Open Beach law: NI. Beach camping prohibited.

Energy problems: No effect seen, no changes planned.

There are twenty-three parks in the system with camping at nineteen (one primitive); twenty-two recreational areas with camping at sixteen.

GEORGIA

Department of Natural Resources, Parks and Historic Sites Division, 270 Washington St., S.W., Atlanta, Georgia 30334

Location

Population centers: Within fifty miles of every community in the state.

Natural features: Considered, but main criteria for selection is sufficient acreage, suitable topography, and a "manifest need for a park in that particular area."

Physical Facilities

Acreage range: .03 to 5,800 (12 to 2,343 hectares); most under 250 (100 hectares) are for day-use only.

Campsite terrain: Varies from mountain to swamp. Level and raised for drainage.

Tentsite ground: Mostly compacted earth. A few fine gravel.

Wood availability: Commercial fire logs for sale.

Fireplaces: Fire rings at tentsites. Some waist-high. A few three-wall still used at a couple of parks.

Cabins: Log cabins, wood and cement-block cottages, home-type houses, and mobile homes on permanent bases. Fees vary with type and place.

Trailers: Twenty-nine-foot (8.8 m) maximum, $3.00 per night. No extra charge for connections. Facilities for self-contained plumbing.

Motor homes: Twenty-nine-foot (8.8 m) maximum.

Transportation: One airstrip, no other forms.

Utilities

Toilets: Flush.

Sanitary dumps: Yes.

Water: Piped in toilet buildings, pumped elsewhere. Hot showers.

Electricity: Outlets at buildings and at campsites. No extra charge.

Grocery: Staples only. *Ice, Restaurant, Gasoline:* No. *Laundry:* Tubs, automatic washers. Few parks have driers. Policy is not to compete with private business within reasonable radius.

Activities

Museums: Two archeological, twenty historical (various periods), one excavated Indian mound.

Trails: Two self-guiding trails, one guided combination boat-and-nature trail. Guided boat tours at Okefenokee.

Boating: Restrictions depend on the size of the lake. Small lakes are restricted to fishing and swimming only. A few lakes are restricted to motorless boats, some for rent.

Swimming: At lakes and pools, designated areas only.

Fishing: No trotlines, seines, spears, etc., permitted. State license required—must be sixteen or older.

Hunting: Prohibited. No firearms permitted. Bows restricted to archery ranges.

Horses: No.

Playgrounds: Mostly city-park type; some with themes now being built.

Other Rules

Camping fee: $3.00 per night per site. Must get permit by 7:30 P.M. Check-out time, 5:00 P.M.
Time limit: Two weeks.
Reservations: No.
Fires outside fireplaces: Prohibited.
Pets: Dogs only, on six-foot leash. Continuous barking or menacing attitude grounds for removal.
Motorcycles, trail scooters, etc.: Restricted to paved roads.
Gate locked: 10:00 P.M. to 7:00 A.M. Keys available at most parks; arrangements may be made with superintendent at remainder.
Alcoholic drinks: Prohibited.
Minors camping: Regular campsites limited to one family; primitive campsites to organized groups led by responsible adults. Ratio at discretion of superintendent.
Energy problems: Because of proximity of parks to population, no plans are being made to cater to low-energy consumption camping forms.
Roadside camping: Roadside park system is for picnicking—camping is prohibited.
Open Beach law: "No knowledge of one. Doubtful, however, that unsupervised camping would be allowed."
Camping is permitted at thirty-nine of fifty-four parks in the system.

HAWAII

State Parks Division, Department of Land and Natural Resources, Box 621, Honolulu, Hawaii 96809

Location

Population centers: Has not been a major factor in the past, but is an increasing factor now.
Natural features: Of prime importance, both as a protective device (especially with new parks in Oahu where urban sprawl is a problem) and as an interpretive factor.

Physical Facilities

Acreage range: 1 to 5,000+ ($\frac{1}{2}$ to 2,000+ hectares); smallest with camping is 7.6 (3 hectares); most are fairly small.
Campsite terrain: NI.
Tentsite ground: NI.
Wood availability: NI.
Fireplaces: NI.
Cabins: $3.00 per person (maximum six in group) increasing 50¢ increments for each less in group, $8.00 for one person; $70.00 per week per unit

maximum. NI on extent of cabins; utensils, bedding, and household equipment provided.
Trailers: At two.
Motor homes: At two; considering banning all camping machines as "inappropriate."
Transportation: A foot/bicycle trail from one park to a nearby airfield is planned. Buses to several parks, but schedule changes rapidly. No railroads in state.

Utilities

Toilets: At all with camping; NI on type.
Sanitary dumps: No.
Water: At all with camping, NI on system or showers.
Electricity: NI.
Grocery, Ice, Restaurant, Gasoline, Laundry: NI.

Activities

Museums: NI, historic importance of many implies there are.
Trails: At several.
Boating: Salt water at coastal parks, NI on inland.
Swimming: At ten, NI on fresh or salt water.
Fishing: NI.
Hunting: NI.
Horses: NI.
Winter sports: One ski area with portable rope tow, no cross-country trails needed (no trees).
Playgrounds: NI.

Other Rules

Camping fee: None.
Time limit: One week.
Reservations: Required one week in advance.
Fires outside fireplaces: No, but camp stoves and warmers may be.
Pets: Not permitted to run at large in park grounds and buildings.
Motorcycles, trail scooters, etc.: NI, *Snowmobiles:* "not practical."
Gate locked: NI.
Alcoholic drinks: Prohibited to "drink or display to public view."
Minors camping: NI.
Roadside camping: NI.
Open Beach law: NI.
Energy problems: Mass transit bus access encouraged, and recreation vehicles discouraged. Camping machines may be banned because they are "inappropriate to a recreational experience in the natural environment" rather than as a fuel conservation measure. No changes were noticed during the 1973–74 "shortage."
Hawaii has forty-seven parks and historic sites and permits camping at eleven. In addition, the department is planning to double the developed

parks in the next five or six years (from 1975), including at least two undersea parks.

IDAHO

Idaho State Parks and Recreation Department, 2263 Warm Springs Avenue, Boise, Idaho 83720.

Location

Population centers: A system of campgrounds, primarily in the southern part of the state, is being developed accessible to population centers. The major state parks are not close to population centers.
Natural features: The major parks are situated in areas of unique natural features. In the minor campgrounds, natural features are of secondary importance.

Physical Facilities

Acreage range: 11 to 5,505 (4 to 2,202 hectares); those with camping from 142 to 5,505 (58 to 2,202 hectares).
Campsite terrain: Wooded.
Tentsite ground: NI. Photos show natural soil and grass.
Wood availability: Natural wood on site. No policy yet formulated on collection.
Fireplaces: NI. Photos all show gasoline stoves.
Cabins: No.
Trailers: Must fit space, which varies. Sewer hook-ups at two.
Motor homes: NI.
Transportation: NI.

Utilities

Toilets: Flush.
Sanitary dumps: At eight.
Water: Piped at all but one, hot showers at many.
Electricity: At all but one.
Grocery: At one. *Ice, Restaurant, Gasoline, Laundry:* NI.

Activities

Museums: Interpretive program at at least one.
Trails: At half.
Boating: Ramps at most.
Swimming: At one at least.
Fishing: At most; ice fishing at one-quarter.
Hunting: Prohibited.
Horses: NI.
Winter sports: Sledding at one-third, ice skating at one-fifth, snowmobiling at one-fifth, and a photo shows cross-country skiing.
Playgrounds: NI.

Other Rules

Camping fee: NI. (None had been set in 1968.)
Time limit: At an as-yet-undetermined time in the future, there will be a limit.
Reservations: NI.
Fires outside fireplaces: NI.
Pets: On leash or in tent or vehicle at all times.
Motorcycles, trail scooters, snowmobiles, etc.: NI.
Gate locked: NI.
Alcoholic drinks: NI.
Minors camping: NI.
Roadside camping: Yes. At least in the southern part of the state, these are excellent facilities with flush toilets and are extensively used by camping machines, but few tents are seen (the wind is high and cold much of the year).
Energy problems: Three parks are experimenting with a tent rental program in which the site, tent, two cots and pads, ice chest, stove, and lantern are available "for a minimal fee." This program is both to allow people to try camping without investing in equipment and also to provide overnight accommodation for travelers without equipment. Figures weren't available at deadline, but the impression was that attendance was showing more residents of the state and a shorter distance traveled. Coordination of information with private campgrounds and trailer parks near camping areas is attempting to use these facilities for trailer storage and thereby cut gas consumption to and from the camping areas.

Camping is permitted at eleven of the nineteen state parks administered by the department.

ILLINOIS

Department of Conservation, Information/ Education Division, State Office Building, Springfield, Illinois 62706

Location

Population centers: NI. Fairly even geographical distribution.
Natural features: Important. Historical factors are also important. Some parks are on artificial lakes.

Physical Facilities

Acreage range: Parks from 22 to 3,026 (9 to 1,222 hectares) most over 100 (40 ha); conservation areas from 87 to 8,680 (35 to 3,507 ha), most 500 to 3,000 (200 to 1,200 ha).
Campsite terrain: Varies.
Tentsite ground: Varies.
Wood availability: Camp stoves or charcoal only.
Fireplaces: Mostly camp stoves.

Cabins: Few.
Trailers: NI on size limits; electricity at half.
Motor homes: Same as trailers.
Transportation: Very small airstrips in few.

Utilities

Toilets: Flush at very few. Privy at rest.
Sanitary dumps: At half.
Water: NI on system. Tested water available at all sites. Hot water, NI. Showers at very few.
Electricity: At half. 25¢ per night.
Grocery, Ice: NI. *Restaurant:* At one-quarter. Refreshment stands at most parks and conservation areas. *Gasoline:* NI. *Laundry:* No.

Activities

Museums: At very few.
Trails: Naturalist tour at at least one. Nature and hiking trails mentioned at several, but not enough information to determine proportions or trends.
Boating: At most. One-quarter of these prohibit motors. Another quarter restrict power to a maximum of $7\frac{1}{2}$-horsepower, and a few more restrict to 10-horsepower. Ramps at a third. Rental at almost half of those permitting boating. NI on rates.
Swimming: At only two.
Fishing: At over three-quarters. State license required.
Hunting: At most conservation areas and a few parks.
Horses: NI.
Winter sports: Varies, contact individual campground.
Playgrounds: NI.

Other Rules

Camping fee: $3.00 per night at A campgrounds (showers, flush toilets); $2.00 per night at B (vehicular access); $1.00 per night at C (tents, primitive sites, no vehicular access).
Time limit: Fourteen nights; checkout 3:00 P.M.
Reservations: No.
Fires outside fireplaces: NI.
Pets: All pets on leash.
Motorcycles, trail scooters, etc.: NI.
Gate locked: NI.
Alcoholic drinks: No.
Minors camping: NI.
Roadside camping: NI.
Energy problems: Campers are coming from a shorter distance, but no changes are contemplated.

Camping is permitted at forty-one out of sixty-five state parks, seven out of twenty-four conserva-tion areas, none of the twenty-three state memorials, and three of the four state forests.

Pamphlets on individual state parks and memorials (historical parks) are published by the Department of Conservation.

INDIANA

Department of Natural Resources, Indianapolis, Indiana 46204

Location

Population centers: Generally near population centers.
Natural features: Important; wide variety of types preserved.

Physical Facilities

Acreage range: 22 to 22,697 (9 to 9,168 hectares); most between 1,000 to 8,000 (400 and 21,319 hectares).
Campsite terrain: Generally level.
Tentsite ground: NI other than "level"; illustrations show grassed.
Wood availability: For sale at most parks. No collection at parks. Collection permitted at state forests and fish and game areas.
Fireplaces: "Some provided"; NI on type.
Cabins: At a few parks.
Trailers: Electricity maximum twenty amps where available.
Motor homes: NI.
Transportation: NI.

Utilities

Toilets: Flush at most parks. Vented pit at remainder of parks, state forests, and all but one fish and game area.
Sanitary dumps: At a few.
Water: At all campgrounds. Hot water and showers at most parks and one forest.
Electricity: At class A sites only.
Grocery, Ice: At some parks, but NI on number. *Restaurant:* NI. *Gasoline:* Available at some in connection with boat fuel but NI on number. *Laundry:* Tubs at about half of parks.

Activities

Museums: Nature at two, historical at one.
Trails: Naturalist program at two-thirds of the parks in the summer, at six parks year 'round. Hiking trails at all but one park of the entire system. Horseback trails at just over half of the parks and almost all of the forests.
Boating: At two-thirds of the parks, three-quarters of the forests, and all but one of the fish and

game areas. For rent at all parks with boating, at a few of the forests, and at almost all the fish and game areas. Rent varies with the size of the lake and the boat type. Motors prohibited on lakes of less than 100 acres, electric motors only on lakes below 100 acres.

Swimming: At three-quarters of the parks and two forests. Three parks have pools with 50¢ fee, 25¢ for lockers. Remainder is in lakes (free).

Fishing: At all forests, all but one park.

Hunting: At forests and fish and game areas.

Horses: Rental at a little over half of the parks and almost all of the forests. Special camping facilities for campers with horses. Prohibited on hiking trails.

Winter sports: Skiing, skating, and tobogganing at one park. Equipment for rent. Toboggans for rent. NI on rate.

Playgrounds: At almost all parks and forests and at two fish and game areas. NI on type. Slides and swings; timber forms for climbing.

Other Rules

Camping fee: Class A: $3.00 per night in season, $2.50 in winter; Class B: $2.50 in season, $2.00 in winter; Class C: $2.00 in season, $1.50 in winter; Horses $1.00 per horse, year 'round. A and B both have plumbing, A has electricity at the site; C is primitive with pit toilets.

Time limit: Two weeks; season Memorial Day to Labor Day.

Reservations: In fourteen parks and six recreation areas.

Fires outside fireplaces: Only in designated spots.

Pets: On leash.

Motorcycles, trail scooters, snowmobiles, etc.: License required, restricted to roads.

Gate locked: NI.

Alcoholic drinks: NI.

Minors camping: At least one in group over eighteen years old or special permission from property manager.

Roadside camping: NI.

Energy problems: NI.

Camping facilities are at all sixteen parks, one beach, six out of seven recreation areas.

IOWA

State Conservation Commission, 300 4th Street, Des Moines, Iowa 50319

Location

Population centers: Irrelevant. Distribution is quite even throughout the state.

Natural features: "Upon the shores of lakes, streams, or other waters or at other places within the state which have become historical or which are of scientific interest, or which by reason of their natural scenic beauty of location are adopted therefore."

Physical Facilities

Acreage range: Parks from 442 to 1,600 (178 to 850 hectares); figures not given on all. One state forest, 5,000 (2,000 hectares).

Campsite terrain: Varied, mostly flat.

Tentsite ground: Grassy to lightly graveled.

Wood availability: For sale at 25¢ per bundle. Damaging trees prohibited. NI on gathering dead or down wood.

Fireplaces: Fire rings and waist-high.

Cabins: At seven parks; $10.00 per day, $50.00 per week; reservations required; open shelters at half.

Trailers: Same rate as camping. No full connections. Electrical connections at less than half. 50¢ extra for electricity, no water or sewer connections.

Motor homes: Same as trailers.

Transportation: Airstrips at three; no other forms.

Utilities

Toilets: Flush at two-thirds, chemical or privy at remainder.

Sanitary dumps: At one-quarter.

Water: Mostly piped. A few wells. Hot water at most with showers. Showers at two-thirds.

Electricity: See *Trailers.* A few additional parks have electric lighting.

Grocery, Ice: At few; *Restaurant:* At three, snack at most; *Gasoline;* No; *Laundry:* Tubs at few.

Activities

Museums: Not at any parks which allow camping.

Trails: Naturalist tours on request, self-guiding nature trails in two-thirds; hiking trails in three-quarters of the parks and two-thirds of the forests; horse trails in two areas.

Boating: At two-thirds. Motors prohibited at lakes under 100 acres, 6-horsepower or less at artificial lakes over 100 acres. No limit on motors on natural lakes. NI on boat rental but "boat and bait concessions" are at half of the parks.

Swimming: Supervised at one-third, unsupervised at one-fifth of the parks and one-third of the state areas under local government management. Supervised swimming fees 50¢ for over twelve years old, 25¢ for those under.

Fishing: At most of the parks and state areas under local government management, and at two-thirds of the forests. Ice fishing at most.

Hunting: At the one multiple-use area and all forests. Firearms prohibited in parks.

Horses: Trails in two parks and one forest; no rental.
Winter sports: Ice skating and sledding at one park, no formal facilities.
Playgrounds: None, "against concept of state parks."

Other Rules

Camping fee: $2.00 per night without showers, $2.50 per night with; 25¢ per person in excess of six. No charge in forests.
Time limit: Two weeks. One week in forests. Season starts from April 15 to May 1, ends between October 15 and November 1, depending on campground. Camping permitted in off season, but utilities are generally turned off. Checkout 3:00 P.M.
Reservations: No.
Fires outside fireplaces: Prohibited.
Pets: On leash or in vehicle only.
Motorcycles, trail scooters, snowmobiles, etc.: On roads only.
Gate locked: 10:30 P.M. to 4:00 A.M.
Alcoholic drinks: None permitted.
Minors camping: NI.
Roadside camping: NI.
Energy problems: People coming from shorter distances, but no changes contemplated.

Camping is permitted at fifty-one out of ninety-five state parks (including the only multiple-use area), at five out of eight state areas under local government management, and at three out of seven state forests.

The Commission publishes leaflets on individual parks and forests.

KANSAS

State Park and Resources Authority, 801 Harrison, Topeka, Kansas 66612.

Location

Population centers: NI.
Natural features: NI.

Physical Facilities

Acreage range: 493 to 2,733 (177 to 1,104 hectares); all but one below 1,700 (680 hectares).
Campsite terrain: NI.
Tentsite ground: NI.
Wood availability: NI.
Fireplaces: Mostly waist-high.
Cabins: NI.
Trailers: At one-third, connections at one-third of those.
Motor homes: Same as trailers.

Transportation: "Some" private aircraft facilities; no bus or rail service.

Utilities

Toilets: Flush at most. Some privy used between October and April.
Sanitary dumps: In all but two.
Water: Piped; NI on hot water; showers at all.
Electricity: At very few.
Grocery, Ice, Restaurants: NI, snacks at most; open varying lengths; *Gasoline, Laundry:* NI.

Activities

Museums: NI.
Trails: Nature trail at one park.
Boating: At all but two, marinas at half, rental at half.
Swimming: At all but one, in lake. Glass, metal, and plastic containers prohibited on beaches.
Fishing: At all. State license required. Fishing from boating docks or in swimming areas prohibited. Cleaning fish restricted to posted areas.
Hunting: Firearms, including air guns, prohibited.
Horses: Restricted to designated trails. NI on rental.
Playgrounds: At only one park.

Other Rules

Camping fee: $1.00 per day or $5.00-per-calendar-year vehicle permit. $1.50 per night camping charge at developed campsites.
Time limit: Two weeks.
Reservations: NI.
Fires outside fireplaces: Prohibited.
Pets: On leash. Not allowed anywhere on beaches.
Motorcycles, trail scooters, etc.: NI. *Snowmobiles:* Restricted.
Gate locked: NI; quiet time 11:00 P.M. to 6:00 A.M.
Alcoholic drinks: NI. Intoxication or drinking on beaches prohibited.
Minors camping: NI.
Roadside camping: Prohibited.
Energy problems: No changes planned because most of users are from fifty-mile (80 km) radius. Camping is permitted at all eighteen parks.

KENTUCKY

Department of Public Information, Capitol Annex Building, Frankfort, Kentucky 40601

Location

Population centers: NI on policy. Location is away from major cities.
Natural features: Of prime importance. Some are on artificial lakes.

Physical Facilities

Acreage range: 90 to 51,000. Only three are over 3,330.
Campsite terrain: NI. Photos show flat and wooded.
Tentsite ground: NI. Photos show natural ground.
Wood availability: Collection permitted. Some for sale.
Fireplaces: Indicated at over half. Photos show do-it-yourself, three-wall.
Cabins: Extensive supply at several parks. Rates vary with size. Cottage-type.
Trailers: At about half. No connections other than electricity. Fifty-foot combined length maximum.

Utilities

Toilets: Flush except at two primitive campgrounds. NI on these.
Water: Piped. Hot water and showers (hot) at all with flush toilets.
Electricity: At all except primitive camps. Free.
Grocery: At one-third. *Ice:* At two-thirds. *Restaurant:* At two-thirds. *Gasoline:* NI. *Laundry:* At six.

Activities

Museums: At one-third. Mostly historical.
Trails: Hiking trails at most. Naturalist-guided trails at one-quarter.
Boating: At most. Ramps at about half. Rental (including motors) at most of these. Fees vary with horsepower. Out-of-state boat registration honored.
Swimming: At most. Bathhouses at most of these. Mostly lake. NI on fees. Pools at resort lodges (probably for lodge guests only).
Fishing: At most. State license required.
Hunting: Prohibited.
Horses: Rental at over half. Own permitted.
Playgrounds: Directed recreation in summer at three-quarters.

Other Rules

Camping fee: $2.00 per day plus 25¢ per person when there are more than six. $1.00 per day at primitive camps with no extra charge when there are more than six.
Time limit: Two weeks. Season April through October.
Reservations: For cabins and lodges only.
Fires outside fireplaces: NI. Photos show only open fires.
Pets: On leash.
Motorcycles, trail scooters, etc.: "Probably [will be] prohibited."
Gate locked: No. No definite quiet time—"nine or ten."
Alcoholic drinks: Permitted.

Roadside camping: Tents prohibited. Almost fifteen per cent of the roadside parks have water and rest rooms, and about eight per cent have water only. The remainder are merely tables with trash facilities.

There are twenty-seven state parks, nineteen with established campgrounds and two more which permit primitive camping. There are airstrips at almost one-quarter.

LOUISIANA

State Parks and Recreation Commission, Drawer 1111, Baton Rouge, Louisiana 70821

Location

Population centers: Irrelevant.
Natural features: Major factor. Parks are spread fairly evenly through the state. Some are on artificial lakes.

Physical Facilities

Acreage range: NI.
Campsite terrain: NI. Photos show mostly wooded.
Tentsite ground: NI.
Wood availability: NI.
Fireplaces: "Pits."
Cabins: At most parks. $7.00 to $12.00 per night.
Trailers: Water and electrical connections.
Motor homes: Same as trailers.
Transportation: No.

Utilities

Toilets: Flush.
Sanitary dumps: Yes.
Water: Piped. Hot, NI. Showers present or under construction.
Electricity: At all sites, no extra charge (unless you have an air conditioner).
Grocery, Ice, Restaurant, Gasoline, Laundry: NI.

Activities

Museums: At one-third; mostly historical; 50¢ adult charge except for $1.00 at one.
Trails: Nature trails at at least two, NI on hiking.
Boating: At three-quarters. $1.00 launching fee. $1.50 per day rental. Launching from approved ramps only.
Swimming: At over half. Pool or lake. Charge for use of pools and/or bathhouses. Swimming at designated locations only.
Fishing: At most parks.
Hunting: Firearms prohibited.
Horses: NI.
Playgrounds: NI.

Other Rules

Camping fee: $3.00 per night ($4.00 with air conditioners).
Time limit: Two weeks.
Reservations: For cabins only.
Fires outside fireplaces: Prohibited.
Pets: Five-foot (152 cm) leash.
Motorcycles, trail scooters, etc.: NI.
Gate locked: NI.
Alcoholic drinks: NI.
Minors camping: At the discretion of the superintendent.
Roadside camping: NI. Information regarding fires, permits, etc., indicate it is prohibited.
Open Beach law: NI.
Energy problems: Less from out of state, but no changes are planned.

Camping is permitted at nine developed parks and two undeveloped ones out of twenty-two parks, monuments, and commemorative areas.

MAINE

Department of Conservation, State Office Building, Augusta, Maine 04330

Location

Population centers: State parks and forest campsites are located throughout the state. Forest campsites are in unorganized wilderness areas.
Natural features: Of prime importance—especially the state forest campgrounds, which are in the wilderness areas.

Physical Facilities

Acreage range: 55 to 201,018 (22 to 81,274 hectares); next smallest is 5,004 (2,000 ha); most are between 175 and 1,000 (70 and 400 ha).
Campsite terrain: Mostly wooded. Some open. NI on terrain. Photos show flat.
Tentsite ground: Natural soil.
Wood availability: For sale at a few.
Fireplaces: Usually rock or concrete block three-wall, waist-high.
Cabins: In one, $4.00 per person per night. A few Adirondack shelters in some others.
Trailers: One park limits trailers to nine feet (2.73 m) high, seven feet (2.12 m) wide, and twenty-two feet (6.67 m) long or a forty-four-foot (8.35 m) combined length. NI on others.
Motor homes: Length requirement same as trailers.
Transportation: NI.

Utilities

Toilets: Mostly vented pit or chemical; some flush.
Sanitary dumps: NI.
Water: Mostly piped. Some hot water and hot showers.
Electricity: NI.
Grocery: NI. *Ice:* NI. *Restaurant:* Snack at some.
Gasoline, Laundry: NI.

Activities

Museums: No.
Trails: Extensive trail system at Baxter (largest); naturalist tour at two, hiking at many.
Boating: Ramps at most. Rentals at some, $1.00 per hour or $4.00 per day.
Swimming: At about half. Lake or ocean. Lifeguards at some. No extra charge for campers.
Fishing: At most. Fresh and salt water. Nonresident license required for over sixteen years old fishing in fresh water, from $6.50 for three days to $15.50 per season.
Hunting: Specific parts of one park only; prohibited elsewhere.
Horses: None.
Winter sports: NI.
Playgrounds: At some.

Other Rules

Camping fee: $2.50–$4.50 in season, $2.00 off season. Baxter $1.00 per person, $2.00 minimum.
Time limit: Two weeks; season May to between October and December, closed in off-season.
Reservations: Baxter only.
Fires outside fireplaces: Permits only.
Pets: Prohibited at two, "suitable restraint" at others.
Motorcycles, trail scooters, etc.: Prohibited at Baxter, restricted at others; *Snowmobiles:* NI.
Gate locked: 10:00 P.M. to 6:00 A.M. at Baxter; 11:00 P.M. to 7:00 A.M. at others.
Alcoholic drinks: No.
Minors camping: One adult per five at Baxter, one per eight at others.
Roadside camping: NI.
Open Beach law: NI.
Energy problems: NI.

Camping is permitted in fourteen of the twenty-five parks. In addition, there are 175 Bureau of Forestry campsites in unorganized areas, many accessible only by water or trail. These have fireplace, table, and privy.

The department publishes a Forest Campsites brochure and the Department of Commerce and Industry publishes "vacation planners" on parks, historical sites, hiking, canoeing, etc.

MARYLAND

Department of Natural Resources, Maryland Park Service, Tawes State Office Building, 580 Taylor Avenue, Annapolis, Maryland 21401

Location

Population centers: Widely dispersed through the state but still within four and a half hours drive from the Washington-Baltimore metropolitan area.
Natural features: Prime consideration is the ability of the area to support the type of recreational facilities offered. Historical significance, danger of destruction by suburban expansion, highway construction, existing highways, natural beaches, etc. are also factors.

Physical Facilities

Acreage range: 99 to 9,923 (40 to 4,000 hectares); most 350 to 3,000 (141 to 1,200 hectares).
Campsite terrain: Varies, most wooded.
Tentsite ground: Natural and improved.
Wood availability: For sale. NI on collection.
Fireplaces: Mostly three-wall and stone fire rings. Some waist-high, but they are restricted to charcoal only.
Cabins: At a few. Cottage-type. NI on fees.
Trailers: Twenty-three foot (8.96 m) total combined length; no connections.
Motor homes: NI.
Transportation: No.

Utilities

Toilets: Flush at most; privy in unimproved areas.
Sanitary dumps: At a few.
Water: Piped at parks, hot water at most, showers at all "improved."
Electricity: No.
Grocery, Ice, Restaurant: snack at one-third; *Laundry:* tubs at improved sites.

Activities

Museums: Historical at five.
Trails: Naturalist tours at two-thirds, self-guiding same. Hiking trails at two-thirds.
Boating: At over half; rental at one-third; motors prohibited at a few.
Swimming: At over one-third, some pools, NI on charge.
Fishing: At almost all. State license required of all over sixteen for fresh water.
Hunting: Permitted in nine parks; state and Park Service licenses required.
Horses: No.
Winter sports: No organized winter sport facilities. Ice skating at a few. Cross-country ski and snow-mobile trails in state forests in western part of state.
Playgrounds: At all parks. NI on type.

Other Rules

Camping fee: $3.50 for improved ($4.00 at Assateague $2.00 for unimproved.
Time limit: Two weeks. Season from April 15 to October 31. Camping permitted out of season, but no water or toilet facilities are available. A few campgrounds are winterized and permit year 'round use of facilities. Checkout 3:00 P.M.
Reservations: At three parks, for one week between last week of May and mid-September. One week per park per season maximum. $1.00 reservation fee plus $7.00 ($8.00 at Assateague) nonrefundable deposit.
Fires outside fireplaces: Prohibited.
Pets: Prohibited.
Motorcycles, trail scooters, snowmobiles, etc.: All off-road vehicles prohibited.
Gate locked: No. Camp must be erected between 9:00 A.M. and 10:00 P.M. Quiet time 11:00 P.M. to 7:00 A.M.
Alcoholic drinks: Prohibited to minors.
Minors camping: Minimum sixteen years old and maximum of four per campsite.
Roadside camping: Prohibited.
Open Beach law: NI.
Energy problems: NI.

Camping is permitted at fourteen improved parks and four unimproved parks out of thirty-two operational parks in the system.

Pamphlets are available for individual state parks.

MASSACHUSETTS

Department of Natural Resources, Division of Forests and Parks, Leverett Saltonstall Building, Government Center, 100 Cambridge Street, Boston, Massachusetts 02202

Location

Population centers: NI.
Natural features: NI.

Physical Facilities

Acreage range: NI.
Campsite terrain: NI.
Tentsite ground: NI.
Wood availability: NI.
Fireplaces: NI. Photo shows do-it-yourself.
Cabins: At three. One room $6.00, three rooms $8.00, electricity 50¢ extra per day.

Trailers: Only if it can fit space. $4.00 with water and sewer, at one park only.
Motor homes: Same as trailers.
Transportation: No direct service, but bus service near some eastern parks.

Utilities

Toilets: Flush at most, unstated other at one-quarter.
Sanitary Dump: NI.
Water: Piped at most, NI on rest; Showers at most.
Electricity: NI.
Grocery, Ice, Restaurant, Gasoline, Laundry: NI.

Activities

Museums: NI.
Trails: Hiking and horse at most, recreational vehicle trails at almost all.
Boating: At over half; registration required of those over 5 horsepower.
Swimming: At almost all; designated areas only.
Fishing: All but two; third Sunday in April to February twenty-eighth next year; $14.25 per season, $8.25 for seven days; all fifteen and over require license.
Hunting: At all but three; $16.26 for fifteen years old and older, those 15 to 17 must pass test; bow deer-hunting license $5.10 extra.
Horses: At most, NI on rental.
Winter sports: Cross-country skiing at four-fifths; NI on other forms.
Playgrounds: NI.

Other Rules

Camping fee: $4.00 per day with sewer and water connections (at one park); $3.00 with flush toilets and showers (at most); $2.00 without flush toilets (at one quarter); $1.00 at backpacking campsites; $1.00 car parking fee.
Time limit: Two weeks in season; season last Saturday in June to Saturday before Labor Day; pay for intended length of stay, reregister (for longer) by 5:00 day before end, checkout time (and for refund if cutting stay short) 1:00.
Reservations: No.
Fires outside fireplaces: No.
Pets: Leash or cage; horses in designated areas; no animals in swimming areas or unattended in campsite.
Motorcycles, trail scooters, snowmobiles, etc.: Designated trails only; snowmobiles in daylight only except at few areas.
Gate locked: NI; quiet time: 10:00 P.M. to 7:00 A.M.
Alcoholic drinks: NI.
Minors camping: Family units only (except in group camps one adult to ten minors) except by advanced permission of supervisor. Children twelve and under may not be left unattended.
Roadside camping: NI.
Open Beach law: NI.
Energy problems: No changes yet, but it may result in reduction or curtailment of winter camping activity (camping is permitted only when rest room facilities can be operated) and some fee increase for electrical outlets at campsite.

There are ninety parks in the system, of which twenty-six permit camping.

MICHIGAN

Department of Natural Resources, Park Division, Lansing, Michigan 48926

Location

Population centers: NI.
Natural features: NI.

Physical Facilities

Acreage range: 32 to 58,323 (13 to 24,062 hectares); most below 5,000 (2,000 hectares).
Campsite terrain: NI.
Tentsite ground: NI.
Wood availability: Concessionaire.
Fireplaces: NI.
Cabins: In two, but not state operated.
Trailers: NI.
Motor homes: NI.
Transportation: NI.

Utilities

Toilets: Flush at three-quarters, privy at over half.
Sanitary dump: At a few.
Water: Piped at most; hot showers at most.
Electricity: At three-quarters.
Grocery: At a few developed parks. *Grocery, Ice:* NI. *Restaurant:* Snack at over half. *Gasoline, Laundry:* NI.

Activities

Museums: At five parks. Outdoor centers at a few parks and half the recreation areas.
Trails: Hiking trails at over half; park naturalist at one-quarter; horse trails at six.
Boating: Launching at over half; rental at one-third (NI on notes); canoeing at half.
Swimming: At two-thirds.
Fishing: At most.
Hunting: At half.
Horses: At very few; NI on rental.
Winter sports: Cross-country trails at very few; power vehicles (including snowmobiles) excluded from several.
Playgrounds: At most.

Other Rules

Camping fee: $1.00 per day or $5.00 per year entry fee; camping fee $3.00 per day with electrical service at site, $2.00 at those with flush toilets and no electricity or vented pit toilets and electricity, $1.50 no facilities or in backpacking campsites.

Time limit: Fifteen days in season (June 15th to Labor Day). Checkout 3:00 P.M.

Reservations: In season only; at least four nights, maximum fifteen; $2.00 plus total cost of camping fee for duration of stay plus entry fee, paid on arrival.

Fires outside fireplaces: No.

Pets: Dogs on six-foot (182 cm) leash, none unattended; prohibited on beaches.

Motorcycles, trail scooters, etc.: Prohibited in "quiet areas"; NI elsewhere.

Gate locked: NI. Quiet time 10:00 P.M. to 7:00 A.M.

Alcoholic drinks: NI.

Roadside camping: Prohibited.

Minors camping: NI.

Energy problems: Coming from shorter distances, no plans.

Camping is permitted at 75 out of 79 parks, and almost 600 water-access sites.

The Department distributes an American Automobile Association book of campgrounds in the state.

MINNESOTA

Minnesota Department of Natural Resources, Centennial Office Building, St. Paul, Minnesota 55155

Location

Population centers: NI. Distribution is fairly even.

Natural features: NI. Most are along rivers or lakes.

Physical Facilities

Acreage range: 31 to 29,124 (31 to 11,766 hectares); most between 200 and 3,00 (80 to 1,200 hectares).

Campsite terrain: NI.

Tentsite ground: NI.

Wood availability: Bundled wood for sale "where available." NI on cost or collection.

Fireplaces: "Usually well marked and may have a grill."

Cabins: NI on number, but some present.

Trailers: Permitted, but no connections.

Motor homes: NI.

Transportation: NI.

Utilities

Toilets: Flush at half, rest vented pit; "primitive" at state recreation areas and state forest campgrounds.

Sanitary dumps: At one-third of parks.

Water: Available at all. Hot water and showers at half of parks. NI on hot showers.

Electricity: 50¢ per day per outlet.

Grocery, Ice, Restaurant, Gasoline: NI. *Laundry:* At half of parks, NI on type.

Activities

Museums: At one-eighth of parks.

Trails: Nature trails at over half of the parks. Hiking trails at almost half.

Boating: At almost half of the parks, one-third of the forests. Rental at one-quarter. NI on type or restrictions.

Swimming: At less than half of the parks, one-third of the forests. NI on type, presumably lake.

Fishing: At over three-quarters of parks (evenly divided, stream and lake).

Hunting: NI.

Horses: At three parks.

Winter sports: NI.

Playgrounds: NI.

Other Rules

Camping fee: $3.00 per night plus $3.00 per year or $2.00 per two days Motor Vehicle Permit sticker.

Time limit: Two weeks per park. Emergency camping in parks not having regular camp areas.

Reservations: No.

Fires outside fireplaces: Not permitted.

Pets: On six-foot (182 cm) leash and attended.

Motorcycles, trail scooters, etc.: Not on trails. *Snowmobiles:* NI.

Gate locked: Not locked; closed 10:00 P.M. to 8:00 A.M.

Alcoholic drinks: NI.

Minors camping: NI.

Roadside camping: NI. State parks are close enough together to enable camper to reach one for emergency camping.

Energy problems: NI.

Camping is permitted at forty-three out of eighty-seven state parks, all twenty-two state forest campgrounds, one out of eight wayside parks, and three out of five state recreation areas.

A municipal and private campground directory is published by the Division of State Parks.

MISSISSIPPI

Mississippi Park Commission, 717 Robert E. Lee Building, Jackson, Mississippi 39201

Location

Populction centers: NI. Appear to be fairly evenly distributed.
Natural features: NI. Pictures show considerable natural beauty.

Physical Facilities

Acreage range: 200 to 2,442 (80 to 987 hectares), fairly evenly distributed. Island park was recently destroyed in a hurricane and will probably be used only for a wildlife refuge with no camping, because of upkeep costs.
Campsite terrain: NI.
Tentsite ground: Natural soil.
Wood availability: For sale (NI on charge). Collection prohibited.
Fireplaces: Three-wall.
Cabins: At all parks, $20.00 to $40.00 per weekend, $60.00 to $90.00 per week.
Trailers: At all parks, one historic site.
Motor homes: NI.
Transportation: NI.

Utilities

Toilets: Flush.
Sanitary dumps: NI.
Water: Piped. Hot water, NI. Showers.
Electricity: Being installed. 50¢.
Grocery: Concession stands at all. *Ice:* At most. *Restaurant:* NI. *Gasoline:* At most, NI on type. *Laundry:* Being built, NI on type.

Activities

Museums: No.
Trails: Being developed for hiking.
Boating: At all parks, one historic site; rental $2.00 per day, launching $1.00 for 10 hp or less, $2.00 for over.
Swimming: At all but one park, at one historic site; children under twelve 25¢, adults 50¢, free to those in cabins and group camps.
Fishing: At all parks and one historic site; "up to 25¢ per day."
Hunting: Prohibited.
Horses: Prohibited.
Playgrounds: No.

Other Rules

Camping fee: $2.50; $3.00 with electricity.
Time limit: Two weeks.
Reservations: No.
Fires outside fireplaces: NI.
Pets: On five-foot (1.5 m) leash.
Motorcycles, trail scooters, etc.: No restrictions until trails are built.

Gate locked: No.
Alcoholic drinks: Prohibited.
Minors camping: NI.
Roadside camping: Permitted.
Open Beach law: No.
Energy problems: NI.
   Camping is permitted at all fourteen parks and at one of the four historical sites.

MISSOURI

   Missouri State Park Board, Box 176, Jefferson City, Missouri 65101

Location

Population centers: NI. Map shows them fairly removed.
Natural features: Important.

Physical Facilities

Acreage range: 38 to 16,335. Most are between 75 and 6,000.
Campsite terrain: NI. Photos show level ground and fairly heavy woods.
Tentsite ground: NI. Photos show natural soil and turf. (This state was the site of my first encounter with cobblestone paving for tentsites.)
Wood availability: For sale, 25¢ per bundle.
Fireplaces: Three-wall and two-wall. Waist-high.
Cabins: At one-fifth. NI on fees.
Trailers: Full connections at one-fifth. $1.50 per day. Dumps at less than half.

Utilities

Toilets: At all. Flush.
Water: Piped. Hot water at all. Showers at all (or under construction) with hot at most.
Electricity: At one-third. 25¢ per day.
Grocery: At almost one-half. *Ice:* NI. *Restaurant:* At one-third. *Gasoline:* NI. *Laundry:* Coin-operated at most.

Activities

Museums: Nature at two, one with naturalist. Archeological digs and similar points of historical interest outside museum setting at a few others.
Trails: Nature trails at almost two-thirds.
Boating: At less than half. Horsepower restrictions on a few. Some rental.
Swimming: At two-thirds. One-tenth in pools, rest in streams. (Many of the streams are cold-spring fed and are uncomfortable except in summer heat.)
Fishing: At most. State license required of all over sixteen.

Hunting: Prohibited. Possession of firearms is considered evidence of intent.

Horses: Rental at one-fifth. Use restricted to designated areas.

Winter sports: Ice boating at one.

Playgrounds: At a few.

Other Rules

Camping fee: $1.00 per unit per day. Check-out time, 3:00 P.M.

Time limit: Fifteen days. Camping permitted year 'round, but water and toilets available only between April 15th and October 31st.

Reservations: No.

Fires outside fireplaces: Prohibited. No fires at all after 10:00 P.M.

Pets: On ten-foot (3 m) leash.

Motorcycles, trail scooters, etc.: Prohibited.

Gate locked: No.

Alcoholic drinks: Permitted.

Roadside camping: "Frowned upon."

Camping is permitted at thirty-one out of thirty-seven state parks. There is an airstrip at one park.

MONTANA

Department of Fish and Game, Division of Recreation and Parks, Helena, Montana 59601

Location

Population centers: Within reasonable distance of population centers.

Natural features: Mostly of prime importance. Some are located on artificial lakes. Camping is permitted at two state monuments (historic reason highest).

Physical Facilities

Acreage range: 1 to 2,800 ($\frac{1}{2}$ to 1,131 hectares). hectares).

Campsite terrain: From harsh barren areas to heavily wooded.

Tentsite ground: Natural soil.

Wood availability: Not generally available.

Fireplaces: Three-wall plus waist-high.

Cabins: At one park.

Trailers: Permitted. No connections.

Motor homes: NI.

Transportation: NI.

Utilities

Toilets: Chemical. Flush beginning to be installed.

Sanitary dumps: NI.

Water: "Mostly from wells." Hot water in two parks, no wells.

Electricity: None.

Grocery: No. *Ice, Restaurant, Gasoline, Laundry:* NI. In one recreation area.

Activities

Museums: Two.

Trails: Self-guiding in six recreation areas.

Boating: At over half. Ramps at most. Boat rental at concession areas in two parks.

Swimming: At about half. Mostly lake. Some river.

Fishing: At over half.

Hunting: Not permitted.

Horses: Restricted; no rental.

Winter sports: None.

Playgrounds: At two.

Other Rules

Camping fee: Ranges from $1.00 to $2.00 per vehicle or $10.00 per season.

Time limit: Fourteen days. Season May 1 through September 30.

Reservations: No.

Fires outside fireplaces: Prohibited.

Pets: On leash.

Motorcycles, trail scooters, etc.: "Restricted."

Gate locked: No.

Alcoholic drinks: Permitted.

Minors camping: NI.

Roadside camping: Prohibited.

Energy problems: NI.

Camping is permitted at twenty out of twenty-one parks and at two out of five monuments under state authority.

NEBRASKA

Nebraska Game and Parks Commission, Lincoln, Nebraska 68509

Location

Population centers: Irrelevant.

Natural features: A major factor. State parks have substantial part of their acreage in a "relatively undisturbed state." State recreation areas are primarily for heavy daytime recreational use, but camping is permitted at most. State wayside areas are roadside parks. Special-use areas are mostly game management areas.

Physical Facilities

Acreage range: 3 to 6,726 (1 and $\frac{1}{2}$ to 2,576 hectares) land, 0 to 34,700 (13,918 hectares) water; most at lower end of both scales.

Campsite terrain: NI.

Tentsite ground: NI.

Wood availability: Free and available at most campgrounds.

Fireplaces: Fire rings, waist-high, or metal three-wall.

Cabins: Concessionaire-operated at two, state-operated at five; NI on rates.

Trailers: Special areas at eight parks. NI on connections. Those over forty feet (12.14 m) long or eight feet (2.43 m) wide require highway permits.

Motor homes: NI.

Transportation: NI.

Utilities

Toilets: All but two permitting camping; NI on type.

Sanitary dumps: At four.

Water: "Drinking water" at all, NI on system; showers at a few.

Electricity: 50¢ per night extra.

Grocery, Ice, Restaurant, Gasoline, Laundry: NI. "Concessions" at fifteen.

Activities

Museums: At three.

Trails: Hiking at all.

Boating: Nonpower only at one-third, all types at over half; 5 mph (8 km/h) speed limit at three; rental at five, NI on rates.

Swimming: Unsupervised at half, supervised at five.

Fishing: At all but three.

Hunting: Varies with area and time.

Horses: At four.

Playgrounds: NI.

Winter sports: NI.

Other Rules

Camping fee: $1.00 to $2.00 per night at ten grounds, free at rest.

Time limit: Fourteen days in any thirty-day period; two days in wayside areas; NI on checkout.

Reservations: Yes; contact local park superintendent.

Fires outside fireplaces: NI.

Pets: On leash and under physical restraint. Health certificates required for dogs and cats brought into state.

Motorcycles, trail scooters, etc.: NI.

Gate locked: NI.

Alcoholic drinks: Prohibited, as is intoxication.

Minors camping: NI.

Roadside camping: At all but one wayside area. $2.50 at two, primitive (no facilities) at two others).

Energy problems: NI.

Camping facilities are at four of five state parks (primitive camping at the fifth); sixty-one of sixty-four recreation areas (two of the remainder with primitive camping); and eighteen of twenty-three wayside areas (two of the remainder primitive).

NEVADA

Department of Conservation and Natural Resources, Nevada State Park System, 201 S. Fall Street, Nye Building, Room 221, Carson City, Nevada 89701

Location

Population centers: Irrelevant.

Natural features: Important. Historical significance has equal influence.

Physical Facilities

Acreage range: 2½ to 34,000 (1 to 13,817 hectares); smallest with camping 40 (sixteen ha), rest over 200 (eighty ha).

Campsite terrain: NI. Photos show park terrain varies widely.

Tentsite ground: Coarse gravel topped with fine gravel, river gravel, or pea gravel and clay mix.

Wood availability: For sale. Bringing own advised.

Fireplaces: Three-wall.

Cabins: None.

Trailers: No connections.

Motor homes: NI.

Transportation: NI.

Utilities

Toilets: Flush at three, vented pit at rest.

Sanitary dumps: NI.

Water: Some piped, some spring, some NI. Hot water and showers at one. NI on hot showers.

Electricity: No.

Grocery, Ice, Restaurant, Gasoline, Laundry: None.

Activities

Museums: Historical at two. Nature center at another.

Trails: Hiking trails at three.

Boating: At seven, no rentals.

Swimming: At half.

Fishing: At seven, state license required.

Hunting: No. Firearms prohibited except during open season in vicinity.

Horses: Prohibited at most.

Winter sports: NI.

Playgrounds: No.

Other Rules

Camping fee: $2.00 per night.

Time limit: Fourteen days per season per party per park.

Reservations: No.
Fires outside fireplaces: Prohibited.
Pets: On six-foot (182 cm) leash.
Motorcycles, trail scooters, etc.: All vehicles restricted to roads and parking lots only. *Snowmobiles:* NI.
Gate locked: No. Quiet time 10:00 P.M. to 7:00 A.M.
Alcoholic drinks: NI.
Minors camping: NI.
Roadside camping: Prohibited.
Energy problems: Increase in use of those close to urban areas with a decrease in use of those in remote spots; drop in nonresident use; no plans for changes in facilities.

Because most of the state parks are off paved highways, the Department urges travelers to check on the conditions of the roads before attempting to reach a park. Also, desert-driving provisions (food, water, fuel, etc.) should be carried.

There are sixteen state parks, thirteen of which have camping facilities.

The Department publishes leaflets on individual parks.

NEW HAMPSHIRE

Department of Resources and Economic Development, Division of Parks, Concord, New Hampshire 03301

Location

Population centers: NI. While state parks are more numerous in the populated southern part of the state, few of them permit camping. Parks permitting camping are fairly removed from population centers.
Natural features: NI. Descriptions seem to emphasize natural features.

Physical Facilities

Acreage range: Listed acreage ranges from 300 to 6,552 (121 to 2,647 hectares), with smaller ones not permitting camping. However, acreage figures were omitted for most of the parks.
Campsite terrain: Wooded. Photos show flat terrain.
Tentsite ground: NI. Photos show natural soil with sparse or worn grass.
Wood availability: "Available at all campgrounds." NI on details.
Fireplaces: NI. Photos show a free-standing cast-iron grill with large rocks around it on two or three sides.
Cabins: No.
Trailers: No connections. Permitted "only if they fit conveniently into available tentsites. There are no special facilities for them."

Motor homes: Same as trailers.
Transportation: NI.

Utilities

Toilets: Flush.
Sanitary dumps: NI.
Water: Piped. NI on hot water or showers.
Electricity: NI. Probably not, considering trailer situation.
Grocery: "Bread and milk" at one. "Limited provisions" at another. *Ice:* At one-third. *Restaurant:* At one. Refreshment stands at one-third. *Gasoline:* NI. *Laundry:* At one, NI on type.

Activities

Museums: Nature centers at one-fifth.
Trails: Hiking trails at three-quarters.
Boating: At half. Rentals at one-quarter. NI on fees or type of boats. Unlimited power at one. "Trolling speed" at one-third, no motors at rest.
Swimming: At two-thirds.
Fishing: At two-thirds. State license required.
Hunting: NI.
Horses: NI.
Winter sports: Downhill and cross-country skiing at one. Snowmobile trail at one.
Playgrounds: NI.

Other Rules

Camping fee: Varies from $2.50 to $4.00 for state residents, $3.00 to $5.00 for nonresidents; NI on primitive areas.
Time limit: Two weeks.
Reservations: No.
Fires outside fireplaces: Permit required, including for camp stoves.
Pets: On leash. Prohibited at beaches and in water.
Motorcycles, trail scooters, etc.: NI.
Gate locked: NI.
Alcoholic drinks: NI.
Minors camping: NI.
Open Beach law: NI. Three parks (not permitting camping) are on the coast.
Energy problems: NI.

The Department publishes a pamphlet listing privately-owned campgrounds in the state, and a snowmobiler's guide is published by the Bureau of Off Highway Vehicles (same address as Parks), which give the finer details of regulations of these vehicles.

NEW JERSEY

Department of Environmental Protection, Division of Parks and Forestry, Bureau of Parks, Box 1420, Trenton, New Jersey 08625

Location

Population centers: NI.
Natural features: Of prime importance. None in heavily urbanized areas.

Physical Facilities

Acreage range: 80 to 99,639 (32 to 40,256 hectares); most in 1,000 to 10,000 (400 to 4,000 hectares) range.
Campsite terrain: Wooded and level.
Tentsite ground: Mostly grassed or natural soil.
Wood availability: "Not furnished." Charcoal for sale at some parks. Bringing own advised.
Fireplaces: Mostly three-wall. Some fire rings and waist-high.
Cabins: At six, $10.00 to $18.00 per night.
Trailers: At all forests and all but one park. No connections.
Motor homes: NI.
Transportation: NI.

Utilities

Toilets: Flush at most, "pit" at rest.
Sanitary dumps: NI.
Water: Piped at over half, pump at rest.
Electricity: NI.
Grocery, Ice, Restaurant, Gasoline: NI. *Laundry:* At two forests.

Activities

Museums: At some.
Trails: Hiking at most, naturalists at half, nature area at over half, horse trails at one-third.
Boating: At all, over half for boats without motors. Ramps $1.00. Rental at a third, 75¢ per hour or $3.00 per day for canoes, hourly only on holidays and weekends.
Swimming: At half.
Fishing: At almost all, no breakdown into fresh and salt water.
Hunting: Not in parks, but permitted in other areas.
Horses: Trails, but NI on rental.
Winter sports: NI.
Playgrounds: At most parks and forests. NI on type.

Other Rules

Camping fee: $2.50 or $3.50 per night.
Time limit: Forty days; checkout 3:00 P.M.
Reservations: One-third of sites between June 15 and Labor Day, for seven-or fourteen-day period (if space is available, may be extended to forty-day total), nonrefundable reservation fee $3.00 to Treasurer, State of New Jersey.
Fires outside fireplaces: Prohibited.

Pets: Prohibited.
Motorcycles, trail scooters, snowmobiles, etc.: NI. One forest has a wilderness area accessible by off-the-road-type vehicles.
Gate locked: NI. Quiet time 10:00 P.M. to 7:00 A.M.
Alcoholic drinks: Prohibited.
Minors camping: NI.
Roadside camping: Prohibited.
Open Beach law: No.
Energy problems: NI.
Camping facilities are at seven of nineteen parks, seven of ten forests, and two of three recreation areas.

NEW MEXICO

Department of Development, State of New Mexico, State Capitol, Santa Fe, New Mexico 87501

Location

Population centers: Irrelevant.
Natural features: Some have unique features. Other are located at large artificial lakes.

Physical Facilities

Acreage range: 19 to 5,000 land and 17,000 water. water.
Campsite terrain: NI. Photos show some woods, much in desert.
Tentsite ground: NI. Photos show natural soil.
Wood availability: NI. Probably not available at desert campgrounds.
Fireplaces: NI. None visible in photos.
Cabins: At several parks. Range from Adirondack to cottage-type. NI on fees.
Trailers: Connections at some parks. NI on fees.

Utilities

Toilets: Flush.
Water: Piped. Hot water and showers at Destination Resort types, NI on others.
Electricity: See *Camping fee.*
Grocery: At most parks. *Ice:* NI. *Restaurant:* At Destination Resorts. *Gasoline, Laundry:* NI. Most parks are reasonably close to a fair-sized town.

Activities

Museums: One historical.
Trails: NI.
Boating: $3.00 per calendar year under 10-horsepower, $5.00 for over. $1.00 per day for all types. For rent on most lakes. One natural lake has rowboats, pedal-boats, and kayaks for rent (NI on using your own).

Swimming: Destination Resorts usually have pools. Others use lake, or no swimming facilities are available.
Fishing: At artificial lakes. State license required.
Hunting: NI.
Horses: Several parks have saddle horses for rent. NI on using your own.
Winter sports: No facilities.
Playgrounds: At most parks. NI on type.

Other Rules

Camping fee: $1.00 per day and $5.00 per week without electricity, $1.50 and $7.50 with electricity. Organized youth groups free.
Time limit: Fifteen days.
Reservations: No.
Fires outside fireplaces: NI.
Pets: "Restricted in such a manner that they do not run loose."
Motorcycles, trail scooters, etc.: NI.
Gate locked: NI.
Alcoholic drinks: NI. However, cocktail lounges would indicate permission in Destination Resorts at least.
Roadside camping: Permitted. (Same paragraph in literature mentions that "carrying firearms is permitted in cars but not on person.")
Rock Hound State Park permits limited collection of agate.
Camping is permitted at all twenty-one state parks.
The Department publishes booklets on publicly owned campgrounds, boys' and girls' camps, golf courses, guest ranches, mountain lodges, and resorts in the state.

NEW YORK

State of New York Conservation Department, Division of Parks, State Campus Site, Albany, New York 12226

Location

Population centers: Parks located close to population centers do not permit camping.
Natural features: Of prime importance.

Physical Facilities

Acreage range: 10 (an island) to 2,294,853 (Adirondack Forest Preserve). Most are fairly small (under 1,500).
Campsite terrain: NI. Most photos show dense woodlands.
Tentsite ground: NI.
Wood availability: NI. Since most heavy-use areas prohibit camping, it should not be a problem.

Fireplaces: NI.
Cabins: Mostly in Finger Lakes region. Cottage-type, one to four rooms. Adirondack shelters throughout system.
Trailers: Electrical connections only. Mostly in Finger Lakes, Thousand Islands, and Central region.

Utilities

Toilets: Mostly flush. Some privy and do-it-yourself at wilderness areas and canoe regions.
Water: Piped. NI on hot water. Showers available.
Electricity: Mostly for trailers only.
Grocery: At a few. *Ice:* NI. *Restaurant:* Most have refreshment stands. *Gasoline:* NI. *Laundry:* At very few, almost all in Central region.

Activities

Museums: A few.
Trails: A few self-guiding nature trails, mostly in Finger Lakes and Palisades regions. Most parks have hiking trails.
Boating: Several parks have boats for rent. A few (mostly in Central, Allegheny, and Forest Recreation regions) have canoes for rent. Several have launching ramps for 50¢ fee. A few canoe routes.
Swimming: A few pools. Mostly beaches (ocean or lake). NI on fees. Swimming not permitted after dark.
Fishing: At almost all parks. State license required.
Hunting: NI. Firearms prohibited except during hunting season.
Horses: Trails at very few. Rental in only two parks.
Winter sports: At a total of twelve parks, skiing at seven, skating at seven, tobogganing at two, bobsled run at one.
Playgrounds: NI. Athletic fields at practically all parks over twenty-five acres.

Other Rules

Camping fee: $1.50 per night. 50¢ for additional vehicle with same party.
Time limit: Two weeks from the Saturday before July 4th through Labor Day. Period begins at 3:00 P.M. on day of arrival and ends at 11:00 A.M. on date of expiration. Camping season Memorial Day to mid-September.
Reservations: For group camps only.
Fires outside fireplaces: Prohibited. In fuel-scarce areas, restricted to cooking and anti-insect smudge only.
Pets: Restricted to leash and tentsite area of owner.
Motorcycles, trail scooters, etc.: NI.
Gate locked: NI. Quiet time 10:00 P.M. to 7:00 A.M.
Alcoholic drinks: Prohibited on beaches. NI on rest.
Boys camping in a group must include one who is at least eighteen; girls must be accompanied by

one who is married and over twenty-one or unmarried and over twenty-five.

Glass is prohibited at beaches.

There are over 100 camping areas in the system, some of which offer more than one campground.

Pamphlets are published by the Department covering individual parks and forests by regions.

NORTH CAROLINA

Department of Conservation and Development, Travel and Promotion Division, Raleigh, North Carolina 27611

Location

Population centers: Irrelevant.
Natural features: NI. Of considerable importance at several parks without camping.

Physical Facilities

Acreage range: 572 to 17,360 (231 to 7,013 hectares).
Campsite terrain: NI. Photos show flat and wooded.
Tentsite ground: NI. Photos show natural soil worn bare.
Wood availability: At some parks, small fee.
Fireplaces: One for each tentsite, three-wall.
Cabins: At two campgrounds. $65.00 per week.
Trailers: No connections. Not permitted at one (mountain top).
Motor homes: Same as trailers.
Transportation: NI.

Utilities

Toilets: Flush.
Sanitary dumps: At three.
Water: Piped, with showers. NI on hot water.
Electricity: No.
Grocery, Ice: NI. *Restaurant:* Refreshment stands at all but one campground. *Gasoline:* No. *Laundry:* Washtubs.

Activities

Museums: At two campgrounds and some other parks.
Trails: Both nature and hiking trails at five parks, more at other parks not permitting camping. Naturalist tours in the summer are listed at six parks.
Boating: At most. Several for rent. Permit required.
Swimming: Three campgrounds permit swimming in lakes, at designated areas only.
Fishing: At most. State license required.
Hunting: Firearms prohibited.
Horses: At designated areas only.

Playgrounds: NI. Athletics in designated areas only.

Other Rules

Camping fee: $2.50 per day per campsite plus 50¢ per person in excess of four (limit six per site).
Time limit: Two weeks. Season about April 1st to November 1st.
Reservations: For one or two weeks only, camping fee in advance.
Fires outside fireplaces: Prohibited.
Pets: Dogs only, on six-foot (182 cm) leash; no other types of pets.
Motorcycles, trail scooters, etc.: On regular roads only.
Gate locked: 8:00 to 9:00 P.M. closing time (depending on month), 8:00 A.M. opening. Quiet time 10:00 P.M. to 6:00 A.M.
Alcoholic drinks: Prohibited.
Minors camping: One adult per group.
Roadside camping: Prohibited, but roadside rest areas system for picnicking offers toilets and drinking water.
Open Beach law: NI.
Energy problems: NI.

There are camping facilities at nine out of twenty state parks. Camping is permitted (but there are no facilities) at two more.

A directory of privately and publicly owned campgrounds is published by the Department.

NORTH DAKOTA

North Dakota Travel Department, State Capitol Building, Bismark, North Dakota 58501

Location

Population centers: Irrelevant.
Natural features: Of major importance. Historical importance in some.

Physical Facilities

Acreage range: NI on state parks. 54 to 5,178 in Game Management Areas, which permit camping but have no facilities.
Campsite terrain: NI.
Tentsite ground: NI.
Wood availability: NI.
Fireplaces: NI except that all parks have them.
Cabins: NI.
Trailers: Sixty-foot limit. NI on fees or connections.

Utilities

Toilets: Present at all parks. NI on type.
Water: "Drinking H$_2$O" at all parks, NI on system. NI on hot water or showers.

Electricity: At only one, NI on fees.
Grocery, Ice, Restaurant, Gasoline, Laundry: NI.

Activities

Museums: NI.
Trails: NI.
Boating: At all except one park. NI on fees on rental. One wilderness area has a canoeing trail.
Swimming: At about half.
Fishing: At all except two.
Hunting: NI.
Horses: NI.
Playgrounds: At one. NI on type.

Other Rules

Camping fee: 50¢ per day or $2.00 per year vehicle permit, plus $1.00 per night or $3.50 per week camping fee.
Time limit: NI.
Reservations: NI.
Fires outside fireplaces: NI. No alternative in wilderness areas.
Pets: NI.
Motorcycles, trail scooters, etc.: NI.
Gate locked: NI.
Alcoholic drinks: NI.
Roadside camping: Prohibited, but roadside parks have drinking water and rest rooms.

There are seven state parks in the system, all permitting camping. In addition, there are nine game management areas and one historical site which permit wilderness camping but have no "man-made facilities or even good roads leading to the areas."

OHIO

Ohio Department of Natural Resources, Division of Parks and Recreation, Building C. Foutain Square, Columbus, Ohio 43224

Location

Population centers: "Our policy is to limit state park development to sites outside major metropolitan areas, leaving the development of close, day-use areas to Ohio's many fine metropolitan park districts and city park and recreation departments."
Natural features: A major factor. Many are on artificial lakes.

Physical Facilities

Acreage range: 32 to 13,849 (13 to 5,595 hectares). Some smaller areas do not permit camping.

Fourteen are adjacent to sizable state forest or wildlife lands.
Campsite terrain: NI. Photos show flat and wooded.
Tentsite ground: NI. Photos show natural soil with some grass.
Wood availability: Natural firewood "occasionally provided in small amounts," concession.
Fireplaces: Fire ring or three-wall in Class A and B. Do-it-yourself in primitive.
Cabins: At fourteen; basic (four rooms, sleeps six) $17.00 daily, $85.00 weekly; deluxe (all twin beds, electric heat, complete cooking facilities, screened porch) $21.00 daily, $110.00 weekly.
Trailers: Thirty-five foot (10.31 m) maximum length, NI on connections.
Motor homes: Three-hundred-square-foot (27.87 m²) maximum floor area.
Transportation: Landing strips at four; NI on other systems.

Utilities

Toilets: Flush at Class A; chemical at Class B; privy at primitive.
Sanitary dumps: At Class A.
Water: Piped, showers at Class A; piped or well, no showers, at Class B.
Electricity: At Class A, 25¢ per night where available.
Grocery, Ice: At Class A; *Restaurant:* Snack at most Class A; *Gasoline:* NI; *Laundry:* At most A, few B.

Activities

Museums: Nature programs at most.
Trails: Hiking trails at most; riding trails at very few.
Boating: At most; ramps at over half, docks at over half; rental at half, NI on rates.
Swimming: At most; NI on type.
Fishing: At all except one.
Hunting: NI; firearms prohibited in campgrounds.
Horses: Horse camping at two; trails at very few.
Winter sports: Tobogganing, ice skating, and sled riding at one; snowmobiles at ten.
Playgrounds: At most.

Other Rules

Camping fee: Class A with electricity $2.50 per site per night during season, $1.50 off season; Class A without electricity $2.25 during season, $1.25 off season; Class B with electricity: $2.00 in season, $1.50 off season; primitive campsites, no charge any time. Visitors $1.00, refundable on leaving.
Time limit: Fourteen days within a thirty-day pe-

riod. Season from March 31 to November 1, year 'round where heated washhouses are provided. Visitors during 6:00 A.M. to 10:00 P.M. only.

Reservations: At twelve parks, through Ticketron, Box 2501, Cincinnati, Ohio. $1.50 reservation fee ($1.75 through mail), no more than ninety days in advance.

Fires outside fireplaces: No.

Pets: Prohibited in designated camping areas.

Motorcycles, trail scooters, snowmobiles, etc.: "Motor vehicle operation within the camping area shall be restricted to that necessary for direct transportation to and from a campsite." Some snowmobile areas.

Gate locked: NI. Quiet time 10:00 P.M. to 6:00 A.M.

Alcoholic drinks: NI.

Minors camping: "Any person under eighteen years of age and desiring to register for a campsite should have a letter of permission with a statement of responsibility signed by the camper's parents."

Roadside camping: NI.

Energy problems: More use by state residents; reservation system helping; plans for mass transit developed but won't be formulated completely until the situation "stabilizes and can be evaluated thoroughly."

Camping is permitted at forty-four out of sixty-two state parks.

OKLAHOMA

Oklahoma Industrial Development and Parks Commission, Suite 500, Will Rogers Memorial Building, Oklahoma City, Oklahoma 73105

Location

Population centers: Away from large ones, but fairly close to county seats or major farm-market towns which use the facilities extensively.

Natural features: Of major importance.

Physical Facilities

Acreage range: Parks from 200 to 11,802 (most in lower thousands). Recreation areas from 28 to 8,098. Most have lakes in tens of thousands of acres in addition.

Campsite terrain: Varies widely.

Tentsite ground: Most is grassy.

Wood availability: Provided.

Fireplaces: Three-wall, waist-high.

Cabins: At two-thirds of the parks.

Trailers: At all but two parks. $30.00 per month. Free for a short time.

Utilities

Toilets: Flush at all but one (privy).

Water: Piped. No hot water. Showers.

Electricity: At some.

Grocery: At half. *Ice:* At at least one. *Restaurant:* At two-thirds. *Gasoline:* Some for boats, at least one for cars. *Laundry:* Tubs at rest rooms at all. Automatic equipment at two resorts.

Activities

Museums: At two.

Trails: A few.

Boating: At two-thirds. Rental at two-thirds.

Swimming: At all except two. One-third pool, one-third beach, one-third both.

Fishing: At all except two. State license required.

Hunting: Firearms prohibited.

Horses: Rental at one-third. Own permitted.

Playgrounds: Children's playgrounds at all but three. Golf at one-third. Light sports (shuffleboard, badminton, etc.) at half.

Other Rules

Camping fee: None.

Time limit: At discretion of park superintendent. Two weeks at some.

Reservations: For trailers only.

Fires outside fireplaces: Required in some parks.

Pets: On leash.

Motorcycles, trail scooters, etc.: Prohibited.

Gate locked: No policy.

Alcoholic drinks: Permitted.

Roadside camping: Prohibited.

Oklahoma permits camping at all twenty-two state parks and thirteen recreational areas. The recreational areas are quite similar to the parks but are mainly situated on major lakes with proportionately little land area.

OREGON

State Highway Division, Salem, Oregon 97310

Location

Population centers: NI. Map shows distribution coincides with population, plus extensive parks along the Pacific Coast.

Natural features: Important. Most of the parks not having camping facilities are for the purpose of natural or historical preservation, or future park expansion.

Physical Facilities

Acreage range: 1 to 8,302 ($\frac{1}{2}$ to 3,354 hectares) evenly distributed. Most of the small-acreage parks are lake or ocean coasts or are on mountain peaks.

Campsite terrain: Varies widely.

Tentsite ground: Natural soil at most, "improved" at some.

Wood availability: Furnished free.

Fireplaces: Three-wall.

Cabins: No.

Trailers: In trailer spaces only; water, electricity, and sewer at several, water and electricity at several; full utilities $4.00 per night, water and electricity $3.00 per night.

Motor homes: Same as trailers.

Transportation: No.

Utilities

Toilets: Flush at most. At unimproved sites, distance to them may be great.

Sanitary dumps: At two-thirds (those with trailer facilities).

Water: Piped. Hot water and showers (hot) at most campgrounds.

Electricity: At trailer facilities and electric stove shelters.

Grocery, Ice: NI; *Restaurant:* Snack at several; *Gasoline:* NI. *Laundry:* At trailer sites.

Activities

Museums: At two parks.

Trails: Hiking and nature trails at several. System is expanding.

Boating: At one-third. Boats for rent at two. Large number of coastal parks makes this percentage smaller than in most states.

Swimming: At almost half. Mostly ocean or lake.

Fishing: At over half. Both fresh and salt water.

Hunting: All parks are game refuges.

Horses: On designated trails only. No rental.

Winter sports: No. (most suitable parts of state are under National Forest administration).

Playgrounds: At very few.

Other Rules

Camping fee: $4.00 for full hook-ups, $3.00 for partial hook-ups, $2.00 for tents, $1.00 for primitive sites (few).

Time limit: "Seven out of any ten days in the same park." Checkout 2:00 P.M., 4:30 P.M. Sundays and holidays.

Reservations: At eighteen; $1.00, no advance.

Fires outside fireplaces: Prohibited.

Pets: On leash.

Motorcycles, trail scooters, snowmobiles, etc.: On designated roads only.

Gate locked: No.

Alcoholic drinks: Not prohibited.

Minors camping: NI.

Roadside camping: "May be occupied only eighteen hours out of any twenty-four-hour period. Setting up campsites, tents, etc., is prohibited, although visitors are permitted to sleep in their cars or trailers if they become fatigued while traveling."

Open Beach law: No.

Energy problems: Hot showers reduced to 6:00 A.M. to 9:00 A.M. and 6:00 P.M. to 9:00 P.M.; limits on firewood supplies; three-wheelers replacing cars for park patrol.

Camping is permitted at fifty-four out of 235 parks.

PENNSYLVANIA

Office of Public Information, Department of Environmental Resources, Box 1467, Harrisburg, Pennsylvania 17120.

Location

Population centers: NI. Distribution of parks is fairly even throughout the state.

Natural features: Of prime importance. Some are of primarily historical interest.

Physical Facilities

Acreage range: 50 to 20,075 (20 to 8,110 hectares). Some smaller parks do not permit camping.

Campsite terrain: NI.

Tentsite ground: NI.

Wood availability: "Cutting of standing trees and shrubs" prohibited—this presumably includes dead wood. NI on rest.

Fireplaces: Fire rings.

Cabins: At eleven, two of which don't permit camping. One to four rooms, $22.26 to $37.10 per week.

Trailers: Tent and camp trailers only, no connections. "Discharge of trailer sewage or sink waste on or into the ground" prohibited.

Motor homes: No.

Transportation: No.

Utilities

Toilets: Flush at one-quarter. Rest "pit." The current program is to increase the number of flush.

Sanitary dumps: At a third.

Water: Available at all campgrounds. Piped where

flush toilets are, NI on rest (presumably pump since it is tested). Hot water, NI. Showers at campgrounds with flush toilets.
Electricity: No.
Grocery: At most. *Ice:* NI. *Restaurant:* Very few. *Gasoline, Laundry:* At a few.

Activities

Museums: At one.
Trails: Nature trails at very few. Hiking trails at most. Snowmobile trails at some.
Boating: Motorboats at half, nonmotor at remainder. Ramps at one-third. Rowboats, canoes, sailboats and some inflatable craft. NI on rates. $2.00 state annual launching fee, $5.00 mooring fee. Federally-approved state registration required.
Swimming: Pools at very few. Beaches at most. Swimming prohibited without lifeguard or outside designated areas.
Fishing: At all but two parks. State license required. Ice fishing permitted.
Hunting: At most in season. Firearms, bows, and slingshots prohibited at other times. State license required.
Horses: Trails at a few, prohibited in beach and picnic areas, NI on rental.
Winter sports: Skiing at six, ice skating permitted.
Playgrounds: Play areas available.

Other Rules

Camping fee: $2.00 and $3.00.
Time limit: Fourteen days. Forty-eight hours must pass before using the same park again. Season second Friday in April to third Sunday in October. Checkout 4:00 P.M.
Reservations: Yes, NI on details.
Fires outside fireplaces: Prohibited.
Pets: Prohibited.
Motorcycles, trail scooters, etc.: NI.
Gate locked: NI. Quiet time 9:00 P.M. to 8:30 A.M.
Alcoholic drinks: Prohibited.
Minors camping: One person over eighteen in maximum of five nonfamily group.
Roadside camping: Prohibited.
Energy problems: Instituted reservation system as a result.
Camping permitted at forty-four out of 123 recreational areas and two out of forty-two state forest picnic areas.

RHODE ISLAND

Rhode Island Development Council, Roger Williams Building, Hayes Street, Providence, Rhode Island 02908

Location

Population centers: Irrelevant. Size of state makes all campgrounds close.
Natural features: Of major importance. All are in heavy woodlands.

Physical Facilities

Acreage range: NI. One park is listed as 2,100 acres (848 hectares).
Campsite terrain: Level and wooded.
Tentsite ground: NI. Photo shows natural soil.
Wood availability: NI.
Fireplaces: Three-wall. See *Camping fee.*
Cabins: One park has only cabins, fee $1.00 per person per night. Another has two Adirondack shelters only, fee $2.00 per night for both shelters as a unit.
Trailers: NI.
Motor homes: NI.
Transportation: No.

Utilities

Toilets: Vented pit.
Sanitary dumps: NI.
Water: Pumped. No hot water or showers.
Electricity: NI.
Grocery: No. *Ice, Restaurant, Gasoline, Laundry:* NI.

Activities

Museums: NI.
Trails: At most. Unguided.
Boating: At two parks. Ramp at one. Two others accessible only by canoe.
Swimming: Pool at one park. Lake at two others.
Fishing: At most.
Hunting: In season.
Horses: NI.
Winter sports: NI.
Playgrounds: Athletic fields at half.

Other Rules

Camping fee: $2.00 per night for tent campgrounds. Permit obtained in advance from Division of Parks and Recreation, 83 Park Street, Providence, Rhode Island 02903. No charge for use of the canoe campgrounds. Fire permit required.
Time limit: Permits have a two-week limit.
Reservations: One park reserves some tent spaces.
Fires outside fireplaces: NI. Probably not, since fire permits are required for any fire.
Pets: On leash.
Motorcycles, trail scooters, etc.: NI; *Snowmobiles:* Restricted.
Gate locked: NI.

Alcoholic drinks: Prohibited.
Minors camping: NI.
Roadside camping: Prohibited.
Energy problems: NI.

Out of five state parks, camping is permitted at three, cabins are at one other, and Adirondack shelters at still another. Two canoe campgrounds each are on two management areas.

A directory of privately owned campgrounds is published by the Council.

SOUTH CAROLINA

South Carolina Department of Parks, Recreation, and Tourism, Box 113, Edgar A. Brown Building, 1205 Pendleton St., Columbia, South Carolina 29201

Location

Population centers: Most in rural areas or close to small towns.
Natural features: Major factor.

Physical Facilities

Acreage range: 35 to 7,361 (14 to 2,974 hectares); most under 1,000 (400 hectares).
Campsite terrain: Mostly wooded; level on gently sloping.
Tentsite ground: No prepared sites, natural ground.
Wood availability: Dead wood only, no cutting.
Fireplaces: Waist-high, some fire rings.
Cabins: At twelve parks; $9.00 to $25.00 per night or $55.00 to $150.00 per week.
Trailers: At all permitting camping; full connections, no extra charge.
Motor homes: Same as trailers.
Transportation: No.

Utilities

Toilets: Flush at all.
Sanitary dumps: At entrance of all camping areas.
Water: Piped, hot showers in all.
Electricity: Connections at all developed sites.
Grocery, Ice: At several; *Restaurant:* At three, snack at most; *Gasoline:* NI; *Laundry:* At two.

Activities

Museums: Interpretive center at one-third.
Trails: Hiking trails at most. Nature trails at most; mini-bike trails at three; horse trails at four.
Boating: At all except four; ramps at a few; rental boats at half; pedal-boats at half.
Swimming: At most, mostly lake, some ocean, very few river or pool. Memorial Day to Labor Day, 50¢ for adults, 25¢ for children, salt water free.

Fishing: Fresh water at most, salt water at three, state license required.
Hunting: No.
Horses: At five, rental at one.
Playgrounds: At all.

Other Rules

Camping fee: $4.50 per site per day at coastal parks; $3.75 at others.
Time limit: Seven days, year 'round season.
Reservations: No.
Fires outside fireplaces: No.
Pets: On leash only.
Motorcycles, trail scooters, etc.: NI.
Gate locked: Dark to daylight, except in emergencies.
Alcoholic drinks: "Public display not permitted."
Minors camping: No restrictions.
Roadside camping: NI.
Open Beach law: NI.
Energy problems: Additional emphasis on trail development; possible backpacking facilities; no mass transit yet; attendance down 1974 vs. 1973, but unusually wet summer may be part of problem.

Camping is permitted at twenty-seven of thirty-three parks.

SOUTH DAKOTA

Department of Game, Fish and Parks, State Office Building, Pierre, South Dakota 57501

Location

Population centers: Irrelevant.
Natural features: Of major importance. Some are historical.

Physical Facilities

Acreage range: 10 to 72,000 (4 to 29,000 hectares).
Campsite terrain: Prairie to hill.
Tentsite ground: Level, NI on soil cover.
Wood availability: "Available" at most campgrounds. NI on details.
Fireplaces: In all campgrounds; NI on type.
Cabins: At four parks; NI on type or rental.
Trailers: NI.
Motor homes: Same as trailers.
Transportation: Airport at one park.

Utilities

Toilets: Flush at all but one park, several recreation areas; NI on rest.
Sanitary dumps: In one and near another.

Water: At most; developed campsites have hot water and showers.
Electricity: At half. NI on fee.
Grocery: At about one-quarter. *Ice, Restaurant, Gasoline, Laundry:* NI. "Information signs at park entrance provide local information."

Activities

Museums: At one park.
Trails: Hiking at all but one park, at only one recreation area.
Boating: Parks: all but one, ramps at all but one, docks at most. Recreation areas: at most, ramps at most, docks at half; NI on rental.
Swimming: At most.
Fishing: At most. Ice fishing.
Hunting: NI.
Horses: Rental at some parks. Trails at some parks.
Winter sports: Cross-country trails at two, downhill at seven.
Playgrounds: At most.

Other Rules

Camping fee: $2.00 per night.
Time limit: Five days.
Reservations: No.
Fires outside fireplaces: No.
Pets: On leash.
Motorcycles, trail scooters, etc.: License required; *snowmobiles:* NI.
Gate locked: 11:00 P.M.; NI on opening.
Alcoholic drinks: NI.
Minors camping: No restrictions.
Roadside camping: "Camping is allowed in all park areas, including roadside parks."
Energy problems: No plans for change.

Out of twelve parks and thirty recreation areas, developed campgrounds are in ten parks and twelve recreation areas.

TENNESSEE

Division of State Parks, 235 Cordell Hull Building, Nashville, Tennessee

Location

Population centers: All are within forty miles of an urban area, most much closer.
Natural features: Important.

Physical Facilities

Acreage range: 52 to 42,000. The majority are between 1,000 and 10,000.
Campsite terrain: Most wooded, lake, or river areas.

Tentsite ground: NI.
Wood availability: NI.
Fireplaces: At some.
Cabins: NI.
Trailers: At ten, with future plans at four other sites.

Utilities

Toilets: At most.
Water: At most.
Electricity: At most. 25¢ per day, 75¢ with water and sewage (where available).
Grocery, Ice, Restaurant, Gasoline, Laundry: At or near most.

Activities

Museums: At one.
Trails: Nature at some.
Boating: At most.
Swimming: At most.
Fishing: At most.
Hunting: No.
Horses: At three. NI on rental.
Playgrounds: At some.

Other Rules

Camping fee: $2.00 per day plus 25¢ per person when there are more than four. Children under six free.
Time limit: NI.
Reservations: NI.
Fires outside fireplaces: NI.
Pets: NI.
Motorcycles, trail scooters, etc.: NI.
Gate locked: NI.
Alcoholic drinks: NI.
Roadside camping: NI.

There are twenty-one parks with another in the planning stage.

TEXAS

Parks and Wildlife Department, John H. Regan State Office Building, Austin, Texas 78701

Location

Population centers: Only one is presently located near a major urban center, but there is a possibility of establishing new parks in these areas.
Natural features: Of major importance in recreational park selection. Many have historical importance as well and a few are located on old Indian campgrounds.

Physical Facilities

Acreage range: 13 (primarily historical with camping permitted, but undeveloped) to 15,103 acres (9 to 6,112 hectares); most between 300 and 700 (120 and 280 ha); only two over 2000 (800 ha).
Campsite terrain: Mostly level and wooded.
Tentsite ground: Mostly natural soil. Some grass.
Wood availability: NI. (Collecting prohibited.)
Fireplaces: Mostly three-wall. Some waist-high. Some do-it-yourself.
Cabins: Cottage-type at a few $6.00 per night for two, $1.50 per additional adult, 75¢ per additional child six to thirteen years old. Screened shelters at several, $3.50 per night first car, $1.00 per additional car. Open shelters at some, $2.50 and $1.00 per car; both shelter types limited to three cars.
Trailers: At most. Connections at most: electricity $1.50, electricity and water $1.50, electricity, water, and sewer $1.75.
Motor homes: NI.
Transportation: Airstrip at one, NI on other systems.

Utilities

Toilets: Flush.
Sanitary dumps: At half.
Water: Piped. Hot water, NI (personal experience shows them increasing). Showers at most.
Electricity: 50¢ fee. Available at rest rooms.
Grocery: At several major parks. *Ice:* NI (at a few at least). *Restaurant:* Snack bar at a few. *Gasoline, Laundry:* NI.

Activities

Museums: At several, mostly historical, some nature.
Trails: Self-guiding nature trails at a few, more being built. Nature centers at several. Hiking trails at a few.
Boating: Ramps at many. Rental at a few. Boat motors over 12-horsepower and water skiing prohibited on lakes less than 225 acres (100 hectares) surface area.
Swimming: A few pools (fee). Mostly lake. Some salt water. Lake swimming in designated areas only.
Fishing: At over half. State license required.
Hunting: Firearms prohibited in parks.
Horses: Rental at very few. Own permitted in designated areas only.
Playgrounds: NI.

Other Rules

Camping fee: $1.00 per day or $12.00 per year entry fee at all but two (50¢) parks with camping (25¢ for thirteen or older other than by car, bus, or aircraft), no entry fee at undeveloped parks. Camping fee $1.00 per night.
Time limit: Fourteen days in season, twenty-eight days out of season; one Saturday must pass before returning in season, two Saturdays out of season; however, this is only if the demand on the park requires it. Any stay over one week invokes this time period rule. Season May 1 to September 15. Checkout time 2:00 P.M.
Reservations: Cabins and shelters only; write to park concerned, enclosing one night's fee.
Fires outside fireplaces: No.
Pets: On leash only, prohibited in public buildings and swimming areas; horses, stock, poultry, or other livestock prohibited as are dangerous or disturbing animals.
Motorcycles, trail scooters, etc.: Restricted as to location, time, safety standards, etc.
Gate locked: NI. (One park did at one time.) Quiet time 10:00 P.M. to 7:00 A.M.
Alcoholic drinks: Sale and public consumption prohibited.
Minors camping: Under eighteen prohibited except with written permission of parents or in group supervised by adult.
Roadside camping: NI.
Open Beach law: Yes, although they will seldom admit it.
Energy problems: NI.

Camping is permitted at forty-four out of fifty-eight parks, three of which are undeveloped.

UTAH

Division of Parks and Recreation, 1596 N. Temple, Salt Lake City, Utah 84116

Location

Population centers: NI. Map shows even distribution throughout populated areas.
Natural features: Important at most. Artificial lake is a factor at some.

Physical Facilities

Acreage range: 10 to 22,000 (4 to 8,900 hectares); most between 100 and 3,000 (40 and 1,200 hectares).
Campsite terrain: NI.
Tentsite ground: NI.
Wood availability: NI.
Fireplaces: NI.
Cabins: NI.
Trailers: Connections at one. Hook-ups at four.

Motor homes: NI.
Transportation: None.

Utilities

Toilets: Flush at developed, privy at undeveloped.
Sanitary dumps: At eight.
Water: Piped at over half, NI on rest. Hot water, NI. Showers at three-quarters.
Electricity: NI.
Grocery, Ice, Restaurant, Gasoline, Laundry: NI.

Activities

Museums: At one-fifth.
Trails: Hiking trails at several.
Boating: At half, ramps at half, decks at just under half, rentals at seven, NI on rates.
Swimming: At half.
Fishing: At half.
Hunting: In season. Firearms prohibited at other times.
Horses: NI.
Winter sports: "No formal facilities as yet."
Playgrounds: NI.

Other Rules

Camping fee: Entrance fee: $10.00 per year, $1.00 per day per car, 50¢ per day per person (walk-in), no charge for under sixteen years old, $5.00 per year for senior citizens and physically handicapped. Camping fee: (in addition to entrance fee) $1.00 at primitive sites, $2.00 at developed sites, $3.00 with hook-ups. Utah Fun Tag (annual entrance permit) carries a $1.00 per site per night reduction. Fees during season only.
Time limit: Fourteen days in any thirty-day period, shorter at the discretion of the campground director. Season varies with campground. Check-out 4:00 P.M.
Reservations: Required for groups of ten or more; none for less.
Fires outside fireplaces: NI.
Pets: "Under control and on leash at all times."
Motorcycles, trail scooters, etc.: NI. *Snowmobiles:* Registered vehicles on designated trails only.
Gate locked: NI; quiet time 10:00 P.M. to 6:00 A.M.
Alcoholic drinks: NI.
Minors camping: No restrictions.
Roadside camping: NI.
Energy problems: No effects (use still growing) other than longer stays and higher percentage from state. No changes contemplated.

Camping is permitted at thirty-eight out of forty-four parks; thirty-one are developed, seven undeveloped. Those without camping are mainly historical.

VERMONT

Agency of Environmental Conservation, Department of Forests and Parks, Montpelier, Vermont 05602

Location

Population centers: NI. Evenly distributed through the state.
Natural features: A large part of all parks.

Physical Facilities

Acreage range: 20 to 20,936 (8 to 8,578 hectares); most between 100 and 600 (40 and 243 hectares).
Campsite terrain: NI.
Tentsite ground: Coarse sand added at some, turf at others.
Wood availability: Furnished. Cutting prohibited. NI on gathering down wood.
Fireplaces: Three-wall.
Cabins: No.
Trailers: No connections. On same basis as tents.
Motor homes: Same as trailers.
Transportation: No.

Utilities

Toilets: Flush.
Sanitary dumps: NI.
Water: Piped. Hot water and showers (hot) at all.
Electricity: NI.
Grocery, Ice: NI. *Restaurant:* Refreshment stands at one-third. *Gasoline, Laundry:* NI.

Activities

Museums: Nature museums in larger parks.
Trails: Hiking trails at all parks; self-guiding nature trails and evening programs in larger parks.
Boating: In all parks; rental at half; ramps at most water-oriented parks, no launching fee, NI on rental fee.
Swimming: At over half, lake or pond.
Fishing: In or near all parks; license required of fifteen years and older; ice fishing at some.
Hunting: Firearms and bows prohibited in developed areas between May and October inclusive. NI on other times and places.
Horses: Restricted in parks; rental near most parks.
Winter sports: Skiing: downhill at several, concession lifts at some, cross-country trails at many; tobogganing; ice skating; snowmobile trails in or near all. In all day-use parks.

Other Rules

Camping fee: $1.00 per adult with minimum of $2.00. Children under eighteen free when part of a family unit. Youth groups 40¢ each.

Time limit: Three weeks.

Reservations: Minimum six nights, maximum three weeks. Usually needed between July 1st and Labor Day.

Fires outside fireplaces: Prohibited.

Pets: On leash. Dogs must have proof of vaccination.

Motorcycles, trail scooters, etc.: No restrictions "yet."

Gate locked: Closed, not locked. Quiet time 10:00 P.M. to 7:00 A.M.

Alcoholic drinks: Permitted.

Minors camping: One of group must be over eighteen, one per ten in large groups.

Roadside camping: No.

Energy problems: Plans are to continue reservations as the trend is to longer stays and travel directly from home to one campground. Trails program is stepped up, as is the interpretive program, and more attractions will be provided at the park. Camping is permitted at thirty-six out of forty-three state parks and forests.

VIRGINIA

Division of State Parks, 1201 State Office Building, Capitol Square, Richmond, Virginia 23219

Location

Population centers: Distributed throughout state.

Natural features: All state parks offer natural features of unique interpretation and are so preserved for scientific, educational, and recreational purposes.

Physical Facilities

Acreage range: 130 to 4,934 (53 to 1,993 hectares); most are between 1,000 and 4,500 (400 and 1,200 hectares).

Campsite terrain: Wooded, fairly flat ground.

Tentsite ground: Natural soil at all, prepared pads at one.

Wood availability: Concessionaire sales in season, NI on out of season.

Fireplaces: Grills.

Cabins: At eight parks, May to October, two weeks maximum; rates vary with size.

Trailers: Thirty-five feet (10½ m) maximum some back-in; connections at some.

Motor homes: Same as trailers.

Transportation: NI.

Utilities

Toilets: Flush.

Sanitary dumps: At all with camping.

Water: Piped; hot. Showers at all but one.

Electricity: 25¢ per day.

Grocery, Ice, Restaurant: In season, mostly snacks. *Gasoline:* At some. *Laundry:* Tubs at all, no machines.

Activities

Museums: At most.

Trails: Hiking at all; self-guiding nature trails at half; bicycles at one-third.

Boating: Electric or manual at most, motors at five; rental at all; launching at most.

Swimming: At all; lifeguards at all but two. Fee, but NI on amount.

Fishing: At all. License required in fresh water.

Hunting: At some.

Horses: Rentals in four in season; private horses permitted in two of those at all times and other two only in off season.

Playgrounds: Playfields at all, equipment at four.

Other Rules

Camping fee: $3.00 per night year 'round.

Time limit: Fourteen days, season from Memorial Day to Labor Day.

Reservations: Virginia State Park Reservation System, Box 62284, Virginia Beach, Virginia 23462; or Ticketron offices. $1.50 fee in addition to camping fee.

Fires outside fireplaces: Prohibited except in charcoal grills or stoves.

Pets: On maximum six-foot (182 cm) leash.

Motorcycles, trail scooters, etc.: Same as automobiles (including license and roads).

Gate locked: No; attendant on duty twenty-four hours, year 'round; day use 10:00 A.M. to dusk.

Alcoholic drinks: Prohibited in public.

Minors camping: NI.

Roadside camping: Prohibited.

Open Beach law: NI.

Energy problems: NI.

Camping is permitted at fourteen out of twenty parks. Pamphlets are published on individual parks, guides to nature trails, and museums.

WASHINGTON

Parks and Recreation Commission, Box 1128, Olympia, Washington 98504

Location

Population centers: NI. Map shows distribution of parks coincides with distribution of population.

Natural features: Important.

Physical Facilities

Acreage range: 1 to 20,931 ($\frac{1}{2}$ to 8,456 hectares); most between 100 and 1,000 (40 and 4,000 hectares).
Campsite terrain: NI.
Tentsite ground: NI.
Wood availability: Furnished "for a small fee." NI on collection.
Fireplaces: Present. NI on type.
Cabins: At one-tenth. Shelter-type at half. NI on fees.
Trailers: Sites at one-third. Water and electricity. Sewer connections at "some." $3.50 per trailer per night where full hook-ups are provided.
Motor homes: If they fit in trailer space.
Transportation: No, but one "fly-in" campground is being developed.

Utilities

Toilets: Flush at four-fifths. Privy at three-quarters including all without flush toilets.
Sanitary dumps: At some.
Water: NI, but probably piped where flush toilets are. Hot water, NI. Hot showers at two-thirds.
Electricity: See *Trailers.*
Grocery: At one-third. *Ice:* At one-quarter. *Restaurant:* At one-fifth. Snack bars at one-quarter.
Gasoline, Laundry: NI.

Activities

Museums: Interpretive centers at a few.
Trails: Hiking trails at one-quarter. Nature trails at two. Horse trails at one-twelfth.
Boating: Launching facilities at over one-third. Rental at one-eighth. Half salt and half fresh water. One-eighth of state parks accessible only by boat.
Swimming: At two-thirds. Mostly fresh water.
Fishing: At five-sixths. Equal fresh and salt water. State license required for fresh-water fishing. Salmon license free. Salt water does not require license. Clams and oysters have limit but require no license. Ice fishing at one.
Hunting: No.
Horses: At one-twelfth. Rental at two. Restricted to designated trails.
Winter sports: Skiing at four; slopes, tows, and lifts at three; skating at four; sledding at four (overlapping nine parks).
Playgrounds: NI.

Other Rules

Camping fee: $2.50 per site per night.
Time limit: Seven days if overcrowding occurs.
Reservations: No.
Fires outside fireplaces: With a permit.

Pets: Prohibited in dining rooms, kitchens, swimming areas, and trails. Otherwise permitted, on leash no longer than eight feet (244 cm).
Motorcycles, trail scooters, etc.: Permitted on roads only. *Snowmobiles:* Only in designated parks and only registered vehicles.
Gate locked: Closed, not locked. 10:00 P.M. to 6:30 A.M.
Alcoholic drinks: Still officially NI, but a cryptic comment implies it is a problem.
Minors camping: No restrictions.
Roadside camping: NI.
Open Beach law: NI.
Energy problems: Coming from shorter distances, no changes planned.
Camping is permitted at seventy-five out of ninety-five staffed parks.

WEST VIRGINIA

Department of Natural Resources, State Capitol, Charleston, West Virginia 25305

Location

Population centers: NI. Map shows fairly uniform distribution.
Natural features: Of prime importance.

Physical Facilities

Acreage range: Parks from 355 to 10,057 (143 to 406 hectares) (smaller ones without camping); forests from 5,000 to 13,043 (200 to 5,269 hectares).
Campsite terrain: NI. Photos show level woodland.
Tentsite ground: NI. Photos show natural soil.
Wood availability: For sale. NI on collection.
Fireplaces: NI. Photos show three-wall.
Cabins: At most parks permitting camping, few forests.
Trailers: Water and electricity at a few.
Motor homes: NI.
Transportation: None.

Utilities

Toilets: Flush at all parks and most forests. Privy at rest of forests.
Sanitary dumps: At eight parks and two forests.
Water: Piped at parks and most forests. Pumps at rest of forests. Hot water and showers (hot) at several.
Electricity: At a few parks and no forests.
Grocery: At a few parks and no forests. *Ice:* NI. *Restaurant:* At almost all parks, no forests. Refreshment stands at all parks and half the forests. *Gasoline:* NI. *Laundry:* Coin-operated at parks with hot water.

Activities

Museums: None.
Trails: Hiking trails at all parks and forests. Naturalist tours at half of the parks.
Boating: At almost all parks, one forest. Docks at a few parks. NI on rental.
Swimming: At all parks and half of the forests. Mostly pools (fee) but some lake and stream.
Fishing: At all but one park and one forest. State license required.
Hunting: At all forests. Firearms and bows prohibited in parks.
Horses: Rental at a few parks and one forest. NI on using your own.
Winter sports: Downhill skiing with lifts at one park.
Playgrounds: At all parks and forests. NI on type.

Other Rules

Camping fee: $3.00 in standard campgrounds (all but one park and in three forests), $2.50 in rustic (privy toilets—one park and five forests), $1.50 in primitive campgrounds (state public hunting and fishing areas).
Time limit: Two consecutive weeks. Season May 1 through October 15. Checkout 3:00 P.M.
Reservations: No.
Fires outside fireplaces: Prohibited.
Pets: On leash.
Motorcycles, trail scooters, etc.: NI.
Gate locked: No. Quiet time 10:00 P.M. to 7:00 A.M.
Alcoholic drinks: NI.
Minors camping: NI.
Roadside camping: Prohibited.
Energy problems: "No adverse effect." Campers coming from shorter distances.

Camping is permitted at nine out of twenty state parks, eight out of nine state forests, and on a primitive basis at nineteen public hunting and fishing areas.

Pamphlets are available on individual state parks.

WISCONSIN

Department of Natural Resources, Box 450, Madison, Wisconsin 53701

Location

Population centers: Irrelevant.
Natural features: Of prime importance.

Physical Facilities

Acreage range: 9 to 196,000 (3½ to 79,184 hectares); most between 300 and 4,000 (120 and 1,600 hectares).

Campsite terrain: Generally wooded.
Tentsite ground: Varied with improved drainage where needed.
Wood availability: For sale (50¢ per bundle). NI on collection.
Fireplaces: In picnic grounds.
Cabins: No.
Trailers: Electricity 50¢ per day. Sewer 50¢ per day. NI on water.
Motor homes: NI.
Transportation: NI.

Utilities

Toilets: Flush at campgrounds. Privy at primitive and canoe campsites (accessible by hiking or canoe only).
Sanitary dumps: NI.
Water: Piped at campgrounds. Natural sources at primitive areas. Hot water, NI. Showers at campgrounds. NI on hot water.
Electricity: 50¢ per day.
Grocery: Concessions at major parks and forests. *Ice, Restaurant, Gasoline, Laundry:* NI.

Activities

Museums: Three formal and three informal nature centers; displays at other "selected" parks/forests.
Trails: Self-guiding nature trails at twenty-nine parks/forests (few with more than one); guided nature trail hikes at seventeen; bicycle trails at four.
Boating: Complex rules regarding motorboats and sailboats. (Get "Wisconsin Boating Regulations" from Conservation Department.) Boating permitted at about half. Ramps available where recreational water is. Several areas have canoeing waters (information available from Conservation Department).
Swimming: At over two-thirds. Mostly lake.
Fishing: At all.
Hunting: In season at state forests and one state park. Firearms and bows prohibited outside established target areas.
Horses: Restricted to designated trails and areas. No rental although some commercial rental adjacent to parks/forests.
Winter sports: Cross-country ski trails at fourteen; winter nature observation points at some.
Playgrounds: NI.

Other Rules

Camping fee: Admission sticker required for entrance to almost all parks and forests; residents $1.50 daily, $5.00 annually; nonresidents: $2.50 daily, $8.00 annually. Admission fees required year 'round at some, in season only at most.

Camping fee $2.75 per day in modern, $2.25 per day in primitive and canoe campsites, in season only.

Time limit: Twenty-one days in a four-week period. Season April 1 to October 31.

Reservations: At eighteen parks and forests. Reservation form from DNR office, send to park involved. Minimum two days for reservation. Reservation must be in at least seven days and at most sixty days before use. All fees plus $2.00 reservation fee with application. Refunds for cancellation.

Fires outside fireplaces: Prohibited.

Pets: On leash. Prohibited in public buildings, picnic grounds, and on beaches.

Motorcycles, trail scooters, etc.: Prohibited on trails. *Snowmobiles:* NI.

Gate locked: "It shall be unlawful to enter any state park or any camp or picnic area in any state forest between the hours of 11:00 P.M. and the following 4:00 A.M. No camping party shall start setting up or taking down its camping unit between the hours of 10:00 P.M. and the following 6:00 A.M.

Alcoholic drinks: "Unlawful to drink or possess any intoxicating liquor or fermented malt beverage in any state park, or Kettle Moraine and Point Beach state forests (except in family campgrounds by registered campers) between March 31 and May 29." NI on other times and places.

Roadside camping: Prohibited.

No information was received on the number of parks and forests in the system or the number permitting camping.

WYOMING

Wyoming Travel Commission, 2320 Capitol Avenue, Cheyenne, Wyoming 82001

Location

Population centers: NI. Map shows even distribution.

Natural features: One major factor (recreational opportunities another).

Physical Facilities

Acreage range: NI.
Campsite terrain: NI.
Tentsite ground: NI.
Wood availability: NI.
Fireplaces: Three-wall at two-thirds of the parks and half of the Game and Fish Commission campgrounds. None or NI at rest.
Cabins: NI.
Trailers: At all. Connections at one Game and Fish campground, under construction at two state parks.

Motor homes: NI.
Transportation: No.

Utilities

Toilets: Do-it-yourself at a few parks and all campgrounds. NI on type at most parks.
Sanitary dumps: NI.
Water: At all parks, one Game and Fish campground; NI on type. Showers under construction at one park; NI on hot water.
Electricity: NI.
Grocery: At one park. *Ice, Restaurant:* NI. *Gasoline:* At one park. *Laundry:* NI.

Activities

Museum: NI.
Trails: NI.
Boating: At all but one park and two Game and Fish.
Swimming: At almost all parks, one-third of campgrounds.
Fishing: At all parks and all Game and Fish.
Hunting: At all parks and all but two Game and Fish.
Horses: NI.
Winter sports: NI.
Playgrounds: NI.

Other Rules

Camping fee: $2.00 at parks (except one which is free); free at Game and Fish; $5.00 per year for any one park, $10.00 per year for all parks.
Time limit: Fourteen days at all but one park, five days at all but one Game and Fish (no limit at the two exceptions). Season varies, some year 'round.
Reservations: NI.
Fires outside fireplaces: NI.
Pets: On leash. Not permitted on trails and in boats.
Motorcycles, trail scooters, etc.: NI.
Gate locked: NI.
Alcoholic drinks: NI.
Minors camping: NI.
Roadside camping: Prohibited.
Energy problems: No effects.

Camping is permitted at all eight parks and ten Game and Fish campgrounds.

The Commission publishes a directory of motels, hotels, resorts, dude ranches, and outfitters.

NATIONAL PARK SYSTEM OF CANADA

Parks Canada, Department of Indian Affairs and Northern Development, Ottawa, Ontario K1A 0H4

Location

Population centers: Irrelevant.
Natural features: Of prime importance.

Physical Facilities

Acreage range: 594 to 17,300 (240 to 7,000 hectares).
Campsite terrain: Varies widely.
Tentsite ground: NI. Photos show natural soil and grass.
Wood availability: Supplied.
Fireplaces: Fire pits to grills and stoves.
Cubins: At most, prices vary.
Trailers: Fifty-foot combined length except for forty-foot on Banff-Jasper Highway and Cabot Trail. Restricted to designated areas in parks. No drainage directly onto ground. $2.00 per night unserviced; $3.00 electricity only; $4.00 water, electricity, and sewer.
Motor homes: NI.
Transportation: Aircraft prohibited; train service to some; NI on buses.

Utilities

Toilets: Flush at "serviced" campgrounds. Flush or privy at "semi-serviced." Flush, chemical, or privy at "primitive."
Sanitary dumps: At many.
Water: Piped in serviced. Piped, pump, or stream in semi-serviced and primitive. Hot water in serviced. Showers in some serviced.
Electricity: Included in fee at serviced and semi-serviced.
Grocery, Ice, Restaurant, Gasoline, Laundry: Varies widely; some form at most.

Activities

Museums: Interpretive centers or interpretive exhibits at most.
Trails: Naturalist tours at all; self-guiding interpretive trails at most; hiking trails at most; horse trails in some.
Boating: Permitted at almost all parks. Motors prohibited on some small lakes. Boat and canoe rental at many, charter boats at some, NI on rates.
Swimming: At most, fee only for pool or hot mineral springs.
Fishing: At most parks. $2.00 annual license required for fishing within the national parks. Provincial license required for adjacent waters.
Hunting: With one exception, none at all; all firearms must be sealed while within park boundaries.
Horses: Designated areas only. Rental in some.

Winter sports: Downhill skiing at four, cross-country at most; toboggan at one, curling at two.
Playgrounds: "Day use areas" at most.

Other Rules

Camping fee: Entry fee varies from 25¢ to $1.00 per day or $2.00 to $5.00 per season. $2.00 fee for unserviced sites, $3.00 with electricity, $4.00 for water, electricity, and sewer connections.
Time limit: Usually two weeks. Season from mid-June to Labor Day, minimum facilities from late May to mid-October. Winter camping in some parks.
Reservations: One campground in one park, plus group campgrounds.
Fires outside fireplaces: No. Camping outside campgrounds also possible with a permit. All garbage must be packed out.
Pets: Dogs only.
Motorcycles, trail scooters, snowmobiles, etc.: Designated roads only.
Gate locked: No. One park is day-use only.
Alcoholic drinks: Provincial laws apply.
Minors camping: NI.
Roadside camping: No.
Open Beach law: No, but effect of one in Pacific Rim National Park.
Energy problems: No effect, so no change is contemplated.

Registration is required for mountain climbing.
There are eighteen national parks permitting camping. The government accommodation guide lists twenty-one serviced campgrounds, four semi-serviced, one primitive, and eighty without designation but presumed primitive. Wood Buffalo, the largest in the system, is not yet developed for tourists. In addition, permits to camp outside of campgrounds are easy to obtain and open an endless supply of campgrounds to the skilled camper. Trans-Canada Highway campgrounds offer even more camping space as many are on the edge of national parks.

A directory of Trans-Canada campgrounds is available, as is a booklet of scenic tours off the Trans-Canada Highway. Pamphlets on individual or regional groups of national parks are available. Accommodation guide lists facilities and prices at concession facilities in all parks.

For entry, U.S. citizens need identification papers (birth certificate, voter registration, etc.). Mexican citizens must show passports. No visa is required.

ALBERTA

Travel Alberta, 10255–104 Street, Edmonton, Alberta T5J 1B1

Location

Population centers: NI. Distribution appears fairly uniform. Highway campsites are located forty miles apart, closer on heavily traveled highways.

Natural features: A factor in some. Available recreation is the prime reason, although natural beauty is considered in locating them. Highway campsites are located in woods and near watercourses, if possible.

Physical Facilities

Acreage range: 43 to 49,620 (17 to 20,000 hectares); most under 2,000 (800 hectares).

Campsite terrain: NI. Highway campsites wooded when possible.

Tentsite ground: NI. Highway campsites are grassed.

Wood availability: NI.

Fireplaces: Three-wall at highway campsites.

Cabins: NI.

Trailers: Permitted at all permitting camping. Connections at very few, sewer and water at only one.

Motor homes: NI.

Transportation: NI.

Utilities

Toilets: Dry chemical in most, flush in very few. Dry chemical at highway campgrounds. Privy at forests.

Sanitary dumps: At several parks; NI highway; none at forests.

Water: Wells on half, piped on most; pump at most highway but some pipe and cistern; pump at forest.

Electricity: Very few parks, no highway or forest.

Grocery, Ice: None at highways or forests. NI on parks. *Restaurant:* At one park. Refreshment stands at over half. None at highway or forests.

Gasoline, Laundry: NI.

Activities

Museums: NI.

Trails: Hiking at eight parks, NI on forest, highway too small.

Boating: At over half of parks, half of forests, few highways; rental at few parks, negligible highways, no forests. NI on cost.

Swimming: Over half parks, several highway, NI on forest.

Fishing: At most parks, half highway, NI on forest.

Hunting: In forests. Prohibited in parks and highways. Guide required for non-residents hunting big game. Provincial license required.

Horses: NI.

Winter sports: NI.

Playgrounds: Most parks, no highway or forest.

Other Rules

Camping fee: Parks have fees, additional for hookups, but NI on amount; free camping in forests, free in season in highway.

Time limit: Fourteen days in parks. Season from May 24 to Labor Day.

Reservations: NI on parks. None in highway. NI on forests.

Fires outside fireplaces: Prohibited on highways. NI on parks or forests.

Pets: No restrictions on highways. NI on parks and forests. Prohibited on beaches.

Motorcycles, trail scooters, etc.: NI on parks or forests. No restrictions on highways—"however, excessive noise . . . is not tolerated at night."

Gate locked: NI on parks or forests. No on highways.

Alcoholic drinks: "In tents or trailers providing they do not create a disturbance" on highways. NI on parks and forests.

Minors camping: NI.

Roadside camping: NI, highway campgrounds are close together.

Energy problems: NI.

Camping is permitted in forty-four out of forty-seven Provincial Parks, fifty of sixty-three Forest Service Recreation Areas, and all 234 Highways Campsites.

Travel Alberta also publishes an accommodations directory (*Let's Do It*) and a canoe facilities booklet (*Canoe Alberta*).

BRITISH COLUMBIA

Provincial Parks Branch, Parliament Buildings, Victoria, British Columbia.

Location

Population centers: Those close provide extensive recreational facilities; those in remote areas are primarily wilderness preservation areas.

Natural features: One of the most important considerations in both types of parks.

Physical Facilities

Acreage range: Less than 1 to over 37,000 ($\frac{1}{2}$ to 15,000 hectares).

Campsite terrain: Designed to use natural terrain with the least disturbing.

Tentsite ground: Natural soil.

Wood availability: Furnished in developed campgrounds. Cutting trees prohibited.

Fireplaces: Design varies.

Cabins: No.

Trailers: Twenty-foot (6 m) maximum.

Motor homes: Same as trailers.

Transportation: Aircraft generally prohibited; bus goes by or through many; trains go by or through some.

Utilities

Toilets: Vented pit in all developed parks, flush replacing or augmenting in many.

Sanitary dumps: NI.

Water: Pump or pipe; no hot water.

Electricity: No.

Grocery, Ice: NI; *Restaurant:* At motel complex in one park; *Gasoline, Laundry:* NI.

Museums: Historical at five, nature houses in five with more planned or under construction.

Trails: Naturalist tours in many, self-guiding nature trails in many; hiking trails in most and back-packing trail system outside parks; bridle paths in one.

Boating: Power prohibited at some; ramps in some; rental in few, NI on rates.

Swimming: Permitted where suitable areas exist.

Fishing: At most. Provincial license required.

Hunting: Prohibited in most parks.

Horses: Prohibited or restricted; no rental.

Winter sports: Downhill skiing at two; no others on an organized basis.

Playgrounds: At some.

Rock hunting is listed at one, mountain climbing at another.

Other Rules

Camping fee: $2.00 per night at most, free at rest.

Time limit: Fourteen days per park per year. Season April 1 to September 9. Checkout 12:00 noon.

Reservations: No.

Fires outside fireplaces: No.

Pets: "Permitted unless they become a nuisance."

Motorcycles, trail scooters, etc.: "Prohibited except on normally traveled vehicle roads." *Snowmobiles:* Prohibited.

Gate locked: 11:00 P.M. to 7:00 A.M. during season.

Alcoholic drinks: Permitted subject to provincial laws.

Minors camping: No restrictions.

Roadside camping: No.

Energy problems: "Irrelevant."

Camping is provided in 150 parks out of 314 parks and recreation areas.

The province publishes an accommodation guide of all facilities in the province, a guide leaflet to each major provincial park, a booklet listing the full text of all roadside interest markers (valuable in traffic), and a leaflet with charts to all provincial marine parks.

MANITOBA

Department of Tourism, Recreation, and Cultural Affairs, Parks Branch, 1981 Portage Avenue, Winnipeg, Manitoba R3C 0V8

Location

Population centers: Provincial parks are all located in the populated southern part of the province, although there is a very extensive network of canoe trails in the lakes of the northern three-quarters of the province.

Natural features: Of major importance. Natural lakes are found in all but two, and they are on rivers.

Physical Facilities

Acreage range: Over 5,000 to over 640,000 (over 2,000 to over 25,850 hectares); half are over 100,000 (40,000 hectares).

Campsite terrain: Flat, in organized lots. Mostly wooded.

Tentsite ground: NI. Photos show natural soil and grass.

Wood availability: Supplied.

Fireplaces: NI. Photos show elaborate three-wall.

Cabins: Not operated by government; some private cabins are rented.

Trailers: At most. Trailer hitches must attach to frame. Safety chain must be used. Sixty-foot combined length limit at most provincial parks.

Motor homes: Same as trailers.

Transportation: No restrictions on aircraft; NI on airstrips, but extensive water indicates floatplane operation. One park is serviced by scheduled bus, other bus lines go through parks on regular roads. NI on trains.

Utilities

Toilets: Flush at most, but some still have privies.

Sanitary dumps: NI.

Water: Piped. NI on hot water. Showers at most.

Electricity: At most, no additional charge.

Grocery: At a few. *Ice:* At very few. *Restaurant:* Snack bars and concessions at very few. *Gasoline:* NI. *Laundry:* At very few.

Activities

Museums: No.

Trails: Self-guiding and non-guided nature and hiking trails at most parks.

Boating: Not allowed in one park; boats classed as having living accommodations not permitted in parks or recreational areas. Ramps at most. Canoe trails in northern and eastern part of province.

Swimming: Lake beaches at all parks.
Fishing: Lake or stream at all. License $3.00 for Canadian, $10.00 for foreign. Required for all over sixteen.
Hunting: Subject to changing provincial hunting regulations.
Horses: Designated trails in parks and recreation areas having stables only.
Winter sports: Downhill and cross-country skiing at one each, tows operate on weekends and holidays only.
Playgrounds: At a few. NI on type.

Other Rules

Camping fee: $1.50 ($2.00 with electricity, $2.50 with full connections) per day; $9.00 ($12.00 and $15.00 per week.
Time limit: Three weeks (ten days at one, one week at two, and one day at two); Season June 15 to August 15. Checkout 6:00 P.M. (5:00 P.M. at ten-day limit, noon at shorter limits); no renewal for forty-eight hours.
Reservations: No.
Fires outside fireplaces: Prohibited.
Pets: On leash and under control at all times.
Motorcycles, trail scooters, etc.: Licensed and on roads only. *Snowmobiles:* Designated trails only in southern half (northern is their proper habitat anyway).
Gate locked: Returning campers only after 11:00 P.M.
Alcoholic drinks: In tent or trailer only.
Roadside camping: There are twenty-one roadside campgrounds outside the provincial parks for camping. These have the same camping facilities as the parks, but lack the recreational facilities. In addition, there are several roadside picnic areas.
Minors camping: No restrictions.
Open Beach law: NI.
Energy problems: "Only effect was reduced percentage of U.S. visitors." No changes contemplated.
    There are camping facilities at eleven parks, six forests, eighteen campgrounds, eleven recreation areas, and four beaches; all except parks are generally unserviced as are camping areas in the extensive network of canoe trails.
    The Department publishes an accommodations guide for the province and a set of "canoe trail maps" which, with their marginal sketches, make good wall posters.

NEW BRUNSWICK

    Department of Tourism, Box 1030, Fredericton, New Brunswick E3B 5C3

Location

Population centers: Irrelevant.
Natural features: Of primary importance. Other recreational needs are a major factor.

Physical Facilities

Acreage range: 1 to 42,800 ($\frac{1}{2}$ to 17,291 hectares).
Campsite terrain: Varies.
Tentsite ground: Sand, gravel, or grass.
Wood availability: Provided free; no collecting.
Fireplaces: Sheet metal stoves.
Cabins: No.
Trailers: Electrical connections at most, 50¢; no other connections.
Motor homes: Same as trailers.
Transportation: No.

Utilities

Toilets: Flush and privy.
Sanitary dumps: Yes.
Water: Piped or pump. Hot water and showers at some.
Electricity: See *Trailers*.
Grocery, Ice, Restaurant, Gasoline, Laundry: No. Some canteen concessions, one store concession.

Activities

Museums: One auto.
Trails: Hiking; naturalist tours scheduled and on request, self-guiding nature trails.
Boating: No power restrictions; ramps (NI on ramp fee), rental at one, NI on rate.
Swimming: NI.
Fishing: Fresh and salt water, ice fishing.
Hunting: At one park.
Horses: No.
Winter sports: Cross-country ski trails, downhill skiing, tows and lifts; tobogganing; ice skating.
Playgrounds: In most, city-park type and athletic fields.

Other Rules

Camping fee: $2.50 or $3.50 per day, depending on facilities.
Time limit: Fourteen days, checkout 3:00 P.M.
Reservations: No.
Fires outside fireplaces: Prohibited except in areas specifically designated.
Pets: Under restraint.
Motorcycles, trail scooters, etc.: No. *Snowmobiles:* Designated trails only.
Gate locked: No.
Alcoholic drinks: No regulations other than provincial Liquor Control Act.
Minors camping: No restrictions.

Roadside camping: No.

Open Beach law: No.

Energy problems: Fewer from U.S.; other than some encouragement of mass transit, no plans for changes.

There are twenty-nine camping areas in the Provincial Parks System. In addition, there are thirty-nine picnic grounds administered by the Department, most of which have drinking water and privy toilets.

The Department publishes a list of all publicly and privately owned campgrounds.

NEWFOUNDLAND AND LABRADOR

Department of Tourism, Parks Division, Box 9340, Station B, St. John's, Newfoundland A1A 2Y3

Location

Population centers: Evenly distributed; trend is toward developing more destination facilities near urban centers.

Natural features: Unique natural features high priority; "good quality recreation land" also important consideration.

Physical Facilities

Acreage range: 2 to 8,640 (1 to 3,491 hectares); evenly spread.

Campsite terrain: Wooded and as much as possible flat.

Tentsite ground: Mostly natural soil; topsoil and seed or sod introduced where natural soil is inadequate for sustaining grass.

Wood availability: Woodyard with saw and ax furnished. However, in periods of fire danger wood fires are banned, so campers are advised to bring gas stoves in case. Collection (outside woodlot) prohibited.

Fireplaces: Concrete block with metal grate; on ground.

Cabins: No.

Trailers: No connections.

Motor homes: Same as trailers.

Transportation: "Private aircraft access—no restrictions where opportunity exists"; NI on strips, so probably means float planes. NI on bus or train.

Utilities

Toilets: Pit. Vented pit.

Sanitary dumps: At two parks on Trans-Canada Highway.

Water: Gravity-fed pipe or pump; no hot water or showers.

Electricity: No.

Grocery, Ice, Restaurant, Gasoline, Laundry: No.

Activities

Museums: Interpretive program; logging exhibit at one park.

Trails: Seasonal naturalists at two parks; hiking trails at a few.

Boating: Power prohibited at two, private boats prohibited at one (rental facilities there), ramps at several. Rental $1.00 per half day, one park only.

Swimming: Fourteen public beaches; swimming in parks, mostly fresh-water ponds; no designated swimming areas.

Fishing: No license (except for salmon) required of residents; nonresidents must have license for fresh water but not for salt-water. Ice fishing.

Hunting: No. Hunting and target shooting weapons (including BB or bow) prohibited within a park.

Horses: No restrictions, no rentals.

Winter sports: Organized facilities just getting started, but exists on informal basis now.

Playgrounds: At two.

Other Rules

Camping fee: Entry permit 50¢ per day or $2.00 per season; camping fee $1.50 per party per night.

Time limit: Ten consecutive days. Season May 15 to September 15. Checkout 3:00 P.M.

Reservations: No.

Fires outside fireplaces: Prohibited.

Pets: On leash or in cage.

Motorcycles, trail scooters, etc.: Only those licensed for highways; *Snowmobiles:* Restricted to unplowed roads only.

Gate locked: Closed (hooked gate) all the time to keep out noncampers. Quiet time after 10:00 P.M.

Alcoholic drinks: Tolerated.

Minors camping: No restrictions.

Roadside camping: Mainly as an overflow when camping areas are full.

Open Beach law: No.

Energy problems: No effects felt or anticipated.

Camping is permitted at thirty-five out of forty-six parks but at none of the fourteen beaches.

NORTHWEST TERRITORIES

Division of Tourism, Government of the Northwest Territories, Yellowknife, NWT X0E 1H0

Location

Population centers: Located on highways (as are population centers) but little correlation except for Community Parks.

Natural features: Of highest priority in Natural Environment Recreation Parks, minor in Outdoor Recreation Parks, incidental in Community Parks and Wayside Parks.

Physical Facilities

Acreage range: 2 to 182 (1 to 74 hectares).
Campsite terrain: NI.
Tentsite ground: NI.
Wood availability: NI.
Fireplaces: NI.
Cabins: No.
Trailers: NI.
Motor homes: NI.
Transportation: No.

Utilities

Toilets: Privy.
Sanitary dumps: No.
Water: In half, NI on system or showers.
Electricity: No.
Grocery, Ice: At two; *Restaurant:* No; *Gasoline, Laundry:* At two.

Activities

Museums: No.
Trails: No.
Boating: Launching at two, rental at one, NI on rates.
Swimming: At two.
Fishing: At two.
Hunting: No discharge of guns in parks now in operation although will be permitted in Outdoor Recreation Parks.
Horses: Not permitted to roam at large.
Winter sports: No formal facilities.
Playgrounds: No.

Other Rules

Camping fee: $5.00 per year (April 1 to March 31).
Time limit: Fourteen days.
Reservations: NI.
Fires outside fireplaces: NI.
Pets: On leash or direct physical control.
Motorcycles, trail scooters, snowmobiles, etc.: In designated areas only.
Gate locked: NI.
Alcoholic drinks: NI.
Minors camping: NI.
Roadside camping: NI.
Open Beach law: NI.
Energy problems: No effect, no plans.

Camping is provided at nine of nineteen Wayside Parks. No Natural Environment Recreation or Outdoor Recreation Parks have been built at this time. NWT is just getting into the parks field—in the first edition they had no parks and an address in Ottawa.

NOVA SCOTIA

Nova Scotia Travel Bureau, Department of Tourism, Box 130, Halifax, Nova Scotia, B3J 2M7

Location

Population centers: Close to population centers.
Natural features: Of considerable importance.

Physical Facilities

Acreage range: 62 to 1,220 (25 to 493 hectares).
Campsite terrain: All wooded. Most are on a lake, river, or ocean.
Tentsite ground: Grassed.
Wood availability: Yes; NI on method.
Fireplaces: Yes, NI on type.
Cabins: No.
Trailers: At all. Fee same as tents.

Utilities

Toilets: Vented pit.
Sanitary dumps: Yes.
Water: Piped at two-thirds, pump at rest. No hot water or showers.
Electricity: No.
Grocery, Ice, Restaurant, Gasoline, Laundry: None at present.

Activities

Museums: No.
Trails: At some; NI on types.
Boating: Ramps at some.
Swimming: At two-thirds.
Fishing: No license needed for salt water. $5.00 per year for trout and salmon.
Hunting: No.
Horses: No.
Winter sports: No.
Playgrounds: No.

Other Rules

Camping fee: $3.00 per day.
Time limit: Fourteen days.
Reservations: No.
Fires outside fireplaces: No.
Pets: On leash.
Motorcycles, trail scooters, etc.: Yes. *Snowmobiles:* Restrictions.
Gate locked: 11:00 P.M.
Alcoholic drinks: Permitted.
Roadside camping: In an emergency only.
Open Beach law: "With very few exceptions, such as privately owned beaches, all beaches in Nova Scotia are open to the public."
Minors camping: No restrictions.

Energy problems: No effect, no changes contemplated.

Camping is permitted at eighteen provincial parks.

A list of privately operated campgrounds is published by the province, as is an excellent tour book.

ONTARIO

Ontario Ministry of Natural Resources, Whitney Block Queen's Park, Toronto, Ontario M7A 1X5

Location

Population centers: Within two hours' drive of population centers for Recreation Park campsites; deep in vast wilderness for Primitive and Wild River Parks.
Natural features: Of total importance in Primitive and Wild River Parks; of some importance in Recreation Parks.

Physical Facilities

Acreage range: 10 acres to 2,910 square miles (4 to 75,369 hectares), two parks are over 1,000 square miles (2,590 hectares).
Campsite terrain: Varied.
Tentsite ground: Varied, mostly sand.
Wood availability: Furnished free. Collection discouraged. Cutting prohibited.
Fireplaces: Metal grates.
Cabins: No.
Trailers: Restricted at some wilderness campgrounds.
Motor homes: Same as trailers.
Transportation: Aircraft prohibited except on designated floatplane lakes in Quetico and Algonquin parks; NI on other forms.

Utilities

Toilets: Flush at over half, vented pit and privy at rest.
Sanitary dumps: At several.
Water: Piped at over one-third, well and stream at rest. NI on hot water or showers.
Electricity: At one-fourth, 50¢ extra.
Grocery: At a few. *Ice:* At very few. *Restaurant:* One. Refreshment stands at a few. *Gasoline, Laundry:* NI.

Activities

Museums: At less than ten per cent. Evenly divided between historical and nature.
Trails: Hiking trails at one-third. Naturalist-guided nature hikes at the two largest parks. A few self-guiding nature trails.

Boating: Launching facilities at almost all. Canoe trips at a few. Two parks are restricted to boat campers only. Boat rentals rare in parks but, especially canoes, available nearby.
Swimming: Prohibited at a few.
Fishing: Nonresident license required. Those under seventeen don't require a license if accompanied by someone with one. Ice fishing at a few.
Hunting: At a few. Waterfowl only. License and special permit required. Air guns and bows prohibited.
Horses: No.
Winter sports: Cross-country skiing and snowshoeing at over half, downhill skiing at very few; tobogganing at a few; ice skating at very few; snowmobiling at just under half.
Playgrounds: At a few.

Other Rules

Camping fee: $3.50 per day; boats in Quetico $15.00 per season water entry fee (if enter by road, included in car fee). $2.00 per canoe per night in canoe campgrounds.
Time limit: Twenty-eight days; checkout 2:00 P.M.
Reservations: No.
Fires outside fireplaces: No.
Pets: On six-foot leash.
Motorcycles, trail scooters, etc.: Prohibited in Primitive Parks (as is all motorized equipment). NI on rest. *Snowmobiles:* Designated trails only.
Gate locked: No.
Alcoholic drinks: On campsite only.
Minors camping: NI.
Roadsid camping: No.
Open Beach law: NI.
Energy problems: NI.

Camping is permitted at ninety-five out of 116 parks.

Special guide books and canoe trail books are published for Quetico and Algonquin Provincial Parks winter recreation on public lands in the province, campgrounds (including privately-operated) of the province which also provides information on the three long hiking trails (Queenston-Tobermory, Kingston-Ottawa, and Port Hope-Glen Huron [under construction]).

PRINCE EDWARD ISLAND

Prince Edward Island has one national park but no provincial parks.

QUEBEC

Ministère du Tourisme, de la Chase et de la Pêche, Hôtel du Gouvernement, Québec, Québec G1A 1R4

Location

Population centers: Direct correlation between population and campgrounds, but not necessarily near population centers.
Natural features: Primary criterium in provincial parks; in campgrounds outside parks, convenience to travelers is more important.

Physical Facilities

Acreage range: From not stated to 13,123 square miles (3,398,857 hectares); most are large enough to be measured in square miles rather than acres.
Campsite terrain: NI.
Tentsite ground: NI; but guidebook *Camping Quebec* lists the percentage of shade.
Wood availability: NI.
Fireplaces: "Fireplaces" at very few, "campfires" at most, photos show do-it-yourself.
Cabins: At almost all; $6.00 to $14.00 per day.
Trailers: In camping units.
Motor homes: NI.
Transportation: Airport in one, floatplane facilities in another; NI on bus or train.

Utilities

Toilets: Flush at most, privy in several.
Sanitary dumps: In half.
Water: In most, NI on system; showers in most, NI on hot water.
Electricity: In several.
Grocery, Ice: In several; *Restaurant:* In few; *Gasoline:* NI; *Laundry:* In few.

Activities

Museums: NI.
Trails: Nature study at several; hiking trails in most.
Boating: Canoeing in several.
Swimming: At most; mostly lakes; beach, river, and pool at few.
Fishing: At half, ice fishing at a few; $2.00 per day for residents, $5.00 for nonresidents.
Hunting: Small and big game at a few.
Horses: At a few; NI on rental rates.
Winter sports: Cross-country skiing at several, downhill at very few; snowshoeing at a few; snowmobiling at a few.
Playgrounds: At very few.

Other Rules

Camping fee: $2.00 to $5.00 per day depending on facilities.
Time limit: Fourteen days, checkout 2:00 P.M.
Reservations: No.

Fires outside fireplaces: No.
Pets: Dogs on leash only.
Motorcycles, trail scooters, snowmobiles, etc.: Not in campgrounds, in designated areas only.
Gate locked: NI; Quiet time 11:00 P.M. to 7:00 A.M.
Alcoholic drinks: On tentsites only.
Minors camping: NI.
Roadside camping: NI.
Open Beach law: NI.
Energy problems: No problems.

Camping facilities are at fourteen out of nineteen provincial parks.

The Ministère publishes a guidebook (bilingual) of all campgrounds (including privately-run) in the province.

While not absolutely required, a knowledge of French is helpful outside the major population centers.

SASKATCHEWAN

Department of Tourism and Renewable Resources, Administration Building, Regina, Saskatchewan S4S OB 1

Location

Population centers: Irrelevant. Small parks in populated areas, large ones outside.
Natural features: A major factor.

Physical Facilities

Acreage range: 17 to 387,520 (7 to 156,558 hectares); most are over 1,000 (400 hectares).
Campsite terrain: NI.
Tentsite ground: Mostly gravel. Some grass.
Wood availability: Free.
Fireplaces: NI. Photos show three-wall and mortared-stone fire rings.
Cabins: At four; $7.00 to $21.00 per day; check-in 4:00 P.M., checkout 12:00 noon.
Trailers: At most.
Motor homes: NI.
Transportation: No aircraft; one park with bus; no trains.

Utilities

Toilets: Flush at highly developed campgrounds. Pit at rest.
Sanitary dumps: At several.
Water: Piped. NI on hot water or showers.
Electricity: At most Provincial and half of the Regional parks; $2.00 per day additional.
Grocery: At a third. *Ice:* NI. *Restaurant:* Coffee shops or snack bars at most. Cafés at a few.

Gasoline: NI. *Laundry:* At Provincial and Trans-Canada campgrounds.

Activities

Museums: A few.
Trails: Self-guiding nature trails at all but two Provincial, interpretive programs at several, nature trails at a few Regional; NI on hiking.
Boating: At almost all. Docks at a few. Rental at several. NI on rental. Horsepower restriction at two lakes. Living aboard prohibited at all Provincial parks.
Swimming: NI.
Fishing: At almost all.
Hunting: Firearms prohibited except for game harvesting under special conditions.
Horses: Rental at four parks. NI on using your own.
Winter sports: Downhill with T-bar or rope lifts at three Regional; two Provincial (T-bar at one, rope at both); cross-country trail at one Regional; skating rink at two; toboggans at two.
Playgrounds. Formal, directed recreational program (city park type) at all Provincial; playground at almost all Regional.

Other Rules

Camping fee: Entrance fee $1.00 per day or $4.00 per season. Camping fee $1.00 per day at unserviced sites or $3.00 per day with electricity. Campgrounds without an attendant (unserviced) are free.
Time limit: NI.
Reservations: No.
Fires outside fireplaces: Prohibited.
Pets: "No dogs on beach and no free roaming of domestic animals."
Motorcycles, trail scooters, snowmobiles, etc.: NI.
Gate locked: NI.
Alcoholic drinks: Sale prohibited.
Minors camping: NI.
Roadside camping: NI; extensive pattern of regional and private parks on highways make this a moot point.
Energy problems: Has had a minor effect on travel patterns of tourists, but not enough to change methods.

Camping is permitted at sixteen out of seventeen Provincial Parks, seventy-eight out of eighty-four Regional Parks (with five still under construction), and all four Trans-Canada Highway Campgrounds, and at over 100 provincial campgrounds outside the Provincial Park system.

A directory of privately owned tourist accommodations is published by the Department, as well as pamphlets on individual Provincial parks.

YUKON

Government of the Yukon Territory, Tourism and Information Branch, Box 2703, Whitehorse, Yukon Y1A 2C6.

Location

Population centers: Irrelevant.
Natural features: Less important than locating on major roadways.

Physical Facilities

Acreage range: NI; relatively small campgrounds administered by the Department of Tourism, no large parks comparable to provincial parks yet.
Campsite terrain: Two photos show flat terrain, one sparse woods, the other heavy conifers.
Tentsite ground: NI. Photos show natural ground.
Wood availability: Furnished.
Fireplaces: Barbeque-type made from oil drums.
Cabins: No; kitchen shelters at half.
Trailers: No connections.
Motor homes: NI.
Transportation: No.

Utilities

Toilets: Privy.
Sanitary dumps: At several.
Water: Well at a few, stream at most, no water at two.
Electricity: No.
Grocery, Ice, Restaurant, Gasoline, Laundry: No.

Activities

Museums: No.
Trails: NI.
Boating: At half.
Swimming: Beach at one-quarter.
Fishing: At three-quarters; license $3.00 per year for Canadians, $10.00 per season or $3.50 for five days for foreigners.
Hunting: Prohibited in campgrounds.
Horses: NI.
Winter sports: NI.
Playgrounds: No.

Other Rules

Camping fee: $5.00 per year sticker.
Time limit: NI; season May to October.
Reservations: No.
Fires outside fireplaces: No.
Pets: NI.
Motorcycles, trail scooters, etc.: NI.
Gate locked: NI.

Alcoholic drinks: Permitted.

Minors camping: NI.

Roadside camping: The system is basically roadside camping facilities which are located reasonably close together along most of the highways (exceptions being new highways in the far north where they haven't expanded into yet).

Open Beach law: NI.

Energy problems: NI.

Camping facilities are provided at forty-four of the forty-seven campgrounds and lunch-stops (a "lunch-stop" lacks the campground's facilities, but may or may not permit camping).

MEXICO

Secretaria de Agricultura y Ganaberia, Tacuba No. 7, Mexico, D.F. Mexico

Location

Population centers: A large number are located around Monterey and Mexico City. Like all development in Mexico, they are more numerous in the south than in the arid north.

Natural features: Both historical and scenic areas are included in the national park system. The natural features are unique.

Physical Facilities

Acreage range: 1 to 67,000 hectares (A hectare equals 2.471 acres). The smaller ones are mainly historical. There are twenty-four over 1,000 hectares.

With the exception of one in 1898 and another in 1917, the national parks were all established after 1936. Efforts in this regard have thus far been mainly in simply preserving these areas of unique scenic and historic value, and practically nothing has been done toward developing them as camping facilities as the U.S. and Canada have done. Now that Mexico has been successful in the development of economic and social services, which have taken such a large part of its national budget, the development of these areas for tourists will probably be undertaken in the near future.

While Mexico is quite bilingual in the tourist centers, anyone attempting to camp in the national parks should have a good working knowledge of Spanish. In some wilderness areas, even Spanish is a secondary language to various Indian languages and dialects. Camping in the national parks is totally primitive camping with no facilities at all provided. The desert areas of the north will require fuel to be brought in, and in all areas assume the water to need purifying.

Camping is permitted at all forty-seven national parks in Mexico. At present, there are no state parks.

For entry, U.S. citizens need an International Certificate of Innoculation and Vaccination only if they have visited a country other than the U.S. or Mexico within fourteen days before entering. A Tourist Card (obtained at Mexican consulates, tourism offices, immigration offices at the border, and some airlines) is required. Canadian citizens need a passport (visa not required) to obtain the Tourist Card.

KAMPGROUNDS OF AMERICA

Kampgrounds of America, Inc., P.O. Box 1791, Billings, Montana 59103

The crowding of public campgrounds has produced, in an attempt to meet the need for camping space, the privately owned campgrounds, open to the general public. Kampgrounds of America is a franchise operation and in many ways is typical of this type of campground.

Location

Population centers: "Preferably near population centers, but far enough away to reduce the noise, such as five to eight miles and/or adjacent to heavily traveled highways or inter-state systems."

Natural features: "Being primarily an overnight accommodation, the natural features do not enter too strongly except in the event the location is near or adjacent to national or state parks or other large tourist attractions."

Physical Facilities

Acreage range: Minimum of 5 acres required to obtain a franchise; 10 acres preferred, to allow room for expansion from the minimum of 50 tentsites.

Campsite terrain: Level.

Tentsite ground: Grass required.

Wood availability: For sale. While some may have woodlots, the very intensive (ten tents per acre) use of the facility makes on-the-site wood supplies most unlikely.

Fireplaces: Twelve waist-high units are furnished with the franchise. Operators generally add three-wall fireplaces for the rest.

Cabins: None at present although some campgrounds may rent permanent tents in the future.

Trailers: No connections are required although most operators will have electrical connections available.

Utilities

Toilets: Flush.
Water: Piped from well or municipal supply. Hot water and hot showers.
Electricity: See *Trailers.* Also available in rest rooms.
Grocery: Staples. *Ice:* NI. *Restaurant:* Not required. NI on any providing it. *Gasoline:* White gas required. *Laundry:* Coin-operated washers and driers required.

Activities

City-park-type playground required. All others optional. NI on extent they are offered.

Other Rules

Camping fee: Minimum of $2.00 per night. The average is $2.50.
Time limit: None.
Reservations: Yes.
Fires outside fireplaces: Prohibited.
Pets: On leash.
Motorcycles, trail scooters, etc.: NI. Small size makes this a road situation rather than one of trails.
Gate locked: "Very seldom." All traffic in and out passes through a check point at the main facility building.
Alcoholic drinks: No restrictions "although we do keep a close watch so that the national image of KOA would not be damaged by such things as indiscriminate drinking and partying."

KOA has regular inspectors who travel to make sure the camps are operating according to the advertising.

BOISE CASCADE

Boise Cascade, One Jefferson Square, Boise, Idaho 83728

Location

Population centers: NI. About half are located on or quite near highways. The rest are reached by a network of county and logging roads.
Natural features: A factor in some. Several Minnesota campgrounds are on canoe portages.

Physical Facilities

Acreage range: NI; 2,264,424 total acreage (914,827 hectares).
Campsite terrain: Most have creek or river frontage. Wooded, of course.

Tentsite ground: NI.
Wood availability: Provided at heavily used sites. Gathering at rest.
Fireplaces: Provided, but NI on type.
Cabins: No.
Trailers: Permitted. No connections.
Motor homes: Same as trailers.
Transportation: Float planes in northern Minnesota only. No other systems.

Utilities

Toilets: "Pit."
Sanitary dumps: No.
Water: Piped at a few, well in some, stream in rest. No hot water or showers.
Electricity: No.
Grocery, Ice, Restaurant, Gasoline, Laundry: No.

Activities

Museums: No.
Trails: Hiking is a major activity.
Boating: None in Northwest. Canoeing in several in Minnesota.
Swimming: At most, in lakes.
Fishing: At most in both areas.
Hunting: At most in Northwest. NI on Minnesota.
Horses: NI.
Winter sports: Snowmobile trails.
Playgrounds: No.

Other Rules

Camping fee: None.
Time limit: NI.
Reservations: No.
Fires outside fireplaces: With proper safeguards.
Pets: NI.
Motorcycles, trail scooters, etc.: NI. *Snowmobiles:* Restricted to marked trails.
Gate locked: No.
Alcoholic drinks: NI.
Minors camping: No restrictions.
Energy problems: No changes anticipated.

The Boise Cascade Corporation operates thirty-eight campgrounds in Washington, Oregon, Idaho, and Minnesota. The Corporation also publishes maps to trails and portages in their grounds.

WEYERHAEUSER

Recreation Planning Supervisor, Weyerhaeuser Company, Tacoma, Washington 98401

Weyerhaeuser is typical of the lumbering companies who are concerned with the image of the lumberman as a practitioner of cut-and-burn lumbering and a creator of eroded hillsides. As low-pressure advertising, some of these companies have established campgrounds on their tree farms.

Location

Population centers: NI. Because of the nature of the land, few are very close to major centers.
Natural features: Forest areas which have already had some public use.

Physical Facilities

Acreage range: 1 to 28. Most are under 10.
Campsite terrain: "Level but unimproved. Drainage is adequate during normal camping months of June through September."
Tentsite ground: Natural soil.
Wood availability: Furnished.
Fireplaces: Three-wall.
Cabins: No.
Trailers: No connections.
Motor homes: Same as trailers.
Transportation: No.

Utilities

Toilets: Privy.
Sanitary dumps: No.
Water: Well at one-fifth. Rest pump, except one spring and one with no water. No hot water or showers.

Electricity: No.
Grocery, Ice, Restaurant, Gasoline, Laundry: No.

Activities

Museums: NI on tours of operations, etc.
Trails: At one.
Boating: At very few. No rental.
Swimming: At one-fifth. No lifeguards.
Fishing: At three-quarters. State regulations apply.
Hunting: State regulations apply.
Horses: Permitted. None for rent.
Winter sports: NI.
Playgrounds: At one.

Other Rules

Camping fee: None.
Time limit: "A forty-eight-hour limit is encouraged, but not rigidly enforced."
Reservations: No.
Fires outside fireplaces: "Discouraged. . . . Prohibited during state-enforced fire seasons." Camping outside campgrounds on same basis.
Pets: No restrictions.
Motorcycles, trail scooters, etc.: "Discouraged, particularly during dry, dusty weather." *Snowmobiles:* NI
Gate locked: No.
Alcoholic drinks: No restrictions.
Minors camping: NI.
Energy problems: NI.

Weyerhaeuser operates nine campgrounds in Oregon and Washington.

CHAPTER TWENTY-TWO

Housekeeping

The selection of equipment and the campsite is important in camping, but it is not camping. It is only preparation. Camping is living with the equipment on the campsite. It is also challenging yourself to expand your knowledge and skills—to undertake activities which will enable you to get to know yourself better.

Yet in order to do these activities, a certain amount of time must be spent in what can only be termed "housekeeping." These routine activities of running a camp must be done, and the women-folk who do similar tasks all year should not be excused on the grounds that "this is a vacation," although they should, in all fairness, have a lighter job of it than at home. Because of the challenge of camping, children will often insist on helping in tasks that they almost have to be forced to do at home. Many men who never enter the kitchen pride themselves on their ability as camp cooks.

These factors help reduce the housekeeping tasks of the woman of the family. It also constitutes a major part of this challenge—those who wouldn't be caught dead doing certain tasks at home do them in camp without realizing that they are the same jobs.

Like any housework, housekeeping in camp is far easier using certain procedures and equipment. This chapter, then, is a study of those aides to easier camp housework.

MAKING AND BREAKING CAMP

Making and breaking camp is much easier and efficient with a set procedure. When you arrive at the campsite, unload all of the gear you will be using (in the case of backpacking or horsepacking, unload everything and give your transportation a rest). Keep the gear in one spot until it is used.

Normally, you should set up your tent first. If there is a heavy rain expected and the drainage is poor, keep ditching tools handy. Don't ditch unless it is actually needed.

Next, move the gear into the tent in its proper place. The gear should be protected from rain, and besides it is handier to have it inside. Your food supply should be cached outside (to keep animals from coming inside), but that is the only exception other than your transportation system.

If it will be a while before mealtime, set up the beds and other items of the tent. If not, start to work on the fireplace next. The firesite should be cleared of all vegetation (including humus soil) for at least six feet (2 mm) around. The firewood supply should be collected and at least one day's supply put under a weatherproof shelter. Unless you are at this stage long before mealtime, start the fire for supper.

Next, build the latrine and dig the garbage pit and grease trap. Set up the inside of your tent (if you haven't already) and unpack the ingredients and utensils for supper.

By the time you have the food prepared for cooking, your fire will have died down into a good bed of coals for cooking. Your camp is now in operation and the total time elapsed has been fifteen to thirty minutes. If you have help in tent erection and divide the other tasks, the total will be ten to twenty minutes.

When leaving the campsite, pack all your gear for transportation. Cover the tent ditches (if any), and the fire, latrine, garbage, and grease-trap pits with dirt. Pile the dirt up in a mound over the holes; the next rain will settle it. Place two sticks in an X on each mound. Future campers will know not to dig there and unearth garbage, charcoal, or worse when trying to make a fireplace. These X-markers are the only signs anyone should find to know that you have been there. Leave a clean campsite for the next campers.

In campsites that permit wood fires, however, there is one other thing to leave—a neat pile of firewood for the next camper.

Never let your gear get scattered while you are in camp. You should have everything together so that you can pack it in a few minutes. If you have a certain order for packing everything, you won't be as likely to leave any of your equipment at the campsite.

The custom of a bag for each piece of equipment helps. The item should be in its bag whenever it is not in use. To pack, you only have to find the relatively large bags, and not the small items in them.

CARE OF THE CAMPSITE

Keep things clean in camp. The Japanese custom of removing your shoes before entering is an excellent way to keep the inside of your tent clean, especially in rainy weather and/or if you have a tent floor. Any mud or bits of vegetation you find on your bedding should be removed immediately, before it has a chance to work into the fabric and become difficult to get out.

This attitude of cleanliness applies outside the tent too. Not only should you avoid scattering litter, you should also avoid damaging the natural surroundings. Of course, a slight amount is inevitable—cutting firewood, and the general trampling of the grass—but this should be reduced to a bare minimum. In grasslands, don't walk by the same way each time as this soon wears a smooth trail which invites erosion in wilderness areas. On the other hand, where prepared trails exist, stay with them and reduce the damage to the vegetation off the trails.

CAMP FURNITURE

The longer you stay in one spot, the more elaborate you can make your camp. "Elaborate," as it applies to camping, is a term completely unrelated to "better"—it may or may not be. This will depend, in the case of camp furniture, on what you make and what your preferences are in camping activity.

You can build furniture from materials found on the site. These are on the order of those made by Boy Scouts to demonstrate their lashing ability at Scout Expositions and camps. They aren't necessary to the running of an orderly camp, and for less than a week they are a definite waste of time unless you get enjoyment out of such things. A large (and somewhat heavy) supply of binder twine is required for this sport.

The trend toward actual camping in organizational camps is most commendable. However, give a camp counselor a roll of binder twine and he often does (or directs) some mighty odd things with it. While nearly every campsite in such a camp has tables, chairs, washstands, and several other special-purpose creations, the cooking fire is still on the ground. The campers sit on chairs at tables to eat the food, but they bend and squat to cook it. With the exception of the latrine bench, which is made even in camps where there is no other lashing done, an altar fire should be the first thing made with binder twine.

Actually, with the exception of these two items, camp furniture can be made without lashing. (So can these two, but it is usually easier to use lashings than to improvise without them.) A convenient stump or boulder, or a section of a large log rolled into position, is just as good for sitting or eating. It takes far less time to make, it serves just about as well, and when you strike camp it can disappear into the surroundings better than an odd-length pile of stout sapling poles.

In addition, fifty to a hundred feet (15 to 30 m) of parachute cord is all that is required for a latrine seat and an altar fireplace. It weighs only a few ounces (about 200 g). For elaborate lashing work, you will need at least two pounds (1 kg) of binder twine, and more is needed if the required number of these elaborate items of "temporary" equipment is very great.

CACHES

In camp, you must store your food out of reach of insects, rodents, and larger animals. In bear country, the cache should be at least ten feet (3 m) off the ground and five feet (1½ m) from the nearest large limb. It should be suspended from a tree, since a bear can knock down a tripod cache and even rip open a locked car trunk. The rope should be tied high on the tree trunk or the bear will knock down the rope. Six feet (2 m) is high enough. A bear literally can't figure out these things unless they are in front of his face.

Outside of bear country, almost any means you can devise to keep your food off the ground will do.

When you cache food for several days in the wintertime, be sure to hang the cache ten feet (3 m) above the highest possible snow level. Otherwise, a heavy drifting snow can make your cache available to a rabbit.

Campsites, especially the public ones in state or national parks, which are crowded to capacity most of the year, are terrible fly attractions. In these campsites, a fly cabinet is one of the most useful types of cache. It is a box, usually suspended because of ants, covered with netting to keep the flies out.

One variation employs a pan of water on top of the box with the water being syphoned down the sides by the capillary action of the netting. This forms an evaporative cooler which keeps the food up to ten degrees F (6°C) cooler and thus fairly fresh even in hot weather.

When food is cached for several days in the summertime, ants often become a problem. You can prevent this by using an antproof hook. Weld, braze, or solder a cup to the hook in a leakproof manner. Attach the hook between the cache and the suspending rope, then fill the cup with water. A light film of oil on the surface of the water will retard the evaporation.

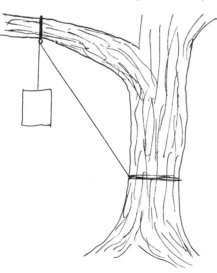

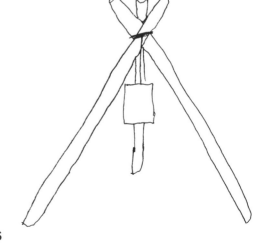

CACHES

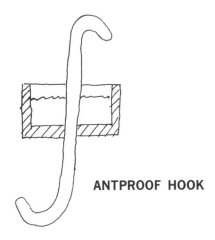

ANTPROOF HOOK

Dampening the rope with kerosene will also antproof it for several days. However, kerosene will taint food and if you use too much you are in trouble.

DISH-WASHING

The most unpopular part of camping is dish-washing. It is bad enough at home (except possibly with an automatic dish-washer), but it is much harder in camp. This is because of the trouble in getting hot water and because most of the cooking is done over open fires which blacken the pans. In spite of the problems, there are several ways to reduce much of the work.

One way is to avoid blackening the bottoms of the utensils. Mix a thick paste of soap and water, or use liquid detergent, and cover the outside of the pot with a thin coating. If the coating is not broken (it scratches off easily after it dries in the fire), the blackening will wash off the utensil without scraping or scrubbing.

Another good way is to forget about the blackened outside, saving both the weight of carrying the detergent and the time it takes to apply it, and just clean the inside (plus any food particles on the outside). Let the blackening build up. This helps increase the efficiency of the utensil by absorbing more heat and transmitting it evenly over the blackened area.

If you cook over softwood flames, you will have a certain amount of trouble from this deposit

because it will be heavy and almost fluffy. Because this coating of soot is so fluffy, it holds quite a bit of trapped air and actually has an insulating effect. While use of very hot flames or coals will, in turn, burn this fluff off, you generally have to clean it off with vast quantities of elbow grease. If you have to use softwoods, use soap coating, as the soot will be working against you, not with you.

This problem with blackening can be avoided by only using coals or stoves. However, even with coals a certain amount of blackening occurs. While this is a beneficial amount, it will rub off and you will need to protect the insides of the pots around it in the nesting set from getting dirty. The best way is to use individual bags for each utensil in the nest. While this means another ounce (25 to 50 g) of weight, and a long session at the sewing machine, it does have other advantages (see Chapter 6).

A third way is to avoid the use of regular utensils by using aluminum foil. Its use in baking is quite well known to most campers, who generally use it for baking potatoes or for one-"pot" hamburger and vegetable combinations. It is, however, quite useful for cooking other foods too. Its main advantage, even over the avoidance of dish-washing, is that it retains all the juices of meat, and only the driest of vegetables need water added. All the vitamins are retained instead of being cooked away as happens in an open pot. However, it is fairly expensive since the foil generally can be used only once.

Aluminum foil from a roll is not the only way of using aluminum foil in camp cooking. Frozen foods quite often come in aluminum-foil pans—not only the shallow (often too shallow to use in camp cooking), divided pans for TV dinners, but also the deeper and more versatile round and rectangular pans for meat pies and cakes. If you use these foods very often, the number of little pans mounts up quickly. By taking several of them, along with freeze-dried food, the entire food supply for a one-week camping trip will weigh less than ten pounds ($4\frac{1}{2}$ kg) for two people (and still equal the traditional two and a half pounds [1 kg] per person per day of food). After the pans are used, they can be thrown away.

Another way is to line the inside of a nesting-set pot with aluminum foil and put foil or soap over the outside. This is too wasteful for normal use, but if you have more aluminum foil than time, it might be worth it.

When you finally face the fact that you will have to wash dishes sometime (even if only the insides), you will need the proper equipment. The best item is several of the small, throw-away scouring pads with soap in them. A sponge and a good, grease-cutting powdered cleanser is also useful. The cleanser should be kept in a waterproof can or large pill bottle to prevent hardening or the loss of chlorine.

Always use hot water for washing. Build the fire up, if necessary, and put some water on to boil while you eat. Use your largest pot (already cleaned) for this. All utensils should be scraped as clean as possible before wetting. Put a little of the water in the utensil you are cleaning and scrub it with the scouring pad. Do not mix soap with the supply of boiling water (such as by dunking the pot you are cleaning), but keep it clean.

Using the soapy water in the utensil, wash the inside and, if needed or desired, the outside. Rinse with just enough clean cold water to get all the soap off. Then give it a final rinse in the boiling water. Put it aside, upside down, to drain. By rinsing in boiling water, it will drain dry without streaking or spotting.

If you are backpacking, or if your supply of detergent has run out, you will need a substitute. The best one, both for the availability of the materials and the chemistry involved, is ash from the cooking fire. Ashes have long been a source of alkali for making soap. If there is any grease in the pot, you will have a crude lye soap automatically. Get ashes that have turned white, indicating that the charcoal has been completely burned out. A little fine sand or charcoal will furnish abrasive to help in the scouring action.

Don't use too much ash. Especially with aluminum utensils, the resultant lye will etch it deeply enough to ruin it. Also, too high a concentration will ruin your hands as well. Even this crudely made lye is quite caustic. Use only enough to combine with the fat to be changed into soap. In this form, it is relatively harmless and an efficient cleaner.

LAUNDRY

Since camping clothes are usually the washable type, laundry in camp is just a matter of hand-scrubbing. While this is hardly like dumping them in a washing machine, it is not too difficult.

The chemical detergents, as opposed to old-fashioned soap, makes laundry easier, and, thanks to a hard battle, laws now require biodegradable detergents and pollution is no longer the camp problem it once was. However, the precautions formerly required with the old polluting detergents should still be followed as a good conservation practice: use as small an amount of low-sudsing detergent as you can, and don't dump the wash water into standing or flowing water. Even though, unlike the old stuff, it will decompose, it still makes the water taste bad until it has completely decomposed. Also the phosphates in many high-suds detergents fertilize the pond sufficiently that algae growth is stimulated to the point that the natural bogging cycle is accelerated to a matter of years rather than centuries.

Dig a pit, far from water, and dump it there. Your latrine is as good as any place. Fill in enough dirt to absorb the water.

An adequate supply of hot water is all the remaining washing equipment needed. A tent guy or length of parachute cord supplies the clothesline. If you are far away from a plentiful water supply, wash only your socks and, possibly, your underwear.

On the other hand, if you are car camping, get a large plastic bucket with a water-tight lid. This makes an excellent washing machine on the back roads. Start out with hot, soapy water and the clothes. After a while on the road, empty the soapy water, rinse the bucket and the clothes, and add hot, clear water and drive on. After a while longer, change the water again and give it a final rinse. Finally, hang them up somewhere to dry (while eating lunch at a roadside park perhaps). Laundry completed. The bouncing of the car furnishes the agitation.

When getting a supply of hot water for this is a problem, the cold-water detergents can be used.

It is often possible to combine the use of a commercial washateria with some other in-town activity such as grocery shopping. Many of the privately owned public campgrounds have such facilities, and more of the publicly owned ones are putting them in.

SANITATION

Sanitation is always a camp problem. Even in campsites where you have plumbing, you will still have no other means of refuse disposal except garbage cans. These are emptied with varying efficiency.

In wilderness areas, you are usually on your own for practically all your sanitation operations. Therefore, the few simple skills needed in this department must be known by any camper who enters these areas.

Garbage

In wilderness areas, where there are no garbage cans, all garbage should be buried. Bury aluminum foil the deepest since it decays very slowly. With tin cans, open them at both ends, put the ends inside the can, and flatten the can. They will rust away in a couple of years. Then put the rest of the garbage in the pit.

If the pit is to be used several times while you are at that particular campsite, cover the garbage with at least three inches (75 mm) of dirt after each time the pit is used. The last layer of garbage in the pit should be at least one foot (30 cm) below the surface and covered with a mound over the top or all sorts of interesting creatures will visit your cafeteria—especially skunks.

Mark the filled mound with an X of sticks. Use sticks at least one inch (25 mm) in diameter for two reasons. First, they are more visible than smaller ones. Second, by the time they rot away, the garbage inside will have rotted too.

In areas that are frequently used, but don't have garbage cans, never bury metallic waste. Clean and flatten foil and cans and carry them out to dispose. They weigh very little. The metal takes a long time to decay—especially aluminum. There have been several popular wilderness areas ruined because too many people buried their garbage there in too short a span of time. Bury metal only in places which will not be used by more than three or four groups per year. If you can't find out how many use the area, take it out as a precaution.

No matter how seldom used the area is, never bury glass or plastics, as they practically never decay (although sometimes you can burn the plastic). Fortunately, glass is seldom used in wilderness camping because of its breakability.

Where they are supplied, always use garbage cans. If they are full, report it to the campground authorities.

Grease

Grease is usually just thrown on the ground, in the fire, or poured in the trash can in public campsites. Every campsite should have its own grease trap. They are easy to make and operate. Even where garbage cans are furnished, the fly problem is much less when they are used. The secret is in making a tight enough screen of grass over the top. You should not be able to see the bottom of the pit through the grass. The grease sticks to the grass as the water goes through. After an hour in the sun, burn the grass. Use dead grass, of course. It is needed both for the absorption of the grease and the burning of the grass. Make a fresh screen daily.

In most cases, straight grease will not be involved in the use of a grease trap since it will usually be saved for use in cooking. The grease that a grease trap catches is what is loosened in the dish-washing process, although some will often be drained from a skillet which is set to drip on the trap awhile after

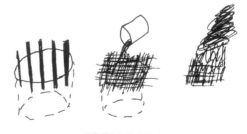

GREASE TRAP

most of the grease is poured off. Burned food particles in the skillet make the grease supply an unsuitable place for this final dripping.

Latrines

Toilet facilities are always a problem. Public campsite toilets are much like the garbage cans—some places they are immaculate, in others they are dangerous. In fact, the garbage cans are often a good indication of the condition of the restrooms.

Other than the standard plumbing, there are several solutions to the problem. By far the best one is a chemical toilet with a vent. The toilets empty directly into a tank of chemicals (usually a chloride-of-lime solution or similar disinfectant) with a vent in the roof to carry the gases out. The typical method is with a turbine at the top of the vent. It works well whenever the wind is blowing, but without a wind, the odors may start coming back up the toilets.

One answer to this problem works well on small units (up to four toilets). A small flame, usually butane, in the vent sets up the needed convection currents. Sometimes the particular section of vent pipe at the flame is clear plastic, so it also acts as a night-light for the inside of the building. Another advantage of the flame is that it destroys the odors, although they seldom reach the ground again after being vented the usual way.

Next down the scale of quality comes the un-vented chemical toilet. This is the type often used on construction sites for the workmen. They are usually adequate if the building is vented and the holding tank is emptied often enough. They have a definite odor, but it is usually the chemical, and, while strong, it is not really unpleasant.

The old-style privy, with nothing to kill the odor, is the worst of all. It is, of course, much worse in warmer weather. Sprinkling lime in the pit after using will keep down the odors, but this is not done in public campgrounds because people tend to waste the lime by putting in too much. Therefore, the problem continues.

The final form seems worst of all, but, because of the conditions which permit its use in the first place, it is not nearly as bad as the privy. That is a do-it-yourself latrine which every wilderness camper will have to construct at some time in his camping career. It really isn't difficult. First you need to locate it carefully. The campsite should definitely be up-wind from it. It should be well screened with brush or canvas for privacy. It should be free of standing water after a prolonged rain, and no nearer than two hundred feet (60 m) to any stream (because of pollution) if you stay at that campsite for more than a day or two. It should be far enough from camp that it doesn't draw flies to the living and cooking areas, yet be close enough for convenience in an emergency. The path should be easily negotiated in the dark. The paths should be cut or tramped in the grass. Never pull up grass to make a path—it will be muddy if on level ground and will cause erosion if on a slope. Also, don't pack the grass so much that it kills it.

There are two types of improvised camping latrines. One is the cat-hole. It is so called because it is simply a hole in the ground which you cover after using once—just as a cat does.

The other is a little more elaborate. It has some sort of seat, a deep hole, a pile of dirt, and some means of scraping the dirt back in the hole. The

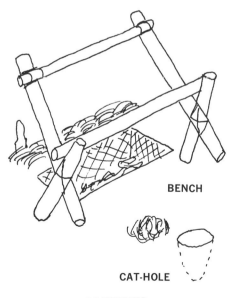

BENCH

CAT-HOLE

LATRINES

seat is usually a one-pole arrangement, lashed together with binder twine or parachute cord. If you stay long, chlorinated lime should be sprinkled in the trench before covering with dirt in order to reduce the odor. A small wooden paddle, whittled out of a suitably large piece of wood, can serve as a shovel for pushing the dirt back into the hole, thus freeing your usual digging implements for other duties.

There are folding toilets on the market which have a standard seat and a disposable bag underneath. Where weight and bulk are of no concern, you might try them, either with the bag or over a pit. Generally, however, they are even too bulky for cars. Probably station wagons are their best use, since trailers and camping machines can take a water toilet with a built-in holding tank.

Regardless of the toilet system, the flat kind of toilet paper, such as is used in public restrooms, is best, especially when going light. It not only fits in the pack more compactly, you can take only a part of the package and not have the bulk of a whole roll. Be sure, however, to take more than an adequate supply.

There should be some container (a large tin can on a stand is excellent) to keep the toilet paper dry in wet weather. You can fit the roll type with a can on a string to keep it waterproof. However, the hole in the can should be drilled rather than punched, to keep it from sawing the string in two.

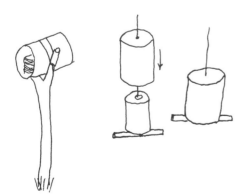

TOILET-PAPER SHELTERS

A bucket of water nearby for washing hands will help maintain home sanitation standards.

When camping with babies, diapers are a problem. The commercial disposable ones are good for very young babies, but lack the "capacity" of the cloth types. Washing diapers in camp is not only difficult, it is no vacation. This problem can be solved by buying used diapers from a diaper service. These are a bit threadbare in places, but still quite as good as the new ones. They are generally in better condition than your regular ones are before they are finally converted into dust rags, wipe cloths, or whatever you do with old diapers. What's more, they actually cost less than the commercial disposable ones. It takes will-power at first, but you simply throw them away after use. Bury them deeply, the same as the latrines. In developed campsites, check with the management about how to dispose of them.

WATER SUPPLY

Many campsites have a water system—a purification plant and hydrants. Others have a pump and a pure-water well. Still others, usually the remote and/or desert ones, do not have any system at all. In these wilderness areas, the problem of adequate water is left up to the camper.

There are two solutions to this problem. First, you can bring in the fresh water with the rest of your gear. It has the advantage of being pure, the disadvantage of being limited in capacity and therefore impractical for long periods. However, in desert areas this is usually your only choice.

The second method is to purify the water in camp. It has the advantage of an unlimited supply of raw water, the disadvantage of being a bother to use.

There are three standard ways to haul water, although almost any container will do the job. These are the canvas water bag, the rubberized bag, and the jerry can. They were discussed in more detail in Chapter 9.

The canvas bag is perfect in camp, even if you use other methods for the actual transportation of the water. Hanging from a tree or tripod in a shady area of the camp, it will keep one to five gallons

(4 to 20 liters) of cool water at the cost of only about a half-pint of water per day to the evaporation that cools it.

Where water is available in streams or a lake, it may be better if you purify your own on the spot. The most common method of water purification is to boil it for at least five minutes—twenty is often recommended. Allow it to cool. Then aerate it by pouring it from one container to another to get rid of the flat taste that the boiling produces.

While boiling won't remove solids such as salt or silt (in fact, it concentrates them), it will kill the bacteria. Obviously, it is of use only when you have adequate fuel.

An ideal method of purification and clarification combined is to rig a small still. The still is the only way you can get drinkable water from brackish or sea water.

Another advantage of distilling your water is that it removes most of the bad taste that water often has. It will also give you clear water from muddy water, although your boiler will be a mess when you finish.

If your water supply is dirty, and you don't use a still, you will need some way of clarifying the water. Filtering is the easiest. Use a filter from a chemical supply store or one made for a type of coffee maker. These are disks of porous paper which are folded to fit the inside of a funnel. The water is poured in the funnel and drips through the filter into a suitable container below. The chemical filter does a more thorough job, but takes quite a long time. The coffee filter will do it faster, but you may have water that still looks like it has coffee in it.

A length of kerosene-lantern wick used as a siphon is a good filter. Soak it first in water and then set it up as you would any other siphon. The water rises by capillary action but soon drips out the lower end, leaving the mud behind in the top container.

If the water has a bad taste or odor, boil some charcoal with it and let it stand overnight. Remove the charcoal and treat it with your usual purification and clarification method. If the taste and/or odor is due to animal or vegetable matter, instead of dissolved minerals, they will often carry through the distillation process, so, even with a still, use the charcoal first with bad-smelling water.

Regardless of the method you use, if it involves heating, aerate the water after treating to restore its taste.

Chemical purification methods, such as Bursoline tablets, iodine, or chloride-of-lime, are useful in areas where fuel is scarce. Acid is helpful if the water is extremely alkaline.

With normal activities and temperatures, an adult needs two quarts (2 liters) of water per day. With strenuous activities and/or high temperatures, the needed amount is higher. With exertion, the salt requirements also rise, so increase that intake also with salt tablets or extra salt on your food. Up to forty per cent sea water may be mixed with fresh water and drunk without harm.

PART VI

The Extra Benefits

No one goes camping just to stay in a tent — you can do that in your back yard with much less cost. There is always something to do. Sometimes it will be as intangible as Thoreau's meditations at Walden Pond. Sometimes it will be as tangible as an addition to the menu. It can be an activity or a new experience which enriches the total man—which is the purpose of camping anyway.

Two activities which are essentially means of transportation and are covered in Part IX are hiking and canoeing. Even when you hike and canoe for pure recreation, without the burden of camping gear, the techniques are basically the same—therefore, they won't be duplicated here.

With the exception of swimming, all of the activities discussed in this part require a camp setting to enjoy them to the fullest extent. This does not mean that you have to *be* camping; you can just go out for the day. And it does not deny the potential for nature study and photography in the back yard or the city park; but the potential in these places is greatly reduced and an expert is often required in order to find anything at all. Few cities have fishing facilities in which you really have much chance of catching anything except "rough" fish and garbage. Very few have climbing, even a fifty-foot (15 m) cliff for rock-climbing practice. And probably none have caves worth exploring which are not commercially exploited. None permit hunting, although some do have target ranges and trap and skeet ranges.

Because of such restrictions, many people consider these activities to be the only purpose of camping. As a result, they seldom think of trying any others. Camping for them is simply living in convenient proximity to a trout stream, game country, or mountains. While these are perfectly valid reasons for camping and I would hardly discourage them, these people are usually in a rut. The hunter, for instance, may also photograph. The bird watcher often does, but he will seldom regard a mountain as anything but a nuisance to be avoided if possible, and he will consider canoeing useful only because a canoe is quieter than a motorboat and doesn't scare the animals as readily.

None of the activities in these chapters are particularly hard for the beginner. They have been sufficiently developed so that their gradations of difficulty are firmly established and recognized. The beginner can start on something within his ability and progress to more difficult aspects as his skills and interests develop. There are hard and easy mountains, caves, and white-water streams; plentiful and rare plants and animals; easy and difficult techniques in hunting, fishing, and swimming; easy and difficult conditions for wildlife photography. As a result, the well-rounded camper will want to try them all, at least to some degree. There are several benefits from this attitude. You may find a new field of interest that you will want to pursue to the point of excellence. In adopting the viewpoints of these other activities you will understand why certain things should be preserved which you would otherwise consider unimportant. You will learn skills in that particular field that will be useful in other fields. And it is good discipline to try something new.

A basic knowledge of the skills of hunting and fishing is invaluable in the unpleasant circumstances of survival conditions. A knowledge of backpacking and canoeing add a greater dimension to the camping possible with the easier, and therefore more popular and overcrowded, transportation systems. A knowledge of nature adds immeasurably to your camping enjoyment, and skill in wildlife photography enables you not only to recapture these moments but also to share them with others. Climbing and spelunking not only challenge the mind and body, they also teach you the skills of developing a light pack and reducing your equipment to the maximum comfort in the minimum weight and bulk. And swimming is not only a valuable camp sport in its own right, it is a necessary safety skill for the canoeist, boat camper, or fisherman.

The activities discussed here are skills which must be developed. As with all such skills, they can't really be learned from a book. The purpose of including them is to show those of you who have not had extensive experience in them what equipment is needed, what skills must be learned, what conditions are needed to participate, what laws concern some of them, what the dangers are and how to avoid them, and what sources you can call upon to assist you in developing these skills.

With these skills, the whole range of camping enjoyment will open up—easy in the basics, difficult to master. Generally, the cost of the equipment is low and the rewards are great. They are a great stimulus toward real camping. Typical overnight picnickers refuse serious camping on the grounds that they "don't want to go out under all those primitive conditions," they "like comfort." Frankly, so do I. I see no reason to undertake the harder forms of camping, such as backpacking, just to be doing it. On the other hand, I would again, as I did once, hike across Grand Canyon—a substantial part of the way on a six-inch (15 cm) water pipe—if that is the only way I can see the great beauty of that area unspoiled by the legal vandalism of dam builders and concessionaires.

CHAPTER TWENTY-THREE

Nature Study

Nature study is probably the most popular camp activity. It is often enjoyed by people who would deny it is even what they are doing. ("Come look at this funny-looking bug!" "What is that grey bird that goes down a tree head first?") It is also enjoyed by dedicated amateurs (in the original sense of the word) who come equipped with a portable library of field guides, checklists, high-powered binoculars, photographic equipment, and even high-fidelity tape recorders and parabolic reflector microphones.

Nature study may be casual or it may be the entire purpose of the camping trip. But even if it only amounts to admiring pretty scenery, it is a reason campers will travel for miles to an out-of-the-way campsite (civilization having an unfortunate habit of destroying natural beauty).

Nature study includes not only the most popular, bird watching, but a wide range of other wildlife, from the smallest moss to the giant redwoods. It also covers rocks, minerals, fossils, weather, and many other fields. The study of weather is useful in all forms of camping. Snow is a topic of concern to mountain climbers since techniques vary on different types of snow. Geology is important to climbers and white-water canoeists, and it is the total reason for the sport of spelunking. Nature study involves reading tracks and other signs as well as simply recognizing animals. Nature is a perfect subject for photography, a shy subject which is always changing, creating the challenge of diffi-cult lighting conditions in addition to the standard problems of photography itself.

Equipment and techniques will vary with the field of study, but the cost of the equipment is low compared with that for other activities and the basic techniques are easy to learn. On the other hand, the skills of the expert are developed over a lifetime and the serious student will never fail to be challenged. In addition, there are many excellent books on specific areas of nature, and field guides to help you identify your finds.

EQUIPMENT

Although much of what you need in the way of equipment depends on what phase of nature study you are interested in, two items are needed regardless of the field—a small notebook and a pen or pencil. The pen should be the ballpoint type with an extra cartridge. These do not smear or leak if they get wet. In the notebook you will record your field observations. Field guides for identification will be needed, but keep the weight down. If you are going light, you can record a full description of the specimen in your notebook and look it up when you get back. A basic sketching ability is valuable as I have found that I normally fail to record the critical field mark in my verbal description. Particularly pay attention to the number and location of stripes or color patterns. Size is also important in narrowing down the list.

While the equipment comparatively is low, it is not cheap and must be selected with care. While much of it can be made or improvised, the items you must buy often vary widely in price, which only slightly reflects quality. This is especially true of binoculars and cameras.

Binoculars

For studying wild animals, you will need optical help. Binoculars are standard, but if you are going ultra-light a monocular will do. The monocular has the further advantage of being usable as a telescopic lens in a single-lens reflex camera. For most uses, however, the small-size (but fairly high-powered) binoculars will generally be better. They weigh under a half-pound (225 g) for six or seven power. Achromatic lens are a must to prevent the halation or rainbow effect around the edges.

Don't get field glasses. The difference between field glasses and binoculars is simple — binoculars use both lenses and prisms, while field glasses use only the lenses. The prisms produce the effect of very long field glasses without the extra bulk or weight. They give a clearer image and are sturdier.

Binoculars are rated by power—the number of times the object is magnified. This is given as a number followed by x (meaning "times"). The second number given is the diameter of the objective lens (the one farthest away from you, and thus closest to the object, as you look through it) measured in millimeters. The most common size, the 7 x 35, would magnify the image seven times and have an objective lens with a diameter of thirty-five millimeters.

The field-of-view figures are quite valuable in choosing binoculars. Around 375 is average. This means that you can see an area 375 feet wide at a range of one thousand yards. Generally, the larger the objective, the larger the field of view. However, there are many exceptions. The featherweights, with their small objective lens, are quite competitive in the field-of-view category with the larger binoculars. Wide-angle binoculars, with fields of view over 425 or so, often gain this figure at the cost of sharpness, and their image is sometimes distorted in the pin-cushion effect (a checkerboard pattern that tends to flare out at the edges).

Another valuable point in choosing binoculars is their relative light efficiency. This will give you an idea of how well you can see with them in dim light. Since animals are most active at dawn and dusk, this is important. Relative light efficiency is determined by dividing the objective number by the power and squaring the result. For coated lens, add fifty per cent. The ideal minimum is twenty-five or an objective diameter five times the power. As you can see, the little 6 x 15 featherweights lose out here despite their other excellent features. In the case of coated lens (which are the most common, though you should nonetheless make sure they are when you buy), the featherweight would have a relative light efficiency of only 10.675 while the 7 x 35 would have a 37.5. This difference shows up quite noticeably at dusk if you compare the two.

High power is a mixed blessing. The higher the power, the better detail you will get of distant objects. But you also get a smaller field of view and a greater problem of wobble. A slight movement of the instrument will produce a large movement of the image. A seven-power instrument is about the highest that can be hand-held in the field—eight-power if you are very steady. Any higher power needs a support, such as a stick or a steady upward pull on a cord held under your foot. These are a bit awkward to set up under field conditions. When you get above twelve-power, a tripod is all that will work. This obviously makes high-powered binoculars inconvenient in the field, especially when trying to pick up the image of a running chipmunk fifty feet away.

For general nature study, 6 x 30 or 7 x 35 binoculars are the best. For hikers, the 6 x 15 is excellent. It weighs only seven ounces (200 g) and will fit comfortably in your pocket, whereas the larger ones weigh a couple of pounds (about 1 kg) and require a sturdy carrying case to protect them. If you are watching a certain area from a blind, twelve-power is the top limit. Above that, the field of view and the wobble make it too unwieldy for most wildlife study.

The comparatively new "zoom" binoculars are variable-power binoculars running from seven to twelve or more power. You change the power while using the binoculars by rotating a knob similar to the focus adjustment. The ones currently on the market have two serious drawbacks, as far as their use in camping is concerned. The first is their weight and bulk, which makes them a little cumbersome for nature study. The other problem is the power. They would be better for camping if the power varied from three to eight rather than upward from seven.

As every child soon finds out when playing with one, when you look through binoculars from the objective lens, things appear greatly reduced except when the object is very close. Binoculars make an excellent magnifying glass for studying plants and mineral specimens, extracting a splinter, or any other use you may have for a magnifying glass. The featherweights are especially valuable since you conveniently hold them with one hand. I have stopped carrying a hand loupe when camping because of this versatility of the 6 x 15

In selecting binoculars for camping, your first and best guarantee is the place where you buy them. All of the major camping and climbing outfitters carry excellent binoculars. The ones you get at major department stores are usually of good quality, but they are also heavier than is really needed, marketed for those who fallaciously think big size means high power.

Test the glasses carefully. A modern, box-type skyscraper is an excellent subject, being a grid of intersecting vertical and horizontal lines. If possible, be well above ground level or at a considerable distance from the building to reduce the effect of perspective on the parallel lines. This particular pattern may also be found inside the store somewhere—in an air-conditioning grille, shelves, etc. It will best show up any lens distortion caused by trying to build in more magnification or relative light efficiency than the size of the binoculars would otherwise handle. Sweep it slowly from side to side, watching the lines at the edge of the image. If they move relative to one another, the image is distorted.

Also consider weight carefully. Binoculars don't feel particularly heavy in the store, but how heavy will they feel when hiking a considerable distance, or when holding them for prolonged periods in a blind?

Finally, what is the packaging? The feather-weights are easy—I carry mine in its flexible case (to keep out dust), in my shirt pocket, with the cord around my neck to reduce the danger of it coming out and dropping. The large ones must be carried from the shoulder under the opposite arm and therefore they tend to be banged around a bit by the arm. The best binocular case is made from very heavy leather with a plush inside. Leather is fairly rigid, yet it will flex enough to help absorb the shock of banging. The plush is needed both to further cushion the instrument, and to keep out dust from the lens.

A small seam is a good place to keep the stub of a small brush (number 3 watercolor) to clean the lens. A bulb-type camera lens brush is even better if you have the space in the binocular case for it. These brushes will reduce the chance of accidentally scratching the lens as opposed to simply rubbing them with a tissue.

Botanical Equipment

For most camping areas, the total equipment needed for plant study is a magnifying glass. The ideal is a folding, three-lens magnifier giving five through twenty power. A jeweler's loupe is also useful. Many plants are quite small and the lens is needed in counting stamens and gaining the necessary data in order to key out its identity.

Since specimen collecting is outlawed in most campsite areas except by special permit, collecting cases and plant presses will not find much use with the average camper. However, if you should have the opportunity to build your own herbarium, these two items are not hard to make.

The collecting case is typically a cylindrical can with half of it, down the length of the cylinder, forming the lid. This is fitted with a shoulder strap for ease of carrying. The cylinder is about six inches (15 cm) in diameter and a foot and a half to two feet (45 to 60 cm) long. This permits the collected specimen to be transported with a minimum of damage.

You can make a plant press from some scrap half-inch (12 mm) plywood, several desk blotters, and some old newspapers in a sandwich arrangement, with a couple of light webbing straps or leather post-office straps to bind the whole thing together. The plant goes between two sheets of newspaper, between the blotters, and the whole thing is squeezed together for a couple of days.

The dried specimen is then mounted, with mucilage, on light poster paper, using narrow strips of tape or thread stitching to reënforce it at various spots. Put a label giving information on the plant at the bottom of the paper.

For conservation reasons, never take more than one specimen from a group of at least ten.

Mineralogy Gear

The geologist's pick is basic for rock hounds. A half-inch (12 mm) cold chisel is also good for removing samples, especially delicate crystals which would be damaged by heavy hammering to remove them from their matrix. Old dental picks are excellent for cleaning up a specimen, but are more valuable in fossil preparation.

Almost as necessary as these tools of removal is a good assortment of cloth bags. These will vary from the size it takes to hold a cubic-inch (10 cm^3) specimen on up to a fifty-pound (22$\frac{1}{2}$ kg) feed bag to hold the other bags. If you won't be collecting very many specimens, you can use your pockets, although this gets them dirtier than is really necessary.

An elaborate Mohs' scale is unnecessary for field identification. A basic field form of the kit is: fingernail 2$\frac{1}{2}$, penny 3, knife blade 5, glass 5$\frac{1}{2}$, and a piece of file 6$\frac{1}{2}$.

A small piece of unglazed porcelain will do for smear tests. A three-quarter-inch (2 cm) square of mosaic tile or ceramic floor tile is excellent. Just be sure that the back is unglazed. A magnifier, similar to that used in the botanical equipment, is useful for making out the crystal structure of small veins or grainy rocks. Ten-power is the highest necessary. A three-quarter by one-inch alnico magnet is useful in distinguishing between the many forms of black, grainy rocks between six and seven on the Mohs' scale. Just keep it away from your compass.

While hardly necessary, Estwing's Gem Scoop is a useful gadget to avoid backache from prowling over the ground. It is also useful and safe for turning over rocks which may have snakes or wasps'

nests under them. A gold-pan is useful for panning, not only gold, but other heavy minerals from stream gravel. Shovels, picks, screens, and other tools of minor earth-moving operations are useful if you are collecting for sale or trade.

There are two items of mineral-hunting gear which begin to run into money but add flexibility to prospecting and the greater enjoyment to be had in a serious collection of mineral specimens. The first of these is the Geiger-Müller counter, which provides certain proof of radioactivity in minerals. Probably even more valuable for the average rock hound is the ultra-violet light source, or black light.

The black light comes in two different types—long wave and short wave. Because everything but the power source must be different, they are rarely available in the same unit. The short wave is the more useful, although both will find service. The black light performs two duties for the rock hound. First, it is an aid in identification. Many types of rocks look alike—they have the same color, crystal structure, hardness, etc.—yet they react differently to ultra-violet light, glowing with entirely different colors or not at all. As a result, portable lamps are extremely valuable in prospecting tungsten ores and other commercially valuable minerals. The second use of the black light is purely for show. Fluorescent rocks are beautiful, glowing with bright and eerie colors. They enhance any display.

Finally, although they cannot be considered field gear, a bunsen burner, charcoal block, blowpipe, and specific-gravity scale are all useful in a small laboratory back home. These, plus a few chemicals, will enable you to positively identify any mineral.

For lapidarists, there is a good rule of thumb concerning rocks: if it is solid rather than cracked, compact rather than grainy, and a knife blade won't scratch it, it will take a polish. (As with most rules of thumb, there are exceptions. Some cracked and even grainy rocks polish beautifully.)

Paleontology Equipment

A geologist's pick is helpful for fossil hunting, but hitting the matrix with another rock will often dislodge the fossil just as well—if you know how. An old paste brush, with the bristles cut down to an eighth-inch (3 mm) in length, is good for cleaning the dirt off a specimen. An awl, a dental pick, an ice pick sharpened to a thinner point, or a small cold chisel is useful for chipping away bits of matrix and the chisel is required for dislodging them from a large matrix. A magnifying glass is all else that is needed, with the possible exception of small bags for the specimens if you don't want to carry them in your pocket.

Universities, museums, and local rock clubs are the best sources of field guides to local fossils.

HOW TO SEE THE ANIMALS

With camping areas becoming more crowded, wildlife is being more cautious, if not forced out completely. As a result, it is becoming more difficult to even get to see any wildlife.

Stalking

It is tragic that the Boy Scouts dropped their old Stalking merit badge from the list. It was a tough badge, involving the photographing of wild animals in difficult circumstances with normal snapshot-type equipment. It was dropped because "not enough passed the requirements," yet the boys who did struggle through and pass got far more than a small patch of embroidered cloth for their uniforms. They learned the most important part of nature study—how to meet the animals on their own terms and win. As a result, they were not only more knowledgeable about the wilds and better photographers because of what they had learned about lighting, they learned the self-discipline required in staying absolutely still for an hour at a time, and were better conservationists because they became part of the ecological structure, not merely somewhat interested observers.

Animals rarely pose. If you want more than just a fleeting glimpse through binoculars, you will have to learn how to approach an animal without alarming him. This is doubly difficult because all animals are preyed upon by some other animal, and most of them are preyed upon by man. As a result, the animal you want to watch will probably have very good reasons why he does not want you to watch him.

The first rule in stalking is to see him first. Observation is the secret of wildlife study. Always keep on the look-out for anything. If the animal sees you first, he will probably leave so quietly you will be convinced that there are no animals in the area.

This brings up a corollary to this rule: consider yourself watched at all times. If you do, you won't be tempted to make such unsound moves as darting across a clearing instead of working around it. If you are seen in this rather unskilled attitude, the animals will definitely become alarmed and not only leave immediately, but the crows, jays, squirrels, and other "warning" animals will publish up-to-the-minute bulletins on your exact whereabouts for the rest of the day.

Sir Robert Baden-Powell, founder of the Boy Scouts, was once asked, in reference to the Scout motto, "Prepared for what?" Baden-Powell replied, "Why, just anything!" This applies to stalking. Expect the unexpected and you will probably get to see it—and if you are skilled, you will probably get a treasured photograph of it too.

The second rule is to move slowly and quietly. Most animals have fairly poor vision, but they generally have excellent senses of hearing and smell. Do not, however, try to move in absolute silence. In the first place, it can't be done. In the second place, the snap of a twig, the crunch of a dry leaf, or the roll of a dislodged rock will alarm animals far more than an occasional slight noise.

The corollary to this rule is to move in spurts, as herbivores do. (They move slowly, feeding as they go, periodically—thirty seconds to a minute—raising their heads to look, listen, and sniff, while swallowing the food they have been chewing.)

The skilled stalker, then, will move up-wind in spurts, stepping on rocks or hard, bare ground in preference to leaves and on leaves in preference to sticks, and be ready to stop, completely motionless, at the least sign of nervousness on the part of his quarry.

The third rule is to blend with your background. Animals have a poorly developed sense of color, so color itself is not much of a concern. However, pattern is. While an animal cannot tell between a couple of blocks of color in the lab, other than that one is lighter than the other, a light-colored jacket will outline the unmistakable shape of *Homo sapiens* against the underbrush to any nervous animal.

Stalking animals rarely requires slithering around on your stomach. However, there are many times when crouching is necessary and occasionally times when you will have to slither or give up the stalk.

Use backgrounds and foregrounds as much as possible. The less of you that is visible to the quarry, the less you will risk having the quarry catch you moving. However, still consider yourself watched at all times. The "warning" animals don't care whether you are stalking them or not, they let everyone know about your presence. Once you set them off, you might as well sit down and make yourself comfortable, it will be at least an hour before you can start moving again.

When you choose your surroundings carefully, freezing will make you disappear into the background. When you freeze, look around by moving your eyes — not your head. If you spot something, make every move very, very slowly and be ready to freeze again at the slightest sign of nervousness on the part of the quarry.

In wooded areas, stalking is difficult because of the noise factor of the underbrush, but quite simple from the aspect of background. To a deer or similar animal, a person, perfectly still, doesn't look very different from an old tree trunk. Skilled stalkers have been able to actually touch a wild deer by moving up when it was feeding and freezing when it raised up. This takes considerable skill and practice, of course, but anyone can stalk a deer and get close enough so that its image will more than fill the field of view in a camera without using special lens.

The Blind

The blind required simply for observation does not have to be as elaborate as the one used for photography since in the latter you need some concealment of the movement of changing film and lenses and some shading of the brighter parts of your equipment.

Actually, you have only two considerations: the location and its comfort. You will need a location which gives a wide view of the surrounding area, yet does not stretch so far away that the animal in the distance is practically out of sight. You should have a fairly uniform background if you want to take photographs. And you should be downwind of the spot you view.

Your blind should be concealing, without obstructing your vision. You should, as with stalking, blend into your background. It should be comfortable in that you can maintain a comfortable position without having to twist and crane to see out.

To use such a set-up, you should go where the animals go, and get there ahead of them. Ponds are excellent places to watch. In the first place, they form the water holes for the larger mammals; in the second, they have their own very interesting wildlife all day long. Lush pastures are also good, especially if well shaded. They are used even in the heat of the day when most areas are practically deserted. Mornings and evenings between dark and sun-up or sunset and dark are the best times of the day.

There are many ways to lure animals to your blind. Garbage pits and salt blocks set for cattle will attract many types of animals. However, the blind itself should still be chosen with care. You cannot depend entirely on the lure, you still have to use the stalker's skills.

One of the best lures is "squeeking." After waiting anywhere from ten minutes to half an hour, depending on how much the animals were disturbed by your arrival, you can start squeeking. There are two ways to produce the squeek. The first is to put your finger (the base joint) over your mouth horizontally, and suck. Get a high-pitched squeek, not a smack. The squeek is not loud—it doesn't have to be. Repeat it in a chattering pattern for about thirty seconds, then stop for about fifteen—unless you have visitors.

Mechanical squeeker produces a wide variety of sounds which attract birds and mammals.

The second method is with a squeeker. This is a piece of wood with a hole in it. A pewter plug is coated with rosin and put in the hole. Turning the plug produces the squeeks. With a little practice, you can produce a wide variety of tones and patterns.

When you get an answer—usually a bird about ten feet (3 m) away looking completely puzzled—keep it up as long as he shows an interest and stop if he gets nervous. At all times, don't make a perceptible move.

Some of the commercial predator calls will attract a large variety of animals. Check about the legality of game calls. In some areas, possession is considered evidence of intent to hunt. The recorded waterfowl calls are in this category. In other areas, they are completely illegal. This is especially true of phonograph records of game birds. However, the records are most valuable in learning the calls.

It is tempting to put food out as a lure for animals. Resist this temptation completely. About the only animals you can rely on attracting by this means are the skunk, the bear, the raccoon, the field mouse, and occasionally a deer. Only the coon will give you a show worth the problems that come with it although the deer will sometimes give you some good photographic subjects. Animals poaching off people are one of the biggest problems in many of our parks. With bears, this is absolutely dangerous. These are wild animals and not tame at all. The problem of destructive bears in our parks could be completely remedied within five years if people would obey the rule: Do not feed the animals. Most people give food that is nutritionally bad for the animals as well.

PRACTICE

Like all skills involving a wide variety of the senses, stalking requires practice. Just reading this chapter or any other written source on the subject is not going to do more than give you an intellectual acquaintance with a few of the techniques. You have to learn to read the scene yourself. Much of this can be done in an area no wilder than a large city park, provided it has not been too carefully manicured.

The number of stalking games which can be used in these surroundings is endless. The Boy Scouts have collected quite a few, but anyone with a little imagination can think up more. A group of adults on a picnic trailing a whiffle-poof (an irregular log or piece of wood full of nails, dragged over the ground thirty minutes to an hour before trailing) is no more foolish-looking than a group of overweight businessmen playing touch football. As the skills are developed, the trail can be made more difficult. I once had a group of Scout leaders successfully follow a bare-log whiffle-poof trail which jumped ditches, backtrailed, and performed every other trick I could think of (without actually picking it up)—and the trail was four hours old.

The basic skill you need in order to see the animals is keen powers of observation, and this includes hearing as well as sight. Studying bird-song records (see Chapter 55) is excellent home practice in identifying the sounds of nature. You should have someone skip back and forth across the record so that the order in which they appear won't subconsciously aid in your identification.

A high-fidelity portable tape recorder, a good microphone, some earphones, and an old thirty-inch radar reflector for the mike will enable you to record some sounds of nature of your own. Birds aren't the only producers of melody in the wilds. Frogs have a wide variety of calls, especially in the spring. If you really want a challenge, try collecting mammal calls.

This sound-chasing is not only a great application of stalking techniques, it will open up a whole field of nature study, not only to you but to your friends.

The old Cub Scout standby, Kim's Game, can be adapted to increase your powers of observation. This is the game in which several objects are placed on a tray. You look at them for a half-minute or so and then they are covered and you are asked to list the items you remember. With skill, the viewing time is reduced, the number of objects increased, and/or you are required to describe them in greater detail.

The armchair camper's version of this game uses a photograph of a wilderness setting (a snapshot, an ad in a magazine, etc.). You get to look at it for one minute, then you list as much about it as possible, using a rough sketch or diagram. This should include the terrain, soil type, vegetation, animal life, compass-bearing of the camera, weather, best place for the tent, caches, latrine, and other aspects of camping life. Quite obviously, much of this you will only know from logical deduction. If there are no animals in the picture, your description of the wildlife must come from your knowledge of that particular habitat. If the soil doesn't show, the terrain and vegetation will have to give you the clues. The active camper might wish to start a file of such photographs, on the back of which he has listed, from personal observation of the actual site, the factors which must be deduced from the picture so that there are no arguments.

With practice, more information can be gained in a much shorter time. Finally, the skills of observation will be developed to such an extent that in fifteen seconds all the information can be gathered at a subconscious level, only to be developed in detail after the picture is removed. With this kind of training, you will be able to observe much more closely in the wilds.

CHAPTER TWENTY-FOUR

Photography

While the skills are different, it requires no less skill to photograph wild animals in their habitat than it does to participate in mountain climbing or white-water canoeing.

Nature photography is one of the most challenging forms of photography. In addition to dealing with the usual problems, the wildlife photographer must cope with vast differences in light and shadow, weather, the difficulty of getting his subject to pose in a realistic attitude, the remoteness of the scene, and the fact that the entire operation must be done not only from a camping situation but also from one in which the transportation is vastly restricted in weight and bulk.

Both the equipment and the skills must be keyed to these problems. The photographer must, for the most part, be completely self-contained in both his photographic and camping equipment. Because of the weight limits imposed by the photographic equipment, the normal camping equipment must either be reduced to the bare minimum or extensive trips from base camp to the shooting site must be made—often in the dark of the morning in order to be at the blind at the time which is least disturbing to the subject.

While anyone can get a recognizable shot of some of the semi-wild animals in our national parks, the other extreme of wildlife photography is so difficult that there have been only a handful of experts in the art. This expert level was gained through the exposure of miles of film, total dedication, and a considerable basic talent to start with. However, any camper can learn to do far better than he is now doing.

CAMERAS

For the serious nature photographer, the camera used must meet several rather rigid requirements. These requirements apply to still and movie cameras alike. First of all, it must be ruggedly constructed. Naturally, no one in his right mind is going to abuse a camera, if for no other reason than that they are expensive. Still, the camera used for nature photography is subject to being hit by branches as you go through the underbrush, to moisture, to dust, and to other conditions not encountered in a studio.

Obviously, with these conditions being the norm rather than the exception, the camera itself must be built sturdily, and the moving parts, especially in the shutter mechanism, should be as simple as is compatible with a wide range of flexibility in its performance.

The first line of protection is a good camera bag. This will typically be an over-the-shoulder, carry-all bag which holds not only the camera but film, lenses, lighting, tripods or similar supports, and all the other paraphernalia that goes with serious photography. This should incorporate the proper balance between rigidity, to preserve the contents from distortion, and flexibility, to absorb the shocks rather than transmit them to the contents.

Within this bag—or by itself, if you are traveling light—is the camera case itself. This is the one that comes with the camera. It is fairly tight-fitting, but should be lined with a usable thickness of foam rubber and/or a plush fabric so that the camera is not really in tight contact with the case except at the tripod screw (which holds the camera and case together).

In addition to this protection, the lens, the most delicate of the more rigid parts, must be kept protected with a lens cover whenever you are not actually using the camera.

These simple precautions of proper packaging will do a great deal to keep your camera from harm.

The second requirement for a nature camera is that it must be relatively light in weight. Even when auto camping, you must consider weight. This rules out the large press and portrait cameras unless landscape photography is the whole purpose of your trip. For still cameras, this leaves only 35 mm and the $2\frac{1}{4}$ x$2\frac{1}{4}$ or $2\frac{1}{4}$ x $3\frac{1}{4}$ from 120 film. Backpacking rules out movie cameras—again, unless photography is the whole purpose of the trip.

While not absolutely required, several other features are worth having if you can have them without the loss of the more important ones. Ease of loading will be appreciated when you have to load with cold fingers. A cartridge load which will permit a partially exposed roll to be removed will give your camera added flexibility since you can change from color to black and white as conditions warrant.

Quick changeability of the lens is another useful feature. Cameras which will permit you to remove one lens and put a telephoto or wide angle directly into a lens retainer are far more flexible than one requiring a screwdriver to remove and attach the lens. A bayonet lens mount which requires only insertion and a slight twist to lock is better than the threaded mounts which require careful alignment to prevent cross-threading and several turns of the lens to secure. A turret or a zoom lens is better in a movie camera than a fixed lens which requires tools to change.

Other features are more in the nature of accessories and will be discussed under the proper heading.

Range-Finder Camera

The 35 mm still camera is the type under discussion here. These cameras focus through a split-image viewer although some models will have a ground-glass focusing attachment which may be used as well. However, these generally are more for the purpose of permitting a lower-angle shot than for accurate focus since the image on the glass is usually quite small. A reflex housing is often used on a range-finder camera for use with a telephoto lens, but the reflex is in the lens itself rather than in the camera.

There is some criticism of 35 mm film size (usually by $2\frac{1}{4}$ x $2\frac{1}{4}$ fans) that the small negative will not permit large enlargements. True, you have to have your lens clean or the dust will look like an out-of-focus log jam when the picture is blown up over twelve inches (30 cm), but usually the range-finder is an adequate focusing device. The sharpness of the lens is more important. The main exception comes with the ultra-close-ups that border on photomicrography. In these cases a focusing frame will be better since parallax is a major problem as well.

The greatest advantage of the 35 mm, whether range-finder or single-lens reflex, is its light weight. It is a rugged, compact camera that you can carry all day, hanging around your neck, ready to shoot, without getting a sore neck from it. Almost all wildlife photography done in the field today is with the 35 mm, usually a SLR.

The range-finder camera still has its advantages, the greatest of which is cost—which is about half the price of a comparable SLR. And for the beginner who will use it as much or more for shooting the kids or Aunt Minnie's birthday party as for the inhabitants of the neighboring swamp, it is just as good. As skills (and bank account) develop, you can always buy a more versatile camera. In the meantime, you can learn a lot with the range-finder.

Its main disadvantages (with standard lens) are parallax and the problem of sharp focusing on close-ups. With different lenses, you are out of focus unless you have adaptors, reflex focusers, and a lot of other items which a SLR avoids simply by being what it is.

Single-Lens Reflex

The single-lens reflex has many advantages and some disadvantages over the range-finder cameras. Its main advantage is that you see the picture you are going to take—not one a little way above it—so the problem of parallax is cured, and this feature holds true regardless of what lens you put on, so focusing is far easier.

The main disadvantage of SLR is the cost, which is almost twice as much as a comparable range-finder model. But for the serious photographer, the advantages are worth it. And with the SLR you won't forget and leave the lens cover on—you can't sight the camera if you do.

The 35 mm SLR cameras on the market all have the advantages of portability and rugged construction that the range-finder models have.

Many reflex cameras take the larger film sizes. These are usually twin-lens reflex, so parallax is a problem. With them, you get the advantage of the larger negative size. This will permit clearer enlargements and the pictures are large enough to crop out rather large areas. On the other hand, the $2\frac{1}{4}$ x $2\frac{1}{4}$ cameras do weigh a bit, and hold fewer frames of film at one time. You don't go tromping through the underbrush all day with one of them hanging from your neck unless you are also the type who carries a three-hundred-pound (135 kg) Duluth pack by its tumpline alone.

Movie Camera

The 16 mm is still to be preferred over the 8 mm camera for wildlife photography despite the technological advances made in 8 mm cameras in recent years. While both the camera and the film are more expensive (with the accessories required for nature photography, they cost as much as a small car), you will get a better-quality picture with the 16 mm, although, like the range-finder 35 mm still camera, the 8 mm does make an inexpensive training camera for the occasional wildlife photographer. The quality of the 8 mm cameras is increasing rapidly and the skilled camper can take acceptable pictures with cameras now on the market.

Not to be overlooked is the fact that, if you become proficient enough, there is a fairly good market for high-quality wildlife films, both for projected movies and for television. The public-relations-type films that companies make for service-club audiences are in 16 mm, as are most television commercials before they are taped. Commercial films can be blown up from 16 mm to the 35 mm size to be used in theaters, but 8 mm is too big a jump. Television-projecting devices will take only 35 mm or 16 mm film sizes.

The number of 16 mm cameras on the market is quite small compared to the days before the emphasis on 8 mm. However, most of them are of good quality. The types designed for television news cameramen are rugged and rather quiet in operation, but don't have a very wide range of lenses, especially in the telephoto area. There are also a few being made primarily for commercial-movie hand-held units. They are quite useful for wildlife photography, complete with zoom lenses and stocks. They are expensive, but everything you could ask for in a nature camera.

ACCESSORIES

The list of photographic accessories is quite long. However, they are rather light in weight, so this is not too much of a problem if discretion is used in their selection.

Bulk, once again, is almost as important a factor as weight. Photographic equipment is easily scattered and the usual photographer's bag is awkward to carry with a backpack. Some small-size container (a belt pack is ideal) is needed to carry the equipment needed for one day's shooting away from base camp.

LENSES

The lens that comes on your camera—a regular, three-feet (1 m) -to infinity-type lens—will be the one that gets the most use. Therefore, it should be selected with care and not bought simply because it comes with the camera.

The selection of a lens is a compromise between three factors: speed, sharpness, and price. Since motion is often a part of the subject matter in wildlife photography, a fast lens is a great help. However, once you get below f/2.8, another problem comes up—a three- or four-element lens won't produce as sharp an image. The six- or seven-element lens will handle speeds down to f/1. something, but the cost is outrageous. However, with better automated lens-making equipment now in use, lenses are one of the few items that is holding its own or even dropping in price. Used lenses from reputable dealers are another source of quality equipment at a lower price. They generally come from customers "trading up" to a more exotic lens. For the amateur, a good f/2.8 or f/3.5 lens will handle anything he is capable of handling anyway, so the problem is not as great as it seems at first. Just don't buy your lens by the f number alone.

Wide-angle lenses are quite common in the three-lens turrets of movie cameras, but not as common as they should be in still photography. Good composition virtually requires the use of a wide angle in many woodland shots of larger animals.

While rather expensive, a telephoto lens is a must for the serious nature photographer. A 135 mm to 300 mm is standard here. There are several ways to avoid much of the expense of the telephoto. A zoom lens is one answer. Originally developed for sports television, the zoom was quickly adapted for movie cameras in place of the three-lens turret. You can get them to fit still cameras as well. However, with still cameras, a single-lens reflex is a necessity in order to get the proper composition and focus for your picture. They do have a problem in that they must be focused at the smallest magnification and when "zoomed" the image is then out of focus as viewed through the viewer. At the extreme other end of the magnification range, this may well be enough out of focus that the proper moment to shoot may not be intelligible. In such instances, two camera operators may be needed—one to hold the camera so the subject is properly framed, and the other, using binoculars if need be, shooting with the aid of a cable release. This quickly gets to something almost as clumsy as several different lenses and juggling back and forth between them. The zoom lens functions as a standard lens, in-finitely through the magnifications to the peak power of that particular lens.

A third way is with a monocular. They are fairly low in cost, and can always be used as a monocular without the camera. The finest example of the monocular is the spotting scope used by target shooters to see where their shots hit. Again, a SLR is a must in order to get the proper focus and an adapting ring is needed to make it fit the lens opening. Typically, the camera lens is set on infinity and the focusing is done to the monocular.

Carry a portrait (close-up) lens or two, especially when doing color work. Wild flowers or mineral specimens are just as challenging as animals and a good color close-up is quite rewarding.

The lens, regardless of the type, should fit a filter retaining ring over the basic lens, or quickly change with it, rather than necessitating the partial dismantling of the camera every time you change lenses. The possible pictures available to you in the field change so quickly, you need to be able to change your lens fast, and with no tools.

FILM

The choice of film depends on the subject you shoot. If you shoot animals, in poor light you will need as fast a film as you can regularly buy. This usually means Triple X Panchromatic film since faster film is rarely available. Plus X is perfectly adequate if your subject is more cooperative in regard to light and motion. It produces a better-quality image than the faster film, all other things being equal.

You should try to stick as much to one speed of film in color and in black and white, since it is hard to get to "know" more than one speed unless you are able to shoot as often as a professional.

If you do your own developing, be sure to use as fine-grain a developer as you can get. With a small film size such as is used in nature photography, the size of the possible enlargement is more often determined by grain than by such normal factors as enlarger capacity, size paper available, and aesthetics. With coarse-grain development, a 35 mm enlarged to 6 x 8 inches (15 x 20 cm) may look like a mosaic!

When going light in the field (no camera bag), film is most easily carried in the little metal film cans taped onto the camera strap. Four is most convenient, but six or eight can be attached with a resulting difficulty in getting film in or out. Keep a regular order so you won't open a can with already-exposed film in it. The usual camera bag trick of turning the cartridge over doesn't work here as they only fit into the can small-end-up. The lack of a leader will keep you from double exposing, but there is still the wasted time—time that can be particularly valuable when trying to change film before the subject spooks.

FILTERS

A small collection of filters weighs only a few ounces (about 100 g), yet makes the difference between a snapshot and a photograph. With few exceptions, they are simply pieces of colored glass or plastic (originally gelatin) mounted in a metal ring which force-fits on an adapter ring which, in turn, usually screws into the end of the lens housing. They are generally quite low in cost and present no technical problems other than that you must watch the "filter factor." This is the number by which you must multiply your shutter speed (or enlarge your iris opening proportionately) to compensate for the amount of light which the filter absorbs.

Lens Shade

While not a true filter, the lens shade does exclude unwanted light and typically fits on an adapter ring (although some may screw into the lens housing or even be built into the lens housing itself). Its principal function is to keep incidental light out of the lens, thus fogging a picture shot at a fairly close angle to the sun.

The inside of a lens shade should be a flat black paint or even a flat black flocking to absorb most of the unwanted light. The paint absorbs less of the light, but the flocking requires more delicate treatment as it rubs off fairly easily.

Color Filters

The old reliable K2 yellow filter is a must in the nature photographer's filter collection. It is a

standby for bringing out clouds or cutting haze. It is also used when yellow colors (green, yellow, or orange) dominate the picture—as is typical with vast amounts of vegetation. It is also good for bringing out the texture of snow.

Because it has a low filter factor of two, there are not too many pictures its use will exclude because of poor light.

Similarly, low filters in red and green are good where those colors dominate. However, these will compliment rather than replace the K2.

Because of the subtleties of light and shadow which make up most woodland scenes, filters should be used which have only a slight effect on the finished picture. They should heighten contrast in order to make the photograph (which is on film that is sensitive to light the eye cannot see) more in accord with the actual scene the eye sees.

Polarized Filters

The polarized filters consist of two filters of polarized material which can be turned to vary the amount of light admitted. It excludes light evenly across the entire spectrum. This is most useful when photographing around water, which has an excessive amount of glare and reflection. It is also useful in cutting the reflection from snow, trees, or rocks.

Quite logically, the polarized filters are the most expensive of the filters, and unless you do an extensive amount of photography around water, you can generally manage quite well with no other help than your colored filters and your f openings. On the other hand, if you want action shots of trout taking the fly and other fishing scenes, it may well be worth it.

Again, keep the filter factor low in order to keep your photograph realistic. If you can't find the filter factor, cover your exposure meter with the filter and read it directly—the meter will automatically compute the filter factor into its reading.

EXPOSURE METERS

In the rapid changes from light to dark that typify the habitat of the nature photographer, a good exposure meter is a must. The coupled light meters which automatically adjust the camera for the light reading pose quite a problem in nature photography. The subject is rarely in the brightest part of the picture. As a result, the coupled meter records the brightest light (which is nearby the subject) and not the light of the subject, which is in the shadows trying to remain camouflaged. As a result, your subject is underexposed.

A behind-the-lens meter (but one not coupled to the camera) offers a possible solution—especially with a tight shot or a telephoto or zoom lens, since they generally record a fairly narrow area in the center of the picture. Still, a separate meter and a good ability to estimate the light in a shadowy area of the picture is more valuable.

The problem is that the average meter does not restrict the angle close enough. Special meters which can take spot readings, the sort used by movie producers and resemble odd-shaped cameras with long, shaded eye pieces, not only are difficult to use in the field, they cost over a hundred dollars.

I find the most convenient exposure meter is the one which mounts on top of the camera but has no connection with the camera mechanism. It is considerably lighter in weight and you don't risk losing it or having it banging around on your camera strap or neck. It has the same problem with the angle of reading, but that is something you have to put up with.

Regardless of the meter type, be sure and add the filter and lens factors to your meter reading.

LIGHT

While sunlight will be your usual light source in nature photography, there are times when artificial aids are needed.

Reflectors

Reflectors use sunlight (although they can be used with artificial light as well) to fill in deep shadow with a soft light. The best reflector is made by wadding up a piece of aluminum foil and then unfolding it and glueing it to a flat surface. The reflector should not bounce a definite beam of light that creates its own shadows; it should help soften shadows of the main light source.

Reflectors are a bit bulky for most field photographs, but aluminum foil is light in weight and a frame can be improvised on the spot. White shirts or even rocks can be utilized as improvised reflectors.

One advantage of reflectors is that nesting birds will get used to them (if they aren't glaring) just as they do blinds and won't panic during photography as they will if a flash goes off to fill the shadow.

Flashes

Flash units used to be about twice the size of a large flashlight and about as heavy. Now they are down to where the wildlife photographer can consider using them as a shadow eliminator in the field.

First of all, the fold-up reflector is definitely an asset. It takes up less space in the pack, and it doesn't have the searchlight gleam from reflected sunlight which often convinces the animal you are stalking that whatever is coming toward him isn't going to do him any good.

An accessory flash unit, connected to a synchronizing jack in the camera, is far more versatile because the flash does not necessarily have to point in the direction of the camera aim, but can be off to one side as a fill-in light source.

Power is still something of a problem in flash photography. You have to have fresh batteries, and toward the end of their life they will sometimes work and sometimes not—you never know until it is too late. A capacitor helps. This is an electronic item which builds up a charge slowly (from the batteries) and releases it all at once (when you fire the bulb). Weak batteries simply take longer to charge the capacitor.

Kodak once came out with a gadget which could certainly be of help to the wildlife photographer (or anyone else). This used a capacitor, but instead of batteries you turned a knob twenty times to generate enough current to charge it. The knob should be replaced by a crank, but the idea of never having to worry about batteries is a good one.

You still need a separate bulb for each shot, however, unless you use the multiple-unit flash cubes, which don't have quite the output needed for nature photography. You need blue bulbs for color film to avoid the orange tint caused by the film's sensitivity to certain light put out by a clear bulb, but the clear bulbs are brighter for black-and-white photography.

Large areas, such as caves, can be photographed by opening the camera on a time exposure and setting off a series of flash bulbs in sequence to illuminate all the details.

Strobes

Strobe light is a variant of the flash with its own particular advantages and disadvantages. Its disadvantages concern its weight and bulk, particularly its battery pack, which is quite large. However, it will produce a brilliant light in such a brief time that it, rather than the shutter, will often determine the exposure time. As a result, you can catch the leap of a fish or stop the wing action of a hummingbird.

REMOTE CONTROL

Remote control rigs in nature photography permit the photographer to be somewhere else, including in the picture. They constitute an alternative to the blind as a means of photographing animals without disturbing them.

Cable Release

The cable release is the least remote of the group. Its principal use is in slow-speed work with a tripod or similar support, the cable release simply being a device to dampen the natural motion of the photographer, which may cause blurred images.

The cable release, like the shutter release itself or a gun trigger, should be squeezed, not pushed.

With the addition of an air release, you can then move a hundred feet (30 m) from the camera and still be able to snap the shutter. This is quite useful in situations such as at the entrance to a den, where a blind is not usable because of the scent.

Timer

The timer is designed for one purpose, to let the photographer get in the picture. For the solo canoeist or hiker wanting to record his exploit on film, it is quite useful. The imaginative wildlife photographer can probably figure out some other purpose.

Mousetrap Rig

Small animals can often take their own pictures with a mousetrap rig of some type. The trigger is usually either a bait on the end of a string or a trip string across a run. In either case, the string is pulled, ultimately setting off the camera, and, since this is usually done at night, the flashbulb. Between the string and the shutter release is one of the wildest Rube Goldberg-like devices used in photography.

With two methods, the string sets off a mousetrap. The striker of the mousetrap will then hit one of two items, a button or a toggle switch, which

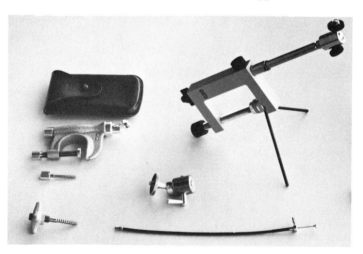

Camera supports include gadgets which clamp onto things, screw into trees, or double as both clamp and tripod. A cable release is needed to use them.

sets off the shutter release through a solenoid, and the striking of the shutter release directly or through a cable extension. Since the impact is usually enough to jar the camera some, the cable is generally used.

Another method uses the solenoid actuating the shutter release, but the string actuates a microswitch to start the current—without the mousetrap.

A tarp should be put over the rig if rain is likely.

MOUNTINGS

Poor light requires a slow shutter speed. A telephoto lens has a wobble factor which excludes the usual hand-holding. A movie camera needs something to smooth out a long pan shot. In all of these cases some type of support is required on which to mount the camera securely.

Legs

The standard mounting for a camera is the tripod. It is a completely rigid unit, yet a pan head at the top will permit adjustment of the camera in both vertical and horizontal planes. Tripods can be bought for a fairly low price which will permit a wide degree of adjustments, for uneven ground and odd camera angles, and still be light in weight and collapse into a convenient package for carrying.

Not used as much, but quite often just as good, is the monopod. You are required to hold it steady, but the fact that the weight of the camera is supported makes this far easier.

The monopod principal is used in many improvised set-ups. A simple loop of parachute cord forms sort of a monopod turned inside-out. You hook one end of the loop under your foot and the other end over the camera and pull upward. Your muscles do not have to balance the weight of the camera exactly and so you can hold it steady with a minimum of trouble.

There are a wide variety of clamps and screws which will make most anything into a monopod. These are C-clamps or screws which drive into trees. Many of them have pan heads, extensions, and many other features which make the rigid mounting of the camera easier.

Stock

A great help in animal photography is a gunstock rig. With this, you aim your camera like a rifle. It is adaptable to either still or movie cameras and is almost required for telephoto work without a tripod. With a movie camera, a stock is absolutely necessary to get the full potential out of your equipment.

There are many excellent commercial stocks available, the most common one being the hand grip with a trigger operating a cable release. However, this compares to the big ones about the same as a pistol does to a free rifle. Many of the commercial camera stocks look more like pieces of abstract sculpture than rifle stocks, in order to save weight. Plans for making one to fit various types of cameras appear occasionally in photography or home-workshop magazines, or you can design your own.

BLINDS

Blinds have long been a traditional aid to the wildlife photographer. The only real requirement is that they must blend in with their surroundings, hide the person in them, and be relatively comfortable. Any other feature is just that much extra. Funeral grass has been used, but it is too hot, and animals don't notice their surroundings that much anyway. The best material is an old camouflage-pattern tarp or parachute. With this hung over a frame of saplings, brush, or pipe, a small canvas seat, slits for viewing and cameras, and adequate ventilation, the blind is in business. However, fabric blinds should be stretched tight enough that there is not a noisy flutter in wind.

TIME LAPSE

A movie-camera shutter release which will enable you to take only one frame at a time will find additional use in the interesting field of time-lapse photography. Although this is a studio operation, its close relationship to nature photography makes it a logical side field.

The only technical problems are involved in setting up a timer to automatically trip the shutter at the prescribed intervals and a control of the lighting. Many time-lapse photographers use a box with shutters which remain open except when a picture is being made, then they shut, artificial lights come on, the picture is taken, the lights go off, and the shutters open again. This permits the plant to grow naturally, the blossoms to go through their natural cycles of opening and closing, without having the problems of light readings every time, or of uneven lighting in the finished film.

TECHNIQUES

Finding the Subject

There are three common ways to photograph animals. The first is by stalking. The stalking is no different than that described in Chapter 23. However, you must have your camera ready with the proper changes in light in mind to adjust your camera. You must get closer to photograph an animal than simply to observe him. This is true even with a telephoto lens. Such a rig is not easy to use when stalking because of the wobble problem mentioned in the discussion of binoculars. A telephoto lens requires a firm support and that is rarely available when "shooting from the hip" with a camera, even when you have the assistance of a well-fitted stock mounting.

The most common technique used by professional wildlife photographers is the blind. Set it up near a nest, mating grounds, water hole, or whatever attracts the animals, and leave it for at least a full day. The next day, get in it at the time of least animal activity and wait. Be sure to pack a lunch and take a couple of books with you because you will be there for a long time. However, the results are usually well worth it.

The third technique is the remote-control rig described earlier. This is a hit-or-miss proposition, with the only real skill involved in the selection of the background and in using obstacles to make the subject approach from the desired direction. The rest is just a matter of luck. Still, it is an interesting little grab bag.

Plants and minerals, fortunately, require little skill in getting them to pose—they are there, immovable and waiting. The only thing you have to be concerned with are such matters as composition, lighting, angle, exposure, etc.

Composition

Volumes can be written (and have been) on the subject of photographic composition, yet it finally boils down to a matter of an artistic eye and lots of practice. Still, there are words for the novice that are well worth reviewing by the veteran.

You should have a center of interest—something upon which the eye of the viewer immediately focuses—the subject of your photograph. On the other hand, don't fail to observe the entire picture in the viewer. Is there some part that distracts from the subject? Try changing your angle or tightening your focus so that it is out of focus. Take particular care about the "Men from Mars" effect of trees growing out of heads, etc.

Make sure of your background. While you can usually reduce it to an out-of-focus blur, it is far better to utilize it to emphasize your subject. The first way is to be sure the background is either substantially darker or lighter than your subject. With people, this is easy; with wild animals who need to blend with their background for protection, it is harder. A low angle (silhouette it against the sky) is usually the easiest, although a pond or patch of sunlight will often do the same thing.

Give some reference as to size and direction. Include trees, canyon walls, people, camping equipment, or something else to give effect of size and distance.

Finally, make sure your subject is completely in the picture. This is especially a problem with rangefinder and double-lens reflex cameras in which parallax is a problem. When in doubt, take more area than is necessary. You can always crop out the rest later, but you can never put in a part that is outside the film.

These are the basics. The rest is a matter of practice—and very stern self-criticism. Don't try to neatly center the subject in the photo or cut it in half with the horizon, but try to imagine the factors in the pictures as having weight—massive objects having heavy weight, small objects light weight, subject heavy, background light, etc. Try to make the picture balance in the center.

Lighting

Lighting is always a problem with the beginner who has just graduated from the just-press-the-button snapshot to one of the fine-quality SLR's with all its dials on f openings, shutter time, ASA numbers, and a lot of other bewildering information he didn't even know existed, much less that he needed.

The problem finally resolves itself to a fairly broad band of coupled numbers: f numbers on one side and speeds on the other. He realizes that he can choose any number of these combinations and still get a photograph that is correctly exposed.

The choice is really this: the faster the shutter speed, the less blur you will get and the faster action you will be able to stop, but on the other hand you will have to open your aperture more to let the light in for this shorter period of time. This means that you are going to lose detail, your focus will only include a very narrow portion of the picture. Conversely, a tight opening, approaching a pinhole (in which, incidentally, everything is in perfect focus—even without a lens), will permit more of the depth to be in focus, more of the picture will show up in nice crisp detail, and the longer you will have to hold your shutter open in order for the needed amount of light to come in—thus very little motion can be permitted.

Actually, this is not a hard decision to make. Generally speaking, unless you are taking a picture of a moving animal or one which is sufficiently nervous that you suspect he will start moving as soon as he hears the shutter click, take as slow a picture as possible. This is especially true with landscapes or pictures which have a definite element of landscape in them. The one exception to this is when you are moving, such as in a boat or some other vehicle. In this case, don't drop below 1/250 second or the whole thing will blur. On the other hand, in Grand Canyon use the highest f number your camera will reach—comparatively speaking, nothing is moving down there.

Artificial assistance was discussed under equipment. Use discretion. It often helps more than hinders. Portability is more often the deciding factor.

Dawn, dusk, campfires, or electrical storms are excellent times to experiment with time exposures.

Here bracketing exposures is almost a necessity since you are working with light too dim to work an exposure meter. Bracketing (taking adjacent exposures or speeds of the same subject to ensure one of them being correct) is good insurance in any type of photography, but is often beyond the budget of the occasional photographer. Knowledge of exposure will save just as many pictures, and you can bracket only those you feel will be exceptionally good (in composition and subject matter) or about which you are particularly doubtful.

CARE OF EQUIPMENT

Photographic equipment is expensive, yet it is often mistreated. Heat and moisture are the main villains. Most professional nature photographers use a surplus waterproof bag to store their cameras in. Properly packed in one of these rubberized bags, even going overboard in a boating accident won't hurt them. Photographers further pack them in old sweaters, foam insulation, or some other material to equalize the cold of the night and the heat of the day, and to keep it from damaging their film.

The neck strap is a simple safety device, yet it is probably the best one developed. However, the strap should be checked periodically as perspiration and abrasion can weaken it considerably, especially if you are carrying a heavy lens. Lens covers should be used at all times when not actually shooting.

The lens is the most easily damaged part of the camera. Fingerprints can etch it, dust or tree limbs can scratch it. The camera kit should include the following cleaning equipment:

lens tissue
lens cleaning fluid
a camel-hair brush

These can be obtained from a photographic supply house or optical lab.

Do not tinker with the insides of the camera. It is a delicate mechanism and strictly for the expert. This goes for do-it-yourself lubrications too.

Keep each piece of equipment protected from each other and from the elements. It takes very little more trouble to do so, and it pays off in the long life of some very expensive equipment.

CHAPTER TWENTY-FIVE

Pot Shooting

A proper discussion of hunting would fill a whole book. This chapter will discuss only a very small aspect of hunting, but one which will probably be of most interest to the camper. This is pot shooting, in the original meaning of the word—hunting for the pot. This is different from trophy hunting, hunting for the freezer, varmit hunting, or any of the other aspects of this varied sport.

Shooting techniques for pot shooting are fairly much the same as for any hunting, although the line between pot shooting and survival hunting may grow thin enough at times to permit the shooting of stationary animals. The guns are fairly standard light-caliber rifles and shotguns. The animals are those which are, for the most part, ignored by the average hunter, who is usually out for deer, waterfowl, or upland birds rather than the more lowly edible rodents.

Yet pot shooting is not a sport to be despised. It has its challenges which, while not as technically difficult as big-game hunting, have the added factor of affecting the quality of the menu that very night.

LEARNING TO SHOOT

Pot shooting is often practiced by persons who care very little for the other forms of hunting, but do like to vary the camp menu. As a result, many of them are not what the more avid hunters would consider expert shooters. Therefore, a few words

are in order for the camper who would like to participate in this form of the sport without getting into the more intricate fields.

Anyone with reasonably good coordination can learn target shooting. It is simply a matter of putting the bull's-eye on top of the front sight post or centered in the cross-hairs of a telescopic sight, holding your breath, and squeezing the trigger. With practice comes accuracy; that's all there is to it. The trouble comes in translating this skill into a meat course for the evening meal without wasting meat or making the animal suffer. The problem is that the animal in question generally doesn't want to be a part of this scheme and will take all kinds of fast evasive action to avoid it. As a result, the marksman who can drive nails at 100 yards, or even 100 meters, often misses hitting a rabbit (which is almost 100 times the size of the nail) at twenty yards (18 m).

What you need to learn is one of several closely related systems which have grown up either reducing the dependence on sights or doing away with them entirely. The idea is that if you fire as soon as your gun comes up and the sight picture is there, you will hit the target. As with anything, this requires practice, but it is worth it.

One system, Instinct Shooting, is normally taught with BB guns. After only one or two hours of instruction, most students can regularly hit coins thrown up like clay pigeons, and a few can even hit BB's with enough regularity to show it isn't an accident. Instinct Shooting is based on the principle that if you point your finger, with both eyes open and not sighting down it, you will automatically point directly at your target, as can be proven by holding your finger there and having someone else sight down it for verification. As a result, with a short amount of practice, you can learn to point a gun at a moving target and hit it. This is typically taught indoors or in some vacant lot with a BB gun with its sights removed.

An older and less radical method uses the standard post front sight, but the rear sight is simply a flat bar—the idea being that you can automatically find the center of a short length (about one-half to three-eighths of an inch [1 cm]) just as you can automatically find the little hole in the center of a peep sight.

Regardless of the system, the idea is to try to get off the shots as quickly as possible. This does not mean to rush it or you will never hit anything. Simply get the gun up, point or aim (depending on the system used), and squeeze the trigger.

Learning uses a lot of ammunition (therefore the use of BB guns in Instinct Shooting), but there is no other way to learn. Animals, unlike clay pigeons, move irregularly. One old method, which is still good for deer hunting, is to put a target inside an old tire and roll it down a hill. The tire will bounce irregularly, just as a deer bounds along. However, this does little good, other than as a first step, for the would-be pot shooter. Something more the size of the pot meat is a tin can. Tie it onto the back of a car with a fifty-foot (15 m) length of reasonably stout string (seine cord is good). Drive over rough ground at about fifteen to twenty miles per hour (25 to 30 km/h) about fifty yards (45 to 50 m) away from the shooter. The bouncing can is a close duplication of the size and action of a rabbit.

In all these practice sessions, be sure of your backstop. Be certain that the bullet can't ricochet over the countryside.

When shooting at these bobbing targets, the technique is the same as you used on the still targets. Pull the gun into position, sight or point it at the target, and pull the trigger. Shoot as soon as the gun is in the correct position. Don't dawdle over the exact position, shoot. Make your shooting a reflexive matter so you don't have to think consciously what to do next. With this practice (and you must keep practicing or you will lose accuracy), you will always have an ample supply of rabbit, squirrel, or similar small game on your camp menu.

CHOICE OF GUNS

In this country, pot shooting is generally done with one of two types of guns—a shotgun of .410 to 20 gauge, or some form of the .22 rifle. Of the two, the shotgun is the less desirable because of its shorter range, reduced killing power, and heavier ammunition. In addition, a single cartridge for the gun will weigh as much as a half-box of .22 long-rifle cartridges, no small matter to consider when weight is a major factor.

Still, hunting laws in many states prohibit the use of rifles in hunting—even for deer—and the rifled slug will tear up too much meat to use it against the rabbit-size animals that constitute the principal pot game in this nation. (A rim-fire .22 is usually permitted, however, and should be used whenever possible.) When using a shotgun, use at least a number four shot for these animals. Anything lighter runs too much chance of crippling the game. While the cripples are usually recovered if you have a dog, there is no sportsmanship in using light loads which make the animal suffer unduly. If you want to give it a "sporting chance," use a rifle, or a muzzle-loader, or even a bow and arrow. All of these will kill cleanly if they hit, but require greater skill and accuracy than a shotgun.

There are two basic types of .22 rifle—the standard rim-fire guns and the center-fire varminter rifles, which have a very flat trajectory. The rim-fire .22 has the advantage of being cheap to keep in ammunition and is comfortable to use. Under fifty yards (45 m), it is an excellent snap-shooting rifle and while the bullet can travel a full mile (more than 1½ km) under ideal conditions, it is still about one-third the range of the varminter guns.

A .22 pistol, shooting .22 long-rifle ammunition, has the advantage of being relatively lightweight, but it requires considerable practice to be able to hit reliably with it. Even with practice, it is basically in the survival-gun category. The .22 pellet guns with CO_2 cartridge power are improving rapidly and there are now several with enough muzzle velocity to kill cleanly. However, because of the lightweight bullet, they are strictly short-range guns.

The varminter rifle uses a larger case (such as a 30-30 or 30-06) necked down to take a .22 or so caliber bullet. (For the purposes of this discussion, .22 will include the whole range up to the .243.) With all that power, flat shooting is accurate, with telescopic sights, up to 300 yards (275 m). It uses a heavier bullet than the standard .22 long rifle, so the killing power is greater, even at the end of its range. Because of the fantastic muzzle velocity, the need of a good and safe backstop is of the first importance.

These guns were designed for the woodchuck, an animal which does not permit close stalking. As a result, they are more often used from a stationary position rather than the stalk-and-snap-shooting tactics of the rim-fire .22. Still, the skills of snap-shooting apply to the telescopic sight just as much as they do to the open sights. One of the problems of varmint gun shooters is that they tend to treat the animal as a paper target and often it has gone back into its burrow before they decide that they have it in their sights well enough.

While not really designed for it, the varminter guns are quite adaptable to the stalk-and-snap-shooting tactics—if the proper backstop is there. This problem of hunting both a safe backstop and the game may be more than the average hunter's concentration will permit, but it must be done to avoid hitting someone in the next county.

Because of the tremendous power of these varmint calibers a hollow-point bullet will literally blow up a rabbit at short range. A sharp-pointed, jacketed bullet is better for small meat animals. Under fifty yards (45 m), aim for the head. As long as you are going to blow something up, hit an area with little meat on it. Beyond that range, let your marksmanship determine your point of aim. A head shot is always preferred if you can hit it.

For these guns, a telescopic sight is well worth its weight, especially when hunting chucks or over ground which has been rather heavily hunted (with the resulting shyness of the quarry). Two and a half

to four power is best; either of these will permit both snap-shooting and careful aiming from a stand. Variable power scopes have the advantage of being useful, in their higher powers, for big-game hunting, but they will have little use in pot shooting. When stalking, leave them at base camp or at home; open sights are faster.

All firearms, including pellet guns, should meet federal and state firearms laws—even when they are to be used for target shooting. This includes laws regarding transportation as well as use.

GAME

Don't be afraid to branch out in the selection of meat. In most areas, rabbits and, if game laws permit, squirrels are the only off-season game animals. Yet there are many more edible animals which are not normally classified as game animals but still provide not only a welcome addition to the menu but a measure of sport as well.

Raccoon and possum are common meat animals in many areas, especially in the South. The armadillo is spreading its habitat from the Southwest into many parts of the country east of the Mississippi and north into Kansas. (However, recent evidence is that air pollution is lowering the temperatures and the range is again shrinking.) It has long been used as a meat animal in some areas where it is sometimes referred to as "poor man's pork" because of its taste. Others consider it to taste more like dark-meat chicken. It is an excellent source of fat in the camp diet since it is high in that factor without being greasy.

Although I haven't tried them, I understand that the woodchuck and the nutria are good to eat. Porcupines are too, but should be left alone to provide survival food since they can be killed with just a stick. Singeing the quills is not a very reliable safety measure and destroys some of the food value. Just skin them carefully. Since they are generally up a tree, they may be difficult to take.

Most people don't like the idea of eating rodents, presumably because of the mental association with rats; but rabbit, squirrel, chuck, porcupine, muskrat, nutria, and beaver are all considered delicacies in one geographical area or another, and all are rodents.

Also often omitted strictly because of psychological reasons are rattlesnakes. They can be easily skinned, cut into sections, and fried like fish. However, any more unlikely dishes must come under the subject of survival food and not voluntary additions to the camp menu.

With most of these animals, practically any meat recipe can be used for preparing them. However, most, if not all, should be soaked overnight in salt water, and older specimens should be parboiled before cooking to reduce the "gamey" taste to reasonable limits.

HOW TO FIND AS WELL AS HUNT

Rabbits are easy to find. Usually you can flush one by walking across a field. Be ready—you never know they're there until you see their powder puff growing smaller in the distance. This is where snapshooting practice really pays off. If you don't find any by walking across a field, look for game runs. You often find them by moving up or down the run.

Rabbits have definite territories. If you don't hit one when you flush it, keep following it. It will eventually circle around to keep out of another's territory. Keep this up for a while and it will tire so that you can get quite close to it and even get a good shot at it while it is standing still. This is often the only way a fair marksman can get one with a rifle.

Squirrels are usually in trees and rather hard to find there as you walk through the woods. You can often find at least one on the ground. If not, keep still and listen. After a while, they will come out and start chattering. Then you will be able to see them. Since they usually stay on the wrong side of the tree if they see you, have a partner circle around to run them back to you. If you are alone, throw rocks to the other side of the tree. If that doesn't fool them, leave your hat or jacket on a bush and move as inconspicuously as possible to the other side of the tree.

Woodchuck is easy to find in its habitat but quite a problem to get within range. A varminter rifle, a telescopic sight, and a concealed stand are usually required. Nutria is most easily hunted from a canoe, the shooter in the bow with a single paddler in the stern. Backstops are of concern here since water will deflect a bullet as easily as it does a skipping stone.

Raccoon and possum require dogs or pure luck to locate with any degree of regularity. They are commonly found at night in trees, two conditions which make it very difficult for the unaided hunter.

Armadillos are also found at night, but they are fairly easy to locate with the aid of a flashlight. However, check the jacklighting laws first or you may be accused of something you weren't doing at all.

Muskrat and beaver are plentiful in some areas, extinct in others. Unless you find their lodges, don't depend on finding any. Since these latter two are legally furbearers rather than game, check the laws on them first.

The rules for pot shooting are quite simple, yet require practice to master. Hunt only one animal at a time, know its strong and weak points, its habitat, and what part of that habitat will enable you to gain the greatest advantage over your quarry. Work into or across wind. Move as quietly as possible, in spurts, and prepare to freeze instantly. Try to see your quarry before it sees you. Keep calm, make sure of your target and backstop. Always fire the best shot you possibly can under the circumstances and reload immediately. Wait a few minutes before trailing a wounded animal unless it is so slightly wounded that it moves off immediately. Don't give up if you have no luck. Hunt with an expert as much as possible to learn the finer points of the sport.

Finally, learn several recipes for preparing each animal. Rabbit can become quite tiring if prepared the same way every day.

CHAPTER TWENTY-SIX

Pan Fishing

Pan fishing does not refer to the smaller members of the perch family called pan fish; this is a type of fishing for immediate needs—fishing for the pan. It is the most common type of fishing, falling roughly between the "anything goes" techniques of survival fishing and sports fishing with a mountain of fine equipment.

Because of the weight limits of camping, the equipment you bring will be a little different from that used by the fisherman who goes out for "a day on the lake." Except for car or boat camping, both the weight and the bulk must be watched. Also, since there is a limit to the amount of equipment you can carry, you are going to have to select your fish and fishing waters carefully and match the equipment to it, instead of taking all your gear and matching it to the stream or lake.

Fishing is probably exceeded only by hiking as a camp sport. With the modern equipment now available, it is a sport which can be enjoyed by the backpacker as well.

EQUIPMENT

Obviously, you can't take all your fishing equipment on a camping trip unless that is the sole purpose of the trip. Many campers like to fish and to eat fish, but they also like to do other things that also require equipment. Many campers like to fish and to hike in with just a backload of gear.

The weight and bulk limits in these instances severely restrict the amount of fishing equipment. In such cases what is needed (and useful regardless of your transportation and lodging) is a complete fishing outfit weighing under two pounds (1 kg), complete.

There are rods on the market in fly, spinning, and baiting-casting models that weigh only five and a half ounces (150 g) and break down to two-foot (60 cm) sections—a feature possessed by none of the featherweight fly rods. They don't have the sport of the two-and-a-half-ounce (75 g) fly rods, but you are fishing primarily for your food and only secondarily for fun. If you get an eight-inch (20 cm) small-mouth bass on one, you will think it is light enough.

While the fly and spinning rods are excellent for camping, the same cannot be said for the plug casters. There is nothing wrong with the rods, but the weight and bulk of an adequate assortment of plugs make them out of the question for going light. They were developed in the short-folding models principally for businessmen who want to fish on business trips and can't very well be seen with a load of fishing tackle. This way they can put it in a suitcase or attaché case and look every inch the respectable businessman.

With the fly and spinning rods, the rod, case, reel, line, and a full assortment of flies or spinning lures will round out a complete fishing outfit with only one and a half or two pounds (under 1 kg) of weight and 3 x 6 x 24 inches (7½ x 15 x 60 cm) overall. The flies or bugs should duplicate a wide variety of natural food and hooks for natural bait should be included as well. Separate lines for dry and wet flies are welcome; separate reels weigh only a few ounces (100 g) more and lend far more flexibility for changing from one to the other.

Another form of camp fishing, which should not be overlooked is hand fishing. This is the most common in survival fishing, but it is not to be frowned upon either for the sport or for the fish it produces. It can be done either with an improvised pole (any supple sapling will serve the purpose, although willow will probably be the best available) or simply with a hand line. Natural bait rather than artificial baits are used.

The system has two very definite advantages: it is inexpensive and it is quite often legal without a fishing license. All you need is some line, an assortment of hooks, several sinkers of the split shot and eared variety, and a float or two. (Although it would seem that any old piece of wood would do the job, it is usually too hard to find one with the proper action.) A smaller edition of this outfit is found in most survival kits.

TECHNIQUES

Each form of fishing has its own techniques, each fish having its own habits which must be taken into account in attracting it to your hook. Fly and spin fishing have certain skills which are needed in order to make a cast. Both of these and hand fishing as well have the problem of selecting the bait. While whole books can be written on these subjects, the bare outlines are presented here.

Hand Fishing

Very little skill is required for hand fishing. That is one reason it is so popular. It is excellent for introducing children to the sport—they gain a feeling of self-sufficiency because they can do practically all of it themselves. It is popular with campers because it permits them to get a chance to fish with only a small box of equipment—a box that can easily be slipped into a pocket for carrying on the trail.

The combination of hook, sinker, and float should be adjusted for each type of bait. Frogs and mature insects such as crickets and grasshoppers should be permitted to float on the surface. Most other bait should be sunk to a point where they are only a few inches (10 to 20 cm) off the bottom. The sinker should be far enough away so that the bait has a chance to move about in a realistic manner.

Poles have a considerable advantage in catching larger fish. The pole bends, gradually increasing the drag on the fish, protecting the line from being broken. Fishing with a hand line requires quick action to haul the fish in before he takes off with the line (and perhaps breaks it).

Fish eat almost anything and therefore you have a wide variety of choices to offer them. Most can be easily found with a minimum of work. Grubs can be found in most rotting logs. Lift the log (checking first for snakes, scorpions, etc.) or kick it apart with the heel of your shoe. Tent caterpillars make excellent bait and are quite obvious in their thick webs. Simply cut off the branch near the edge of the tent. You not only get a good supply of bait, you also help reduce this menace to the trees. Wasp larvae are also irresistible to fish, although you must convince the wasps they should be elsewhere before you stand much chance of getting the nest. Knocking it down with rocks and picking it up after the wasps scatter is the safest method.

Worms are traditional, and most deservedly. However, you have to dig in humus soil. They won't be in clay or sand. Crickets and grasshoppers will catch bass and larger perch and are fairly easy to catch, especially if you use an improvised butterfly net made from mosquito netting and a light branch.

Fish, being aquatic animals, eat aquatic animals. A little wading will uncover a host of excellent natural bait. Crayfish can be caught with a minnow seine or simply by pinning them down against the rocks. This is obviously restricted to the smaller ones, as the pinchers of the large ones will tell you. You can also catch them on hooks baited with pieces of earthworm. It is best to remove the pinchers of the larger ones so they don't scare away the fish. Hellgramites are found in much the same habitat as crayfish. Pinning them as you turn over the rock is far easier then with the crayfish.

Minnows can be caught by either seines or traps, although the latter is a little too bulky for the average fishing camper. Clams and mussels can be opened and cut into pieces to provide bait for a wide variety of fish.

Several not so natural baits can be tried by the hand fisherman. Bread or raw dough is found tasty by several varieties of fish. Catfish like cheese and even strong laundry soap. Fishermen after these critters are infamous for their various blood and stink baits. However, these are used mainly on trot lines, probably because even the most ardent fisherman can stand to be around them only so long.

When you catch a fish, find out what he has been eating by making a little autopsy of its stomach contents. Catch some of that kind of food and you will catch much more fish, since that is obviously what they like that day.

Fly Fishing

Fly fishing is not difficult but it does take a certain amount of practice to make a cast. Practically all the work is done with the wrist, just a little with the forearm.

Start with the rod thirty degrees above horizontal. Quickly raise it to vertical. Wait until the fly is about a foot from straightening out the line behind you (this is the tricky part), then lower the rod to almost horizontal. Never snap the rod down, just lower it. Pull some more line from the reel and repeat until your fly is where you want it.

The difficulty that beginners have is in timing the backcast. If you start the forward motion too soon, you may pop the fly off into the grass behind you and cast only the leader. If you snap the rod down, you will certainly lose the fly. On the other hand, if you start too late, the fly will drop and you will lose distance or may even catch yourself with the hook.

Practice fly casting without a fly (for safety reasons). You should be able to get distance on the cast without having it pop as you start the cast. A pop (as with a whip cracking) is caused by the tip actually breaking the sound barrier. With the inch or so (last few centimeters) of tip traveling almost a thousand miles an hour (about 1,500 km/h) and then suddenly stopping, it is no wonder that it will break.

Once you learn how to cast, the hardest part is in selecting the proper fly. Since the object of fly fishing is, for the most part, a surface feeder, watch to see what the fish are eating and offer them the nearest thing you have to it in a fly.

Since fly-fishing reels are fairly light, you may wish to take two: one loaded with dry line and the other with wet. This will permit you to adapt to the fish's diet with either dry flies or nymphs. Fly reels and spinning reels are made with interchangeable spools. These extra spools, loaded with lines of different pound-tests, make it possible to carry only one reel of each type, reducing total weight.

Trout, as well as panfish and bass, prefer the swifter parts of the stream where the water is oxygenated and choice items of food come drifting downstream. Cast to these spots as well as to brush piles and lily clumps to convince the fish that the fancied-up hook you are plopping before them is really a poor, helpless, tasty insect driving by or just fallen in the water.

Spinning

Spinning is halfway between fly fishing and plug casting. The lures are lightweight like the fly-fishing bugs and even a dry fly can be spin cast a short distance. Yet the ease of casting, especially for the beginner, is more like plug casting. The main difference in casting technique between spinning and plug casting (other than such details as the reel being on the bottom of the rod, the left-handed crank, etc.) is that you don't have that pause every so often between the cast and the retrieve to take out the bird's nest from your reel.

Spinning outfits are only slightly heavier than the fly-fishing rigs. This permits you to take a wide variety of lures on your camping trips without losing the ability to do it while backpacking.

Spinning is one of the easiest techniques to master. Start with the rod slightly over your shoulder. Swing it forward, releasing the line at a little past vertical as you go. Let the line go as far

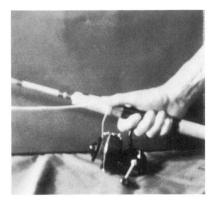

Those who learned with a bait-casting reel will find this method of casting with a spinning reel easier than using the little finger.

as you want it to go—or as far as it will go—whichever comes first.

The usual method of handling the line during the cast is to hook it over your index finger. This is fairly awkward to release. Plug casters especially will prefer another method. Take the bight of line up to the top of the rod and hold it with your thumb. The reel and guides are still on the bottom, only a bit of the line goes to the top of the rod and back down again on the same side. In this position, the release of the line is the same with a plug-casting rod.

The molded-rubber artificial lures are tops on a spinning rod and bring the eating-size fish quite well. Spoons are another good spinning lure. An assortment of these, with a popping bug or two and possibly a wet fly, will get you a nice supply of fish for your dinner—and a lot of fun while you are doing it. An extra spool with a different-strength line will add flexibility where the weight is not a factor.

Plug Casting

While plug casting is too heavy with its accoutrements for most forms of camping, it is still a possibility for car or boat camping where there is provision for the tackle box full of lures. Casting is easy and probably known by people—even those who have never tried it. The selection of the plugs is strictly a matter of practice.

It is given a once-over-lightly here not because of the bulk of the equipment but because the technique is practically restricted to the bass-size fish, which are at the large end of the range of fish sought in fishing for the pan.

Spin Casting

Spin casting is a hybrid of the plug-casting rod and the closed-face spinning reel. The reel is mounted on top of the rod and has a thumb-rest which controls the action the same as the thumb action on the cylindrical reel.

Despite the differences in spool alignment, there is no practical difference between this system and the more standard plug casting except for the absence of backlashes and the ease with which the lighter lures may be cast.

CHAPTER TWENTY-SEVEN

Climbing

A trail, by definition, is not wilderness, even though wilderness is within reach on either side. A trail, by being man-made, cannot be wilderness which is pure nature. For the most part, however, trails are the best way to see the wilderness since they destroy far less nature than a road does and they can cover far more area than can be covered by canoe.

Yet when a camper wants to get into the wilderness on foot, it usually involves climbing. This chapter will not discuss the more difficult forms of climbing, such as rope work, rock and snow climbing, mountain rescue, and such, other than on a survey basis. It would take far too much space and, besides, this advanced phase of climbing is not learned from a book. Either you know how, and such a discussion would be on the fine points, or you would need the services of an experienced mountaineer anyway.

This type of mountain climbing is a separate sport and, while well worth trying, it is not the kind the off-the-trail camper will be concerned with as he tries to get deep into the wilderness areas. The type of climbing discussed in this chapter is for him, and for the camper who wants to climb that hill near the camp to see the view, but can find no beaten path to the top.

HILL CLIMBING

Although not as difficult or expensive as mountain climbing, hill climbing also has its fine points

of technique, its sense of accomplishment, and its breathtaking view at the summit.

One of the peculiar dangers of this type of climbing, as opposed to rock or snow work on the more famous climbing mountains, is the fact that they are usually covered with loose dirt rather than any secure foothold. This must be considered by the climber, as should the fact that where it is not loose dirt it is an almost impenetrable tangle of saplings, underbrush, and vines—usually of the cat-brier variety.

Brush

The problems of brush in hill climbing vary with the part of the country. At the timberline it may be simply a dense belt of conifers which are brush because climatic conditions won't let them become trees. In the valleys of the big mountains, it is deciduous trees kept small by winter avalanches stripping off their tops. In the Appalachians, it is rhododendron thickets. In the Pacific Northwest, it is salmonberry. In the river bottoms of the South, it is cat-brier or canebrake. Regardless of what it is, it is usually between your camp and the hill or mountain you want to climb.

The first rule in brush travel is to use trails as much as possible. These are not only the trails laid out by the Rangers or hiking clubs, but also fire-breaks, trappers' trails, and even game trails.

Second, try heavy timber. Dense forests are rather free of underbrush except in the clearings since the trees keep out the necessary sunlight that is needed by the young trees which form much of the brush.

In mountainous regions, stay out of avalanche areas. They are certain to contain brush since the avalanches have knocked down the trees.

Finally, use one extreme or the other in regard to water. Stay away from it to the extent of traveling on the ridges since the streams often become almost swampy in regard to encouraging brush. If this is not possible, wade upstream along the creek bed, avoiding the brush on the banks. Such hillside creeks are usually quite shallow. I have climbed many along exposed rocks in mid-channel without taking off my boots or getting them wet.

If none of these methods are possible, and you are in an area where such tactics are permitted, get a machete and bushwhack your way through. It is hard work, but in some areas it is the only possible way to get through.

Dirt, Talus, and Scree

Hill climbing rarely involves rock climbing in the sense that mountain climbing does. The loose dirt of well-timbered, steep hillsides is the most common terrain problem encountered by the hill climber, but in the lower levels and foothills of mountains, talus and scree are also a problem.

The main danger in all of these is in the hillside losing its balance rather than the climber losing his. Talus and scree are at the maximum angle for stability, and the dirt is often exceeding its angle because the trees prevent it from sliding. The dirt isn't too bad when it gives way because you can always catch a passing tree. Talus can easily become a rock slide and falling boulders are neither a good foothold nor a pleasant prospect for those below. Scree has not only the disadvantage of dirt, but a very nasty ability to get between your sock and boot with a discomfort far out of proportion to the actual size of the rock.

Regardless of which of these problems you are facing, the cardinal rule of climbing definitely holds true—keep vertical. When you try to use your hands to climb (other than on a fairly sheer cliff), the force on your feet is directed backward slightly as well as downward. This, coupled with the slope

of the hill and the natural instability of the surface, reduces friction considerably and greatly increases the chance of slipping. If you have a tendency to slip, climb with your feet cross-ways to the slope to increase your friction and side-step up the slope.

Don't depend on small plants to anchor you as you pull up. Nothing smaller than a two-inch (5 cm) tree trunk should ever be trusted. Especially on rocks, watch where you put your hand—you might grab a sunbathing copperhead by mistake.

Scout your pathway in advance. In dirt climbing, avoid exposed rock strata more than four feet (125 cm) thick. Even limestone, with all its nice footholds, will have at least one overhang which makes falling a distinct possibility. If you follow these strata far enough, there will be a safe way over them. Remember, you don't have the safety of a rope belay like rock climbers have.

On talus, stay to the edge of the talus slope. If a rock slide should start, you would at least have the chance of jumping off the talus instead of going down with it. Talus, however, is rarely so unstable that knocking loose one rock will take the rest of the slide with it.

Movement on talus is best made with kind of a float, in which the foot comes in contact with the rock but never seems to really bear down on it, and is very quickly followed by the next step. Steps are naturally fairly short and the floating periods are rapidly alternated by rests on obviously secure boulders.

Vegetation through a talus slope will indicate stability. The presence of flowers and similar-size plant life indicates that some dirt has formed under the boulders, cementing them together into a fairly stable slope. Moss will indicate some degree of stability since rolling stones obviously gather none.

Scree is like talus only more so. Some avalanching is practically inevitable so the group must take care that there is a clear path down the slope for the rocks to roll without hitting anyone. A warning should be shouted the instant any rock is dislodged to warn those below.

On loose dirt, coming down is the hardest. The common habit of catching a passing tree with one hand and swinging around it is extremely dangerous, especially if it has rough bark. I have heard, from an eyewitness, of a severed wrist artery from this. If you have to use trees to break your speed, never have more than a six-foot (2 m) space between you and the tree when you start moving and hit it head-on, with your arms absorbing the impact. A far safer way when you can't simply walk down is to sit down and slide, using your heels to keep from going too fast.

Descending on talus is about the same as going up with a little longer period of floating permitted between the security of large boulders. You must, however, be careful never to build up speed as this is a good way to lose your balance should you step on a precariously balanced boulder and have it go down the slope ahead of you.

Coming down scree, on the other hand, is not only easy, it is practically a side sport in mountain climbing. In screeing, the object is to start a small slide of pebbles and then ride down the slide. The pebbles are acting as ball bearings between you and the slope. Keep shuffling your feet to keep them from sinking into the slide. By adjusting the angle of your feet to your direction of movement, some directional control can be gained. Be ready to jump out if you get up too much speed or a boulder is ahead. Gloves are helpful in case you do lose your balance and fall down.

A geologist's pick makes a good hillside version of the ice ax. It makes a good brake going downhill sitting down. It will furnish a hand-hold in climbing a slippery, humus-covered slope. It is handy for cutting steps in a scree slope which has grown thick with grass or flowers. However, as with the alpenstock, you climb the slope with your feet, don't climb the pick with your hands.

Because gravity is overeager to help you coming down, scout your descent with all the skills you used on your ascent. Coming down safely is harder than going up. The expectation of the view is no longer present and you are generally in a hurry as well. Your footholds are now far down the hill rather than just below eye level as they were when you were going up. Don't over-extend yourself in your climbing, or you may be like the cartoon couple standing on top of an extremely thin pinnacle. One is saying, "Doesn't a view like this make you realize how insignificant man is; and how stupid we are because we don't know how to get back down?"

MOUNTAIN CLIMBING

Like most difficult sports, you can't learn mountain climbing from a book. The best way is to get with a group which has both the equipment and the skilled personnel to teach you. Of course, a general familiarity with the items of equipment and their use makes the job of learning much easier.

There are two surfaces which you will encounter in mountain climbing: rock (which includes plain dirt) and snow (which includes ice). Each has different techniques and, to a considerable extent, requires different equipment.

Rock Climbing

This is the sort of climbing that the average person thinks about when he hears the term "mountain climbing"—pitons, rappelling, rope work, and climbers clinging to what looks like a sheer cliff. It is also the sort required in advanced spelunking.

Fortunately, there is no such thing as a sheer cliff (except some flowstone formations in caves, which are really a separate form of mountain climbing anyway). All rock has cracks, ledges, chimneys, and other irregularities which enable the climber to form an anchor.

The secret of rock climbing is careful selection of the route. For this reason, above all others, rock climbing is not something to teach yourself. Go with an experienced group and learn properly. Balance is critical. The climber who is well balanced on the slope, who has three secure holds at all times, and who moves smoothly will negotiate a cliff in perfect safety without alarming the belay at all. Incidentally, the rope is strictly a safety device. You climb the mountain, not the rope. The only exceptions to this are in techniques too advanced for our purposes here.

Footholds should be close enough together to make the steps comfortable. Use definite ledges if you can. If there are none, use the small ledges which will permit only the edge of the boot or its toe to get a grip. Climbing boots are a must here since they are the only thing that will grip such a ledge in safety. When traversing (going horizontally along the slope), shuffle rather than crossing the legs.

Since rock climbing assumes a steep slope (otherwise it would involve the techniques of hill climbing or even hiking), hands are also used for support and stability. Just as the big ledges (or "buckets") are preferred for foot placement, the ideal hand-hold is a doorknob-shaped projection that you can really grab. (Naturally, all footholds and hand-holds should be tested with pressure before depending on them.)

The doorknobs, unfortunately, are quite rare and you will generally have to be content with the same kind of little ledges that you use for your feet. Hand-holds should be between the head (for visibility) and the waist (to prevent bending and reducing foot friction).

When the going gets really tough, the technique called counterforce is required. In balance climb-ing, gravity holds you on the slope. In counterforce, you jam some part of your body into a fairly large crack and the pressure between one side of the crack and the other will hold you in place. This is done by jamming a foot in, either between the sides of the boot or between the heel and the toe, or with the hands as though trying to pull the crack wider apart. On a ridge, you squeeze the two sides with your knees and your hands. One counterforce, the cling hold, seems impossible but is actually fantastically effective. Stand on the thin ledge and pull up with the hands from under a higher rock. Chimney stemming involves jamming the entire body between the two walls of the chimney.

Snow Climbing

While rock climbing uses little more than good boots and muscle for the actual climbing (the rope equipment being strictly for safety), snow climbing requires a couple of additional items: crampons

Crampons are required on ice and frozen snow. One on lower left is adjustable to size. Point covers save wear and tear on packs.

and an ice ax. It is interesting that while the person not familiar with mountain climbing thinks of rock climbing as typical of the techniques, he thinks of snow-climbing gear as typical of the equipment.

Crampons are spikes which lace onto the boot for breaking through the ice crust which is on most snow slopes (often under a thin crust of more recent snow). These can have as few as four points and fit in the instep of the boot. They are used mostly where there is very little snow and their lighter weight on the pack is preferred. They are also useful in hill climbing, where dirt or bracken-fern-covered slopes counter the lug sole's superiority on rock with a slippery performance.

Where there is extensive snow climbing, the standard crampons are needed. These have either ten or twelve points (depending on whether or not they have two points which extend basically forward, just under the toe of the boot). In any case, they must fit to the boot size so that the instep of the crampon fits the instep of the boot and the front (vertical) pair of spikes are just under the forward edge of the toe of the boot. When not in use, they are usually carried on the outside of the pack against a fairly large patch of leather to prevent damage to the pack fabric.

The ice ax has three primary uses. The first is in cutting steps in a steep snowbank. The steps should have enough vertical slope to clear the ankle and, if the bank is steep enough, the knee so you don't have to lean outward (and thereby imperil balance). The line of steps should move up the slope on the diagonal. If the slope is slight enough for a head-on attack, you don't need steps, the

Ice axes are used in cutting steps, as hiking staffs, and as belaying points in snow. The one on the left disassembles for ease in packing. The curved slot in the center one fits the ax blade of a similar one to join them as an aid in climbing.

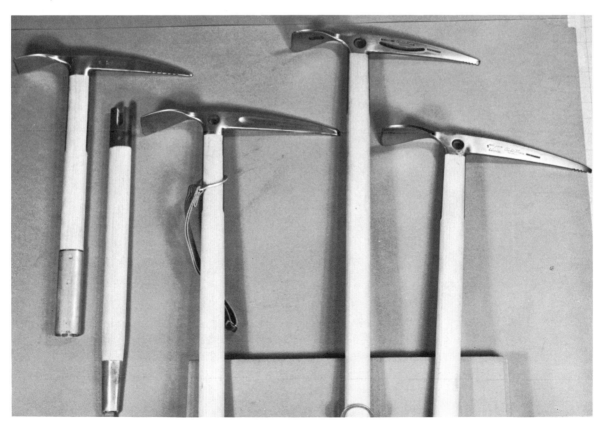

crampons alone will hold. The step for a turn in the zig-zag diagonal should, of course, be made for the outside foot and be slightly oversize since this is a good place to stop and rest awhile with both feet in the step. In snow, you can usually kick your steps without using the ax (one purpose of the twelve-point crampon).

The second purpose is in arrests, in which a slide down the mountainside is stopped by planting the pick in the snow. The pick should be firmly planted in the ice and you roll on top of the handle to keep it from popping out.

The third purpose is as a third leg. The spike is used as a hiking staff for walking on snow. It will drag in the snow for balance in glissading (the controlled sliding down a snow slope, much like skiing without skis, except that it is often intentionally done sitting down). Or it is used for clawing—a process by which you employ the horns of a twelve-point crampon and the pick of the ax to fight up an ice-covered slope without cutting steps.

ROPE WORK

To be perfectly frank, mountain climbing is a bit dangerous. Yet, with the exception of major peaks, accidents are completely preventable without recourse to the ultimate prevention of staying at home (the most dangerous spot on earth in terms of statistics). Proper use of the rope is the best way to prevent accidents from becoming injuries.

Of primary concern, obviously, is the rope. Just any rope won't do, even if it has a sufficiently high breaking-strain figure. The best type is Goldline, a synthetic rope used exclusively in mountain climbing. The standard size is 7/16-inch diameter (a figure which makes more sense in its original size of 11 mm), 120 feet (36 m) long. The next best is mountain nylon. Beyond that, forget it. Manilla will work as long as it doesn't freeze, but it is like lead if it gets wet and is hard to manage as well.

The problem to consider in a rope is that its purpose is to absorb the force of the fall. A rope therefore must not only be strong in that it doesn't break easily, it also has to be elastic. An inelastic rope would be worse than hitting since it would not only stop the falling climber as abruptly, it would, because of its size, concentrate that force on the chest as the rope snapped into the rib cage. The Goldline and nylon will stretch half of their length in stopping a fall. Therefore, the stop is only uncomfortable (which I doubt is even noticed in the relief of no longer falling).

Since a life may literally depend on it, the rope should be free of abrasions. It should always be carried coiled up and inside a pack for protection. The rope should be tied to the climber with a bowline knot (except for the middle climber who should have a butterfly). The ends should be whipped to prevent unlaying.

The belay is the most important man in climbing because he is responsible for the safety of the person doing the actual climbing. Belaying is, of course, rotated, although a beginner will usually

Climbing ropes, rappel slings, and a ladder for extremely difficult passages (such as a crack-free sheer cliff) or spelunking.

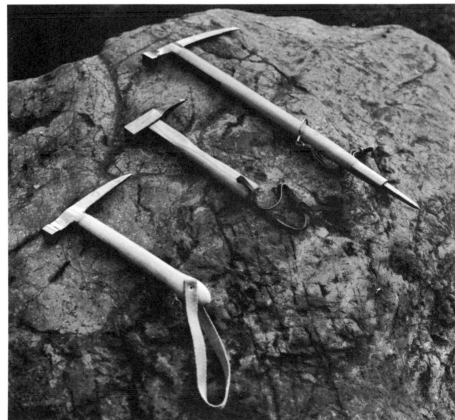

Pitons come in a wide variety of shapes to fit different-sized cracks, different directions of stress, and sometimes with rings to help clear small overhangs, although sometimes more than one carabiner will be needed to keep the rope from wearing against the rock.

Piton hammers are required to drive the pitons into the rocks. They usually have a pick opposite the head. One also doubles as an alpenstock.

be placed in the middle of the rope and be excused from such duties.

The belayer should have a secure position. It is obviously important that the belayer not be dislodged from his position while stopping a fall. He should be free to move about. He should be protected from falling rock (especially if he is belaying the leader who is therefore above him and likely to dislodge rocks if he starts to fall) by being under an overhang or around a corner from the leader. And, finally, he should be comfortable, especially if two must be belayed from his position.

The strongest belay is sitting down. The rope passes around the belayer's waist to gain friction. The hand on the side opposite the climber controls the tension. This position is improved when possible by sitting behind a tree or standing behind a tree or standing behind a boulder. If the belayer is simply sitting on the wide ledge, he should, in turn, be anchored by a piton to the wall. The rope should pass around the belayer so that the controlling hand is on the opposite side of the belayer from the climber.

At times, belaying directly is not possible because of the lack of ledges close enough at hand. In such cases, the rope must be passed through a piton to reduce the distance of the fall. Pitons are wedges which are hammered into small cracks in the rock to anchor a rope. They come in a vast assortment of sizes and shapes, each to fit a different-size crack, direction of crack, or depth of crack. Regardless, they should hammer in with a ringing sound, give resistance all the way to the end, and the eye should be hanging down. They should be removed when finished. Tap them back and forth sideways until they pull out.

Where there are no cracks, an expansion bolt must be placed in a hole drilled with a star drill. This is a time-consuming practice and is needed only on the most difficult slopes.

The rope does not pass through the piton eye, but through an appendage of it called a carabiner. The carabiner is sort of a cross between a chain's link and a safety pin. It is an oval of metal with a gate in one side of the oval. This gate swings inward to permit attaching it to the piton and the

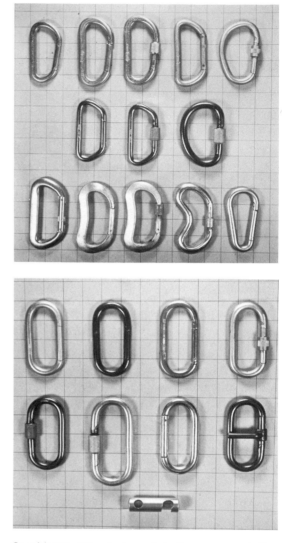

Carabiners are used to link the rope and the piton. The bar at the bottom attaches to a carabiner for use in rappelling as a brake.

rope to it, and fastens securely to prevent it from opening when it is in use. Carabiners are sometimes used with a small rope-sling for rappelling. The rappel rope is taken a full turn around the carabiner for friction.

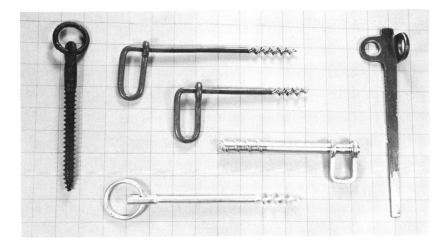

These pitons are for use on ice instead of rock.

The rappel is that spectacular drop you see in pictures of mountain climbers hanging from a rope while sliding down a mountainside. It isn't usually done that way. Normally, the rappel is aided by a belay from above. The dulfersitz is the standard rappel when the carabiner isn't used. The rope passes between the climber's legs, front to back, around to the left, across the chest, over the right shoulder, and the speed is controlled with the left hand while the right hand maintains balance.

The climber leans back until he is almost horizontal and walks backward down the mountainside. The spectacular version you usually see is very hard on the rope and the anchor and you don't see the accident that often results.

Belaying is also used on snow work, especially on glaciers where the problems of ice bridges and hidden crevasses make belaying a necessity. The ice ax makes an excellent belaying point with the handle struck into the snow and the rope wrapped a couple of turns around the head. The belayer's foot keeps it in place. Special ice pitons are used with regular carabiners to help. The rope is also handy for getting out of crevasses with prussik knots.

Regardless of the ground type, safety is the most important part of mountain climbing. With it, the climber can see the breathtaking view at the summit and still get to tell his friends about it.

CHAPTER TWENTY-EIGHT

Spelunking

Spelunking is becoming a popular camping activity in areas where there is an abundance of caves. Spelunkers have always been big campers, so if you are one who needs an excuse to go camping, here is one.

The principal cave areas in this country are in the Appalachians (principally the Great Smokies), the Ozarks, and the Hill Country of Texas. Mexico offers many possibilities that should not be overlooked. The best area is the Sierra Madre Oriental in Tamaulipas, San Luis Potosí, and Nuevo León. Trans-Pecos (Texas), New Mexico, Arizona, and Utah have many shallow caves which are of interest to archeologists because of artifacts, burials, and pictographs. Canada and most of the northern part of the United States are without many caves because of the scouring and filling action of the glaciers during the Ice Age, although there are some spectacular exceptions known to spelunkers.

Most of the more spectacular caves in this country are commercially exploited and the chances of finding such a cave for the first time is slight. Still, there are some caves, known to spelunkers, that are quite beautiful and not exploited. One spelunker has said that every cave has at least one feature that is not found in any other. No cave should be ignored because it is not world-famous.

Most of the caves not open commercially but still of great interest to the spelunker are those with narrow passages somewhere, usually at the entrance, those which require crawling on the muddy cave floor, or those requiring a rope descent of thirty to two hundred feet (10 to 60 m). These caves are rarely visited but are of great beauty.

Needless to say, you don't just walk into these as you would Carlsbad Caverns. You will require proper equipment and a thorough knowledge of proper techniques if you are to have a successful trip. The National Speleological Society Grottos (local organizations) are the best sources of information on techniques and cave locations. Visit one of their trips to learn the techniques and you will probably want to join. They can teach you all the skills.

EQUIPMENT

Clothing

Cave temperatures usually range in the fifties. Because of the humidity, the cold is quite penetrating. Also, the cave floor is usually quite slippery because of mud. The ceiling is often low in places, and it is absolutely dark. Despite this rather discouraging list of features, it is possible to explore wild caves in a degree of relative comfort if you are properly equipped.

Footwear used in spelunking is often the same as for hiking or rock climbing. Sometimes, in the case of caves which are particularly muddy, smooth-soled boots are preferred to the lug sole or nails since they don't pick up the mud as easily. Hip boots are sometimes used for wading underground streams. The usual hiker's two pairs of socks are worn both for the usual cushioning and for insulation.

The choice of underwear depends on the temperature of the cave and the amount of exertion done. As a result, it will vary from thermal to normal.

Heavy coveralls are practically the spelunker's uniform. They should be at least one size too large to permit jackets, etc., to be worn under them. On the other hand, they should not be too baggy as they will bunch up when you are in restricted passages. Ankles and wrists should bind snugly to keep out mud, sand, or whatever is loose in that particular cave. Rappel patches are welcome if any rock work is being done. Knees should be protected by the rubber pads made for scrubbing floors without developing "housemaid's knee." Some spelunkers prefer to use large pockets over the knees stuffed with large rubber sponges. These pockets should fasten to keep their contents in, but don't use safety pins as they can be worked open in a narrow crawlway.

Gloves are often worn, not so much for insulation as to keep the hands clean in a muddy cave. They are absolutely necessary if you plan to do any photography since muddy hands will ruin a camera. Cotton work gloves are quite adequate although wool ones may be desired in wet caves.

Like the baggy coveralls, a hard hat is part of the uniform. It is usually either a miner's hat with the bracket for the carbide lamp or a football or crash helmet modified to take the headlamp. The hat should have a chin strap to keep it from falling off when bending over. The strap should be fastened with a snap fastener so that if it becomes caught, you can pull out of it.

Light

Spelunkers traditionally carry three light sources. The main one is the carbide miner's lamp. It has the advantage of being the cheapest to operate, it has a variable flame, it is reasonably foolproof, and it is lightweight enough to fit on the hard hat. Additional carbide is carried in a watertight container and water to add to it in the lamp is taken from the canteen or the cave stream.

A two-cell flashlight is the secondary source since it has about the best light output to weight ratio. The batteries, of course, should be fresh.

The last source is a plumber's candle and waterproof matches, both in a waterproof container.

The carbide lamp will burn for four hours at a low level and two or three at normal brightness. The flashlight will go for two hours continuously and for about three burning hours if given periodic rests. A plumber's candle burns at a rate of one inch (25 mm) per hour and an eight-inch (20 cm) candle is the standard carried in.

Several candles can be pooled to heat soup or coffee in the cave for both energy and warmth.

Water

The usual military-type canteen is all wrong for spelunking—it sticks out and can snag on anything reasonably well anchored down. Plastic bottles are preferable and the bota is even better because of its flexibility. Some cavers take two plastic canteens, one for drinking water, the other filled from the cave water for use in the carbide lamp. However, some definite means of distinguishing one from the other, even in the dark, must be employed. Cave water is no more to be trusted than surface water, for the same reasons. Halizone tablets may be used for purifying it.

Miscellaneous Gear

Miscellaneous items should usually be carried in a waterproof container inside the coveralls. A watch is helpful since you can easily lose track of the time. A compass and a map of the cave is helpful, although the compass can be useless if there is iron ore in the area. A whistle for signaling should be carried in an accessible but safe place. Scotchlite triangles for route marking should be carried in a small box. A small first-aid kit should be carried by each person and a more fully equipped one by one person in the group. A knife is useful for many small jobs.

Rock-climbing equipment (pitons, carabiners, piton hammer, rope, expansion bolts, etc.) are often needed. Since in spelunking, rock work is simply a way to get over or around an obstacle rather than as an end in itself, portable ladders are considered sporting here and are often needed.

An adequate supply of trail rations should be carried by each person in the group. Spelunking is quite tiring in the chill, and high-calorie food is needed to keep up energy and body heat.

Because of tight places, packs are generally out of the question. Equipment not carried on the individual is carried in a Gurnee can—a bullet-shaped container about a foot or so (30 cm) in diameter and a couple of feet (60 cm) long, made out of sheet metal. A line attaches to the nose and it is dragged over the ground through the lemon squeezers (extremely tight passages), corkscrews (narrow tunnels twisting in three dimensions), and over the bottomless pits that attempt to slow spelunkers in their search for underground beauty.

TECHNIQUES

Techniques in spelunking are concerned not only with the safety of the operation, but with common courtesy too. Most caves are on private property. As a result, you will need to get permission to explore the cave. Many are on farms, which will bring up all the usual rules about camping on farms: leave gates the way you found them, park and camp where you are told, bury or carry out all garbage—especially the slaked-lime residue from carbide lamps. Cows will eat the stuff and even their four stomachs can't hold the acetylene gas that will be generated by what little carbide is left. In fact, the lime doesn't do them any good either.

Never enter a cave, even for a short distance, alone. Three is the minimum number and four is preferred. (In case of injury, someone should stay with the injured one, for first-aid and for psychological reasons, and someone needs to go for help—and that presents a safety problem if he goes alone.)

Because of the cold, the poor footing, and the rugged terrain, spelunking is a fairly tiring activity. Like backpacking and mountain climbing, you need to be in fairly good physical shape to do it. This means well, rested, and sober. It will work

a great hardship on your companions (who will be tired too) if they have to help you out.

A hard hat is necessary, not only because of low roofs, stalactites, and similar fixed objects, but also because rocks and sometimes even gear will come down on your head. The helmet also provides a very convenient place to anchor a light which will leave your hands free and always shine where you are looking.

Always tell someone on the outside when you will be out. Leave yourself plenty of time so that a slight delay in negotiating a tricky passage or gazing at the unexpected beauty of a newly discovered chamber won't bring in the rescue squad, but be sure the leeway is not so large that they won't be able to start in time if you need it. Be sure to report after you get out. With larger parties, one of the group is generally designated to wait outside and make sure all who have gone in come out. This is especially valuable where several small groups are entering at the same time.

As with mountain climbing, the leader must be an experienced practitioner of the sport and, if possible, have been over the route before. At any rate, he should have, in addition, the qualities of leadership, the mature judgment, and a primary concern for the well-being of his group. If he does not meet these qualifications, don't go. If he does, he should be obeyed explicitly because the safety of the entire group depends on it.

There are three reasons for needing help: getting lost, injury, and blackout. Each is handled slightly differently. In all cases, conserve your strength.

The best solution to getting lost is, of course, prevention. Check landmarks from all angles to avoid getting lost. Remember that shadows change the view by moving the light source only a matter of inches. Cave roofs often have more-easily-recognized landmarks than walls or distant formations. The string trail won't work. As one spelunker stated it, "In a small cave, you don't need it, and in a large one, you can't carry enough to do you any good."

The standard directional marking is an arrow, pointing the way out. These are scratched in some temporary location such as mud, or are made with little triangles of Scotchlite tape, one-inch (25 mm) altitude and half-inch (12 mm) base, stuck on the walls with the sharp point showing out. These are, of course, removed as you leave the cave.

If you do get lost, follow the usual rules for getting unlost: sit down and calmly retrace the route in your mind; check for your footprints in the mud, or some other sign. If these fail, blow your whistle three times and wait for an answer. The others will follow the sound to find you (laying a proper trail as they come).

If there is an injury, keep one person with the victim and send the rest for help. Administer first-aid if you have the equipment at hand. Treat for shock.

If you get a blackout in all systems of all the members of the group, blow the whistle and keep calm. Sooner or later, someone will come. If you have to keep in one spot for any reason, conserve your light. Turn down the carbide lamp and have just one or two burning unless you need the light for first-aid or a similar reason.

Never jump in a cave except in carefully controlled situations involving a rope and a secure belay. Walking, crawling, slithering, or wading is the standard means of cave locomotion. Also be careful of dislodged rocks, especially in multi-level caves—someone may be below. This is a fairly standard rule in mountain climbing, but in the reduced visibility of the cave the danger of slipped steps and falling rocks is much more acute. For this reason, safety ropes and a secure belay is standard operating procedure on anything other than horizontal passages.

Always be sure of your passage. Never go down a restricted passage without the safety line—even if it is level. Have it tied securely around your waist with a bowline so it won't be pushed off, either over your head or over your feet. Have a clear set of signals for the belayers to know what to do if you get stuck or fall. Always use the rope when moving on a slippery or steep slope.

Rope work, piton usage, rappelling, and other techniques are the same as in rock climbing. In all spelunking activities, but especially rock work, conserve your strength. Your chance of injury increases as exhaustion takes the edge off your reflexes and your judgment.

Leave everything exactly as you find it. The only exception is collection under the supervision of a scientist. Don't litter with garbage, film boxes, wrappers, or the carbide-lamp residue, which can get quite messy in underground streams and dampness. A small plastic bag will carry the garbage out.

Never, never vandalize. The vanadium mine in Havasu Canyon is tunneled from quartzite with small veins of no-grade jasper relieving the endless sparkle. Being a mine rather than a cave, and not a very deep one at that, there is no danger of getting lost, yet the walls are almost covered with the smudge of candles and carbide lamps. Not one of the smudges has a purpose, such as an arrow pointing out; most of them are simply random lines of the vandals.

One thing you can take from any cave is photographs. A set of good cave photographs is most valuable in a scientific interpretation of the cave's origins, its wildlife, and other important bits of information.

Cave photography is not too different from above-ground photography. You have the obvious problem of light since all light must be artificial, and despite how bright flashbulbs seem when you are looking into them as they go off, the cave's darkness can soak up an astounding amount of that light. Photofloods and similar types of light are best from a photographic standpoint, but are hardly portable by spelunking standards, especially if the cave involves considerable crawling. Flares, flash powder, and similar pyrotechnics are good in theory but tricky to use, and they have a fantastic amount of smoke output for the rather lazy ventilation of the average cave to handle.

Time exposure with various members of the party setting off hand-held flash guns is about the only real way to light a large room.

Some indication of size should be provided since a stalagmite, by itself, has no reference. A piece of equipment is excellent for a small object; a person for a large one.

Because of the humidity and temperature, hold your breath while taking pictures or the lens will fog up. A tripod (or similar support) and cable release will usually be needed because of the exposure time. Also, keep your camera and your hands clean when wallowing in the mud of narrow passages. Most spelunkers pack their cameras in their cases, inside plastic bags, inside cloth bags, inside padded boxes.

Caves are formed by stream action and in many caves the streams are still there, often with interesting fish, crayfish, and salamanders which have totally lost their eyes and skin pigment. These caves can be explored by two methods: boating and swimming.

Inflated rubber boats are best for underground streams but folding kayaks are often adequate. Skin diving requires a scuba rig, including a wet suit and a safety line.

Underground streams vary speed sharply. If the current is over half as fast as your comfortable paddling speed, use a safety rope on the boat. Cave rivers often have sudden waterfalls or places where the surface runs right into a cliff, so keep a sharp lookout and have a clear set of signals to the belay.

A rain will often cause a sharp rise in these rivers. Look for high-water marks. Stay out of caves which have a considerable fluctuation in water level if there is any chance of rain anywhere in the area. In 1961, such a rise in water level caused the first spelunking deaths in this country to occur in a true cave (although abandoned mines and fissures had caused spelunking deaths before).

With safety rules followed in all aspects of spelunking, cave exploration can be an interesting sport for the camper.

CHAPTER TWENTY-NINE

Swimming

Swimming is usually thought of as a way to cool off in the heat of the day, and, as pure recreation, it is of great value. However, there are far more reasons for knowing how to swim than having a good time. Seven thousand Americans drown in an average year. In 1942, more American servicemen died by drowning than directly due to enemy ordinance. The real tragedy of these statistics is that a large number of the victims were good swimmers.

There is a big difference between swimming in a swimming pool, with hand-holds convenient and life guards on duty, and swimming in the middle of a choppy lake with your boat sinking. The main difference, oddly enough, is not in the distance involved; swimmers who have done a mile without trouble in a pool are in serious trouble in a choppy lake a hundred yards from shore. The main difference is psychological.

Ironically, swimming is really not a very efficient way to travel in the water—floating is much better. This does not mean lying down on the water with the face, toes, and chest out of the water, but simply the absence of sinking. The scientific use of this principle was developed at Georgia Tech during World War II, and is well known by the name of "drownproofing." Unfortunately, more people are familiar with the name than with the skill.

Every camper who goes near the water should know the techniques of drownproofing. It helps if they also know how to swim, but that is not essential. Beyond that, diving, underwater-swimming, and skin-diving skills add further horizons, but these are simply icing on the cake, most of the real value comes from the first two.

More places are teaching drownproofing techniques since its publicity by the Peace Corps. Swimming is taught by the Red Cross and the Y's for little or no cost. Drownproofing has the advantage that, if there are no lessons available in your area, you can teach yourself. However, for psychological reasons, if not for safety, it should be in a swimming pool with life guards.

DROWNPROOFING

The relaxed human body, with lungs filled with air and no food in the stomach, is lighter than water. This means that if you don't panic, you can't sink. The problem with most non-swimmers, aside from fear of the water caused by poor introduction to it, is that not everyone can "float" in the swimmer's sense of the word. Men especially tend to float in an almost completely vertical position and women float at a slight angle to the surface (due to the fat on their legs). Yet with very few exceptions, practically everyone will float, in the sense that they won't sink.

Even though practically everyone will naturally float, because of the angle, there is a psychological

DROWNPROOFING FOR WOMEN

problem. People naturally float with only the tips of their heads out of the water. There is no way to breathe, even though they don't sink.

Drownpoofing is a comparatively recent technique to meet this problem. It has been used successfully for over thirty hours at a time, and those who know the techniques can stay up for eight hours with their hands and feet tied in a position rendering them useless (with obvious applications in accidents involving fractures). Even "sinkers" can stay alive for a long time in water over their heads.

Basically, drownproofing is a means of conserving energy. It requires far less work than treading water—ten per cent over basal metabolism for drownproofing *vs.* 100 per cent for treading water. You may or may not try to move through the water—if you do try to move, you will use a slight bit more energy than if you don't, yet anyone (even when tied) can cover a mile (1 or 2 km) by this method and still not be the least bit tired.

While the technique is the same, the basic floating position is different for women and fat men than for men of more normal build. The first group can float easier than the second.

Drownproofing for Women (and Corpulent Men)

The first step is the resting position: arms and legs hanging down. Step two is getting ready: arms raised outward and legs spread for a scissor kick. Step three is breathing: lower the arms and press the legs together (not in a sudden movement which will waste energy, but in a smooth movement) and exhale. You will be rising during this first part. As your head is out of the water, inhale. Step four: go under, using additional thrusts only if necessary to avoid going too deep. In the beginning, resting will be for only a few seconds. As practice builds up, however, ten seconds is average. The point is to get a breath when you want one, not when you have to.

Drownproofing for Men (and Thin Children)

For most men a slightly different resting position is required of the higher specific gravity. They will normally float at an angle to the surface and their resting position is similar to the "jellyfish float" most beginning swimmers do as their first step off

DROWNPROOFING FOR MEN

the bottom of the pool. However, in drownproofing the back of the neck rather than the top of the head should be up. Step two finds the forearms together at the forehead with the palms facing both downward and outward and the legs in a wide scissor-kick position. Exhale here. Exhale only half to three-quarters of your total lung capacity since you need some of the bouyancy to keep floating. Be sure the back of your head is on the surface, not the top of it, just before this step. Step three: move the head quickly, but not violently, up out of the water, the arms and legs still in their same position. Step four: inhale, spreading your arms (the position of the hands exerting an upward force without expending much energy), and closing your legs to help keep you up while doing so. Step five is to go back under. Men have more trouble with this and often a small downward stroke with the hands is needed to keep from continuing to sink after the head starts back down. If this sinking is done too quickly, you can go deep enough so that the pressure makes you lose all bouyancy (Boyle's law, the Cartesian diver, etc.). This is especially critical with athletes who have a marginal bouyancy at best. Rests should be from ten to twenty seconds but, as with the women's technique, get a breath when you want it.

Traveling Drownproofing (for Everyone)

Drownproofing is an obvious advantage when up a lake without a boat, since, even with clothes on, you can keep afloat indefinitely. However, there is a simpler method than just bobbing there, hoping someone will see you (which may be quite difficult). You can head for the shore. If you start swimming, unless you have been swimming quite a bit recently you will tire out very rapidly and possibly not reach the shore at all. On the other hand, an adaptation of the basic drownproofing technique will permit you to travel a considerable distance and not be tired. The first step is the usual inhaling step in the drownproofing cycle. The second step is to get in the position of step two for men. This is done as soon as the head is under and not before, but with one slight difference: the hands rather than the forearms are at the forehead and the whole body is tilted forward so that the back leg is almost at the surface. With step three, the hands are moved forward with the arms now straight as the feet are brought together. Step four starts as soon as the feet are together with the arms swung around in a breast stroke to the side.

By now, you are moving through the water in something resembling the swimmer's front float. Again, remember to take a breath when you want it and not to wait until you are "out of air." This will probably mean that you will "put on the brakes" a little before your forward momentum is used up—by bringing both knees up near the chest and then extending the legs for the scissor-kick position. The body is now in the resting position for men, and, picking up the men's drownproofing cycle, you raise your head for a breath and start the traveling cycle all over again.

The main problems in drownproof traveling are twofold. Women will have some problem learning the second half since their legs tend to float. Keep your back straight when raising the knees to help get the body vertical. The second problem applies to everyone and that is that it takes a little time to develop the proper rhythm. Drownproofing inventor Fred Lanoue sets this point at around 200 yards (180 m)—quite a distance when you are beginning to doubt the effectiveness of the whole procedure. However, it is quite effective and you can't get tired. Cold and boredom are the only real problems and, unless the water is very cold, they are more a nuisance than a danger.

SWIMMING SAFELY

Drownproofing is strictly an emergency procedure and it is frightfully boring, even if it does save your life. If you want to have fun in the water, swimming is still the best way. However, there are certain precautions which must be taken. First of all, learn how to swim. This may sound like stating the obvious, yet it is surprising how many people splash around without knowing the first thing about how to swim. This can be quite dangerous in the camp swimming hole when the bottom drops and rises quite suddenly rather than sloping gently like the park swimming pool.

At the campsite swimming hole, there are rarely life guards. You will have to take that responsibility yourself. Therefore, a few easy rules should be strictly followed.

Never swim alone. This especially true when you are diving into only moderately deep water. It is an absolute requirement in salt water where sharks sometimes add to the earlier problems of jellyfish and sting rays. If you are with a group larger than four, pair off with the buddy system and rotate life-guard duty to make sure that everyone who goes down comes up in a reasonable length of time.

Don't overexert yourself. That island out there may not look far, but it is easy to underestimate distances over water. If you are at a high altitude, don't try to swim far since you can't get as much oxygen in the thinner air. Don't swim for long periods in cold water. It saps your strength quickly without your realizing it.

Horseplay is for the horses. Most campsite swimming holes are rocky and therefore dangerous. Ducking should be absolutely prohibited as it gets out of control too easily. This doesn't mean that you can't try water games. Piggy-back wrestling on sandy bottoms is safe, as are most water sports. It's the pushing and ducking that causes trouble.

Finally, have a mouthpiece for artificial respiration and know how to use it (see page 372).

Follow these rules to the extent that they become automatic and the emergencies will probably never arise. And they won't get in the way of your fun.

The ability to swim should be required in canoe camping. This is especially true if there is any white water involved. If you go over in rapids, drownproofing will be of little use because of rocks, yet the shore will be less than fifty feet (15 m) away. In rapids, swim on your back with your feet downstream. This way, you will absorb the shock of hitting any rocks with your legs rather than your head. Swimming upstream this way will slow the downward speed and make dodging the boulders that much easier.

In all cases of boat upsets, the boat itself is the best flotation aid. A swamped canoe will still support its crew and a swamped wooden rowboat will support over a dozen. Not only is it your best guarantee of reaching shore, you save the boat as well.

LIFESAVING

Because of the nature of camp swimming, the camper must be his own life guard. In groups of any appreciable size at all (eight or more), at least one person should be camp life guard and serve life-guard duty just as he would at a public pool

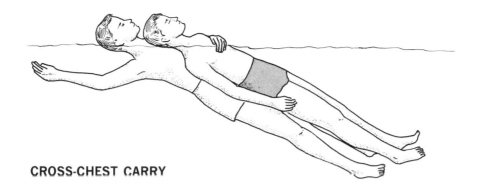

CROSS-CHEST CARRY

or beach. Since this is a good way to spoil the fun for the person delegated to this duty, at least two members of the party should have life-guard training so they can rotate the job.

Lifesaving techniques can most easily be divided into three categories: tired-swimmer assists, rescues, and self-help. The tired-swimmer assists, fortunately, are the most common and the easiest. Most, if not all of these, could be prevented as they are the result of over-extending one's ability.

The legs and feet are only second to the head as the most sinkable part of the body. Since the tired swimmer can be reasoned with and will follow instructions, the easiest tired-swimmer assist is simply to have him float on his back with his feet tucked into your swimsuit or resting on your shoulders. This permits you to use your arms and your legs in swimming while propelling him to the shore. You are simply supporting his legs, which are tending to tire him out because he has to support them. Don't support them so much you get them out of the water, or you may force his head under —otherwise, the technique is fairly easy.

The principal problem with a rescue is that the victim is usually in a state of panic to some degree. As a result, he is more than likely to grab the rescuer desperately, thus pulling both underwater. Lifesaving manuals are full of surface-diving approaches, underwater wrestling matches, and such. Fred Lanoue developed a far simpler way. Approach the victim head-on, and just before you get within reach start circling. If he starts turning with

you, he is still in control to the extent that you can reason with him and at least turn it into a tired-swimmer rescue if you are not actually able to "talk" him to shore on his own physical, if not psychological, resources.

If he does not turn with you but is still thrashing around rather strongly, you are going to be in trouble if you try to haul him in. Wait until he tires a bit. Reason may come with the exhaustion and you can use the tired-swimmer assist; if it doesn't, you at least avoid the fight, and you are there the whole time, ready to move in and grab him if he should go under.

When he is tired enough to be cooperative, whether intentionally or not, a modification of the traditional cross-chest carry is recommended. Unlike the standard form, which is mainly a side stroke, this version is a back stroke which permits one arm and both feet to be used fully for power. Pull the victim (who is pulled to a back-float position) up onto your chest as high as possible and still permit you to move your head freely. This helps keep him from going into a vertical float. Use a back-stroke arm action with a frog kick. Be sure to keep your feet pointed outward or you may claw the victim's legs with your toenails. (I did this once. It has a fantastic, although unwanted, reviving effect on the victim.) A scissor kick can be used if you keep clear of the victim's legs. The victim's lower body and legs should be supported by your upper legs at all times to avoid his going into a drag-producing vertical float.

Self-rescue was discussed in detail a couple of sections ago under Drownproofing. This is by far the best self-rescue known and in its traveling form can cover an amazing distance without tiring. However, there are times when the techniques will have to be used for very long distances or periods of time (such as a boat sinking out of sight of anyone and a long distance from shore). While drownproofing techniques can be used for hours at a time, it is far more comfortable if you have some artificial support to help you. (You should, of course, have been wearing an approved life preserver but, for this purpose, we will assume the worst.)

In such situations, you are usually wearing regular clothes. Wet clothing is air-tight. A life jacket can be improvised by no other method than tying the top button of your shirt and inflating it with your breath. Just roll forward, with your head in the water, and blow into the shirt. The bubbles will collect over your shoulders, making a fairly good life jacket. The shirt will stay wet by wave action and/or capillary action, and you will need to add more air only occasionally.

Far better, however, are long pants. Remove the pants and fasten them back up. Tie the legs with an overhand knot (usually together, making a loop out of the legs) and fill with air. The latter can be done by waving them overhead, filling them like an airport windsock. This requires hard kicking to stay on the water through the swing. In salt water especially, it is easier to hold them on the surface with one hand and splash water into the opening. By splashing the surface, you set up a current of bubbly water which flows through the pants, the water continuing and the air becoming trapped. Finally, you can duck underwater and inflate them with your breath. This takes time, but it is easier for the poor floater or weak swimmer.

With the pants inflated, slip your head through the loop of the legs. Fold the opening shut with a couple of diagonal folds and a cross-fold to seal it. As long as that fold is facing downward and is underwater, the rig will hold air. You can slip your arms through the loop to make water wings, or you can tuck the fold into the top of your swimsuit (women will need a two-piece suit for this), improvising a Mae West-type life preserver.

The main advantage of this rig is that you can even go to sleep in it in perfect safety. The water will splash in your face before you go under, thus waking you up. Also, it is possible for two swimmers to lock arms through the loop in the inflated pants so a single pair of pants can support two people.

Many lifesavings occur outside of a swimming situation. Here neither rescuer nor victim are prepared for the event, and both are generally fully clothed. Oddly enough, many of these are quite close to a steep bank (a car or a fisherman falling into a river, e.g.). As a result, it is possible for the rescuer to reach the victim with some object—a

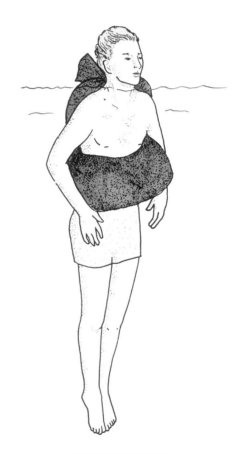

USE OF PANTS FOR LIFE PRESERVER

board, a broken tree limb, his shirt, or simply reaching out with his hand or foot. If he has a rope handy, it can be thrown alongside the victim so he can reach it, even if it doesn't have a flotation device such as a life ring. If none of these are available, he should use a boat, if he can get one quickly (including swiping one temporarily), swimming only as a last resort, after removing his shoes and any outer clothes which may tend to slow down his movement, and using the techniques described above, including inflating his clothing if he is not in condition and may have difficulty in getting the victim back to shore.

More emergency rescues can be made without getting wet than are normally done. Keep your head and consider these before you impulsively jump in.

SKIN DIVING

Skin diving is still fairly rare in camping—mostly because of the weight and bulk of the gear. Yet a fair amount of skin diving can be done with no more than a mask, fins, and a snorkel, which are fairly light and not too bulky. Boat camping, with its fairly heavy weight limits, is an obvious way to combine skin diving with camping.

Snorkel diving is simple and safe for any good swimmer if logical precautions are taken. In addition to the usual rules of safe swimming, don't over-extend your time at depths, as your bouyancy is reduced often past the vanishing point with the pressure of depth and it is quite difficult to come up. This variation in bouyancy does not occur with scuba gear since the air in your lungs is entering at the same pressure as the water at that depth. For this reason, never rise faster than your bubbles, or fail to continue normal breathing when rising with scuba gear, or you will damage your lungs from over-inflation as the outside pressure drops.

Don't try to use any of the scuba devices without instruction. Too many things can go wrong. There are classes held in most large cities and many scuba-equipment stores offer lessons with the equipment. However, the instruction varies widely in quality, so check into that aspect before signing up.

Regardless of the breathing technique, if you are diving in waters where there is any power boating, use the skin diver's flag. It is a red rectangle with a white stripe running diagonally from the point nearest the top of the pole. Incidentally, some flags have either the words DIVER BELOW or a picture of a skin diver on the stripe. While this is to help explain the flag to the uninitiated, it unfortunately more often attracts them closer to find out what's on the flag. All boats (except those tending the skin divers, and therefore flying the flag) should keep clear of the area by 100 feet (30 m). The flag should not be flown while under way unless you are towing a submarine sled. It should be used only when divers are actually in the water.

Develop your skill in this sport in a swimming pool, preferably in a well-taught class on the subject. So far, skin diving has been a relatively safe sport, but it is potentially dangerous. Unskilled divers working in surf, extreme depth, or other difficult conditions, or swimming alone are asking for trouble.

For those who know how, skin diving is a great sport and provides, in addition to the sheer fun of diving, a welcome addition to the camp food supply when near salt water. Spear fishing in fresh water is generally restricted to the relatively inedible rough fish. Needless to say, a loaded spear gun should be treated with all the respect of a loaded firearm.

A well-run scuba club is the best source of help for the diver who is just starting in the sport. You will not only learn new skills under proper supervision, you will generally be able to save money by pooling resources for such needed extras as air-tank compressors, support facilities such as club boats (usually manned by non-diving relatives), and even (if the club is affluent enough) submarines or other more expensive underwater toys.

CHAPTER THIRTY

Other Activities

While the activities just discussed are by far the most common in camping, there are a host of others which may interest the camper—in fact, many of them are often the total reason for the camping trip. Camping is just a convenient and economical way to live while enjoying the activity.

BEACHCOMBING

Beachcombing is probably the most popular pastime of the coastal camper. It rarely requires any equipment, and often requires no skills or special knowledge. Shells are more interesting if some identification is made, but one of the books listed in Chapter 55 will solve that problem. Still, it is enjoyable simply to pick up shells which "look pretty"; after awhile, you will start being more selective (you already have this kind, that one is too damaged by drills, this other is weathered too much).

Just as the study of precious stones is a side field to rock collecting, so lapidary equipment can bring out untold beauty in gastropod (snail, slug, etc.) and cephalopod (the highest class of mollusk) shells. Using a fine saw, a high speed, and a very light feed, slice the shells in half. The spiral cavity of the conches and the involved chambers of the nautilus make most aesthetically pleasing patterns when they are cleaned up and mounted on a black velvet background.

Driftwood has more uses than fueling the campfire. The naturally sandblasted and salt-stained textures of the gnarled limbs make attractive decorations over a fireplace or as the base of a lamp. Artistic campers can develop them into interesting *objet trouvé* sculptures. The unsuitable parts can be most welcome for cooking meals and warding off sea-chill in the evenings.

Other objects of use in decorating are the large glass balls which the Japanese use for fishnet floats. These are quite beautiful and are sometimes found washed up on a beach along the coast. They are becoming more and more rare as the fishermen are now using plastic foam for their floats since it is unbreakable and weighs no more than the glass ones. These beautiful blue spheres will soon become a thing of the past.

Bottles, even without messages in them, make valuable finds. Many old handmade ones have changed from clear to interesting amber tints in weathering.

Another beachcombing target from the past is treasure. This is a complicated sport if you want to find more than an occasional old coin. Most of the treasure found today is obtained by diving rather than digging. It is no job for the amateur with an old map and dreams of sudden wealth. It should be approached strictly as a hobby and nothing more. Still, it is an interesting and occasionally rewarding activity.

When you are not going after a known wreck with proper scuba gear and governmental permission, a metal detector is a useful accessory. This consists of a couple of loops and a small radio transmitter and receiver. When the radio waves bounce off of metal, the second loop detects it and there is a change in the tone heard in the earphones. Surplus mine detectors are about extinct now, but lighter weight (and more expensive) models are on the market. There are quite a few plans for these circulating in magazines. The *Reader's Guide* at your public library will find them for you.

Other than that, all you need is a lot of luck (the detectors will locate vast quantities of old tin cans) and the persistent knowledge that it is only a game, and you will not be too discouraged.

SURFING

Surfing campers can logically be divided into two groups. The first are the surfers who camp as a means of reducing the costs of living until "Surf's up" is sounded. The second group is composed of campers who have gone to the beach for some shore camping and found surfers obviously having fun in an activity with which the campers have had no direct experience. This is a brief survey of surfing for this camper who may be interested in surfing as an in-camp activity but isn't interested in investing heavily in what will simply be an occasional activity, shared with beachcombing, nature study, and camping away from the ocean.

Reading the Surf

The nearest sports to surfing are soaring and white-water canoeing. Both of these, like surfing, depend not only on mechanical proficiency with the vehicle, but on a skilled ability to judge the action of the great forces of nature—unconquerable forces which can only be used by the sportsman in such a refined and skilled manner that the illusion of conquering is created. The sailplane pilot must know the action of the wind, both horizontal and vertical. The white-water canoeist must know the action of flowing water so the surface appearance will give him a clear and instant knowl-

edge of the conditions just under the surface so he can steer his craft through the obstacles. So the surfer must know wave action with enough skill so that he can know which of the peaks of the approaching swell will make a wave he can ride with speed, control, and safety, and how its ever-changing pattern will tip him off to how the wave will be modified by the sea floor, when it will break, and where and how he should move to avoid being wiped out.

The person who visits the coast only occasionally, and therefore has little opportunity to watch surf, should spend several hours simply watching the surf, how it forms, how it behaves, how it is affected by tide and wind patterns. And considerable time should be spent in watching surfers, preferably both body and board surfers.

Waves are not as simple as they appear. In the first place, there is very little movement by a given molecule of water in a wave. The water is not moving forward with the wave, but in a vertical circle, the diameter equal to the distance from trough to crest. The horizontal movement of the water is a slight forward movement as the wave rises, and a slight backward movement as it subsides.

This knowledge is of prime importance to the surfer since he is being moved over the water just as surely as if he were in some more conventionally powered vehicle. This, of course, enables him to steer since, if he were not moving relative to the water, he could have no rudder action from the fin, his hands, or the turning effect from his banking the board.

Strictly speaking, surf is the breaking action of the waves as they come into shore. The unbroken peaks and valleys of water which do not break are swells. There are two types of breakers—plunging and spilling. Waves which don't break, even though they come up on the beach, are too weak for surfing.

The plunging breaker is the type which curls over as it breaks. It has a very steep side and thus produces good speed on a surfboard. It is quite dangerous in larger sizes and can cause the "over the falls" condition in which the surfer is carried over the top of the wave instead of in the tube, and dumped into the water. As we shall see, the bottom can easily be hit when this happens: because of the steep wall, pearling, or catching the nose of the board in the trough, it is quite likely to happen unless the board is controlled quite parallel to the wave. This is the main reason for the wave breaker on surfing kayaks—to keep the bow from plunging too deeply.

The spilling breaker doesn't curl over with a resounding crash, but simply slides down its own face, making a lot of "soup" when it does. Soup, incidentally, looks foamy, but it is still quite hard water, as any surfer discovers when he tries to shoot through it going out. The spilling breaker doesn't have as steep a wall and so you can't get as much speed. On the other hand, it is far easier to control and therefore better for beginners.

Two factors affect breaking: bottom and wind. On a smooth bottom, gently sloping, with no wind, waves will break at a trough depth (distance from trough to sea bottom) of about one and a third times the pitch (distance from trough to crest level). Where there are bars, reefs, or other unevenness of the bottom, the depth may be as much as twice the pitch. A wind blowing off-shore will delay the break of a plunging breaker and an on-shore wind will hasten it. Wind has much less effect on spilling breakers, but it is still a noticeable factor.

Bars or submerged reefs will cause waves to break twice, once over the bar, and again as they approach the beach. The second break, of course, is much weaker since the wave has expended energy in the first break. This kind of beach is excellent for beginners since they can get the experience of breaking waves without the danger caused by the breaking of large waves. Under all other conditions, beginners should learn by riding the soup of expended waves—there is still plenty of energy left in them to move a surfboard.

A knowledge of surf is helpful in getting out to the surfing areas. Especially in big surf, outward progress is difficult because of the waves attempting to surf you back in again. Even in lighter surf, this is a tiring process. There are two ways to reduce the problem, using the waves themselves.

A child might ask, "With all those waves coming in all the time, what keeps the water from piling up?"

The small amount of water running back out to sea after a wave comes onto the beach is insignificant compared to the force of the breakers coming in. A popular theory used to explain it is the undertow—that mysterious and menacing current of water returning under the breakers. The only problem is that it doesn't exist.

Where the water does go is into the rip current. This is an actual current, quite visible even to the novice surf-watcher by the fact that the surf is very small, if present at all at these points. In a cove, the rip current will generally follow the sides of the U since the bottom breaks up the power of the surf there anyway and the rip can move out more easily. Where there are artificial beach preservers, such as jetties, groins, or piers, the rip will form along them for the same reason. Even in a perfectly straight beach, a rip current will develop in several spots.

A rip current is generally quite narrow, often only ten or twenty feet (3 to 6 m) wide, yet it flows quite rapidly and a swimmer can be swept out to sea with panic-producing speed. The logical solution is to swim at right angles to the current until you are out of it and back in full surf, but the tales of undertow are quite strong and the mind does not always come up with this simple solution. To the surfer, however, the rip is a rapid-transit system to the breaker line, called "escalators" in some surfing areas.

Rips are formed by the very factor the child was trying to have explained. The water literally does pile up on the beach until the weight of the water becomes enough to force a rip path through the breakers and drain it out. The pressure then becomes less and the rip vanishes.

The second easy way through the surf is to wait for the lulls. A typical cycle or "set" of waves will be a fairly large one, then a still larger one, then possibly an even larger one, then a gradual decreasing of wave size until the surf is almost glassy. The surfer should head out during these lulls so that he will be past the breaker line when the next big ones come.

This cycle of waves and lulls had a considerable bearing on the 1966 surf-dory championships in which the winning boat always seemed to catch the last wave of the cycle into shore and to tag, turn, and be outward-bound during the lull, while the competitors kept running into heavy surf when outbound. The meet was close because the winner hit a calm stretch going into the finish and three others came riding in on the same set.

The surfer should always try for the largest wave of the set for several reasons. For the expert, it provides the most power and the greatest chance to do something on the wave. For the beginner, it provides the safety factor of altitude in that there is more time to correct before the nose pearls in or the wave wipes him out. For everyone, there is better visibility and therefore a greater margin of safety—and that is a goal for any surfer.

Body Surfing

The obvious major requirement here is an ability to swim in salt water. In fact, the only other equipment besides a bathing suit is the possible use of swim fins to assist in getting up sufficient speed to get into a surfing position.

In most of the Atlantic and Gulf Coast surfing areas, the bottom is relatively smooth and the surf relatively small. You can wade out anywhere from fifty yards to a full mile (45 to 1,500 m). In these areas (and many Pacific areas too, especially when the surf is low), you can wade out to a spot where the water depth in the trough is only waist-to-chest-high (four feet [120 cm] or so) and still catch three-foot (90 cm) waves. This is the area where non-surfers go to "ride the waves." In fact, this type of body surfing is a modified form of riding the waves, different only in that, instead of the strictly circular movement with the water as the wave goes by, the body surfer will catch the wave and move over the water.

Where the surfer is standing on the bottom, it is simply a matter of timing a forward jump so that his body will be supported by the upward motion of the forward edge of the wave in balance with the gravity slide down the front of it. While learning this balance, while getting the "feel" of waves, the surfer is basically in a horizontal, front-float position, but, because of the slope of the wave, only his head and the back of his shoulders are out of the water, and his arms are resting on the surface for stability.

With practice, the surfer will be able to get his head completely out so his arms can be used for steering.

In water over his head, the procedure is the same, except that the surfer must be able to swim fast enough to keep the wave from overtaking him before he gets into the balance point which enables him to truly ride the surf. Here, obviously, swimming fins will help him get up that speed.

When competence is reached, the body surfer will be able to surf within the wave, arms at his side, with only his head out of the water. The arms are brought forward (or outward) only for control. Again, this is for the low surf encountered along most of the nation's coastline. For heavy surf, one or both arms, the hands forming small diving planes like a submarine, are used as outriggers or even as forward probes and bumpers if the water is crowded.

For reasons of safety, body surfing should be done far away from board surfers. The danger is too great. Many learn this the hard way with bad bruises, and worse, from runaway surfboards.

Today, with improved techniques in body surfing permitting far more than the old beginner routine of catch-a-wave-and-ride-it-straight-to-shore, bailing out before wiping out, the body surfer can do as many maneuvers as the board surfer (omitting tandem surfing, of course). After you learn the basics of body surfing, try to find a good body surfer on the beach and ask for help. Now that the fad is over, surfers are quite willing to help beginners who are serious and not wanting to look like someone in a surfing movie. In fact, since the surfing movies all used boards, the body surfers were this way even during the fad—the faddists thought body surfing was beneath them. True surfers, even those who personally prefer the board, know better.

Mat Surfing

Mat surfing is simply using an air mattress (preferably the shorty variety) for a surfboard—or, more properly, for a median between body and board surfing.

Mat surfing, of a very primitive nature, was done on the Atlantic and Gulf back in the 1930's when surfboards were considered strictly Hawaiian, although some was being done in California.

Like early body surfing, it was a matter of catching the wave by fast swimming, and riding it straight into shore. Because the surf in these areas was quite gentle, the wave could usually break with the mat surfer in it and still not produce a wipe-out. High surfs in these areas were not fashionable for swimming (and body and mat surfing were considered basically show-off swimming techniques). Besides, such surf was usually the result of storms and the high wind made them dangerous.

Now that board surfing has made these waves respectable, and has produced enough techniques to reduce the danger to a thrilling rather than a menacing level, mat surfing should make a comeback. Unfortunately, it hasn't yet, except in small areas on the West Coast.

The air mattress should be inflated hard, so it cannot be bent without extreme force. With the shorty mats, the technique is like body surfing while the ride is on top of the wave as in board surfing. Here, the legs will be totally submerged, the arms in an outrigger position, the chin buried in the mat, and the after-edge of the mat coming to about the waist.

With a full-length air mattress, if it can be inflated hard enough, you can actually stand on it in moderate surf—if you weigh under a hundred pounds (45 kg). Because of this, most of the development of mat surfing has been done by kids barely, if at all, into their teens.

For lying-down surfing, even a shorty mattress can support a 200-pounder (90 kg) in a surfing attitude.

The main problem for the mat-surfing camper is the condition of the air mattress. Salt water, oil (often on the surface), and the abrasive effect of beaches are not conducive to a good sleeping air mattress. If you do much mat surfing at all, it would be well to buy one for the purpose. Two feet (60 cm) of width when over-inflated is the maximum since wider ones interfere with arm action. A loose rope attached all around the edge makes the mat easier to catch if it gets away. This means you will probably need to buy a special

surfing mat instead of just any shorty mattress, unless you can figure a way to attach a rope to the air mattress firmly without damaging the air-holding qualities.

Since this section assumes that you are not a confirmed surfer, but merely experimenting with the idea, you are not likely go out and buy a surf mat unless you have some extra money. You can still get some idea of mat surfing from a camping air mattress, but be sure to use an old one. One which, perhaps, has been patched so many times it is lumpy, but still holds air well, is the ideal. Inflate it with a hand pump or as hard as you can by mouth without damaging your eardrums. When it is taken out to the surf, the warmth of the sun will make it a bit harder and thus better for surfing.

Getting out to the swells is more difficult with the mat than in any other way because the mat simply won't "dive" under the approaching wave and, if there is a wind blowing in-shore, it will be difficult to get the mat over the top of a breaking wave. Here, the rope is a necessity. Often the best way is to wait until the last minute, throw the mat over the wave, and let the wave ride over you. Hang on the whole time though, or you might come out the other side minus your mat.

In more gentle surf, the best way is the same as with a board, a kayak, or any other surf vehicle. Simply get up speed and ride up and over the wave. The only problem you may encounter is soup—the foamy crest of the wave which is easily disturbed and seems to take perverse delight in hitting the faces of outbound surfers.

Other than simply letting the soup hit you like a slapstick pie, you have two alternatives. The first is to wait until you are going up the wave and then, at the last minute, bury your face in the mat, letting the soup hit the top of your head instead of your face. The second is to jump on the mat with your knees and hands and let the soup break between you and your mat. This second method requires considerable agility and timing, but you don't have to shake the water off your face as you come up on the other side. For those who surf as well as swim with their glasses on, it is the best way in that it reduces the distortion of wet glasses.

Even if you plan to take up board surfing, mat

surfing is good training since it has the same relationship to boards as sailing does to power boating or sailplanes do to powered aircraft. You are in closer contact with the elemental forces of the wave and have less maneuverability built into your vehicle. As a result, you will learn more ways to get out of bad situations than simply banking out of the way.

An excellent transition from the mat to the full board is the belly board. This is about as long as a mat and as wide as a full board, with a little fin at the back, just like the full boards. In heavy surf, it is even possible to stand up on them, but generally they are ridden with most of the techniques of body surfing and thus fins are recommended. Basically, belly-board surfing is body surfing with many of the full board's controls.

Board Surfing

Because of a series of atrocious movies, this is the most common form of surfing. And because of its mass appeal, it is, unfortunately, practiced by many who should be restricted to body or mat surfing until they learn enough about surf to get on the boards. The power and maneuverability of the modern surfboard makes it no less dangerous than turning a sportscar over to someone who can't handle a regular car.

The typical surfboard (strictly speaking, the Malibu board) is made from plastic foam covered with fiberglass and weighs between twenty-five and thirty pounds (11 to $13\frac{1}{2}$ kg). A small fin at the stern permits its extreme maneuverability. It is quite sharp, to reduce drag in the water, and therefore provides something of a problem while carrying it. It is best to carry it stern first.

The movies always show the surfers riding enormous waves effortlessly to shore. The facts of surfing are quite different. Aside from the fact that these waves are too dangerous to any but the most skilled surfers, they have distorted the picture in another matter too—in reality, most surfing time is spent in paddling. Paddling is a swimmer's breast stroke with the board under the paddler and little or no leg action used, except occasionally for steering by dragging in the water. This is modified somewhat on the West Coast where the cold waters of the California Current make it advisable to keep as much of the body out of the water as possible and the kneeling position is used more—with the resulting "surfer's knots" below the knees.

This stroke is, of course, one of the most tiring in the swimmer's repertoire and the beginner is warned that while board surfing is enjoyable, it is also mostly plain hard work for people in good physical condition.

The board should be paddled with a fore-and-aft trim which puts the bow about an inch (25 mm or so) out of the water and the stern not yet awash in totally calm water.

Except in the case of large waves, going out on a board is strictly a matter of getting sufficient speed and hitting the waves head-on so that the soup is splashed to the side of the board.

The beginner, especially in high surf, is advised to ride waves which have already broken. They have lost most of their energy and, if they should break for a second time, there is little danger involved, whereas the big ones can be quite dangerous to the novice. Therefore, the beginner should stop his outward progress just short of the breaker line. In light surf, of course, he should continue on out to the point where the swells are just becoming surf since they are quite small. Three feet, trough to crest, is the maximum surf the beginner should try.

Turning is a problem on the flat surfboard, but there are easier ways. The easiest is to move back so that you are sitting over the fin. This will make the bow slant steeply out of the water, but not so steeply that you are likely to be spilled off the stern. Either by kicking your feet in opposite directions to paddle the board around, or simply by "swivel-hipping," the board is turned to a position roughly parallel to the shore. In this position, the build-up of waves may be watched comfortably, and you will still be able to turn the board the rest of the way in time to start paddling to get speed to catch a suitable wave.

With the wave selected, the procedure is to start paddling toward shore as though you were trying to get away from the wave. Since waves travel close to ten miles per hour (15 km/h), you are unlikely to be able to paddle faster just using your hands. You will feel it when the wave is actually giving the forward motion and you are surfing.

The beginner should get up to hands-and-knees position until he learns the feel of a wave and the basics of steering. Steering, at least for the beginner in light-to-moderate surf, is simply a matter of banking—the low side is the inside of the turn. The object in surfing is to run as parallel to the wave as possible (to prolong the ride) without slowing the speed in the direction of the wave to the extent that the wave overtakes you.

After a few such rides, the surfer is ready for a standing position. By moving forward or backward, the standing surfer can regulate his speed relative to the wave. He has much more flexibility in his ability to tilt the board and thus change direction more easily. And it is easier to simply step back to get out of a wave than it is to crawl back. The final step, coupled with a pivot around, enables the surfer to sink into the back of the wave with his board swinging around at a slant so the board is practically turned around before the next wave comes by. With practice and help, progress is made in more advanced skills.

The prime safety rule in surfing is to stay with the board. In all but the heaviest surf, there is no excuse for not maintaining full control of the board under any wave condition. Anyone who gets wiped-out in less than three-foot (1 m) surf should go back to the kneeling position and learn the waves better.

However, since this does sometimes happen, usually from pearling (having the nose catch in the trough, flipping the board), you should know the proper way to get out. Jump clear of the board and roll up in a ball with your hands behind your head and your elbows together covering your face. As you start to come up, extend one arm upward as a bumper. Stay under as long as possible to get out of the wave. If you have any control whatsoever left over the board before diving, try to kick down the stern so that it leaves that particular wave. An unmanned surfboard riding a wave is a dangerous thing.

Kayak Surfing

I was rather surprised when I started my research on kayak surfing, hoping to get the benefit of other viewpoints, to discover that in all the surfing books I could find, only two made mention of kayak surfing. One of these simply mentioned that kayaks were used for surfing, the other had about half a paragraph stating that it was done by only a few on the West Coast and that one surfer had been able to surf in the Canadian canoe. That was all. I first read about kayak surfing in *White Water Sport* (see Chapter 54), which had a bit over two pages with several illustrations on kayak surfing, and it was a book on white-water canoeing. From this I assumed it was a specialized but somewhat normal surfing form, much like the Australian surf boats or surf skis (a thick surfboard with double paddles), and so I proceeded to convert a non-white-water cruising kayak over for surfing (see Chapter 15).

After doing some kayak surfing, I am even more puzzled as to why it is not more common. It is the easiest method for getting out, and in the moderate surf which is the heaviest found in Atlantic or Gulf waters except from a hurricane, it is practically devoid of all danger, even to the beginner. Of course, a good degree of proficiency at normal smooth-water kayaking is required and some white-water experience is helpful. However, outside of the heavy surf of the Pacific (which I have not experienced except in the sheltered waters of Georgia Straits—which on an exceptional day has a surf equal to the average Gulf of Mexico waves), there is no problem for the skilled kayaker in a well-modified boat.

While the slalom single-seat kayak is best for surf (as it is for any purpose other than camping), I have had good success with my eighteen-foot ($5\frac{1}{2}$ m) twin-seat cruising model—the same one I use for canoe camping. The only changes I make are to fasten a wave breaker under the bow ring and flagpole mounting and, of course, to use a spray cover. An advantage of a homemade spray cover, like a homemade tent, is that you can include features lacking on commercial models. The circle I cut out to form the cockpit hole can be replaced with a zipper when the hole is not used. This is quite useful in surfing as the water tends to come over the cover with a bit of force and the usual sleeve cannot always be fastened tightly enough at the vacant position to keep water out.

Normally, when using the two-seat kayak and only one surfer, the front seat is used and the aft one is sealed. This helps get the weight forward so that the normal surfing balance is maintained. However, in heavy surf the aft seat may be preferred since maintaining speed when surfing won't be a problem, but a lighter bow may be desired for going out.

The properly fitted surfing kayak goes through the usual Atlantic and Gulf surf quite easily, the water rarely breaking over the bow. In Pacific surf, however, the wave breaker is required to punch a hole in the water (although it is quite easily done). In fact, the wave breaker is definitely recommended for all rough water as insurance. Because the back of the wave is longer than the steeper front, going out is actually easier in terms of physical exertion than coming in, although of course it takes longer. The surfing run is done just as with a board, timing the approach of a good wave, paddling to build up speed, and catching the forward slope of the wave. Leaning forward helps maintain this speed at the critical point when paddling stops and surfing begins.

Steering can be done in four ways: (1) by use of a pedal-operated rudder, (2) by using the paddle as a rudder, (3) by paddling on the opposite side to turn, and (4) by banking the kayak toward the direction of the turn by shifting the body weight. Normally the fourth way is the easiest and most effective. In light surf, the third is often required since the drag of the kayak, especially a large tandem cruising model, does not permit enough speed to keep up with the smaller waves. If the paddle rudder is used, it should be used on the wave side of the boat since on that side the water is rising and it will provide a secure brace point for the paddle if bracing is required. When the paddle is not being used for steering or for propulsion, it is often useful to hold it horizontally, about chin-high, and use it as a tightrope walker uses his balance pole.

One of the main advantages of kayak surfing is that it can be done in surf which is too weak for board surfers. It is excellent in the normally weaker Atlantic and Gulf surf although quite exciting (or is it panicking?) in the heavy surf of the more famous surfing spots seen on television sports shows. In the tamer waters, anyone who has mastered the kayak in fresh water and has had the psychological conditioning of paddling across motorboat wakes to be convinced of the stability of the kayak can handle light surf the first time out. (This is, of course, assuming the kayak is properly fitted with a wave breaker and spray cover.) Turning is the only part which is harder than lake paddling since the waves tend to weathercock the boat evenly across the front of the wave and are quite powerful, especially in the inland part of the circuit where the soup of the broken wave makes a more vertical wall than the slope of the swell farther out.

Turning out of a surfing position can generally be avoided by simply bracing on the opposite side of the wave and simultaneously leaning toward the wave, pivoting around the paddle. You will pull out quite easily and the wave will turn you a quarter to a third of the way around in the process. A stroke of the paddle on the opposite side of the kayak from the brace will generally complete the turn since the next wave will generally weathercock the stern the rest of the way around—especially if you are still in your paddle stroke when it hits.

The spray cover shown in Chapter 15 is quite effective. About a half-cup of water is shipped each trip out—mostly forced under the extreme forward edge of the cockpit coaming when the wave breaks over the entire length of the kayak. Time has to be taken occasionally to empty the pocket of water which collects in the bight of the sleeve around the paddler. Simply pulling up the elastic part when you reach calm water will allow it to pour off, as will any which manages to collect in the middle of the spray cover between the hatches.

The great advantage of the kayak, even over its ease in paddling out, is its ability to pick up speed easily. Therefore you can catch waves too small for board surfers to use for more than a straight run in.

While definitely on the spectacular side, the ability to do an Eskimo roll (see Chapter 45) is invaluable if you work in heavy surf, since, even if a wave wipes you out, you can still pop back up to the surface without either having to leave your kayak or even getting water in your craft. It is a good intentional tactic if caught broadside by a plunging breaker to roll toward it and, if the upcurrent isn't strong enough to right your craft, simply roll on around and pop up when it is past.

SKIING

Since this is a camping book, the discussion of skiing will be restricted to the form of skiing most adapted to the camper—cross-country. Since the development of the ski tow, downhill skiing (including slalom) had almost totally eclipsed cross-country (or x-c) skiing in popularity. However, this is now beginning to change and x-c is becoming the biggest boom in outdoor recreation. Still it is a minority form of skiing and probably will be for another five or ten years. Like the Canadian canoe and the kayak, this preference for downhill is at least partially the result of fallacies which are only now beginning to be cleared up.

X-c is considered a frightfully athletic sport and downhill a more leisurely activity. Actually the contrary is true. In fact, even on the competition level, the prime for x-c skiers approximates the time downhill skiers are ready to retire. Indeed, many Scandinavians (where x-c is a major means of transportation) are skiing x-c long after sixty.

The equipment and the techniques for x-c are different from the more familiar downhill, but the equipment is finally becoming available on a reasonably widespread basis, and more ski trails are being laid out to accommodate skiers who want more than the slopes. Even a few x-c instructors are beginning to appear, although it is still pretty much a teach-yourself sport outside of competition.

Equipment

When x-c equipment is compared to downhill, several differences are immediately noticed. First off, the price for full equipment (skis, boots, bindings, and poles) is less than half as much—even a third as much for comparable quality if you know where to shop. And you won't have the expense of lifts and tows.

The ski is quite different. It is only a couple of inches (5 cm) wide at the foot and a half-inch (1 cm) wider at the tip and tail. Its length should be to your palm or wrist when holding the ski vertically as high as you can comfortably reach. It has no metal anywhere except for the binding, and it is much more flexible than the downhill ski. Because of these differences, it weighs only about one-third as much (four pounds [1.8 kg] vs. twelve pounds [5½ kg], average).

The boots are considerably lighter, resembling a light rock-climbing boot without the treaded sole. In fact, many rock-climbing boots have a grooved heel for this very reason—a factor which makes ski mountaineering so much easier to equip.

Instead of all manner of lashings and quick-release mechanisms, the x-c bindings are attached only at the toe either with a metal strap going around the heel to hold the boot on the clamp, or an attachment which clamps the toe itself down. The sole is flexible enough that normal walking action is done with the skis on. A pin (or pins) on the ski and corresponding hole(s) in the heel of the boot permit the foot to stay rigid on the ski for sideways control when the weight is on the heel, but pop off in case of falling. The heel is quite free to move vertically. This is to prevent the tendon damage or blisters on the heel you would get from using downhill bindings for x-c (unless, of course, they have the heel release for this purpose).

Cross-country does not involve the speed and shifts, etc., of downhill so the extra side bracing is that much extra weight. Because x-c skis are so light and all wood, they will break before a leg does in case of a fall, so even safety bindings are not necessary, although they are available (and may save your skis as well). A heel pop-up (a piece of rubber under the heel) keeps the snow from packing around it in a ball.

The poles are about four inches (10 cm) longer than downhill poles and the straps permit a couple of inches (5 cm) variation in grip position and thus the most effective pole length. Normally they should fit under your armpits. The basket is about the same as downhill poles. The tips are the main difference: x-c tips are curved forward so they will pull out more easily, while the downhill tips are straight.

Clothing for x-c is much like downhill ski clothing, although, because of the greater exertion, it is a bit lighter. One of the main savings in x-c is that, even in the resorts, the x-c skier shuns fancy, expensive ski fashions. Any winter clothing which permits free movement is fashion for the x-c skier—in fact, it is often the badge of the sport. Also, since speed is rarely developed to any great degree, goggles are unnecessary. (Most x-c skiing is done in wooded areas which cut glare to tolerable levels. Inuit slit-goggles may help in open places.)

A normal assortment of wax and rags, corks, blowtorches, or whatever you use to put wax on with, completes the equipment. Even that load can be reduced by using the skis with mohair strips on the bottoms. These are simply sprayed occasionally with silicone boot spray. This eliminates any need for waxing as they will always have the right slide/stick characteristics regardless of the snow. However, the strips wear out in a season or two of week-end skiing and will cost more in the long run than the wax. A belt pack is adequate for any day tour and a small ski pack will take care of equipment for an overnight tour. A spare ski tip, which simply clamps onto a broken ski, is also recommended for the rare emergency.

Techniques

This is the main difference between x-c and downhill skiing. In the latter, the problem is stability and control while descending a slope powered mostly by gravity. In cross-country, you are fighting gravity more than you are going with it. Therefore, most of the time you need to plant your ski flat into the snow so it won't slip as you move forward. As you move forward, your heel lifts from the back ski, but the ski stays firmly planted in the snow until you take the weight off that foot to move it forward. During this process, your poles are helping you by giving balance and by pushing back. Since the opposite arm to the foot moves forward each time, the basket should be planted even with the foot so that, since you are leaning forward somewhat, the force will be directed back as well as down.

The idea is to develop a coordination of feet, arms, and body so that you are striding forward in a purposeful manner, taking care to plant the ski flat each time.

Going uphill is the same as in any other form of skiing. The side-step, herringbone, and traverse are used to overcome the back-sliding effect of gravity. However, there is another method, peculiar to cross-country: skiing up. This takes an extra coat of wax, powerful arms, and considerable practice, but it is basically no different from level x-c skiing—plant the ski carefully and use the poles. The body attitude is an exaggerated knee bend and forward lean, as if you were stalking something.

Downhill skiing on x-c skis is quite different from downhill skiing on downhill skis. Because of the peculiar nature of x-c bindings, wedeln and other forms so effective on the edged skis just don't work very well on the rather laterally sloppy x-c skis. Most downhill running in x-c is simply straight running. Body position is slightly different, however. Remember, nothing is holding your heels down, so keep the weight rather evenly distributed on your feet to keep from falling on your face. If you have already developed skill as a downhill skier, you may even have to lean back slightly to overcome habit. The knees should be only slightly bent. Keep the points of the poles back slightly, but not straight back since you may need to use them as outriggers. If you are in wooded areas (as most good x-c trails are), don't use the straps on the poles so you won't be jerked back if the basket should catch on some underbrush.

The best turn for these skis is the old step turn since it produces practically no side force on the ski. Stops are generally not much of a problem in x-c because you either are going slowly enough in the first place, or you will soon run out of downhill anyway. If worse comes to worst, the sit-down stop is still a very effective brake.

Waxing is a critical factor in x-c because you have to have the bottoms both slick for downhill and sticky for uphill. Actually, this is a problem of individual conditions and it is best to get an assortment (they don't cost much) and try to find out from other skiers which are best until you learn to judge for yourself. When in doubt, put them all on, starting with the hardest. The snow will remove all that are too soft and leave you with the right one. It is wasteful and after awhile you will get the general idea about the best wax for the conditions. Cross-country skiers are most generous with this information—outside of competitions.

As with any other sport, find those who know how and try to learn from them. That, and practice, will always help you become an expert.

WATER SKIING

Boat campers especially, but to a great extent any lake camper with a suitable boat, will be interested in water skiing. There are so many places selling water-skiing equipment, including stores which specialize in it entirely, that you will not have any trouble finding equipment or advice in outfitting for this sport. Since it is so widespread, you probably have several water-skiing friends who would be willing to teach you the techniques.

The stores will be able to fit you with the proper-size skis for your size and ability, as well as with a life jacket, which should always be worn when water skiing. Except for the tow rope, also available at water skiers' stores, all else you need is a boat.

The Boat

Any boat capable of maintaining a speed of at least twenty miles per hour (32 or 33 km/h) with the skier can be used for towing. This is possible with as little as $7\frac{1}{2}$-horsepower in an outboard if the boat design is ideal, but generally 10-horsepower is the minimum. More power is needed if the boat is designed for more purposes than simply water-ski towing. Also, more power is needed for slalom or jumping (where a speed of 35 mph [55 km/h] is needed) or for more than one skier.

The ideal boat design for water skiing (and it is just as good for fishing, but too small for much camping) is an outboard between fourteen and sixteen feet (4.2 and 4.8 m) long and four to five feet (1.2 to 1.5 m) of beam at the transom. Below that length and beam will be unstable with a powerful engine and above that length and beam wastes power because of hull drag.

A pop-out plug is excellent for the tow-rope attachment. These are two-piece attachments—the socket attaches through the transom and a plug fits in it. A force just under the amount which would cause injury to the skier's arms or shoulders will pull the plug free. This is especially valuable for helmsmen without much ski-towing practice. If the speed is too great, the plug will come out instead of damaging the skier's arms.

A rear-view mirror is a necessity. While some states permit skiing without one, especially if an observer is riding in the boat, the helmsman will generally feel better if he can watch directly while still keeping a proper lookout ahead. Without the observer, there is no excuse for not having a mirror. It should be wide enough in field of view that the helmsman can see the skier in any position without having to move from side to side to find him.

Ideal, but not required, a steering arrangement from a front cockpit rather than a stern seat and tiller control makes a safer lookout position.

The outboard motor should be at least 25-horsepower since this will permit towing two or even three skiers, and skiing is more fun when there is company at the end of the tow rope.

A center anchor point for the tow rope, aft of the motor, makes tangled tow lines far less likely.

The hull plan of the boat should be a modified V, of a planing rather than a displacement type. Catamarans of either two or three hulls are even better for speed and stability.

Other Equipment

The main item of equipment, of course, are the skis themselves. Until you have gained enough skill for slalom, jump, or short skis, stick to the standard size of $5\frac{1}{2}$ to $6\frac{1}{2}$ feet long and six inches wide. Be sure to check the condition of the fin—the most likely spot to break. Hold the ski upright and flex downward at the foot position. If the fin tends to separate from the ski at the leading edge, you may have trouble from it later.

The best tow line is quarter-inch (6 mm) polypropylene or manilla. Polypropylene costs more but it will float and is a little stronger. Polyethylene also floats, but it is much weaker and stretches unreliably. Manila is inexpensive but it should be broken in first by towing behind the boat (without a skier) for a few minutes. After it dries out, singe off the hairs and you will have a perfectly adequate rope.

A single handle is best for beginners since the wider trick bar and double handles for slalom skiing are more confusing to the beginner, who has enough to be confused about for the moment.

SAILING

Sailing the usual one-design classes will not be considered here since there is not much likelihood that the camper will be using one. They are not really large enough for camping gear in a boat-camping situation, though there is no reason why they can't be used for camping since they are both roomier and more stable than the canoes and kayaks which are used both for camping and for sailing (although seldom at the same time).

This is to cover two types of sailing—the canoe and the surfboard. In both cases, there is considerable modification to the craft to make it sail. The Canadian canoe is generally sailed backward, since the stern thwart makes an excellent step for the mast and the bow thwart is too far aft for the job. The tandem kayak is better designed for it, the forward point of the cockpit being the right position for the mast. The surfboard has been modified for sailing so much that it is really a totally new craft—the sailfish. It, in turn, has been modified into the sunfish and the porpoise, which have small cockpits.

The Canadian canoe and the sailfish both use a lateen rig, while the kayak generally uses a marconi-rigged sloop arrangement although a sliding gunter has advantages in folding to a smaller package for transport. Both canoes use leeboards, while the sailfish uses a daggerboard for lateral stability. All types are fairly widely available, and there are excellent plans for a Canadian-canoe sailing rig in the Red Cross *Canoeing* book (see Chapter 54).

Leeboards should be placed so that there is a slight tendency to come into the wind when sailing close-hauled. The depth of the daggerboard should be adjusted to get the same effect.

Except for stability, these little sailers are handled just the same as the more conventional sailboats. There are fairly inexpensive courses offered in sailing in most good sailing waters. It is strongly advised that you take one of these to get the fullest enjoyment out of your camping sailboat.

ANIMAL COLLECTING

Children, especially, want to catch anything they see moving in the wilds and make a pet of it. While this has the obvious danger that most animals do not like such treatment, and are inclined to prove it with tooth, claw, sting, or whatever defense they have developed, there should be something said about the subject other than simply "don't."

Close contact with wild animals is an educational opportunity which no child should be denied. However, this should be done under proper supervision since many animals do have dangerous aspects, and it should be done with a proper regard for the safety of the animal as well as for the safety of the child.

A good example of this is in the problem of visitors feeding the animals in the more popular parks. The danger in feeding park bears is obvious (although for some reason it never seems to stop those who continue to feed them). Yet there is also a danger in feeding park deer. Deer are a lot smaller than most people imagine (they are closer to a large dog than to a small horse in size), and therefore are "so cute." They are even cuter when you hold the food up so that they raise up on their hind legs to get it. The problem is that deer don't like to have their front legs off the ground and will try to rest them on something handy. The only "something handy" is the person holding the food. A deer's hooves are its main defensive weapon and are razor-sharp at the tips. With nothing but the best intentions of stability, the deer proceeds to severely cut the person holding the food.

This problem is coupled with the fact that the average person does not feed the animals food that is good for them. No wild animal can easily digest a candy bar, even the highly omniverous raccoons.

While a truly wild animal will not let you get near enough to pet it (even if it has never seen a human before), the semi-wild animals of the parks will, because they associate it with food. They are so accustomed to sponging off tourists, they will snap angrily if you don't have any. Couple this with the possibility of rabies, especially in the smaller animals, and the fact that it is unlikely that you can catch the animal to keep it for observation, and the problem becomes more severe. Then the assumption of rabies must be made and the painful Pasteur treatment begun.

Reptiles and amphibians are a little more receptive. Taking proper precautions against being bitten, you can handle them with ease. Again, consideration of the animals' welfare is in order. They should be captured only to "show the kids" or to take to the Ranger for positive identification, then taken back to where they were found, and released.

It is the rule in all national parks that the wildlife has priority over the people. The parks are set up for them and the other natural features of the area which, otherwise, would be destroyed. You are simply permitted to visit—so act as a guest. Under no condition, should any wildlife be removed from the area.

ARTS

There are many art forms which adapt themselves quite readily to the camping situation. Many of these are done elsewhere, some can only be done in nature. Many of them are fairly simple in the degree of skill required and children will find them most interesting, while others are quite complex and require a considerable amount of skill. One or more would be of interest to any camper and they provide a good recreation activity for periods of bad weather.

Painting

Painting is one of the more popular art forms (and here we would include sketching, pastels, and other forms which, while they don't use paint, do use similar techniques and subjects). In a camping situation, it is much like photography in that it requires a bit of weight and bulk invested in it and often it will be the main purpose of the camping trip.

I have always been disappointed to note that at such major scenic wonders as Grand Canyon there are photographers in abundance, but few painters. Here are areas of great physical beauty and artistic challenge, yet few seem willing to accept the challenge. On the other hand, go to any oil-painting class in a community recreation center and you will find the students painting the Maine Coast, Havasu Falls, the Adirondacks, and Mount McKinley—all from pictures cut from magazines.

A sketch pad and a set of charcoal pencils, erasers, and blenders take up no more space than a reflector oven, and they weigh considerably less. A full load of equipment for several finished oil paintings take up no more space than a card table. These can easily be fitted into a camping situation if the artist is willing to put forth a little effort on behalf of his hobby. It also might result in some good art.

Music

It may seem strange to find music included in a book which attacks overnight picnicking, yet there is a definite place for this art form in camp. Bulky instruments are out of the question, of course, since you cannot carry them conveniently except by car and the campsites used by auto campers are far too crowded for much increase in the sound level.

Instrumental music is no stranger to the history of camping. Thoreau took his flute to Walden and found it fitted into the scene quite well. Jean Sibelius would often go camping with a violin to help him create the great melodies that reflect so beautifully the lake shores of Finland.

Recorders (the straight flutes, not the tape machines), harmonicas (if played well), and even the fretted strings go well with the camp setting. Soft music around the campfire in the evening, unobtrusive yet heightening the mood, does much to increase the enjoyment of camping.

Nature Crafts

The term "nature crafts" is a catch-all for several media which use items found only in nature as an essential part of their creation.

One of the most complex and difficult of these

is part of another craft—that of gathering wild sources of natural dyes which are used to dye yarn for hand-weaving fabrics. These dyes are still not totally replaced by the artificial ones. Most of them are completely color-fast. The possible range of colors goes from the brightest to the most muted, all around the color wheel. This is one of the best examples of a hobby which combines operations which can only be done in the wilds, and those which cannot be done there. It is also one of the most rewarding nature crafts to the hand-loom artist.

At the opposite end of the spectrum of difficulty is one which even a child can do, and will enjoy doing. This is plaster-casting animal tracks. The procedure is quite simple. After a band of paper is placed around the track to be cast (an optional step), a buttermilk-consistency mixture of plaster of paris is gently poured in and allowed to harden.

A more advanced method is to pour just enough of the mixture to get the track well coated, sprinkle on a light coating of grass (not enough to cover), and then another coating of plaster (just enough to cover the grass). This permits you to have a very thin shell of plaster and still not lose much strength. It keeps down the weight until you can get home for the next step. The finished cast is sprayed with some of the spray-on stuff used to keep food from sticking to the pan. Another collar of paper is put tightly around it, and a one-inch (25 mm) -thick layer of plaster is poured into the collar. Tap it several times to get the bubbles out and let it dry.

After separating it, spray it with a dirty-looking flat enamel to protect the plaster from atmospheric moisture and to make it look more natural. Put a label on the back giving information on the animal, where the mold was taken, etc. These not only make good paperweights, bookends, and such, they are also a valuable educational tool in track identification.

Those who dry flowers to use as wiltproof arrangements will find a wide variety of subjects in wildflowers. You might carry along some drying compound to get the colors while they are fresh. However, the weight of this stuff makes a car necessary and most places a car can go restricts or prohibits wildflower picking for conservation reasons. Planning ahead will do much to alleviate this difficulty. As a matter of good conservation practice, never pick more than ten per cent of those within range of visual identification without moving. If that ten per cent is less than one flower, don't pick any—the plant is too precariously situated in that environment.

There is one nature craft which can be developed to a high degree of sophistication. That is using twigs, seeds, leaves, and other bits of vegetation, in their natural shape, as ingredients in small sculptures. This requires the touch of a model maker, the searching ability of a botanist, and the imagination of a child. The results are often amazing. Spatterprints, gravel mosaics, and other such "art" forms are widely covered in the lower-age Scouting books.

PART VII

Emergencies

The treatment of camping emergencies falls into two categories: prevention and cure. Logically, the former is vastly superior to the latter. Some topics in this part, such as navigation, are almost exclusively prevention; others, such as first aid and survival, are primarily cure. The wise camper will not neglect either.

The beginning camper is hereby warned that reading this part may not encourage him to camp. He will imagine all the problems of major first-aid practices, living off the country, and the multitude of pests affecting him directly the first time he ever goes camping. Thus, his worst fears will parade out to haunt him: camping is obviously a danger which no sane person would dare undertake.

This, of course, is the wrong approach. Most of the first-aid procedures will never come up because the beginner will be camping in highly developed public campsites in which the situation is almost like that of a city as far as emergency facilities are concerned. Survival will be strictly of academic interest until he progresses far enough in his camping skills to move into the true wilderness. Pests will be strictly that—pests—not a menace, and can be controlled by following the simple steps outlined in that chapter.

Only the section on navigation will be of direct interest to the beginner. Unfortunately, most beginners (and some who call themselves campers but who have never left their camping machines in a fully developed campsite) don't venture onto the nature trails of even the more highly developed campgrounds. This is despite the fact that these trails are quite well marked and it would be very hard to get lost on them. The basics of navigation are useful if only to give them confidence in their ability to see what the campgrounds are there for in the first place.

For the experienced camper who likes the challenge which camping has to offer, the situation is considerably different. He will be going into the wilderness with no more assistance than his equipment and the members of his group. Other than the fact that they have left word with the Rangers, other officials in the area, or simply those at base camp (which may be home) about their itinerary and could reasonably expect help to be on its way if they do not show up within a certain time, they are strictly on their own as far as meeting any emergency needs are concerned.

For these campers, this part is of the utmost importance. Like any situation of this type, the need is never expected, yet the skills and knowledge could quite literally be a matter of life or death if it should arise.

Pertinent parts of the first-aid and the survival chapters should be written on waterproofed paper and put in the first-aid and survival kits. Paper can be waterproofed by three methods: ironing waxed paper over it, taping it with transparent tape, or placing it in a sealed plastic envelope (after the information is typed or written in waterproof ink, of course). It is also possible to have the paper laminated in plastic, but this is too expensive, thick, and heavy for my tastes.

However, this should be restricted to such matters as the head and spinal injury checklist and the manual and marker signals, both of which are fairly complex and must be exact if the emergency arises. All the rest of the information should be planted firmly in the brain and constantly reviewed and practiced so that it will be an automatic response if the need arises.

Even for the experienced camper, this part could give a false impression of danger. The wilderness is less dangerous than city streets, but both require a basic knowledge of the dangers and how to deal with them.

Camping is a safe activity. Most of the deaths and serious injuries in camp are not due to camping itself, but to some other sport, such as climbing, boating, swimming, or hunting, which are just as dangerous when not done from a camp setting. In fact, for several reasons, they may be less dangerous in camp. The participant is not tired from a long commuting from home to the area of the sport. The camper is more likely to be in better physical condition than the non-camping participant. And because he is daily dealing with open fires, edged tools, and uneven terrain, the camper is more careful than the person who has automatic gadgets to do all of these things for him.

This part on emergencies, like the subject itself, is something that probably won't come up, regardless of where you camp. It is included as the camper's best insurance policy, costing nothing but a little time to learn the skills.

CHAPTER THIRTY-ONE

Navigation

While the term "navigation" conjures up images of sextants and chronometers, it also applies to the camper's problems of how not to get lost in the wilderness, the use of maps, and direction-finding with and without a compass.

While compasses and maps are the only instruments used, a surprising number of the techniques closely parallel the navigation techniques of the ocean—especially those used in the days before electronic or even celestial navigational instruments made the job so much easier.

HINDSIGHT

This does not mean the ability to discover what you did wrong after it is too late. Hindsight is a form of observation that is an essential skill of the camper. As you move about in the wilderness, look behind you from time to time. Landmarks appear quite different from the other direction.

With the constant use of hindsight, if you should become temporarily befuddled, you can more easily recognize a landmark you recently passed. This hindsight is necessary if you are to return the way you came on an unmarked trail, unless it is the only trail in the area.

Especially note trails entering your trail. On the way back, these forks are apt to be confusing if you didn't remember which to take. In areas with many trails, a map is useful; if not a printed one,

then one you make as you go along. Then you can mark your route and not get lost at the forks.

USING THE COMPASS

The best way to keep from getting lost is to get a good compass and map and know how to use them. In the absence of the map, a compass alone is invaluable.

Alone, the compass is useful in ded reckoning. Ded (short for deduced) reckoning is quite accurate in skilled hands. This is a very reliable navigational method when used correctly, and it is not very difficult to learn. It was the chief means of ocean navigation until a century and a half ago, and most of the age of exploration had taken place long before that time.

In ded reckoning, you know where you are by knowing your direction of travel (which is where the compass comes in) and your speed (which you generally learn by experience). It is more often done in the opposite manner; you know where you are and where your objective is, and simply set a compass course between them and take out, correcting as obstacles require you to deviate from this course.

The pedometer is a great gadget for flat land, where your stride can keep fairly constant, but in rough terrain it will be of virtually no use at all. As a result, you are better off without one because you will then cultivate skill in ded reckoning, which can be used in any terrain.

Ded reckoning really doesn't even require a compass if you have a good feel for finding north (or, for that matter, just a feel for the direction in which you are presently going in relation to the general direction you have to go to get there) and you are headed toward a target sufficiently large so that you are not likely to miss it.

There is, therefore, a lot of nonsensical folklore about this feel for finding north and for other navigational talent. There is no built-in compass. The talent is developed over a period of time, even though it is usually developed unconsciously and practically always works on that level. There have been countless tests that show that a person cannot find his way in a straight line on a flat terrain with no wind on a totally overcast day or while blindfolded. Even the best backwoodsman would experience extreme difficulty navigating in unfamiliar territory since he depends to a great extent on memorized landmarks (to the extent of certain strata or biological zones if not specific trees, boulders, or such).

Most of this feel for finding north is really a subconscious celestial navigation based on the position of the sun, stars, wind, or similar more or less reliable factors which can be observed as a part of the situation without actually stopping and thinking, Well, the sun is still a bit to my right but in an hour it should be behind me because it will be solar noon and I am traveling north. The human mind is a great computer and is perfectly capable of processing that kind of information without any strain—provided it has been "programmed" for the task. The best way to program it for this often vital job is by constant practice.

This is quite an interesting sport to enjoy in your car in a city with which you are unfamiliar. Sometime when you are in no hurry, try getting there by ded reckoning. (It can be quite a thrill when all the suburban streets slowly start curving the wrong way or a stream begins to make dead ends.)

With the help of a map, the matter is much easier, although often just as challenging—much more so in the wilds than in the urban sprawl. If your compass has a means of correcting declination,

set it first. If it does not, compensate accordingly each time you take a reading. Never overlook this; you could be twenty-five or more degrees off course, even in the United States (excluding Alaska), and a full 180° in some parts of the Arctic and Antarctic.

In using the compass, hold it flat, wait for the needle to stop swinging, and slowly rotate the compass until the north of the correction dial is under the blued end of the needle. North on the reading dial is true north.

If you have no correction on your compass, line the needle up on the degree of declination (e.g., 15°W would be fifteen degrees west of north, or 345°). North on your dial will be true north.

If you don't know the declination for that area (a rather unlikely circumstance since most topographical maps show it), you can find it if you have a clear night. Make a sight from sharpened sticks and sight it on Polaris. Check this direction with your compass's magnetic-north reading. The difference is the declination for that area. Simply have your reading dial pointing north along the sticks while the correction dial is lined up with the needle.

Generally speaking, any map that doesn't show declination isn't accurate enough to worry about. You will probably be on ded reckoning anyway and aiming for something big like an intersecting road, railroad, or river to find your way out.

There are pitfalls in this process which you must watch for. There are often duplicating landmarks. You may be on the crest of a hill and on either side you can see a creek meandering down, apparently joining. Watch out; check a map; take great caution—they may also flow away from each other just out of sight in those woods on the horizon and be part of an entirely different river system by the time they empty into the ocean.

Again, you may sight a bend in the river ahead. A slowly meandering stream may have several of these ox-bows a few hundred yards (or meters) apart but a couple of miles (3 or 4 km) apart by river. Is this one the bend above your camp or below it, or the one next to it?

Or you see two hills with cliffs facing you. Which one is the cliff visible from your camp?

These are situations where a good topographical map will be well worth its small cost. Most non-topographical maps won't show hills or creeks, and the ox-bows they draw in the river only mean the cartographer thought it meandered there—most rivers do somewhere along the way. With a good map, you simply take bearings on any prominent landmark and find your position by triangulation. With a good map and compass, you will be within a hundred yards (or meters) of your precise spot. Then, knowing your exact location, the rest is easy

You can follow the creeks on the map and see where they go. You can sight the ox-bows by compass and know which is which. And you can recognize the landmarks on the other side of the mountains by looking at the contour lines, or, if they are too much alike to recognize, you can take compass bearings on them and the camp and work it from there.

With your present location known and your camp's location known, by using the map and compass together you can pick out the best route to get there—one which is not only short, but avoids difficult terrain.

Take your sighting along the line of travel indicated by your map. If the terrain won't permit a single straight line of travel for the distance, break it into several parts, checking your map and compass as you go to make sure of your exact position.

The map-making compasses have an arrow the length of the card to line up with the bearing on the compass dial. You sight along this arrow. With the lensatic compass, line up the hairline on the lens with your bearing and sight along the hairline.

The cruiser compass (the one with backward markings) is handled the opposite way to others. Orient your needle on your degree reading and the lubber line is lined up in the proper direction. The sighting mirror of the Silva Ranger map-making compass reverses the dial for this feature, while preserving the more normal compass set-up for other uses.

The only compass I ever saw that combined the map-making and lensatic compass was an old military compass that weighed half a pound (about 225 g). Silva makes a couple of models (Ranger and Prospector) which use a mirror in connection with a sight to line up the compass dial and the line of sight. These are rather expensive as compasses go, but for the serious camper are well worth the money when you are off the beaten path. They are used as either the lensatic or the map-making type, depending on the situation.

Keep the compass away from iron or steel while using it, as this throws the needle off considerably. Also keep it away from magnets at any time, since it could weaken the magnet in the needle—slightly, but enough to reduce the accuracy of a precision instrument. Protect it from sudden jars—keep the needle locked (if it has this provision) when it is not in use, and keep it in a shirt pocket and on a lanyard around your neck or pants belt-loop as added protection (you are least likely to land on your shirt pocket in case of a fall). The compass is a fairly delicate instrument. Treat it well—your life may depend on it.

MAPS AND THEIR USE

In most areas, the U.S. Geological Survey (or the Geological Survey of Canada) has made excellent topographical maps which cost 50¢ or less. These use standard markings and are usually in the same few scales.

The scale will either be stated as a ratio (SCALE 1:24,000) or as a fraction ($\frac{1}{24,000}$). In this case, one unit (whether it is an inch, centimeter, or kumquat seed) on the map equals 24,000 of the same unit in the wide open spaces. Under the scale figure are three rulers: the top one measuring miles, the second measuring feet, and the third kilometers. You measure the distance you want on the map with the ruler on your compass and transfer this distance to the scale ruler at the bottom of the map to find the actual distance.

The contour interval is also given in the lower margin. On all topographical maps, the closer the contours are together, the steeper the hill. However, you must know the contour interval to know exactly how steep in vertical distance the slope really is.

A third item to notice is the revision date. If you find an old road which isn't on a recently revised map, you are probably off the trail. On the other hand, a new road which is not on an old map is nothing to worry about—you might as well pencil it in for future reference.

It is a good practice to inquire ahead of time, from someone who knows the area and can also read a topographical map, about what changes have occurred which are not on the map. This information can be most reassuring when something pops up that you haven't been warned about by the map. Park or Forest Rangers, campground superintendents, etc., are the best sources for this information.

The only other item on this margin that you need to notice is that little angle, the declination angle. The top of the map points to true north—the North Pole, the ninetieth parallel north. The compass, however, points to magnetic north—the North Magnetic Pole, which wanders around Greenland and the Canadian islands just north of Hudson Bay. The angle shows the difference between your compass needle's north and the real direction of north, or the "approximate mean declination" given in degrees east or west and followed by the date on which that was the declination. This wandering of the magnetic pole will amount to less than a degree in the United States.

The maps of both the U.S. Geological Survey and the Geological Survey of Canada are topographical maps (as are most other nations' official maps). These show contours, bodies of water, buildings, and other landmarks. They are also to an accurate scale. Road maps you get at the corner service station are not accurate since they have no scale (and even the road mileage is only approximate).

If you are traveling by boat along the coast, the U.S. Coast and Geodedic Survey or Canadian Hydrographic Service charts are what you need. They will give you the depth of the water, the bottom material, and the location of bouys, lights, etc., as well as the channels, and points for getting supplies. They show very little detail of what is on the shore except for such prominent landmarks which are aids to navigation. If you plan many trips ashore (as most campers do), a topographic map of the same area will be most welcome.

All topographical maps use the same standardized symbols. These are usually, but not always, shown on the right margin of the map. Whether they are or not, it is best to learn them so you can read the map more rapidly. They are quite easy to learn since most of them are quite obvious.

All maps follow the same color code. Cultural (man-made) features are in black ink. Hydrographic (water) features are in blue. Vegetation is in green (a solid light-green overlay is wooded areas, dotted green is scrub brush). Hypsographic features (contour lines, bench marks, altitude figures, etc.) are in brown. (A dotted brown shaded area indicates sand dunes which, because they move and are constantly changing their shape, cannot be accurately shown in coutour lines.)

Now you know how to read a map, how do you use it? Let's say you want to get from base camp to a good fishing spot across the hill, and back again. You can see the hilltop from your camp and hike directly there on a visual reference. Checking your map, you see that the fishing hole is along

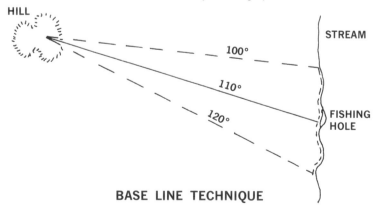

BASE LINE TECHNIQUE

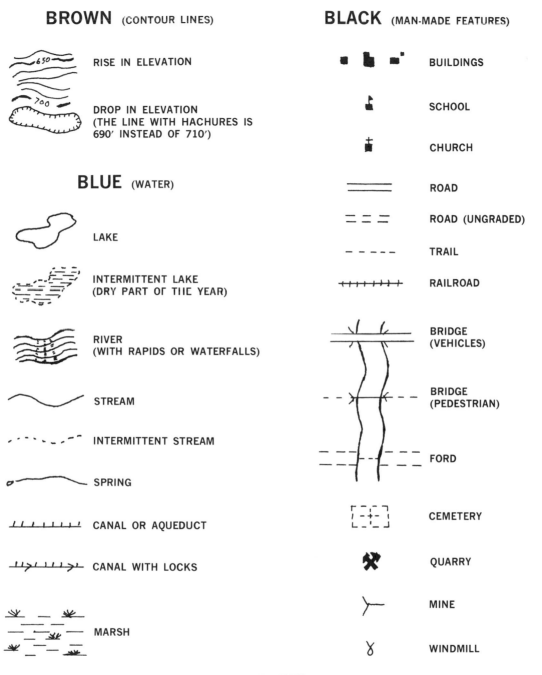

BROWN (CONTOUR LINES)

RISE IN ELEVATION

DROP IN ELEVATION
(THE LINE WITH HACHURES IS
690' INSTEAD OF 710')

BLUE (WATER)

LAKE

INTERMITTENT LAKE
(DRY PART OF THE YEAR)

RIVER
(WITH RAPIDS OR WATERFALLS)

STREAM

INTERMITTENT STREAM

SPRING

CANAL OR AQUEDUCT

CANAL WITH LOCKS

MARSH

BLACK (MAN-MADE FEATURES)

BUILDINGS

SCHOOL

CHURCH

ROAD

ROAD (UNGRADED)

TRAIL

RAILROAD

BRIDGE
(VEHICLES)

BRIDGE
(PEDESTRIAN)

FORD

CEMETERY

QUARRY

MINE

WINDMILL

MAP KEY

a compass course, or azimuth, of 110° from the peak of the hill. Since the slope of the hill is wooded, you can neither see the fishing hole nor go to it in a straight line. So you take a general course of 100° or 120° and hit the creek either upstream or downstream from that favorite spot. Then you follow the stream in the correct direction until you get to the fishing spot. This procedure is called a "base line reference"—the base line in this case being the stream. On other occasions, it may be a road, trail, fire break, power line, or lake.

Other times you may use an offset course. You know the direction and distance, and have translated the latter into paces (a form of measurement not requiring instruments). Counting the number of paces, you come to an obstacle—a hill, swamp, lake, etc. Turning at a right angle to it, you count (from zero) the number of paces it takes to get around it. Take another right-angle turn (to get back

on your original azimuth) and walk past the obstruction, counting off the paces from your original distance. Then take a right-angle turn to remove the distance of your first detour and you are back on course again.

This sounds, at first reading, very complicated. Actually it isn't. You only have two sets of figures to worry about: the length of your azimuth and how far on it you have gone, and the length of your detour and how much of it you have corrected. With a little paper work, you can often substitute other angles for those right angles and save on the distance traveled. Plot your course on your map, using only straight lines, around obstacles, to your goal.

Because of the problems in using pace measurements, the course itself should be along fairly smooth terrain (although it can slope upward or downward if it does it to a constant degree).

When moving, your compass bearing should be

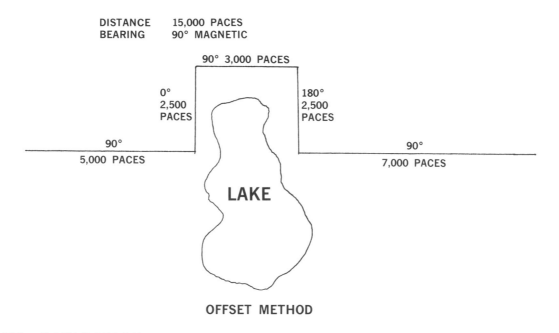

OFFSET METHOD

maintained by heading toward some landmark in the line of sight along your heading. In the absence of these landmarks (such as in a dense forest or on open prairie or desert), check your compass often to prevent circling.

Don't be afraid to mark your map with these bearings, especially the ways you travel most often. A soft-lead pencil is good for trips off the normal paths since you can later erase the marks with an art-gum eraser without damage to the map.

MAP MAKING

Often you cannot find a map with as much detail as you would like to have. If this is the case, you can make your own fairly easily.

Start with a topographical map of the area—the contour lines will be quite far apart on the map scale you use, but they will be accurate, which is more than you will be able to do without a transit and other surveyor's instruments.

Your first coverage of the area is called "traverse." Traverses come in two varieties, open and closed, depending on whether your starting and ending points are the same or different. The closed traverse checks itself to a great extent since, if your error of enclosure (the difference on the map of your start and end) is small, your map is accurate.

It is best to use roads to establish your traverse, but if roads are few, use any other fairly straight reference point, including simply a compass bearing across an open space. A clipboard, with two plastic clothespins replacing the clip (since the metal clip would affect the compass), mounted on a camera tripod is ideal for map making since you can line your map up with the land each time you turn and mark the new azimuth directly with the map-making compass.

At each turn in the traverse, mark the intersection on the map with the azimuth and distance (probably in paces). A landmark off of the traverse, such as a hill, a house, or some other feature, should be located by taking bearings from two separate points (preferably at intersections) and locating it by triangulation.

Make notes on vegetation, soil type, terrain, water, etc. The probable reason you are making

this map instead of using the ready-made ones is that you want more information that the larger-scale topos have. Give more information than you can conceive of anyone ever needing. That way you will be sure of having the information you need in the future.

After checking your traverse by going over the route a second time, gathering still more notes and checking all data gathered the first time, redraw the map in the finished form. Leave the error of closure on the finished map; don't try to bend lines so that it disappears, you will only be making the map intentionally inaccurate, and probably more so than with the small, but highly conspicuous, inaccuracy of the error of closure. The error of closure should, however, be kept down to the point of being less than a hundred feet per square mile (15 m per km^2). If it isn't that accurate, do it over.

Make sure you draw the map accurately. Add up all the angles in your traverse which turn in the same direction, subtract the total of all the angles which turn in the other direction. The answer should be 360° for no error of closure.

CELESTIAL NAVIGATION WITHOUT INSTRUMENTS

A compass and ded reckoning is the preferred method of navigation without a map, but when you have no compass the problem is increased considerably. However, it is still possible to find north. The only real problem is that, if you want to get within twenty degrees of an accurate direction, you will need clear skies, dawn, sunset, night, and/or several hours' time (during which you can be doing other things, fortunately).

The "moss on the north side of trees" method is often inaccurate. Moss grows on the coolest side and this is not necessarily north. Also, some types of lichens look like moss and prefer the sunny side. The sun and moon only rise in the east and set in the west twice a year, during the equinox. All other times they are a bit north or south of due east and due west. Still, they indicate the general direction—except in polar areas.

It takes a while to see it, but star motion is a rough indication of direction. Line up a fairly bright star near the horizon with the tops of a couple of stakes or other fixed objects. After about an hour, check on its movement from the stakes. Stars seem to rise in the east, set in the west, move right in the south, and left in the north. This is in a rather arcing movement and only of general accuracy, but it is helpful when some of the more accurate stars are obscured by clouds, trees, or some other opaque objects.

Polaris

The region around the North Celestial Pole is a maze of stars which are neither bright nor dim. There are a few first-magnitude stars in Ursa Major (the Big Dipper) and one of them, with an adjacent third-magnitude star, is useful in finding Polaris, the polestar. These two are at the end of the bowl of the dipper (or the middle of the back of the bear, depending on whether you can see the whole constellation or not). Polaris is at the tip of the handle of the Little Dipper and varies between first and second magnitude.

The center star of Cassiopeia's M or W points in the general direction of Polaris.

(In the case you are ever really lost, you can find your latitude by measuring the altitude of Polaris in degrees with a plumb line and protractor.)

Because of a wobble in the earth's movements, the North Star changes on a 25,800-year cycle. It is now about ten minutes (one-sixth of a degree) off and is getting worse. The next North Star will be Gamma Cephei in 4000.

Southern Cross

In the Southern Hemisphere, there are no bright stars right over the pole, so finding south by the stars requires the cooperation of two constellations, and even then it is a bit inaccurate. Fortunately, all the stars you need to work with in this situation are of first magnitude or brighter.

Sight down the line between the brightest two stars in the Southern Cross (in the upright of the cross), and intersect it with a perpendicular line from the two brighter-than-first-magnitude stars in nearby Centaur, Agena, and Alpha Centuri. (The latter, incidentally, is the closest star to the sun.) Somewhere in the general area of the intersection of these two imaginary lines is due south.

The Southern Cross is fairly small as constellations go, but it is easily recognized as it appears on the flags of Australia, New Zealand, and Western Samoa.

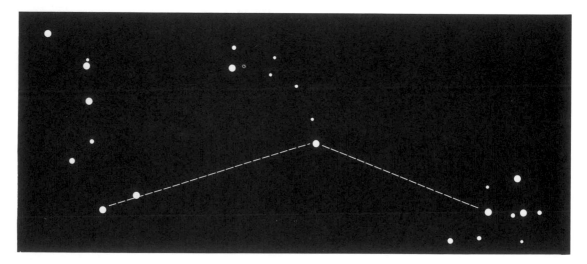

POLARIS

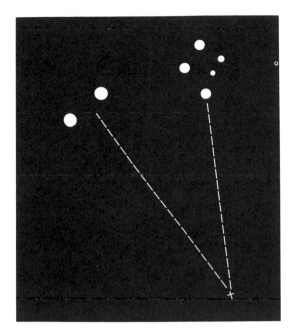

SOUTHERN CROSS

Orion

At any latitude, Orion's knife is on the south side of his belt, and the belt lines up nearly vertically in the east or west when rising or setting. Mintaka, the belt star on Orion's left as he faces you (and the first of the three to rise or set), is only twenty minutes south of the celestial equator—the nearest star to it—which makes it practically due east or west on rising or setting and far more accurate than a compass with only a slightly inaccurate declination setting.

Orion is probably the easiest constellation to find. It is large, has two brighter-than-first-magnitude stars and two first-magnitude stars (the arms and legs) with three second-magnitude stars in a straight line (the belt). In the Northern Hemisphere summer, it is seen in the morning; in winter it is seen in the evening.

STICK AND SHADOW METHODS

With the exception of the watch compass, the stick and shadow methods take too long to be of best use. However, with clear days and cloudy nights, it may be the best method. All references to noon mean mean solar noon, so turn the watch back one hour to get off Daylight Saving Time during the summer (or whenever DST is being tried).

Short-Shadow Method

This method takes at least two hours on both sides of noon if you have no watch and must guess at the time. If you have a watch, it will take about half an hour or so, starting about that long before noon.

Place a pole in level ground. Mark the end of the shadow with stakes (twigs will do) as it moves along. The point where the shadow of the pole was the shortest is solar noon. (The reason you had to start a half-hour before noon was to provide for watch error and the difference between standard time and solar time.)

The line from the short-point stake and the pole is north and south—the pole at the south and the stake at the north in the Northern Hemisphere,

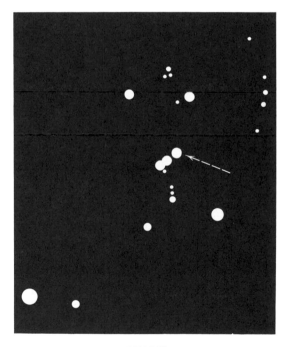

ORION

SHORT-SHADOW METHOD

reverse for the Southern. The method is completely ineffective in the tropics because the shadow will be too short to be accurate and the effective "hemisphere" will change during the year.

Arc Method

The arc method has much the same problems of geography and time as the short-shadow method. However, it is a good method to use when you will be away from your camp during the day, trying perhaps to catch some fish or find some edible plants in a survival situation. It takes a few minutes in the morning and a waiting time in the evening.

Set up the pole as with the short-shadow method and put a stake at the end of the pole's shadow. With a length of rope, draw an arc around the pole, the distance from the pole to the first stake.

When the pole's shadow again touches this arc, plant another stake. Now connect the two stakes with a line. Find the mid-point on this line. (You can do this by the method you used in high school geometry for besecting a line, but it is usually easier to measure the line with a length of rope. Hold both ends, letting the middle fall in a bight. Take the bottom-most point with your other hand, and use that distance to find mid-point on the line.) Mid-point connects with the pole as does the "shortest point" stake of the short-shadow method.

One That Doesn't Work

There has been considerable publicity lately about a system which uses a line of stakes laid out much like the short-shadow method. It is claimed that you only need to set out a couple of stakes and take the line from that as an east-west line. It is further claimed that this is quicker since it can

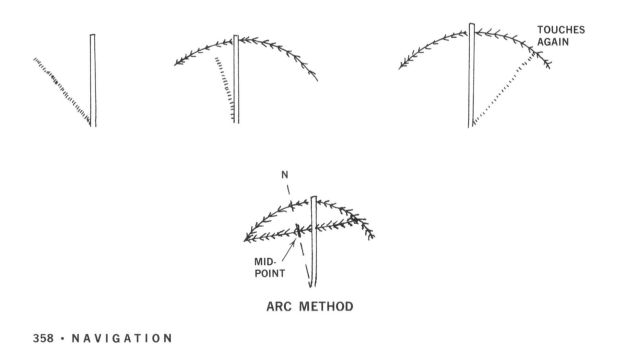

ARC METHOD

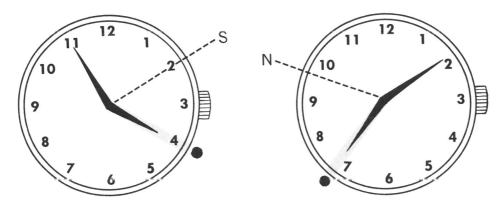

WATCH METHOD

be done in the morning or evening instead of both times or at noon.

Unfortunately, it doesn't work, as you can easily prove by continuing to lay out stakes at the tip of the pole's shadow throughout the day. You will find that they do not form a straight line at all, but a parabola. What's more, they are farthest off in the early morning and evening, especially near the solstices when the sun rises and sets farthest from the cardinal points.

WATCH COMPASS

An old woodsman's trick for finding north uses only a wrist watch and a short length of match-size stick. It will be accurate within eight degrees if the watch is correct. If you are on Daylight Saving Time, move it back an hour to sun time. (The mnemonic for moving a watch for Daylight Saving Time is: spring forward, fall back.)

Hold the watch level, with the stick over the center of the watch. Turn the watch so that the shadow of the stick lies along the hour hand. South, not north, will be directly between the hour hand (and the shadow) and twelve on the watch, within the acute angle formed by the two, between 6:00 A.M. and 6:00 P.M. North will be within the acute angle between 6:00 P.M. and 6:00 A.M. (The mnemonic for this is: N for north and night, S for south and sun.)

If you have a compass, you can also use this trick in reverse to set your watch.

CHAPTER THIRTY-TWO

First Aid

Probably no camping trip lasts over a week without someone requiring some form of first aid. Usually it is of a very minor sort, a slight cut or burn or splinter, but because of the isolation, any injury is potentially dangerous.

For the car camper in a state or national park, a Red Cross first-aid handbook is all that is needed other than an assortment of bandages and a snake-bite kit. You can always climb in the car and get the victim to a doctor in the nearest town. For this kind of camper, the Red Cross book is completely adequate and this chapter is not for you.

But for the wilderness camper, another technique is needed. The first aid required in the wilderness, far from any medical help, is quite different from the first aid taught by the Red Cross, which is strictly temporary and assumes that a doctor will be with the victim within a couple of hours at the most. In a wilderness camping situation, a doctor is rarely handy. Sometimes he is several days away. Also, in camping there is often the need to move the victim. Unless the injury is critical, he will have to get out, at least in part, on his own power. Therefore, the first-aid supplies and the techniques must be prepared with this in mind.

In Red Cross first aid, the purpose is to keep the victim from dying from shock or loss of blood, and to make him as comfortable as possible until the doctor comes. In remote areas, the primary purpose of first aid is to get the victim back in operation; fractures must be set (or at least im-mobilized), bleeding stopped, burns soothed, and wounds cleaned up as best as possible. After return-ing to civilization, fractures can be rebroken and reset, skin grafts performed to cover burns, and antibiotics given to counter any lingering infection. If the earlier makeshift techniques are not used in the wilds, the chances of returning to civilization for the expert medical treatment may not even be possible.

In the wilderness any injury is serious. Even a simple cut should be watched for signs of infection. Head for a doctor any time any of the following occurs:

a fever lasting more than one day

recurring fainting, especially after a fall or a head injury

vomiting for more than a few hours

diarrhea if accompanied by severe abdominal pain, fever, evidence of internal bleeding, or if it continues for more than one day

an eye irritation that does not quickly subside after irrigation with cool drinking water (it must be pure water to avoid the chance of an infection if the eyeball is scratched)

a fracture or dislocation

a sprain that is especially painful or shows bleed-ing under the skin

poison-ivy irritation over large areas of the body

a bite by a poisonous snake

a bite by a wild animal

any cut severe enough to require suturing

an earache, other than from a loud noise or a blow, lasting over a few hours, or over one day if caused by a noise or a blow

burns, even first-degree, over large areas of the body, and any third-degree burns other than highly localized ones (larger than a tack-head)

All of these are signs of severe danger and the victim must be moved out (applying proper safeguards, such as immobilizing fractures, etc.) as quickly and as gently as possible.

In case of very severe injury, such as spinal or skull fracture, a gunshot wound in a body cavity, severe loss of blood, or extensive burns, when in remote areas (over three days from medical help) send for help by use of marker panels, signal mirror, and/or smoke columns. This should not be done except in an absolute emergency or you may find yourself with a very expensive bill from the rescuing agency.

The items of first aid least likely to be needed in camping are the ones which are most complicated and will therefore take up the most space in this chapter. The simple and common needs can be disposed of in a short time. A slight cut? Clean and bandage. A slight burn? Cool and protect the skin. But a spinal fracture or a gunshot wound, unheard of by the average camper and practically never encountered by the mountain climber or hunter, takes a lengthy description. Don't let the space taken up by these rare misfortunes discourage you from camping, even in the more remote areas. Camping is one of the safest of sports. Minor cuts and burns are due to the fact that the average person seldom uses a knife or an open fire any more, rather than from any inherent danger in camping itself. Actually, mountain climbing is not often done away from medical help and there is greater danger of being shot by a poor hunter on a friend's farm than in the remote areas of a national forest.

FIRST-AID KIT

Your camping outfit should include a small but well-equipped first-aid kit. Since the type of first aid required in remote areas is quite different from the first aid practiced in a city, the kit must be equipped accordingly. My own kit is based on an article by Dr. E. Russel Kodet, M.D., which appeared in the October 1962 issue of *Outdoor Life*. To his recommended list, I have added a few items I have found useful and made one change, on his advice, in the medications listed. However, the kit is my own, based on Dr. Kodet's article, the Red Cross handbook, the *Army Field Manual*, and other first-aid literature, as well as my own experience in camping.

Your first-aid kit should be in a metal or plastic box or a leather or cloth bag and it should include the following items:

Teflon gauze pads in sterile packages

prepared bandages with Teflon gauze pads, in all sizes

half-inch adhesive tape

Kling roller bandage

triangle bandage

sutures (sizes 000 and 5-0) in sterile packages with needle attached (one of each or two of the 000)

butterflies (large and small sizes)

snake-bite kit

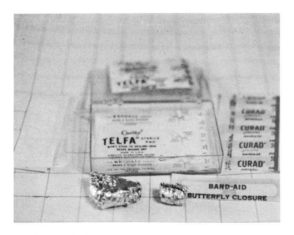

Hiking first-aid kit.

Camp first-aid kit, packed . . .

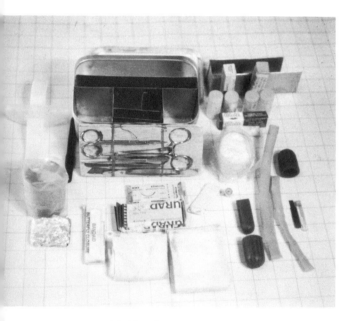

. . . and laid out.

scalpel blades (one round, one pointed), handle optional
needle-nose forceps
scissors
mosquito-clamp hemostat
aspirin tablets (or stronger substitute)
Metycaine ointment
neomycin-and-gramicidin ointment
Tridol (5 mg tablets)
Lomotil (2.5 mg tablets)
antibiotics (penicillin, or broad-spectrum drugs)
Blistex
pHisoDerm (or equivalent)
thermometer (in protective case)
roll of elastic bandage (optional)
resuscitation tube (optional)
special medicines for hay fever, motion sickness, etc. (optional)

All of these together will weigh under a pound (1 kg) (container included). Mine fits in an aluminum box 3 x 4 x 6½ (75 x 100 x 150 mm).

Enough to take care of minor cuts can be packed in a 35 mm film can or 2 x 3 x ½ inch (50 x 75 x 10 mm) plastic box for hikers.

The Teflon gauze pads and prepared bandages (available under a variety of trade names) may be used instead of the usual gauze to prevent a bandage from sticking to a wound. The adhesive tape should be split since a quarter-inch (5 mm) -wide piece will often do the job as well. Also, to save space, wrap the tape around a section of matchstick or toothpick rather than the spool it comes on.

The Kling bandage will stick to itself (by interlocking fibers) but has no adhesive to stick to anything else. Use it for binding the Teflon bandage to the wound when tape is unadvisable. The triangle bandage is for a sling or for use as a head bandage. Make it out of rip-stop nylon (parachute cloth) so it will not take up much space in the kit.

Butterflies may be bought or made. They are made by taking a three-inch (75 mm) length of half-inch (10 mm) adhesive tape or a two-inch (50 mm) length of quarter-inch (5 mm) tape. At the corners of the center one-third of the length, make an angled cut (about a 45° angle) toward the center, about one-third the width. Fold the center

BUTTERFLIES

section inward on the sticky side. This gives you a butterfly-shaped piece with the adhesive covered in the center. Protect the exposed adhesive with plastic (like the prepared bandages) until you need it. In case of a bad cut, it will often function as a suture to close the cut.

I agree with Dr. Kodet that the inclusion of sutures in a camping first-aid kit seems a bit in the do-it-yourself doctoring category. Yet I also agree that when you are in an isolated area, you may have to suture a severe cut to keep it from starting to bleed again or to avoid a disfiguring scar. The little needle and monofilament nylon or braided-silk suture packets are both sterile and compact. Normally, however, the butterfly will do the job. Certainly they should be given a try, even when the cut looks bad. The butterflies are an amazing device—easy to use and they usually work. Whether you can use the butterflies or have to suture, the bleeding should be stopped first.

The snake-bite kit should include the following items:

a constriction band
a scalpel blade
antiseptic (for the scalpel and the bitten area, not for the wound after cutting)
suction cups for both flat and curved surfaces

The Cutter snake-bite kit is the best because of its compactness. However, it does require a slight modification to be even better. The kit comes with a cloth webbing tape for the constriction band. This is hard to tie properly—especially with one hand when you have been bitten on the other. The best constriction band is one and a half feet (50 cm) of surgical rubber tubing (the same kind as is used for dilating a vein to take blood for a lab test or transfusion). It is easier to get the proper tension with rubber tube than with the web band. If necessary, you can tie it with one hand and your teeth. (You will have a struggle cramming it into the Cutter kit, but it will almost pop out by itself when

you open the kit. The best way to get it in is to spiral it tightly inside the small suction cup—around the scalpel and antiseptic—on out and into the larger one that fits over it. When so modified, it lacks an eighth of an inch or so [3 or 4 mm] of closing completely—but it is enough to hold it together, even when loose in your pocket.)

In snake country, each individual in the group should carry a snake-bite kit if he will be going more than two minutes' distance from the base camp's first-aid kit.

Memorize the instruction sheet that comes with the kit and discard it. The room it takes can better be filled with a rubber constriction band.

As for the "hardware" in the first-aid kit, the scalpel will remove the dead flap of skin from an angled cut better than scissors. For broad areas, the rounded blade is better; for confined areas, use the pointed one. By clamping a scalpel blade in the hemostat, you can get the benefits of a regular scalpel without the half-ounce (15 g) weight of the scalpel handle.

The scissors are used to cut bandages, tape, or even broken fingernails. A hemostat is a clamp built like a pair of scissors, with a locking mechanism to hold it closed. You will need it to tie any sutures since you can't push the needle accurately with just your hand. Both the forceps and the hemostat are useful for pulling splinters although the forceps are far better. The hemostat makes a good small vise for repairing equipment.

Sterilize all instruments by boiling before using them.

The Metycaine is an anesthetic and the neomycin-and-gramicidin ointment is an antibiotic to be used in case of eye injury. The eye must be kept covered after medication since it loses its blinking reflex. In such a case, start for a doctor immediately. Vision is nothing to play doctor on.

The Tridol tablets are for nausea or cramps that persist undiminished. Lomotil is for diarrhea. The antibiotics are for very high fever (other than from sunstroke).

Blistex is for fever blisters or the badly chapped lips so common in high, cold, or windswept camp-sites.

With the exception of the aspirin tablets and the

Blistex, all the drugs will require a doctor's prescription, so see your doctor. An explanation of what you want them for should be enough. He may recommend some newer drugs—the development is so rapid, these may well be obsolete.

With the exception of the antibiotics, all the drugs listed are stable and will last indefinitely. The antibiotics will last a couple of years, and after that time they should be renewed.

The resuscitation tube should be carried if you will be doing any swimming or boating, and the elastic bandage should be carried if you will be hiking on rough terrain or doing any climbing.

GENERAL RULES

The first rule in first aid is to keep calm. A relaxed but quick manner is far better than a tense, hurrying-off-in-all-directions approach which not only is inefficient but does little to calm the victim. This is most critical when you are both the victim and the medic. Some degree of shock is present in any injury and this must be fought with calmness if you have to do the treating on yourself.

The priorities in first-aid treatment are: (1) stop any serious bleeding, (2) restore breathing, and (3) counteract any poisons. Since poisoning is rather unlikely in camping, that is usually one less worry you will have. In any injury, treat for shock.

Shock is far easier to prevent than to treat, so fast work is of utmost importance. Keep the victim warm. This means to conserve his body heat by proper insulation; it does not mean to add external heat, such as building a fire or applying a hot-water bottle. Lower his head to bring more blood to the brain. The only exceptions to this are in the case of a head or chest injury, when the increase of blood pressure in the head may cause bleeding or the pressure on the lungs may make breathing difficult, and in the case of spinal fracture, when the victim should not be moved except under very strictly controlled conditions. It does no good to give stimulants since they have no effect on shock as formerly believed. Never give a drink to an unconscious or semi-conscious accident victim as he can't swallow and may choke on it. *Under no circumstances, give alcohol: it is a depressant and would only increase the depth of shock—possibly to the point of death.*

Always check for fractures before moving the victim. Make sure you have found all points of bleeding. This is especially necessary in cases of shotgun accidents or tumbling falls.

In all cases, keep the victim calm and assured that he will get over it. Ideally, don't let him watch you treat him if he is bleeding or suffering from a burn. But don't force the issue.

OPEN WOUNDS

Since the terms vary in first-aid books in the classification of wounds, I will define my terms now to save confusion. "Cuts" refer to all types of lacerations and incisions—both the clean cuts made by sharp-edged objects and the ragged cuts made by rocks, thorns, etc. "Punctures" include any open wounds that are deeper than they are long. "Abrasions" are the scraping injuries that take off the skin but do little or no damage to the tissue under the skin and have only a slight bleeding or flow of lymph.

Cuts

While cuts are the most common type of injury, they are usually the easiest to treat. The wound should be cleaned of any foreign matter by washing it with antiseptic liquid soap, such as pHiso-Derm, and water, and, if deep, it should be bandaged. If there is any severe bleeding it should be stopped before treating. The procedure will be discussed under Severe Bleeding, the section following this one.

In the case of a deep cut, close the cut with a butterfly tape or two to speed the healing. This will prevent the cut from working open and starting to bleed again. The butterfly is almost always adequate.

However, in the rare case that is too severe for the butterfly, suturing is necessary. The 000 size is the most common and, while the finer 5-0 is preferable on the face to reduce the scar, the 000 is adequate for all camping needs since any suturing job is reason enough to head for a doctor who can patch up the needlework to more professional standards.

A mosquito-clamp hemostat is practically required for suturing, and a pair of forceps not only saves thread but makes tying easier as well. While the idea of suturing without anesthetic sounds horrible, the pain of a surface cut severe enough to require suturing in camp has already anesthetized the area so that the needle is more irritation than pain.

Clamp the needle in the hemostat. Hold the hemostat like scissors with your thumb and middle finger and support it on the side with your index finger, close to the needle.

Swing the needle in an arc corresponding to the curve of the needle, into the skin, but not into the tissue under the skin, and out the other side of the cut. (A whole roasting chicken is excellent for practice. You can stuff the fowl before practicing and

pop it into the oven when you finish.) There should be an equal distance from the cut to the needle holes on each side.

The suture is tied in a surgeon's knot with the help of the forceps. In this technique, you never need to touch the needle or suture. Grasp the loose end (about one inch [35 mm] long) of the stitch with the hemostat and wrap the suture loosely two full turns around the shank with the forceps. Pull the hemostat out with the loose end still clamped in it. This forms the two ends into a double overhand knot. Snug this knot against the skin at one side of the stitch, being careful not to distort the skin, but completely closing the cut. This is important in determining the size of the resulting scar.

Keeping the hemostat clamped around the loose end, tie an overhand knot by wrapping the suture one full turn around the hemostat, and pull through as before. Slide this down on the first knot to secure.

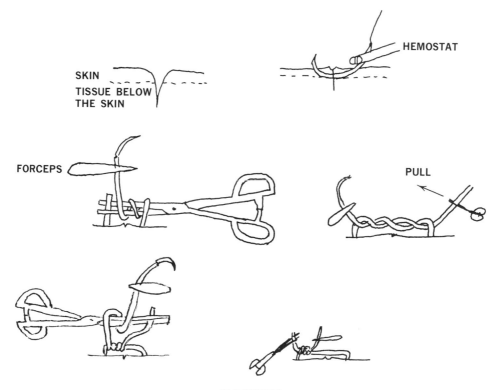

SKIN
TISSUE BELOW THE SKIN

HEMOSTAT

FORCEPS

PULL

SUTURING

Cut both ends with scissors or scalpel about a quarter-inch (5 mm) from the knot. Make the next stitch, if needed. When finished, bandage loosely. If it is on a large joint (knee, elbow, etc.), bandage with an elastic bandage under slight tension. Make sure that all implements and bandages are sterile before working by boiling the instruments five minutes and keeping the bandages in their sterile packages until they are ready to apply; and make sure that they continue that way throughout the operation.

Normally the sutures will be removed by a doctor. If you still haven't gotten to one, you will have to do this simple job yourself. It should be done about ten days after the suturing. When removing the stitches, lift one up and cut the vertical part at the hole under the knot. Pull the knot to remove the suture. It hurts some, but not as much as you might think.

REMOVING

Do not suture near the eye—you might distort the eyelid. Because of the protection of the skull, cuts are seldom very deep there anyway. A butterfly or two should handle them easily.

Punctures

In camp, punctures usually come from two sources: splinters and fish hooks. Splinters can be removed with a needle or forceps. If they come out cleanly, they require little attention. If they don't, the flesh is usually torn up enough to be treated as a cut.

Because of their barbs, fish hooks present more of a problem. If the barb is not embedded, treatment is not too difficult: remove it (if it is not already out) and clean it up with soap and water.

If the barb is embedded, push the hook around until the barb is pushed out of the flesh. It hurts a lot less if you do this in one quick, smooth

motion; a slow, deliberate push is unnecessarily painful. Cut off the barb with wire cutters and remove the rest of the hook by pulling it back out the way it entered. (You should carry compound-action pliers with wire cutters in your repair box. They are useful for many camp jobs, and essential for this one.) Allow the wound to bleed as much as possible. Such a puncture is quite contaminated by the hook and bleeding helps clean it. The bleeding will stop soon. Suction of the wound with a snake-bite kit's suction cup may help if it refuses to bleed. Finally, clean with soap and water, and bandage.

FISH HOOK REMOVAL

Abrasions

Abrasions are easy to treat but hard to heal. Wash the area until it is clean, using forceps, if necessary, to remove embedded pieces of dirt (but use a delicate touch), and leave the wound open to the air. Bandages (except for the Teflon ones) stick to the wound and prevent the formation of a scab. This retards the growth of new skin. While the Teflon bandages don't stick to the wound, they do keep the air from circulating around the area as freely and thus they retard scab formation too.

If the gnats are heavy, put a little bug repellent around the wound (on the uninjured part). To prevent clothes from irritating the wound, make a wire guard (see next page) and tape it to the sound skin around the wound.

SEVERE BLEEDING

In any bleeding injury, the priorities are: (1) stop

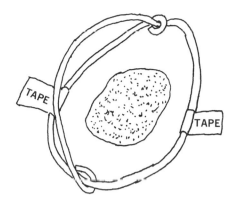

ABRASION GUARD

the bleeding, (2) protect the wound, and (3) treat for shock. The best way to stop bleeding is by local pressure. Take a gauze pad and press it against the wound. This closes the capillaries in the immediate area (which are supplying the blood to the wound) and holds the blood in the wound until it can clot. It will take from five to ten minutes to control bleeding enough to release the pressure. Elevation of the injured part helps as it reduces the blood pressure at the spot. However, do not elevate if a fracture is involved until the bone has been splinted.

Sometimes the bleeding cannot be readily stopped by local pressure. This is fairly common when a major vein or artery has been cut, or in the case of a fracture. However, even in these rather rare cases, the bleeding can usually be stopped at the pressure points. These are located in various parts of the body where large arteries come to the surface. Here you can feel the pulse. Pressure on these points will stop the flow of blood on the side of the point opposite the heart. To reduce discomfort to the patient, use a pad of cloth over the pressure point. The heel of the hand is best below the heart, but fingers must be used on the points above the heart.

Pressure Point	Where to Press	Bleeding Controlled
temple	against the skull	upper head on that side
neck, between the neck muscles and the windpipe	into the neck muscles	entire head on that side
under the jawbone, halfway between the chin and the ear	into the jawbone	lower face on that side
above the collarbone, between it and the shoulder muscles	into the shoulder muscles	shoulder and entire arm
inside the arm, near the armpit where the armbone can be felt	against the upper armbone	lower two-thirds of arm
inside the wrist, on the thumb side of the tendons	against the wristbones	hand
pit of the leg, at the groin	into the leg muscles	entire leg
behind the knee, between the tendons	into the joint	lower leg

When the pressure-point method fails, a tourniquet is required. This is very dangerous to use and all attempts to stop bleeding by other methods should be made first. In fact, some authorities insist that any bleeding can be stopped by pressure points and direct pressure alone.

The tourniquet is, of course, useful only on the arms and legs. It should be applied close to the wound, but there should be unbroken skin between it and the wound. If there is a joint in the way, place the tourniquet above the joint. Be sure it is tight enough to stop the bleeding. If not, it will simply stop venous flow and, by increasing the local blood pressure, make bleeding more intense. (This is done intentionally in snake-bite treatment where bleeding is the object, but in no other case.) Use a material between one and a half and two inches (4 or 5 cm) in width for the tourniquet to prevent damage to deep tissues from the intense contraction by a narrower material.

Slowly release the tourniquet after fifteen minutes. If it looks as if the bleeding will start again (the clot becomes shiny, starts swelling, etc.), retighten the tourniquet slowly until the clot appears secure again. (The wound should be cleaned of blood right after the bleeding is stopped so that the clot will be as small as possible and therefore stronger.) It is often possible to have the tourniquet only partially tight and still control the bleeding, after the bleeding has been stopped. This should be done whenever possible since the limb needs all the blood it can get in order to fight infection.

Don't allow free bleeding, even for a short time. There is much more danger from bleeding to death than from gangrene. Antibiotics will usually prevent the loss of a limb from gangrene, but nothing will prevent bleeding to death except stopping the bleeding.

Regardless of the method used, the bleeding stops easier if the bleeding area is elevated above the heart to reduce the blood pressure at that point.

Small wounds can be bandaged with a prepared bandage after the bleeding is controlled. They have a mild butterfly effect and are quite good for the purpose. However, even on a minor injury, preserve the sterility of the bandage. After opening the package, bend the top back so you can pull loose the plastic backing without touching the gauze. Holding each piece of backing, place the gauze pad firmly on the wound and pull away the plastic while sticking the adhesive tape to the skin. After the plastic is removed, smooth down the tape.

Gauze flats should be handled only by the smallest portion of the corners. Apply them snugly to the wound and tape or bind with roller bandage. In all cases, clean up the area with soap and water as soon as the bleeding has stopped and before bandaging.

Again, shock is present in all injuries, no matter how slight. In a cut finger, it more often appears as anger at oneself for being so stupid. In a serious injury, it is often unconsciousness. Usually, however, it is a faint feeling, a slight but controlled panic, and a "sick all over" feeling. It is a normal reaction and no cause for alarm if handled properly. Always treat for shock.

BLISTERS

Blisters are a common problem to the hiker who has not properly conditioned his feet and/or does not have the proper-size hiking shoes. Obviously, prevention is the best treatment—hiking shoes that fit with two pair of soft and fairly heavy socks on, and feet that are accustomed to hiking.

If you should get a blister, immobilize it with a piece of adhesive tape while it is still small. The fluid will then be absorbed back into the tissues and the skin will not have to be broken, exposing the tissue to bacterial invasion.

A large blister should be opened. You can't just jab a pin in it, but it is not hard to do. First, wash the area thoroughly, with soap and water as an antiseptic. Take a sterile needle (the finer the better) and push it into the tissue just to one side of the blister, preferably on the lower edge, and then up into the blister from the sound tissue under the bubble. Let the lymph drain naturally or apply very gentle pressure to help it come out. Do not drain it flat, just relieve the pressure. Immobilize the skin with a piece of adhesive tape, preferably running in the direction of the rub that caused the blister.

Do not attempt to drain blisters caused by burns.

BURNS

After cuts, burns are the most common form of camp injury. This is partly because of many camper's unfamiliarity with open fires, and partly because of sunburn.

Burns are classified into three degrees. First degree is the "boiled lobster" look of bright-red. Second degree is covered with "water" (actually lymph) blisters. These blisters range in size from a pin head to a quarter. Third degree is charred black, with considerable tissue damage.

The main problem with burns is that of infection. If they are extensive, there is a secondary problem of dehydration. The problem of shock is more severe in the case of burns than in any other type of injury, for the amount of damage.

Do not pull clothes over a burn. Cut them loose and lift them off. Do not try to pull off a piece of cloth which has stuck to a burn, but trim around it to remove all the loose material possible. Do not try to clean a burn or break blisters. Use no medications on extensive or second- or third-degree burns. Cover lightly with sterile gauze. Teflon is excellent.

If minor in degree and area, a burn may be left exposed. Cooling with water or ice is helpful in case of minor burns which have not broken the skin. Thirty minutes of cooling immediately after the burn will usually prevent blistering and promote healing. Burn ointments give some relief in minor, first-degree burns, but they are a danger when used on extensive first-degree or any more serious burns.

Other than shock (which is severe), the danger with third-degree burns, and to some extent with second-degree ones, is the drying out of the tissues. They can be kept at their proper water and salt levels with normal saline solution, which is .9 per cent salt solution. A teaspoon of salt to a pint ($\frac{1}{2}$ liter) of water is a fair roughing. Lacking measuring devices, you can estimate it fairly well by taste. You should be able to tell that something has been added to the water, but not quite be able to identify it as salt. The victim should drink small amounts of the solution to prevent dehydration. Make sure it is cool or even cold, to prevent vomiting. If the victim shows any tendency toward vomiting, substitute plain drinking water.

Sunburn is treated as any other burn.

A rope burn is really an abrasion and should be treated as such.

HEAT

Too much heat can produce one of two conditions—heat exhaustion or sunstroke. Both the symptoms and the treatment are different. Heat exhaustion is a form of shock caused by the loss of body moisture and salt, and is treated the same way as shock. The symptoms are:

color: pale
pulse: weak and rapid
skin: moist and clammy
temperature: low

Lower the victim's head and keep him warm. If he is conscious, give salt tablets and water or cold normal saline solution. The heat-exhaustion victim is very rarely unconscious.

Sunstroke is the opposite. The heat from the sun has actually raised the blood temperature to a dangerous degree. These are the symptoms:

color: red
pulse: strong
skin: dry with no perspiration at all
temperature: very high

The victim is often unconscious. Raise his head and do everything possible to cool him off. Call a doctor. The sunstroke starts with a headache and a strong, throbbing pulse, so prevention is usually possible. *But sunstroke is often fatal.*

Accurate diagnosis and prompt treatment are required. Memorize the symptoms and the treatment for each. This is really not too difficult; just remember that the treatment should do the opposite of the symptoms.

The best preventative for both heat exhaustion and sunstroke is to drink plenty of water, increase your salt intake, and wear cool clothing. Don't stay in direct sunlight more than necessary. Rest frequently in the shade. Don't overexert.

COLD

Cold can produce three problems, but, unlike heat, they are not opposites.

Frostbite

Frostbite is not as common as sunburn but it is more dangerous. Treatment has changed in the last few years as the result of more study. Many of the old methods, such as rubbing with snow, have been found to be quite dangerous.

Frostbite usually strikes the parts of the body which have a greater surface area to give off heat—feet, hands, ears, and face. The feet, hands, and ears can usually be protected, if you don't get them wet, but a full face mask usually gets in the way too much to justify its slight protection. The pull-over ski caps which cover the face except for the eyes and nose are of some help, especially if there is not a high wind blowing through them, but my glasses won't fit under them because they pull it away from my face, nor over them because my ears are inside.

Extremely cold weather is no time to be camping alone. Be with at least one other camper and watch each other. Frostbite first shows up as a white spot, usually on the ear, nose, or cheek. If this happens, cover the area immediately to thaw it out. Keep your head warm at all times in cold weather, because of the large radiation area (especially the ears) and the lack of an internal heat-regulation ability in the head such as the rest of the body has.

You are in severest danger of frostbite when you fall through ice into the water below. When the temperature is quite low, this can be serious. The obvious first rule is to get out of the water as fast as possible. Next, dry off quickly. If only your foot has gone through, this is fairly easy—poke it in the nearest snowbank. A dry snow (the most common at temperatures low enough to make this accident dangerous) is an excellent blotter.

If you should have to cross stretches of ice, a sheath knife or, even better, ice awls should be carried—in the hand if the danger is severe. If you should go through, the point of the knife or those of the awls, driven into the ice as far out as you can reach, will greatly aid your getting out. Flutter-kick your feet to the surface and, pulling on the awls, if you have them, roll onto the ice.

If there is any danger of the ice breaking again if you stand on it, pull yourself to the nearest snowbank and roll in it to blot off most of the surface moisture.

The snowbank will do the job almost completely if you have been able to get out quickly enough so that you are not soaked through and have water-resistant clothing on to retard the water's movement through the clothes. The remaining water will probably quickly freeze, giving you a good windbreak, a costume about as flexible as poorly made plate armor, and a serious insulation problem if you don't do something fast.

The best thing, if you can, is to change out of the wet clothes as quickly as possible. If you don't have a change, or if it got wet too, start to work on a fire at once, before your hands get stiff. Here, waterproof matches in a waterproof match safe are crucial. Build a windbreak as soon as the fire gets started to get the maximum effect of the fire. Don't get too close or you may damage your clothes before the ice underneath is melted enough for you to feel the heat. This is a long process, so if the windbreak and fire combination are doing the job, get out of your clothes while they are thawing.

If frostbite really sets in, the treatment is harder. Handle the frostbitten areas carefully. The greatest danger in frostbite is gangrene. This is bacteria and it can't get in the body except through a break in the skin. But frozen skin breaks very easily (just as you can break frozen steak easier than you can cut it). Also, the circulation is impeded and the natural resistance to bacterial invasion is sharply reduced.

Thaw out the frozen part in warm water (up to blood temperature of 98.6°F [37°C]). After feeling has returned to the area, exercise it. (Making faces will work if that is the region affected.) If there is no water available, keep the victim as warm as possible and carry him (if the legs or feet are affected) or immobilize the affected areas and get him back to base camp for treatment as soon as practical. If it is quicker, build a fire and heat some water (snow, ice, etc.) for treatment in the field. While the thawed areas should be exercised, they should not be used extensively (walking, etc.) until it is determined that there has not been any tissue damage. (This will take a couple of days.)

Treat second-degree frostbite (blisters) as second-degree burns and get medical help as soon as possible.

Hypothermia is most like frostbite in treatment (keep warm to prevent, warm up to treat), but is quite different in symptoms. Hypothermia is literally what it says: the lowering of body temperature. "Exposure" and "freezing to death" are hypothermia. It is dangerous mainly because it has already done much of its deadly work before the victim even notices it. Then it is often too late.

The body can tolerate the loss of a few degrees of body temperature provided that the deep organs are not chilled and warming is immediate. It cannot tolerate extreme loss or prolonged loss of even a few degrees that are affecting the deep tissues. Therefore prevention is of utmost concern. Hypothermia can be prevented by application of heat (getting near a fire), retention of heat (dress warmly), generation of heat (both from food or exercise). The latter, however, must be watched so that too much of the blood isn't working on digestion instead of temperature regulation or that you chill too rapidly after a hard session of work.

Two areas are particularly productive of hypothermia: wind and water. Wind can best be controlled by watching the wind-chill tables carefully and dressing accordingly. Water is particularly deadly as hypothermia can strike a swimmer on a very warm day if the water is cool. For this reason, survival technique in cold water calls for as much clothing as flotation will permit and the least amount of moving.

Treatment calls for immediate warming. Dry if wet, use a fire, rotating like on a rotisserie before it using a reflector, a second fire, or a blanket on the opposite side. Warming the inside with a hot drink helps. Treat for shock.

Trench Foot

While it sounds like something out of the First World War, when it was a leading cause of casualties, trench foot is still a danger when the ground is wet and cold. Though it is caused by nothing more than these two factors of weather, it can be serious enough to necessitate amputation.

Yet the prevention is quite simple. Keep out of mud and standing water as much as possible. Keep exercising your feet by any means, from hiking to just wiggling your toes. Avoid cramped positions. An altar fireplace is especially welcome as it keeps the fire out of the ooze and keeps you from the cramping position of squatting to tend the fire, which impedes the circulation to your feet and lower legs. Massage your feet for about five minutes at least once a day. Keep your feet dry, especially between the toes, and have an ample supply of dry socks. Keep your feet and your socks clean. Finally, wear shoes that are loose-fitting enough to allow you to wiggle your toes while wearing two pair of socks but are still snug enough at the ankle and heel to prevent blisters.

ARTIFICIAL RESPIRATION

The best method of artificial respiration is mouth-to-mouth resuscitation. While it is harder than you might think, it is fairly easy to learn. First, lay the victim on his back. Clear his mouth of any foreign matter and pull his tongue forward. Now, here is the only tricky part. Tilt his head back (your fist under his neck may help, as will a rolled-up blanket or towel if there is one handy) and, with your other hand, hold his nose shut. This is to keep the air from going in his mouth and out his nose without going to his lungs. Cup your mouth tightly around his, leaving no place for the air to leak.

Inflate the victim's lungs completely each time. With adults, this requires a fairly forceable blowing, much like inflating a rubber balloon. If the chest doesn't rise, hold the jaw higher and blow harder. Allow the lungs to deflate naturally. If the deflation is noisy, raise the jaw some more. The speed should be about twelve to fifteen cycles per minute after the first five or ten cycles, which should be rapid to reoxygenate the lungs more rapidly. Take a deep breath while the victim is exhaling. If he doesn't exhale readily, press on his chest.

After treating for a while, the victim's stomach

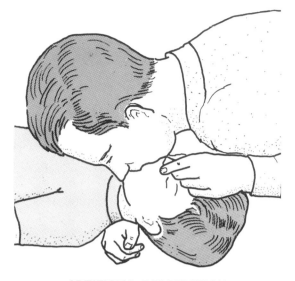

ARTIFICIAL RESPIRATION

mouth, securely sealing it. Seal your mouth around his nose and proceed as with the mouth-to-mouth method. The mouth-to-nose technique is obviously not as efficient as the mouth-to-mouth, but it is sometimes the only method under the circumstances.

When you are treating small children, hold your mouth over both mouth and nose. Use twenty cycles per minute and in small puffs. Take a breath for yourself periodically if you start to get dizzy from the short breaths. Otherwise the techniques are the same.

There is an S-shaped tube on the market which fits down a victim's throat. The tube handles the problem of the tongue sliding back, so you don't need to tilt his head back. All you have to do with your hands is to hold his nose shut and keep the little shield-shaped piece tight against his mouth. This method is more sanitary as well as easier to use. When you will be swimming or canoeing much on your camping trip, it will be worth carrying one in your first-aid kit. It weighs under two ounces (about 50 g).

Keep it handy. It is of no use if you have to do without it while someone goes to dig it out of the first-aid kit at base camp. Obviously, don't delay treatment to get it, even if it is only a few yards away. You can always change over to it during treatment.

may start bulging. This is from some of the air being forced into it. While there is no danger from this, it will make inflating his lungs more difficult. So when it starts bulging noticeably, press gently on it with your hand during the deflation part of the cycle.

Keep the air passages clear at all times.

Keep up the treatment until the victim can breathe by himself or is pronounced dead by a competent medical authority. It sometimes takes hours to restore breathing. When the victim does start breathing, synchronize your breathing with his for a few minutes before stopping the treatment. Keep him quiet for at least fifteen minutes—and preferably longer. Any sudden exertion could stop his breathing again. Loosen his clothing and treat for shock. Keep him under close observation for at least an hour to make sure that his breathing doesn't stop again.

On rare occasions, jaw injuries prevent the use of the usual mouth-to-mouth resuscitation techniques. Move the jaw forward by the angle under the ear instead of sticking your thumb in his mouth and pulling. This will move the tongue into the proper position. Place a hand over the victim's

CHOKING

Choking on food can generally be stopped by bending the victim over so that gravity helps the coughing get the particle up. A sharp pound between the shoulder blades synchronized with the cough will help. If the victim is unable to cough (called restaurant syndrome because it is the cause of so many sudden deaths there) because the food is completely blocking the air passage, another treatment is called for. Grasp the victim around the chest from the back, gripping your own wrists at the base of the chest. Squeeze suddenly and hard and the particle will pop out like a cork from the sudden compression of the air in the victim's lungs. After removal, give the victim a sip of water (or milk, if you have it) to reduce the throat irritation, and check for signs of shock.

HEART STOPPAGE

A man who has worked at a desk all year, getting little exercise, starts on a backpacking trip with little toughening up and, without warning, he gets hit with a heart attack miles from a roadway. A drowning victim, under artificial respiration, begins fibrillating. Lightning strikes near a climber and his heart stops from the shock.

Until the early 1960s, the only thing that could be done in such cases of heart stoppage was to cut open the chest cavity and massage the heart directly by hand. Needless to say, few persons were willing to try such an operation without medical skills.

Now there is a method that anyone can do—even while someone else is giving artificial respiration. However, the heart must have actually stopped before this technique should be used. In case of a heart attack in which the heart is still functioning, put the victim in a sitting position and keep him warm. Do not let him exert.

In the case of heart trouble, check to make sure the heart has really stopped. Heart massage can complicate a heart attack, but with heart arrest it is the only treatment. The carotid artery in the neck is a more reliable indicator of a pulse than the wrist. (See the pressure-point chart, page 367, for neck pressure point.) If no pulse is felt, check the eyes; if they are dilated, the heart is stopped.

Place the victim on his back and treat for shock. Put your off hand (the one you don't write with) on the lower end of the victim's sternum (the breastbone), palm down. Put your other hand on top of it—the heel as near the wrist of the other one as you can and still permit the wrist to bend fully. Use the heel of the hand only—don't let your fingers touch the victim as they will reduce the pressure. One hand is adequate for children.

With heavy, but not extreme, pressure, push down on the chest and release the pressure. Do this about fifty to sixty times a minute, or slightly slower—but stronger than your own heartbeat which will beat in the lower seventies normally, and probably in the upper seventies during this rather strenuous activity.

Keep up this pumping until his heart is beating again, or until ten minutes have passed without the victim's color returning. After that time, it cannot

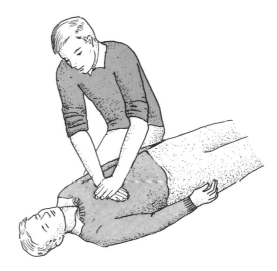

HEART MASSAGE

be started. There is an increasing amount of permanent brain damage from lack of blood after four minutes of stoppage, so speed is critical.

If the color returns, keep at it until the heart starts. This may take over an hour or even require taking the victim to the hospital to use electrical shock to start it. As with the lungs in artificial respiration, the heart is functioning but not on its own.

External heart massage can be combined with mouth-to-mouth resuscitation by a smoothly working pair. One person does the heart massage and the other the artificial respiration. Since the heart massage is rather strenuous, they may wish to change places every few minutes. The cycle is ten pumps on the chest and then a full inflation of the lungs taking about the time of one chest pumping.

It is far more difficult, but still possible, for one person to do this dual job. In this case, the cycle is fifteen pumps and two breaths, each taking the usual time for that number when each is done alone. The movement from one area to the other should be fast but smooth, using as little energy as possible to make a fast transit.

Keep the victim quiet after the heart starts again. Relapse is quite easy in such cases. Continue to treat for shock.

STROKE

Apoplexy or stroke is another circulatory disorder which may attack a camper who tries a too strenuous form of camping without getting in condition first. It is a rupture or clogging of a blood vessel in the brain. The symptoms are:

color: usually red but sometimes grey

pulse: strong but slow

pupils: unequal in diameter, at least one often severely dilated

body: one side more limp than the other, even when relaxed

breathing: difficult

occasionally distorted mouth

complete unconsciousness

To treat stroke, raise the victim's head. Cool his head but not the rest of the body. Keep him quiet, move him only if necessary, and don't give stimulants. Get a doctor even if by use of air rescue.

POISONS

This is another area in which you are far safer in camp than at home. Camping uses very few poisons. Petroleum and alcohol products for stoves and lanterns, insect repellents, and some medicines —that's about the extent of it. Practically nothing compared with the gallons of cleaners, insecticides, solvents, etc., which fill the space under the average sink.

Prevention can take care of all camp poisoning cases. Keep the poisons in well-marked containers out of the reach of children, but make sure that the children know what they are so that curiosity won't be fatal if they should happen to get to them anyway.

With most poisons, vomiting is the best treatment. However, there are three exceptions to this: acids, alkalis, and petroleum products. The first two are neutralized by each other. For petroleum (kerosene, gasoline, etc.), give large quantities of milk and get to a doctor. The problem with the first two is corrosion of the throat, which is serious enough as a result of the stuff going down without a second treatment coming back. The problems with the fuels is that the fumes can get into the lungs, where they are most difficult to remove, and in high enough concentrations they can cause inhalation intoxication. In extremely high dosages, it can cause suffocation.

Insect repellent is not likely to be swallowed— even small children seem to know it is needed more on the outside. Aspirin may be a danger, especially the flavored children's aspirin that tastes like candy and can kill like the poison it is.

While not normally thought of as a poison, the biggest danger of poisoning in camping is carbon monoxide. This gas is colorless, tasteless, and odorless. It is produced by the incomplete combustion of fuels—either in a motor vehicle's exhaust or from open fires, lanterns, and stoves. Charcoal fires give off a heavy concentration.

The symptoms are nausea, headache, and dizziness. But the worst symptom is the psychological inability to do anything about getting out. Prevention is the only answer. Ventilation will take care of the problem completely. Never build a fire in a tent that is not open at both top and bottom for this ventilation nor a charcoal fire in any tent.

Food poisoning (which is not really true poisoning since it is caused by bacteria rather than chemical action) is a more common camping problem. This is typically caused by using ice chests which are not adequately insulated and therefore don't keep the food as cold as it should be, or by attempting to keep food without refrigeration that is not processed for any other means of preservation.

With the exception of some of the more virulent forms not likely to be encountered in camping unless they were already present in the packaging, food poisoning in camp is more likely to be an agonizing day of vomiting and diarrhea. This is the body's natural way to get rid of poisons. Unless it continues for more than one day, diarrhea should not be treated, but allowed to run its course.

CRAMPS

Cramps are one of the most painful injuries in camp and, for the occasional camper suddenly involved in strenuous activities, a rather common one too. The treatment is almost as painful as the injury. Usually cramps occur while swimming or hiking and are either in the stomach or the leg or foot.

If you have a cramp in your leg or foot, grasp the cramped muscle and knead it vigorously. When the cramp is out, try to relax the muscle. If it is in your stomach, draw your legs up. If you are swimming, use the backstroke to get to shore, using your arms only. Don't panic. This is the real danger of cramps. While cramps are extremely painful, they are not dangerous by themselves.

Heat is often a help with leg cramps from strenuous hiking. I crossed Grand Canyon while they were putting in the water pipe line. As a result, I spent most of the first day getting in and out of trenches and climbing over pipes. A hard hike was made almost impossible by this construction. At the Ribbon Falls campsite, my legs started cramping up and I couldn't even lie down. Massage helped only while I was sitting up and massaging. Even though it was still quite warm, I zipped my mummy bag up to my waist. Although I was sweating a lot, the cramps quickly subsided, and after a while I was able to get a good night's sleep in complete comfort. Because it warms evenly, a sleeping bag is far better than a fire when simple massage does no good.

For abdominal cramps not resulting from exercise (such as eating or menstruation), take a Tridol tablet. However, this should be done only if the cramps are persistent and an hour's rest gives no relief at all.

SPRAINS

Sprains are pulled or torn ligaments. The only treatment is to rest the sprained part until it heals. Hot-water soakings help. If there is blood under the skin (other than lightly ruptured capillaries) or difficulty in healing, you should see a doctor.

If it is a sprained ankle and the victim must walk, tie a support on the ankle. It should be an inch to an inch and a half (25 to 35 mm) wide, and should be tied over the shoe. This must be done immediately since the swelling starts right after the sprain. With high-top shoes, loosen them slightly before tying the support. The treatment is intended to reduce the swelling, not prevent it. After tying, the weight should be put evenly on the injured foot when walking.

A sprained wrist requires only rest, although a sling will make it more comfortable. No other support is necessary.

If you are carrying an elastic bandage, it is far better, no matter where the sprain is, to use it to bind the sprain. Wrap the sprained joint with the bandage under a comfortably tight tension.

FRACTURES

Fractures are quite rare in camping outside of mountain climbing, but because of the isolation they are quite serious. The first rule is to make sure that it is a fracture. Sprains and bad bruises often feel like fractures to the victims. On the other hand, a fractured toe often feels like a bruise or dislocation. The signs of a fracture are:

tenderness at the break
discoloration
unnatural shape (a bend where there is no joint, etc.)
difficulty or impossibility of movement

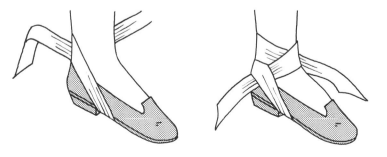

SPRAINED ANKLE SUPPORT

when movement is attempted, a grating of the fracture may be felt or even heard

Never try to set a fracture. It is too easy to break off a piece of the jagged edge. The muscles pull against a fracture reflexively and it is impossible for the victim to relax them.

Splint fractures where they are. Do not move the victim until the fracture is splinted, and be sure additional fractures are not overlooked. Always pad the splint. You can make the splint from a couple of boards, slabs, well-padded sticks, a hiking staff, or anything that is long enough and reasonably rigid. The splint should be longer, on both ends, than the bone that is broken. It should totally immobilize the fracture, but it should not be tied so tightly that it interferes with the swelling that results from the fracture.

An easy temporary splint for a fractured leg is to tie it to the other leg with several ties both above and below the break. Also tie the feet together across the instep to keep the foot from rotating.

The best splint, however, is a traction splint. For it, you need a forked stick, about a foot (30 cm) longer than the leg and at least an inch and a half (35 mm) in diameter. Pad the fork and cut a notch in the opposite end. Tie a sprained-ankle support to the foot and tie a loop of cloth to it under the instep. Put the other end of the loop in the notch and make a tourniquet tie with a short, stout stick. Twist the tourniquet tie until the leg is straightened out and the pull of the muscles is counteracted by the traction. Anchor the stick to keep the tie from unwinding.

The traction splint can also be used on a broken arm, the tourniquet tie attaching to a bandage around the wrist. However, it is often easier to use a regular splint so the arm can be kept in a bent position in a sling.

A broken elbow should be immobilized by taping the forearm to the upper arm and taping the whole unit to the chest to keep it from swinging about.

A kneecap fracture is splinted by straightening the whole leg and splinting.

A fractured collarbone can be felt by running a finger over the bone. The victim is unable to move that arm and supports it with his other hand to relieve pain. If not supported, the injured shoulder

is lower than the other. To treat, support the arm in a sling around the neck and tie it against the body to keep it from moving. The sling should be tight enough to take the strain off the fracture.

A rib fracture causes severe pain at the point of fracture when breathing deeply or coughing. It can often be felt by touching. Breathing is usually shallow because of the pain. The victim may hold his hand over the spot to immobilize the fracture, and he will cough frothy, bright-red blood if the lung is punctured (this fortunately is extremely rare). A normally fractured rib should be immobilized by tying a bandage snugly around the chest, knotting it on the side opposite the fracture. Pad under the knot to prevent irritating pressure. If a lung is punctured, do not bandage the rib. Immobilize the victim as well as possible and get him out as quickly as is safe. If there is no spinal damage, raise the upper body in case of any chest injury to make breathing easier.

Except for lung punctures, these fractures are not particularly dangerous considering their severity—if they are properly immobilized. Head and spinal injuries are far more critical. In the wild places, you can't just call an ambulance. The victim often has to be moved even while waiting air evacuation. As a result, many mountain climbers keep a list of symptoms in their first-aid kits for determining diagnosis of such injuries. A more extensive discussion of the following checklist may be found in *Mountaineering* (see Chapter 54). If you do any mountain climbing, the book is most valuable.

For head injuries:

(1) Control surface bleeding (a normal first-aid priority).
(2) Loss of consciousness indicates a probable concussion; fracture may or may not be present.
(3) Look for blood or other fluid running from ears, nose, or mouth. Elevate the head and wipe it off. If it collects again, there is a fracture at the base of the skull.
(4) Examine pupils for uneven dilation or no reaction to light change (indicating brain damage) by covering and uncovering the eye, or the use of a flashlight.

(5) Very slow pulse or fluctuating respiration indicates brain hemorrhage.

(6) If the victim is conscious, check for nausea (without having an abdominal injury) or a general headache (as contrasted to one strictly at the point of injury).

(7) See if the victim knows who and where he is.

(8) Test for loss of movement or feeling on one side.

(9) If he has none of these symptoms (other than number one), have the victim stand with his eyes closed. Instability indicates inner-ear damage.

(10) If he has none of these, he can get out on his own, otherwise he must be carried out on a stretcher—even if he wants to walk. If he walks, he should be kept under close observation for at least six hours for drowsiness, nausea, or increased headache.

Two fractures of the head which are not in the critical category are nose and jaw fractures. A nose fracture will be deformed, swollen, and bleeding. Apply cold to ease the pain and get to a doctor. Do not treat in any other way as it could cause permanent deformation. A broken jaw shows pain of movement, possible loose teeth, bleeding from gums, and even a mouth hanging open with heavy salivation. Immobilize it by tying it to the head with the bandages tied to the top rather than toward the back, to prevent distorting the jawbone.

Head injuries are often accompanied by neck injuries. The checklist for cervical (neck) fractures is as follows:

(1) Find out if the victim's neck hurts. If there is severe pain without bruises, it is either a fracture or hemorrhage in the spine.

(2) Muscle spasms and an unwillingness on the part of the victim to move his neck are typical of cervical fractures.

(3) If no other injuries prevent it, test for loss of movement by asking the victim to move each arm and each leg. Test for loss of sensation by touching various parts of his body. If any doubt remains, treat for a fracture.

Turn the victim on his back, keeping his head in perfect alignment with the rest of his body. The person turning the head should exert a slight traction while doing so. Put a pad under the victim's neck to keep its proper curve and one on each side to prevent movement. Bind them snugly, but not tightly, in place with a belt. Any moving must be done with a rigid stretcher.

Spinal fractures are usually in the small of the back—the lumbar or last two thoracic (chest) vertebrae. The checklist is:

(1) Check for loss of movement and sensation as for cervical fractures.

(2) If pain is two or three inches off the centerline, it is probably a fractured transverse process (the bony horn-like projections which anchor some of the back muscles). If the pain is on the centerline and feels deep, it is the main part of the vertebra.

Turn the patient over slowly and keep his legs in alignment. Put a small pad under the small of his back to slightly exaggerate the curve. Any movement should be by rigid stretcher although a lower-back fracture can be transported face down in a blanket. (This is not advisable over rough ground since it is hard to keep it straight.)

Further details on moving are given in the section on Transportation later in this chapter.

Hip fractures are treated as thigh fractures if one leg can move, as a spinal fracture if no movement is possible.

Compound fractures (those in which the bone breaks through the skin) should be treated as simple fractures and the wound as a cut. Do not, under any circumstance, get antiseptic on the bone. It will destroy the red-blood-cell-making capacity of the marrow and lead to serious complications. If the distance to move is far, keep the bone moist with a sterile normal saline solution and protected from contamination, or use a traction splint to withdraw the bone into the muscle again.

In all fracture cases, treat for shock. In the case of a spinal fracture, do not lower the head but keep the victim warm.

DISLOCATIONS

The symptoms of a dislocation are:

intense pain
deformity of the joint
extreme swelling
shock (often severe)
usually complete loss of movement

With only a couple of exceptions (jaw and digits), dislocations cannot be reset by the first aider. Also, in these cases, the similarity of fractures on and near the joint is far too close to distinguish without X-rays. Even when the joint of the bone can be felt, there is occasionally a fracture present as well.

A jaw can be reset by hand. First pad your thumb or it may be amputated as the jaw slips back into place. Grasp the jaw by the angle below the ear and pull down, gently but firmly. The muscles will pull it back into place. Try to reduce the impact as much as possible as it could damage the cartilage which forms the bearing surface of the joint, as well as your thumb.

A finger or toe is simply grasped firmly in the hand and traction is applied. Do not attempt to reset if the dislocation is near a cut.

A dislocated arm or leg should be splinted the same as a fracture and help sought at once.

EYE INJURIES

Injuries to the eye itself are always serious—even damage to the area around the eye should be treated with caution.

The most common form of eye injury is a foreign substance between the eye and the eyelid. Gently blinking will generally produce enough tears to wash the matter out. If not, it is fairly easy to remove. Place a matchstick or similar-size object fairly high across the upper eyelid. Take the eyelashes and pull the eyelid back, over the stick, to expose both the underside of the lid and the entire eyeball. Find the irritating object and remove it with the corner of a piece of sterile cloth. Take care not to use a hard substance which might damage the tissues of the eye or lid.

In the case of dust, sand, or other fine particles, wash the eye out with clean (drinking) water or normal saline solution.

If the eye itself is actually scratched, cover the eye and start for help immediately. If the distance is great and the pain is severe, pull back the eyelid as noted above and spread some of the Metycaine and neomycin/gramicidin ointments on the lid, taking care not to touch the lid with the tubes themselves. Carefully fold the lid back over the eye and cover it with a bandage to keep it closed.

GUNSHOT WOUNDS

Gunshot wounds are complicated puncture wounds. With superficial wounds on the arms or legs, where bleeding is slight and the shot or bullet is visible, remove it with forceps. If it is not visible without probing, or if the bleeding is severe, leave it in. The rest of the treatment is like any puncture wound. Clean it thoroughly. Allow superficial wounds to bleed, to clean themselves out internally—there is a great chance of infection from the lead, powder, grease, dust, and whatever else was forced into the wound with the shot. Do not, however, allow heavy bleeding to continue. Stop it as you would any other severe bleeding.

The main danger in chest wounds is the collapsing of the lung due to air entering the pleural cavity between the lung and the inside of the chest. Have the victim exhale as completely as possible. Cover the hole with a thick pad of bandage, pressing as hard as possible without causing undue discomfort to the victim. Bind it in place with a strap, belt, or padded rope in a taut-line hitch to maintain pressure. Have the victim lie down on his injured side so that the healthy lung can get as much air as possible. Treat for shock, but with the head somewhat higher to make breathing easier.

Gunshot wounds in the abdomen are the worst to treat since there is usually severe internal damage. Cover the wound loosely, do not try to replace dislodged intestine or other organs, treat for shock, and get him to a doctor as fast as is comfortable. As usual in serious injury, take proper precautions against shock.

The problem of gunshot wounds in the neck or jaw is that the victim may choke to death on blood. First, stop the bleeding by local pressure. Rarely will pressure points be needed—and obviously a tourniquet is out of the question. Second, check the inside of the mouth for dentures, or loose bits of teeth, bone, or tissue. Third, bandage—and, if needed, tie for fractured jaw. If the victim is unconscious, turn his head to one side to allow any internal bleeding to drain out of his mouth. Treat for shock, omitting the head-low position.

If it is not fatal, a gunshot wound on the head should be treated as a head fracture or concussion, following the same checklist procedure outlined in the section on head fractures, pages 376–77.

In all cases, stop the bleeding, prevent infection, treat for shock, and get the victim to a doctor as quickly as practical.

In any case of gunshot wound, whether accidental or self-inflicted, you are required to notify a law-enforcement officer.

POISONOUS PLANTS

The best thing to do about poisonous plants is to recognize them and keep away from them. Poison ivy, oak, and sumac are unmistakable (see Chapter 33). These plants are nothing to fool with. Even if you are immune, you can lose that immunity overnight.

If you are exposed to their poison, the best treatment is to take a bath immediately with strong soap, lathering as thickly as you can. There is, unfortunately, no other treatment. Pills which were once on the market were found to be totally ineffective. However, see your doctor. It is possible that by the time you read this, a pill may have been developed which really does give immunity.

After rash appears, washing with strong soap is not recommended since it irritates the blisters. About all you can do then is to reduce the itching and try not to scratch. Both of these are very hard to do. Calomine lotion or tannic acid (10 per cent solution) is about as good treatment as any, although none give complete relief.

SNAKE BITE

There are many kinds of snakes and only a few are poisonous. All snakes will bite if forced to do so. If the bite is by a non-poisonous snake, no treatment is needed except to clean up the wound with soap and water. A poisonous snake's bite can be fatal if not treated. However, the treatment is serious in itself and should never be given unless the bite is from a poisonous snake. Therefore, you should know how to identify snakes—at least the poisonous ones and their non-poisonous imitators (see Chapter 33).

The most common poisonous snakes in the Western Hemisphere are the pit vipers. North of the Rio Grande, this group includes rattlesnakes, copperheads, and water moccasins. Their name comes from the heat-sensing pit between the eye and nostril which enables the snake to find rodents in underbrush or poor light. All pit vipers have the same kind of poison and the same antivenin will work in the case of a bite by any of them. The poison attacks the red blood cells which carry oxygen and food to the body's cells and carbon dioxide and wastes from them. With these red cells out of action, the body suffocates.

To treat a bite by a pit viper, loop the constriction band snugly around the part of the body bitten, about four inches toward the heart from the bite. The constriction band is not a tourniquet. It does not cut off the circulation. It only stops the flow of blood to the heart (and from there to the rest of the body). The arteries still bring blood to the injured areas. This is important; the area must bleed. Keep the bitten area lower than the heart to increase blood pressure at that point. To test the constriction band for tightness, you should barely be able to force your finger under a surgical rubber constriction band. The veins below the band should stand out prominently. If the bite is not on an arm or leg (including hands and feet), skip this part and go quickly to work on the rest.

Over each fang mark, cut an X-shaped incision at least an eighth of an inch (3 mm) deep and a quarter-inch (5 mm) long to produce bleeding. (Some more recent sources say the incision should be two parallel cuts, one through each fang puncture, but agreeing on the size. It is supposed to make a smaller scar.) Be careful that you miss the big veins when cutting. They will show up like a road map with a properly applied constriction band.

Apply suction to the cut. If you don't have a snake-bite kit with its suction cups, use your mouth. It won't hurt you if you swallow any of the venom.

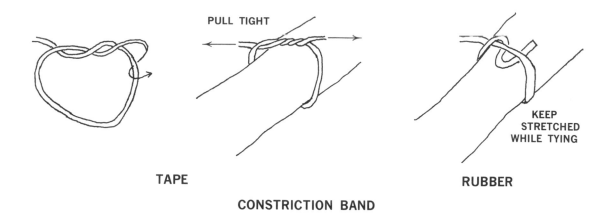

PULL TIGHT

KEEP STRETCHED WHILE TYING

TAPE

RUBBER

CONSTRICTION BAND

The hydrochloric acid in your stomach destroys it. Don't pay any attention to the "sores in your mouth" warning. If you are treating yourself, you have enough poison in your system already. A little more absorbed in the mouth is insignificant compared with the amount you can remove that way. If you are treating someone else, the small amount you absorb won't even be noticed. Besides, the victim may die if you don't.

The wound will start swelling. Make more cuts around the swollen area and apply suction to them too. If the swelling should reach the constriction band, move it another four inches (10 cm) up the limb. Do not release it except to move it up. The tissues below it are still getting enough blood. Continue suction until the swelling subsides noticeably.

As always in the case of injury, treat for shock. Ideally, don't let the victim watch. Get a doctor with antivenin. Don't move the victim unless absolutely necessary, in which case carry him.

Do not give stimulants. Depressants, such as aspirin, may help a little. The traditional "snake-bite oil," alcohol, is dangerous since it dilates the blood vessels. Ice, if you have it, applied to the wound, greatly reduces the swelling and other side effects. There have even been some tests which have used ice alone and no cutting. However, this involves getting the body temperature at the bite down to around 50°, which is hardly possible outside a hospital. Bleeding is still the best treat-

ment in camp. In fact, more recent reports have questioned the whole practice of using ice for treatment except by trained medical personnel as there have been some rather nasty cases of severe frostbite damage to deep tissues—something that can't happen with the more easily learned bleeding treatment.

If you go into snake country where you will be a week or so getting out, get some antivenin and hypos. This is too bulky, heavy, and expensive to take on the usual camping trip, but in remote snake country it will be worth taking the precaution. First aid for snake bite is only the *first* aid to be given. Antivenin is required for a quick recovery. However, antivenin is a horse serum, so watch out if you have reactions from horse-serum vaccines.

The only poisonous snake in North America which is not a pit viper is the coral snake. It is a cobra. Its poison attacks the nerves from the nerve endings at the bitten area, through the nerves, to the spinal cord and the brain. Breathing is paralyzed. The treatment is the same as for pit vipers except that the constriction band is an unnecessary waste of time. The coral snake's venom works faster than the pit viper's, so the less time wasted the better. Keep calm, but work fast. The correct antivenin is that for cobras so tell the doctor that it was a coral-snake bite. Generally, however, the antivenin is not available and must be flown in. Artificial respiration is often required in severe cases.

Fortunately, the chance of being bitten by a coral snake is very slight, since they are fairly small and are active only at night. Also, their diet, unlike the rodent-eating pit vipers, is not helped by the presence of man, so they keep away. You will probably never see one, even when camping in their habitat.

INSECT BITES

Victims of bites by the more dangerous members of *Arthropoda,* such as the black widow spider and (in the case of children being stung) scorpions, wasps, bees, and kindred insects, should be treated for shock. Ammonia or baking soda over the wound helps.

Bee stings are left (along with the poison gland) by the bee and should be removed by forceps. A magnifying glass helps in seeing the sting. You should grasp the sting, not the gland, with the forceps. A daub of mud placed over the sting will help if you have no forceps. Let the mud dry and pull it off. The sting will come with it. In case of severe swelling, get a doctor.

Ticks should be removed before they bury themselves under the skin (see page 386). The bite itself requires no treatment if the tick is removed properly, but a thorough soap-and-water washing is good insurance.

Bites by insects that are more pesky than dangerous (mosquitoes, chiggers, etc.) should be left alone or treated with ammonia, soda, or isopropyl alcohol.

MAMMAL BITES

If you have done nothing to provoke the animal and it bites you, there is the danger that it is rabid. This often strikes wild animals such as foxes, skunks, and bats, as well as feral domesticated animals such as dogs and cats. If you are bitten by any such animal, try to capture it or kill it without damage to its brain so it can be studied for rabies. If it isn't rabid, the study will save you some very painful shots. The incubation time is longer in humans than in other animals so there is plenty of time to make sure. Once developed in an animal (humans included), there is no cure. Incidentally,

any mammal can become rabid. There has even been a case of a rabid whale.

An infected animal may run wildly, frothing at the mouth, or it may sulk quietly but be irritable. Contrary to popular belief, you can't tell a rabid animal by looking. An unprovoked attack is the best presumptive sign, but even it is not a positive indication.

In any case, wash the wound, try to get the animal, and see a doctor.

OTHER ANIMAL TROUBLE

This is another catch-all section of items too minor to warrant a separate section for each.

Aquatic Poisons

Jellyfish, men-of-war, sting rays, sea urchins, and such can easily be avoided by the careful beach camper. However, accidents do happen to those who, while normally very careful, occasionally relax their caution. The poisons carried by these are quite deadly, although fortunately they lack the injection mechanism of the poisonous snakes.

The first two attack the skin with sticky tentacles, the latter two use a puncture wound to help them. The poison produces extreme inflammation, sharp pain, and even, in extreme cases, paralysis. In any case beyond a surface inflammation, get to a doctor. Shots may be needed to counteract the effects. Even in severe cases, the paralysis will let up in a day to two weeks. Although extremely painful, they are rarely fatal. Treat for shock, and apply soda or ammonia.

Porcupines

The quill of a porcupine is quite a problem to anyone stuck with one because the moisture of the body swells it, making it harder to remove. The pliers used in fish-hook removal makes the job less difficult. Grasp the quill, as close to the skin as possible, and pull quickly, smoothly, and with a rotation to help both in collapsing the barb somewhat and in enabling it to cut its way out easier.

Treat the wound as a puncture. If there are quite a few quills to remove, treat for shock.

Skunks

The only real problem of skunk musk in first aid is the rare case when the victim gets so close that the musk is sprayed in his eyes. As with any foreign liquid in the eye, flood with clean water. Give the victim plenty of rest and keep the eyes covered as much as possible for a couple of days.

TRANSPORTATION

Most of the first-aid situations in camp are only a bother—a cut finger or burned hand is treated and the camp routine resumes as though nothing had happened. Even when the situation is such that the camp must be stopped and medical aid found, the victim usually gets out basically under his own power, although his gear is often split up among the rest of the group for carrying out. Only very rarely will you have to carry out one of your group—and the instances of air evacuation are so rare that they automatically make all the newspapers in the country, even if only as a filler on an inside page.

However, when these rare situations arise, the proper knowledge of transportation techniques is as important as the first-aid treatment itself. Always move the victim carefully, with the least jarring possible. Considering the distance, speed is of secondary importance to comfort. Take all of the first-aid steps possible before moving—this especially applies to splinting fractures, controlling bleeding, and treating shock. Except when the face is red and the body hot, keep a blanket or an equivalent around him during transportation, and this means under as well as over him. Except when chest injuries makes breathing difficult, the victim should be in a lying position. When unconsciousness makes diagnosis difficult, assume there may be a neck fracture and move him accordingly.

Stretchers

A stretcher is not standard equipment. Therefore, any case needing a stretcher requires one to be improvised.

In cases not involving spinal fractures, a fisherman's litter (see page 446) is probably the best. It is as serviceable as the stretchers improvised from blankets that are shown in the first-aid books. However, rope is usually available in camp and blankets have been replaced by sleeping bags, which make poor improvised stretchers, though a sleeping bag under the victim makes the fisherman's litter more comfortable as well as providing warmth under him.

In cases requiring a rigid stretcher, take two poles the same size as you use for the fisherman's litter, and lash a platform of one-inch (25 mm) -diameter sticks to it. Pad it with a sleeping bag and remember to put pads under the small of the victim's back and the bend of his neck to keep his spine in a slight backward bend.

Carries

There are two types of first-aid carries. The first group are basically lifts designed to get the victim off the ground and onto a stretcher. The second group is used to get the victim over a moderate distance and are for much less serious injuries.

The basic lift to get a victim on a stretcher is the three-man carry, which in many cases really requires four people. The three get on the uninjured side, one at the shoulders, one at the hips, and one at the knees. They kneel on one knee, and at the command of the one closest to the victim's feet, they support him as evenly as possible. Working together, they lift him up and either move him to the stretcher or to some other means of transportation. The fourth man (necessary only in cases of fracture or dislocation) either lifts the splinted limb or applies traction to a fractured spine by gently pulling on the victim's head while being careful to keep it in perfect alignment with the rest of the body.

Carries involving as many as eight persons (four on each side, alternating hands down the line) is useful for fairly long distances (if the ground is reasonably level) since with a two-hundred-pound (90 kg) man each lifter only has to support about twenty-five pounds ($11\frac{1}{3}$ kg).

In the second group of carries are the two-man and single carries and the assist. In one of the two-man carries, the carriers grasp wrists and shoulders with opposite hands and form a seat (over the wrists) with a backrest. In another, a "pack

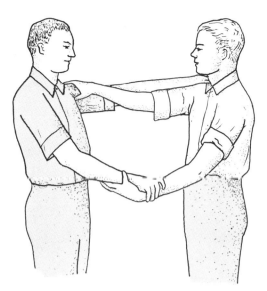

TWO MAN CARRY

FIREMAN'S CARRY

saddle" is made by each carrier holding his own left wrist with his right hand and the other's right wrist with his left hand. This makes a seat which is fairly comfortable for both the victim and the carriers.

Single carries include the piggy-back and the fireman's carry, in which the victim is carried over one shoulder, seat first, with one of his arms over the other shoulder. He is secured in this position by the carrier reaching between the victim's legs and holding the wrist or elbow of the victim, pulling the victim's arm across his (the carrier's) chest.

The assist enables the victim to use the carrier

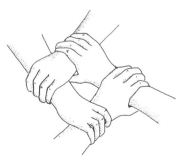

PACK SADDLE

as a crutch with his arm around the carrier's neck. The carrier holds this arm downward, enabling the victim to relax his arm, and steadies the victim by holding him around the waist. This situation presupposes the victim can walk, even with some difficulty, but needs help in taking some of the weight off his feet or in keeping his balance. (This is in the absence of head injury. A head injury producing imbalance always requires a stretcher.)

PREVENTION

Any accident or illness spoils a camping trip. Practically all of this chapter can be unnecessary if proper preventive steps are taken. You can also prevent most illnesses. Before going on your camping trip, have a complete physical check-up with special attention to teeth, appendix, and anything else that could go wrong.

Vaccine is another good preventative. A camper should have, in addition to the usual shots for smallpox, diptheria, etc., the permanent (toxoid) tetanus, polio, and typhoid shots, and any others that might be helpful in the area where you are going.

Top physical condition is an excellent preventative of disease and injury in camp—and this doesn't mean that you have to be an athlete nor does it have anything to do with physical handicaps. I know of one man who camped from a wheelchair. He was in top physical condition in spite of a polio attack in his youth.

Flabby muscles can take all the fun out of a backpacking or canoe trip and reduce the fun of even an auto-camping trip. Exercise before you go and it will be easier when you get there.

Camping accidents are almost always preventable. Selection of good campsites will prevent accidents from natural causes such as lightning and flooding. Careful selection of routes (out of thick underbrush, away from loose rocks, etc.) and care in walking (never step on anything you can step over, nor over anything you can conveniently step around, and be sure of your footing) are the most effective ways to prevent sprains, fractures, lacerations, and other equally serious accidents. And being sure where you put your feet (or hands, if climbing) will be the best safeguard against snake bite.

Proper sanitation practices will greatly reduce the chance of dysentery as well as preventing strength-sapping "bugs" that don't actually show up as illness. Care of the feet is especially important in keeping your body at peak efficiency.

Knowledge of first-aid techniques is a necessity for the camper in wilderness areas, but care and observance of safety rules will make this knowledge just a pleasant feeling of competence rather than a life or death matter.

CHAPTER THIRTY-THREE

Pests

The reluctance of many people to try camping is centered on the problem of camp pests.

By pests, I don't mean the litterbugs or the unthinking people who keep you awake half the night in public campsites. These are indeed pests, but while litterbugs are all too common, noisy campers are fortunately quite rare. A quiet word to the Ranger or camp superintendent will insure that your next night will be peaceful.

The pests that concern this chapter are those of the wildlife, both flora and fauna. The tenderfoot is usually full of dread at the prospect of encountering them, yet they are simply pests. Few of them are dangerous under any circumstance, and even these can be kept away with the exercise of a few simple rules.

To a certain extent, you will have to curtail your activities in order to avoid some pests, especially if you insist on going to certain places. You may have to simply endure them—it can be done, especially if your love of the outdoors is tempered with reason and you realize that nature is not all peace and quiet. While there will be other times when the wee beasties make life perfectly miserable, there will be other times when the great experience you get will be vividly remembered long after the battle with mosquitoes and such is forgotten.

In most camping situations, pests are either non-existent or strictly due to the presence of man. Moving into the more remote areas will free you of most of them. Insects can be avoided by camping in the winter—a most enjoyable season as long as there isn't a fresh cold front coming through.

The skilled camper will not be bothered by pests, because he knows how to deal with them or even to avoid them entirely. The beginner will learn with amazing rapidity during his first encounter. If he learns from his experience, the pests will become a minor problem in relation to the beauty nature offers.

MOSQUITOES AND SUCH

Mosquitoes are the most common form of camp pest, and one of the most persistent. With the exception of the *Aëdes* and *Anopheles* genera which carry yellow fever and malaria, the bite of a mosquito, in and of itself, is the only thing to worry about. (The two disease-bearing genera are not too common in America north of the Rio Grande and must have first bitten someone with an active case of the disease before they can transmit it at all. In any case, you are safe from the diseases if you are far from any human habitation.)

While the most common genus, the *Culex,* does not transmit any disease other than a rare outbreak of encephalitis now and then (usually in urban areas), it is by no means harmless. The bites inflicted by the larger species are quite painful. Also there is the subsequent danger of infection due to a too vigorous scratching of the bite.

You can avoid the mosquito problem in one of two ways. The first is in the selection of the campsite. A campsite far removed from swampy ground, stagnant pools, and dumps where water can collect after a rain will almost always be free of mosquitoes. An exposed campsite with a steady breeze will have few mosquitoes, even if they are fairly heavy in the area.

The second way is with a good mosquito dope. The best has an active ingredient of N,N diethyl metatoluamide. Like all bug dopes, it generally has to be reapplied every couple of hours, especially if you are sweating a lot.

Remember, mosquitoes can bite through clothing, so treat your back as well, unless you are wearing a pack which will protect it. It usually takes a while for mosquitoes to work through the cloth, so you can usually swat them in time if you see them. In groups, check each other constantly in heavy mosquito country.

Use a spray cautiously inside the tent, making sure you keep it off the tent fabric since it can destroy the waterproofing.

If worse comes to worst, you will need a head net and gloves. This arrangement is hardly comfortable and is generally unnecessary, but when it is necessary there is no substitute.

There are a host of smaller relatives of the mosquitoes and flies which infest the northern canoe country in the late summer which make mosquitoes seem lazy by comparison. These are the various deer flies, midges, and no-see-ums. The main problem, especially with the last named, is that they are so small, swatting is a very inaccurate method of dealing with them.

Bug dope works well, but quite often, in the cool of the evening around the campfire, the best cure is a thick smudge on the fire. At times, they will be so bad that the smudge will have to be carried through the night.

Flies (the house-fly and horsefly varieties) are basically a man-made problem. They rarely exist in the deep wilderness in bothersome quantities, but they are a major problem in crowded campsites. There are really only two things you can do about

them. The first is to check the garbage cans in the campsite to see how regularly they are emptied, and move somewhere else if they are not. The second is for wilderness camping: keep your horses as far from your camping area as is convenient.

TICKS

In hardwood forests, ticks may be a problem. Although decreasing in occurrence, there are still several diseases transmitted by ticks, so there is more than just a painful bite to be avoided. Antibiotics will take care of the various fevers, so they are no longer fatal, but they are quite agonizing and no one would willingly risk them.

There is only one way to handle the problem of ticks—constant watching and removal. Examine your body at least every twelve hours. This includes the hairline, folds of the skin, and other hard-to-see places. It takes quite a while for ticks to bury completely under the skin. The best way to get them out is to touch them gently with your finger. Usually they will pull out and drop off fast.

If they have their mind too much on food to notice, try again—this time by applying alcohol or something hot (a cigarette, a smoldering piece of punky wood, a just-blown-out match, or heated metal). The idea is to make them so uncomfortable that they move, not to kill them in there. Never try to pull the tick out, with or without twisting, or the head or mouth may break off under the skin and cause a severe infection. Force them out and stomp them.

Ticks can be kept off pets by using a tick powder.

CHIGGERS

Chiggers are mites that are six-legged bloodsuckers in their larval stage. When they get to the adult phase, they acquire some manners and an extra pair of legs and feed only on plant juices. In the more familiar larval stage, they burrow under the skin and produce the most irritating, itching welts.

Generally, they get onto the body from grass. Then they crawl on the skin until they reach an obstruction, such as socks or a belt, and there they burrow. Powdered sulphur or bug dope applied to these spots helps convince them that they are unwanted. Tucking the pants legs inside the socks or using gaiters made for keeping scree out of mountain climber's boots also helps since the chigger will rarely crawl higher than eighteen inches (45 cm) above the landing site without finding skin. If he doesn't find something edible by this time, he generally drops off.

SPIDERS

With the exception of the black widow and the brown recluse (which can be quite painful), spiders are harmless. Running into webs is the worst thing that is likely to happen to you in camp.

The black widow is easily identified. She is about a half-inch (1 cm) long, jet-black, with an almost spherical abdomen. The underside of the abdomen has a characteristic red-orange hourglass marking.

The brown recluse is actually more of a danger than the black widow although it was only in the late 1950s that its danger was recognized. The brown recluse is slightly smaller than the black widow, and has an oval body (contrasted to the spherical black widow) and a dark violin-shaped spot on the cephalathorax (the first of the two body parts, the abdomen being the other).

Fortunately for the camper, neither is often found far from human habitation. They feed on the fly-to-cockroach-size insects man seems to attract with his food. You are in more danger of encountering them in your garden than in your campsite unless it is an established campground, in which case caution is definitely recommended.

The tarantula strikes fear in many, but it is really all bluff. I was bitten at least ten times playing with them as a child. The bite is not nearly as painful at first as a bee sting and has none of the after-effects that the sting does. However, sometimes they have gas-gangrene bacteria on their fangs (they dig as well as bite with them), so wash the wound with soap and water as a precaution. A healthy person can counteract this rather weak bacteria and need not fear even this rare side-effect.

When you are going through underbrush, hold an arm upright in front of your face to keep webs from hitting you. You can get them off your arm easier than out of your hair. Swinging a hiking staff cures the problem of webs. In the early morning, after a heavy dew, they are beautiful, glistening in the sunlight, so learn to enjoy them—they do tend to keep down the fly population around camp.

SCORPIONS

Scorpions can inflict a painful sting. However, they will not bother you if you don't bother them. Just be sure to shake out your shoes and clothes before putting them on in the morning. This will be the only time you will see one unless you turn over a rock and one is under it. They are really quite good around camp, since they eat cockroaches, crickets, and other insects of that size which can damage your food supply or your clothes. I have camped in areas full of scorpions but the only time I have ever been stung was when one was in a hand towel in my own house.

ANTS

If an ant is under a quarter of an inch (5 mm) in length, its bite will be of no great concern. Aside from putting your camp away from the top of any large anthills, protecting your food supply will be the only problem. An antproof hook (see page 276) is valuable if you need to cache your food for any prolonged period.

With the larger ants, keep more than twenty-five feet ($7\frac{1}{2}$ m) from their hills and food trails (streaks of bare ground radiating from the hills) and keep food off of the ground at all times.

SNAKES

There is probably more unfounded fear of snakes than of anything else. There are many kinds of snakes; all are beneficial to man and only a few of them are poisonous. However, the bite of a poisonous snake is a dangerous situation, so you will have to know how to identify at least the poisonous snakes and their non-poisonous imitators. Unfortunately, there is no sure short-cut to this.

Folklore contains several commonly accepted methods to use in distinguishing poisonous from non-poisonous snakes by just a few features. Like most of folklore, they are a mixture of half-truth and total fiction. None of them work, although some are helpful in a limited way in identifying the pit vipers, which are the only kinds of poisonous snakes which are likely to strike a camper. Although only a slight danger, the coral snake is still a danger.

Probably the most common folklore is the theory that poisonous snakes have diamond-shaped heads while the harmless ones have heads little larger than their necks. By this method, not only would the deadly coral snake be judged harmless, the harmless hog-nosed snake would be considered poisonous.

Another way, so says folklore, is to look for the pit between the eye and the nostril. If it is there, it is a poisonous snake. This is a sure and foolproof way to identify the pit vipers; no other snake has this pit. But again, the coral snake escapes identification.

This pit-identification method prevented a mild catastrophe in my younger days as an amateur herpetologist. I had cornered a light leafy-green snake with a white underside. It looked like a yellow-bellied water snake (a non-poisonous species). I was about to grab it behind the head when I saw the pit. It was an extremely light-colored water moccasin.

A third way, tradition says, is by looking at the eyes. True, pit vipers do have elliptical pupils while the rest have round ones—including the harmless-looking coral snake. In poor light, however, the pit viper's pupils have dilated to an almost circular shape.

A fourth way, according to folklore, is by looking at the bite. A poisonous snake will leave two large punctures from the fangs and a horseshoe-shaped row of small punctures. The non-poisonous snake will leave only the horseshoe-shaped row.

This method might be accurate if snakes left a perfect toothprint. However, nature is rarely textbook-perfect in anything, and this is no exception.

The fang marks may be no larger than the others. Only two teeth of a harmless snake may break the skin. A poisonous snake may have broken a fang and the reserve hasn't worked down yet. In such cases (all rather common), appearance is dangerously deceptive.

Most non-poisonous snakes *and the coral snake* will grab hold and chew. This will mess up any set of toothprints. In fact, you can rarely see the skin, if the snake is large, because of the bleeding. While this bleeding stops quickly—much as with a bad scratch—in the case of non-pit vipers, it would be a waste of valuable time to wait to find out. The pit viper's poison has an anti-coagulant in the venom and bleeding will continue since the blood can't clot.

Usually (but again, not always), the pit vipers will strike and then recoil quickly for another strike. (The term "coil" here refers to a striking position, usually the S-shaped position, and not necessarily a strict spiral coil.) Unless they are sunning in that position, a snake will rarely go into the spiral coil to strike, but rather the quicker S-constriction. Also, contrary to popular opinion, the snake doesn't have to strike to bite. It can just reach over and chomp down.

The only safe defense is to learn the differences between the various snakes. The pit vipers are fairly well described by the first three "folklore" methods. Besides the light-colored water moccasin which can look like a yellow-bellied water snake, there are two non-poisonous snakes that will cause some confusion here. The hog-nosed snake, sometimes called a spreading adder or puffing adder, despite the fact that adders are Eastern Hemisphere poisonous snakes, is one. But it not only lacks the pit, it also has an unmistakable upturned nose. Also, if he sees you first, he will spread his neck and hiss. He will flatten out so thinly that his spine will show. If you attack him, he will usually turn over and play dead. (He is a poor actor, though, because if you turn him right-side-up, he will turn back over again.)

The gopher snake looks a lot like a rattler. It even shakes its tail when disturbed. However, it has a checkerboard back rather than a diamond pattern and, of course, the tail makes no sound by itself. But if it unintentionally rattles its tail against something like a piece of sheet-metal roofing lying on the ground, it can sound very convincing.

The coral snake presents a different problem. Shape is no help at all here. Not only that, there are two harmless snakes with the same general color pattern—yellow, red, and black bands, a narrow band of one color separating wide bands of alternating colors. This color scheme makes the coral snake very easy to notice.

The difference between the coral snake and the coral king snake and the scarlet king snake is one of order and proportion. The head of the coral snake is black and the narrow bands are yellow. The king-snake imitators have red heads and yellow bellies and the narrow bands are red or black.

The chance of being bitten by a coral snake is very slight. They are active only at night and the king snakes are active in the daytime. Coral snakes are small—rarely over two feet (60 cm) in length. Their fangs are only one-eighth inch (3 mm) long, while the rattler has fangs over a half-inch (1 cm) long if he is full grown. It is possible for a coral snake to strike without breaking the skin—especially because most areas of the human anatomy are too flat for it to bite since it doesn't open its mouth very wide (unlike the pit viper, which can hit a completely flat surface).

Unless you corner or surprise a snake, he will rarely strike. Usually, if he doesn't try to escape, he will try to bluff you into retreating. Go ahead and retreat, even from a non-poisonous snake. There's nothing cowardly about it. It is only observing a basic courtesy of nature: don't bother the residents any more than is absolutely necessary, they were here first.

The snake will then probably leave. If he doesn't, toss a piece of gravel or dirt on him. He will leave then. Don't kill even a poisonous snake unless it is in a very thickly inhabited area, and then catch it, if possible. If you kill it, the mouse or rat it would have had for dinner will be in your gear. Never kill a non-poisonous snake under any circumstance.

A snake-bite treatment is not the prettiest thing in camp, so give the snake a chance to keep out of your way. It will. It is a lot more afraid of you than you can possibly be of it—and with far better reason.

MAMMALS

There are only four wild mammals that will give you any real trouble: the bear, the porcupine, the field mouse, and the skunk. Any other visitors should be welcome for the change they bring as long as you cache your food properly.

The bear is the one who will try to get into your food supply no matter what you have done to keep him out, and it takes a good cache to frustrate him. A loud noise (pounding on a pot, e.g.) or a sudden flash of light accompanied by throwing rocks or pine cones is the best way to get rid of him. Because of those who continue to feed them, national park bears don't scare very easily and do considerable damage to campers' gear. Strong support of the Park Service's campaign against feeding bears is necessary if the problem is ever to be solved.

The porcupine is usually after salt. For this reason, he will ruin canoe paddles, gun stocks, ax handles, and anything else with sweat on it. He is also fond of bacon. Tin cans piled on top of your gear will scare them off if they try digging into the pack. Cache your food. You can chase them off with sticks or small rocks. They can't throw their quills, but their tails have a longer range than you might think, and the quills are quite loose.

Caching food will keep field mice away. They may come inside your tent (if you don't have a floor or sod cloth) but they will leave if they find no food. They are clean, rather interesting creatures, unlike their urbanized relatives.

Skunks are usually after garbage. They will leave you alone if you burn your garbage and bury it well enough. For obvious reasons, don't antagonize a skunk. The musk has a range of ten feet (3 m) for temporary blinding and a quarter-mile ($\frac{1}{2}$ km) for detection.

If you are the victim of the musk-spraying apparatus of a skunk, don't bury your clothes. Wash everything thoroughly. If they have sprayed musk in your eyes, wash them out by pouring water in them. Do this quickly or you will be blinded for a week or so.

The best way to get the smell out of animal fur—when your dog comes back with his tail between his legs and his nose pushing dirt—is to soak the fur with tomato juice. Wait a short while to let the juice absorb the musk, then wash it out with water.

The only other danger from wildlife is the extremely rare rabies (see page 381), and there is a much greater chance of being bitten by a rabid animal in the city than in camp.

POISONOUS PLANTS

There are two common types of poisonous plants: the poison ivy or poison oak and the poison sumac. While these two differ in appearance, they are from the same genus and have the same poison. The dead plants are just as deadly as live ones. A case was contracted from a twenty-five-year-old pressed specimen in the S.M.U. herbarium!

Poison ivy and poison oak are basically the same plant through most of the country—one is a vine and the other is a bush (western poison oak is a separate species). This plant is unmistakable in all its forms. It has a cluster of three leaves. This cluster as a whole is symmetrical, although the side leaves by themselves are not. The poison-oak leaves are deeply notched, and look more like oak leaves, but they still have this form of symmetry. The berries are translucent, waxy, white clusters.

The nearest imitator to poison ivy are the Virginia creeper, which has five leaves to the cluster and no berries or visible flowers, and several wild berry vines which have spiny stems, small leaves, and/or large blue or black berries.

The problem identifying poison sumac is its close resemblance to the staghorn sumac, to which it is related. It differs from the non-poisonous sumacs

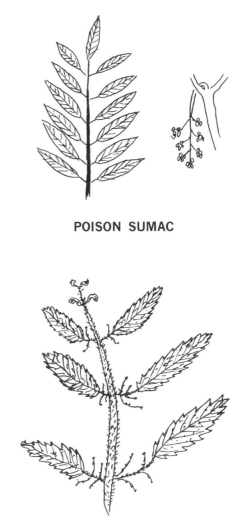

POISON SUMAC

POISON IVY

AXIS OF SYMMETRY

STINGING NETTLE

in that the edges of the leaves are smooth instead of notched and the berries are on hanging stems at the forks of the branches instead of on spikes at the ends of the branches. The berries are white or greenish grey instead of dark red.

Nettles are not, strictly speaking, poisonous, but they are extremely irritating. They can only cause irritation if you get scratched by the plant, as contrasted to the poisonous plants which affect you only if you are touched by the smoke of the burning plant or by the plant itself. If you wear long pants, you run little chance of having trouble with nettles. Oddly enough, when boiled, they are edible greens.

CHAPTER THIRTY-FOUR

Survival

Every year in our national parks and forests, people get lost. Some of them are good campers who took a wrong turn in the trail. Others haven't learned to follow a trail at all. With the rapid increase of air travel in light aircraft, there will be a natural increase in forced landings in sparsely settled areas. This will happen in spite of a greater number of passenger-miles flown without mishap. If food supplies are low toward the end of a camping trip, or lost in a canoe accident, survival becomes a serious problem.

An adequate treatment of the problems of survival would require a full book. For full detail, I recommend one of the books in the survival section of Chapter 54. This chapter is just a once-over-lightly guide for campers who get lost in state or national parks or forests and, if proper action is taken, will not be under survival conditions for more than twenty-four hours before they are back in civilization.

Many car campers think that the more extreme techniques in this chapter are strictly for the backpackers and canoeists who venture deep into the wilderness and not the concern of those who stick to the established campgrounds of our state and national parks. Yet how important a basic knowledge of survival technique is to even these campers was illustrated on August 17, 1959, at 11:37:15 P.M. At that time, an earthquake hit an area near Yellowstone National Park, vastly changing the

geyser pattern there. Rock Creek campground was buried in the landslide which created Earthquake Lake. Cabin Creek campground at the other end of the instantly formed lake was flooded.

Here were car campers, in highly developed state park campgrounds, who were without their camping equipment. Some of them were injured, and all of them were without any resources other than what they had within them for a day or two until help arrived. If it weren't for the facts that Yellowstone National Park was just twenty miles (30 km) away and the center of the quake quickly was determined, they would have probably been in there considerably longer.

At the more casual level, emergency navigation should be known by anyone who gets out of a car in a campsite—especially the children, who are more likely to have the urge to wander.

Likewise, car trouble on remote stretches of road or light-plane forced landings require the means to get help quickly. A survival kit is as important a requirement for the camper (or even the traveler who doesn't camp) as a first-aid kit.

NAVIGATION

When you are lost, your first problem is to get "unlost." If you can do this, the whole problem of survival is usually avoided (although a long hike may still be required).

The quickest way to find your location is with the navigational techniques discussed in Chapter 31. When you have found north and oriented your map, you are ready to get your bearings. Using the map, locate as many landmarks as possible—hills, lakes, buildings, etc. Find the direction to each of these points. Plot the bearings on your map and the intersection of these bearings will be where you are on the map.

Then act accordingly.

If you are lost and either don't have a map or you can't find any landmarks, sit down. This works wonders in preventing panic. More people are lost through panic than through an actual lack of knowledge about their location. The old verse "When in danger or in doubt/Run in circles, scream, and shout" has no place in camp survival techniques, even that mildest of "survival" conditions—getting unlost.

After you sit down and calm yourself a bit, start going back over your trip in detail. Try to remember the turns you made, the landmarks you saw, the streams or roads you crossed, etc. When you have remembered as much of it as you can, go back over it, drawing a map of it on a piece of paper or on the ground. After you have drawn this, compare it with your map, if you have one. Find where you went off the correct trail and backtrack to that spot.

Ded reckoning helps even when you are lost. Since you can hardly be traveling lost for over an hour and three or four miles per hour (5 or 6 km/h) is the absolute top speed you can walk for any length of time in the wilderness, even if you are in the best physical condition, you are probably within three or four miles (5 or 6 km) of a known location. In populated areas or in most state parks, you can reach a road within a half-hour by traveling in a straight line.

If you are still completely lost after sitting awhile, you can start trying to get help.

Remember, it is all a matter of viewpoint. In a sense, you are not lost at all—your camp is. If you are a prudent camper, you will have at least a hiker's-model survival kit with you (weight: two ounces [60 g], in a 35 mm film can). If you know the basic skills, you can live indefinitely with this equipment, so you might as well enjoy the challenge. By taking it easy, adjusting yourself to this new way of living, you will be in fine condition when your rescuers finally find you—or you finally find them by staying put.

GETTING HELP

In most survival situations, it is far better to stay put and try to get help to come to you rather than to try to get out on your own: they know the area and are not as likely to get further lost. Therefore, you should know several means of attracting attention to your situation—several, because no one system will work in all cases.

On federal or state land, where most camping is done, the quickest way to get help is to clear some space and build a bonfire. Keep it under control, but make it as hot as possible. A log-cabin fire is best. Pile on plenty of green leaves or grass to produce dense smoke. The nearest fire-observation tower will see the smoke and someone will be there in a short time. However, take proper fire safeguards and always be able to put it out.

One dense column is adequate in controlled forests. Use a clearing both for conservation and fire-safety reasons, and because trees tend to diffuse the smoke instead of letting it rise in a distinctive column which can't possibly be confused with mist, low clouds, or dust.

In complete wilderness (far from fire lookouts and other probable witnesses), in the desert, or in areas where camping outside the developed campgrounds is permitted, use three columns about one hundred feet (30 m) apart or use a blanket for Indian-style smoke signals. The idea is to make it clear that this is not just another campfire or a dust-devil. (Smoke signalling requires two people to hold the blanket and let it balloon upward until the smoke is spilling from under it, then slide it off the smoke bubble to let it rise in a distinct puff.)

If you are hunting, fire the traditional three shots, ten seconds apart. If you get no answer, wait. They either didn't hear you or they are coming. They should answer you with two shots, but not many hunters know this, so don't depend on it. Many use only a single shot, which is confused with the normal hunting sounds. Don't waste your ammunition on signalling, you may need it later to get some food.

A whistle is the best emergency signalling device. It carries farther than your voice and you won't get laryngitis using it. It is better than a gun because it won't be confused with the normal hunting sounds, nor can it get out of control like a fire. It is easy for children. Its range is only a couple of hundred yards (75 m or so) in dense woods in the daytime, but it can be heard three or four miles (5 or 6 km) on a calm night in flat desert. It can be carried in the pocket and, in the metal forms, is unbreakable.

If you are in an isolated area and your absence is noted, an air search will usually be made. The reflection from a signal mirror will attract its attention from a great distance. The best material to have is ferrotype tin, which is used in darkrooms for drying prints and is available at most camera stores. The second best is the polished stainless-steel metal mirror which is available from camping outfitters.

Regardless of the material, both sides must be shiny. It should be fairly small to store easily. Cut a small hole in the center of the mirror. It is best to make this hole cross-shaped since a cruciform spot of light can't be confused as can light from more usual holes.

When the aircraft and the sun are within 90° of each other, look at yourself in the mirror with one eye and at the aircraft, through the hole, with the other. Move the mirror so that the spot of sunlight on your face will disappear through the hole. If the angle is greater than 90°, hold the palm of your hand under the mirror. The spot of sunlight you need to make disappear through the hole will be on your hand rather than on your face. Otherwise, the procedure is the same.

You can use a car headlight at dusk or even at night with much the same effect. Remove the sealed-beam bulb from its socket in the car, but do not disconnect it from the wires. It will then be able to be pulled out almost a foot (around 30 cm), giving you considerable flexibility in how it can be pointed. While one of you aims the light at the plane, the other should turn the light switch on and off (an SOS signal, three short, three long, three short flashes, is best but not absolutely essential).

You should attract the attention of the plane to more than just your presence. There are two internationally standardized codes for signalling aircraft in emergencies. One uses panels of brush, tracks in the snow, cloth, or any other material at least three feet (1 m) wide and twenty feet (6 m) long. The other is based on the way you stand. It can only be used with slow, low-flying aircraft and it is harder to "read" than the panels.

A radar reflector (or any large piece of metal, such as a fuel can) mounted high on a boat will make it visible on a radar screen.

If at all possible, stay put. Especially in the desert, stay with, but not in, your car. It is not only a lot

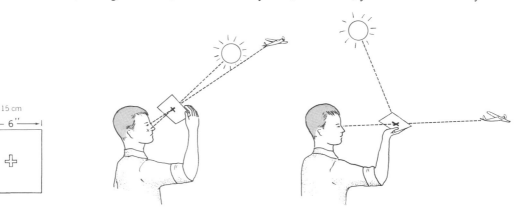

SIGNAL MIRROR

easier to find a car than a wandering individual, the shade of the car makes a fair shelter from the heat and the inside will stay warm deep into the cold of the desert night as well as providing fairly soft seats for a bed. Put out panel signals to show your condition.

If you absolutely must move, leave a note at the last firesite telling your plans and direction of travel. Be sure and date it in order to save confusion if someone finds it ten years later. If you don't have any paper, use a slab of bark, or scratch it in the ground or on a rock. Just make it noticeable. At the first clearing, make a signal giving the direction of travel, along with any other pertinent information, to any aircraft. Even if you are not known to be missing, the pilot will report the signal to the proper authorities.

In the United States, outside the Western mountain ranges, if you don't know the direction out, the best way is to go downhill. Keep going downhill until you come to a stream. Follow the stream on down. This has two advantages. First, settlements are often near streams; second, you can get a better food supply there. (In the Western mountains, however, this process can lead you down some of the most inaccessible canyons in the world.)

In Canada, this method has some severe limitations in that outside of the valleys of the Red River of the North, St. Lawrence, Columbia, and Fraser, most of the waterways head north—away from civilization—and the latter two go through some very rugged country before reaching habitation. Most mountain streams head into dense woods as soon as they hit timberline. The going is quite difficult under these conditions and the chance of anyone finding you in there is quite slim—you have to get out on your own, or else.

On a large lake, the deepest dip in the horizon usually indicates the exit point of a stream.

If you come to a road or railroad, follow it. There is a far greater chance of someone picking you up, or at least seeing you. When a dirt road intersects another road, you can tell which way the settlement is by noting which way any tire marks turn. (This trick is used by sociologists to determine which town a rural area trades in.)

However, be sure the roads are still in use.

Abandoned roads sometimes literally have no source (a landslide five years ago may have wiped out a half-mile [1 km] stretch just before the intersection and this has now grown over with scrub brush) and no destination (the logging camp, which was the reason for the road in the first place, was abandoned seven years ago).

On the other hand, a dirt road can look abandoned from no other cause than a heavy rain or dust storm the day before. Vegetation is the best clue. While it will take years for a well-packed rut to grow anything but an occasional patch of grass, the grass in between the ruts will be darkened from grease rubbed off the underside of a car for no longer than a week. The fresher the grease stains, the more heavily traveled it is.

Whenever you are traveling in wilderness areas under such survival conditions, leave a trail that can be followed by a search party. There are several standardized systems for marking trails. Blazes on trees, however, should not be used for conservation reasons—it makes the trees vulnerable to disease. In addition, several well-maintained hiking trails use a blaze system (with tree paint on the blaze both for visibility and to keep out anything harmful to the tree). These should not be messed up with a confusion of lost-person trails.

Other methods, however, can be used since they can be "erased" with no more effort than a kick, a scrape, or a pull.

The big problem with using trail markers is that the same systems of trail markers are often used in many areas to mark hiking trails, portages, and other routes. Thus, as with the blazes, the lost wanderings of a "befuddled" camper will make a mess of a well-marked trail system. As a result, someone is likely to take off on your trail (which may now be several years old if you managed to get out without someone having to trail you and thereby erase your trail), thinking it leads to a fabulous fishing spot, and wind up in a barely populated mining town instead.

Obviously, some system of differencing is needed. Since you are in trouble, and the standard sign for trouble is three of something, simply surround your sign with three of whatever it is you make your signs out of. This way somebody will realize that

MARKER SIGNALS   # MANUAL SIGNALS

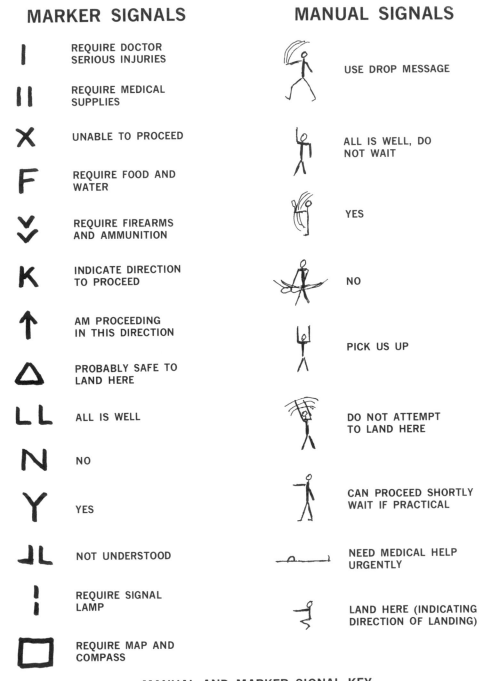

I	REQUIRE DOCTOR SERIOUS INJURIES
II	REQUIRE MEDICAL SUPPLIES
X	UNABLE TO PROCEED
F	REQUIRE FOOD AND WATER
VV	REQUIRE FIREARMS AND AMMUNITION
K	INDICATE DIRECTION TO PROCEED
↑	AM PROCEEDING IN THIS DIRECTION
△	PROBABLY SAFE TO LAND HERE
LL	ALL IS WELL
N	NO
Y	YES
⌐L	NOT UNDERSTOOD
!	REQUIRE SIGNAL LAMP
☐	REQUIRE MAP AND COMPASS

USE DROP MESSAGE

ALL IS WELL, DO NOT WAIT

YES

NO

PICK US UP

DO NOT ATTEMPT TO LAND HERE

CAN PROCEED SHORTLY WAIT IF PRACTICAL

NEED MEDICAL HELP URGENTLY

LAND HERE (INDICATING DIRECTION OF LANDING)

MANUAL AND MARKER SIGNAL KEY

MARKER SIGNALS (Cont.)

⌐↘ WILL ATTEMPT TAKE-OFF

□ AIRCRAFT SERIOUSLY DAMAGED

L REQUIRE FUEL AND OIL

W REQUIRE ENGINEER

this is a wandering trail out and not the one they should be following in. If it is fresh, they may start down it and catch up with you and show you the way out.

Under walk-out survival conditions, travel slowly for several reasons. First, it has a calming effect when you need a calming effect the most. Second, it gives any following group a chance to catch up with you. Third, under survival conditions, it is best to make camp in the early afternoon since you can't always find the ideal cave or other natural shelter and it takes awhile to find the next base. It also takes awhile to set out snares for game or go fishing to supplement your food supply. Finally, it conserves your energy under conditions which will tend to tax it to the utmost.

LIVING OFF THE LAND

There are always some foolish hunters or fishermen who will go off into the woods with just a little food. The rest, they explain grandly, is waiting for them in the woods and streams. Rarely do they manage to get an adequate diet this way, even in open season, and even if they do a steady diet of game and fish gets tiring.

A weekend camping trip on this basis does offer a considerable challenge. (After all, you can go this

TRAIL MARKERS

MESSAGE	ROCKS	GRASS (TIED IN OVERHAND KNOT)	STICKS	PEBBLES	SCRATCHES
THIS IS THE TRAIL					
TURN RIGHT					
TURN LEFT					

long without food and not suffer any effects worse than a growling stomach.) But longer periods should never be undertaken voluntarily without considerable practice. On the other hand, under survival conditions, you may be forced to do this. If you have no gun, you will need alternative skills in catching the game in addition to finding it. If you have no ax, a shelter involves some special skills if anything has happened to your tent. Fire making (or conserving) becomes a problem as your matches are used up.

While these extreme forms of survival camping come up quite rarely, you must have the knowledge of how to cope with them if you are to survive.

There are four essentials to a survival camp. The first is a water supply, which will be discussed later in more detail. The second is a fire as even in the desert nights are cold, and it also has its use in cooking. The third is a shelter—at least a windbreak to concentrate the fire's heat and to keep the cold wind out—and with a waterproof roof if precipitation is likely. And finally a bed that is reasonably soft—both for a restful night's sleep to restore vitality for the day ahead, and because a soft one will have the necessary dead-air-space insulation to keep the chill of the ground off you.

Many of the techniques used in survival camping, such as the bough bed, are not recommended as a normal camping procedure. Of course, many practices which are frowned upon by true woodsmen today or are even illegal may be used under survival conditions since the survival of the individual is the important thing. Even so, conservation should be practiced as much as possible under the circumstances.

SHELTER

Often under survival conditions you will not have a tent with you. In this case, shelter is a major problem.

In clear weather, you can sleep in the open. If the weather is cold, build a reflector fire on both sides of you, about ten feet (3 m) apart. When you are between two such fires, you will be warmer in the open than you would be in a tent without a fire.

If there is a wind, a simple windbreak is often all that is required. Make your bed in the lea of a large boulder, or build a screen by lacing brush between saplings.

If you do need shelter, start looking for it right after noon. Caves, overhanging rocks, and other natural shelters are rarely around when you need them.

If you are able to stay put, you had better prepare for a long wait before the search party gets there. Any sort of lean-to will give you adequate shelter if it is windproof. This can be done by plastering a thatched roof and walls with mud or clay. Another layer of thatch over this will keep the rain from washing it off. Evergreens make the best lean-to roofing, but any very leafy branches will do. Lap the upper rows over the lower ones like shingles. It is possible to make a roof without any leaves by weaving a large number of finger-diameter sticks to form a sort of wicker-work which is then plastered with clay. A reflector fire at the entrance will heat the shelter adequately in the coldest weather.

You can stay warmer if you eat just before going to bed as it steps up the metabolism of the body.

In survival camping in snow, the problems of maintaining heat are naturally magnified. Make a shelter first of all and then build a fire. Stay as dry as possible to avoid loss of body heat. You can often make a comfortable shelter by digging into the snow at the base of a large evergreen. Dig to the ground, piling snow up on the sides. The shelter can be roofed with evergreen branches and the bottom should definitely be floored with them for insulation and bedding. A small fire may be built at a lower level than the beds (so it will go out before carbon dioxide or carbon monoxide builds up to a dangerous level), but leave adequate space in the roof for the smoke to leave. An air passage (made by poking a hiking staff through the snow from the surface to the base of the fire) improves draft considerably.

If the snow is hard enough, a snow cave can be dug in the side of a drift. Insulate it with evergreen branches, leaving adequate air holes, and leave some kind of conspicuous marker outside so that searchers will know you are in there. It is possible to make a snow-block door to cover the entrance and let body heat warm up the inside. Snow is a good insulator—the interior of an igloo is often as high as sixty degrees above zero Fahrenheit (15°C).

The problem in desert survival shelters is double that in snow. In the desert the days are quite hot and the nights are cold. Since the dehydration problem requires any movement to be done at night, if you are moving you will need only protection from the heat of the day since your exertion will keep you warm at night.

The best shelter is to dig into the sand and put a tarp (weighted with rocks to hold it in place) over the top of the hole, with another tarp or a fold of the same tarp about six inches (15 cm) over that.

If you are under survival conditions because of a car breakdown or a forced landing, build a shelter alongside the vehicle for use during the day, and sleep in the warmer vehicle at night.

If you are adrift in a boat, a boat cabin is the best protection. Stay inside with the windows open for ventilation. If you have no cabin, or perhaps in addition to it, rig an awning from a sail, a blanket, or any other large cloth to shade the boat. Because of the reflection of the water, the sun is the main problem in boat survival. In cold weather, keep out of spray and stay as dry as possible.

CORDAGE

One of the great advantages of carrying a good bit of parachute cord is that it can be modified for almost any situation. It can be used for lashing, snares, fishing line, and a multitude of other uses.

A lean-to will not require heavy lashing cords if the cross-piece is laid in the stubs or forks of branches on the uprights. As a result, the cords from within the parachute-cord sheath will be more than adequate. They have a thirty-pound ($13\frac{1}{2}$ kg) breaking strain, more than will ever be encountered on a lean-to. In fact, you can often even separate these into their three basic strands. Several lengths of parachute cord then yield a large amount of cord for lashing or other emergency uses.

If you don't have any, or enough, such cord, you can make your own. It is time-consuming, although not really difficult. The fibers can be gathered from long grass leaves, fibrous vines, or similar vegetation. Yucca fibers from the dried leaves are excellent, being used for this purpose by most of the Southwestern tribes.

After separating the individual fibers, or at least separating small clusters of them, no larger than heavy thread, start braiding them together. The four-plait round, so favored by the lanyard makers and children's camps is far superior to the three-plait flat which is best known from hair braiding. The first braiding should be less than a sixteenth-inch ($1\frac{1}{2}$ mm) in diameter.

Splicing additional strands to the braid can be done by overlapping the strands a couple of inches (about 5 cm) and braiding them as one. Don't have more than one splice under way at a time.

Stronger rope can be made by braiding smaller sizes together in the same fashion. While this rope is a little on the stiff side—slightly more so than fresh hemp rope—it is quite serviceable, and, under certain conditions, well worth the time spent making it. It is an excellent duty for any member of the party who is injured and cannot help with the more normal camping activities as it gives him something to do instead of lying there feeling helpless, and it enables him to make a real contribution to the survival of the group.

WATER

Many people are surprised that there is no mention of food listed under the four items under Living Off the Land. Even under survival conditions, a healthy person can go for a month without food, if he conserves his energy. On the other hand, even under ideal conditions, a person can't last a week without water—in desert heat, a couple of days is closer. As a result, the need for water is given this high priority.

Getting water under survival conditions is not always as easy as it would seem to be. Streams are, or course, the most likely source. If there is no human habitation upstream, the water is usually pure. If you are not absolutely certain, however, be sure to purify it before drinking.

Some water holes in the desert are actually poisonous. These can be easily discovered by the bones of animals and the absence of plant life around them. Since these poisons cannot be removed by normal methods, it is best to avoid all water sources without vegetation except for snow and the rain water trapped in solid rock.

Conserving Water

There is a threshold of body-water level below which it is dangerous to stay and much more water is required to regain the normal balance than simply to regain the level above this amount. As a result, rationing water may be dangerous if the ration is not enough to maintain this level. Also, it is better to drink a small amount whenever you feel thirsty than a large amount periodically, disregarding any feelings of thirst. (This is one reason I like the bota—it wets the throat with a small amount of water, giving the feeling of more water than has actually been used.)

The best technique in survival conditions is to reduce the sweat rather than the water. The amount of water needed depends on the amount used. The major use of body moisture is in keeping cool by sweating. If you can reduce the amount of sweating, you can save water without ill effect.

In the desert, this is most critical because of the extremely high temperature during the day and the low humidity, which tends to dry out the body rapidly. As a result, it is practically required that any travel in the desert on foot be done at night. Two similar experiences proved this vividly to me.

My first trip to Grand Canyon was an overnight in-and-out from South Rim to Phantom Ranch and back. The trip out was made during the day. I used a full liter (1.1 quarts) of water coming out of the inner gorge to Indian Gardens and filled an empty bota there. It was almost empty at Three Mile House, where it was again filled. At One and a Half Mile House, it was about half empty, and again filled. At the Rim, it was half empty.

The second time I covered this stretch of uphill desert was the last day of a hike which had started on the North Rim. We made the final leg from River House, which is a couple of miles ($2\frac{1}{2}$ km) shorter than Phantom Ranch (but we were much more tired). It was full moon. This particular stretch is not too spectacular, and I wanted to photograph the sunrise from Three Mile House, so we started at moonrise (in the canyon, about midnight). At Indian Gardens, I added about a cup to the bota and took a long drink directly from the fountain. At Three Mile House, the water tasted hard, so I simply spit it out and took a few squirts from the bota while photographing. At One and a Half Mile House, the water had the same taste, so I still used the bota. At the Rim, I was surprised to find I had about two-thirds of the liter I left Indians Gardens with.

The weather was the same on both trips. I was much more tired on the second trip, yet I only used a little over $\frac{1}{2}$ liter at night contrasted to over $2\frac{1}{2}$ liters for the same trip in the daytime.

In boating, canoeing, or simply by water you will be much more comfortable by spending as much time in the water as possible, taking care to stay in the shade to avoid sunburn. In the case of a boat disabled in salt water, this technique is as important as night travel in the desert as a means of conserving fresh water. However, keep attached to the boat with a line to avoid being left behind in case a wind comes up and blows the boat away.

In all cases of water scarcity, avoid dehydrating agents. Alcohol is normally used in industry as a drying agent, and it works the same way in your body. Most medicines act the same way, as well as probably having harmful side-effects if used as a survival substitute for water. Smoking will do the same thing. And since digestion also uses water, reduce eating as much as is practical.

Dehydration will cause a slowing of bowel action. This is a normal reaction of the body to conserve water. Do not use laxatives under these conditions as they may dehydrate tissues to the danger point.

The body is the best place to store water. If moving requires leaving a water supply, drink as much as is physically possible before moving out, and carry as much as possible too. If you have been without water for quite a while and come upon it, take a little at a time over a fairly long period. Otherwise, drinking a lot in a hurry will probably cause nausea and will quite literally run right through you, thus wasting most of it.

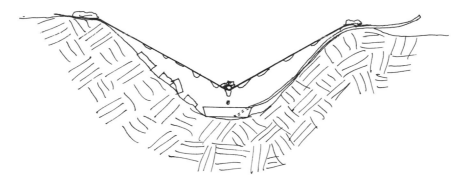

SOLAR STILL

Precipitation and Such

Two forms of precipitation have value as emergency water supplies, rain and snow, as does one "and such": dew.

Rain can be collected in any large cloth—tent, tarp, plastic sheet, boat sail, blanket, etc.—and thence be funneled off one side into any appropriate storage container. As long as the collecting and storage facilities are uncontaminated, rain is pure water.

Snow has the added advantage of being, to a great extent, its own storage container. It is best to melt snow and aerate it before using it since it tastes quite flat in its melted form. Snow can be used directly if it is melted in the mouth before swallowing. It can be eaten in moderation, like ice cream, but this will usually create a problem of maintaining body heat since the cold will then be inside as well as outside.

Dew can be collected from leaves, but the best way is to set out metal such as pots, reflector ovens, etc., to collect dew. Any object with a temperature below the dew point will condense the moisture out of the air.

Artificial "dew" can be created with solar stills. If you will be boating in salt water, one or two of these picked up from the surplus store will be a welcome addition to the survival kit. They will produce a quart (1 liter) of fresh water per day, even on a cloudy day.

Even the desert will yield drinking water with a solar still. Dig a hole about three and a half feet (1 m) in diameter and about a foot and a half (50 cm) deep. In the bottom of this conical hole, place a can, or a small pot, a cup, a foil container, etc. Over the top of the hole, sagging close to the walls of the cone, place a six-foot (2 m) square of thin polyethylene, firmly attached to the sides with the dirt which was dug out of the hole, and weight it at the bottom with a rock. A tube may, if desired, connect the container in the bottom with the surface.

Since there is moisture in the desert sand, it will evaporate when exposed to the air. Hitting the plastic, it will condense back into liquid and run down the plastic and drip into the container. The rig will make about a quart (1 liter) of water in a day. After that, it should be rebuilt in another spot as it has taken most of the water from that hole. Vegetation may be used to line the hole to increase the water. Cactus is best because of its high moisture content. To assure purity, nothing in the hole should touch the plastic.

It will require hunting, but Du Pont Tedlar 100BG-30, one mil thick, is the best plastic for the still.

Finding Water

Quite often, the obvious sources, such as streams, lakes, snow, ice, rain, etc., are not available. In such cases, you will have to find water—sometimes when it is not even to be found at the surface at all.

Other than in the desert or on beaches, fresh water can be found within a day's hike of most spots. If you are in the mountains, it is almost certain that there is a stream in any deep ravine, especially if the slope of the mountainside itself is not so steep that it runs off quickly. At higher altitudes, the snow on the mountain peaks can be used, although most of the year the little run-off streams from the bases of these snow masses is a better source because of the problems in using snow directly. Mountain meadows contain water almost to the point of being swampy. If a stream is not actually flowing through the meadow, a small amount of digging will create a catch basin which will fill in a couple of hours.

In either prairie or semi-desert, a band of trees is an indication of a creek. These are thick stands of cottonwood or even willow, thick with under-brush. They are seldom over fifty feet (15 m) wide, but extend for miles.

The typical sandy beach presents more of a problem. Sand, being porous, will have few creeks flowing through it—usually nothing smaller than a small river will have enough water to soak the sand sufficiently to flow through it at the surface or even near it. As a result, it will be quite a distance from one such stream to another and, considering the hiking qualities of loose sand, practically impossible on short-water supplies.

You can get fresh water on almost any salt-water beach by a trick of specific gravity. Salt water is heavier than fresh and, under sand, they don't mix readily. All that you have to do is to dig a short distance inland from low tide. If you don't have a shovel, use a shell or simply your hands. As soon as you dig deep enough to get a seepage, stop digging and let the water flow in. Test it by wetting a finger and tasting it. If you didn't dig too deeply, the water will be reasonably fresh. While this takes quite a while to fill up, it is unadvisable to dig any deeper until you have collected an adequate supply because if you dig too deep the salt water will flow in and ruin everything. You could also use a solar still in the hole.

Desert also presents its problems since water is usually underground. Where it is underground, it is usually too far under to be within reach of the entrenching shovel and bare-hands technique of the survival camper.

The problem, then, is how to find the under-ground sources which are close enough to the surface to reach. As a rule of thumb, if you can't reach damp sand by the time you are six inches to one foot (20 or 30 cm) deep, you won't be able to get water at any depth you can dig with your equipment.

The most likely place is where there is dense vegetation—mesquite, cottonwood, live oak. While an occasional large tree or evenly scattered small ones will dot the desert regions, a large clump of large trees requires an extensive supply of water the year around. If you don't find a flowing stream, you will usually find a distinct stream bed mean-dering along. The logical site for your well is at the base of the bank on the outer side of a bend, or anywhere you see damp sand. Failing to get a seepage from the damp sand, your trusty solar still can extract it.

In a sand desert, things are much harder since dunes cover vegetation, even where there is enough water. The foot of the steep side of a sand dune usually has water, although it will often be too alkaline to drink straight. Vinegar, lemon juice, or a few drops of hydrochloric acid will counteract the base and give a more neutral pH reading and the water will be quite potable. A bit of litmus paper might be in order in such regions.

Even in sand desert, if you see a moderate-size plant still holding its own against the dunes, it has the help of adequate water. Digging a well at the base of this plant (being careful not to uproot the plant) will often tap a slow flow of water into a collecting basin.

In most cases of needing water in the desert, the solar still described earlier is far more efficient, especially if you make three or four of them and then dig a nice long east-west trench and lie down in its coolness and shade and sleep until evening.

Grassy strips along the face of a cliff will often indicate small springs. Although their flow is not very fast, a small catch basin dug or attached to the side of the cliff will catch an adequate supply over a period of time.

The same technique used on seashores can be used at the edges of swamps if the water is brackish or too high in tannic acid to be potable. However, there is less chance of success and the still may be needed there too.

Binoculars are well worth their weight in finding the visible signs of water. In many areas, getting across rough terrain to them is more of a problem than finding the water itself. Again, the glasses help in scouting a route before you trap yourself on a hillside with no up or down possible.

Game trails will deepen and begin converging as you near a water hole. This will often lead you to a water hole whose vegetation is hidden by a hill or other obstruction. In swampy areas, the trails will lead you on solid ground through the swamp where otherwise you would literally bog down.

Streams are often muddy and the water you get from these shallow wells is almost always that way. Techniques for clarifying this water are found in Chapter 22 under Water Supply.

Vegetation

Plants will often contain a drinkable sap. The succulents are the best source for this and the barrel cactus is such a good supplier that it is protected for this reason. To get water from the barrel cactus (which is fairly large as cacti go and is shaped like a keg), cut the top off and mash the pulp against the sides. The water will collect in this cavity. Since this will kill the cactus, it should never be done unless the need is genuine.

While not as efficient as the barrel cactus, practically any cactus will serve the same purpose with a bit of equipment. Simply remove the hard, waxy skin and mash the pulp in a container. Naturally, the larger the cactus, the easier this is. A chunk of prickly-pear stem can be trimmed of its spines and the inner pulp cut into bite-size pieces and chewed directly for the water.

Grapevine will serve as a water source. Cut through the vine with a diagonal cut. Then cut several feet (1 or 2 m) above it and let the sap drip into your mouth or a container. This is even more effective in the tropics with the lianas.

Many plants have highly saturated fruit. Watermelon is the obvious example, but it is rarely encountered in survival conditions. However, in season, prickly pears have only slightly less water, and I think they taste much better. They should be a dark red-purple. Scrape off all the little fuzzy thorns (which fester badly if they get into your skin—you can't remove them). Peel off the hard skin and eat the pulp inside. The seed are a lot like blackberry seeds; you can chew them up or spit them out.

In woodlands, the situation is a lot better. Wild plums and various wild berries are not only high in moisture content, they serve well as a source of quick-energy sugars. There are usually one or more ripe all seasons except winter and early spring.

FIRE WITHOUT MATCHES

Usually your match supply runs low when your food supply does. While you should always carry a small amount of waterproof matches as a reserve supply, there are times, especially under survival conditions, when they are used up or must be severely rationed.

There are several ways to save on matches, or even of doing without them altogether. The first way is to keep the fire going. Use only hardwoods for the campfire. They burn down to coals which stay alive for hours. Put a tarp a few feet over the fire in case of rain. A ditch around the fireplace, as around a tent, will prevent flooding in a prolonged rain. Build the fire up before going to bed and there will be coals the next morning for building a new fire.

In dry weather, another method is useful. Lay the fire so that it will burn into a large log. Cover the coals with ashes and then with dry dirt. The next morning, dig it up and use the smoldering coals to start a new fire. Keep the covering loose as it should be able to get some air—just not enough to permit it to burst into flame.

In the absence of matches, there are still several ways to make a fire. The old reliable flint and steel is one of the best match substitutes. A good set

FLINT AND STEEL

should include a piece of flint, a piece of steel, and a piece of charred wicking.

The flint should be as small as can comfortably be held while using. To really conserve space, a musket flint is good. These are, oddly enough, still available from dealers serving muzzle-loading-gun enthusiasts. They will cost about fifteen or twenty cents and be of the best grade flint obtainable. It is difficult to hold the small flake of flint in your hand, but you can pad the jaws of your repair-kit pliers with cloth or leather and hold it in that. This is similar to the hammer arrangement of a flintlock gun.

The steel should be about four inches (10 cm) long, one inch or less (2 cm) wide, and an eighth-inch (3 mm) thick. It should be hardened, high-carbon steel. Test several specimens on a grinding wheel to find one which really kicks out the sparks.

The wick of a jeweler's alcohol lamp is the best spark catcher. It is big enough to hold easily. The more traditional charred cloth is too flimsy to survive the shaking the average survival kit gets in the course of an average camping trip, much less until the time comes that it is actually needed. The wick should be one to one and a half inches (25 to 35 mm) long. Light one end. Blow out the flame and smother the sparks. Dip the other end in glue to keep it from fraying.

Extra fine steel wool is another good spark catcher, as is a mouse nest if you can find one.

With a good set, flint and steel is a reasonably quick way to start a fire. Hold the steel upright with the wick at the base, charred end up. Strike a glancing blow down the steel. When you catch a spark on the wick, blow on it gently. Let the glow brighten. Light your tinder from this. Shredded cedar bark, pussywillow fuzz, birch bark, milkweed, or even dried pine needles serve ably as tinder. When the tinder catches, quickly put it into the fire to catch the kindling.

A cigarette lighter is a good match substitute. A lighter, fueled and sealed with waterproof tape, is a good reserve match supply. Even if the fuel is gone, you still have an inferior flint-and-steel set. A carbide lamp has the same mechanism. Some match safes have a strip of sparking material along the sides or bottom, so they will spark a knife.

The old hunters with their flintlocks never had trouble starting a fire. All they had to do was to put a piece of cedar bark in the pan with the priming powder and pull the trigger. The bark lit. In those days, the standard way to get a light was with a gadget resembling a pistol without a barrel and with a tinder box in place of the priming pan. The flintlock was the same as the gun's. Flint and steel is quite reliable if you know how to use it.

The metal match is a more modern device and is used much the same way, cutting off long pieces in a whittling action with a knife. The whittled pieces take the place of the charred wick.

Quite often a camper will have neither matches nor flint and steel for starting a fire. Under these conditions, the camper's imagination and a few old techniques will have to do the job. Lenses are an often overlooked way to start a fire. Tinder, much like that required for flint and steel, is needed in order to ignite easily. A lens from binoculars, telescopic gun sights, or a strong magnifying glass will ignite paper or natural tinder. You can even make a lens from clear ice by scraping it with a knife and smoothing it in your hands.

Electricity is another method. A car or airplane battery can supply the current. Connect an insulated wire to each terminal. Scratch the free ends together to get a spark. Light the tinder from that.

A couple of flashlight dry cells and some fine steel wool will start a fire. Hold the batteries tightly as they would fit in the flashlight. Hold one end of the steel wool under the negative pole at the bottom of the stack and hold the other end against the small positive button (not with your finger directly on top!). It will start to glow at the positive end and you will be able to light tinder by blowing on the glowing steel wool.

In the case of a magneto-ignited outboard motor, remove a spark plug with the high-tension wire attached. Ground the base of the plug against the engine block and crank the engine to get the spark. The cigarette lighter of a car is another way to get electricity translated into enough heat to light a fire. In all of these, an old rag soaked in gasoline will make the ignition much more dependable as well as easier.

It is possible to start a fire with a gun. Remove the bullet or the shot and wadding from a shell

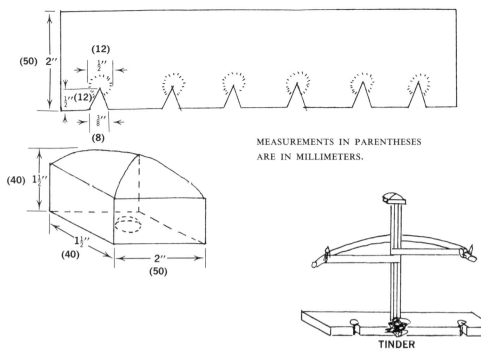

MEASUREMENTS IN PARENTHESES
ARE IN MILLIMETERS.

TINDER

FIRE BOW

and sprinkle part of the powder on the tinder in a well-built fire. Put a piece of frayed cloth into the cartridge and fire it upward. It will come down smoldering, if not actually in flames. Blow on it to build up the glow and touch it to the gunpowder-primed tinder to light the fire.

The cliché formula of rubbing two sticks together is all folklore. It is quite unlikely that a fire could be built by this method even if you didn't tire out first. However, there are wood-against-wood-friction fire starters. By far the best of these is the fire bow, from the Southwestern indians. It works quickly for a wood-against-wood friction although not as fast as flint and steel.

The critical aspect in the mechanism is the angle and depth of the notch in the fire board. The drill should be octagonal instead of round. Be sure to lubricate the spindle at the top of the drill to keep it from catching fire. Use soap or candle wax. The drill and the fire board should be made of the same material. The best woods are yucca, cottonwood, aspen, cedar, cypress, and elm, in that order. The cottonwood root is better than the trunk wood. (This applies to any use of cottonwood.)

Put the bow, together with a loose pile of tinder, in the notch (but not covering the base of the drill itself). Move the bow in smooth, full arcs back and forth. Press down on the spindle as much as possible without slowing down the drill action.

When the drill starts smoking, speed up the action and possibly press a little harder. When the smoke indicates that you have a spark, remove the drill and blow gently on the hole until it glows brightly. Push a bit of the tinder into the notch to catch the spark. When the tinder starts glowing, take the fire away and blow on the tinder until it flames up and you can put it in your fire.

EDIBLE ANIMALS

Animals provide a wide range of emergency food. North America has very few animals that are

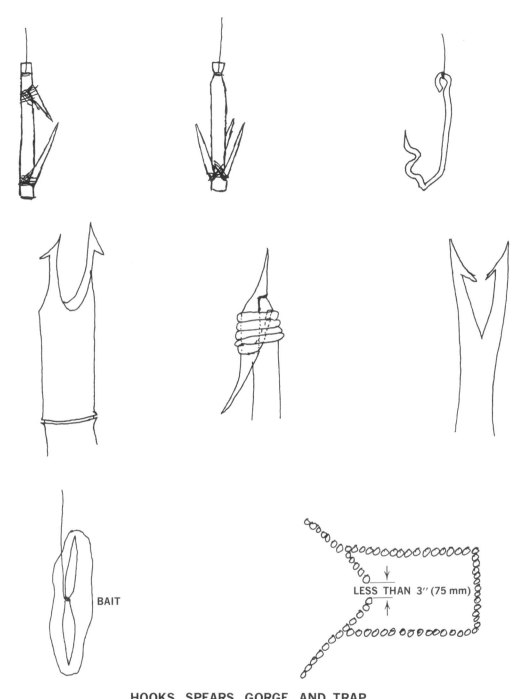

LESS THAN 3" (75 mm)

BAIT

HOOKS, SPEARS, GORGE, AND TRAP

poisonous to eat. All mammals are edible, except for the livers of the polar bear and the ring and bearded seals, which contain toxic amounts of vitamin A. The rest of their meat is edible. Since they are limited to the arctic regions, the problem will probably never arise.

All reptiles are edible. The rattlesnake, iguana, sea turtle, and snapping turtle are considered in the gourmet category, but the others are edible in an emergency.

Although all birds are edible, some (like the buzzard, spruce grouse, and loon) may not particularly taste it.

All amphibians are edible, but since many (such as toads and some salamanders) have poison glands in their skin, you should skin them before cooking.

Except for a few rare salt-water fish found occasionally on the Pacific Coast (these few are rather strange-looking, so that is a warning sign), all fish are edible. Fresh-water fish especially should be cooked thoroughly to kill parasites.

All mollusks (shellfish) are edible except for the black meat of mussels and clams found on the Pacific Coast from May to October. At other times, and in other places, even it is edible.

Crustaceans are an excellent supply of edible meat. Crayfish and crabs are especially easy to catch.

In salt water, a wind-drifting boat and a plankton net will supply an abundant amount of a fish-tasting paste, as well as an occasional crab or shrimp which may be eaten or used as bait to catch fish.

Insects are edible too, with some exceptions. Don't bother with caterpillars nor with moths or butterflies. Most beetles are too bitter. Grubs (insect larvae, not worms) are edible, as are grasshoppers, cicadas, and crickets.

Watch for animals such as raccoons, badgers, and bears to see what they eat. Humans can eat almost any food that they eat. However, stay clear of carrion.

FINDING AND CATCHING ANIMALS

Streams are the best source of food. Most small ones have crayfish. These are quite good and easily

caught. However, it takes several to make a meal. Fish are found in most sizable bodies of water that are not polluted. You can make fishing equipment with a pocket knife if you have to, and bait can be found in, or alongside, the water.

A bundle of sticks shaped into a hollow cone, pointing downstream in an opening in a dam, will trap fish. Spears and traps should be used only in case of absolute necessity as they are usually illegal except for rough fish. With the spears, remember the refraction of the water and aim a bit below the fish.

The gorge is baited with the gorge parallel to the line. When the fish swallows it, it pulls loose and goes crosswise and catches in the throat or stomach. A barbless hook is easily made from stiff

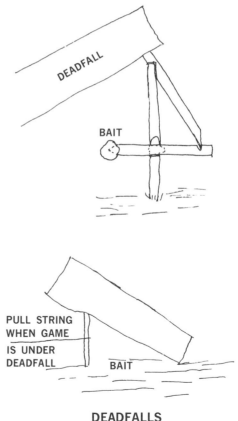

DEADFALLS

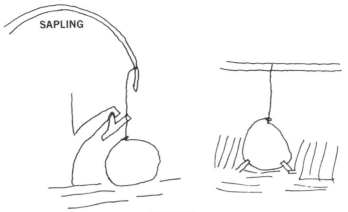

SNARES

wire and is legal most anywhere. However, you have to keep a tight line on it at all times to keep the fish from throwing it.

When you catch a fish, open up its stomach and see what is in it. Since you know what the fish are eating, your chances of catching more are better. Catch some live ones to use for bait.

Aside from projectile weapons (firearms, bows, slings, blowguns, boomerangs, etc.), the best way to catch mammals is with snares. They are easy to make—the hard part is in getting the animal into the snare. You will need to set at least six or eight to have a good chance of catching something. They should set overnight in game runs or the entrances of burrows.

You will lose less of your catch to predators if you set the forms which pull the victim off the ground by means of a bent sapling, a dead weight, or a similar force.

For rabbit, a four-inch (10 cm) -diameter loop a couple of inches (5 cm) off the ground will do the job. Three-inch (75 mm) loops mounted on a pole leaning against a heavily used tree will snare squirrels as they use the pole to mount the tree faster. Snares along game runs can be made more effective if the trail is narrowed so that there is no opening except the noose. However, make the obstruction look natural or even a rabbit will get suspicious.

Most areas are full of abandoned burrows and game runs. Make sure that the spot is in use before

wasting a snare on it. Look for fresh tracks in game runs, bits of fur on thorn bushes, or actually observe an animal using it. Look for fresh dirt at the entrance of a burrow, diggings or droppings a few feet away, or see it used by the occupant.

Birds will rarely be taken in snares, even baited ones. You will have to creep up on one sleeping and use a stick or throw net, or else use some type of projectile weapon. There are, however, some types of traps which work, although they require baiting—if you have plenty of one food which will make a good bait but are tired of it and want some variety in the menu, this may be a good idea. Most upland game birds, particularly quail, will fall for a trap which spirals inward with a stick wall about a foot and a half (50 cm) high. Bait the trail and they follow it around and around until, when they are in the small space in the center, you can catch them with your bare hands.

The Indians of Mexico use a large gourd, with peep holes, fitted over their heads. With this over their heads, they tread water over to a flock of ducks and quickly pull one under, wring its neck, tie it on a belt, and go after another. You might be able to improvise a substitute. The critical idea is that it should appear to be drifting so it doesn't alarm the ducks.

Insects represent a good (and very little used) food source. Grubs (beetle larvae) are quite edible when roasted. You can find them in rotting logs. Grasshoppers are the best for several reasons. They are large as insects go. They are easily caught. Their food value is as high as peanuts (one of the highest in calories for the weight). The migratory grasshopper (locust) is eaten as a staple in many parts of the world, notably the Near East. In fact, the people there wonder why we have such a strong feeling against eating them. They point out that the locust eats only good, clean grain and we refuse to eat the locust, yet we will eat the meat of a hog that has had nothing but garbage since it was weaned. Legs, wings, and the hard, chitinous skin of insects are inedible. The skin, however, is usually removed after cooking.

EDIBLE PLANTS

The utilization of the flora of the region for survival food depends on one of two things: being in the area in the proper season, or liking greens. For a complete discussion of plant survival food, see one of the survival books in Chapter 54. An adequate treatment of the subject would take a disproportionate amount of space—especially the illustrations.

However, a few generalizations are in order.

Never eat a plant that has a milky sap. (The exception is the dandelion which makes good greens when the tender shoots are boiled.)

Do not eat plants, especially grains, which are spoiled or have a mottled or speckled surface, as they are probably diseased.

Never eat mushrooms. Many are incurably poisonous, and the food value of the non-poisonous ones is not worth the bother of picking them.

A plant is generally safe to eat if it is eaten by rodents, or omnivores such as the raccoon, bear, or badger. Birds are not good test animals; some will even eat poison-ivy berries.

If you are not sure about a plant, cook it and sample it in very small quantities until you are certain it is edible. Wait at least twenty-four hours after the first pea-size piece before trying another. (The exceptions are the water hemlock and poisonous varieties of mushrooms which are fatal even in very small doses.)

All nuts are edible, and most are nutritious and quite common in many areas. Acorns must be cooked and made into flour, but the other nuts may be eaten raw or roasted. Not to be overlooked are the piñon pines of the Southwest which have a delicious nut-like seed.

Most leafy plants may be made into greens if they are not spiny or stiff. (Another exception: the stinging nettle is edible if dropped into boiling water and allowed to cool.)

Plant food has many advantages over meat for the camper under survival conditions. It is rich in vitamin C, an item almost lacking in any meat other than liver. You don't have the difficulty in collecting plants that you do in bagging an animal. Many plant foods may be eaten raw—an advantage when your matches are gone or in wet weather.

SURVIVAL KIT

The weight—a pound or so ($\frac{1}{2}$ kg)—invested in a survival kit will be welcome if the need arises and will be helpful in varying the menu. The kit should include the following:

40 yards (35 m) of 10- to 15-pound ($4\frac{1}{2}$ to 6 kg) -test monofilament fishing line*
fish hooks
split shot sinkers
a small float
a metal signal mirror
a polyethylene or Tedlar sheet (four-to-six-foot [1 or 2 m] diameter) for solar still
an orange smoke flare (optional)
a folding radar reflector (optional) for boats in salt water
a second compass (a reserve to your regular one)
a key to manual and marker signals (on waterproof paper)
waterproof matches and/or a fueled and sealed cigarette lighter
a parachute cord
hydrochloric acid in a taped bottle with a dropper (optional) for desert alkali water, and possibly a bit of litmus paper strip

*In addition to the regular use, this is also excellent for making snares (almost invisible) and even emergency sewing.

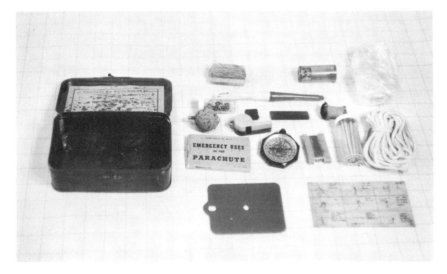

A well-equipped survival kit is necessary when camping in deep wilderness.

A smaller version of the survival kit can be packed into a 35 mm. film can.

a flint-and-steel set (optional)
a plankton net (optional) for boats in salt water
jerky and/or penole in air-tight packages—pemmican may be substituted for the jerky in cold weather (optional)

Some writers on this subject have recommended the addition of small wet and dry fishing flies to this kit. For the sportsman who is primarily fishing anyway, this is a good idea since tackle boxes can get lost along with other camping equipment. However, for the average camper they could cause a bit of legal difficulty since in many areas the possession of artificial lures is considered evidence of intent to fish, and unless you also have a valid fishing license you could be in trouble. Natural bait will take fish more reliably anyway. This is for survival, after all, not sport.

The entire survival kit should weigh less than a pound (200 g) and fit in a cloth bag or metal box to be carried in the pack.

Even this could be too big for the hike or the hunting trip from base camp in a wilderness area if you are carrying other gear. Under these circumstances, you don't expect to be under survival conditions. Yet bad weather (or an earthquake such as marooned several campers just outside Yellowstone in 1959) can make even a couple of miles (3 km) to base camp too far if it is over a suddenly flooded stream or rain-slickened rock slide.

A miniaturized version, developed by the Boy Scouts, will fit into a 35 mm film can or 2 x 2 x $\frac{1}{2}$ (5 x 5 x 1 cm) plastic box such as package fishing equipment. It contains the following:

2 fish hooks
10′ (3 m) of fishing line wrapped on a match stick
2 split shot sinkers
2 aspirin tablets wrapped in aluminum foil
2 prepared bandages
3′ (1 m) of adhesive tape wrapped on a toothpick
a scalpel blade protected with adhesive tape
10′ (3 m) of fine steel wire (for snares)
8 waterproof matches
a compass

The compass is the small type often inset into gunstocks. It is hardly a precision instrument, but will do as a reserve.

One of these small kits, plus a snake-bite kit, is all the emergency gear required for such hikes from base camp.

CHAPTER THIRTY-FIVE

Measurements

The average camper, in the normal course of his camping, will have no need to make precise measurements of anything. Therefore, carrying around accurate measuring devices on the grounds that "it might come in handy sometime" is carrying around so much extra ballast. Yet there are situations where the skill is most useful.

In building a bridge across a chasm on your vacation land, you need to know how wide the span must be when you cannot go across it with a tape measure to find out. You will also need to know how tall a tree is so you won't chop down one that is too short for the job.

The fine camp sport of orienteering requires as much skill in measuring distance accurately as in using a compass with precision.

Making an accurate map of your favorite camping grounds requires the knowledge of several measurements, vertically and horizontally, that can't be obtained with either tape measure or pacing. For this you have to be your own transit.

When you need to know whether to start something which has to be finished before dark, you have the problem of finding out how long until sundown. This can be done without knowing what time sunset is. Without a watch at all, you can still get within ten minutes of accuracy.

These problems require a certain knowledge of simple techniques. But they cannot be solved in any other way practical in camping.

TOOLS

The basic unit of measurement in this system is you. I happen to be a perfect size for this since my stride is two and a half feet (75 cm), my shoe is one foot (30 cm), and the last joint of my index finger is one inch (25 mm). You might not come out with such even divisions, but all it requires is a little more math work.

The second item of equipment is a stick or two. These should be measured to get a known size from them, but they can be found on the site and measured there just as easily as carrying them in. A hiking staff, however, is most useful in this regard. In my younger, Boy Scout days, when I had more need to practice these arts than I do now, I had my hiking staff marked, by wood-burning, in one-inch intervals.

Occasionally a piece of rope tied into a ring with twelve equally spaced knots will be useful. This is a completely accurate method of finding a right angle without using a compass (the circle-drawing or the magnetic kind). Form it into a triangle, three, four, and five units on each side. Pythagorean formula (the square of the hypotenuse, etc.), nine plus sixteen equals twenty-five, does the rest. Actually, this is far older than Pythagoras. The ancient Egyptians used it to resurvey the farm lands after the annual silt deposit from the Nile flood. However, if you have one, a magnetic compass will be quicker.

And finally, an assistant, holding things, moving things, or just standing in the right spot is often useful.

DISTANCE

The obvious way to measure distance is to pace it off and multiply the length of your pace by the number you took to cover the distance. Be sure to compensate for steps which were undersize or oversize because of obstacles as well as for outright detours. Other than that, pacing is a fairly accurate method. Jogging at the same stride as walking will speed up the process of measuring a large distance, or in orienteering against the clock. Alternating fifty to a hundred paces of each is the fastest with the least energy consumed. It is also a good physical-conditioning exercise.

The problem in measuring distance is when you can't pace it off. Then you have to resort to more indirect methods.

One of the more common needs for measuring distance is in getting the answer to the question, "How far away is the storm?" By getting this answer over a period of time, you also answer, "How fast is it coming?" and "When will it get here?" and "Is it going around?" This is really fairly easy. Simply time the interval between the lightning and the thunder and figure four and half seconds to the mile (just under 3 seconds [2.8] to the kilometer). Anything over twenty-five seconds probably won't be heard anyway. If you don't have a watch, count chimpanzees ("One chimpanzee, two chimpanzees, three chimpanzees. . .") to roughly approximate the seconds.

A smaller distance to be measured is "How far is it across the lake (river, canyon, swamp, down-fall, rock slide, etc.)?" Here we get into the proof of the imagination of the human brain, because there are countless ways, ranging from a sight-and-pace instead of the transit-and-chain survey-or's technique to a carefully controlled look.

The carefully controlled look is quick, but not too accurate. It is called the Napoleon method, although I haven't been able to find the connection with Bonaparte. To measure with this method, tuck your chin down to your chest. Look at the point in the distance and pull your hat down so that it covers to that point. Next, slowly turn, keeping the hat, your chin, and your body in approximately the same position relative to each other, and face across a stretch of reasonably flat terrain. Pick out a spot which your hat position will indicate as being the same distance away as the point you are measuring. Pace off the distance and convert it to feet or meters. Be sure the distance you are pacing is fairly level or you will get a false reading.

Technique number two involves the use of right triangles and it is amazingly accurate. To find the distance (X), sight an object (a tree) and then along a flat area ninety degrees from the first line of sight. Pace off an arbitrary distance (A) and place a stake. For accuracy, it should be at least one quarter the distance across whatever you are measuring. Continue in exactly the same direction for one half that distance ($\frac{1}{2}$A) and place another stake. Move out at a right angle from this second stake (away from the distance being measured) until the target spot (the tree) is lined up with the first stake. Measure the distance from that spot to the second stake, multiply by two, and convert to feet or meters. That is your answer.

A third method requires a map-making compass and a piece of paper. It is basically a fast version of the triangle method. Take a bearing on the distance you need measured and draw a line on the paper the proper angle from "north" on the paper (the azimuth of A-C). Pace off an arbitrary distance (A-B) in any convenient direction and mark it on the paper. This line should be drawn to scale. At this point (B) take another bearing on C and draw that on the paper. Using the scale, measure the distance you need to know.

HEIGHT

Measuring vertical distances without instruments is even harder than measuring horizontal ones. The big problem is that of perspective. A good illustration of this is the artist's paintbrush method. This involves holding a stick out at arm's length and moving it so that your hand is at the ground and the tip is at a known distance as you sight over it. By moving the sighting along the stick upward, inchworm fashion, the error starts creeping in. Try

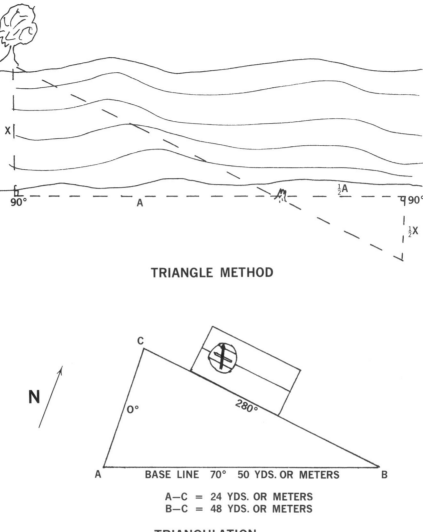

TRIANGLE METHOD

TRIANGULATION

BASE LINE 70° 50 YDS. OR METERS

A—C = 24 YDS. OR METERS
B—C = 48 YDS. OR METERS

it against a skyscraper office building and see how, by that method, if the distance from the third to the fourth floor is ten feet (3 m) (probably accurate), then the distance from the thirty-fifth to the thirty-sixth floor is two feet (60 cm) (preposterous).

Obviously, any system for measuring height must automatically compensate for the perspective. The only real problem is that practically all of the accurate methods require a large amount of clear, flat, level terrain under the item to be measured. While this is good for flagpoles, buildings, and smokestacks, it is often impossible for trees and cliffs, and the latter is more often what we need to measure. However, one or more of the following methods will generally work out.

The first is the shadow method. The sun's rays

being essentially parallel, the shadow is proportional to the object. Measure the length of the object's shadow by pacing; measure the length of your own shadow. Divide the length of the object's shadow by the length of your own and multiply by your height. This will give you the height of the object.

Method number two requires a stick or an ax handle. It is a lumberman's method for measuring a tree. Sight the tree (or whatever else it may be) on the stick (the same as the artist's brush) and pivot it down until you are measuring a length of ground also at right angles to your line of sight. This is away from you, so it preserves the same perspective as the object. Make sure the point on the stick is still lined up with the base of the object. Go to the place indicated by the end of the stick and pace the distance from that point to the object.

The distance is the same as the height.

The inch-to-foot method is the reason my old hiking staff was marked off. Pace off any distance from the object (the farther, the more accurate, within reason) as long as it is some multiple of eleven. At the end of this distance, place a staff or pole. Pace off one-eleventh that much farther. You now have twelve of these units between you and the object and the pole is one unit away from you. Get down on the ground and sight at the top of the object. Note where, on the pole, the line of sight hit. Measure the distance from that point to the ground, in inches. The number is the height of the object in feet. For metric system, pace out nine units plus one unit beyond the pole. A centimeter on the stick gives you ten centimeters on the object.

PART VIII

Ropework

For the purpose of this section, the term "knot" will have a somewhat restricted definition—hitches, splices, and lashings will be considered separately. Under this definition, a knot is a means of forming a rope in a certain pattern to do a specific job, which holds by its own friction, and does not unlay the rope. A hitch depends partly on the friction of the rope against an object other than itself. A splice requires unlaying the rope. And a lashing is a way of fastening an object by wrapping it with some form of cordage, depending almost entirely on the friction with the object lashed.

A good knot or hitch should be easy to tie, should hold under the conditions desired, and should be easy to untie. The splices are permanent, and lashings, while improvised, are assumed to be permanent.

In the long and complex history of ropework, different names arose for the same pattern of knots and hitches. Some of these (which were based on the different uses of the knot or hitch, its origin, or some other reason not related to the actual pattern) are still in use and the expert in ropework will undoubtedly protest that the term I have given is incorrect. In this section, I have generally used the same name for the same pattern, regardless of the use. For instance, I call a larkshead pattern a larkshead even though technically speaking it is a cow hitch, girth hitch, bale sling, or whatever.

On the other hand, some names are too well established to use the same name. Typical of these are the sheet bend and bowline. The latter is tied with the bight, the former is tied onto the bight. Although the finished pattern is exactly the same, one is used to tie unequal-diameter rope together, the other to make a fixed loop in itself.

Also, when a knot is capsized (changed in shape without actually being untied, usually by a strain in a different direction from the usual), it changes its name. In a sense, a larkshead is simply a capsized square knot, and a granny knot capsizes into two half-hitches (which is a vast improvement).

417

While many knots and hitches can be used interchangeably, there is at least one purpose for which a given knot or hitch is vastly superior to all others. In this book, I have restricted the examples to one of each category. The basis of selection was that it be a commonly known knot, easy to tie, and better than any other commonly known knot for the purpose.

CHAPTER THIRTY-SIX

Rope

There are three basic kinds of rope—layed, braided, and combination. The layed rope is made by twisting the fibers in the same direction into strands. Three (or, rarely, four) strands are likewise twisted together to form the rope. Braided rope, as its name implies, has several strands which are braided together. Sash cord is an excellent example of this type. The combination has several small ropes (made up of layed strands) enclosed in a braided sheath or cover. Parachute cord is the best example of this type.

While braided and combination ropes wear better, this difference is of little concern in camp ropework. In fact, layed rope is better in the quarter-inch or larger sizes since it is practically impossible to splice a braided rope. Parachute cord is an exception in desirability because of its high strength-to-weight ratio and its versatility. Binder twine, which is used mostly in lashing, is simply a layed strand—it is not even a rope, although three of them can easily be made into a rope if the need arises.

The strength of a rope is also important. Nylon is probably the best from this standpoint as it also stretches quite a bit and helps absorb shocks which would otherwise break a rope. Hemp is adequate for most uses and, because it is more economical, it is often the best choice.

The twistings of the rope into knots, hitches, and such weakens the total strength because of the strain put on the individual fibers. The amount of this weakening depends not only on the material the rope is made from, but also on the type of knot, hitch, or whatever, and the direction of strain in relation to it. A clove hitch on the opposite side of the rail from the strain has almost ninety per cent of the rope's strength preserved, while one with the strain coming out at a right angle has only half that much. This is because of the sharpness of the bend. A tourniquet tie, which has the most and the sharpest bends of all, weakens the rope so much that it can easily be broken with just a twist of the wrist. Interestingly enough, the knot itself is fairly strong because of the compacting of the fibers in the knot, so the rope breaks just outside the knot itself.

Even with the number of items of ropework being kept down to a one-to-one ratio with the uses, some will not be needed by the average camper. A bowline on a coil is a necessity only to mountain climbers, although it is nonetheless useful for keeping coils of rope neatly stored without tangling and therefore not limited to the climber. The camper who knows all the items of ropework in this part will always have a technique to fit every situation, without being a walking encyclopedia of ropework either.

Additional knowledge of ropework can be gained

by using one of the books in Chapter 54. Many a sailor's knife sheath and handle were decorated with knotwork as were many of his other tools. Knotting, like leathercraft, is a useful craft for the camper to use to decorate his gear. Unlike leathercraft, it is one which can be worked in camp on a rainy day or when it is too hot for other activities. It requires few tools and the material is easily stuffed into a spare corner of the pack when moving on.

I have left out one very standard knot, the sheepshank, simply because there is a better method. It is designed to shorten a rope without cutting it, but it holds only as long as there is a strain on it. A far more logical method would be to untie one end of the rope and retie it shorter. For some reason, this logical approach is overlooked. Also, this "new" method puts far less strain on the rope, since the sheepshank is one of the roughest of all the knots on the rope fibers.

LAYED ROPE

There are two materials commonly used for camping rope: hemp (including its allied fibers) and nylon. Hemp (plus sisal, ramie, and similar plant fibers) is the most common and the cheapest. It is a good, serviceable rope, and with proper care will last several seasons. However, it tends to have loose fibers which stick out from the rope and will often stick in your hands like small splinters when you work the rope. If you keep them singed off, the rope is easily worked.

Nylon is a bit more expensive, but it lasts longer. Its best representative, other than parachute cord which is not layed, is the 7/16-inch (11 mm) mountain-climbing rope. However, other nylon ropes are better suited for general camping use since they are far cheaper than the highly elastic mountain ropes.

Other materials, such as polyethylene (which floats), cotton, Dacron, and similar substances are either too expensive or too weak for use in camping. A fairly new material, polypropylene, combines the floating ability of the polyethylene rope with a strength between that of hemp and nylon.

PARACHUTE CORD

The cord from parachute risers has a versatility that earns it discussion apart from the other ropes. This particular rope has a parallel-layed center (the strands are not twisted around each other) and a braided outside. The entire rope can be used for anything that can be done with a five-hundred-pound (225 kg)-test line.

The core cords have a thirty-pound (130 kg) test and are ideal for lashing or any other use requiring stout twine. They make good snares for small game.

The core cords are layed of three strands which, naturally, have a ten-pound ($4\frac{1}{2}$ kg) test each. Usually at least one of these is black and will give you, when unlayed, three good fishing lines. The others may be darkened with dirt, nut husks, or any other substance you have at hand.

The braided sheath, by itself, makes a good shoestring.

The parachute cord is easily kept from unlaying by burning the ends to fuse the fibers together.

CARE OF THE ROPE

Most people have rope or other cordage around the house—and this is the problem. Nothing much ever happens to the stuff. As a result, they get the idea that rope is pretty durable material. In the house, where the only problems it faces are a bit of strain now and then and frequent tangles, it can hold up well, treated any old way. In camp, however, it is a different matter.

First of all, there is the ground, usually slightly damp after a night of dew, and always teeming with fungus spores which would dearly like to nestle in the fibers of a good hemp rope. Then there is the pack that the rope gets crammed into, while slightly damp, to cook awhile and let the mildew go to work. And there is the dirt, sand, and other abrasives which gnaw at the fibers of the rope. No wonder the average camp rope looks like something off an old shipwreck. And some people blame the rope for not holding up.

Care of a rope is really no harder than the care of a tent or any other piece of camping equipment of vegetable origin. First, whip the ends. This keeps it from unlaying, fraying, and generally coming apart at the ends. Second, keep the rope neatly coiled and off the ground when it isn't in use. Neither of these precautions is difficult. Whipping is a once-only chore with most ropes, and coiling becomes second nature when you have learned how.

Keep the rope out of the rain unless it is an essential part of the tent or other outdoor gear. If it is used for guying, slack the rope before it gets drenched. Always let it dry out before packing, or if this is impossible, dry it out at the first chance, the same as you would a tent.

Don't use a load-bearing rope (such as a tent guy) after it shows signs of breaking, as it can't be trusted. Retire it to some duty more in keeping with its condition, such as a stake loop for the tent. Often, if the rope is in otherwise good condition, the worn part can be cut out and the remainder can still be used for normal purposes. If it has finally worn out completely, the frayed-up remains of a hemp rope makes excellent tinder for starting a fire.

CHAPTER THIRTY-SEVEN

Knots

LEARNING TO TIE KNOTS

It is difficult to learn to tie knots by reading a book. The typical explanation requires previous knowledge of knots and a good imagination as well. Some writers have given up entirely and just used pictures. If you have good visual perception, this is adequate.

I don't say that the method I am using here is the best for everyone, but I have success with it. At best, though, it will only show you how. The only way to really learn to tie a knot is to practice.

Get about three feet (1 m) of venetian-blind cord. Whip the ends (see Chapter 41). Learn the parts of the knots; all explanations will be given in these terms rather than "go around the part you just went through." Follow both the text and the drawings, checking as you go. If this doesn't help, find someone who can tie the knot and have him teach you.

Practice the knot several times with the book, then try it from memory. Try it with your eyes closed; you may have to tie it in the dark sometime. Then to test your ability, try to teach someone else (but not necessarily in writing). If you can do that, you really know how to tie it. The Seattle Mountaineers claim that the true test is to tie it in a cold shower with your eyes closed, since you will encounter these conditions on the mountain sometime. I think an even tougher test is to tie it dry, pull it very tight, and then try to untie it in a cold shower with your eyes closed.

PARTS OF A KNOT

The parts of a knot or hitch have names. These names go back to the days of sailing vessels when sailors prided themselves on their ability to tie complex knots. Even the most complex ones can be described by using only these few terms.

The end of the rope used in the tying is called the "running end." The rest of the rope, from the part of the knot being tied to the opposite end, is called the "standing part." The tip end of the standing part is called the "bitter end" and has entered our common language along with "at the end of my rope." When the running end is bent back on

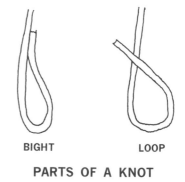

BIGHT   LOOP

PARTS OF A KNOT

itself without crossing, it forms a "bight." When it crosses, it is a "loop." When the running end is on your side of the standing part, it is an "overhand loop"; if it is on the opposite side, it is an "underhand loop."

These, plus the "turn," which is a 360° turn around the rope or object, are the basic parts of any knot or hitch known. In the descriptions of the various knots, however, the turn is often referred to as a "spiral" since the direction, toward or away from the standing part, is often a factor in the way the knot is tied.

END KNOTS

The overhand and figure-eight knots are the most useful end knots for camping. Their primary use is to prevent the end of the rope from unlaying. The overhand is more compact, but can work loose under strain. The figure-eight knot is only slightly less compact, but has considerably more strength.

Other, more specialized knots are used to prevent the end of a rope from coming out of a block on a boat rigging, for instance, but they are of little use to the camper because of their complexity.

Overhand Knot

To tie an overhand knot, make a loop and pass the running end through it. As with all knots, finish by pulling it tight. The problem with the overhand knot is that with heavy use it will capsize off the end or become too tight and difficult to untie.

OVERHAND KNOT

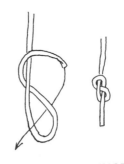

Figure-Eight Knot

The figure-eight knot is tied in the same way as the overhand knot, except that you give the loop a half-twist before you pass the running end through. Just be sure you don't twist it the wrong way and turn the loop into a bight.

The figure eight is a bit easier to untie after hard use and has a little more bulk, which is helpful in keeping the rope pulling out of a hole.

ROPE-TO-ROPE KNOTS

These are various means of tying two pieces of rope together. They each have a different use.

Square Knot

The square knot is the standard method of tying two ropes together. However, it can only be used on ropes of approximately the same diameter.

Take the two ropes and tie them in an overhand knot, left over right. (For the loop of the overhand knot, imagine the standing parts to be joined together, forming the loop.) Then tie another overhand knot, right over left. Remember: the same end is on top each time the overhand knot is tied—just on a different side. When the knot is finished, the short ends (a and b) are both on top and the ends of the same rope (a and c, or b and d) are on the same side of the bight formed by the other rope.

The granny knot is often tied by error when trying to tie a square knot. It is formed by tying both overhand knots left over right (or both right

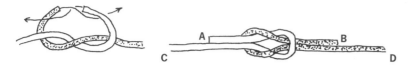

SQUARE KNOT

GRANNY KNOT

over left). The ends of each rope are separated by the bight of the other. The granny knot will not hold reliably and is often hard to untie.

Sheet Bend

The sheet bend is used to tie a small-diameter rope to a large one. Make a bight in the large rope. Run the small rope through the bight, from the back toward you. Then take it around the bight at the point where the large rope lies parallel to itself. Next, tuck the running end of the small rope under its own standing part, staying on top of the large rope's bight.

Like the square knot, both standing parts on the sheet bend are on the same side.

For a double sheet bend, take the small rope around the large rope's bight twice. This is not really any stronger, but it is less likely to come untied in use. However, it is rarely even worth the extra effort.

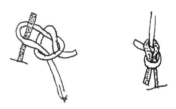

SHORT-END BEND

Short-End Bend

Sooner or later we run across a situation when we need to tie onto a rope, but there isn't enough of it sticking out to get a good hold on it. Tying onto this short piece is fairly simple with the short-end bend.

Push the short piece through the loop of a slip knot. The slip knot should be tied loosely, but still tight enough to hold its shape while sliding it. Capsize the slip knot (tighten it until the loop is pulled through the knot) and the short piece will become the bight of a sheet bend.

SHEET BEND

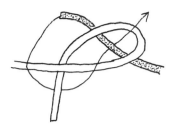
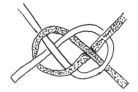

CARRICK BEND

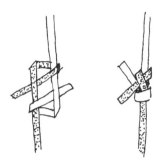

STRAP KNOT

Carrick Bend

Especially with boats, you may have a rope that is too thick to bend sharply enough to tie in a square knot. Here you need a carrick bend. This is also useful when you are under survival conditions and have to use green vines until you can make some more serviceable rope.

Take one of the ropes and make an underhand loop. Take the second rope and put it under the first rope's loop, perpendicular to the central axis of the loop. Now take it over the first rope's standing part under the running end, and over the loop. In going over the loop, it should be passed under its own standing part and back up again so that it is on top of both sides of the first rope's loop.

Strap Knot

The strap knot's chief use is in tying two straps together. It may find use if some webbing straps break on your pack. It is also a good method of joining grass or vines together as emergency rope and it is a bit easier to tie than the carrick bend. However, it won't hold on rope.

Each strap is tied in an underhand loop around the standing part of the other strap.

FISHING KNOTS

Fishing knots are given separately because they are used to tie line (usually gut or monofilament nylon) that is too smooth to hold with other knots. They are so hard to tie and untie that they have no use with regular rope.

Fisherman's Knot

The main advantage of the fisherman's knot is that, as fishing knots go, it is fairly easy to untie.

Take the two lines and lay them parallel, the running end of one against the standing part of the other. With the running end, tie an overhand knot with the loop around the standing part of the other line. Repeat with the other line. Pull tight and pull the two overhand knots together.

To untie, pull the two knots apart and untie each overhand knot separately.

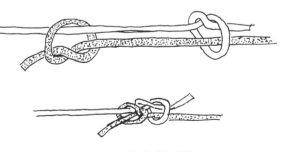

FISHERMAN'S KNOT

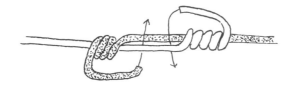

BARREL KNOT

Barrel Knot

The barrel knot is the strongest of the fishing knots—and the hardest to untie.

Lay the two lines parallel, as with the fisherman's knot. Spiral the running ends around the other lines' standing parts away from the center knot for five or six turns. Bring the ends between the two lines in the center of the knot. Pull tight.

To untie, pull on both coils until they separate; pull out the running ends and uncoil. It is harder to untie than the fisherman's knot because of the frictional resistance to pulling the coil apart. As a result, it is more often simply cut. You waste little line if you cut it where the running end lies over the coil. Only one side needs to be cut.

Leader Loop

The leader is used to tie a fixed loop in a low-friction line. Make a bight and tie the whole bight into an overhand knot. If it slips (which is rare), untie it and tie it again—using a figure eight (twice around the standing part) or stevedore (three times around the standing part) knot.

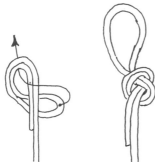

LEADER LOOP

LOOP KNOTS

Loop knots are divided into two classes: running and fixed. In the running loop, the size of the loop can be changed without untying the knot; in a fixed loop, the size of the loop cannot be changed without untying it.

Slip Knot

A slip knot is the standard running loop. To tie, make a loop in the running end. Pass a bight of the standing part through the loop. That bight forms the loop of the knot. To untie, pull the standing part until the knot disappears.

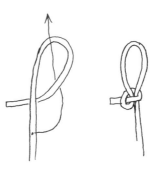

SLIP KNOT

Running Sheepshank

The running sheepshank, or Baker's bowline, is primarily a block and tackle improvised entirely out of one piece of rope. It gives a two-to-one mechanical advantage, minus the considerable friction loss.

First tie the bitter end (of the standing part) to a secure anchor. Next, a suitable distance from this, tie the rope in a fixed loop such as a butterfly loop or leader loop (the resulting loop does not have

RUNNING SHEEPSHANK

to be very large). Take a bight in the running end around the object you are moving, the running end through the loop, and pull the running end.

This moving can be continued as long as there is another anchor point to move to each time the rope is used up.

Bowline

The bowline (pronounced bō′lin) is the standard fixed loop. The easiest way to remember how to tie it is by the "rabbit analogy." Make an overhand loop in the standing part. The rabbit (the running end) comes out of its hole (the loop), goes around the tree (the standing part), and goes back into its hole again.

A variation starts with an overhand knot with the running end pulled up and back to form the rabbit hole and tree. The completion is the same as the more usual method.

A third method is essentially a composite of the

first two methods, but it is done with one hand. This method is quite valuable in tying a bowline around yourself in a rescue situation since your off hand holds the standing part throughout, both keeping you from falling and slacking the remainder of the rope to tie the knot. The first step is identical with the other systems except that the "hole" is made by twisting the rope around your wrist while holding the running end. This both makes the "hole" and gets the "rabbit out of the ground." Next comes the tricky part: the running end is manipulated around the standing part with the fingers while the rest is held between the little finger and the palm. After passing it around the standing part, it is grasped again in the hand and the running end and your hand are both pulled out of the loop. Test the knot before putting your weight on it.

Bowline on a Bight

Three other forms of the bowline are also useful, especially in climbing. One is the bowline on a

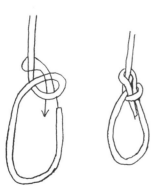

BOWLINE 1

BOWLINE 2

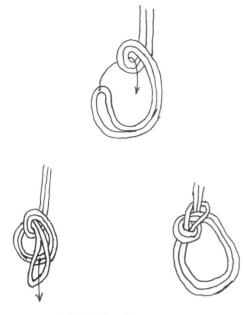

BOWLINE ON A BIGHT

Spanish Bowline

A second form of the bowline is also a double-loop knot. Unlike the bowline on a bight, the Spanish bowline has its two loops separated. It makes a good rope with one loop used for the seat and the other the backrest.

Start with a slip knot almost twice as large as you will need each of the finished loops to be; twist the loop one half-turn so that the standing part crosses in the back. Keeping the running end of the slip knot tightly against the standing part where they are parallel, and holding the turn in the back of the knot, slide the bight immediately next to the running end outward until it forms a loop the same size as the one in the original slip knot (which will be shrinking) so that you have what amounts to a larkshead with a one and a half turn around the standing parts.

Slide the X up the loops until they are both fairly small. Reach through both of them from the back and take the bight below the X and pull it through. This will form your two loops and the X will remain between them. To untie, pull the two small loops at the base of the large loops, changing it back to the larkshead pattern, and slip the larkshead off the end.

Bowline on a Coil

The final useful form of the bowline is tied on a coil of rope. This is a good knot to use to keep your small coils of rope neat in camp as well as to keep climbing rope untangled, which is its essential purpose.

bight. Make an overhand loop (like the "hole" in the usual bowline's rabbit analogy). Take the bight (which forms the running end in this knot) through the loop. Pull the bight down to the end of the large loop formed by the running end, separate the bight and put this large loop through it, and slide the running-end bight up so that it is around the standing part. Pull it tight before using it since it can slip before the friction of the knot takes over.

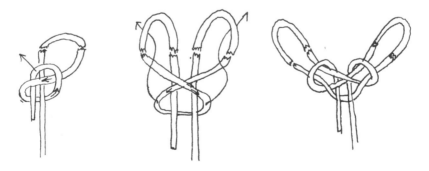

SPANISH BOWLINE

  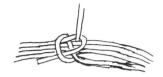

BOWLINE ON A COIL

In this knot, the standing part is where the rope enters the coil, the running end is the bitter end within the coil. These must be at the same point on the coil to tie it. Pull up a bight on the standing part within the coil and give it a half-twist to form an underhand loop. Take the running end through the loop, around the standing part, and back out the loop at the same point. Pull on the standing part to tighten.

If the coil will be handled roughly, tie the running end into a couple of half-hitches around the coil. If there is no appreciable length outside the coil (the coil is used for storage rather than simply taking up the excess length at the end of a climbing rope), tie the standing part in half-hitches around the coil the same way on the other side of the knot.

Taut-Line Hitch

Despite its name, the taut-line hitch is not a hitch but a running loop that holds under strain, but can be changed after releasing the strain. It is most commonly used to tighten tent ropes. The pattern, tied around a pole instead of its own standing part, is called a magnus hitch. However, a good clove or timber hitch does the job as well and is easier to tie.

First, form the loop around the anchor. Take the running end and make two small turns around the standing part, spiralling it toward the inside of the loop. Then tie a half-hitch around the standing part, outside of the large loop.

Prussik Knot

The prussik knot is a good example of the futility of trying to divide these twistings of rope into neat categories called "knots" and "hitches." Mechanically, the prussik knot is quite similar to the taut-line hitch—a knot for a running loop that holds under strain. However, in its usual function, it is a hitch made on another rope. It could be used in place of a taut-line hitch, except that it is too hard to tie to make it worthwhile under conditions of light to moderate strain. Under heavy strain, though, the taut-line hitch will slip. This is where the prussik knot is required.

Its main use is in mountain-climbing rescue work or technical climbing up cliffs without any hand- or footholds. Three short lengths of rope are tied to a regular mountain-climbing rope with prussik knots. (Sometimes the one for the body is omitted and a carabiner or belt holds the climber to the main rope.) The other ends of these ropes are tied in bowlines—a large one supporting the body under the arms, and a small one for each foot. The foot ropes come from the prussik knot, through the waistband (if any), between the legs and one around each leg, so that the bowline knot is on

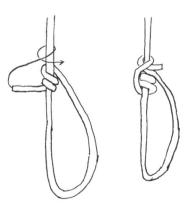

TAUT-LINE HITCH

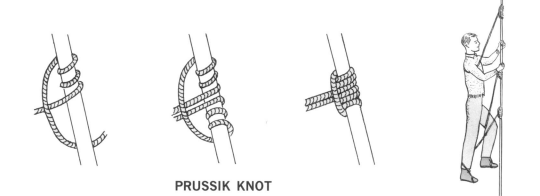

PRUSSIK KNOT

the forward, outside part of the ankle when the foot is in the loop.

One at a time, slack is made on one of these ropes and the prussik knot is slid up the climbing rope. The same process is repeated with each of the two or three prussik knots in rotation until the climb is completed. This requires far less strength and balance than is required to climb hand over hand (and the 7/16″ [11 mm] climbing rope is almost impossible to climb this way, anyway).

You can tie the prussik knot the same way you would tie a larkshead on a bight, going around twice instead of once. If this will not hold your weight, loosen up the knot and go around once more. More than three turns are rarely required. Yet this is too cumbersome with a fairly long rope. A faster way is to spiral the running end around the large rope two or three times, over its standing part, and then two or three more times inward toward the standing part so it ends adjacent and parallel to the standing part.

This knot has more uses than just getting out of a crevasse or up a sheer cliff. A tree without

low limbs will often make a good deer blind, and this is an easy way to climb it. Also, if you happen to have the rope with you, it is a good way to climb such a tree as a lookout point if you are temporarily befuddled as to your precise location. Throw the main rope over a secure limb above the lowest one, secure the rope to the limb, attach your small lines, and climb to the lowest limb. Then climb by more normal methods as high as you need to go.

Butterfly Loop

The butterfly loop was primarily designed to make a fixed loop for the middle person on a climbing rope. It is a good way to make a fixed loop in the middle of a rope to make a harness for dragging heavy loads.

Take a bight, the size you want the loop to be, and twist it one full turn to form a loose figure eight. Fold this double loop back over the standing part to form two intertwined loops. Pass the bight (the tip of the original bight) through both loops where they overlap and pull on the bight to tighten.

 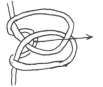 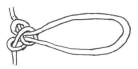

BUTTERFLY LOOP

CHAPTER THIRTY-EIGHT

Hitches

Because hitches, by definition, require friction against an object other than the rope itself, many hitches are quite complex. Probably the best ex ample of this is a circus tent pole, which has a considerable strain running parallel to the pole (you will probably have to see it in a photograph, tent circuses are so rare these days).

However, in camping, a half-dozen will serve for any use you may have outside of fishing.

BAR AND RING HITCHES

These are the most common hitches. Most of them are actually called "hitches" although some of the ring hitches are often called by the nautical term of "bend." Bar and ring types are somewhat interchangeable in usage, although the ring hitches are really too complicated to replace good bar hitches on bars, and the bar hitches will usually slip on a ring.

Half-Hitch

Two half-hitches are the easiest of the hitches to tie. Tie an overhand knot with the object through the loop. Then make an overhand loop around the standing part with the running end passing between it and the previously tied single half-hitch. The second half-hitch is on the opposite side of the first half-hitch from the object. Two half-hitches are needed as only one rarely has enough friction

to hold. The single half-hitch is most often used to finish a knot by keeping the running end against the knot so it won't loosen the knot from hitting obstructions.

Properly tied, there is a clove hitch on the standing part. If it is a larkshead, it is technically called "reversed half-hitches" and is slightly weaker.

A sub-type is the pipe hitch, which is useful in tying onto slick metal. Instead of circling the object once, the rope is spiralled around it several times before tying the half-hitches. Otherwise it is the same.

Clove Hitch

The clove hitch is the strongest hitch of all. It is easy to tie once you learn it. It is stronger if it is tied on the opposite side of the object from the strain, or at least at right angles to it.

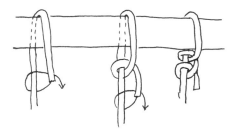

TWO HALF-HITCHES

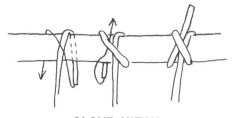

CLOVE HITCH

Make a loop around the object with the running end on top of the standing part. Make another loop beside it and tuck the running end under the standing part between the two loops. Remember, both ends (standing and running) are in between (end-between) the two loops.

Constrictor Knot

The constrictor knot is even more secure than the clove hitch, although, of course, a bit harder to tie, so the clove hitch is still the best under most conditions.

The first turn of the constrictor knot is tied exactly the same way as the clove hitch. After the second turn around the object is made, the running end crosses the standing part (instead of moving up parallel to it without crossing) and tucks under the diagonal of the turns and then under the standing part just past the spot where the diagonal crosses over it. This gets the running end back between the two turns and both ends are still on the inside (end side) of the two coils as on the clove hitch. The constrictor knot just tucks the ends under each other as well as under the coils to increase friction.

It is not very easy to untie, especially when wet, so if you don't need a considerable amount of strength to hold the object, use the clove hitch.

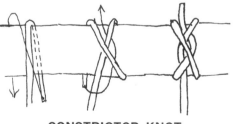

CONSTRICTOR KNOT

This knot is easy to tighten by pulling on the two ends and it has many points of friction so that it doesn't loosen readily; therefore it is an excellent way to tie temporary whippings and anti-unlaying bands for splices. It also makes a good vise for tightening joints to be glued or for starting parallel lashings. It is more efficient than the miller's knot for tying sacks closed.

Timber Hitch

The timber hitch is a development of the half-hitch. Tie a half-hitch. Spiral the running end back around itself to gain friction against bark or similar rough surfaces.

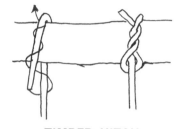

TIMBER HITCH

Fisherman's Bend

While the fisherman's bend, or "anchor bend," can be used equally well on bars or rings, it is too complicated to replace the good bar hitches like the clove and timber hitch, Its holding power on smooth metal rings, however, in unsurpassed.

Make two turns around the ring. Tie a half-hitch with both the standing part and the center of the double turns within the loop of the half-hitch. Another half-hitch finishes it.

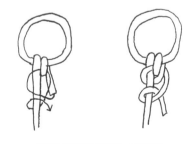

FISHERMAN'S BEND

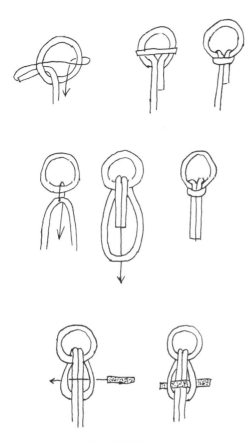

LARKSHEAD

Often this hitch is tied with the load more or less equal on both ends. When tied that way, pass the bight through the ring and both ends through the bight.

Occasionally a toggle is used since it is impractical to tie it with a bight on a very long rope. For this method, pass the bight through the ring and put the toggle behind the bight and in front of the standing part.

FISHING HITCHES

The fishing hitches are various means of attaching lines to flies, plugs, or fish hooks. While it could logically be argued that these are really running loop knots tied around the eye of a hook or plug, their specialized nature and the fact that none of them are ever used without the eye of a hook or plug make them hitches in practice if not in design. Their design also shows through in the fact that they always have "knot" in their name.

Wemyss Knot

The wemyss knot (pronounced weems) is a figure-eight knot with the shank of the hook through the loop and the standing part through the eye of the hook. Its main advantage is that it doesn't mess up the feathers of a fly.

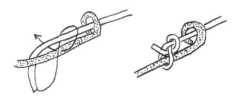

WEMYSS KNOT

Turle Knot

The turle knot is a slip knot over the shank with the standing part through the eye. While it may mess up the feathers of a fly, it is a stronger hitch than the wemyss knot.

Larkshead

The larkshead is really a combination of various knots and hitches. However, it has an identity all its own as a hitch. It is usually tied with a wide strap on a saddle and is called a "cinch knot" or "girth hitch." When it is tied with a rope, a half-hitch is usually needed to keep it from slipping.

To tie it by the end on a ring, take the running end through the ring and over to the left. Bring it around the left side of the ring and across the front to the right side. Then bring it through the ring and under the horizontal part of the knot. Slide the horizontal part of the knot down to the bottom of the ring while pulling the running end tight.

TURLE KNOT

Clinch Knot

A clinch knot is the strongest, but also the hardest to untie. It is quite similar to the barrel knot in construction and, like it, is often cut rather than untied.

Pass the running end through the eye of the hook. Then wrap around the entire loop and through the loop at the eye of the hook.

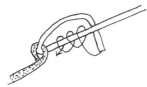

CLINCH KNOT

CHAPTER THIRTY-NINE

Lashings

Lashings are relatively permanent ways of holding wood together with rope. Binder twine is the best material for lashing, although parachute cord may be better for the average camper as binder twine has little use other than for lashing. In an emergency, any flexible rope will do the job.

In lashing terminology, "wrap" means to make one complete circuit of the wood according to the pattern of that particular lashing. "Frap" means to go one complete turn around the wrapping (but not the wood) to tighten the wrapping. Both wrapping and frapping should be done as tightly as possible.

Lashings are all started and ended with a clove hitch. The clove hitch should be on the top of the piece as you look at it. The rope should be taken around that piece and the wrap started from the bottom. Likewise, the frap should end by going under the piece and around to the top for the final clove hitch. This is because the strain on the hitch would otherwise be slightly diagonal to the clove hitch, weakening its holding power somewhat. With the extra half-turn at the beginning and end, the clove hitch has its maximum strength (ninety per cent of rope strength—the highest of any knot or hitch) to hold the strain of a well-tightened lashing.

SQUARE LASHING

The square lashing is so called because the rope is wrapped at right angles to the wood, inscribing a square. It is used to join two pieces at right angles to each other.

Start on the leg with a clove hitch. Wrap under the leg and over the cross-piece. Wrap three times. Frap three times. Finish on the leg opposite the starting hitch with another clove hitch.

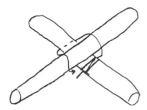
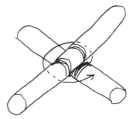

SQUARE LASHING

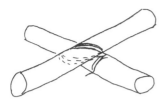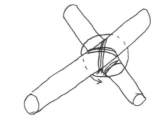

DIAGONAL LASHING

DIAGONAL LASHING

The diagonal lashing is used where there is an angle other than ninety degrees or where the wood is sprung apart so that the lashing must pull them together as well as hold them there.

The start is made on the bottom leg. Wrap diagonally under this leg, and over the top one. Wrap this way three times. Take the rope under the bottom leg (and at right angles to it, along the starting clove hitch) and wrap across on the other diagonal three times. Frap three times. Finsh with the usual clove hitch on the bottom leg, opposite the starting point.

Whenever the spars are bent so that they don't meet readily, use a timber hitch or constrictor knot to pull them together before starting the usual diagonal lashing pattern. Finish with a clove hitch as usual.

SHEAR LASHING

This is a flexible lashing for shear poles. Start with the legs together and parallel. Tie the clove hitch on one of the legs. Wrap loosely seven times with

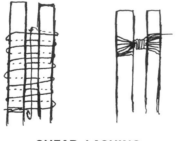

SHEAR LASHING

about three or four times the rope's diameter distance between the poles. Frap tightly between the legs three times. End with a clove hitch on the other leg. Take care that the rope doesn't cross over itself where it lies on the poles.

TRIPOD LASHING

This is the Indian way. Place the poles on the ground, two poles together and the other one at an angle to them. The intersection of the poles is the lashing point. The distance between the base ends of the poles is equal to the base spread of the erected tripod.

Tie a clove hitch around all three poles and wrap tightly four times around the whole cluster—don't weave in and out. Don't frap. End with a clove hitch on the single pole as close to the first hitch as possible.

To erect, lift the center so that the poles are upright. Take the outside one of the paired poles and move it around to place.

For four legs, use two pairs of poles. Move the outside poles at the same time. This requires an additional person. The tripod can be erected by one person although it is easier with two. The tetrapod requires two and is easier with three. The tripod is a far sturdier structure than the tetrapod.

For more than four poles, stack them like tipi poles over the basic tripod or tetrapod. Use a longer rope to tie the basic tripod and let it hang down rather than tying the final clove hitch. After you stack the additional poles, wrap the rope around the whole thing four times, snaking the rope up and pulling tight every quarter to half circuit around the stack.

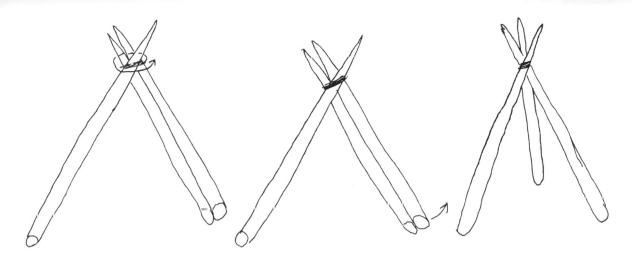

TRIPOD LASHING

PARALLEL LASHING

Parallel lashing is used to join two parallel spars, either to reënforce or to splice. Wedges hammered between the poles and the lashing make the lashing tighter. On a broken canoe paddle, using a strip of rawhide and no wedges, this lashing can be most valuable. Soak the rawhide after tying and you will have a mend that is almost as strong as the unbroken paddle.

Start the lashing with a clove hitch or constrictor knot around both pieces. Wrap as far as the rope will allow, and end with a clove hitch, also on both pieces. Since there is no frapping, the wrapping and the hitches must be tight. Nylon rope is especially valuable here since it is somewhat elastic.

CONTINUOUS LASHINGS

These are ways of joining a succession of pieces which otherwise would require an astronomical number of square lashings and an endless amount of cordage.

There are a wide number of these continuous lashings, reflecting the inventiveness of the many of the world's cultures which have developed lashings, in the absence of metal nails, for fastening their houses and furnishings. The two given here were chosen because they represent the two types of continuous lashings, those with and those without spars, and of those two categories these are the easiest to tie.

Paling Lashing

This is commonly used for making flat surfaces from many cross-pieces close together, such as an alter-fire platform, table, chair, bridge, etc.

Start with a clove hitch on the spar. Go under the spar to the far side of the first cross-piece, diagonally over it back toward the clove hitch, under the spar, onto the far side of the next

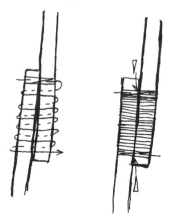

PARALLEL LASHING

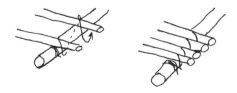

PALING LASHING

cross-piece, and so on. End with a clove hitch on the spar.

Malay Lashing

This is a quick way to make a screen for a latrine, a windbreak for a survival shelter, or even one of those old-fashioned straw mattresses. Grass or poles may be used in this lashing.

Start in the bight of a long cord. Put in a pole or bundle of grass and switch the upper and lower lines. Put in another so weave the entire piece. A loom makes the procedure much faster.

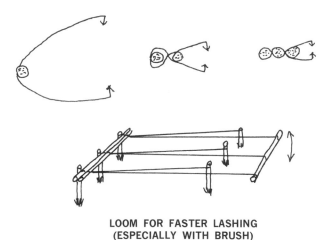

LOOM FOR FASTER LASHING
(ESPECIALLY WITH BRUSH)

MALAY LASHING

PACK LASHINGS

While the obvious use of pack lashings is to secure a load to the pack saddle of one of the equine breeds, it also can be used for lashing a pack onto a pack frame or attaching any other more or less square-shaped bundle to a rigid framework for transportation.

One-Man Diamond Hitch

The diamond hitch in either the single or double diamond patterns has long been standard. The double diamond presupposes a barrel as the central item of the cargo, which shows how old the pattern is. The diamond is easily tightened and, with a little skill, can be tied by one person standing in one spot (on the left side of the animal).

As with any pack-animal lashing, the pack should be fairly compact, covered with a tarp or other waterproof, rugged material, and the belly band should have a ring on one end and a hook on the other.

Start the tie with the ring of the belly band attached to the lashing rope. Lay the rope toward the animal's tail and bring a little loop toward you. Throw the rope with the belly band across the pack, over the rope, so that as it swings under the animal you can catch it. Keep holding the little loop with your left hand (assuming you are right-handed) so the whole pattern doesn't go over with the belly band.

Hook the belly band over the loop and pull it snug. Make another small loop on the other side of the fore-and-aft line and tuck a bight of it under the crossing line, being careful not to disturb the bight around the hook. Feed enough line into the tie to form a loop large enough to throw under the bundle on the off side and pull it tight.

Reach into the bight you formed under the crossing line and take a bight from the fore-and-aft line and pull out a bight big enough to pass under the bundle on the near side. Ideally, this should use up practically all the lashing line. Tie the remainder back on itself with a taut-line hitch. This will enable it to be tightened on the trail.

This tie makes a good pack-frame tie using a bowline in the end of the line instead of the belly band. The bowline, however, must be tied around the first bight after going around the frame (in place of the hook of the belly band) rather than tied at the start.

Box Hitch

Although not as secure as the diamond hitch for loose loads, and requiring two people to tie instead of one, the box hitch is considerably easier to tie. It is tied much as a parcel for mailing.

Start by throwing the belly band over the animal and catching it when it comes under. Hook it over the line and pull it snug. Make an underhand loop

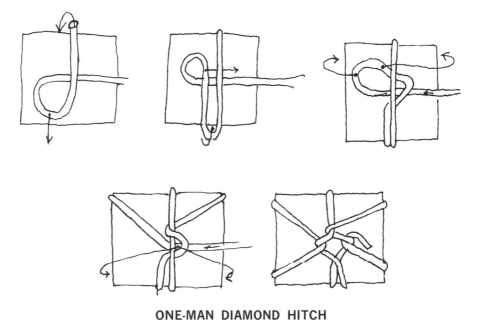

ONE-MAN DIAMOND HITCH

in the line and pull it under the bundle on your side while your partner holds the loose end. He then makes a similar loop on his side and pulls it under the bundle there. The free end is then tied to the cinch ring of the belly band or through it and back onto itself with a taut-line hitch.

SNOWSHOE LASHING

Aside from improvising an emergency harness for a snowshoe, there is not really much use for this lashing. On the other hand, when it is needed,

← — HEAD

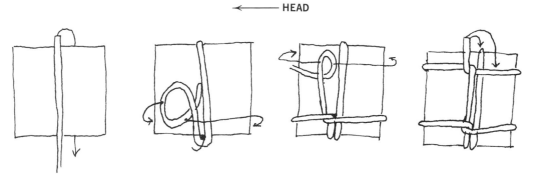

BOX HITCH

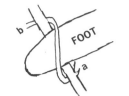

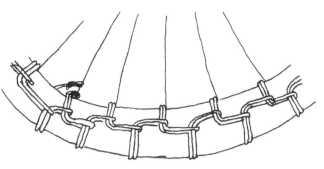

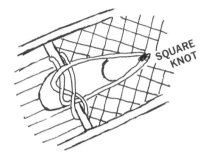

SNOWSHOE LASHING

there is no substitute. You need a piece of rope about three feet (1 m) long for each shoe.

It is easiest to tie using both ends at the same time, so we will call one running end a and the other b to save confusion. Each goes around the foot bar of the snowshoe, a from the front to the back and b from the back to the front, the bight lying loosely on the webbing; a goes under this bight and forward so that both ends meet in front of the bight.

Put your foot in the correct position on the snowshoe, under the bight, and tie the two ends together in an overhand knot to hold the proper tension on your foot. They are then carried back, a over the crossed part and b under it, to the heel of

TIRE-CHAIN LASHING

your boot, where they are tied in a square knot.

This holds the snowshoe to your foot and still allows your foot to pivot in the usual way.

TIRE-CHAIN LASHING

While this trick is designed for a bicycle, it can be worked on a car tire if you have wire or mag wheels.

Tie the end around one spoke with a bowline. Pass a bight through the spokes to the other side and take it around the tire. Take another bight at the point between the next pair of spokes, on the near side, and pass it through the first bight, pulling the first bight tight as you do so. Continue on alternate sides, on around the wheel until the last spoke. On it, take the end through the previous bight, around the first bight, and back through the previous one to complete the chain all around the wheel. Tie it to the first spoke with a bowline.

If the rope is longer than needed, take the loose end after tying the final bowline and run it in and out of the spokes, around the wheel, until it is used up. Then tie it to the nearest spoke with a bowline.

Splices

There are three splices that should be known by the camper: the short splice, the eye splice, and the end splice. They are all done essentially the same way by weaving the strands of one rope (or part of a rope) against the lay of the strands of the other.

The ends of each strand should be whipped for easier handling. Instead of whipping the usual way, tie a constrictor knot with fishing line, or use adhesive or masking tape. Let the tape extend past the end of the rope and twist into a point to make the tucking easier.

After completing a splice, trip off the projecting ends of the strands and roll the rope under pressure (between two boards or between your foot and the floor) to smooth and "set" the splice.

A fid is most useful in splicing, to open the strands, but if you don't have one, you can open them by twisting the rope against the lay. This does, however, distort the rope and weaken it somewhat, so the fid is definitely preferable.

SHORT SPLICE

The short splice is used to join two pieces of rope, end to end, permanently. The length of the splice is six times the diameter of the rope. Tie a piece of fishing line around each rope, three diameters from the end. A constrictor knot is best for this.

Unlay the rope this far and tie or tape each individual strand to keep it from fraying.

Mesh the strands of the two ropes together. The strands of each rope will go in the direction of its lay, and therefore in the opposite direction to the lay of the other rope. Always go in this direction and you will not get confused. Take a strand over both the fishing line and the first strand of the other rope. Then go under the next strand. Do this with each of the other strands of the first rope; then do the same with the other rope. Pull the splice tight after each set of tucks, but don't pull either rope out of shape.

Continue this weaving, alternating ropes, one tuck at a time, until all of the strands have only a short end left sticking out. Cut them off as close to the rope as possible. Cut the fishing line that prevented the rope from unlaying and remove it. Roll the splice until it is as smooth as the rest of the rope, although it will be larger in diameter.

While totally unnecessary for strength, it is neater if, about two tucks from finishing, the tie or tape at the tip of the strands is removed and about a third of the fibers are cut off at the rope. The strand is again tied or taped and another tuck is made. The process is repeated with half of the remainder removed. After the next tuck, all the remainder is removed. This makes a taper rather than an abrupt change of diameter at the splice and will work on

SHORT SPLICE

each of the three splices included here. The advantages, however, are strictly aesthetic.

EYE SPLICE

The eye splice is the way to make a permanent loop without seriously weakening the rope as a knot does. It is fixed and cannot come untied. If a rope is to run through the eye, a metal thimble should be inserted. This prevents the running rope from sawing through the loop.

Unlay three or four diameters from the end of the rope and tie it with a fishing line to prevent unlaying. Make a bight the size you want the loop to be. With a pencil, mark the standing part and pull one of the strands of the running part through it. Do the same around the standing part with the rest of the running strands. Keep them properly spaced and all running in the same direction—against the lay of the standing part. Take one strand for one tuck and then the next strand one tuck and so on, being careful not to distort the standing part in a lopsided or twisted manner. Weave over one, under the next, until finished. Trim the ends of the strands close to the rope, cut the anti-unlaying tie, and roll the splice until it is smooth.

If you will be needing a thimble in it, insert it last. You should have a slight difficulty in forcing it in the eye. A leather sleeve, sewed on the loop, will serve the same purpose as the thimble as well as letting the loop stay flexible. This flexibility is required on a lariat to avoid choking the animal.

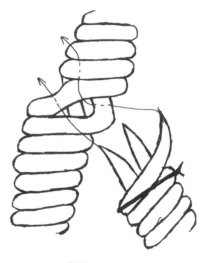

EYE SPLICE

END SPLICE

The start of the end splice is the crown knot. This is a means of weaving the strands together on the end of the rope to prevent unlaying. (However, it won't hold up in use, so something more is required as an end knot.) To tie the crown knot, fold each strand across the end. Tuck each strand under the one it crossed in the pattern. In this way, each strand holds down another one so the pattern stays tight. Don't try to pull a crown knot tight—it simply starts untwisting the rope in a distorted way and does no good at all. Keep it tight enough to avoid coming apart, but no tighter.

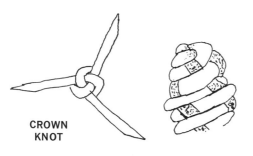

CROWN KNOT

END SPLICE

The strands are now in a horizontal position. Bend each one down, in turn, over the adjacent strand of the rope proper, and tuck it under the next strand. After you have done this with all three strands, the familiar splicing pattern has emerged. Continue weaving the strands until you are finished. Cut off the short ends and roll smooth as with all splices.

CHAPTER FORTY-ONE

Other Techniques with Rope

This chapter will include practically anything about ropes not covered in other chapters.

WHIPPING

Rope should be whipped to prevent unlaying (unless you use it enough in one length to merit end splices). Whipping is done by wrapping fishing line or similar strong twine around the end of a rope. There are two methods of whipping, each with its advantages and disadvantages.

In the first method, lay a bight of the whipping line at a point three or four diameters from the end of the rope; take a bight from that point to the end and back again. Start wrapping the twine around the rope from the first point to about one quarter-inch (5 mm) or one half-diameter (which-ever is larger) from the end. Wrap the twine tightly and as closely as possible, but don't get it on top of a previous turn. The end of the whipping should be tucked in the bight and pulled under to prevent loosening. Trim the end of the whipping cord sticking out so that it is flush with the whipping.

The second method is currently being taught by the Boy Scouts. It is admirably suited to this age group since it is easier to tie strongly. However, it wastes far too much of the whipping cord. First, make a loop in a length of whipping cord and hold it on the rope, with the two ends parallel and in opposite directions. Start about two diameters from the end and wind it toward the end. After one or one and a half diameters of whipping, hold it to keep the whipping from loosening and pull on the two ends. Cut the ends off flush with the end of the wrapping when you finish.

The nylon ropes can be fixed without whipping or end splices. Take a lighted match and burn the end. The fibers will fuse together to form a solid mass at the end which will prevent unlaying. This is especially good with the versatile parachute cord. However, let it cool before handling and don't, as my father once did, try to mold the still-soft mass into a point for lacing. (The zipper on his sleeping bag broke and he was still half asleep when he did it—but not afterwards.)

Other ropes can be sealed by dipping them in

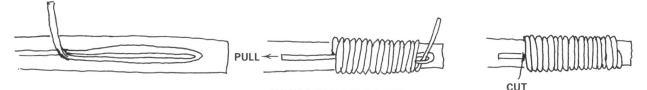

PULL ←

WHIPPING WITH END

CUT

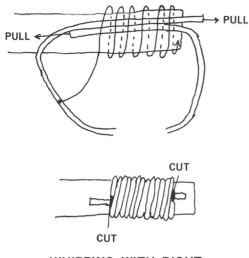

WHIPPING WITH BIGHT

a plastic resin glue. However, it will be stiffer and rougher at the tip than if it is whipped. Adhesive tape can be used for a temporary whipping but it comes off too easily for anything more permanent.

PARBUCKLE

The parbuckle is a method of rolling heavy loads by using the load itself as a pulley. The pulling force is doubled, minus the friction involved.

Anchor the bight of the rope around a stake or tree. Pass it under the object, spreading the two ends as much as possible. Pull on the ends.

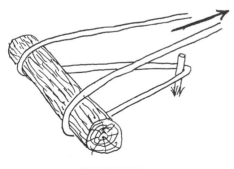

PARBUCKLE

For all practical purposes, this method is limited to rounded objects, although occasionally you will be able to scoot a non-rolling item across hard, level ground by this means.

SPANISH WINDLASS

The Spanish windlass is an easy way to make a windlass from two poles without any carpentry at all. The smaller the windlass pole and/or the longer the crank pole, the stronger the mechanical advantage. The larger the windlass and/or the shorter the crank, the faster it will operate.

Place the crank at a right angle to the windlass. Put the crank through a bight of the rope, on the opposite side of the windlass from the standing part of the rope. Turn the crank so that the rope is wound up onto the windlass.

Allow the short end to wind up on the windlass with the standing part to keep it from slipping, but for greater strength do not let the rope being wound cross itself at any point as this puts a slightly increased strain on the rope. If the rope is wound with no gaps, you can let it put another layer of turns on top of it with no loss of strength.

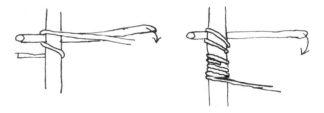

SPANISH WINDLASS

TOURNIQUET TIE

Far from being merely a first-aid device, the tourniquet tie is a method of applying a great force over a short distance. It is useful for bending poles and tightening ropes, although a Spanish windlass is usually better. You can use it to make a vise or clamp for emergency repairs. Use two sticks or boards connected by the tourniquet.

The tourniquet tie is easy and quick to rig. Make a loop around the two objects. Put a strong stick

TOURNIQUET TIE

in the loop and twist a part of it into a smaller loop. Keep twisting the stick so that the larger loop is contracted. Exert as much pressure as is needed or as your rope will stand. This rig produces so much pressure that there is always the danger of breaking the rope. The sharp twist weakens the rope considerably.

HOBBLE TIE

This could have been included in the chapter on knots, but since it is nothing but square knots it seemed that its use gave it a somewhat distinctive position.

The hobble tie is simply a method of hobbling a horse for the night so it can feed and still not wander too far to find the next morning. It is worked from the mid-point of the rope, with the horse standing in a normally relaxed position (this may be a bit hard until the horse knows what you are up to, so soft words are in order to avoid having the front hooves land in your back).

Using a square knot, tie the rope around one leg, snug enough so that it won't slip over the hoof or catch on a stick easily, but not tight. Leaving a judicious amount of slack, move over to the other foot and tie another square knot. Tie a final square knot on the outside of the leg, making it as snug as you did on the first leg. The horse can still walk to feed, but can't run or move very fast.

It is possible to capsize this rig and a smart horse may figure out how to do it. If you find one or both of the inner knots capsized or almost so, he is learning. If this happens, add an overhand knot on top of the first square knot and just before tying the second one. This won't capsize. Just be sure the overhand is tied so it forms a square knot,

instead of a granny knot with the existing square knot.

HOBBLE TIE

FISHERMAN'S LITTER

While the obvious use of the fisherman's litter is as a stretcher for first-aid use, it is also a good method for moving firewood into camp from a somewhat remote chopping yard, or for carrying game out after a successful hunt.

All it takes is two stout poles and fifty feet (15 m) of quarter-inch (5 mm) manilla or eighth-inch (2 mm) parachute cord. Tie a clove hitch around one pole to start and, keeping the poles the same distance apart (two feet [60 cm] is good for a stretcher), wrap the rope around it for about six to ten feet (2 or 3 m) down the poles, and tie it onto the other pole with another clove hitch.

Short poles wedged or lashed between the main ones at each end may make it a little easier to handle and a bit more comfortable, but they are not really needed.

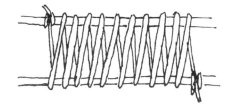

FISHERMAN'S LITTER

CHAIN KNOT

There is probably only one use for the chain knot, but that use makes it worthwhile to know. The chain knot is a method of reducing a long piece of rope to a short length so that it doesn't get tangled as a coil will. Its one practical use is in lifesaving in which a strong swimmer ties a bowline over his shoulder with one end of the chain-knotted rope while his partner stands on the shore, pays out the line by raveling the knot, and then hauls both the swimmer and the victim back to shore.

The chain knot starts out as a slip knot. The standing part is pulled through the loop of the slip knot, the loop is reduced so that it fits snugly, but not tightly, against the parallel parts of the bight in the standing part. This bight then becomes the loop of another slip knot and the process is continued until the line is used up. The last slip knot is pulled tightly so the bight doesn't fall out and the knotted line is coiled in a ready position until it is needed.

If all the members of the group are about the same size, the bowline may be tied at this time.

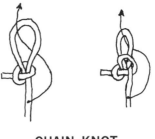

CHAIN KNOT

This will speed matters when the time comes. However, it is better to tie the bowline at the time if there is any chance that it would be difficult to get on or that it would possibly come off during the towing.

PART IX

Transportation

Transportation is the determining factor in much of camping. It determines the weight, bulk, and amount of gear that you can carry as well as the type of each item. By its restrictions on the permissible weight of the food supply, it determines how long you can camp without having to go and buy more provisions. It determines the territory that can be seen, since much of the more beautiful wilderness areas can only be seen by backpacking, horsepacking, or canoeing. A backpacker must be in good physical condition; horses are very expensive; and a canoeist must know how to swim. These three requirements can exclude an amazing number of people.

Still, there is much to be seen by those who aren't in top physical condition or who are still in their infancy as far as camping skills are concerned. Anyone who can walk at all can walk a couple of miles without any real discomfort. Even in our most overcrowded national parks, you can get away from the crowd by walking a short distance.

As the authors of *Going Light* discovered, "the crowd diminished according to the square of the distance from the highway and according to the cube of the elevation above it." As Americans become more dependent on the automobile for going to the corner grocery, we can assume the Sierra Club's formula may have to be revised to read "the cube of the distance and the fourth power of the altitude."

A check of the trail registers at Grand Canyon will show only about one-third of the hikers on the trail are Americans. The rest come from all over the world. There are places where, if you hear anyone at all, they are probably speaking French or German; even the English is with a British accent.

While there is a little more outdoors activity in Canada than the United States, there is not much. The statement that "the average 60-year-old Swede is in better shape than the average 30-year-old Canadian" can be explained to some extent by my experience in doing a trail guide for the Baden-Powell

449

Trail. If it weren't for the trees, the whole of this 35-mile (56 km), 19 road-heads trail would be visible from the urban sprawl of Vancouver. Yet in covering the whole of the trail, except for road-heads, I only saw twenty people—and twelve of them were in one group! Yet it was on week-ends in good weather.

The study of camp transportation, therefore, is more than simply a study of the different means of transportation; it is a survey of the various forms of camping as well.

The big paradox of camping is that the more complex your transportation system is, the less flexible your camping activities can be. The only real advantage of a car over the backpack and hiking boot is that it gets you there quicker. What can be done when you get there is greatly restricted unless you leave the car and adopt another means of transportation.

The big bus-type "land yacht," which isn't camping by any stretch of the imagination, is restricted to paved roads. Any site off the paved roads may as well be on the next planet because you simply cannot get there in one. On the other hand, while it would take a ridiculous length of time, you could cross the continent on foot. It has been done many times. Also, and more important, on foot you can visit parts of Grand Canyon where Fred Harvey's trail-polluting mules don't go, the top of Mount McKinley, the entire length of the Appalachian Trail, or some back trail where the beauties of nature are still unharmed by the destructive ravages of "civilization" and "progress."

With a canoe, you can get into the deeper parts of the Quetico-Superior region where not even airplanes are permitted, or take a leisurely float-fishing trip down an Ozark river which winds its way miles from any road or trail.

Yet the equipment needed on these canoeing and backpacking trips can easily be carried on the camper's back or tossed into the trunk of the family car to get to where the camping starts and in the safest time possible. With a camping machine, you can camp along the road without having to make and break camp every day and thus get there faster and start your real camping sooner than with just a standard automobile.

Regardless of your transportation method, you should make sure that the people you leave behind, either at home or at base camp, know where you are going and at least the basic route you will take getting there. The slower your transportation method, the more important it is to have some system of checks by which those at home base can send out help if you don't return by a certain time.

CHAPTER FORTY-TWO

Backpacking

An old story tells of a cowboy who rode his horse everywhere except indoors (which was frowned upon in even the wildest Western towns). One time a group of fellow cow-punchers had him go across the street on some contrived errand. Sure enough, he went outside, unhitched his horse, mounted, rode across the street, dismounted, tied his horse, ran the errand, and reversed the procedure coming back. When the friends laughed at him for this, he said, "If God had meant for man to walk, He would have given him four legs!"

The modern American substitutes four wheels and an internal-combustion engine, but his attitude is the same. As a result, walking is avoided whenever possible and hiking is regarded in the same light as mountain climbing, sky diving, and scuba diving—something that a few athletic nuts may enjoy, but nothing for the ordinary person. This attitude is bad enough among those who think using elaborate camping machines is "roughing it," but among campers it is ridiculous. Yet many fairly competent campers are convinced they are physically unable to take a backpacking trip.

Backpacking is the only way you can really see the scenery. All other transportation devices, with the exception of canoes in certain areas, are just too fast and/or too limited as to where they can go. Hiking, with an occasional assist from its cousin, mountain climbing, is the only transportation system that can literally go anywhere on earth. As areas of true wilderness become more and more remote, this most primitive of all forms of transportation will be more and more an essential skill of the true camper.

Hiking is nothing but walking with a purpose for a fair distance. Almost everyone can walk, therefore almost everyone can hike. Backpacking is simply hiking equipped for a longer period or distance. With proper conditioning, almost everyone can backpack.

Roy McCarthy, in his excellent little book, *Tackle Camping This Way,* mentions encountering backpackers with small children, leg braces, and even artificial legs on the mountain trails. True, Britishers still know how to walk and a fairly large portion of the population does so quite regularly; it seems reasonable that Americans can be expected to do as well. The rash of fifty-mile hikes during the early 1960s proved that—an alarming portion of them made the hike even without conditioning.

However, this is not to give the impression that backpacking is the same as walking to the corner and back. Without proper skills, equipment, and conditioning, backpacking will be almost as bad as the prisoners of the automobile claim it is. Getting into the proper physical condition, learning the proper skills, and using the proper equipment, backpacking is really quite simple, tolerably comfortable, and aesthetically the most rewarding way to travel with the possible exception of the canoe.

Who says backpacking is for athletes? Author models pack-frame pack. Note bota hanging from frame upright just over side pocket.

As with all skills in camping, you have to start off simply and build up your reservoir of information, but there is no reason at all why a healthy person can't learn enough about backpacking in a couple of seasons to be able to take a two-week backpacking trip in comfort. First, you start at a couple of overnight camps using backpacking equipment but normal transportation. This is to get accustomed to the lightweight gear first. Next, take a couple of overnight hikes. Twenty pounds (9 kg) of equipment (plus the clothes you wear) is completely adequate. Finally, to cap off the season, take a one-week backpacking trip. Next season you can take that two-week trip in some area of incredible scenery. This, of course, assumes that you will keep in shape with a simple program of exercise (not necessarily calisthenics) all through the year.

PHYSICAL FITNESS

Backpacking is rather demanding on the physique, although not nearly as much as the average non-hiker thinks. Proper conditioning is essential to all forms of camping if you want your trip to be as enjoyable as possible. While these conditioning activities are most essential in backpacking, they are useful in other forms of camp transportation too—especially bicycling and canoeing.

The first rule in conditioning is to start early—you are asking for trouble if you wait until the week or two before you leave. You may get the muscular stiffness that follows hard, sudden exercise just when you need to have the most mobility.

The second rule is to start easy and build up slowly. This means that the best time to start getting into condition is after you get back from the previous year's trip.

But let's assume that you are new to backpacking. You have taken a couple of weekend backpacking trips but they really weren't very hard—you only hiked about five miles (8 km) from the road-head to your camp and a couple of days later hiked the same distance back again. How then do you start getting in shape?

Actually, getting in shape is no different than keeping in shape. What's more, there is a wide variety of activities that you can use to get or stay in shape and most of them are fun in themselves.

Calisthenics

The most useful and the least enjoyable way to condition yourself is calisthenics. Setting-up exercises have been regarded as the favorite pastime of health nuts and school physical-education classes—not voluntarily indulged in by normal people—but a well-balanced program of calisthenics is about the only way all your muscles will be properly developed—and camping activities have an efficient way of letting you discover muscles you didn't know you had.

The problem with calisthenics is that they are usually overdone. With a good program of physical activities, which will be discussed later, the average person needs calisthenics mainly to work muscles that are seldom used outside of some camping activities. A good program of calisthenics is one which takes a short time each day but still works out all your muscles. Fifteen minutes per day is adequate, done in an unhurried manner but without resting, in order to build up your endurance.

I usually start about a month before a trip because I am lazy.

The first set I use is for the legs. This starts with kicks, first one leg in one direction, then the other in the same direction. Then kick in another direction. Kick forward, out to the side, and back. Keep the knees stiff, and kick as far as you can. After each kick, return to a standing position but don't put your weight on that leg until you finish the series with it. Start at twenty kicks of each leg in each direction and increase by ten each week until you reach fifty.

The next set is deep knee bends—the same number of times as the kicks—but they should not be so deep that they stretch the vital Achilles tendon.

Next, rest the legs and give the arms and shoulders a workout. Hold your arms out at your sides and run them rapidly in small circles twenty times in one direction, then twenty in the other. Increase by ten each week until you reach fifty.

Next, swing them in a horizontal plane, clapping them in front and in back the same number of times as the other arm exercise. Then swing them vertically the same number of times.

Now work on the part in between. A slant board is best for sit-ups—start with six and increase one per week until you reach ten. If you have no slant board, do them flat on the floor with someone holding down your legs or hook your feet under a bed or some other piece of heavy furniture and triple the number. Pull up slowly rather than snapping up. It is not only easier on your muscles, if you use furniture to hold you down it is easier on the furniture.

Next, give the back a workout by bending over and touching your toes. Again, start with twenty and increase by ten each week until you are doing fifty.

Finally, jog, starting with a quarter-mile ($\frac{1}{2}$ km) and adding that amount each week until you

reach a full mile (2 km). The odd part about this routine is that, not counting the jogging, it takes no longer to do at the end of the month than it did the first time, despite the fact that you are doing about three and a half times as much work. (If you are in top physical condition when you start, this statement won't apply, but it is true of the average person who does little physical work on his job.)

A physical-culture faddist would consider this far too little calisthenics, but it will keep you in top camping condition all year long. They should, however, be supplemented with other physical activities. You should walk every weekend during the final month of training. Running is good. Simple jogging is just as effective as it does the same work as walking, but does it in a shorter time.

Riding

A bicycle is not only good for exercise, it is also a good camp transportation method and one that is sorely neglected in this country. (See Chapter 43.)

Just as running is more efficient in relation to the time spent than walking, there is an analogous item to the bicycle—the unicycle. These are becoming more available as automotive supply and cycle shops stock them along with bicycles, tricycles, and tetracycles (a bicycle with training wheels). It is a fantastic leg and endurance conditioner.

"Exercise" Games

Sports are usually the most enjoyable form of exercise, yet for the purposes of the camper some sports are more effective than others. Most American sports, such as football, baseball, and basketball, are too erratic in their action to be effective. Soccer is a good exercise sport, but it is still too rare in this country despite the rise of professional soccer, although both soccer and rugby are growing as adult sports in Canada. Individual and doubles sports, however, are very suitable exercise.

Tennis has most of the qualities needed as long as too much of your time isn't spent serving. Handball and related sports (squash, etc.) are usually better since the action usually continues longer. Swimming is great for endurance but leaves much to be desired as a leg conditioner—at least the way most people swim. The children's playground game of four-square ball, in the hands of young-adult experts, can become as good a conditioner as handball.

Of course, diet plays an important part in all of this, but the calisthenics and regular participation in some of the other exercise activities listed will enable you to take out on an extended backpacking trip at a moment's notice. You will enjoy it more too.

HOW TO WALK

The average person really does not know how to walk on rough ground, on steep slopes, or for any distance over a mile (1½ km). It is torture for him, not because of anything built into the situation, but because he simply doesn't know how to walk properly. He plops his feet down any old way, generally pointing out too far, and without a proper sense of speed or rhythm.

The only real problem with walking as a means of transportation is speed. In all other aspects, it is far superior to any other form. It is the most inexpensive, it can cover almost any terrain, there are practically no upkeep or maintenance problems, and it is totally enjoyable if you know how.

Rhythm is critical in walking, and the longer the distance the more important it is. It should be fitted to your individual body and you should stick with it. If you are in a group, modify your stride but not your rhythm.

You find your proper rhythm mostly through trial and error. If you are in average condition (healthy, but no trained hiker), you can walk about a mile (1½ km) and not feel it, regardless how badly you walk. Somewhere in the second mile, you will begin to feel it and start compensating for it. Count the number of steps per minute just before the second milestone. Make this count over, say, a five-minute period. After making the count, stop the hike for the day.

The next time, start off at this pace and keep it quite steady. (This should be the next day unless you were so far out of condition that your legs are sore, in which case wait until they loosen up a little.) It will seem frightfully slow at first, but most good hikers are somewhat slow in their walking. Modify your pace a bit here and there, always after you have covered at least a full mile (1½ km). By then, the actual number of steps per minute is of no concern; you will be able to feel it kinesthetically without any help from a stop watch.

The next important item to master is the stride—the distance between one foot and the other in a step. As with pace, the beginning hiker starts off too enthusiastically. Again, find out what kind of steps you are taking at two miles (3 km). The stride should be the kind you normally take when you are in no particular hurry. This is your natural stride and you shouldn't tamper with it.

There is one modification, however, that is beneficial and not tiring—swivel your hips forward with the foot. This adds about two to three inches (50 to 75 mm) to your stride without noticeably increasing the work. Multiply this small amount by the number of steps you take on a hike and you can see how much distance you gain. This is in a horizontal, not vertical, plane, and after a little practice it requires no conscious effort. Long-distance walkers, such as in the Olympics events, do this to an exaggerated degree, but they are worth watching for pointers. The records for running and walking the mile in competition are just a couple of minutes apart.

Another factor that makes a trained walker move faster and farther with less effort is that he keeps his legs far straighter than the untrained person does. While, as we shall see later, this must be modified by terrain, it holds fairly true. Most hiking is done on reasonably smooth and level ground, even in the mountains.

The knee should bend just enough to clear the foot off the ground so it doesn't shuffle in the dust. The hip swings forward in a comfortable pendulum arc and plants the foot, heel first, at the end of the stride. The other leg now pushes off with a spring at the ankle and repeats the cycle. When the ankle is springing, the knee is straight but relaxed.

The feet should be kept as parallel with the

direction of motion as possible—any deviation will reduce the effective energy from the ankle spring. If, because of a lifetime of incorrect walking, your ankles simply won't permit this without pain, then try to have them as nearly parallel as possible without conspicuous discomfort. Hopefully, this problem will ultimately disappear as an obstacle to hiking skill.

Rough terrain presents more problems than smooth and level ground. First of all, the stride has to be modified with each change of terrain. It is doubly important on uneven ground to keep the rhythm as much as possible, although when the hiking involves climbing, this is impossible. The knee has to bend more as the heel hits the ground to absorb the greater shock of going downhill or to shorten the stride when going uphill. Ankle spring needs to be greatly reduced when climbing since it puts a heavy strain on the calf muscles and Achilles tendon—instead, use the thigh muscles and the knee joint for this lifting.

When climbing, a new type of rhythm is needed. A short (one- or two-second) pause after each step or every three or four steps is needed to keep from getting winded. Here again, there is the temptation to move at top speed in the beginning. Do not yield to this temptation or you might not make it at all.

Long rests are not needed more than two or three times a day (and these for meals or snacks). Brief rests of five minutes or so are useful when climbing, but I personally prefer "tripod rests" when hiking, even up steep hills. The tripod consists of the hiker's two legs and his hiking staff, the staff taking most of the load of the pack. Long rests, especially in hard climbs or steep hikes, tend to cramp (or at least stiffen) the leg muscles while keeping going or taking a tripod rest results in no discomfort.

In the longer rests, lie down with your feet higher than your head for about ten minutes. Take off your boots and change socks. Treat any incipient blisters. Try to relax completely. After about ten minutes, get up and "bile the kittle" (fix lunch). The normal moving around required for this task will massage out any approaching leg cramp or stiffness. Make sure the trail meal is a high-energy, easily digested one. After resting about five minutes after the meal, head back on the trail again.

EQUIPMENT

The most important item of gear for the backpacker is a good pair of hiking shoes. In addition, you need to wear two pairs of socks and carry at least one pair to change during a long hike. (If you just change one pair of the two, put the new pair on the inside and move the previously inside pair to the outside. The previously outside pair contains most of the dirt which destroys the cushioning effect of the two pairs. If the previously inside pair is damp with perspiration, let it dry out before putting it on again. As mentioned before, the lunch hour is the best time to make this change.) What to look for in a good hiking boot is discussed at length in Chapter 10.

Next to foot gear, the most important item in backpacking is the pack. If you have a heavy load (over twenty-five pounds [11 kg] is a heavy load in backpacking), this means a pack frame or ski pack. It should have wide shoulder straps to help keep the weight of the pack from cutting into your shoulders. Trailwise makes a pack frame with a sponge-rubber and leather yoke instead of shoulder straps which, with a waistband, is the most comfortable strap arrangement on the market.

If you are accustomed to it, a tumpline helps; otherwise you will only get a sore neck. It is of great value in situations such as with the Duluth pack where very heavy loads are carried for fairly short (one mile or less—1½ km) distances.

A heavy waistband on your pack will take some of the strain off your shoulders and put it directly on your pelvis instead of transmitting it through your spine. The waistband also keeps the bottom of the pack from flopping against the small of your back (or the top of your pelvis, if you like your pack low), greatly increasing the comfort of the pack. The waistband should be nylon webbing rather than leather so it will flare out at the hips. Otherwise, you will develop blisters or bruises on top of your hip bones. Also, a quick-release device should be used to tie the waistband so you can shed it quickly in case of a fall.

All backpacking equipment should be light in weight. A tab tent or a mountain tent made of lightweight fabric is the only possible tent type other than the improvised shelter of the poncho.

All others are too heavy. A short-model air mattress is the heaviest you can carry and even it may be too heavy if the distance is far and food takes up much of the weight. Polyethylene ground cloths will only last a week before they get torn up, but since they only weigh a few ounces (less than 100 g), they are ideal. They have a horrible habit of sticking to your face so be sure they are completely covered by your bedding to prevent being suffocated. The build-up of static electricity in these things is amazing, especially on cold, dry nights. Cleaners' bags provide a ready and cheap supply.

The food should be dehydrated or naturally dry. Watch the bulk limits of the food as well as the weight. A bulky pack, even though fairly light in weight, can be uncomfortable to carry. An adequate supply of water should be carried to get from one water source to another; consider the high rate of water consumption when hiking and the water needs of dehydrated food. The bota (see page 90) is the best water container for backpacking. It is light, it is flexible and it rations the water in a very efficient way.

If you are backpacking at fairly high altitudes (where most backpacking trails are), you must take an adequate supply of clothing to conserve your body heat. Even in dry weather, ponchos make a good windbreak against the cold of mountain tops. If you do enough backpacking under these conditions, however, windproof pants and an anorak will be much more efficient.

ORGANIZING THE PARTY

Regardless of the size and experience of the group, some organization is required. In a large group, or with a large percentage of inexperienced hikers, or over fairly dangerous terrain (mountain climbing, spelunking, etc.), a rather complex organization is required. In a small group of experienced campers, the organization is so informal that it appears to be non-existent.

In any case, the leader has the important job of coordinating the operation. His job is to see that the weight of the packs is kept within proper perspective (a task with beginners), that the community gear is properly distributed among the group according to their strength and ability, and that all necessary items of equipment are included and no unnecessary ones are taken. I have a friend who delights in asking anyone who has just been on a camping trip, "Did you forget the toilet paper?" Generally he gets a sheepish, "How did you know?"

The leader is also responsible for getting the slower hikers toward the front and the faster ones toward the back of the line on the trail. To do otherwise is to have the group spread over a couple of miles with the ones in the lead unhappy because of the ones lagging, and the ones behind unhappy because the rest of the group has run off and left them. It is also a good idea to put the photographers with the slow group since, even if they are expert hikers, they do stop frequently for their shutter-bugging.

It might be useful to divide a fairly large group into two separate groups with the slower hikers in the first group. The faster hikers could finish breaking camp after the slow pokes have left and start considerably after them. (Since the expert hikers are both fast and can carry a greater load, they are the ones who carry the tents anyway.) This could be timed so that both groups reach the next campsite at the same time or so that the slow group will reach it slightly ahead of time and start wood gathering before the fast group arrives with the tents.

Under no circumstances, other than going for emergency help, should any member of the party leave the main group by himself. Sometimes, in case of injury, someone will have to be sent for help, but even then, if the numbers permit, two should go as insurance. The fact that conditions are difficult enough for an injury to occur is indication that the danger of injury may be greater than usual and the securing of help should not depend on one person.

Generally speaking, the hiking should be done in the morning. Break camp shortly after daybreak, allowing enough time for a leisurely breakfast and to let the sun get up high enough to dry out the tents (another reason for having the tents with a late-starting, speedier group). The cooler part of the day is in the morning and the hikers can walk faster with no more expenditure of energy and water than in the heat of the day. Ten miles (16 km) is generally the distance for one day's hike unless the terrain is fairly level. This would put lunch at about the seven- or eight-mile (12 km) point and the next campsite would be reached by two in the afternoon. After camp is set up, there is still quite a bit of daylight left for photography, fishing, laundry, improving the campsite, or fixing an extra-special dinner. Going to bed shortly after dark will permit full rest before arising at the next dawn.

ROUTING

Routing on well-marked trails is no problem unless some vandal has removed a critical trail marker. All you have to do is get a good map of the trail and follow it and the trail markers. Navigation is simple and you can use all your time enjoying the scenery.

Off well-marked trails, however, things are considerably different. If at all possible, get a map of the area from the Geological Survey and find someone who has been there before and get him to mark out the route on the map for you. If the route departs from hiking and gets into mountain climbing, it is best not to go at all except with a leader who has been over the route before. This is especially critical on talus, scree, and rock chutes where there is danger of an avalanche, of a rock slide, or of falling.

Aside from the terrain, the most critical problem of the leader is in locating campsites and water supplies. The campsite should meet the requirements listed in Chapter 21, yet it should be within a reasonable hiking distance from the previous camp. If the hiking conditions are particularly hard, there should be a water source along the trail between the campsites for refilling.

Fortunately for the leader, most of the hiking trails in the country, even those which are not traveled much, are adequately marked and usually have well-written guides for them. These guides cost less than a dollar in most cases and are well worth it. They not only show you every step of the trail (including places you are most likely to take a wrong turn), but also where the outstanding scenic views are, as well as historical, geological, or biological data on the trail.

SKIS AND SNOWSHOES

Backpacking does not have to be abandoned when snow has made walking difficult. Several million of the world's population live where there is practically no other form of transportation during much of the winter.

Most of the techniques and equipment for ski camping are described in Chapter 30. However, there are a few differences between cross-country ski trips during the day and using x-c techniques on a weekend or longer camping trip.

The procedure is basically a cross between the techniques of backpacking, already discussed, and the techniques of cross-country skiing discussed in Chapter 30.

The pack for skiing should be, logically enough, a ski pack. While it is usually better to keep the load fairly high on the back when hiking, when skiing, especially downhill, the center of gravity should be kept low for good control. This further restricts the weight of the camping gear, since the ski pack is not roomy, but it is much safer than using a pack frame or other heavy-load pack.

If you will actually be camping on the snow, you will need several other items of gear in addition to the usual winter camping equipment. Obviously, your tent should have a waterproof floor or you will have a mess inside. And you will have to use the pitching techniques shown for soft ground on page 37.

A sleeping-bag shell will practically be required. This is an outer bag with a foam-plastic bottom to kill some of the heat-sink tendency of the snow below. It not only replaces the air mattress, it also provides another layer of windproofing to keep out cold air circulation. Your body heat warms it the same as the sleeping bag, giving you double insulation on the bottom where it's needed most.

It is wise to carry a clamp-on ski tip in case of damage to a ski. This will permit you to get back with a broken ski instead of having to improvise a set of snowshoes and hike out over fairly rough terrain. On terrain with long, steep climbs, ski climbers attached to the bottoms of the skis will be welcome.

The best showshoes are the Alaskan design, a compromise between the long, thin Maine style and the short, wide bear paw. These will give satisfactory use in both woods and open travel.

Walking in snowshoes is fairly much like hiking. The shoes are shuffled over the snow like cross-country skis, using the pointed tail to trail them properly. The main difference is that you have to walk with your legs a bit farther apart (considerably farther in the case of the bear paws) and, since snowshoes weigh five or six pounds (2 or 3 kg), they are a bit tiring to use.

If you will be encountering any ice or very steep slopes, a set of crampons will be most valuable. This applies both to snowshoes and cross-country skis. Unless you are climbing, the instep crampons are best since they are so much lighter than the full-sole climbing versions.

CHAPTER FORTY-THREE

Bicycles

The use of bicycles as a transportation method for campers has never been as popular in this country as in Europe. This has some logical basis since, until recently, the bicycle was as widely used by Europeans as the family car is used by Americans. While cars are becoming more numerous in Europe, the bicycle is still in heavy use there —especially for weekend vacations.

Even in this country, the riding of bicycles by adults has increased to the point where it is at least no longer embarrassing for an adult to be seen on one. Heart specialist Dr. Paul Dudley White is due much of the credit for the popularization of the bicycle as a health-building recreational device. Bicycle clubs are applying the appropriate pressure to get cycling paths in city parks and even some states have managed to divert some of the vast highway funds into building highways for bicycles instead of the more traditional air polluters. Still, it is quite unusual for a camper to use a bicycle in this country—even in the East, where it is ideally suited for back-road travel by campers.

As a camp transport, the bicycle falls between the backpack and the automobile, yet it is quite different from the canoe and horse, which are also in this intermediate state. You can safely carry only slightly more on a bicycle than you can on your back (well under a hundred pounds) but you can carry it farther and faster with about the same expenditure of energy per hour.

The bicycle can't compete with backpacking in mountains or in going across fields, since you end up having to push your bicycle, with its load, up steep hills or over soft ground. However, it is unsurpassed along the scenic back roads and the more level foot and bridal paths within large city parks.

You have to be in condition for bicycle camping, just as you do for backpacking and canoeing. The easiest way is by riding daily. If you live less than two miles (3 km) from work and have been driving, ride your bicycle there and back in good weather. The amount you save on gasoline in one year will pay for much of your camping trip. Besides, it is good, healthy exercise.

THE CAMPER'S BICYCLE

The bicycle that is used for camping should be a lightweight model with a three-speed transmission or a ten-speed touring bicycle. The single-speed bikes are usually too heavy and are unable to handle hills and rough ground comfortably with a full load of camping gear. The eight- to twenty-speed racing models are usually too light to stand up under the rough use that is inevitable in camping and have a poor low-gear range. The ten-speed touring bicycles require more care than the three-speed ones, but they have a good selection of gear ratios. Get the one with the lowest speed ranges—you will be going up steep hills more often than you will be trying to out-run a car.

You must keep your bicycle in top mechanical condition, especially the tires. Then it can easily handle 250 pounds of camper and gear if it is not ridden too roughly over rocky ground. Avoid underbrush wherever possible as it often hides sharp and strong thorns.

The bicycle should have a battery-powered headlight (not one working directly off of a generator powered by the front wheel) and a red tail reflector. Neither should ever be hidden by your equipment.

You should carry a small repair box containing an extra tire tube, wrenches to fit all bolts and nuts, pliers with wire cutters, a spoke wrench, three or four extra spokes, a patching kit for the tires, fifty feet of $\frac{1}{4}$″ (15 m of 5 mm) rope, extra links for the sprocket chain, extra brake and gear-shift cable, a tire pump, grease (preferably in a tube), and extras of the more essential bolts and nuts. You also must have a basic knowledge of bicycle repair!

Should a tire become so damaged that it cannot be repaired by replacing or patching the inner tube, there is a temporary repair which will enable you to get to a store without damaging the wheel rim. Take the rope in the repair kit (it should be as hard as possible, preferably braided, such as heavy clothesline or sash cord). Remove the tire and tube. Push one end of the rope through the valve hold and tie the end in a figure-eight knot. Pulling the rope as tightly as possible, rotate the wheel in the same direction it will rotate when going forward. Take two turns, laying the rope flat and parallel in the inner groove of the wheel. Pull them tight. Next lay three turns in the outer groove of the wheel, nesting in the grooves between the first turns. Pull them tight. Finally, lay two more turns in the grooves between the previous three turns. Tuck the end around the center turn of the three-turn row several times to secure it.

Check it periodically and tighten when needed. It is a rough ride, but better than carrying the whole load or ruining the wheel rim by pushing the cycle. The tire should be put back on over the rope. This technique is useful when the tire is cut so badly that the inner tube would be completely exposed if it were repaired simply by replacing the inner tube. Care in riding on rough terrain will reduce the need for an improvised tire.

A bicycle's kick stand tends to sink into soft ground, and you need to have the bicycle upright to pack it. A small metal plate can be placed under the stand to spread the weight, but there is another method which weighs nothing. Using a stake and rope from the tent you have just struck, take a guy from the cross-bar to the stake and tilt the bicycle slightly away. This European method works as well on muddy ground as a kick stand does on pavement.

EQUIPMENT FOR BICYCLE CAMPING

Just as in backpacking, the proper pack is essential for bicycle camping. These are pannier packs which mount over the rear wheel just as the panniers mount over the back of a packhorse. However, unlike the heavy plywood-and-canvas horse panniers, bicycle panniers are made of regular pack materials and are much smaller. The size of each side should be no more than six inches wide, eighteen inches long, and fourteen inches high (15 x 45 x 35 cm). A lining of $\frac{1}{8}$″ (4 mm) modelers' plywood should be placed in the panniers next to the wheel to keep the load from rubbing against the wheel or spokes.

Smaller panniers (twelve inches long, eight inches high, and four inches thick [30 x 20 x 10]) may be placed on the front wheel, but they should carry very light equipment in order not to interfere with sensitive steering. A single pack can be fitted in the triangle between the bar and main vertical members of the frame, but it should be kept quite thin (three inches [75 mm] at the most) in order not to interfere with pedaling.

A bundle no larger than a backpacking tent may be placed on a rear luggage rack, over the rear panniers, and a sleeping bag may be put in a handlebar basket or lashed to the handlebars if front panniers are not used. Weight is more critical than bulk in front luggage placement, but bulk should be kept down whenever possible.

In all cases, try to keep the center of gravity as

low as possible. This is the main reason against the backpack—it is carried too high up. Another objection is that you will carry a pack load there and fill up the bicycle panniers with still more, and end up with a load fifty pounds (25 kg) overweight.

The weight of your gear should be kept under fifty pounds (23 kg), excluding the bicycle itself. As with backpacking, you can carry more at any instant than you can all day. With a bicycle, an overload seems no harder at first, but you will soon tire out. Headwinds are bad enough without bulky gear forming a sail trying to push you back.

The camping equipment for bicycle camping is basically the same as for backpacking except that a few more luxury items (reflector oven, etc.) can be carried. Tents should be selected so that they need no large poles (which are impossible to carry comfortably on a bicycle) and should be under eight pounds ($3\frac{1}{2}$ kg) in weight. Here again, a roomier style can be carried than when strictly backpacking as long as weight and bulk are kept low.

Clothing should be comfortable and loose-fitting enough not to bind when you have spent several hours on the bicycle. Except for the use of a poncho, and concessions to comfort instead of fashion, your bicycle-camping wardrobe will not differ much from your usual sportswear for the season.

Most bicycle-camping equipment can be modified for use with either the motorcycle or motor scooter, although neither can carry the gear as easily as the bicycle. While side cars are murder to ride in, they do carry the gear quite well.

RIDING TECHNIQUES

It seems that almost as many people can ride a bicycle as can walk—and just as high a percentage do it wrong. The riding style for camping is different from racing and from the usual recreational riding too. While the turned-under bar of a racing bicycle is quite welcome to the camper since it lets him crouch down and thus lower his wind-resistance, the racing style demands a considerable amount of energy in order to get from here to there in the shortest amount of time. On the other hand, the recreational bike rider tends to waste energy with inefficient pedaling.

The pedal should be under the ball of the foot, not the instep. This permits you to use your ankle as well as your leg when pedaling and saves wear and tear on your calf muscles. The seat should be adjusted so that you comfortably reach the bottom pedal position without bending your ankle downward or completely straightening your knee (but almost do so); you can reach the ground with one foot at a time, but not both together.

In order not to have to fight the wind, you should lean down, but not so much that your arms are supporting any major amount of your body weight. You will still need a sensitive control of the handlebars in order to avoid obstacles, despite the weight of the gear on the front. This is a problem racers don't have, so they can support much of their body with their arms and lower air-resistance better than the camper can. On the other hand, the camper doesn't get as tired, even though he has more of a load.

Don't overexert. You are not racing. Gear down, or push the bicycle up steep hills instead of having to "pump" against a speed so slow that you have difficulty steering a straight course. Ideally, keep pedaling at the same speed all the time, shifting up or down as required by the slope to maintain this same pedal speed. The speed should be a bit faster than you would normally think, and should require only slight effort. Three-speed bicycles require considerably more effort in this regard than the ten-speeds. Unless you have been able to coast a lot, rest every hour.

Don't go too fast. This happens quite easily going down a steep hill, but remember: with the load you are carrying, it will take quite a distance to stop. Also, your maneuverability is sharply reduced and it will be harder to avoid obstacles. At high speed, a spill is quite dangerous.

CHAPTER FORTY-FOUR

Trail Scooters and Snowmobiles

Fairly new to camping are a couple of special breeds of the motor scooter. They come in two types, one with wheels and the other with skis and treads (much like the large snow cats used by the snow-survey crews). While they will seldom go over forty-five miles per hour (75 km/h) on level stretches, they can carry a considerable load up a rocky or snowy hillside.

They have wisely been restricted from the wilderness trails of our National Park Wilderness System, but they are of considerable value in the vast areas of private wilderness and on public land where the erosion danger of wheeled vehicles on trails is not as great, where existing roadways are snowed in, and where there are no pack trains to be spooked by the loud putt-putt coming suddenly around a bend in the trail.

These rigs typically have a sturdy luggage rack behind the driver, on which can be lashed a fairly large supply of camping gear. The type of gear is basically like that used for canoe camping, although the snowmobile camper will need a more winterized set of sleeping equipment and clothing.

TRAIL SCOOTERS

Strictly speaking, the wheeled versions are the trail scooters, although the term is inaccurate since they are primarily designed to operate off the trails entirely. While the ski models do leave the trail (since it is difficult to find the trail), people lazy enough to use a wheeled scooter instead of backpack or burro are generally too unadventurous to get off the trail. Lest some true campers get offended by this statement, let me explain. I am talking about the type of person who made necessary the prohibition of trail scooters in wilderness areas—the sort who considers the scooter a status symbol of his superiority over the backpacker rather than as a means of transportation to get him and his gear into an area to start real camping. This type is seldom a camper.

With the early marketing of these scooters, it very quickly became a fad attracting the sort of noncamper mentioned in the previous paragraph. It also attracted a lot of fast-buck boys who put out some inferior products hoping to cash in on the fad. They did, and as the fad passed so did they. However, there are still a few around, so be careful. A trail scooter is fairly expensive compared to other forms of camp transportation in its load class; therefore it should be chosen with care.

Discuss a given model with other owners. How does it operate in loose sand? How is the fuel consumption off the roads? Any such vehicle will get great mileage on smooth and level conditions. Is the fuel tank of adequate size? Even if you carry extra fuel (as you had better), it is a nuisance to have to stop periodically and fill an undersize tank.

Is the engine properly ventilated for hard use in desert heat? Can it take oversize tires for use on sand dunes? Are such tires available in this size? Dune riding is an exciting sport.

Is it easily repaired with a minimum of tools? It is a long walk to a garage in the wilderness. What is most likely to go wrong with it? What spare parts should you carry? Can you get parts easily? Are there any parts of other manufacture you can substitute? (This is very useful in a small town or will permit you to borrow a spare part to another make of scooter in your group.) What are the best accessories (including improvised or homemade ones)?

Only of secondary importance are the features discussed in most of the literature from the manufacturer, such as capacity, accessories, and speed. Most of these figures are given for ideal conditions, and a trail scooter is never used under ideal conditions.

If you are going to operate it on the highways (and they really aren't designed for it) or on any public road, you must have all the required accessories, such as a horn, windshield wipers (most trail scooters don't even have windshields), and license-plate light (with the license plate to go with it).

Generally speaking, it is better if you get two low speeds for your gear ratios rather than one low and one high. You will rarely find terrain off the road which will permit more than thirty miles per hour (50 km/h), even if your scooter will go forty-five (75 km/h), so why lose the ability to climb ten or fifteen per cent steeper grades for a speed feature you can't use most of the time?

Remember to carry tools and extra gasoline as well as essential spare parts such as spark plugs, distributor rotor and points, condenser, several repair links for the drive chain, an assortment of nuts and bolts, and any other item that particular scooter has an appetite for. They don't push easily over those steep hills they climbed so effortlessly with the engine running.

SNOWMOBILES

Another version of the motor scooter uses a pair of skis for the front wheel and a single wide tread for the rear. They are a little more streamlined, both for looks and to give some protection against a cold wind, but they still are basically open vehicles.

When the snowmobiles first came into popular use (mid-1960s) it was thought that their remote habitat would make them less objectionable than the trail scooters despite their noise. Unfortunately this attitude failed to foresee two problems: that the wilderness would soon get recreational pressure in the winter from a sudden increase in cross-country skiing and snowshoeing, and that an unfortunately large number of these snowmobiles would be bought by the same unthinking types who ruined the reputation of the trail scooters. Soon reports came in of fences destroyed and animals killed by running them to death.

Actually, the snowmobile has more validity than the trail scooter—in the proper hands. It has performed valuable service in search and rescue operations and has freed the Inuit and Cree from dependence on dog sled transport in the winter. However, the noise factor is still totally objectionable and deafness is often the cost of this "fun." Adequate mufflers would remove some of the objections. Still, like the trail scooter, they should be outlawed in the deep wilderness where it is desirable to keep the wildlife wild instead of so disturbed by the noise that they finally leave the area or so accustomed to it that they are no longer wild and become pests like the deer and bears in some of our more crowded national parks.

Safety is a problem with these rigs, not because they are dangerous in themselves, but because of their habitat. It is best that you never go out alone; always go with another one so that if anything happens, one can tow the other back. As one manufacturer pointed out, "You can go so far in fifteen minutes, you can't walk back."

Stay out of loose drifts. While the weight distribution is over a large enough area to keep them from sinking in, you can sink a foot and a half ($\frac{1}{2}$ m) into a drift that is not even over your head. Also be careful along ridges. While you are not likely to get into areas where you have a true snow cornice (where the snow has become so thick on the lee side of a ridge that there is literally no mountain supporting it), you will encounter much softer snow there and, if the other side is steep, you could tumble off.

Again, spare parts are essential. A jerry can of properly mixed fuel is a must. (Snowmobile engines are two-cycle since the oil stands the cold better when mixed with the gas.) Spark plugs and other key ignition parts, chain links, a spare belt, and a wide assortment of nuts and bolts should be carried. You may have to make one, since the skis are rather wide, but a spare ski tip should be carried if you have wooden skis. Metal-ski users should carry a fairly heavy hammer to bend one back into shape if it gets bent by a hidden boulder.

If you drive these into high altitudes, be sure you have the proper carburetor jets. Even with the high-altitude jets, a forty-mile-per-hour (65 km/h) snowmobile will only be doing ten or fifteen (15 to 25 km/h) on a Rockies peak. A good cross-country skier could beat it easily.

These rigs have a wide number of uses. Not only as a way to get across snowbound roads to a hunting or fishing site, but as a ski tow to get into the wilderness for cross-country skiing or just for skijoring as a sport in itself. However, remember that some people like their wilderness quiet, so consider them too—even in the winter.

CHAPTER FORTY-FIVE

Canoes and Kayaks

The canoe has been a part of the camping scene in this country from the days of the earliest French explorers. Some areas of great beauty, notably the Quetico-Superior Wilderness Area, can only be seen by canoe since aircraft are prohibited, the vast amount of water restricts backpacking and horses, and the portages rule out motorboats.

The canoe strikes that rare medium between the speed required to get from one place to another, and the slowness needed to fully enjoy the beauty of nature—the reason for camping in the first place.

The canoe's habitat is also the habitat of game fish, water birds, and spectacular scenery. Canoeing is not hard for anyone who can swim, and is one of the most rewarding forms of camping. In some areas, the expense of owning a canoe can be partially avoided by renting one from an outfitter.

A canoe isn't really an efficient means of transportation—an automobile or bush plane will get you to your campsite faster. But those speedsters don't let you see the country as do the hiking boot, bicycle, or canoe, nor do they require the physical work. Nor, most important of all, do they give the deep enjoyment that comes when the individual pits himself against the power of nature and lets that power play the major part in its being conquered.

TYPES OF CANOES

There are basically two types of canoes—the Canadian canoe and the kayak. The Canadian is the type usually used in this continent, while the kayak is more common in Europe.

The Canadian canoe is divided into three types—white-water, river, and lake models. The lake model has a keel projecting about three inches (75 mm) under the canoe. It is strictly for sailing. The most common is the river model, which, because it must go sideways easily to avoid rocks, has a shoe keel a quarter- to a half-inch (5 to 10 mm) thick and two inches (5 cm) wide.

The white-water canoe is a European adaptation of the Canadian canoe by making a pronounced rocker (longitudinal bend) in the keel, rounding the cross-section with a pronounced tumble-home, and making a full-length spray deck with a small cockpit at each end for the paddlers. The result is a white-water boat which, with the proper paddling techniques, can be beat only by a single kayak in white-water meets—it even beats the double kayak.

Because of the rocker, the white-water canoe turns from the middle rather than the stern. As a result, both the bow and the stern men have the responsibility in steering and the paddles are held more vertically because of the extensive use of draw and pry strokes. While the tumble-home would make loading difficult, there is no reason why the white-water canoe couldn't be used for camping too. In some areas of white water, it could successfully compete with the kayak as an alternative to endless portaging.

The load in a Canadian canoe (which will refer to the river model unless otherwise noted) should be placed in the center and kept as low as possible. If you are alone in the canoe, the load should be slightly forward of the center to balance. Otherwise, the bow will rise high and a headwind will catch it and swing the canoe around.

The kayak is not used in camping in this country nearly as much as it should be. It is lower, faster, and more stable than the Canadian canoe. The wind will never turn the bow as it will the Canadian, even when unloaded and with only one person. Kayaks are made both rigid and folding. The folding style is better for camping since you can store it in your closet with the rest of your camping gear.

In the kayak, the load is placed fore and aft (and, to a very limited extent, alongside) the central cockpit. The paddler sits in the cockpit using a double paddle. It is a little harder to load and unload a kayak; sometimes you almost have to stand on your head to get the gear wedged under the decks. However, the decks protect the gear from weather or from loss in case of an upset (extremely rare).

EQUIPMENT FOR CANOE CAMPING

While much of the camping equipment can be taken from your present outfit, the canoe and its accoutrements constitute the major item of equipment.

Canadian Canoe

Unless you are an accomplished canoeist, get an aluminum canoe if you choose the Canadian type. The wood-and-canvas canoes are more aesthetic and handle a little easier, but in rocky shallows they require almost as much care as a sick baby.

If you really want to enjoy canoeing and canoe camping, learn the techniques and develop your skills in an aluminum model—there is less chance of damage to the canoe. When you gain the needed level of skill and are interested in buying your own canoe, those of wood and canvas or molded plywood offer a tremendous advantage in the beauty department, although I am afraid that the wood-and-canvas ones are on their way to extinction along with jerky, tipis, and many other excellent

camping devices. The plywood models, however, are improving in appearance and in design too, influenced by the European racing canoes.

Aluminum canoes require no painting, they are more damage-resistant (you don't have to be as careful with edged tools and hobnailed boots as with the wooden ones), dents usually pound back out, they make a good fire reflector if the fire is not too close, they are about five pounds (2 to $2\frac{1}{2}$ kg) lighter and won't waterlog, and they are unsinkable, even when loaded, unless the air chamber is punctured.

On the other hand, they get unbearably hot when left in the sun—yet they transmit the chill of the water right to your knees. The slapping sound of the waves on the bottom is far too loud for the quiet-loving camper and they are hard to use for wildlife photography for that reason. (The paddles hitting the sides of the canoe are noisy too, but a piece of rubber hose, slit lengthwise, slipped over the gunwale at the paddlers' positions will reduce the noise.) They wind-wander hopelessly when empty and handled by only one canoeist. And the glare of the sun off it makes painting desirable. The fiberglass canoes have the wear advantages of the metal ones, although they damage more easily from hobnails. They are quieter and conduct less heat. They require very little upkeep, even in salt water.

The ideal Canadian canoe for camping is at least sixteen feet (480 cm) long (seventeen feet [5 m] is easier in rough water), twelve to fourteen inches (30 to 35 cm) high amidships, and at least thirty inches (75 cm) in the beam. It should be able to carry about twelve times its own weight and still have six inches (15 cm) of freeboard. It shouldn't have a flat or a round bottom but a slight curve that is somewhere in between. The keel should have a rocker of two or three inches (50 to 75 mm) (the white-water models you see in sports movies have five or six inches [$12\frac{1}{2}$ to 15 cm] for less resistance in short-range turning but sacrifice directional stability on straight stretches). In the wood-and-canvas models, all the hardware should be brass instead of iron or steel to prevent rust damage—especially in salt water (and even instead of cadmium-plated steel, for it can be scratched). Aluminum canoes must be kept out of salt water unless they have been specially treated.

Kayak

If you get a kayak, get a folding one with a rubberized hull. If one person must portage it over a half-mile (1 km), it will be easier to fold it up and carry it that way than in an erected position—especially in the woods or into a high wind.

The ideal kayak for camping is one of the folding, sixteen- to seventeen-foot (480 to 500 cm) double kayaks. If you have kids and are using it primarily for a sports boat in the general area of the camp rather than as a major means of transportation, the eighteen-foot (530 cm) model may be more useful since you can get a couple of kids in with two adults. For transportation, a sixteen-foot (480 cm) double kayak is easier to handle. A single cruising kayak is about fourteen feet (425 cm) long and both single and double models will run about twenty-eight to thirty-two inches (70 to 80 cm) in beam with an additional three or four inches (75 to 100 mm) in those with inflatable gunwale which makes them capsizeproof.

The racing and slalom models are of no use for camping as they are fantastically unstable in all but the most skilled hands, who use this instability for tactical advantage in competition. They have almost no storage space under the decks. In whitewater competition, this narrow volume is usually filled with all sorts of air bags to aid in flotation in case of an accident. They are, however, a lot of fun for sports canoeing from base camp, and an ideal surfing vehicle when properly modified.

The kayak should be made of a laminated fabric and rubber skin over a spruce and/or birch skeleton. Fiberglass kayaks are also good, but few are made for camping and may present a storage problem compared to the folding ones. The best folding kayaks lock together without separate bolts and nuts, which can get lost quite easily. The decking is usually water-resistant canvas since it, like your clothing and tent, must be able to pass the moisture out or the inside will become unbearably damp from sweat when a spray cover is used. The spray cover, which fastens around the paddler(s) in Inuit fashion, is quite useful in rain or rough water, but undesirable for thermal reasons at other times. If you use it, have one you can get out of quickly in case of an upset—or learn the Eskimo roll, which is more difficult in the stable cruising kayak

than in the narrow competition model or the original Inuit kayak.

While you cannot buy a cruising kayak that way, it is definitely advisable to install hip boards, knee braces, and footrests in order to make the paddler more of a unit with the craft. Essential in white water, it is also quite useful in simple, everyday paddling. If you have a double kayak, see if you can't also rig the seat in the middle of the cockpit to have the advantage of a single kayak as well.

The easiest hip board to rig is by simply attaching a high bucket seat made out of fiberglass to the regular kayak seat. This can be molded to your exact shape by someone who knows fiberglass work, or it can be made a bit oversize and padded with a sufficient amount of foam rubber to anchor you in place firmly but comfortably.

Knee braces are also useful. They are essentially overhangs, padded for comfort, which extend into the cockpit opening from the underside of the coaming. In many kayaks, you can simply wedge your knees under the coaming.

Footrests should be fitted so that you will be comfortably wedged between the footrest and the backrest with your knees firmly touching the knee braces. These can be easily built, firmly screwing the footrests to the keel ladder of the fixed kayak or using one which locks on like the seat on the faltboot. If more than one person uses the kayak, the footrests can be mounted on a track, secured by a wing nut with the end of its bolt peened so that the nut won't come off and get lost, which will give you an adjustable setting for the footrest.

The backrest is relatively unimportant above the pelvis since it is used only in relaxed paddling. When driving or in white water, you will lean forward to get all the power of the upper arm's thrust ahead. The part of the backrest touching your pelvic area should be made integrally with the bucket seat.

A spray cover is a piece of waterproof fabric which fits around the cockpit coaming, usually by a spring or elastic holding it against the coaming itself, and fitting around the paddler just under the armpits with elastic. It keeps spray, waves, and rain out of the kayak. The spray cover is standard in white-water work and it is a very valuable addition to the camper's cruising kayak as well, especially in wet weather. Unfortunately, they are seldom made for double kayaks and you will probably have to make your own. For these do-it-yourself kayak features, see Chapter 15.

The faltboot should also have keelstrips—strips of rubberized fabric similar to the hull material (although usually only three-ply instead of five). These are cemented to the hull along the keel and bilge stringers to take the wear of scraping the bottom. They should, ideally, be installed when you buy the craft, but if not, you should put them on. They should be replaced when they start to wear through and before the main part of the hull fabric itself is affected.

Generally speaking, the fewer parts the better. Stay clear of kayaks with a large number of screws and wing nuts and choose instead the ones which lock together. The total weight should be under fifty pounds ($22\frac{1}{2}$ kg) for a single and under seventy (32 kg) for a double, not including extras outside the complete hull, such as paddles, spray cover, equipment bags, sailing rigs, etc.

Paddles

The best paddles for a Canadian canoe are made of maple. Those of ash or close-grained spruce are also good. The blade should not be over six inches (15 cm) wide and not over one-third the length of the paddle. The edge should be thin (about one-eighth inch [3 mm]) to cut water without noise. The grip should be smooth to avoid getting blisters on your hand from a full day of paddling. The shaft should be sturdy but not too thick since this not only adds weight but also makes it unwieldy to handle.

The grain should be straight, especially in the shaft, and there should be no breaks, cracks, checks, or knots in the wood. Sight down the paddle to make sure it is not warped; if it is, it won't be comfortable as a carrying yoke and will twist when you paddle.

The bow paddle should come to your chin when you are standing, the stern paddle to your eyes or the top of your head. An extra paddle should be carried in the canoe (lashed to the inside to prevent loss in case of an upset), and an extra set (bow

and stern) if there will be any rough water (either white water from rapids or chop in a lake).

For the double paddles of a kayak, the plywood spoon-blade paddles are the most efficient. A thin metal or plastic guard over the blade tips helps prevent veneer-damaging wear which is far more rapid in its progress than the fraying of the tip of a solid single paddle. Drip rings are optional; the experts disparage them, but since I don't get to use my kayak as much as I would like to, I find them essential.

The shaft of a double paddle should be about twice the beam of the kayak and the blades a bit less than the beam and no more than eight inches (20 cm) wide. Leave the racing paddles to the Olympics where the distance is fairly short and speed is the most important requirement.

While one-piece paddles are stronger and preferred in white water, jointed paddles are better for camping because of storage, their availability on the deck in an emergency, and their use as a single paddle in underbrush—which the camper will actually encounter in back-creek paddling. For the best service, soak the paddles at the joint overnight at the beginning of the season and a half-hour before using them.

If your kayak doesn't already have them, sew some paddle loops on the deck and keep an extra paddle in each one. Because of its stability, the kayak will probably go where a Canadian canoe will have to be lined from the shore, and the damage or loss of a paddle in rapids is deadly if there isn't one literally within reach.

Other Gear

Canoe camping requires more equipment than just the canoe and its paddles. You need a repair kit, which will be discussed later. You need a painter—a length of quarter-inch (5 mm) nylon rope about twenty to twenty-five feet (6 to 7 m) long—attached to an eyebolt at the bow. This is used for a mooring line, for getting a tow from a power boat, or for tossing out a sea anchor in extremely rough weather. The free end of this line should be within easy reach of the bow man in either type of canoe.

You also need some means of bailing. A large-size household sponge is the best. It holds over a pint (½ liter) of water, it won't sink if you drop it overboard accidentally, and it will get the water that is a quarter-inch (5 mm) deep in the bilge or against the bilge chine or against the ribs, which no other method will do.

A desirable feature in any Canadian canoe is a set of kneeling pads. These are small cushions which reduce the wear and tear on the kneecaps which is especially severe in aluminum canoes, but not much less in wooden ones. The easiest to make is simply a couple of six-inch (15 cm) squares of one-inch (25 mm)-thick foam rubber, covered with a waterproof cover to keep them from soaking up any bilge water. Many canoeists use only one since the knee on the paddle side gets most of the weight. They can be improvised from almost any material, some of the wilder ones being a hot-water bottle filled with sawdust, a beanbag filled with small chips of cork, a two-inch (5 cm) cellulose bailing sponge (a rather soggy thing), and a pair of low-top tennis shoes with the knees fitting into the heels.

There is less need for padding in a kayak—constant practice will enable you to get over the "saddle sores" from the hard seat—but a half-inch (1 cm) of foam is a bit more comfortable than the bent plywood you get with the craft. However, you shouldn't use foam any thicker or it will shift from side to side and you will lose some of your maneuverability since you can't "swivel-hip" the boat sideways as easily.

Camping Gear

As long as you don't take too much, any of the medium-weight camping gear will do. However, if your route has many portages, you will appreciate backpacking gear more. In general, the tents for a semi-permanent camp and normal sleeping gear will be adequate.

In canoeing, a three-quarter ax is so much better than a hatchet that the hand ax is excess baggage. A tree is often found blocking a stream, leaving little choice between chopping it in two so that it falls to the bottom and the canoe can pass over the break and of unpacking the whole load for a portage of fifteen feet (5 m).

Keep the gear together, preferably in a good pack. A pack frame, carried separately in the canoe, is needed for portages if a Duluth pack is not used. However, it is almost impossible to stow in a kayak. The bags used for packing the folded kayak make good packs for carrying the gear when kayak camping. However, this might present problems if you have a portage long enough to require folding the kayak.

In a Canadian canoe, all items of gear should be tied to the thwart to prevent loss in case of an upset. The kayak's decks give this protection and the small items amidship the cockpit are in watertight bags fastened to the underside of the cockpit coaming.

CANOEING TECHNIQUES

The techniques for the two types of canoes are as different as their outward appearance. The modern techniques, like the modern crafts, are only slightly modified from the aboriginal, yet the differences between the two types make it hard to believe the cultures which developed them were actually adjacent geographically—in fact, they overlapped in parts of Newfoundland. Yet both crafts were admirably suited for their purpose—the kayak a seaworthy, highly responsive, fast hunting boat; the birchbark canoe a stable river boat with a large cargo capacity.

While the Canadian canoe is considerably shorter than the thirty-foot (9 m) *canot-maître* of the voyageurs, and the kayak has increased its stability at the loss of some of its speed, differences still remain in technique as well as appearance.

Loading the Canadian Canoe

In loading a Canadian canoe, first pile the gear at the water's edge in as few bundles as can conveniently be handled at arm's length sitting down. The bow man gets in first, facing the shore, and moves to the bow thwart, holding the gunwales as he goes and putting his feet in the center of the canoe with his toes turned either inward or outward (a matter of personal preference which direction, but one or the other is needed to aid in balancing).

The stern man then gets in with the bow man steadying the canoe with his paddle. When the stern man is in, the bow man stows his paddle and the stern man hands him the packs, one by one. When finished, the packs are tied to the thwarts. Now, with the stern man holding the canoe steady, the bow man turns around and climbs over the bow thwart to his normal paddling position. The stern should have floated free by this time because of the weight shift forward and the normal paddling procedure starts.

Unloading is essentially the reverse, with the stern man careful not to have the canoe move up onto the bank far enough so that the shifting weights during the unloading process will put too much stress on the canoe bottom—especially with a wooden canoe and a rocky shore.

If any precipitation or rough water is anticipated, the pile of gear in the center should be covered with a tarp securely lashed down. It also helps if the gear is placed on a couple of fairly large sapling poles so that, as the canoe ships water, the gear will be kept high enough so the water will be bailed out before the gear gets wet.

Extra paddles should be thrust through the lashing ropes, easily accessible, and a repair kit and painter should be kept under the bow wedge, preferably in a specially built bracket to make sure it does not come loose but is still easy to reach in case it is needed.

Loading the Kayak

The kayak is loaded, as it is boarded, parallel to the shore. One man gets in the kayak and the other hands him the packs as needed. The man in the kayak stows them well under the decks, wedging them securely but being careful not to put pressure on the hull skin, just the skeleton—otherwise, hitting a rock could cause serious damage. Normally a kayak will bounce off a rock because of its resilient skin and the water pressure around the rock absorbs most of the impact.

While this wedging is going on, the man onshore is holding the kayak steady. When loading is completed, the man in the kayak holds the craft steady while the shore man gets in. Carefully, not to put too much strain on the plywood blades, they push the craft sideways into deeper water and start paddling.

An Inuit trick is useful in modern kayaks. The Inuit use the side of the paddle blades to scrape the mud off their boots before getting into their kayaks. While the camper's faltboot is a bit easier to get into to clean out mud than the Inuit's craft, this trick will let you avoid the job entirely.

Since the gear in a kayak is carried under the decks, there is not the problem with rain protection there is in a Canadian canoe. However, since the deck is similar to a tent in materials and construction, no item of equipment should be directly touching the canvas as it will create a capillary leak just as it would in a tent.

Canoe Positions

In a Canadian canoe, tradition has the stern man the skipper since he handles the rudder position. The only exception to this is in rapids or similar emergencies when the forward position of the bow man has the advantage of vision of the danger ahead. The stern man calls the side to paddle, direction (and therefore, indirectly, the strokes to use), loading and unloading procedures, launchings and landings. The bow man sets the pace (usually about thirty strokes to the minute in calm water) since he is usually less experienced and more than likely the weakest. The more experienced stern man, however, will exercise a restraint on the eagerness of a tenderfoot bow man who, typically, tries to set too fast a pace to last all day.

In parties, the guide is in the first canoe and the group's leader brings up the rear.

In a kayak, there is not the same requirement for command to go with position since both paddlers are amidships and exerting the same leverage. In this case, command is a matter of personal taste and mutual agreement. The rudder, if used, is controlled by the stern man simply to keep the cables short and cut down on weight. In white water, however, the forward man takes over as in the Canadian canoe, sometimes even standing up to scout the route before entering a particularly doubtful stretch.

In heavy weather, the Canadian canoe is often reversed and paddled stern first. In this case, the bow man kneels against the center thwart and the stern man uses the bow thwart. This places the paddlers closer towards the center, much like

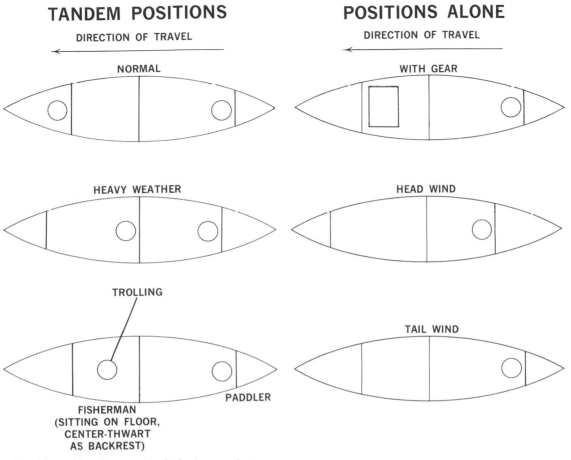

TANDEM POSITIONS

DIRECTION OF TRAVEL

NORMAL

HEAVY WEATHER

TROLLING

FISHERMAN
(SITTING ON FLOOR,
CENTER-THWART
AS BACKREST)

PADDLER

POSITIONS ALONE

DIRECTION OF TRAVEL

WITH GEAR

HEAD WIND

TAIL WIND

CROSSWIND (PADDLE ON LEEWARD SIDE)

CROSSWIND (PADDLE ON WINDWARD SIDE)

a kayak's position. Because both the bow and stern are lighter than if a paddler were in them, they will bob with the waves easier and you are less likely to ship water over the bow. There is less leverage for turning than at the extreme position, but in rough water the gain in fore-and-aft stability more than compensates for it. This position is also good for teaching paddlers since the instructor is closer to the pupil and can move him as well as give verbal instruction.

A passenger can easily be carried in a Canadian canoe, sitting on the bottom, holding both gunwales, and resting against the center thwart. Both the bottom and the thwart can be padded with floating cushions to make the position more comfortable as well as providing an additional measure of safety. The paddlers take their usual position at each end.

It is usually better, however, if the passenger does some paddling. In this case, he will take a standard kneeling position against the center thwart and, in most cases, paddle on the same side as the bow man. In this case, the stern man will use almost a straight stroke, with almost no hook, in order to compensate for the turning tendency of the other two paddlers.

Carrying passengers in a kayak is a little harder, and in most cases it is restricted to children out of concern for the comfort of the paddlers. In any case, it is practically restricted to the longer touring models. A passenger can wedge in between the two paddlers with his legs going around the one in front. A second passenger can wedge into the extreme front of the cockpit (often straddling a mast socket) with his legs under the foredeck. In either case, floating cushions are far more comfortable than the rungs of the ladder keel frame of the kayak, especially since there are no backrests available.

While the kayak offers no real difference in paddling position, the Canadian canoe does, and it will be desirable to change positions from time to time. This is best done at the mealtime break when the canoe is landed, but it can be done in the water. It can be done from either end, but it should be done with care. One paddler, carefully stepping in the center of the canoe and holding both sides, moves to the center, where he sits down on the bottom. The other walks down the center, holding the sides, carefully stepping around the first paddler in a straddling position and taking his place. The first paddler then gets up and completes his move to the new position.

Canadian-Canoe Paddle Strokes

First off, the average person handles a single paddle backward. He reaches as far forward as he conveniently can and pulls the paddle toward him. Actually, the lower arm is a fulcrum and moves only a few inches (10 to 15 cm) (to keep in the same position relative to the water) and only at the beginning of the stroke. The upper arm is pushed away. This method gets considerably more power, not only because of the better leverage but

also because stronger muscles are available for use and you don't get as tired after a hard day of paddling. In fact, the old Indian method involved the whole body moving forward along with the top hand, producing a bobbing effect—and fantastic power applied all day.

The lower hand is held fairly loosely, just above the blade, so the shaft can turn. The top hand is held over the grip and does the twisting of the paddle (as in the J stroke) as well as providing the power.

On strokes parallel to the canoe, try to paddle slightly under the canoe. Don't lean out to do it, just try to do it comfortably. This way you are not wasting any power in swerving the canoe off a straight-line course.

There are three basic types of Canadian-canoe strokes: the cruising strokes (for straight travel), the draws (for turning), and the jams (for stopping or stabilizing). While the degree of twist and the side of the canoe you paddle will vary, there is no real difference between strokes used in the stern with only one paddler.

For purposes of consistency, the sketches of canoe strokes will assume that the bow man is paddling on his right and the stern man on his left, so regardless what side the sketch shows the paddle to be on, the bow man has his left hand up and his right hand down, while the stern man has his right hand up and his left hand down. Paddling on the opposite side is simply a mirror reverse.

The cruising stroke for the bow is the easiest of all. Reach forward as far as is comfortable without bending your back, insert the paddle two-thirds of the blade deep, push the grip away until the blade is even with you, pull out the paddle and start over. Any forward motion you could make by continuing the stroke past you will be canceled by the upthrust in the water forcing the canoe deeper into the

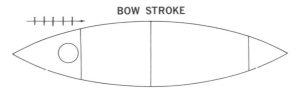

BOW STROKE

water and thus increasing its drag. Save your energy.

Since the stern position is more efficient than the bow position, a straight stroke in the stern would have the effect of turning the canoe away from the side of that stroke. Changing sides every few strokes is a waste of energy since the canoe goes on a slightly zig-zag course and the time and energy of one stroke is totally wasted in the act of changing sides. Because of this, a different stroke is needed in the stern—especially if there is no bow man.

There are essentially two types of stern cruising strokes: The J stroke and Canadian stroke. They both start out as a straight stroke like the forward bow stroke. In the J stroke, when it reaches the paddler, it is turned and forced outward to force the canoe back in line from its turning attitude. (Actually, the J is as viewed from the shore. The canoeist sees it as a rather rounded L, the reverse movement being from the canoe's motion rather than the paddler's effort. If the paddler were to actually form a J from his viewpoint, he would be backpaddling some and would practically kill all the forward speed of the canoe.)

A more efficient variant on the J stroke is the Canadian stroke. The straight part is a little longer than the J, going about a foot (30 cm) past the paddler. Instead of pushing outward after the twist, it is set in a rudder effect and pushed (or rather pulled, since the top arm is doing the work) for-

ward and upward so that it leaves the water about halfway back toward the insertion position. With a little practice, the correct angle of the rudder will come automatically. Naturally, more angle is needed alone than with a paddler in the bow. Despite the fact that the paddle is moving in what appears to be a backpaddle, because it is essentially moving edgeways, very little forward momentum is lost. This is a highly efficient stroke and a surprisingly easy stroke to keep up all day.

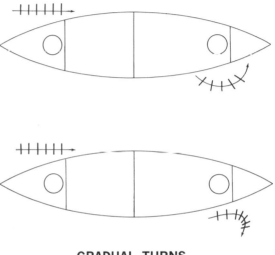

GRADUAL TURNS (BOW AND STERN)

The draws are the most varied because the quickness of turns required under different conditions vary the strokes needed. A very gradual turn can be accomplished by using cruising strokes and varying the size or power of the side force of the J for a stern-side turn, or a semi-circular stern sweep for a bow-side turn.

A sharper turn requires a forward draw in the bow. This is the regular forward bow stroke used in cruising, started diagonally out from the bow and brought in toward the craft rather than simply alongside the canoe. The stern uses a wide stern sweep which moves the paddle in a wide half-circle from the canoe's side, out, and back to the canoe's side. This combination turns the direction of the bow paddler's side.

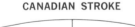

CANADIAN STROKE

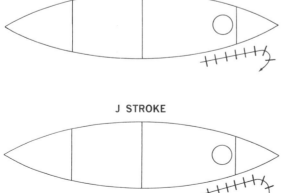

J STROKE

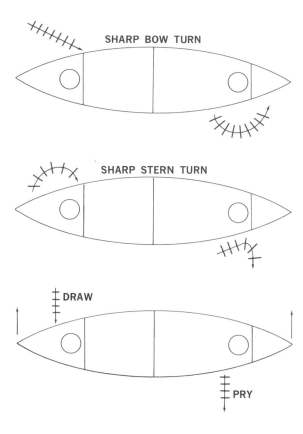

SHARP BOW TURN

SHARP STERN TURN

DRAW

PRY

and the other a pry; the side drawing is the direction the canoe will go.

Both paddlers using either the draw or the pry can turn the canoe around within its own length. This is useful (in a more restrained form) in docking in narrow channels or in cattails.

The jams are generally the brakes of the canoe, but sometimes the rudder or keel. In the quick stop, the blades are held alongside the body, perpendicular to the centerline of the canoe with the thumb of the lower hand holding onto the gunwale so the paddle doesn't move. A canoe moving at full speed can be stopped considerably short of its own length with this method. Trying to stop by backpaddling only wastes energy and splashes water. Because of the part played by the thumb of the lower hand, this stopping jam is often called a thumb lock.

A keel lock uses the same position, but the blade is parallel to the canoe's centerline. This is used to steady the canoe when loading and when in rough water.

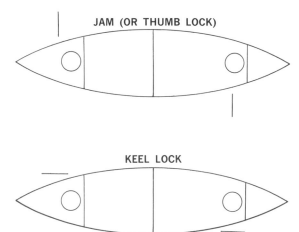

JAM (OR THUMB LOCK)

KEEL LOCK

A turn on the stern paddler's side could be accomplished in the same way by changing sides first, but accomplished canoeists don't like to change sides too often—not only does it waste energy, it destroys the rhythm since the paddlers have to get accustomed to the feel of paddling on another side. For a stern-side turn, the bow uses a sweep, not quite as wide as the stern sweep in the bow-side turn but still a definite half-circle. The stern uses a J with heavy side force.

Moving at right angles to the centerline of the canoe is done with draws and prys. These are done with the paddle blade parallel to the center line and the movement is perpendicular to it. If the movement is done toward the canoe, it is a draw; if done away from it, it is a pry. The two are generally used together, one paddler using the draw

The bow rudder and cross-bow rudder are basically jam strokes since the paddle isn't moved in a horizontal direction. These are generally used in rocky areas or white water with the stern man using a single paddler's J stroke. In these cases, the bow man steers since he can see the rocks sooner than the stern man, and the stern man simply provides the propulsion and occasional direction changes at the bow man's command when the bow rudder will be inadequate. In the cross-bow rudder, the bow man reaches in front of him with the lower hand in order to get the paddle position without having to change hands.

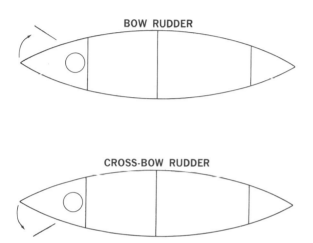

BOW RUDDER

CROSS-BOW RUDDER

Strictly a white- or rough-water stroke is flamming. This requires the bow man to reach over the stem and sweep a hole in an approaching wave for the canoe. This way, the canoe can navigate waves which would otherwise pour over the side amidships. This trick is, of course, for experts who have a good sense of balance in a canoe and skill in timing waves. If you don't have this skill, you had better wait out the storm safe in camp. In parties, use the wake of the lead canoe.

Like a car, a canoe has a reverse gear—and like a car, it is not nearly as efficient as forward. Backwaters are basically light sweeps and back draws done much like the sweeps and forward draws, only in reverse. They are good for nothing except getting out of tight spaces. For any distance over two or three times the canoe's length, turn the canoe around and go forward.

In the camping situation, spare paddles should be carried in case of loss or damage to your regular ones. However, there is one emergency skill which may come in handy in case you lose your paddles—and is fun besides: gunwale jumping. Stand on the gunwales, as far aft as possible while still maintaining good lateral stability, and jump in this position, slowly enough so that you don't actually leave the gunwales but hard and fast enough to push the stern of the canoe deeply into the water. The result is a porpoising motion at about the speed of a leisurely paddling. While this takes a bit of practice to learn, it is often a better emergency system in relatively calm water than paddling with your hands over the bow—especially if the water is cold.

Kayak Paddle Strokes

A double paddle is normally assembled in a feathered position; that is, with the blades at right angles to each other. In this way, the air-resistance of the upper blade is greatly reduced (and this is quite noticeable when bucking a headwind). One hand is held loosely and the other does the rotating of the paddle so the blade is at the proper angle when it enters the water. The rotating hand should be bent back when it is up and pushing, and bent down when it is down and holding. The pushing part is similar to the technique with the single paddle but the double paddle is not held vertically but at a relaxed angle so that it simply drops from horizontal to a floating position in the water. A double paddle can be disjointed in tight spots and one-half used as a single paddle.

With the kayak, the technique is much simpler than with the Canadian canoe. The double paddle, alternating on each side, is much easier to use in steering a straight course. The blade should be as close to the kayak as possible without bringing the other blade so far over the kayak that the water drips off it into the cockpit.

Turns may be accomplished by several means: skipping the stroke on the side of the turn and only paddling on the outside of the turn; extending the paddle farther from the kayak on the outside of the turn but still paddling on the inside (for very wide-radius turns, but it keeps up the speed);

regular strokes on the outside, but backstrokes on the inside (a turn with practically no forward motion); or continuing to make equal strokes on both sides and using a foot-operated rudder to make the turn. The latter feature is used for sailing rigs on kayaks, but it is also useful in regular paddling. Draws, pries, and backpaddles are much the same as with the Canadian canoe.

When two are in the kayak, they use the same strokes, working in unison with one another.

Since much of the enjoyment of kayaking comes in the rough water of streams, surf, and wind-blown lakes, a knowledge of some of the basics of white-water kayaking is useful in increasing the enjoyment as well as the safety. You will have a better control of your craft and you will often avoid an arduous portage simply because the water is a bit rough.

The key to most white-water paddle work, other than the normal straight and draw strokes which are used in calm-water paddling, is the paddle brace. This is one of the more useful techniques of canoeing and an essential preliminary to the more complicated strokes, such as esquimautage (righting a capsized kayak while still in the cockpit) and the slalom tactics (such as the Duffek stroke) possible only with the narrow single kayaks.

The paddle brace enables you to lean your kayak past the point at which it would normally tip over. This makes your hull asymmetrical because the curve of the keel is greater than that of the deck. This gives the water a shape similar to that of the airfoil on an airplane's wing—it will pull one way as the current moves around it. As a result, the kayak will turn around the paddle. The current can be real, as in a stream, or relative, due to the boat's motion on a lake or in surf.

The normal method of the brace is simply to stick out the paddle, blade flat on the water, on the downstream side, to keep the kayak from tipping over. If this were done on the upstream side, the water would flow over the blade, pushing it down, tipping the kayak until the water would flow over the deck and upset it. The force is the opposite on the downstream side since the water is pushing the paddle upward.

The paddle brace is done with the paddle perpendicular to the centerline of the craft or further aft to a point almost alongside the hull. Even when perpendicular to the centerline, it should be held slightly aft of the paddler by bending the upper arm back to hold the paddle behind the paddler's head.

The area in which the paddle is placed will depend on the boat's relation to the tipping force—it will be directly out if the boat is broadside to the current, but it will be almost directly back if it is bracing against a wave kicked up by a rock or a chute working at an angle to the current. The brace is used in an aft position on the back side of a wave to "kick out" in surfing.

While esquimautage is rather useless in the usual camping trip (because of the weight of the gear, if nothing else), for sports kayaking (and this is not necessarily competition) it is quite useful if you want to have the fun of white water and don't want to go swimming each time you turn over.

Esquimautage is harder with the camper's cruising kayak than with the slalom model because the cruising kayak is so stable that it resists turning over, when it is already capsized as well as when it is upright. However, even the full rotation of an Eskimo roll can be done with the cruiser if you practice hard enough.

You need hip boards so that the inside of the craft exactly fits your body at all times and a spray cover so that the water won't flood the craft as you go over. These are good to have in any rough-water kayaking as well as being essential in esquimautage.

CURRENT →

Learn slowly. Rock the kayak over (but not completely inverted) and right it with the paddle on the surface of the water, using a paddle brace. A skin diver's mask may help here. The paddle is held with one hand in the middle and the other at the end of one blade. When you tip over completely, reach up and out of the water with the paddle and lay it, blade horizontal, on the surface of the water, pointing forward. Quickly pull it downward (toward you as you float head downward under your capsized kayak) in an arc around your head. When the arc is amidships, your head will be out of the water although the rest of you will still be on the surface. You are now in a paddle-brace position, so come out of it that way, using your hips to help flip the still-submerged gunwale out of the water if it is reluctant to come.

Even if you can't get all the way up, you will have come out of the water some, so take a deep breath and go under again for another try. If all fails, you can still bail out and swim back up for air.

This maneuver probably won't come up in the average kayak camping trip for a couple of reasons. First, you are unlikely to tip over a cruising kayak except in very white water. Second, with any skill at all, you can stop the tip before you get in the water with a quick application of the paddle brace. If you don't have this much skill, keep out of all white water until you do.

Other Power

A small (under 3-horsepower) outboard motor may be mounted on an outrigger bracket on either type of canoe, although the square-stern Canadian canoe is most common for this purpose. Except for long trips with few portages, they are something of a bother to carry, as well as breaking the quiet that is so welcome in canoe camping.

Sailing rigs are available for both types of canoes, but, again, weight is a problem in portages. Where there are large lakes, they are much better than a long, tiring paddle session, especially if there is a chop on the surface. In rough water and in rainy weather, a spray cover is welcome. Canadian-canoe campers will have to make their own spray covers,

but it is standard optional equipment with the folding kayaks in all but the largest double models.

Lakes

Lake canoeing is probably the most common form of camp canoeing although most canoe campers will do a bit of stream camping too. By far the largest amount of canoeing by the "paddle out from camp" campers is done in lakes, either for pure recreation or for fishing.

The only real problem in lake canoeing is in choppy water. With the exception of sea canoeing (which should not be attempted except with a craft especially modified for surfing), any chop is going to be caused solely by the wind; therefore, get in the lee of islands and points during as much of the trip as possible. This not only gives you smoother water, it also keeps you from bucking as much headwind.

Flamming, described on page 475, helps if you know how. Another tactic requires a good sense of timing on the part of the stern man. He should time the last part of his strokes to coincide with the waves so that they end in an upward flip against the water, depressing the stern and raising the bow just as the waves hit it. The bow will then ride over the waves and not ship water.

Always be able to get to the shore fast if the wind comes up unexpectedly. Shore is the safest place to be in a bad wind. In groups, keep about three or four lengths apart to prevent collisions by the wind-tossed canoes.

Keep the center of gravity low. Sit on the floor of a Canadian canoe if necessary. Paddling is a bit harder with a single paddle from down there, but it is a lot easier than swimming while towing a swamped, loaded canoe with you.

Streams

As you have to worry about wind in lake canoeing, in stream canoeing the problem is current. However, going downstream, this can be a help. Tack back and forth across the stream like a sailboat going upwind to let the current give you a boost.

If you are going upstream, you might make better

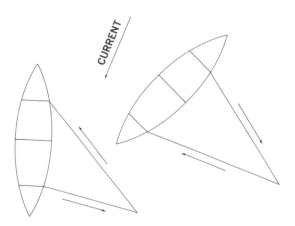

LINING

time by lining if the current is too strong. Keep the bow aimed slightly away from you at all times to keep full control. If there are no rapids, you can leave your gear in the canoes while lining. In rapids, however, the lighter the canoe, the better it will handle. In severe rapids, portage the canoe as well as the gear.

Since fast water is usually quite shallow, you can often make better progress upstream by poling than paddling. Poling is a technique which requires two canoeists. The poles should be long enough to reach bottom with a considerable length to spare. They should be straight, sound, and about a couple of inches (50 mm) in diameter.

One canoeist holds the canoe in the water with one pole while the other gets a good grip on the bottom with his pole. He then pushes the canoe along the length of the pole until he runs out of pole or the angle gets too sharp with the bottom to trust its holding power. He then holds the canoe in place while his partner finds a good grip on the bottom to duplicate the procedure.

For maximum power, the canoeists should stand and really lean into the poles, careful that they keep the canoe pointed directly into the current so that it doesn't swing around.

The pole can also be used in downstream work as a snub to keep the speed from getting too fast. The

stern man does the snubbing with his knees bent against the stern thwart (aft of his usual paddling position). The bow man uses a bow rudder to keep the canoe in line and paddles while the stern man is moving the pole. The snubbing should be a skipping slowing of the canoe rather than stopping action.

White-Water Tactics

While a full treatment of white-water tactics would require a full book and the average camper won't be doing much white-water running anyway, at least a once-over-lightly should be included on this exciting subject.

The primary rule of safety, logically enough, is to learn with an empty boat, a bathing suit, and a life preserver as well as some friends on the bank to wade out and rescue your craft if you have to leave it rapidly.

The first rule to tactics is: never get broadside to the current. The essential way to handle this is with the ferry glide. The term comes from the old ferries which, before an adequate bridge system was constructed, were on almost every river. Their sole motive power was the stream. They would ride across on a cable, with the hull at an angle to the current so that the deflection pushed it across. When across, they would reverse the angle and come back.

In white water, the ferry glide is a system of draws and pries and any other methods you can use to keep your craft parallel with the current while your movement is across it as you weave between rocks which are exposed or barely under water. If you try to steer through the maze as you would in still water, the current will grab your stern and swing it around until you are drifting sideways, almost out of control. When you get to the next rock, you will be in the market for a new boat.

The second rule of tactics is: stay in the main channel. (The few times when this rule must be broken are quite rare and are encountered only in streams too wild for the beginner to be on anyway.) You find the main channel by looking for several things. A glassy spot in turbulent water is deep and therefore safe. A long V pointing away from you and downstream is the channel. Always try to wedge your bow in these V's. When the end of the V has a standing wave, or haystack, crash it head on. It is the main channel and will give you a safe distance between your keel and the bottom even if the haystack does wet your face in the process.

If you do run aground (usually on an almost exposed boulder), try to push straight off in an upstream direction. If the current grabs your stern, let it swing on around. Paddle upstream just fast enough to let the current slowly back you downstream until you can work over to an eddy which will let you turn around again.

A corollary of the first rule of tactics is: never let the water get over your upstream gunwale. If it does, you are going to go over unless you take more action than is usually possible. The easiest way to prevent this (although it takes a proper seat so that the craft is an extension of your body) is a brace. Lean out on the downstream side, extend your paddle blade flat on the water, as far aft as you can, and let the current pivot you around this brace.

Generally, the beginner gets in these situations by violating the second rule of tactics (especially in the kayak, which can handle most white-water problems easier than a canoe). He sees those big waves and tries to thread between them. The waves are big cushions of water and if they are true waves and not just water piling up over a boulder, the water will be fully deep enough there for safety, which is more than can be said about the space in between. (The rocks are usually visible and almost never at the foot of a V.) Hit the waves head on—this is wet and you need a spray cover, but it is safer and more fun.

After you have had a bit of experience in this type of white water, you are ready to tackle the larger currents, to shoot rapids with camping gear, or to try surfing or any of the other things that can be done with the kayak and canoe when the skills have been learned.

Should you capsize and be forced to swim, swim on your back with your feet downstream. This way you will have two advantages: first, you will be swimming upstream (relative to the water) and thus decrease your movement downstream (relative to the bank) while you work your way to the shore;

second, you will be able to absorb the shock of hitting any boulders with your leg muscles instead of your skull.

In severe white water, a crash helmet should be worn.

Portages

Portaging is a cross between canoeing and backpacking with the worst features of both. You not only have to carry all your gear, but a boat as well.

Your gear obviously goes in your packs. Here is where the importance of good packs for your gear shows up. The canoe is what gives most people trouble. In the first place, the occasional canoe camper had better forget about picking up the canoe with a paddle yoke and taking off down the portage trail alone. The balance is a bit too tricky. With both canoeists holding the canoe, it is much easier. They can either pack their gear and take it along with the canoe or cache it and come back for it, as their muscles and energy indicate.

Picking up a canoe, Canadian or kayak, is mainly a matter of timing. Roll the canoe over on its side with the keel toward you. Hold the gunwale (cockpit coaming) on top with your left hand and the thwart (opposite cockpit coaming), as far down as you can comfortably reach, with your right. Pull up with your right hand and push away with your left, raising the canoe. Twist your body and duck your head as the canoe comes up and roll it up over your head.

Watch your step. If the trail is long, you will probably have less trouble with a folding kayak if you dismantle it and carry it in its carrying bags, securely tied to a good pack frame if the bag doesn't have shoulder straps.

A yoke for your canoe will be convenient. In a Canadian canoe, your paddles make a quite serviceable one, although you will probably have to pad the paddles with something if you are not used to it since it puts a lot of weight on your shoulders. Unfortunately not on the market, some kayak campers make a horseshoe-shaped yoke from foam rubber and leather which doubles as a backrest while paddling.

Many portage trails were originally game runs, so don't pitch camp in the middle of one. You will

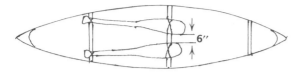

PADDLE YOKE

not only be in the way of other canoeists trying to reach camp, you may have a moose running down it in the middle of the night.

Capsizing and Swamping

If you are close to shore and your swamped canoe is still carrying the load without sinking completely, paddle slowly to shore and empty the canoe there. Sit on the bottom of the canoe while doing this in order to have as much of your body floating as possible.

If you are carrying no load and your canoe swamps, the solution is still fairly easy. Lash the paddles, your shoes, and the kneeling pads to the thwarts or jam them under the bow and stern wedges. Get out of the canoe and capsize it. It will float with a large air pocket under it. You may have to tilt it several times to get all the water out and let the air accumulate under it. Get under one gunwale, and quickly flip it up and over. By the time you come up again, the canoe will be upright with very little water in it. Board it (from one end is the best way as there is least likelihood of recapsizing it or shipping much water) and bail out the remaining water.

If you are carrying a load, the capsizing method won't work. If you are sinking, you will have to jettison something. Yourself is best since you will float. If that doesn't do the job, you will have to dump some of your gear. A float attached to the gear with parachute cord, seine line, or other strong cord will greatly assist in recovering the gear after a crisis has passed. This is a time for quick decisions since you may lose the whole works otherwise. Making these decisions before the need arises is most prudent.

If the canoe remains floating, you can often get the water out by other methods. Get in the water (most rescue methods require swimming) and pull the stern into the water. After the water has drained around the gear from the bow, push the canoe forward sharply. This should slosh out enough water to enable you to re-enter the canoe and bail out the rest.

The easiest method is to use another canoe to help you. Transfer any gear to the rescue canoe. Hold down the stern as with the shoving method and let the other canoeists pull it up over their canoe at right angles to it. Then help them turn yours over to pour out the water. They will ship a little water this way, but not much. They then right the canoe, slide it back into the water, and help you and your gear back in.

The real question in swamping and sinking is: how did you get into the fix in the first place? In all of these rescue techniques, we are assuming that the water is literally over the gunwales. This means that almost all of these cases can be prevented. Bailing is the most logical preventative and will usually work even against a stoved-in hull if you wedge a kneeling pad or some other flexible object in or against the hole.

Stay out of high waves or rapids. This not only prevents swamping from waves, it also reduces the chance of the most likely cause of a flood-out—capsizing. The northwoods experts in canoeing avoid capsizing so well that many of them cannot even swim.

In all cases, stick with the craft, even if you have to swim alongside, holding on. Just be sure you do hold on, especially if there is a wind blowing—otherwise, you may never catch it. Don't abandon ship and try to swim for shore, especially in a lake. In the first place, you will lose your canoe and its gear. In the second, you severely reduce the chance of your reaching the shore at all. As long as it is floating, stay with it; it is your best life preserver.

In cold water, there is the problem of hypothermia—chilling to a dangerous degree. Out of the water, exercise will help maintain body heat in cold weather, but in cold water, the opposite is the case. Reduce the circulation of the water over your body (analogous to the wind-chill factor) by keeping on your clothes and moving no more than is necessary. Here a life-preserver is obviously required since those soaked clothes are going to tend to weigh you down and even drownproofing requires some movement. After getting out of the water, get a fire going and dry out as quickly as possible.

The problem of capsizing is even more unlikely in a kayak. It is almost impossible to capsize a cruising kayak—especially if it has an inflated flotation ring around the gunwales. Keep the heavier items of your gear low in the hull and use a spray cover in heavy waters. If you are securely seated in your kayak, with the load properly placed and a spray cover in place, the proper use of paddle braces will insure safety in all but white water— and if it is all that white, you shouldn't be in it with a load of camping gear in the first place.

A judicious amount of portaging and skill in handling your craft will prevent accidents in either type of canoe.

SAFETY RULES FOR CANOE CAMPING

There is nothing complicated about canoe camping. It is just that water is not man's natural element and there are precautions which must be taken.

The first rule is to keep the load (including yourself) low in the canoe. In a Canadian canoe, kneel, don't sit, on a thwart. Sit on the floor in a kayak.

Second, don't risk an upset. A canoe is reasonably stable if you handle it right. Always go around the edge of lakes, near the shore instead of across the middle, even with a spray cover and/or a sailing rig. The winds will be lighter for sailing, but if you heel over it is a shorter tow to shore.

Scout all rapids from the bank before trying to shoot them. Portage if they are the slightest bit difficult. Don't try to learn white-water canoeing with camping gear. Practice with an empty boat, bathing suit, life jacket, and crash helmet until you can handle your craft under tricky conditions.

White water is doubly hard in a Canadian canoe. Part of the kayak's unwarranted reputation for instability comes from the fact that usually it, and not the Canadian canoe, is used for the rapids-

shooting contests that make the newsreels. (In fact, the white-water canoe hardly resembles the camper's model, while the slalom kayak is only slightly narrower than the camper's cruising kayak.) With either type in white water, a spray cover is necessary to keep from shipping water.

Third, know how to swim. Even then, use a life preserver at all times, especially in white water. The laws of Canada and many states require it. Water-skiing belts are best since they don't get in your way. An inflated Mae West type is good in white water because it is above the spray cover in case of a bailing out. Floating cushions used for kneeling pads are good if you tether them to your waist or ankle so that, in case of need, they won't go drifting out of reach. But it is better to wear them. When using them as a life saver, wear a cushion with your arms through the loops and the cushion covering your chest to hold your face out.

Fourth, watch the weight. On most canoe trips, you will have to portage somewhere. This means you, your gear, and your canoe. Either type of canoe can hold an amazing amount of gear without showing it at the waterline. Don't be tempted to pile on more equipment just because the waterline is still low. Even one mile ($1\frac{1}{2}$ km) of portaging is tiring with an overload. A heavily loaded canoe is more tiring to paddle and much harder to maneuver in a current or rough water.

Fifth, carry an adequate repair kit for the boat. Even the aluminum ones can get damaged. It doesn't need to weigh over a couple of pounds (1 kg) and it may never be needed, but, if it is, there is no substitute. At least one extra paddle is a must.

CANOE REPAIR

Even the aluminum canoes can get damaged. You must be able to make these repairs without help from a workshop full of tools. For an aluminum Canadian canoe, you will need the following items in the repair kit:

2 pieces of a proper-gauge aluminum, one foot (30 cm) square
3 dozen aluminum rivets
a rivet set (or self-expanding rivets)

a keyhole-type hacksaw

a fine metal file

a drill, the same size as the rivets (preferably fitted with a T-handle; if not, include an egg-beater drill)

rubber compound (see page 42)

a hammer (if you don't carry a half-hatchet or geologist's pick)

Damage to an aluminum canoe is almost always a stove-in caused by rocks. After beaching and draining the canoe, cut the jagged hole smooth with the hacksaw and file. Cut and smooth the edges of a patch three inches (75 mm) larger than the hole all around. Place the patch over the hole and bend it to shape if needed, padding it with a piece of wood, if possible, to avoid making the metal brittle. It is usually best to put the patch on the inside of the canoe. Drill the rivet holes in both the patch and the canoe, taking care to have them match exactly. A wooden pin forced into the first three or four holes as they are drilled will keep the patch from slipping. Coat the patched area of the canoe with the rubber compound to act as a water seal and rivet the patch on.

The rubberized fabric of the kayak is not as likely to stove-in, but it can become punctured or ripped. For a kayak, you will need the following items in the repair kit:

pieces of both the rubberized hull cloth and the canvas deck cloth

sandpaper

rubber cement

cold tire patches (a garage roll about three inches [75 mm] wide and a foot [30 cm] long)

waterproof tape

needles (straight and curved) and waxed thread

hull wax

talc

Punctures can often be sealed with the tape until camp is reached and more permanent repairs can be made. Repairs to the deck cloth should be made with a needle and thread rather than cement for a good appearance. In case of a hull puncture or tear, cut away any frayed edges (which will rarely be present). Cut a patch about three inches (75 mm) longer than the tear (three inches [75 mm] square if a puncture). Roughen the rubber coating on the hull and attach the tire patch. Large tears require more work. Stitch the tear together with a cross-stitch (like on a baseball) to keep it from becoming distorted, then patch. If the damage is extreme and a part of the hull must be removed, fit a patch made from the hull-fabric piece into the cut-out area and sew as with a large tear. Small punctures can be sealed with the rubber cement. A tear in the deck is repaired like torn clothing.

Broken ribs or stringers can be repaired by using whittled-wood replacement pieces. They will often do until the end of the camping trip, after which you can order the proper replacement part from the manufacturer. If the stringers are round, a length of aluminum conduit the proper diameter should be included in the repair kit. If you break a stringer, it will generally split along the grain, making a diagonal break. Slip the tubing over the break to hold it in place until a more permanent repair can be made. It is usually possible to glue such a break and avoid the cost of a replacement. Because of the resilience of the skin, this type of damage is almost unknown outside of difficult white-water passages.

For the best protection, the hull of a kayak should be waxed. It makes a much faster craft as well as protecting the skin from abrasions on sandy beaches. Before packing, the hull should be dried thoroughly and dusted lightly with talc to protect the rubber from sticking together in a hot pack. Waxing is also good for the aluminum Canadian canoe as it increases its speed, and thus the ease of paddling.

CHAPTER FORTY-SIX

Boats

As rivers are made navigable to barge traffic and the flood-control and hydroelectric lakes stretch in an unbroken line on other rivers, more and more outboard-motorboat owners are taking up camping in connection with their boats. Secluded coves with sandy beaches dot most large lakes. In all too many, the tops of once scenic canyons despoiled by the dam builders are still visible—a faint remnant of a former area of great beauty. Here camping is often possible, far from crowded public campsites and the roar of other outboards.

The use of motorboats for camping has its own problems of gear and techniques. While the gear must be packed low in the boat and fore-and-aft trim must be watched to keep the boat from becoming either bow or stern heavy, there are few of the weight restrictions found in backpacking, or with bicycles or canoes. Of course, the weight must not be excessive, but large amounts may be carried. Portaging with these boats, of course, is entirely out of the question without car, trailer, and roads. However, in many places a system of locks, canals, and even elevators for boats permit transit from one lake to another.

THE BOAT AND ITS EQUIPMENT

The outboard boat used for camping needs some features that the average weekend-on-the-lake type of boat can do without with no loss of quality.

First, it should be a planing hull. This design is too efficient to be overlooked by the camping boat enthusiast. It should have a broad beam for stability and a low draft for running ashore for the night and freedom from sandbars while under way. It must have adequate freeboard, especially at the transom, for the waters covered. You should be able to clear the propellers of weeds or replace the shearpins without getting into the water.

Since some living will be done aboard (making the boat almost a camping machine in this respect), there must be a shelter—at least a doghouse, preferably a full cabin. The shelter must have good ventilation. It should be large enough for sleeping, be insectproof, have adequate space, and be lockable.

Stoves should either be outside the cabin or adequately vented for safety from carbon monoxide. In either case, a fire extinguisher should be within easy reach. Ice boxes having doors instead of lids should open fore and aft rather than crossbeam so that the rocking of the boat doesn't dump the contents out as the food slides against the door, forcing it open. Never let the ice box drain into the bilge or all sorts of frightful odors and damp rot will result.

The engine should be capable of moving the boat at a reasonable speed. The dual-engine technique is especially valuable in this case. The speed, which is normally the reason for two engines, is not a factor in outboard camping, but the safety factor can be of extreme value since the camper will be getting away from the more heavily traveled boating areas. If one of them should conk out in a way you cannot repair on the spot, the other will get you back to shore for emergency repairs, or even to the next marina if the problem is serious.

The stern-drive engines are well suited for the camping boater. These are the hybrids between inboards and outboards in which the engine is completely inside the boat while the standard outboard type of drive unit is in the water. Their main advantage is that the motor, which is the heaviest part, is in the bottom of the boat instead of perched up on top of the transom. As a result, the center of gravity is lower and the stability is improved. However, the problems of the fixed propeller shaft in the standard inboard engine are avoided by taking the power to the water in an outboard-type propeller assembly. The thrust line of the propeller not only swivels, giving more efficiency in turns, but the whole unit can be raised out of the water like an outboard when running aground. This avoids the danger of bent props and knocked-out rudders which could happen in a true inboard.

Regardless of the type of engine, it should be well ventilated to avoid an accumulation of fumes which can be a deadly fire hazard. Carry more than an adequate amount of fuel on the trip as well as the basic repair parts and tools for the engine and other essential parts of the boat. This is especially necessary on camping trips since you will be traveling away from the assistance of other boaters.

Other equipment should include at least one anchor, preferably two, of a size suitable to the boat and of a type suitable for the anchorage. Fenders on the sides protect the boat when it is tied at a pier. Mooring lines are essential if you don't want to anchor every time (and sometimes you can't). A boat hook is a useful tool in docking and an essential one in picking up a mooring buoy.

A bilge pump is a useful gadget although the large sponge described on pages 468–69 will do the job unless you have a stove-in. An electric pump is best since hand pumps take time best spent at other tasks (especially in case of a stove-in) and engine-operated pumps won't work if the engine has stopped.

Safety equipment should meet the Coast Guard standards for your size boat. This includes navigational lights, fire extinguisher, life preservers for each one on board, and warning and distress signals.

Spare parts and tools for emergency repairs should include shearpins, spark plugs, points and condenser, screwdriver and wrenches for the engine; pieces of two-by-fours (4 x 9s) for wedging a cushion against a stove-in for wooden boats (although fiberglass hulls can also end up this way with careless handling in unfamiliar waters); and some of the new underwater-setting epoxy for boat repairs. Skin-diving equipment (not necessarily scuba) is useful for seeing what is going on down there. Spare bulbs for all lights and similar spare parts round out the list.

Navigational gear should also be carried if you are traveling through the locks of rivers or in the intercoastal waterway. This should include not only compass and charts, but also plotting tools such as a parallel rule, protractor, and dividers. A sounding lead is useful in unfamiliar waters. Instruments may include, in addition to the compass, a tachometer, water-speed indicator, depth gauge, and engine readings such as temperature and battery ammeter. A radio-telephone is useful, especially in commercial waterways.

TRAILER

First of all, a boat trailer should be the proper size for the boat. The rollers should fit the hull contours and the bow eye should be the same height as the trailer winch. If it isn't, both the boat and the trailer risk damage.

Make sure it conforms to state laws as to license, lights, brakes, etc. If the total weight of the loaded trailer is over one ton, it is best to have brakes on the trailer since your car's brake system will have quite a chore stopping the load. In fact, in a sudden stop, such a trailer without brakes is almost sure to jackknife, creating an accident even though no other vehicle is involved.

The trailer should have at least one spare wheel and tire. Typically, boat-trailer wheels are smaller than the car's. This means that they turn more often because of their smaller circumference. As a result, they have a greater danger of overheating, especially on hot summer days. Keep the speed down a bit and your trailer tires will last a lot longer.

The hitch should be a secure ball-and-socket type with safety chains connecting the trailer to the towing vehicle. The car should have a frame-mounted trailer hitch—the weight of the average camping-size boat trailer is too great for a bumper hitch.

Use a lower gear for hills—going down as well as up. Use outside mirrors and check them often; one on each side of the car helps when changing lanes. You can get truck-type outside mirrors which hook onto the window. These are easily removed when you are not towing, but provide a great margin of safety when you are.

Stop and check the load every couple of hours to see that the boat is still riding well with the tie-downs in place, the cover on securely, the hitch holding, the tires still inflated properly, and the trailer lights working.

If you get a tail-gater, get out of his way as soon as possible. Anyone with that poor a sense of depth perception is nothing to have around your bumperless boat stern. When you are passing, make sure you are well around before pulling back into lane.

In backing a trailer, hold the underside of your car's steering wheel but steer it the same as you would the top of the wheel without the trailer—in other words, move it to the left to turn left, right to turn right. This automatically compensates for that turn-the-opposite-way problem of trailer backing which is especially hard for someone who only backs a trailer once a month or so.

LAUNCHING

Line the boat up with the water, about twenty feet (6 m) from the edge. Remove the cover and tie-downs, make sure that the engine(s) are up and the way is clear all the way down the ramp. Back the trailer to a couple of inches (5 cm) more depth in the water than the draft of the boat; set the hand brake and put the car in gear; tilt the trailer and let the boat slide into the water, keeping the bow line attached to the trailer winch. After clearing the trailer, beach the boat, park the car and trailer, board the boat and get under way. Load it in the reverse order of this procedure.

A bumper hitch on the front bumper helps launch trailers in areas where there are no paved ramps and where mud or soft sand reduces traction near the water's edge. Or you could use a front-wheel-drive car. Sand (not containing silt) improves in traction when wet. If you get stuck, take a bucket, fill it with water, and wet the sand. You can use a hub cap if you don't have a bucket.

CAMPING

Camping equipment for boat camping is approximately the same as with automobile camping. Waterproof bags for the gear is a most welcome advantage, not only for protection from rain, but from any bilge water that may get on them while in a low stowage. Plastic cleaner's bags are adequate, although they must be treated carefully to prevent tearing. You will need three, fitted one within the other, to guarantee against leakage.

Check your itinerary carefully before starting a boat-camping trip. You should know ahead of time where you will stop for the night, where you can get supplies, the speed limits along the way (both on the highway and on the water), the purpose of your cruise (sightseeing uses up travel time, but just making speed is rarely of any use on a camping trip), and the anticipated weather and water conditions (you can't travel very fast in rough water or fog).

Provide for emergencies, take plenty of food and fresh water, and made sure your boat is fully equipped and in good condition, and you will have an enjoyable trip.

CHAPTER FORTY-SEVEN

Horsepacking

The people who use pack horses can generally be divided into two groups: those who know the techniques and often use their own animals, and those who hire both horses and wranglers. Horsepacking is expensive. It costs ten to twenty times as much as a canoe or backpacking trip. However, you can have as many "trimmings" as you want.

The gear goes in canvas or plywood boxes called panniers or kyaks (not to be confused with the decked canoes), which are hung on the horns of a pack saddle on the animal. Taking a horse or mule trip without help is definitely for the experienced horseman only. The dude alone will have all his time taken up battling the will of the horse or mule and have no time left to enjoy the camping that these larger pack animals permit.

The burro is somewhat different, He won't carry as much as a horse, but he is a bit easier to manage, despite his reputation for stubbornness. He will rarely run off from you as a horse will—at least not after the first day out. *Going Light* (see Chapter 54 gives all the information needed.

Whether with a horse, a burro, or in between, horsepacking has a definite advantage found in no other form of camping transportation. In a fairly short time, the camper can get into country that a car or canoe can never reach and enjoy the unspoiled beauty of nature which is the *raison d'être* of camping.

SADDLING

Even if you have hired a wrangler, you can still help out with the stock if the wrangler is willing. Currying is something anyone can do, and is an essential part of livestock care. The animal must be clean under the saddle (either riding or pack) and this is done with a curry comb—a sort of sawed-off hairbrush for horses. Simply comb it in the direction the hair grows. Do it gently, especially avoiding the skin at saddle sores. Tell the wrangler about any saddle sores you find on your horse—those on you are your worry.

Make sure the animal's back is free of dirt, sand, salt (from sweat), and other foreign matter, especially burrs. The rest of him should be free of caked mud, but otherwise does not require show-appearance.

Watch out for animals that bite. The first time one tries it, immediately whack him a hard one and bawl him out. Always keep a respectable distance from the rear—this is the dangerous end. A bite will rarely draw blood, but a kick by a healthy mule will break a bone. Watch his ears; when they lie back against his head, the gun is cocked, so prepare to move out if he starts to turn from you.

Saddling takes a little practice, but it is not

difficult. The preparatory step is bridling. More and more, the hackamore bridle is being used rather than the bit. Pack animals almost always work with one. With a well-trained animal, it is completely adequate for a riding animal and a lot easier on the animal than the bit. You just slip it over his muzzle and put the larger loop over and behind his ears. Pack stock is usually tethered with the bridle on rather than a neck rope which can work off or choke, and riding stock using a bit will often be picketed with a hackamore.

Some animals will not respond to the hackamore and a bit is required. The bit applies an irritation in the form of pressure on the soft palate to reën-force the pull of the head by reins. Often an animal (particularly one which has had a rider who jerked the reins rather than pulling them) will refuse to open his mouth to take the bit. When this happens, keep the bridle in place. The horse will toss his head to shake it away, but opens his mouth when doing so. When he does, or if he makes a more vocal protest, slip the bridle into place. The animal is now ready for saddling.

Saddling starts with a saddle blanket. The main purpose of the blanket is to prevent saddle sores by spreading out the pressure of the saddle and cushioning the movement of its load. The easiest way to fold a saddle blanket is to fold it lengthwise once and then crosswise into thirds. Six layers of a good saddle blanket will cushion the load comfortably. Special saddle pads do the same thing without folding.

The blanket is placed on the horse over the withers, which are at the base of the neck (many burros and a few mules have a dark line crossways just behind this point). It is then slid back to a point at which its forward edge is about two inches (5 cm) in front of the saddle (at the dark line mentioned above). This sliding back combs back any hairs which may have been ruffled when placing the blanket on the animal. These could cause irritation which would at least bother the animal, and at most cause saddle sores and remove his load-carrying ability.

Saddling, like packing and mounting, is done from the animal's left. First put the right stirrup and cinch over the seat of the saddle (or, if it is a pack saddle, the cinch over one of the horns). Take it by the horn and cantle (or front and back crosses) and swing it over the animal so that it falls in place without hitting hard. Push the stirrup and cinch so that they slide off without swinging under and hitting the animal's belly.

Tighten the cinch. It should be tight enough so that you can barely get a couple of fingers under it. Sometimes burros especially will take a good lungful of air just before you tighten the cinch. As a result, the cinch will be too loose when they resume normal breathing. Often you will have to resort to trickery (especially when dealing with burros) by appearing to go on to something else and then suddenly tightening the cinch when they don't expect it. The rear cinch should be loose enough to get your entire hand under it.

Breeching and breast-strap harnesses are used on pack animals since an inanimate load tends to shift more readily than a person.

Riding saddles should be properly adjusted to the rider as well. There is nothing more uncomfortable than riding with stirrups the wrong length. You should have about two and a half inches' (6 cm) clearance when standing up in the stirrups.

To anyone with any experience with horses at all, mounting and dismounting seems automatic, yet it is a learned skill. Mounting is done from the left. I will not imply, as some writers have, that off-side mounting is impossible—the Commanches mounted that way and few cultures produced as good horsemen and none better. But very few horses trained by old-time Commanches are still around and it upsets the horse to depart from routine.

If you get a horse who insists on moving out as soon as your foot is in the stirrup (and before you can swing into the saddle), hold a tight left rein to the horn with your left hand. This way, if he starts off, he will go in a tight left circle and practically swing you up if you exert a little pull on the horn as soon as your foot enters the stirrup. If your horse is chronic about this, you may have to start your swing up before you put your weight on the stirrup. It requires a bit of pulling and a hard kick up with your right foot, but it gets you up there—and often noticeably amazes the horse.

Dismounting is just the reverse. Swing your right foot over and onto the ground. Shake your left foot out of its stirrup and flip the reins over the horse's head. Lead the horse away or tie him by the reins to a secure object and you are done.

PACKING

If you are new at packing, get a gentle and experienced animal—to get an inexperienced one will do neither of you any good. Also make sure the saddle is proportioned to fit the animal. Ideally, each animal should come equipped with its own rig, already adjusted so that all you have to do is put it on. Use two blankets for maximum comfort.

The saddling procedure of a pack saddle is identical with the riding saddle except that there are no stirrups to bother with, but there are almost always a breast strap and a breech strap. These should be snug, but by no means tight. Be extra careful about putting on the breeching as this is working quite close to the fighting end, especially with mules. *Going Light* recommends that if the animal won't let you pull its tail out from under the breech strap, leave it there—it will probably get it out by itself, but, if not, the flies will teach it whose side you are really on.

Let the animal remain saddled awhile before loading. This is particularly required with burros faking cinch tightness, but many pack animals try to force off the saddle when it is first put on, yet are perfectly docile after they are convinced that they won't get it off.

Balance the load within three pounds ($1\frac{1}{4}$ kg) between one side and the other. Many campers carry fifty-pound (25 kg) capacity scales to do this accurately. Both panniers should be placed on the saddle at the same time to avoid pulling the saddle to one side. However, since the loops go on the opposite horns, the loops of one usually are placed first, the packer holding them so the weight is applied together. Look from a safe distance behind the animal to make sure the pack holds evenly. Adjust weights or pannier loops if not.

Bedrolls and other more or less flexible items

can be placed on top of the panniers or cradled between them to form a top pack. A manta, or tarp cover, about five feet ($1\frac{1}{2}$ m) square goes over the whole pack to anchor it and to protect it from the elements. This is all lashed tightly into place with a thirty-foot (9 m) lashing rope, using one of the pack-lashing ties shown in Chapter 39.

PACK STRINGS

With more than one pack animal, it is best to put them in strings rather than have each rider look after one or two. First off, this makes it the wrangler's job, which is what he is paid for. Secondly, it gives the riders a chance to be free of such restricting responsibilities. Each animal is tied to the tail of the preceding one. This keeps the pull lower than tying to the pack, thus increasing stability. There should be at least six feet (2 m) between animals so the one in front doesn't kick and the one in back doesn't bite, but no more than ten feet (3 m) so the rope doesn't slack too much or get fouled up on a switch-back. The lead rope should attach to the animal's halter with a snap through a ring so it can be released easily.

Ride with a fairly loose rein. On rocky hillsides, the horse needs all the movement he can get to keep his balance. Lead him up or down steep slopes or across bridges. In areas of unsure footing (sand, snow, fords, etc.), assist pack animals by walking alongside and holding the weight of the pack. Much of the burro's "stubbornness" is simply discretion in places of doubtful footing. If an animal should bog down, unload it immediately and help him out if necessary. You will be a mess, but back on the trail.

Pack stock does better if it keeps moving. If the trail is steep, slow the pace down, but don't stop or they will get restless. On the other hand, don't urge them on if they want to take a break under such circumstances. On stretches which are not difficult, however, keep them moving and don't let them graze unless they can do it and still keep moving. Time out for polluting the trail is another matter. They will stop to do that anyway and nothing will get them moving before they finish the job.

Keep the distance down. Ten miles (17 km) a day is adequate for burros, fifteen (25 km) for horses or mules.

Unpack (but leave the saddle on) when stopping for lunch. Lunch itself should be carried outside the packs so it is easily accessible when you stop. Repacking is fairly quick. Tether the stock for lunch to save round-up time when it is over.

On the trail, keep checking the packs to make sure that they are not coming loose. Don't allow animals to run. Not only will they tire faster but the banging of the packs, especially nesting sets, may excite them to the point of stampeding. Very few packs can hold up under these conditions.

If your mount should spook, jerk back repeatedly on the reins until the bit banging his mouth gets through his panic and he is back under control. Talk soothingly to him after he stops. This is like slapping a hysterical person: it is a bit rough but the most efficient under the circumstances.

CAMPING

Quick planning is the secret of horsepack camping. As soon as you reach the evening's campground, lay it out in your mind as you ride in. Keep the animals out of the kitchen and tent areas, but unload them where the kyaks will be convenient to the cook. Keep everything neat and in a convenient spot for packing the next day.

Line the saddles up as they will be used when packing. Have them readily identifiable as to which animals they fit. Cover them with the saddle blankets, opened animal-side-out to dry and air.

Few burros are accustomed to hobbles and they can hurt themselves on them. Larger animals may or may not be; ask the wrangler or outfitter who rented them to you. Tethering is hard on meadows, especially at high altitudes, but it is often required—especially the first and last days when they try to head home. It is also needed in flat country where they can wander a considerable distance during the night.

The string leaders should be belled. It is a great help in trying to round them up in the morning. If you have horses, it is often valuable to keep one picketed at camp to use to help round up. Quite often, the rest of the string stays within the sound of the bell. The bell should be tied snugly so it stays at the chin. Halters are removed unless they fit tightly enough so that there is no danger of the animals accidentally stepping through them while grazing.

Box canyons are the best camp locations since the stock can be kept penned in by the canyon walls on three sides and the camp on the fourth.

Grain should be carried to help attract the animals within haltering range. A lasso is occasionally needed with horses, but burros can usually be rounded up on foot.

Other than these precautions with the livestock, horsepack camping is about the same in equipment and techniques as boat camping or auto camping with a small car.

CHAPTER FORTY-EIGHT

Automobiles

Today the automobile is the most popular form of camping transportation. The car (and this includes the station wagon) can carry a heavier load farther and faster than any other method except possibly the airplane. It is limited only by terrain and mechanical condition. Even more versatile for camping are the off-shoots of the small military vehicles, pioneered by the Jeep and Land Rover. Now almost all the major automobile manufacturers are bringing out some form.

Despite the capacity and speed of the automobile, you can't just pile in the equipment and head for the nearest campsite. It, like all other methods, has its rules for maximum safety and comfort.

The primary rule is to make sure the car is in top mechanical condition. A car can run perfectly on the city streets, but getting it off onto the unpaved roads of state park campgrounds will show up some rattles you never knew were there. Car trouble in the city is just a nuisance and a delay. In the wilderness, it is a major catastrophe. Before taking your vacation, make sure that every part of your car is checked over carefully and is in top condition.

You should carry a full emergency kit in the car. It doesn't have to be very large; in fact, many cars have totally wasted space in which the kit will fit quite nicely—under a seat, behind the spare, under the dash, or almost anyplace there is room. This kit should include a spare fan belt, fuses, tire-patching equipment, a set of repair tools to fit most bolts and screws on the car, spare spark plugs and possibly points and condenser, flares, tow rope (one of the small block-and-tackle rigs using parachute cord for the rope works well and takes up little room), and about a foot (30 cm) of silver reflective tape (if flying gravel breaks a headlight, the tape will show an oncoming car which one is out).

When you are going into the desert (even along a main highway) or are getting off the trail in a park, always carry at least a day's supply of food and water. If you are getting into the wilderness, such as dune-running or Jeep-trailing, carry twice the food you will need for your plans. The reserve can be trail rations, dehydrated food, or others that will keep, take up little room, and still be nourishing. If you will be away from a safe water source, take adequate water supplies too.

Arrange the equipment in reasonable, systematic order. Items which will be needed first at the campground should be packed last so that they will be on top, easily accessible when you need them. Protect the gear and the car from each other. Do not, under any circumstance, put anything where it will block the rear window or be likely to come forward in case of a sudden stop or wreck. This includes having seatbelts for all occupants.

A set of boxes or other containers will greatly facilitate the packing process. Chuck boxes are old (and too often heavy too) but the basic idea is good.

Units of similar equipment, each in its own slot in its own box, is a valuable system: you won't start clawing through a large mass of gear trying to find an item of equipment which has fallen out of place and is lost somewhere under a great mound of stuff. This should be kept under control—five or six such boxes is the absolute maximum for a station wagon. They should be designed so that they fit into place in the vehicle without rattling or jamming, and they should be easily removed, which means that weight as well as bulk should be kept under control. They should be compartmented so that the contents do not rattle about when taking less than the full load.

If you mount any equipment on top of the car, make sure that it is in a sturdy carrier and securely lashed down. Periodically test the tension of the tie-down straps on the carrier itself as well as checking the lashings and cover for the gear.

If you have only two cross-pieces and no platform, they should still be connected. Under a heavy load, these cross-pieces will move apart and the load will soon be resting on the roof of the car. If you don't have the platform, bolt a metal bar or simply tie a rope between the cross-pieces to keep them from spreading. Actually, a shallow box, no more than six inches (15 cm) deep, is easy to make and increases the value of the cross-pieces. By bolting the box to the cross-pieces with counter-sunk bolts, you can get the advantages of both systems with very little cost.

While the suction-cup rigs are less costly, the gutter clip car-top carrier made for your particular make of automobile is by far the better solution, since it does the least damage to your car. No matter how you clean the suction cups or wax the car roof, they will still scratch the finish of your car.

Roof racks for cars have the obvious advantage of providing a large out-of-the-way place for storing occasionally used items. This is of such an advantage as to make them useful even in the "bread box" camping machines. However, they do have some serious disadvantages. First of all, they raise the center of gravity of the car—perhaps past the danger point in the case of the bread boxes on rough and sloping back trails. Secondly, it is hard to get items out of them in a rain, especially if they are easily damaged by water. Thirdly, there are few roof racks which provide adequate protection against the dust which is often encountered on dirt roads.

Because of these factors, their contents should be restricted to items which are fairly light in weight (you still have to lift them up and get them down regardless of the center of gravity of the car), and not easily damaged by water, dust, and the heat of a sealed container. Most of the items which meet these qualifications are used every day and will usually be inside the car. However, if you have quite a few items which still meet these requirements, a roof rack is most helpful.

SAFETY RULES

Obey all laws. Check with the state highway departments about laws regarding oversize loads before carrying tipi poles, long boats, or any other large, projecting items on top of the car, as well as rules for camping or boat trailers. Highway-department information centers are found on many major highways at the state lines. They are well worth a stop for information on road conditions, special laws, and often information about state parks. They always have a free map which is useful, and usually have literature on many points of interest in the state.

Take it easy on rough, sandy, or flooded terrain. The trip is over if the car breaks a spring or axle, or gets bogged down, or overturns. Overload springs are required if your car has soft suspension and you will be traveling anywhere other than on paved roads. If you have a back end full of camping gear, you may have to have them anyway. Try to keep the load as balanced as possible. Not only will your car ride better, you won't be getting as many dimmit signals after you have already dimmed your headlights.

Whether you are on the road or off, always carry at least a gallon (4 liters) of gas in a spare can. If you are in more remote areas, or have a gas-drinking monster, better make it five gallons (20 liters).

The automobile is a great means of getting to the camping area. Car camping in state parks along a traveling vacation is an excellent way to learn camping techniques. It is about the easiest and most painless way to camp. In time, the desire for more challenge will come but, while you are a beginner, car camping is best.

CAMPING ACCESSORIES

There are many devices which fit on or in a car or station wagon. They are not quite as elaborate as the camping machines, usually providing only shelter and storage for the cooking equipment. The cooking must be done outside the vehicle rather than inside as with a camping machine. They are similar to a small tent trailer in accommodations.

There are basically two types. The first is the type which fits into the back of a station wagon. It provides a double bed on top and a chuck box underneath. Storage space for other gear is provided in the front part of the bottom half, with access from the top. The chuck box slides out for convenience. Sometimes they are fitted with a tent-like boot which fits around the tailgate (which is opened to support it) to give added space. A tarp is definitely recommended to extend it even further

in case of wet weather, so that cooking is still a possibility.

The second type is the car-top tent. It is carried on a roof rack and is usually in a streamlined box. When stopped for the night, the tent is erected and there is space for two. This arrangement is especially good for small families since two can sleep in the back of the station wagon and two up in the tent. The tent is usually for the kids because they can climb better (even though a ladder is usually furnished with the rig) and because kids like the idea of sleeping on top of a car.

Some of these car-top rigs have extras such as water tanks which will provide running water with a usable amount of pressure. Most have folding or detachable legs to permit them to be put on the ground. This not only increases their versatility, but is useful if you want to make a short trip from base camp and still hold your campsite—just take the rig off your car and leave it in the campsite to reserve your spot.

While not offering the challenge of tent camping, nor the luxury of the camping machines, the car-top and station wagon boots do offer a relatively inexpensive way to travel by car even if it is not quite camping.

CHAPTER FORTY-NINE

Camping Machines

With the increase in the use of automobiles for camp transportation came larger and bulkier camping gear. This led to the inevitable problem that setting up and taking down camp was getting to be too much trouble, especially if camp was moved each day. One solution was the sudden rise in other forms of camping. Backpacking increased (aided somewhat by the fifty-mile-hike fad of the early 1960s), as did canoe camping. The early 1970s saw a corresponding increase in cross-country skiing.

Another solution, in the other direction, brought about the development of the camping machine. These are self-propelled vehicles in which you can do all of your eating, cooking, sleeping, and traveling, but they don't have the headroom and other features of the motor coach or the house trailer. They typically have a table and two benches which make into a double bed, a gasoline or butane stove, an ice box, and storage space.

As pointed out elsewhere, they really are not conducive to camping in and of themselves, ads to the contrary. On the other hand, as a combination means of transportation and base of operations while camping, they have much to offer. A good do-it-yourself expert could make a rig to fit a bread-box-type station wagon or pick-up truck for less than the average overnight picnicker spends on his tent and non-essential gear.

One of the primary advantages camping machines have over trailers is maneuverability. With the whole vehicle in one rigid unit, it is easier to turn and to back, you can climb steeper grades, you avoid the problem of fish-tailing in gusty cross-winds, and you can get faster speed on the roads. With a four-wheel drive, all the wheels can contribute to traction, a considerable difference from the one-third pulling with a standard rear-drive (or front only) car pulling a trailer. They are also a lot easier to park.

Both the bread-box station wagons and pick-up-truck camping machines are fairly quickly convertible back into their more normal hauling duties. Thus the family car (or second car, as it more normally is) can perform its usual duties most of the time and still quickly add the camping unit with only slightly more trouble than hitching on a trailer. Also unlike a trailer, it is legal to carry passengers in it while moving. The station wagon type has the added advantage of being the same "room" as the driver's and communications are much easier—the other parent can sit up front as navigator and still be able to move to the back to stop fights and take care of other duties.

The camping machine has the advantage of being set up most of the time; therefore, making and breaking camp is a matter of two or three minutes—a great help where campsites are far apart and time on the road is needed to get to the real camping area sooner. It has the added advantage of being weatherproof. If necessary (and if fully equipped), you don't even have to go outside in a downpour. As a result, it is favored by the overnight picnicker who hates nature in any form, but particularly its unpleasant ones. On the other hand, it is excellent as an intermediate stage in getting a non-camper started in camping since the transition is easier.

Balancing this fine list of advantages are several disadvantages. First of all, it is not camping. The work is done for you and you are never confronted with your own abilities or lack of them. Second, the unit goes with you and this is bad in crowded campsites since your tentsite may not be there when you get back. More and more, the large pick-up camping machines are mounting motorcycles on the front bumper or back porch to use as transportation from the camp to the surrounding spots of interest.

Because the entire unit is carried on or in the vehicle, weight is a problem. Most cab-over pick-up coaches will run a half-ton in weight if they are as much as eight feet (2.75 m) long, and this is empty weight. The capacity of most pick-ups is a half-ton. This means that, for all practical purposes, a pick-up must be a three-quarter-ton capacity if you are to have more than two bunks and a kitchen. The camping station wagons have about the same problem although the weight of the coach itself is saved since the existing car body serves this purpose. Countering that advantage is the low headroom you have in them.

Cost is another consideration. A pick-up unit will cost over a thousand dollars while a station wagon model will add almost that much to your initial cost (and not be removable from it). A unit can be built for just over two hundred dollars. However, except for a water toilet it is not very plush by camping-machine standards. By equipping it with a butane or electric stove, a refrigerator, a hot-water system, 110-v lighting, etc., the cost could easily approach six or seven hundred dollars—and that is on a do-it-yourself basis.

Storage is much more restricted than in a trailer because the vehicle determines the available size of the completed rig—in a station wagon much more so than in a pick-up.

Pick-up camping machines put the weight dangerously far aft in the large models, requiring heavy-duty rear springs. The motorcycles are useful for more than in-camp transportation—they also help keep the front wheels on the road.

STATION WAGONS

The standard equipment in these bread boxes have accommodations for two adults and two children. An adult can use a child's bed if he or she can sleep on a five-foot ($1\frac{1}{2}$ m) -long bed. The rig has a two-burner stove and can be obtained with either a gas or electric refrigerator, although an icebox is standard. It has running water (although generally you have to pump to get it running) and a rather inadequate chemical toilet (often simply a plastic bucket). An awning unrolls from the side of the roof to provide a tent-like porch.

A good worker with wood can get one of these vehicles, and build the accommodations. The savings would be enough to add a water toilet with its own plumbing system under the rear-facing seat. There are directions for making one in Chapter 15. Since you will be off the road much of the time, the rear-engine traction are preferred. High road clearance is welcome on deeply rutted roads, but higher horsepower will be needed if you pull a trailer.

PICK-UPS

Special-model station wagons are not the only form of camping machines. You can get a wide selection of attachments which fit into the bed of a pick-up truck. These are usually made only for sleeping in the half-ton models, but the ones made for the three-quarter- and full-ton pick-ups have all the facilities of a small house trailer. Even the smaller models can be modified to permit cooking. Some on the market are so elaborate that the logical question is: "But is it camping?" The answer, in most cases, is an unfortunate "no." However, as with most camping machines, this is more a question of use than of appearance.

Pick-up coaches are fairly easy to make. The only real problem is in keeping the weight down. As a result, most of them are either aluminum or fiberglass—both materials which are fairly hard to

"Bread box" vehicles make camping machines which are compact on the outside, yet have plenty of facilities inside.

Some of the larger pick-up camping machines fit on regular pick-ups but have almost as much inside as a small house trailer.

learn how to work, although not very hard once you learn. Their main advantage is that, when removed, the pick-up can be used for other duties. As a result, many have folding legs to support them at the correct height when the pick-up is elsewhere. Jacks are available to permit the coach to rest on the ground when not in use (so a high wind doesn't blow it off the legs) and still be easily installed when the time comes. The station wagon models, on the other hand, are generally kept in place, losing one or two seats' capacity and quite a bit of hauling space.

OTHER VEHICLES

You can make a camping machine on a modified scale in almost any station wagon. However, it won't have enough headroom nor can it be a permanent arrangement. It is generally the "double bed and chuck box" arrangement prized by overnight picnickers and discussed in the previous chapter. The VW station wagon holds nine people in its maximum-capacity version; the camping machine holds seven or eight—the same as two other standard station wagon models made by the same company. A permanent rig in a regular station wagon would cut it down to three.

With reclining front seats, even regular automobiles can be made into camping machines. However, they are rather cramping. Yet a few have been built into the standard Volkswagen sedan (beetle version), although they are generally for only one person and at the most for two. So far, I haven't encountered any in the smaller cars, although I have seen the Isetta bubble-cars used for auto camping.

The same problem of space exists in small boats. Most of the larger outboard cabin cruisers have some provision for overnight cruising, but it is another matter with the small craft. I made a one-man unit in my old plywood sixteen-and-a-half-foot ($3\frac{1}{2}$ m) kayak, but it was too cramping to be of any use. On the other hand, a very nice one has been built in the style of the pick-up camping machines, about ten feet long and three and a half feet square (3 x 1 m), for the side-car frame of a motorcycle. Design is far more important than overall size. The real problem is in getting enough empty space where you need it and still keep the outside dimensions reasonably small.

EQUIPMENT

Much of the challenge in camping is in selecting the lightest possible gear for the comfort and money. Equipping a do-it-yourself camping machine is in the same category. Most of the so-called camping equipment on the market today is really good only in the camping machine, which is about the only thing with the power and space to carry it. The equipment is too heavy, bulky, and often delicate for any other use. On the other hand, much very good quality is made especially for the camping machines.

In shopping to outfit a camping machine you are building, remember you are not outfitting a five-room house trailer. Most trailer supplies are totally inadequate for the needs of a camping machine. Just as with backpacking the ultimate might be considered the ability to get enough gear for a week-long backpacking trip into a belt pack, the ultimate in camping machines is getting the functions of a four-room house in a breadbox station wagon or a three-quarter-ton pick-up bed, without going outside the vehicle or climbing up onto the roof.

Actually, the true camper will not put too much equipment in the machine. Just as with backpacking, he knows the lighter the load, the more camping can be done. Give him one of the big city-bus-type motor homes to try out and he will complain about not getting to do any camping. The challenge is gone, he might as well have stayed at home or used a commercial bus tour or the family car and motels. With an overloaded camping machine, everything gets in the way of everything else; there is no efficiency because of all the gadgets. The vehicle is overloaded and therefore can't get onto the back trails which lead to where the scenery is.

The ideal camping machine is something that gets you to the campsite and back without having to use motels. It is a refuge for the family who is just learning to camp during an abominable stretch of foul weather, the kind that causes even the most expert camper to wonder why he didn't check the weather forecasts more closely and go somewhere else.

The camping-machine equipment should be like any other camping equipment, the most comfort in the least weight and bulk.

VEHICLE MODIFICATION

Regardless of type, you will need proper ventilation. This is needed not only to get fresh air when you are sleeping (the vehicle no longer has the ramming effect of its motion to force air through a small opening), but for cooking (carbon monoxide can come from a poorly regulated gasoline stove as well as the car's exhaust) and simply to prevent a musty smell during a wet spell (especially if you have your own sanitary plumbing system).

Screens are useful on all opening windows, especially in mosquito country. If you don't have them, marquisette covers or insecticide or both make satisfactory substitutes.

Items should be accessible with a minimum of disassembling or rearranging. Since a camping machine puts a lot of use in a small space, most of the gear and all of the space must be multi-purpose. With the beds set up, most things are out of reach, so get them before going to bed.

However, you should be able to operate related items at the same time. You should be able to get to your food supply with the table set up and the stove in operation. If your plans won't permit this, replan before you start building. If the commercial unit won't permit it, get another one that will. Likewise, the toilet should be accessible with the beds occupied—especially if you have fairly small children. You should be able to get from one end of the vehicle to the other, while it is moving, without climbing over much gear. This is one area of advantage the station wagons have over the pick-ups. If you have a pick-up, an inter-com is most useful and costs relatively little.

When buying a camping machine, get all the family in and make a dry run of the normal camping procedure to make sure the beds are big enough and no one gets in anyone else's way too much. If you are designing your own, use a modification of the string technique with tents (see Designing Your Own Tent, Chapter 12), using boxes and similar solid blocks instead of the string.

Definitely make sure that items such as toilets fit inside and out before cutting any holes in the vehicle. If you are attaching load-bearing pieces to the car with sheet-metal screws, make sure there is at least a light frame-piece as sheet metal can be pulled out of shape by the load.

STOVES

There are three approaches to the problem of cooking stoves in camping machines. The first is to use a built-in stove designed for a trailer, connected to its butane bottle. While quite fancy, it is really unnecessary.

The second approach is more reasonable and generally the best. Simply mount a standard two- or three-burner gasoline stove in place so it won't slide around. An extra generator and pump is worth carrying. The initial cost is low and fuel is readily available. What is more, it is quite possible that you already have such a stove.

The third approach is an adaptation of the second for the camper whose background is that of the backpacker or canoeist, but, because of a family just learning to camp, or for convenience in travel, is building a camping machine. This involves making a sheet-metal rack to hold two or three backpacking stoves (which the camper will have at least one of if he has done much backpacking). The cost is still lower and, in the case of the Primus 71L and Svea 123, the chances of anything going wrong with them mechanically is slight since they have no pump and are self-pressurizing. Of course, they are a little harder to get lighted.

Regardless of the type of burner unit, the rest of the stove design should follow the techniques used in yacht galleys. Rails should protect the pans from sliding off the stove since this is easier than always having to hunt a perfectly level site to park the machine. Although not a good idea, it will even permit you to cook while traveling. Lids and pots should be securely anchored, a shield provided to keep anything from dumping on a passenger in front (the wind screen on the gasoline stoves, one constructed especially for the backpacker stoves), and a firm rule of no frying established (since fat, unlike water, will ignite if splashed into the stove).

A small fire extinguisher should be mounted within easy reach in case of accident. It should not be directly over or under the stove since this would place it in the path of the heat or the spilling fat in case of a fire.

REFRIGERATORS

A fairly wide variety of camping machine refrigerators are now on the market which use any of a combination of bottled (LP) gas, 12-v car current, or 110-v external power (which is not always available at campsites and never when you are under way). These are between two and four cubic feet (50 to 100 liters) in capacity and some have freezers. The larger ones are far too large for the average camping machine.

Refrigerators are used strictly for milk, meat, and other easily spoiled items and cannot be expected to hold the same proportion of the total food supply as the home refrigerator. As a result, unless there are only two of you, the apartment- or trailer-size models are too small inside for even this reduced portion of the food supply. The larger sizes are usually too large on the outside. As long as you have access to ice (and most campground grocery stores have it), the simple ice chest is as good as any and better than most—there are no moving parts other than the door.

A camping machine ice box should have a drain going through a hole in the floor or at least to an easily emptied holding tank. The drain also has another advantage in using dry ice. Dry ice is available in most towns having a frozen-food locker. Its main disadvantage is that you have to seal everything up air-tight to keep it from affecting the taste. An ice box using dry ice must have a drain since the carbon dioxide will build up pressure inside the box if you don't, and even explode it if the door doesn't blow open first. Plastic wrap will seal the food.

BEDS

There are three approaches to the camping machine bed mechanism. The first is to use the cushions from the seats to form the mattress. This obviously requires seats and backrests to be the approximate size of the bed, not much larger or smaller. In the standard two-adults-two-children models, this usually accounts for only the adults' double bed; the children usually have to use the harder car front seat for their bed or sleep on the floor under the double bed. Some models provide stretcher-type hammocks suspended from the ceiling.

The second approach is to use the platform (usually plywood) that forms the middle and back seats with the table lowered to the same level, or to use part of them in conjunction with the back deck over the engine (for rear-engine station wagons). This is then covered with a standard double air-mattress. The advantage is that everyone has a reasonably comfortable bed (the air-mattress). The disadvantages are what to do with the cushions, and the time it takes inflating and deflating the bed every day.

The third approach uses a seat which has a folding mechanism in it to slide the seat out, the backrest down, and, in the case of the VW camper, raise it to the level of the back deck. This situation is the most common in the pick-up campers which have the seats along the sides which slide out to form a bed the full width of the box. The large cab-over models keep the bed in the overhang permanently set up.

Any or a combination of these methods may be used in the home-built camping machine.

Finally, you could resort to car camping and pitch a tent and beds outside the machine, but then even more time would be wasted, a suitable campsite would be needed, and it would just be evading the issue. However, many camping machines on the market have a built-on tent which is big enough to use for about any purpose, including camping.

PLUMBING

Camping machine plumbing, like a house's, includes two systems: supply and sewage. Supply can be either gravity or pressure. Gravity is the easiest and most reliable, but a water tank on or near the roof raises the machine's center of gravity too much—and is a bit too high to fill easily.

Pressure has two forms: a pump (which can be

either hand-powered or electrically driven) or air-pressure (the water-supply tank has a tire valve attached and is pressurized with a service station's compressed air-hose). The air-pressure method has the advantage of being free of moving parts (which wear) but the disadvantage of requiring the system to be not only water-tight but air-tight as well—and up to a considerable pressure too.

The pump system is, of course, just the opposite. The pump can wear out but anything will serve as the supply system, including simply dropping the pump hose into a five-gallon (20 liter) jerry can below.

The sewage end of the system is surprisingly simple. The sink drains into a bottle which may be poured out on the ground or emptied in a rest room when filled. A plastic bottle is best because of the danger of breakage.

The toilet usually comes equipped with a special hose for connecting to trailer sewage-outlets or has its own septic tank under it (and usually its own water supply too). The septic-tank version is far better because the outlets are rarely available, certainly not while riding down the highway. The septic tank must be emptied and the water tank filled fairly often, but that is a small price to pay for not having to stop every thirty minutes when traveling with small children. The version with its own water supply is an advantage since it avoids the clutter of pipes through the vehicle. In a station wagon, this is of utmost importance since it is rather heavy with water in it and if the camping rig can be removed when not camping, the station wagon has far more capacity for other purposes.

STORAGE

Storage space in camping machines is apt to be just anyplace there is space to wedge something in. Actually, it is not much harder to plan where each thing will go and put it there. At the designing level, this is a matter of personal preference and the mock-up comes in handy here. The commercial units look as though they have quite a bit of space, but much of it is difficult to use (such as closets only nine inches [23 cm] across).

First of all, the car-heater outlets should be left open. This is not only because you will sometimes want the heater on (in high altitudes and during winter trips) but because, having the outlets open, you will avoid having items of equipment get overheated and thereby damaged.

Certain items of equipment should always be available, regardless of the use of the machine at the time. These include car-repair equipment, first-aid kit, toilet, water supply, camera, extra wraps, etc., which are usually needed without warning and should be reached without having to remove stored items to get to them.

For items not needed without advance warning, the vast amount of space under the seats is best. These are entered by raising the seat which forms the lid for the storage bin. Others can be opened at the side or the top, depending on which is more convenient. Vertical doors are a little impractical on the under-seat storage spaces since they typically slope under to gain more foot space.

There should be some storage area which will permit clothes to be hung to avoid wrinkles. However, this does not necessarily mean the full-height wardrobes some commercially built camping machines have. Will the refrigerator door open with the bed down? Make sure that all the doors will open when some other part is in its auxiliary position.

CHAPTER FIFTY

Trailers

Trailers, like camping machines, are almost not camping at all. Yet because they can often be towed by the lightest of cars, they are gaining favor with campers as well as with overnight picnickers. Unfortunately, like cars, each year they get larger and larger so that many currently on the market are easier to tow than small house trailers only because they fold up and therefore have less air-resistance. The other dimensions are about the same.

As for which is better, a camping trailer or a camping machine, both have their advantages. The trailers have the advantage of holding your camp-site in a public campground while you go exploring the surrounding territory; you still have a car with the same capacity as before. And some types readily adapt themselves to large groups in cars, but just one or two trailers.

While the last feature cannot be duplicated in the camping machine, a well-designed one can hold its own in the second: you can always leave a small tent erected on the campsite, or even sometimes (usually only in privately owned campgrounds) simply leave word with the superintendent to keep your spot. Also, trailers are harder to tow than driving a single-piece vehicle, especially when backing or traveling in mountains.

However, the camping machine has its strongest advantage over the trailer in serendipity camping. You park your trailer in the camp and take out to see the country in your car. At the first spot of

interest, you start talking to someone and he tells you about an interesting spot fifteen minutes away. You go there and hear about another spot, and so on, until at the end of the day, you have driven two hours from your trailer with another campsite only ten minutes down the road with another two or three spots of interest within thirty minutes of it. So you are faced with a lot of driving simply to retrieve your trailer before seeing the other spots of interest.

While serendipity camping is often the most rewarding way to spend a car camping vacation, it is very rarely practiced. The average person camps the same way he traveled before he took up camping—on a tight schedule with the distances ten to twenty per cent too far for one day's driving. (This is probably the origin of the camping machine and the trailer. They save setting up camp for the traveler coming in late at night after a long drive.) When the camper's schedule is planned in advance like this, the trailer's disadvantage in serendipity is avoided—but so are the advantages of this lei-surely mode of traveling.

In choosing a camping trailer, the purpose of the trailer should determine the type you get. There are basically three types. The first is the bubble, or small house trailer. There is rarely any camping done in one of these.

The two remaining are more conducive to camp-ing. The first is the familiar fold-the-tent-out-of-the-bed variety. Practically all of these tent trailers are commercially built and the market is crowded enough to make the price competitive with the cost of the materials in a do-it-yourself version.

The other form is almost entirely home-built with a few exceptions being custom-built by firms which do it as a sideline with few assembly-line techniques used. It is typically a large box with a door at the end to get inside to the gear, cabinets built into the side walls, and often one or two tarp tents which unroll from or tie to the roof.

Both types have the same requirements in the construction of the trailer portion. They should have a rigid steel frame, strong suspension, and a sturdy superstructure. They must meet the state licensing requirements, which means lights. And, although rarely required by law, brakes are a valuable addition, especially when traveling in mountains where brake-fade can be a problem for a car alone, but an absolute hazard with a half-ton trailer pushing or pulling it along as well.

When setting up a camping trailer for the night, it should be set as level as possible. A small carpenter's level or, better still, one of the little circular levels used for leveling kitchen appliances is quite useful for this chore. A jack and a large number of reënforced spots on the frame for the jack to attach makes this job easier. A two-foot (50 cm) -long section of 2 x 8 (4 x 18) is useful for wedging under a wheel to aid in the job. Leveling legs at each corner help keep it leveled.

As with the tow vehicle itself, the trailer should be kept in top mechanical condition.

TENT TRAILERS

The tent trailers generally have two ways of opening. The original way was along the centerline with the lid dividing into two halves which formed the beds. This made a tent with an absolute capacity of four and a comfortable capacity of two. In an effort to improve on this, a form of it was developed in which the entire lid went over on one side and the other side became a full tent on the ground. This gave a fantastic amount of space from such a small trailer, but it raised the question: why tow the trailer around since a large umbrella tent was

about the same size, took about as long to erect and strike, but cost much less and could be carried in the trunk of the car?

The designers then figured the whole approach was wrong, so they made a wider trailer so the beds could go cross-ways to the centerline. By keeping the top of the trailer one piece, the slight problem of leakage at the seam while traveling could be avoided. The lid was raised vertically (or one end at a time) to form a flat roof and the tent folded out underneath it. Now some versions have metal roofs on the fold-out parts and even metal or fiberglass walls—it looks as though the ultimate plan is to get rid of the canvas altogether and have a folding house on wheels.

The storage space in these trailers is grossly inadequate. Except in the oversize trailers, it is practically limited to the space under the beds. In the large ones, all the walls are used for storage. In all but the largest, the trunk of the car or the back of the station wagon or pick-up is still needed to carry some of the gear.

Most of the trailers now on the market use aircraft aluminum for the main superstructure although some of the smaller ones use fiberglass. The tent is the weakest part, comparatively as well as absolutely, in the entire trailer and should be carefully checked when buying one. The tent portion should meet all the quality requirements for tents discussed in Chapter 4, although the weight requirements are not quite as stringent. Rarely is there any protection through the netting against a blowing rain.

One of the greatest advantages in selecting a tent trailer is that a fairly wide variety of them are available for rent. By testing several models, you can make a more intelligent choice than by simply looking at them in the showroom. The rent is low enough so that, if you don't do much camping or if you do go on a wide variety of camping trips and only occasionally need such a trailer, rental is by far the wisest choice. Check the trailer carefully before renting it or it may be worn in places and leak.

In any case, renting or buying, choose the trailer with care. Capacity is a relative thing, especially when stating sleeping accommodations. What constitutes a bed will vary from two feet to three and a half feet in width, and many are only six feet long despite the fact that a large minority of the population is uncomfortably larger.

Few trailers provide any real privacy; even the large ones are not subdivided into rooms. This has obvious problems when trying to rig one for a toilet since the curtain arrangement used in the camping machine in Chapter 15 would have to go all the way around since the wall is largely open netting.

BOX TRAILERS

The box trailer is an entirely different concept from the tent trailer. There is far more camping possible since the trailer is, for the most part, strictly a transportation device. It is almost always built by the owner (often using a commercial box-trailer frame) or by some welder using automotive parts for the running gear. If possible, make the trailer use the same wheels and tires as your automobile. That way, you can interchange in case of a flat. However, you should carry a separate spare for the trailer so that even if you have to use your spare, you still have another one for the unlikely but still possible chance of a flat while going to get the first one fixed.

The tent part of the box trailer should be chosen with care since it is a do-it-yourself proposition. The general style of the tab tents in Chapter 12, either with or without the interior tabs, is best, although the actual dimensions will probably have to be modified. While the weight problem of the tent is not as great as with backpacking tents, remember you still have to erect and strike it, and with a small car even the ten to twenty pounds (5 to 10 kg) saved with a lighter-weight fabric permits that much more gear to be carried without danger to the car's drive train.

The box trailer avoids many of the tent trailer's problems, but it does present a few of its own. The capacity is not limited by the size of the trailer since the sleeping is done on the ground rather than in the trailer, and the tent attached to the side of the trailer can be of almost any reasonable size. However, it has the tarp tent's main disadvantage in that the protection from a blowing rain is almost

non-existent. Of course, there is no reason why more standard umbrella, parabolic, and French tents cannot be used with this trailer. In fact, this is the procedure most Boy Scout troops use. (Unfortunately, though, they generally select heavy tents, since the trailer can carry it, and as a result the kids are deprived of any experience in more challenging camping forms, such as backpacking or canoeing where portages are involved.)

However, it is on the inside, rather than the outside, that the greatest advantages of the box trailer are found. By the use of bins built into the walls of the box, equipment can be stored in easy-to-find places with a minimum of rattling around while under way. The front end of the trailer can be curtained off to provide space and privacy for a toilet with a built-in septic tank.

While the fold-out tent trailer is limited to a single family, the box is the domain of church and Scout campers. One of these can handle up to a dozen campers and still not be over four feet wide, eight feet long, and six feet high (120 x 240 x 180 cm). A modified teardrop shape makes it easier to tow, but practically eliminates the tarp-tent-at-the-top method of tentage.

The fact that the box trailer is home-built does not necessarily mean that the design will be ideal—there are still a few things to look for. If a tent is attached to the trailer, there should be a roof overhang or a similar device to prevent the run-off from the trailer going down the trailer side instead of onto the tent.

Bins should open to the outside of the trailer if a tent is used, to the inside if they are not. This is to keep the contents from getting wet while you are looking for something in the rain. The bins should lock with a key (the same key to fit all locks) for when the trailer is parked in the city.

The entire construction, except for the frame, should be kept as light as possible. Aircraft aluminum is best if you have tools for riveting it. Fiberglass is excellent in durability, but a bit on the expensive side, even when you make it yourself. Wood construction should be kept light—quarter-inch plywood is good if you get a hardwood plywood. Make sure it is an exterior grade.

A welded metal frame is best because of the

Here is an elaborate box-style camping trailer. This one has a large ice box in front, cabinets opening on the outside, storage space on the inside with brackets for bow saws and axes, and a matching delivery van to pull it.

weight/strength ratio, but an oak or ash frame is usable, especially with a wooden skin. In any case, the bins should be built into the frame, not just stuck onto the skin. Especially the outside-opening bins should open to two positions, the first all the way open with the door hanging down or swung all the way back, the second (for horizontally hinged doors) restrained with a chain at the horizontal position to form a table for cooking or other work.

As with any trailer, a secure hitch and safety chains should be used, and a frame hitch used on the towing vehicle.

PART X

A Look into the Future

As mentioned in Chapter 1, camping has changed in the last half-century; in fact, it has changed quite a bit since the first edition of this book in 1969. World War II brought the development of many new items of equipment. After that, a torrent of products followed, spurred on not only by the military requirements of the Cold War but by a mobile population that discovered camping to be both enjoyable and economical.

In this half-century, the chemical industries have developed plastics and synthetic fabrics. The large amount of leisure time enjoyed by the public has established a whole complex of industries engaged in making recreational equipment and providing services in that field.

Yet, while this has provided solutions to some of the problems of camping equipment and facilities, too many camping items on the market today resemble gadgets rather than useful equipment. The car and station wagon have replaced the canoe and horse as the main means of camp transportation, and for awhile it seemed that all the equipment on the market was for auto camping. However, lately there has been a swing back with the backpacker finally being recognized by the mass-producers.

Public campsites are more crowded and less attractive with this great increase in campers, but there has been little increase in campsites. Inaction in Congress and in state legislatures, in getting new land and adequate appropriations to develop what we have, seems to be the main problem. Too often they seem to be serving the land-grabbing exploiters than the public who supposedly owns the lands in the public domain. Counter-pressure by campers is the obvious solution.

Because of this crowding of the already inadequate campgrounds in summer, there will probably be an increase in winter camping. If any of the various proposals for year-round school programs are adopted, vacation time may come at almost any part of the year, and the family will certainly be either camping in the winter or restricting their camping to weekends and holidays. There is already a noticeable increase in wilderness camping to the extent that some wilderness areas are threatened by the camper load on them.

With the increase in stream pollution and dams, canoeing may take more to the ocean with a resulting increase in the proportion of kayaks and white-water canoes in the total number of canoes used by campers.

We are in a period of rapid change. In the ten years it took to write and publish the first edition of this book, much has happened to camping and to camping equipment. Freeze-dried foods were perfected and marketed, as were vacuum-dried foods. Gamma-irradiated foods were finally approved in a small number. Thermoelectrics made their first feeble steps out of the laboratory. The parabolic tent reached the market and practically disappeared again. National Park Service campgrounds reached the overflowing stage in the summer. Both the Apache and Navaho tribes started building an extensive system of tribal parks for public recreation and other tribes are starting some degree of park program on their land. The mountain-climbing motor scooter was developed, marketed, created several erosion problems, and was finally banned from national park and forest trails. Part of Grand Canyon was flooded and the National Park and Monument threatened. The term "litter-bug" made the dictionary.

In half that time between editions, other changes took place—also both good and bad. There was a major return to backpacking; cross-country skiing approached a fad in many areas; the fiberglass white-water kayak became established as a major type of recreational boat; the snowmobile became a problem like the trail scooter before it; the manufactured "energy crisis" of 1973–74 became a real crisis in the environmental movement; gamma-irradiated foods still haven't made it to the market yet and the thermoelectrics vanished into the curiosity category again; finally some real camping magazines reached the market (see Chapter 53); and this little effort managed to hang in there long enough to make a second edition.

At this rate, a look into the future is only a look into the next decade or two. Beyond that, no one can predict.

CHAPTER FIFTY-ONE

The Equipment of the Future

We are now at the midway point in the development of camping equipment. There are new discoveries that hold great promise for the camper but are not yet in production. These and others yet to be developed hold the key to the camping of the future. They can continue the trend toward lightweight, quality equipment and techniques in the wild beauty of nature, or they can reverse this new trend and go back to the overnight picnicking in a self-propelled motel.

FABRICS

With the sudden return of the backpacker, the fabric situation has shown the greatest improvement from the previous edition of any item in this chapter. Polyesters in cotton and nylon blends have met most of the clothing fabric needs in all areas except cost, and there it is difficult to judge since the background of prices has risen with inflation too.

The problem of tent fabric is still with us, although it is improving. Lower cost (relatively) nylon tents are now on the market and a favorite of kids spending summers "on the road." They are still a bit heavy in weight (needed because the durability problem isn't quite cured either) and are only used in fairly small pup and mountain tent designs. Because they are so small, they are generally suitable for only one camper in the rain because of capillary leaks and sloping sides.

The coated nylon tent fabrics (see ATC tent, Chapter 12) are excellent, but require a totally different approach to tent design because of their water- and air-tightness. They are not fireproof and if abused will mildew. However, on balance, they may represent the best tent fabric today and potentially (with the fire and mildew problems cured) the best for the future.

With all the "miracle" fabrics that are being developed, there is still nothing to compete with eight-to-ten-ounce canvas in price and, therefore, the lightweight tents are beyond the budget of most of those who can camp only during their summer vacation. New waterproofing compounds on the market are much better than the old paraffin and gasoline methods, but they cost almost one quarter of the total price of the tent.

A synthetic tent fabric is needed to compete with canvas. Nylon and rayon can compete in all but price and the ability to "breathe." A closed tent can't be air-tight or moisture condenses on the inside from the occupant's breathing and sweating. The pre-synthetic era "balloon silk" is hard to get and expensive as well (and really no better than the synthetic fabrics designed for mountain tents). Most long-staple cotton is being used for clothing and other things besides tents. Still, some is available, as are some excellent but expensive cotton and/or nylon mountain-tent fabrics which are probably the nearest we are at the moment to the perfect tent fabric.

The ideal tent fabric would have the air-tightness of ten-ounce canvas, be waterproof against capillary leaks as well as rain, be fireproof against campfire sparks, weigh four ounces per square yard, cost under a dollar per square yard, be light in color and fadeproof, be stable in sunlight, not shrink or mildew, and be highly wear-resistant. A tighter-weave mountain-tent version from the same chemical would have the present mountain tent's air-tightness and would cost about $1.25. If this seems too much for one piece of cloth, remember that the plastics industry as we know it dates only from the 1920s.

Actually, some of the ultra-light tent fabrics now on the market qualify in every way except fire- and mildewproofing, capillary-leakage control, wear-resistance, and cost. The first three problems could be solved by developing chemicals to add to the finished fabric to do the job; a new polymer might meet the durability problem; and the cost would be lowered by mass production made economically sound as the result of a high demand by campers.

CAMPING FOODS

During World War II, there was quite a bit of research done on dehydrated food. Some of it was good enough to pass for whole food. And yet the mass-produced, one-meal package of dehydrated food for campers is generally of poor quality. There is a wide-open market for tasty dehydrated food at a reasonable cost.

Freeze-dried foods and mixtures of freeze-dried and air-dried foods are on the market in limited selections—mostly from camping outfitters. This selection is constantly expanding and the price is either going down or holding its own as other food prices go up. There is even some freeze-dried food making its way into the supermarkets to join the soups, potatoes, and onions that have been the vanguard of the air-dried foods (not considering the only-partially-dried raisins, apples, peaches, apricots, etc.). The quality of these foods is excellent and vastly preferable to some that is mass-produced exclusively for campers.

Another new technique of food preservation is by exposure to gamma radiation. This was delayed for years before being approved for commercial distribution while tests were made concerning possible side-effects. It preserves certain types of food without refrigeration or dehydration with no change in their taste. Other foods, including milk and some vegetables, unfortunately came out with a burned taste.

Now that the Food and Drug Administration has approved a limited variety of these foods for marketing, expense is the main obstacle. With a proliferation of fission power plants and an abundance of highly radioactive wastes coming from them which are almost literally bursting with gamma radiation, it would seem that irradiated foods would have been marketed for years by now. Yet the foods so well preserved by this method are still available only in fresh, frozen, canned, or dried forms. Instead of producing some useful product, the nuclear power plants are being forced on the public with no benefits other than some very expensive electricity and with the hazard of poisons that are proven carcinogens and take two dozen millennia to reduce by only half.

Water is as important a concern as food, especially as the camper is pushed into areas where there is no adequate fresh-water supply. A still, such as discussed in Chapter 15, is one answer, but this requires a fuel supply to keep it going and it is a rather slow method. Possibly some of the other desalinization methods, such as the ionic membrane, may be adaptable to camping needs. Even a modernized version of the World War II life-raft solar still, with its modest but welcome one-quart (1 liter)-per-day output, could be developed and marketed in a small and fairly lightweight model. With these helps, the seashore camper will have an adequate water supply without having to stay near fresh-water streams, or periodically feeding a still, or being restricted to transportation methods which have the capacity for carrying a large amount of water.

Portable generator uses boat-model engine to produce 600 watts of 115-v a.c. Total size about one foot cube.

ELECTRICITY

There are many "comforts of home" which must be left there because there is no electricity in camp. The only practical means of camp electricity today is batteries—either in a car or dry cells. Portable generators are just not portable enough. Besides, they are powered by a little putt-putt engine which is surprisingly loud on a quiet night.

The rechargeable nickel-cadmium batteries help if you are periodically near a recharging place, but any battery is strictly for emergency use only.

As a by-product of research into semi-conductors for transistors, a method was discovered for getting electricity directly from heat. If you put one of these devices in an electrical circuit and heat it, you have a current. So far, the amount of current is small, but there is no reason why it can't be improved at least a small amount. Since the mid-1950s, the Chinese have used these thermoelectric gadgets to operate radios off the heat of a kerosene lantern. True, a radio doesn't take very much current, but then neither does a kerosene lantern give off much heat. Besides, the whole generating system on one of them weighs only a couple of ounces (about 50 g).

These thermoelectric generators could be developed into a generating plant weighing a couple of pounds (1 kg or so) and powered by the campfire or a small bottle of propane gas. It could produce enough electricity to power a small refrigerator and a couple of large flashlight bulbs for light.

Portable generators using fuel cells are being developed for military use. However, they are too big for camping needs and a small one would probably be too expensive as well as too heavy, compared with the thermoelectric generators. Also, you would have the bother of carrying more fuel bottles than the standard one-in-and-one-spare propane tank system since most types need two kinds of fuel at once.

REFRIGERATION

The heat-to-current trick of the thermoelectric generators will work the other way too. Pass a direct current through one of these things and you get heat—far more than with a simple resistor wire or coil such as is used in electric stoves and other cooking equipment. Run it through in the other direction and it gets cold—in fact, it plain freezes up with a nice coating of frost from the atmospheric moisture. With these gadgets, you can have the campfire heating one to produce electricity and the electricity going through another one to cool a portable refrigerator: the campfire will be keeping your meat frozen.

Yet there is an older way to do the same thing. Gas refrigerators in the home are old stuff by now. They have no moving parts to break down. A portable refrigerator like these big ones could run by the heat of the campfire or a propane torch. The propane ones are available now, but are too bulky and heavy for anything except use in a camping machine. What is needed is a collapsible box. It should be light (plastic or magnesium) with fiberglass or vacuum insulation—and under five pounds ($2\frac{1}{4}$ kg) in weight. True, it would be restricted to cars, horses, and non-portaging canoes, but that is some progress.

Union Carbide has come up with a new type of insulation using a laminate of paper and aluminum. An inch (25 mm) -thick bottle of the stuff has kept nitrogen liquified for a month. Snake antivenin requires refrigeration to keep from deteriorating. Outside of the refrigerator, it is about two weeks before it starts losing strength. Packaged in this insulation, it could be kept in the refrigerator until you went camping in snake country—then you could take it out and be gone for a month or two, knowing the contents were still safely around 50°F (10°C). When you got back, you could return it to the refrigerator.

INSECT REPELLENT

Another dream device that science might furnish someday is a chemical to bugproof a tent. The mosquito is my remaining adversary now that I have built up an adequate supply of camping equipment. The insect repellent you put on yourself just doesn't last through the night.

The ideal tent treatment would, of course, be harmless to the tent fabric, people, and pets, and have little or no odor. It would be effective against all types of insects and it would last at least one year despite rain or temperature change. And, above all, it would not kill the insects, only repel them. Insects will develop an immunity to an insecticide through the breeding of the survivors.

Meantime, there is room for improvement on what we have now. Spray cans do a superior job of applying bug dope evenly and it comes in metal rather than glass containers, so there is no danger of breakage.

However, manufacturers would do well to market it in three-ounce-or-less (85 g or less) -size cans—the ten-ounce (285 g) cans are really too big for camping. Room deodorant is available in concentrated three-ounce (85 g) cans with a measuring device in the valve. Samples sent through the mails containing body deodorant have come out in one-ounce (30 g) spray cans which would be perfect for bug dope. Such a dope with N,N diethyl metatoluamide as its active ingredient would sell in small sizes if it were properly marketed. The supermarket crowd wouldn't be snatching it up because of the price, but campers who don't use automobiles would buy enough to make it worthwhile. If it can be done with the relatively expensive miniature salt shakers, it can be done with insect repellent.

CHAPTER FIFTY-TWO

Conservation in the Future

Conservation is an essential duty of the camper since without a vigorous conservation program, the natural beauty that inspires us to camp in the first place will be destroyed and we may as well camp in the back yard. The camper must take an interest in the problems of conservation and work to see that the problems are solved. Therefore, it is necessary that he know the situation and the techniques of doing something about it.

THE DANGER TO OUR LAND

Between the Pentagon, power companies, timber firms, and real-estate promoters, we may lose much of our best scenic land. Some of this land is already legally ours as citizens of a nation holding it as public domain. Other scenic areas are not public domain, but should become so before they are lost forever. Still other areas are essential to science in order to provide "control" areas, where nothing is done in order to compare the effect of experiments elsewhere.

The army's traditional target has been the Wichita Game Preserve in Oklahoma. This is our only national preserve of prairie wildlife. So far, they have been blocked from taking it directly. An attempt to enclose it within adjacent Fort Sill (so they could keep anyone out of it by "reason" of military security) was also thwarted. If either at-

tempts had been successful, the Pentagon brass would have had their private hunting preserve.

In a compromise which kept them from encircling the Preserve, they were given the right to use the Preserve land for firing artillery into target areas within Fort Sill. I discussed the current status of the Preserve with the assistant manager in the summer of 1965. He told me that the citizens of Lawton, Oklahoma, had come to recognize the tourist advantage of the Preserve and were now taking as much pride in the proximity of the Preserve to their city as they were in Fort Sill, and from what I could observe in Lawton, this is true. However, that same day the cannon were loud enough to be felt and despite a no-overflight rule in the Preserve an army helicopter was buzzing a herd of longhorns.

A "buffer zone" of Preserve land is now entirely under army control even though it is still technically under the Department of the Interior. Wichita wildlife is still not safe despite the excellent work by the Department's staff.

The situation at Wichita was repeated shortly afterward when the Air Force tried to get a bombing range in the area adjacent to Aransas Wildlife Preserve in Texas. Aransas is the winter grounds of the whooping cranes and is absolutely essential to their survival. The Bureau of Wildlife tried to enlarge Aransas to include this area which the whoopers sometimes used, but was outside the protection of the Wildlife Preserve. The Air Force quickly blocked it by saying that "in the interest of national security" they would need the area for a bombing range. The situation became complete chaos when the State of Texas entered the picture with a few smoke screens of their own under the "states' rights" label. The Air Force went ahead during all this confusion and started bombing the area and running low-level helicopter flights over it (and Aransas too). This was naturally defended as being "required for national defense" despite the fact that at the time they were spending millions making a practice range out of Cambodia.

The pattern appeared again in 1965 with Operation Long Shot, a study to see if underground nuclear explosions could be detected as distinct from earthquakes with seismographs. They needed an area within the natural earthquake belt. With the help of the militarists (who are their principal beneficiaries), the Atomic Energy Commission stamped the whole project "top secret" to keep the conservationists off until too late. They selected as their site, "in the interest of national security," the breeding area of the almost extinct sea otter.

They used noisemakers to try to drive the sea otters away at the time of the experiment and have clamped a "top secret" tag on what the area (and its inhabitants) looks like now. Sea otters still exist (at least at this writing), but the principal effect of heavy but non-fatal radiation exposure is sterility and extreme mutation.

Not so lucky were the sea otters at the 1971 Amchitka test. The AEC went ahead with this useless experiment despite the danger of starting a tsunami in this earthquake zone, the diplomatic protests of several Pacific nations, and demonstrations by conservationists. Of the 8,000 sea otters, 1,000 died in this stupid stunt according to an actual count by trained biologists in a daring commando operation penetrating AEC's security cordon around the island to prevent this very census.

Lest the remaining service escape censure, the Navy was guilty of this same kind of high-handedness with the people's land in the 1940s. Hahoolawe, an island in the Hawaiian group, was used for scientific research until the Navy began using it for a gunnery range. It is now filled will unexploded bombs and shells. Hahoolawe is not an isolated reef. It is the eighth-largest island in the State of Hawaii—there are several smaller islands with permanent communities on them.

These land grabs represent an attempt to do in America what has been a tragic part of the history of Europe and a current reality in many of the countries of Latin America and Africa. The United States has grown great because its founding fathers feared militarism more than George III and wrote many provisions into the framework of the Constitution to preserve it (the President as Commander-in-Chief of the Armed Forces, the Second Amendment as an alternative to conscription, etc.). But the Pentagon now spends more money in propagandizing for more power "in the interest of national security" than all the money spent to maintain and preserve our system of public lands. The pattern is always the same. The area is absolutely essential for the preservation of certain types of wildlife (in two cases, almost extinct wildlife); the Pentagon "needs" the land "in the interest of national security" even though there is suitable land for their official purpose within a hundred miles (160 km) of the public land they are trying to capture. There is plenty of space to the west and southwest of Fort Sill for expansion. There was an abandoned Navy bombing range on Padre Island, just outside the then only-proposed National Seashore Area, less than fifty miles (80 km) from the land adjacent to the Aransas Preserve. There were countless uninhabited and uninhabitable bays and inlets in Alaska for Operation Long Shot that were far enough away from the sea otters. There were plenty of coral atolls in the Midway chain a couple of hundred miles (320 km) from the island of Hahoolawe.

The attempt to flood Dinosaur National Monument for hydroelectric power awakened the public to the encroachment of the power companies in some of our most beautiful areas. While Dinosaur was saved at the last minute, others have not been so lucky.

After a heated battle in 1913, led by John Muir himself, the cause of conservation was defeated with Hetch Hetchy, and San Francisco went in and built a lake in the Yosemite Valley, even though other areas were available. While this was an unconcealed power grab, similar attempts today offer the excuse that it increases the recreational value of the park. Actually, a water lake's fluctuating shoreline does nothing for any magnificent valley or canyon. They typically have a broad band of bleached cliffs or mud flats around their rims in the late summer when yard sprinkling in the user city and the absence of rain lowers the level. The only water-supply lakes which keep the same level are those near cities, around which the wealthy community leaders have homes or cabins and the level is kept constant by draining other lakes upstream, giving the latter ones even higher fluctuations than normal. A beautiful spot is never enhanced by flooding. The proper site for a water-supply lake is a deep floodplain devoid of any distant view or unusual natural or historical features. There are plenty such sites available, often near the scenic areas the lake-builders are trying to flood.

Today an attempt by a coastal city to flood part of a national park is even more of a crime since desalination is now a possibility. Even though it is more expensive than artificial lakes, it must be considered now or our rivers will never reach the sea but be evaporated and drained in an endless succession of artificial lakes with gradually increasing salt and sewage content so that the lower end of the river will not even be fit for irrigation.

What is more, there will be no wild canyons with their glaciated valleys and geology-textbook stratifications exposed for the wonder of man.

Glen Canyon Dam and the resulting Lake Powell is a monument to pork-barrel politicking at the public expense. There is not enough water in the Colorado System to keep both Powell and Lake Mead (behind Hoover Dam) filled at the same time, yet it was built anyway and the great digging action of the Big Red has now slowed almost to a halt within the world's most beautiful canyon.

Glen Canyon had the best specimens of natural desert-cliff varnish (the big paint-dripping-like coloration on desert cliffs) in the world, but they are now mostly under water (or more precisely, in the water, because it has been dissolved wherever the lake has touched it).

To compound the crime, another dam is being planned just downstream from Grand Canyon National Monument so that the lake would not only flood the Monument, but would back up into the park itself. Figures are hard to get on this project. Several versions of the dam's height have been given, but the largest level would back water halfway up Mooney Falls in Havasu Canyon and be visible from the tourist area at Hermit's Rest on the South Rim. This assumes that they can fill it, which is unlikely unless they both drain Powell and let Mead dry up. Their documentation figures for rainfall would need to go back to the last century and wetter climates to run up a high enough average rainfall to fill all three lakes.

The congressional hearings for this boondoggle were conducted in Northern Arizona (where the water from the lake will supposedly be used for irrigation) during the heat of the 1964 presidential elections, with an Arizona congressman presiding and almost no publicity at all. When it was approved by the committee, the Sierra Club stepped in and mobilized public opinion. The controversy reached such a state that the bill was "defeated" by the Secretary of the Interior withdrawing his approval.

This kind of thing is possible because the old enabling act which established the park and Monument permitted dams within the area (not intending this type, or even dreaming they would be technically possible). A bill to seal this loophole was proposed but died in committee when the idea of the dam was dropped. However, there is currently (1974) talk about reviving the idea (this time for "power generation to fight the energy crisis") and the Grand Canyon is again in danger. The exploiter never sleeps.

The argument that flooding would make the area more accessible was answered with the Sierra Club's counter-proposal that the Sistine Chapel be flooded so that the tourists can get a closer look at the ceiling.

The problem of the timber companies is the problem of the mining outfits and the stock grazers too, although to a more limited extent. The Na-

tional Forest System and much of the crown land in Canada is what is called multiple-use land. It is leased to private individuals and corporations to cut, graze, and mine within certain restrictions. The problems occur at the administration end of the system. These financial interests control the state governments of many of our Western states and the representatives represent them rather than the people. As a result, the administration of the national forests is often dictated by these exploiting groups and as a further result reforestation is limited to certain well-billboarded spots in the forests while mine talings spill down the hillsides out of sight of the roads, and deserts are produced where too many sheep are grazed for too long.

There have even been instances where ranchers cut national forest fences to graze their cattle on your land, depending on their bought-and-paid-for representatives to make sure that not enough personnel would be on hand to patrol the area or that any alert public servant would get a sudden transfer if they were caught. Even when they were caught and convicted, the punishment was insignificant compared to what they gained from violating the law.

While the energies of conservationists have justifiably been concentrated on preserving the national park concept against profit-seeking private interests, the national forests are now in grave danger of being totally destroyed by the very philosophy which up until recently had saved them—multiple use.

Multiple use was Gifford Pinchot's answer to the slash-and-burn foresters prevalent when he took

The color publicity photos of Lake Powell always show a full blue lake contrasting with the reds, browns, and blacks of the cliffs. They are beautiful to anyone who has not seen the way it was before it was flooded. In truth, however, the water is seldom that high, and a high band of bleached rock or mud-filled side canyons line the lake. As the water level fluctuates, this band of destructive ugliness will grow and the desert varnish that made Glen Canyon a place of beauty will progressively be destroyed, a monument to man's destruction in the false name of progress.

over the infant National Forestry Service under Teddy Roosevelt. With his emphasis on sustained yield and controlled cutting and grazing, much land was saved which would have been totally destroyed, as were most of the private timber preserves of that time. In the day of slash-and-burn logging, multiple use had a great value.

Now it is open to question. Timber companies which practice the best of conservation measures on their own land use the most destructive techniques on public lands they lease. Nowhere is this truer on a large scale than in California's redwood forests, where loggers are quickly wiping out every redwood in any area which is even discussed as a possible state or national park. These are some of the slowest-growing trees in the nation. It takes almost a thousand years to get one to maturity, yet within the lifetime of children already born, we may have to do without redwood as a commercial lumber in order to save for succeeding generations the beauty of a living redwood tree. Cypress and even mesquite will meet the redwood's qualities of preservation without painting, and they grow much faster.

The egret was saved from extinction at the turn of the century partly because of the courage of the game wardens in the Everglades (some of whom literally gave their lives for the rookeries), but mostly because the fashion designers stopped using the plumes. A boycott of redwood lumber by conservation-minded people would go far in preserving these majestic trees. While the cut-over redwood groves are being replanted in a redwood-and-fir mixture, the rate of cutting will use up far more redwood than will be ready for cutting a century from now when these few trees are lumber-size.

What has happened with lumbering and the slowest-growing tree has happened with grazing and the slowest-growing non-woody plant, the giant saguaro cactus. Within Saguaro National Monument, grazing and predator control (which has increased the rodent population enormously, and was undertaken to protect the grazing livestock which had no business there in the first place) is seriously damaging the young plants. These plants take twenty to fifty years to grow to the size of an ordinary prickly-pear cactus and a full-grown specimen will be over three centuries old. Saguaros are extremely susceptible to climatic changes and now are on the borderline of survival for this reason alone. Yet the grazers continue to come in—the cactus and the general public just don't seem to matter.

The most flagrant opposition to conservation from timber interests has occurred in the Big Thicket of Texas. Here is the greatest example of Southern hardwood forests blending in with the Western vegetation, and here are found the world's tallest holly, eastern red cedar, Chinese tallow, red bay, yaupon, black hickory, sparkleberry, sweetleaf, two-wing silverbell, and cypress—plus a thousand-year-old magnolia.

In 1966 the cypress was found killed by salt water from an oil well. After Senator Ralph Yarborough introduced the measure to make the Big Thicket a national park, a timber official laughed and said, "The Big Thicket? In four years there won't be any Big Thicket!"

Shortly thereafter, a large rookery of over a hundred nests was found destroyed by aircraft spraying with hardwood-killing spray, normally used to thin out hardwoods for the cash pine woods to be planted. There are no hardwoods in the area and the rookery is plainly visible from the air.

Recently the magnolia, probably the oldest in the South, was found drilled in four places and poisoned with lead arsenate—the usual way to kill a large tree. In their effort to destroy the Big Thicket, the lumbermen have chopped down magnolias in the public domain and protected by state law. No action was taken although the company that did this is well known in the state and the charges connecting them with the crime have been published without any legal repercussions.

Public pressure did force the timber barons to slow down their destruction of the Big Thicket (although not stop it) and part of it is still there. The Texas political machine finally succeeded in their every-six-year slander campaign against Senator Yarborough (just before many of them were sent to prison for corruption) and thereby removed the Big Thicket's ablest spokesman. However, in the House, Bob Eckhardt and Charles Wilson took up the Congressional battle and, at this writing, have saved part of the Thicket; the boundaries are yet to be drawn.

The nestings of several ivory-billed woodpeckers, long thought extinct, have been confirmed in the Big Thicket. I have seen slides of the nests with their distinctive square holes. Ornithologists, obviously, have kept their location secret.

Real-estate promoters have only been a problem to camping and conservation by their opposition to new recreational areas. But this is a real problem because of the rapid increases in population and in campers. Urban sprawl has taken up vast areas of countryside which could be set aside for camping and related outdoor recreation without hurting a growing city—in fact, a vast system of green belts improves a city. Some have even suggested that they may be necessary to provide enough oxygen to maintain life in congested cities. In this era of air pollution, they can certainly do no harm.

The stock answer is that in a culture of rapid mobility, people will be willing to travel several hundred miles for such activities. This is an evasion of the issue and an old one at that. It should be remembered that Central Park in New York City was once opposed on the grounds that one only had to go up to the Bronx to get into the country.

The attempt of promoters around Brownsville, Texas, to block the Padre Island National Seashore Area is a good example of this real-estate opposition. They had delusions of another Miami Beach at the southern tip of Texas and they succeeded in cutting off a fourteen-mile (22 km) strip of the original Seashore Area despite the fact that their dream resort already was over ten times larger than the Florida resort. As a Texan, I can understand the urge to do things in a big way, but this is out of proportion to reality. Actually, their new Miami Beach has turned out to be just another one of those urban sprawls of vacation houses, standing deserted most of the year and kept alive by a vast horde of hard-sell booth operators at fairs throughout North America.

A similar dream on the part of industrial real-estate operators has severely interfered with the saving of the dune lands on the Great Lakes.

The main danger of real-estate promoters and

boost-local-industry politicians is to the thousands of purely local issues, such as city parks which will provide small green belts and homes for birds and small mammals—places where those who don't have the time or the means to drive five hundred miles (800 km) to the nearest public campsite can come and recreate in the peaceful surroundings of at least a microcosm of nature as it really is instead of how man mutilates it to be.

National parks, forests, and monuments, and their state, provincial, and tribal equivalents offer excellent campsites and opportunities for campsites.

When used for all the people and preserved in its natural beauty, the land is not harmed, at least not in a manner that careful management and controlled use cannot prevent or repair. When the vandals of exploitation move in, the land is destroyed for all uses except the exploitation, and when it has served this purpose it is fit for nothing except the desert which is the destiny of all land that is misused by poor agriculture, flooding, or urbanization.

When the account of the conservation movement of the twentieth century is written (assuming the movement wins—otherwise there will be no one left to write it), there will be two pivotal events in the story. The first will be the founding of the movement in the late nineteenth and early twentieth centuries, involving such names as John Muir, Gifford Pinchot, Theodore Roosevelt, etc. The second will be the "energy crisis" of 1973–74. It had no human names, just the largest petroleum corporations in a giant cartel.

This phoney shortage was a masterpiece of strategy on the part of the exploiters. In it they did three things, all to their monetary benefit and the detriment of the consumer and the environment. First, they increased the price of petroleum products from the refinery with little increase to themselves—just a token increase in royalty payments to their puppet governments to take the blame for them—the rest was almost pure profit. Second, they wiped out most of the small, independent service stations whose competition kept the retail prices down. Now they control the whole thing from the exploration to the corner gas station, antitrust and combine laws notwithstanding. Third, they created a climate of panic which wrecked planned air pollution controls on automobiles, branded conservationists as the cause of the shortage because they insisted on environmental controls in exploration and transportation, railroaded their disastrous Alaska pipeline through Congress, and with a massive advertising campaign blinded the public to the real causes, even though the facts were available.

According to Lloyd's List and Shipping Gazette (the standard reference of where the world's merchant ships are and what they are carrying that week), more oil left Persian Gulf ports with oil delivered to the United States during the so-called boycott than in the same period the year before. According to some observers, the reason the "boycott" ended was that the oil companies no longer had any storage space left for all the oil that was backlogged and were even pumping it back into the ground. I traveled through the whole western United States during the "crisis" and the oil fields had the same ratio of pumping to idle wells as before (cartel propaganda claimed that "all existing wells are pumping full time to meet the shortage") and the sky was filled with the trails of jets wasting fuel to show the Pentagon still rules.

The environmentalists were caught in a tactical bind in all this. The advantage of a lie is not only Hitler's point that it is more likely to be believed, but that it can be kept simple to manipulate public opinion in a complex situation. The cartel had a simple lie—it was the environmentalists' fault and we can solve the whole problem by returning all power to the cartel. The environmentalists, on the other hand, had a more complex story: yes, we are running out of fossil fuel energy, but the crunch won't come, at present consumption, until the turn of the century. But if we expect to have any resources for petrochemicals (almost all plastics, including synthetic fabrics) we had better be saving it now. Tanker and Santa Barbara-type spills will kill the sea unless better tanker design and more rigid offshore drilling controls are enforced. The cartel set up a perfect either/or choice when the only safe decision was somewhere in between.

Now that the cartel has convinced the public that fossil fuel is exhaustible (something the environmentalists have been saying all along), they are now pushing fission nuclear power—the dirtiest and most poisonous of all. Now the cartel says the environmentalists are out to destroy the world by depriving it of this nice, cheap, inexhaustible energy source. The radioactive wastes of a fission power plant will create hazards that will make the uncontrolled atom-bomb testing of the 1950s look like a match compared to a forest fire. Fissionable elements are just as depletable as fossil fuel; it will just take longer. Twenty-four thousand years ago, the last ice age was ending; 24,000 years from now, one half of our highly carcinogenic plutonimum supply will have decayed—assuming that no more is made. Who will take care of all that poison in all the changes of history—a poison that is also the prime ingredient of nuclear weapons?

In all this energy issue, the cartel is avoiding looking at energy sources it doesn't control, saying that none of them is the total answer. Of course they aren't. Solar power doesn't work when it is dark, tidal power isn't working at high or low tide, hydroelectric dams have used up most of the streams that can be used without destroying fishing. (In fact, the power dams of the Columbia have already destroyed the world's largest salmon stream and only a change of government in British Columbia kept the Fraser from going the same way.)

One of the causes of the problem in the first place is our reliance on only one energy source—fossil fuel. All of these "inadequate" alternative systems together could meet our needs since the electrical grid can switch from one type of generation to another.

This would open up those already used on a small level to larger use: tidal power, geothermal, solar, wind, methane generation (from sewage or garbage), methanol from lumber mills' wood chips, and even the theoretical possibility of fusion power (whose "waste product" is helium).

To bring in this sensible approach to power sources, public opinion is going to have to stop accepting the cartel's manipulation, governmental corruption, and private armies developing their own foreign policy and put the multinational corporations under the rule of law, stop electing presidents with colossal landslides after Watergates are known, and put the CIA under the control of Congress—the people's elected representatives. Then, when we again have some form of democracy (literally "people rule") we can make the decisions that will safeguard our world from destruction by its own wastes, and even set aside a little bit of nature to show following generations how it was before homo sap slopped it up.

HOW TO HELP

Since the exploiters of our natural resources have vast political power, the citizens whose resources are being exploited must develop political power to counter it. This section, then, is an exercise in practical, grass-roots politics.

You can do far more if you are organized. Lawmakers listen very little to one individual unless that individual has considerable political power. On the other hand, a group, by itself, constitutes political power, and the bigger and better-organized it is the more effective will be its influence on legislation. This is why organized labor is able to counterbalance organized business despite the fact that the net worth of all the unions in the United States, locals and internationals, is only five per cent that of General Motors alone.

This is why such groups as the Audubon Society, the Sierra Club, and the National Wildlife Federation have been able to do the great service in the area of public opinion and legislation that they have. They aren't heavily staffed, but they have a large membership and each of their members has a vote. After the reapportionment decisions of 1964 and 1965, these votes can no longer be outvoted by a few Western ranchers and mine owners.

These conservationist groups have a tremendous array of hard, cold facts. Sheer weight of numbers may prevail for a short time, especially if they are loud and the representative is short on courage, but the side which will ultimately win is the side with the most facts. Unfortunately, conservation often wins after the mob has destroyed the resource so that no one can use it. For this reason, we must have both facts and manpower.

This not only means organizing to the utmost

efficiency, but that liaison with other interested groups is a must. A well-written, objective organizational newspaper is most helpful in advising the members on pending legislation. It doesn't have to be a fancy printing job—a clear mimeographed sheet is adequate if what is on it is good. The editorship is an important job and the member who holds it should be chosen as carefully as the president, if not more so.

Stick to legislation dealing with camping, conservation, and related areas. Dilution of objectives will spoil the effectiveness of your club's voice in camping matters.

It is generally best to avoid endorsing candidates. First, it may divide your membership. Second, it is more effective to deal just with the issues. Third, every candidate does something, sometime, that the majority doesn't like. If they dislike it enough, they will turn against anyone that supported him as well. You are automatically lined up against a large segment of the real estate, power, and military lobbies when you organize. Don't get any more against you than you have to.

Presenting the candidates' platforms on the areas of interest is a good practice, however. Most candidates welcome the opportunity to answer direct questions on issues if they know the answers will be distributed. The League of Women Voters has done an outstanding job along these lines in local elections. A similar questionnaire, dealing only with the area of interest to your group, would help spotlight the positions the candidates are taking in this area.

However, a few tips are in order. Don't load the question. If you can conceal which side you are on, you are that much better off. Keep it short. A few well-chosen questions which can be answered quickly, yet not glibly, are best. Campaign time is not easy on the candidate. And, finally, have the courtesy to supply a stamped, self-addressed envelope.

When presenting an issue to your members, explain it concisely and clearly, give the bill's legislative number, and tell who sponsored it, what committee has it, and who its leaders and members from your area are.

When you are writing to a legislator, refer to the measure by its number—he can check it quicker that way. Don't use form letters in your lobby work. Legislators usually discount them in making up their minds. Give your members ideas and facts for their letters, but not the wording. Also, keep the wording courteous. Give the legislator credit for being able to make up his own mind, even if you aren't too sure he can. Antagonistic letters often have a reverse effect.

When you write, be sure of your facts. A modest, air-tight case is better than a fine-sounding or sensational one that the opposition can easily disprove. Write to all legislators, both for and against your bill, but if you concentrate on any, concentrate on those who are undecided. The ones on your side will probably stay there, especially with a word of appreciation from time to time. The ones opposed will probably stay *there,* but send them word occasionally too so that they can't say, "No one is in favor of this bill."

Use several media. You are not only trying to influence legislation directly but indirectly too, by influencing public opinion. If you must choose one or the other, choose public opinion, because it will ultimately control legislation, even if it does take a long time.

Letters to representatives and key opinion leaders are more effective if supplemented with judicious use of telegrams, phone calls, and personal contacts by personal acquaintances of the target person. Don't forget newspaper letters-to-the-editor columns. The outdoors editor is often more receptive than the regular letters editor—especially on reactionary papers which define exploitation as "free enterprise" and conservation laws as "government interference." However, some of them are strictly hunting and fishing and if the issue is preventing overhunting an endangered species or saying a kind word about natural predators doing the job of preventing varmit overpopulation better than hunters can, they won't help either.

The average representatives in either house on the state or national level are honest. They depend on lobbyists simply because they cannot otherwise do the research. Therefore, we need our lobbyists to be there.

Do not overlook magazines. A first-person account of a vacation, for example, can subtly relay the message that if such-and-such project goes through, the reader will never experience the thrill that the writer had. Any competent writer can produce an article which a Sunday supplement or outdoors magazine will print if the subject is timely and well written. The conservation magazines and, to a lesser extent, the outdoors ones will occasionally publish a "knock them over the head" article if the facts are accurately presented and it is a threat to those who make up the vast portion of their readership.

The equal-time provisions can provide a forum, but unfortunately since the stations generally run the FCC instead of the FCC regulating the stations, this is not always useful in the long run. I had an experience along those lines in the SST battle. The local station said, "We oppose the SST, so in fairness we are asking a supporter to present his views" and thereby presented only the supporting side.

At the time, I was president of the Texas Consumers' Association (which takes environmental stands including this one) and a member of the Texas Aviation Historical Society, so I demanded a chance to reply to the arguments (mostly totally false). The station merely found a professor of environmental medicine to "present the opposed side" and he proceeded to state that the SST was not an environmental issue at all but a political

one and at no time said anything against the SST or its effect on the stratosphere, ozone layer, the economics of supersonic airliners, or any other aspect of this issue.

At this point, I went to the FCC. They finally came through and the night before the crucial Senate vote (too late to affect the outcome) the station ran a taped argument by a congressman against the SST. At no time was I permitted on the air to discuss the excellent way the Concorde SST had performed aerodynamically although it was still financially unfeasible without subsidy either from governments, slower airline passengers, or the above-mentioned ecological factors.

I was then persona non grata at that station and could never get past the receptionist or switchboard again. Also, the news manager who managed this news so skillfully was then promoted to network news chief!

All operations in this field require either complete subtlety so that no one in the medium knows what you are doing (with the risk that the audience won't either) or having enough power to force them to obey the law. It takes a good deal of work and a fair amount of money. But remember, it is your land you are fighting for. It has been taken before and it will be again unless you do something about it.

PART XI

The Camper's Library

Several writers on the subject of camping or the related fields of activities mentioned in Part VI have commented on the fact that the enthusiast can get almost as much pleasure in preparing for an excursion into the wilds as he can from the actual trip. This preparation is done in several ways. There is the obvious way of preparing menu lists, repairing equipment, selecting new gear, and other actual preparations. There is also mental preparation.

The best source of this preparation is a modest but well-equipped library. While magazines and books from the public library will certainly supplement this, a personal library is the best source of spontaneously needed information and reference.

Included in this library should be two or three general references on camping, a campground guide, a few books on the specialized camping activities you prefer, and a modest supply of field guides and other nature references. The whole collection should not cost over a hundred dollars, and will not have to be bought all at once.

This will, of course, be enlarged over the years as you widen your camping horizons to include a larger variety of activities. A clipping file of magazine articles, national park guides, and other useful bits of information not found in books will expand it further. After a few years of camping, you will have an excellent reference library on camping.

The three chapters of this part are not meant to be the last word on the subject. New books are published every season. Magazines are born, improve or deteriorate, and even die (often due to an ill-timed postal increase). Obviously I have not even heard of every book or magazine on the subject, much less been able to evaluate them. The items in these chapters are there first of all because I happened across them and second, because I found them beneficial. Your opinion of a book or magazine may differ as widely as our opinions on any field of camping. However, these are quality publications and, if you find additional ones, enjoy them!

CHAPTER FIFTY-THREE

Magazines

There are a large number of magazines that the camper will find helpful. Many state park agencies or state tourist bureaus publish magazines on either the state's outdoors or a more general coverage of state attractions. Private conservation groups publish excellent periodicals for their members.

Recreational activities of interest to campers are served by a wide variety of major magazines—the hunting and fishing magazines being the oldest. Occasional articles of interest will be found in magazines devoted to photography, boating, skin diving, science (at both the popular and professional levels), and travel. A habit of regular visits to the public library will insure that you don't miss one of these articles before it is too late to buy a copy at the local magazine outlet—finding used magazines is often a hard job. The library routine is also a good way to discover which of the multitude of periodicals are consistently meeting your needs so that a subscription will be in order—so that you can build your own reference file.

In the first edition, I lamented the lack of a real camping magazine. I am happy to say that this has changed and I am now able to have a chapter on camping magazines in this book. Still, Utopia is not here and I am compelled to drag out the old soapbox one more time and expound on my idea of the ideal camping magazine.

While the situation has improved vastly with the addition of the magazines listed later in this section, there is still a large amount of the old overnight picnicking movement left. I still want to see a camping magazine covering the full field of camping: hunting, fishing, mountain climbing, snow camping, skiing, boating, skin diving, nature study, conservation, and photography, as well as the usual line of first-person articles on camping trips and outdoor recipes. It should publish annually a public campground guide, telling not only what the facilities are but what condition they are in, what the weather is likely to be through the year, what the soil type is, etc. It should have do-it-yourself projects for equipment, both permanent and improvised. It should provide a Consumer's Union-type testing of camping equipment on the market to help you choose your gear better. It should have a review of pending legislation, both on the state and national level, so you can act in time and give the professionally staffed groups some popular support in their work to preserve our resources. Finally, it should have reviews of outstanding new books and films of interest to campers. Also I would like to see them do an occasional supplement, such as a catalog of all camp foods on the market (where to get them, their cost, servings, cost per serving, etc.) or similar reference booklets which would be valued by the camper.

The main problem with existing magazines in this regard is that none of them are even monthlies—which, with the lead time required to go to press, is the absolute maximum for getting information on political matters (legislative or administrative) out to the public in time for them to act. Just as the concerned camper must get involved in organized conservation groups to preserve the public land, he must also support these periodicals so that they can grow and become this influence on public opinion that we must have in order for camping to survive.

BACKPACKER. 28 West 44th Street, New York, New York 10036; $7.50 per year, $8.10 in Canada

Backpacker represents probably the best-quality magazine in the camping field. My biggest regret is that it is only a quarterly. Each issue covers not only the expected range of articles, but an in-depth look at some particular item of camping gear—boots, food, packs, etc.—the "supplement" I advo-

cated earlier. Photography is outstanding as is the writing. While it is strictly as its name suggests—hiking, ski touring, snowshoeing, and the related fields of photography, climbing, nature study, etc.—its coverage of equipment makes it a valuable source of information for the canoe, bicycle, and horsepacking camper as well.

WILDERNESS CAMPING. 1654 Central Avenue, Albany, New York 12205; $4.00 per year, $4.60 in Canada

Wilderness Camping is a direct outgrowth of my soapbox in the first edition and I was associated with it in the early days as a contributing editor. Our splitting was strictly in the business end of the publication and not the content. While at times uneven in quality, this publication has come closer than any to meeting my idea of the scope such a publication should cover. It is a bimonthly, which creates problems in the environmental action department, but even there they are trying.

CHAPTER FIFTY-FOUR

Camping

General Resources

CAMPING AND WOODCRAFT. Horace Kephart, The Macmillan Company, New York, 1921

Much of this two-part classic of camping literature has become out of date because of the changing nature of camping areas and technological changes in camping gear. However, much of it is still useful to the camper even though the *Woodcraft* volume was originally written in 1916, and the *Camping* volume in 1917. All of Kephart's earlier book, *Camp Cookery,* is included in the 1917 book.

THE COMPLETE BOOK OF CAMPING. Leonard Miracle with Maurice Decker, Harpers, New York, 1961

This is a good general book on the subject of camping, from a different viewpoint than this one. It strikes a fairly good balance between expensive wilderness camping and glorified picnicking.

THE COMPLETE WALKER. Colin Fletcher, Alfred Knopf, New York, 1968

This is the best book available on the subject of long-distance hikes. The author has impeccable credentials for writing this book. (See Miscellaneous section at the end of this chapter.)

FIELDBOOK FOR BOYS AND MEN. Boy Scouts of America, New Brunswick, New Jersey, 1967

While developed by and for the Boy Scouts, this new edition of the *Fieldbook* is a good introductory book to camping—especially for children. If you still treasure your first edition of *Fieldbook* (1944), you will find very little of it duplicated here. Both are excellent.

KNAPSACKING ABROAD. Herb and Judy Klinger, Stackpole, Harrisburg, Pennsylvania, 1967

Despite its title, this is not a book on camping, but a guide to an inexpensive way to travel—by using a backpack (usually a rucksack or ski pack) instead of a suitcase. In this way, you will blend in with the local tourists and get the better end of the double pricing system practiced in many tourist centers. Whether you camp or not is optional, but the information given is quite valuable for the overseas traveler on a small budget.

ON YOUR OWN IN THE WILDERNESS. Townsend Whelen and Bradford Angier, Stackpole, Harrisburg, Pennsylvania, 1958

I have only one real objection to this fine book. It covers a form of camping which can only be done in the great wilderness areas of the continent which are out of the reach of the wallets of most of us. Still, even for those who do their camping in the state and national parks, it has enough good material to earn it a place in every camper's library.

THE SPORTSMAN'S OUTDOOR GUIDE. Charles B. Roth, Prentice-Hall, New York, 1953

Normally, collected essays are poor additions to the home reference library, though they are interesting enough when checked out of the public library. This one is an exception.

Although it is designed for the hunter, it has very little to do with hunting as such. It covers almost everything that is connected with the outdoors other than the usual camping topics. The author's mention of a mason's hammer got me using the geologist's pick, a tool I have modified and always take on camping trips which will require more tools than just a knife.

It does not cover a sufficient range of camping subjects to stand alone as a camping book, but it is a valuable supplement to any camper's library. The chapters on handguns, knives, walking, running, and tracking are some of the best anywhere.

TACKLE CAMPING THIS WAY. Roy McCarthy, Stanley Paul and Company, London, 1960

This is a look at camping the British way. It contains valuable material on organizational camping, bicycle camping, and short backpacking trips not far from "civilization"—a situation inevitable in most of Britain and in many parts of the Northeastern United States and Southern Canada.

Campground Directories

CAMPGROUND DIRECTORY. American Automobile Association, Washington, D.C., no date

Available only to AAA members, this is a good directory of national, state, and privately owned campsites.

THE HANDBOOK OF WILDERNESS TRAVEL. George and Iris Wells, Harpers, New York, 1959

This is an annotated directory of all wilderness areas with information on the size of the areas and the means of transportation to and in them. It is an excellent reference book. The directory is preceded by a brief discussion of camping and an excellent and comprehensive discussion of travel methods as they relate to camping.

NATIONAL FOREST VACATIONS. U.S. Department of Agriculture, Forest Service, U.S. Government Printing Office, Washington, D.C., 1964

A multi-purpose booklet, this gives information on the types of activities available in national forests, rules concerning camping, and a guide to all national forest campgrounds.

RAND MCNALLY CAMPGROUND GUIDE. Rand McNally, Chicago

This annual gives you excellent road maps showing camp locations and a table showing the features to be found in each campsite in the state. The tabular form makes it much quicker to compare campsites than the usual sentence or key format. A small piece of cardboard, shaped like a carpenter's square, makes the use of the tables easier.

VACATIONING WITH INDIANS. U.S. Department of the Interior, Bureau of Indian Affairs, U.S. Government Printing Office, Washington, D.C., 1965

This is a guide to the campgrounds under tribal control. The system of tribal parks is relatively new and rapidly expanding. This booklet will probably be revised.

A wide variety of information on specific national parks and monuments is available from the Government Printing Office for a nominal charge. These are most valuable for study before a trip so you will know what to look for when you get there. They are available at the Ranger Station and should be obtained as soon as possible after arriving if they were not obtained beforehand. A few states, national forests, and similar campground agencies have similar guides available. Most state park agencies have free directories of their parks.

Backpacking

BACKPACKING, ONE STEP AT A TIME. Harvey Manning, REI Press, Seattle, Washington, 1972

This is a good introduction to the field, covering all the necessary steps in a concise style with cartoon illustrations. It is also available in paperback, but without some excellent photographs.

GOING LIGHT WITH BACKPACK AND BURRO. Edited by David Brower, Sierra Club, San Francisco, 1953

This is the best discussion of lightweight camping available. It will be useful to the camper using heavier forms of transportation as well. Expert campers may find need for the excellent chapter on breaking in non-camping wives to the sport. Aside from its high quality of information, it is written in a lighthearted style that makes enjoyable reading. Its lightweight binding makes it highly portable in the pack.

HOME IN YOUR PACK. Bradford Angier, Stackpole, Harrisburg, Pennsylvania, 1965

This is an excellent basic guide to the sport of backpacking. Selection and care of equipment is ably discussed. It is a bit deficient on pictures, but the word-descriptions are quite adequate. There are some plans for making equipment.

Bicycling

BICYCLING. Ruth and Raymond Benedict, A. S. Barnes, New York, 1944

This book is probably the only one available that fully covers bicycle camping. Because of the technological changes that have come about, both in camping and in bicycle design, there are parts that are outdated. However, these points will be quickly noticed by anyone who is familiar with backpacking equipment and the current market in bicycles.

The book contains many useful plans for making panniers and seats for carrying children safely. These have not become outdated and are still useful today.

Boat Camping

BOATING REGULATIONS. Department of the Interior, National Park Service, U.S. Government Printing Office, Washington, D.C., 1964

Anyone doing boat camping will need this pamphlet to make sure his boat conforms to all regulations. These must be followed in waters under Park Service jurisdiction and are just plain good sense.

THE COMPLETE BOOK OF OUTBOARD CRUISING. Robert Scharff, Putnam, New York, 1960

Almost what its title says, this has excellent coverage of all phases of outboard motorboating. Its discussion of camping is a little weak, but then so is my discussion of outboard boating.

Canoeing

CANOE CAMPING. Carle W. Handel, Ronald Press, New York, 1953

This is a complete guide to the special peculiarities of camping with a canoe. The book duplicates some of the material in the author's excellent book on canoeing (see below), but not enough to make either unnecessary. Selection of equipment, menu planning, and the techniques of handling a fully loaded canoe are among the topics discussed in detail.

CANOEING. Carle W. Handel, Ronald Press, New York, 1956

This little book has the works on the subject of canoeing: strokes, portaging, canoe camping, repairs, navigation, and design. For the beginner, it gives the basic techniques in a simple but complete manner. For the advanced canoeist, it gives information which will result in greater enjoyment and versatility from the canoe.

CANOEING. Joseph L. Hasenfus, American Red Cross, Washington, D.C., 1956

While primarily a book on canoe safety, including rescues, swamping, and all other aspects of canoe mishaps, it also contains some good information on paddles, conversions for rowing, kneelers, and many other items of equipment for both Canadian canoes and kayaks, plus excellent plans for a Canadian-canoe sailing rig.

WHITE WATER SPORT. Peter Dwight Whitney, Ronald Press, New York, 1960

As its title would suggest, this is not strictly a camping book. In fact, the boats discussed are slightly different from those used in camping. However, it has much to offer the canoe camper in its discussion of more efficient techniques. Also, a knowledge of white-water handling is valuable for any canoeist, even if he encounters only a few ripples on the surface of a lake.

Its main feature is that it is the only book available in English with extensive material on the subject of kayaking, and if you know the tricks used with the highly unstable slalom kayak, you can certainly handle the highly stable cruising model used in camping.

THE YOUNG SPORTSMAN'S GUIDE TO CANOEING. Raymond R. Camp, Thomas Nelson, New York, 1962

Despite its title, this is not a kiddie's book. It is an excellent introductory course in canoeing. It also contains a fair portion on the techniques of kayaking.

Climbing

FUNDAMENTALS OF ROCK CLIMBING. M.I.T. Outing Club, Cambridge, Massachusetts, 1956

You can't learn mountain climbing from a book any more than you can learn to fly an airplane that way. Still, some knowledge of the subject before you start is most desirable. This book was written by the Advance Rock-Climbing Committee of the M.I.T. Outing Club to supplement instruction by skilled mountain climbers. It is a good outline of the sport in a small paperback book.

MOUNTAINEERING—THE FREEDOM OF THE HILLS. Edited by Harvey Manning et al., Seattle Mountaineers, Seattle, Washington, 1961

More than just a discussion of climbing techniques, this classic also discusses mountain camping, emergency techniques, route finding, meteorology, etc. Its lighthearted style of writing is similar to the Sierra Club's *Going Light*. It is even illustrated with a subtle sense of humor.

Cooking

THE OUTDOORMAN'S COOKBOOK. Arthur H. Carhart, The Macmillan Company, New York, 1945

This is an excellent guide, especially in the areas of outfitting and preparing food in the field for use later. The recipes are good too.

WILDERNESS COOKERY. Bradford Angier, Stackpole, Harrisburg, Pennsylvania, 1961

Many books on outdoor and camp cooking have good recipes, and this book is no exception. However, it is far more. The information on menu-building, outfitting data, and the wealth of tables and hints for better camp food put this book far ahead of the usual books on camp cookery.

Equipment

LIGHT WEIGHT CAMPING EQUIPMENT AND HOW TO MAKE IT. Gerry Cunningham and Meg Hansson, Scribners, New York, 1976

Gerry Cunningham is the head of Gerry, one of the outstanding camping outfitters in the country. He makes much of the equipment he sells in his stores, so he knows what he is writing about. Meg Hansson is the head designer at Gerry's.

The instructions are clear, even in the more complicated plans. Even more valuable are the specification tables that abound throughout the book on fabrics, fastenings, insulation, etc. Included are the plans for two packs, a sleeping bag, a tent, and an anorak.

Orienteering

BE EXPERT WITH MAP AND COMPASS. Bjorn Kjellstrom, American Orienteering Service, La Porte, Indiana, 1955

Whether for the sport of orienteering, or for more basic camp navigation, this book gives you all the techniques. It also contains problems to test your progress.

ORIENTEERING. John Disley, Faber and Faber, London, 1967

This book covers the sport from an introduction to map and compass, through competition techniques, to laying out an orienteering course. Available in both hardcover and paperback.

Philosophy

THE MEANING OF WILDERNESS TO SCIENCE. Edited by David Brower, Sierra Club, San Francisco, 1960

This is the record of the Sixth Biennial Wilderness Conference, sponsored by the Sierra Club. It contains excellent discussions of the subject and the need for immediate action.

THE QUIET CRISIS. Stewart L. Udall, Holt, Rinehart and Winston, New York, 1963

This case for conservation as being essential to the well-being of a mighty nation is a book to stir you to action, not with emotional phrases, but with cold logic.

WALDEN. Henry David Thoreau. Various editions, including paperback.

The classical discussion of wilderness and its importance to the individual. It is an ideal book to read on a rainy day in camp, letting your mind wander from its pages into your own life and experiences in the wilderness.

WILDERNESS, AMERICA'S LIVING HERITAGE. Edited by David Brower, Sierra Club, San Francisco, 1961

The importance of our system of wilderness areas to the "American way of life" is discussed in detail. This is a potent argument against those who consider only quick profits to be the "American way."

A WILDERNESS BILL OF RIGHTS. William O. Douglas, Little, Brown and Company, Boston, 1965

This is an eloquent plea for the proper legal safeguards for our national wilderness areas, written by a distinguished Associate Justice of the Supreme Court. His pen is strong in defense of nature against the exploiters.

WILDLANDS IN OUR CIVILIZATION. Edited by David Brower, Sierra Club, San Francisco, 1964

This book is a symposium covering the importance of wilderness areas to the totality of society—a wider scope than is covered in *The Meaning of Wilderness to Science.*

Photography

THE COMPLETE BOOK OF NATURE PHOTOGRAPHY. Russ Kinne, A. S. Barnes, New York, 1962

Technical competence in nature photography is built up only by the exposure of yards and yards of film, but the basic techniques are quite easy to learn if they are explained well enough. This book does this and much more. The techniques for various subjects and conditions are discussed clearly and with good illustrations. There are several excellent examples of nature photography to properly inspire you.

HUNTING WITH THE CAMERA. Edited by Allan D. Cruickshank, Harpers, New York, 1957

This book has a chapter on each area of wildlife photography—birds, mammals, reptiles and amphibians, etc.—written by experts in each area. It contains plenty of sound ideas from experienced wildlife photographers.

HUNTING WITH CAMERA AND BINOCULAR. Francis E. Sell, Chilton Company, Philadelphia, 1961

This book not only discusses the techniques of photography itself, it is an excellent guide to buying your equipment. It also has a chapter on "writing" a picture story, and one on darkroom techniques which improve a nature photograph.

OUTDOOR PHOTOGRAPHY. Erwin Bauer, Outdoor Life, Harpers, New York, 1965

This book is an excellent discussion of the subject of nature photography, its equipment, and techniques required for the various forms, including underwater. The idea-checklists for different types of situations—fishing, hunting, boating, camping—in which the author suggests subjects for photographs are well worth purchasing the book.

WILDLIFE CINEMATOGRAPHY. John Warham, Focal Press, London, 1966

This is a guide to the 16 mm photographer of nature. Included is a vast array of techniques, camera and accessory selection, and even tips on editing. Several "assignments" show how a field photographic project is organized and carried out.

Pictures Plus

There are a large number of books on the market which appear to be picture books at first glance.

Yet there is more to them than just pretty pictures. The photographs are masterpieces of photographic art. The texts which accompany them are quite often taken from the masters of nature writing such as Henry Thoreau or John Muir. The coupling of words and pictures capture the feel of the place better than anything short of being there yourself. Some of these books, such as *The Place No One Knew* (Glen Canyon before the Lake Powell flooding), contain the only records left of areas that were once spots of beauty but are now overgrown mud puddles or part of the urban sprawl.

This is a category which is rapidly expanding and would be noticeably out of date by the time the book was published. The best publisher of these is Sierra Club, which averages two new titles a year. Other publishers have produced scattered volumes of comparable quality. They are unmistakable, showing up amid the poorer imitations with a contrast equalled only by comparing an overdeveloped resort with the North Cascades.

Ropework

THE ASHLEY BOOK OF KNOTS. Clifford W. Ashley, Doubleday, Garden City, New York, 1944

Almost 4,000 knots, hitches, splices, and other ropework, both utilitarian and decorative, fill this rather large book. While only a few would be directly of interest to the casual camper, the serious outdoorsman, like the sailor, can find many uses for the decorative knots to embellish his camping gear as well as form a useful in-camp hobby.

FUN WITH ROPES AND SPARS. John Thurman, C. Arthur Pearson Ltd., London, 1964. Available through the Boy Scouts.

For the person who likes to create things with lashing, this book is an excellent source of ideas and projects for all sorts of things.

PIONEERING PRINCIPLES. John Thurman, C. Arthur Pearson Ltd., London, 1962. Available through the Boy Scouts.

While the part on log work won't be of much use to campers, the section on lashing is excellent. Especially valuable are some variations on square and diagonal lashing which do not require clove hitches.

ROPES, KNOTS, AND SLINGS FOR CLIMBERS. Walt Wheelock, La Siesta Press, Glendale, California, 1967

While obviously designed for the rock climber, this makes a good introduction to this specialized field of ropework for the camper who may use the techniques as much for photography, hunting, or nature study as for peak-bagging.

Shooting

INSTINCT SHOOTING. Mike Jennings, Dodd, Mead & Company, New York, 1965

This is the system of Lucky McDaniel which has, unfortunately, been headlined as the method of hitting BB's in mid-air with a BB gun. While many of his students can do this often enough to prove it is no accident, it is not the usual thing either.

Snow Camping

THE COMPLETE BOOK OF FAMILY SKIING. George Sullivan, Coward-McCann, New York, 1966

This is an excellent general introduction to skiing, including both downhill and cross-country. It is designed for family groups including small children.

THE NEW CROSS-COUNTRY SKI BOOK. Johnny Caldwell, Stephen Greene Press, Brattleboro, Vermont, 1974

The main difference between ski mountaineering and cross-country skiing being the proportion of time spent on skis instead of climbing boots, this book is strictly skiing. It is an excellent little source of information on x-c skiing, both recreational and competitive. The section on off-season conditioning is worth the price of the book to anyone with an active Boy Scout troop looking for ideas for combining physical-fitness training with the outdoors. The new version is simply an enlargement of the old one, with even more good stuff inside. Available in hardcover or paperback.

MANUAL OF SKI MOUNTAINEERING. Edited by David Brower, Sierra Club, San Francisco, 1962

For the camper who likes his skiing in more than just the tow-up and ski-down form, or the daily ski tour from the lodge, this book gives the information on characteristics of snow, camping under these conditions, equipment selection, emergencies, etc.

THE SNOWSHOE BOOK. William Osgood and Leslie Hurley, Stephen Greene Press, Brattleboro, Vermont, 1973

This is an excellent little book on a winter sport that is still holding its own in woods despite the inroads of cross-country skiing in the more open areas. The book covers selection of equipment, snowshoeing techniques, handling emergencies, and sport applications both in competition and for the fun of it.

Surfing

SURFING. H. Arthur Klein, Lippincott, Philadelphia, 1965

This book is valuable in that it does not restrict its discussion to surfboards but also includes a couple of forms more in keeping with the camper's equipment—body surfing and mat surfing.

Survival

HOW TO SURVIVE ON LAND AND SEA. Frank and John Craighead, United States Naval Institute, Annapolis, Maryland, 1956

This book has the fault of all military survival books in that it discusses survival in areas of the world we will probably never see, much less encounter under survival conditions. However, it has many valuable sections, especially those on hunting and fishing gear made in the wilderness.

LIVING OFF THE COUNTRY. Bradford Angier, Stackpole, Harrisburg, Pennsylvania, 1956

While no sensible camper would go camping, planning to live off the country for any appreciable length of time, there are emergency situations. This book is a fine guide to the edible and poisonous plants of North America. It goes into detail about techniques which may be the difference between life and death in survival situations.

THE SURVIVAL BOOK. Paul H. Nesbett, Alonzo W. Pound, and William H. Allen, Van Nostrand, Princeton, New Jersey, 1959

Although not a military book and having no discussion of the uses of the parachute in survival, this book is quite similar to the armed forces survival texts. It is excellent on such subjects as water-finding, rescue techniques, and plant life.

The survival textbooks prepared for the armed forces are good for that purpose, but will be of little value to the camper. Since they cover survival techniques usually needed in areas outside this country, much that is in them will be useless to the North American camper.

Also, the techniques are built around the full use of the parachute. While the parachute and its accoutrements provide an excellent supply of survival material, the average camper will not have one unless he is auto camping with a parachute tent, and even then he won't have the pack, webbing, cushion, rip-cord cable, or much of the riser cord; nor would he be willing to tear up the excellent shelter qualities of the paratipi for features that can be made in other ways.

Still, these books do have enough value to make them worthwhile to check out of the public library. The section on rock climbing is one of the best anywhere, and it is in all the armed forces' teacher's manuals on survival, including the Craigheads' book.

SURVIVAL WITH STYLE. Bradford Angier, Stackpole Books, Harrisburg, Pennsylvania, 1972

Unlike most survival books which emphasize food and shelter, this book is best for its coverage of field-made equipment, particularly hunting weapons.

Swimming

DROWNPROOFING. Fred Lanoue, Prentice-Hall, Englewood Cliffs, New Jersey, 1963

While head swimming coach at Georgia Tech, the author of this book developed the concept of drownproofing. It is a must for anyone who does any teaching of swimming and it is definitely recommended for anyone who does any boating, swimming, or other water sports. The book covers such problems as drownproofing for the minority with a specific gravity over 1.00 (those who really, as opposed to psychologically, cannot float), the use of drownproofing techniques in lifesaving, and how to set up a course for teaching drownproofing.

MANUAL OF LIFESAVING AND WATER SAFETY INSTRUCTION. Charles E. Silvia, Association Press, New York, 1954

Being a manual for instructors and written in an academic style, this book is not as enjoyable reading as most of the books in this chapter are. However, it is by far the finest book on this subject published. It covers the entire field in a concise manner and gives lesson plans for teaching the subject.

THE NEW SCIENCE OF SKIN AND SCUBA DIVING. Edited by Bernard F. Empleton et al., Association Press, New York, 1962

This is a revision of the Conference for National Cooperation in Aquatics' first book, *The Science of Skin and Scuba Diving*. New techniques and discoveries have been included in this revision. It is an authoritative discussion of the technical aspects of this sport which should be known by everyone who uses the underwater breathing equipment. Injuries, physiology, and safety rules get the full treatment. There is also a decompression table for the benefit of those who go deep enough for bends to be a danger.

Since scuba diving is not to be undertaken without expert instruction, the book omits the basic points of how to select the equipment and how to use it in both regular and emergency situations. This should be required reading for anyone who uses scuba gear, and it is useful for the mask-and-snorkle diver as well.

THE SKIN DIVER. Elgin Ciampi, Ronald Press, New York, 1960

For once, here is a popular introduction to skin diving which neither tries to make the sport sound so simple that the reader is unaware of its dangers, nor tries to make the author, as a participant, seem more heroic than he really is. The author does not minimize the dangers—in fact, he goes into an adequate discussion of them—but he shows the pleasures of skin diving as a sport any healthy person can engage in with proper training. He discusses all phases of skin diving and includes plans for an underwater case for cameras.

Tents

THE INDIAN TIPI, ITS HISTORY, CONSTRUCTION, AND USE. Reginald and Gladys Laubin, University of Oklahoma Press, Norman, 1957

For anyone wanting to build a tipi, this book is absolutely required. It not only includes plans for making one, it gives many accounts of its use (by the authors and Indians) which will help smooth out the kinks for anyone not familiar with the tipi. It is also of value to anyone interested in Indian lore; its scholarship is excellent.

Miscellaneous

THE JOY OF CAMPING. Richard W. Langer, Saturday Review Press, New York, 1973

This book is listed under miscellaneous rather than general because it isn't a particularly well-balanced coverage of camping in general, but its coverage of the various camping transportation systems and of in-camp sports is one of the best.

THE THOUSAND MILE SUMMER. Colin Fletcher, Howell-North, Berkeley, 1964

This is the account of a hike, the full length of the Pacific Crest Trail, by a solo hiker. The camper who enjoys the backpack and hiking-boot method of camping will enjoy reading this well-written account of an incredible trip, and pick up a few tips as he goes.

THE MAN WHO WALKED THROUGH TIME. Colin Fletcher, Alfred Knopf, New York, 1968

Another solo hike by Fletcher, this one the first longitudinal traverse of the Grand Canyon National Park. Not only will backpackers get many ideas for equipment and techniques from it, his feel for the place is so good that the book could almost be listed in the philosophy section of this chapter as well.

Many other books, such as guide books to certain areas and narratives of travels, will also be included in the camper's library. Because of the regional factor, there has been no attempt to include them here. Getting on the mailing list of the U.S. Government Printing Office will bring you news of countless low-cost, informative publications on all manner of subjects. The list is free.

CHAPTER FIFTY-FIVE

Nature Study

These books have a dual use. The first is as a field guide to help identify individual specimens found in the camping situation. A good book for this purpose should be logically arranged so the particular specimen may be easily recognized. A key chart is often helpful. (This is a means of identification by using a system of features that will identify the specimen in question by a process of elimination.) While the key chart is the only completely accurate method, it is often impractical. It is easy to use a key to identify a tree by its leaves, but it is almost impossible to use one to identify a snake since the only accurate key is based on the number of scales in certain areas of the head and body and capture is, therefore, necessary.

The second use of nature-study books is for home reading. The serious amateur naturalist will almost literally memorize many of these books. This is not only because of his intense interest in the subject, but because there is no room for a small library when camping, especially backpacking.

Probably the best single group of books on this subject is the Peterson Field Guide Series. They use the technique invented by Ludlow Griscom of "field marks," or features found only in that particular species. This method was further developed by Roger Tory Peterson, using clear, colored illustrations, with pointers indicating the distinguishing features. The person who knows how to identify animals looks first for these features, even if subconsciously. Books in this series will be noted as PFGS in this bibliography. Most of these are now available in paperback as well as hardcover, but

the hard use these handy volumes get generally makes the paperbacks wear out too fast.

While the books listed here are restricted primarily to field guides, the serious amateur naturalist will find much of value in the various books of a textbook nature and some of the excellent books on rather restricted areas of study, such as an individual species. In many areas of nature study, these books will be the only source of information, since there are no field books published on such important areas as the tidewater ecology or invertebrates other than insects or shells.

Astronomy

SEASONAL STAR CHARTS, James S. Sweeney, Jr., Hubbard Scientific Co., Northbrook, Ill., 1962

This is the best guide to the skies for the price (under $5.00) for the amateur. The positions of stars down to the seventh magnitude, the Messier objects, etc., are given by coordinates of right ascension and declination. Names and Greek-letter designations are both included. Most important for the camper is a paragraph on each constellation describing objects of interest to the naked eye or with binoculars. Double stars, Messier objects, etc., are described in detail for owners of astronomical telescopes.

THE STARS, A NEW WAY TO SEE THEM. H. A. Rey, Houghton Mifflin Company, Boston, 1962

The author has done a great service to the field of popular astronomy in writing this book. He has taken the constellations and redrawn them, using the same stars, to make stick drawings or cartoon sketches out of what was formerly a jumble of meaningless lines. With this book, I was first able to make out Gemini and all of Ursa Major (not just the Big Dipper). With its help, I was able to give an eleven-year-old astronomer a basic knowledge of sidereal time. It combines the rarely combined—competent scholarship with interesting and easily grasped wording. The 1962 revision includes the Southern Hemisphere as well as the Northern.

However, Mr. Rey has only identified the major stars, the first or brighter magnitudes and the freaks (such as Mira) and some nebulae. An addition of the Greek lettering and the names of all the named stars would make an excellent book even better.

Birds

FIELD GUIDE TO THE BIRDS. Roger Tory Peterson, PFGS, Houghton Mifflin Company, Boston, 1947

See below.

FIELD GUIDE TO THE WESTERN BIRDS. Roger Tory Peterson, PFGS, Houghton Mifflin Company, Boston, 1941

These two books, taken together, cover the full range of bird life in this country. The books are illustrated with color pictures of the birds and distinguishing features are indicated. While the beginner will suffer, for a time, from the lack of a key chart, any bird watcher who can tell a wren from a sparrow can easily use these books to tell what species of either it is.

A FIELD GUIDE TO BIRD SONGS. Peter Paul Kellogg and Arthur A. Allen, Cornell University Laboratory of Ornithology, Ithaca, 1959

See below.

A FIELD GUIDE TO WESTERN BIRD SONGS. Peter Paul Kellogg and Arthur A. Allen, Cornell University Laboratory of Ornithology, Ithaca, 1952

Two twelve-inch LP records in each set make up this extraordinary technical accomplishment. The bird calls and songs are recorded in the field to accompany the two Peterson field guides to the American birds in a page-by-page manner. While this reference cannot be used easily in the field and there are regional dialects of bird "language," as with human language, it is an excellent means of familiarizing yourself with bird songs for better identification in the field.

A GUIDE TO BIRD SONGS. Aretas A. Saunders, Doubleday, Garden City, New York, 1951

Bird songs are virtually impossible to reproduce in cold type. This book gives it a good try, and comes close by giving the call both in lines indicating the pitch and in words indicating accent and timing. Still, it is hard to "read." Start with some you already know until you have fully learned the author's system. A key chart is furnished to help you identify an unfamiliar call when the bird is not visible.

FIELD GUIDE TO THE BIRDS OF TEXAS. Roger Tory Peterson, Houghton Mifflin Company for the Texas Game and Fish Commission, Boston, 1960

For the broad band where the Eastern and Western birds overlap in their ranges, both Peterson books had to be carried in the field. This book is simply a "paste-up" combination of the two books for the birds of this boundary area. While it is designed for Texas, with its amazing total of 542 species, it is also useful in other boundary states, especially Oklahoma and the states of Northern Mexico. The range of each species, however, is given only in terms of the Lone Star State.

BIRDS OF MEXICO. Emmet Reid Blake, University of Chicago Press, Chicago, 1953

This is an excellent little field book covering Mexico and some of the birds of Central America.

BIRDS OF TRINIDAD AND TOBAGO. G. A. C. Herklots, Collins, London, 1961

This field guide not only includes the twin-island republic, but also covers the coastal areas of Northeastern South America as well.

A FIELD GUIDE TO THE BIRDS OF BRITAIN AND EUROPE. Roger Tory Peterson, Guy Mountfort, and P. A. D. Hollom, PFGS, Houghton Mifflin Company, Boston, 1954

For those who live or vacation in Europe, the Peterson method is available for the birds of that continent too.

A FIELD GUIDE TO THE BIRDS OF EAST AND CENTRAL AFRICA. J. G. Williams, Houghton Mifflin Company, Boston, 1964

For the camper with money enough to go on safari, this field guide will add considerable interest. While not subtitled as a part of the Peterson Field Guide Series, it is of the same quality and Roger Tory Peterson did write the Introduction.

Ferns

FIELD GUIDE TO FERNS. Houghton Cobb, PFGS, Houghton Mifflin Company, Boston, 1956

This is a good reference piece to a rather neglected aspect of nature study. With most, a fern is a fern and what's the difference? This book shows you. Unfortunately, it is restricted to the ferns of Northeastern and North Central United States.

THE SOUTHERN FERN GUIDE. Edgar T. Wherry, Doubleday, Garden City, New York, 1964

While the absence of the "field mark" system makes this book inferior to the one above, it does cover the area from the Southeastern states to East Texas.

Fish

FIELD BOOK OF FRESH WATER FISHES. Ray Schrenkeisen, Putnam, New York, 1963

This excellent little book is the perfect solution to identifying that odd thing on your line. It also covers minnows and other non-game fish. The geographic area is north of the Rio Grande.

MARINE GAME FISH OF THE WORLD. Francesca La Monte, Doubleday, Garden City, New York, 1952

While non-game fish are excluded, they are seldom encountered by the average camper unless he is in their habitat, as they rarely take the lures of the sports fisherman. To include all salt-water fish, even of just the coastal waters of the U.S., would require a book too large to qualify as a field guide.

General

COMPLETE FIELD GUIDE TO AMERICAN WILDLIFE. Henry Hill Collins, Jr., Harpers, New York, 1958

This is an attempt to cover all of zoology into one volume to avoid juggling several volumes in the field. It is only partially successful since the total weight of the book is a little on the heavy side for comfortable carrying. It covers the area north of the thirty-sixth parallel (Oklahoma-Kansas to North Carolina-Virginia boundaries) and east of the Rockies.

Insects

A FIELD GUIDE TO THE BUTTERFLIES. Alexander B. Klots, PFGS, Houghton Mifflin Company, Boston, 1951

This handles the species in the U.S.A. and Canada east of the 100th meridian (the eastern side of the Texas panhandle).

FIELD GUIDE TO THE INSECTS NORTH OF MEXICO. Donald J. Borror and Reichard E. White, PFGS, Houghton Mifflin Company, Boston, 1970

This book covers the whole of the class, but unfortunately space restricts it to dividing only down to subfamily except for significant (for man) species which are carried all the way. A once-over-lightly is given at the genus level.

Lichens

LICHEN HANDBOOK. Mason E. Hale, Jr., Smithsonian Institution, Washington, D.C., 1961

Lichens are usually noticed as simply a color pattern on a rock or tree, if they are noticed at all, yet there is a considerable variety in this lowly plant form, and this book helps show you. Unfortunately, it only covers the Eastern United States, and the varieties which lend a bright touch of color to the already colorful desert rocks are therefore omitted.

Mammals

A FIELD GUIDE TO ANIMAL TRACKS. Olaus J. Murie, PFGS, Houghton Mifflin Company, Boston, 1954

With the current crowded-campsite conditions, you won't always be lucky enough to see wild animals, but you will often see their tracks. This little book can open up a whole new activity in nature study—the study of tracks, droppings, pellets, gnawings, and diggings of mammals and some birds. If you know them well enough, you can identify most animals as easily as if you saw them in person.

A FIELD GUIDE TO MAMMALS. W. H. Burt and R. P. Grossenheider, PFGS, Houghton Mifflin Company, Boston, 1952

Typical Peterson Series quality, it provides ready identification for the mammals, including some rare ones. A dentation chart and an excellent set of photographs will enable you to identify skulls you may find, down to genus and occasionally to species as well.

THE MAMMAL GUIDE. Ralph S. Palmer, Doubleday, Garden City, New York, 1954

While the identification method is not as easy to use as the Peterson system, the descriptions are much more extensive, including not only appearance and habitat, but habits and economic function as well.

Mineralogy

A FIELD GUIDE TO ROCKS AND MINERALS. Frederick H. Pough, PFGS, Houghton Mifflin Company, Boston, 1960

This is the best book available for identifying rock and mineral samples. Unlike some of the other Peterson Series books, which are limited to a certain geographical area, this one covers the minerals of the world. A modified key, based on crystal shape, helps narrow down the identification efforts.

While not, strictly speaking, field guides, there are many excellent books and pamphlets showing where to find certain types of minerals—especially gem stones for lapidarists. Some also include fossil beds, but they are usually deficient in this respect, either simply indicating fossil beds without any information on what type of fossil or restricting it to petrified wood, dinosaur bones, or a similar fossil of interest to lapidarists.

Mushrooms

COMMON EDIBLE MUSHROOMS. Clyde M. Christensen, Charles T. Branford, Newton Center, Massachusetts, 1943

Mushrooms have always had a fascination for nature students. Perhaps it is the element of danger which makes mushroom hunting far more developed than berry hunting or the searching for other edible wild plants. This danger is not to be trifled with, however, since with some species a small bite is fatal, delayed in its action, and without a known antidote. There are, however, a few varieties which are quite edible and cannot be confused with poisonous species. These books help you to tell one from the other.

FIELD BOOK OF COMMON MUSHROOMS. William S. Thomas, Putnam, New York, 1948

While it is restricted in its title to common mushrooms, this book covers the entire country with a presentation for the naturalist rather than the cook.

THE MUSHROOM HUNTER'S GUIDE. Alexander H. Smith, University of Michigan Press, Ann Arbor, 1958

A guide to the mushrooms with the skillet in mind.

Paleontology

Like wildflowers, fossils are far too varied to fit into a field guide for a very large area. Many excellent ones are available from universities, museums, and fossil-hunting clubs for surprisingly low cost.

Reptiles and Amphibians

FIELD BOOK OF SNAKES OF THE U.S. AND CANADA. Karl P. Schmidt and D. Dwight Davis, Putnam, New York, 1941

Color and patterns of color are excellent means of identifying snakes, but what if you find an albino? How would you identify it? If you catch one (and if you found an albino, its zoo value would make it extremely worthwhile), you can key it out with nothing to go on but the number of scales around its eyes, nose, body, and tail. It is also good for identification by color pattern as well. This book is a traditional necessity for the serious amateur.

FIELD GUIDE TO REPTILES AND AMPHIBIANS. Roger Conant, PFGS, Houghton Mifflin Company, Boston, 1958

See below.

FIELD GUIDE TO WESTERN REPTILES AND AMPHIBIANS. Robert C. Stebbins, PFGS, Houghton Mifflin Company, Boston, 1966

With the 100th meridian dividing the two volumes, these books cover the identity of all the snakes, lizards, turtles, salamanders, frogs, toads, etc., in the country. A key chart would have helped, but it is valuable anyway.

SNAKES OF AFRICA. R. M. Isemonger, Thomas Nelson, New York, 1962

For those visiting Africa, this book is an excellent field guide for the snakes of Africa south of the Sahara.

Shells

A FIELD GUIDE TO THE SHELLS OF OUR ATLANTIC AND GULF COASTS. Percy A. Morris, PFGS, Houghton Mifflin Company, Boston, 1951

See below.

A FIELD GUIDE TO THE SHELLS OF THE PACIFIC COAST AND HAWAII. Percy A. Morris, PFGS, Houghton Mifflin Company, Boston, 1952

Typical Peterson Series work is done on the favorite nature sport of coastal campers. The field marks are missing as pointers on the excellent photographs, but they are mentioned in the captions. Color and black-and-white photographs make identification easy and are interesting viewing as well.

Spelunking

THE COMPLETE BOOK OF CAVE EXPLORATION. Roy Pinney, Coward-McCann, New York, 1962

This book is an excellent source of information of cave origins, history, and spelunking organization and safety. These two books supplement each other as much, if not more, than they duplicate.

EXPLORING AMERICAN CAVES. Franklin Folsom, Collier Books, New York, 1962

This is an excellent paperback on spelunking. Not only does the author give valuable information on spelunking techniques, but he also presents an account of the history of American spelunking and a listing of the Grottos (local units) of the National Speleological Society, which is the best source of help for the would-be spelunker.

Trees

THE COMPLETE GUIDE TO NORTH AMERICAN TREES. Carlton C. Curtis and S. C. Bausor, The New Home Library, New York, 1943

Subdivided into three large geographical divisions, this book is a key to the native, wild trees of each area.

FIELD GUIDE TO TREES AND SHRUBS. George A. Petrides, PFGS, Houghton Mifflin Company, Boston, 1954

This is an excellent reference book for identification of the woody plants. There is a good key chart in the back.

NORTH AMERICAN TREES. Richard J. Preston, Jr., Iowa State University Press, Ames, 1962

This is an easy-to-use book with an excellent key chart to make identification easier.

Wildflowers

A FIELD GUIDE TO ROCKY MOUNTAIN WILDFLOWERS. John J. Craighead, Frank C. Craighead, Jr., and Ray J. Davis, PFGS, Houghton Mifflin Company, Boston, 1963

A similar volume to the one below, this book covers the mountain region from Northern Arizona and New Mexico to British Columbia.

A FIELD GUIDE TO THE WILDFLOWERS OF THE NORTHEASTERN AND CENTRAL STATES. Margaret McKenney and Roger Tory Peterson, PFGS, Houghton Mifflin Company, Boston, 1954

A comprehensive identification manual for the area east of the 100th meridian and approximately north of the Ohio River.

Many excellent field books are published by state wildflower groups, conservation organizations, and university presses. If you will be doing most of your study in that narrow an area, such a book will be vastly superior to one covering a larger area because of the lighter weight. A book adequately covering the nation would weigh several pounds.

PART XII

Miscellaneous Information

Many beginning campers are at a loss to find such valuable items of information as where to get equipment or where to get help in some of the more specialized areas of camping. This section is something of a catch-all of miscellaneous information. Most campers ultimately find out these things by word of mouth over a few years, but it helps to have all of them at hand. The lists of outfitters and organizations listed here and throughout the book, of course, are not complete. They are merely those with whom I have had some first-hand experience, and that experience has been good.

CHAPTER FIFTY-SIX

Where to Get Supplies

The problem of where to get supplies is one faced by the beginner and seasoned camper alike. The beginner more often faces the problem of quality of design or workmanship. The expert has had enough experience with this factor, but he is still confronted with the problem of getting the best equipment for his money.

Camping equipment is sold in a wide range of places. In addition to these, there is always the possibility of making it yourself, borrowing or buying it from another camper, or, in some areas, renting it.

The so-called surplus stores (which now handle very little government-surplus items) are generally of poor quality. But just as more Stradivari violins have been found in pawn shops than anywhere else, the best buys are sometimes found in these stores. Still, you have to be quite familiar with camping gear not to get "hooked."

Department stores and discount houses generally handle good-quality workmanship, and sell it at a fairly low price, but the items they sell are rather heavy and bulky. They are acceptable for auto camping but rarely for any other method.

This leaves what is probably the safest source of supply for the beginner, and generally the best for all—the specialty houses. These are specialists in camping gear and related items. They generally sell by mail order—a welcome help for those who live outside the areas of extensive camping. The prices are usually higher for a given item than the other sources, but the products are of the first quality and they are designed with an eye to reducing bulk and weight. In the long run, they are usually cheaper than the less sturdy, lower-priced products.

GENERAL EQUIPMENT

There is such a wide assortment of quality camping outfitters that there is no need for descriptive commentary on their lines. They all have a wide variety of equipment of good quality. Get their catalogs and match up the best combination of features and cost for your personal preference.

Alpine Outfitters, 328 Link Lane, Fort Collins, Colorado 80521

Eddie Bauer, 1737 Airport Way S., Seattle, Washington 98124

L. L. Bean, 745 Main Street, Freeport, Maine 04032

Class-5, 2010 Seventh Street, Berkeley, California 94710

Co-op Wilderness Supply, 1432 University Ave., Berkeley, California 94702

Eastern Mountain Sports, Box 9124, Boston, Massachusetts 02215

Frostline Kits, Box 9100, Boulder, Colorado 80303 (do-it-yourself equipment)

Gerry, 5450 North Valley Highway, Denver, Colorado 80216

Don Gleason's, 21 Pearl Street, Northampton, Massachusetts 01060

Holubar Mountaineering, Box 7, Boulder, Colorado 80302

Kelty, 1801 Victory Blvd., Glendale, California 91201

Moor & Mountain, Main St., Concord, Massachusetts 01742

Recreational Equipment, Inc. (co-op), 1525 11th Avenue, Seattle, Washington 98122

J. D. Sachs, Afton Ave., Yardley, Pennsylvania 19067

Sierra Designs, 4th and Addison Streets, Berkeley, California 94710

Ski Hut, 1615 University Avenue, Berkeley, California 94703

FOOD

Chuck Wagon, Micro Drive, Woburn, Massachusetts 01801

Dri-Lite Foods, 11333 Atlantic, Lynwood, California 90262

Freeze Dry Foods, 579 Speers Road, Oakville, Ontario L6K 2G4

National Packaged Trail Foods, 632 E. 185th Street, Cleveland, Ohio 44119 (Seidel)

Natural Food Backpack Dinners, Box 532, Corvalis, Oregon 97330

Oregon Freeze Dry Foods, Box 1048, Albany, Oregon 97321 (Mountain House)

Perma-Pack, 40 East 2430 South, Salt Lake City, Utah 84115 (CampLite)

Recreational Equipment, 1525 11th Avenue, Seattle, Washington 98122

Stow-A-Way Sports Industries, 66 Cushing Hiway, Cohasset, Massachusetts 02025

In addition to these sources, many of these brands are available through the camping outfitters listed earlier. Some of the manufacturers have a minimum order, which does not apply at the outfitter's.

MAPS

UNITED STATES GEOLOGICAL SURVEY

General Services Building
Eighteenth and F Streets, N.W.
Washington, D.C. 20405

U.S. GEOLOGICAL SURVEY

Federal Center
Denver, Colorado 80200

Topographical maps for almost all of the United States and its possessions. An Index is available from the Washington office or the U.S. Government Printing Office. The Denver office handles maps of areas west of the Mississippi River.

GEOLOGICAL SURVEY OF CANADA

Map Distribution Office
601 Booth Street
Ottawa, Ontario K1A 0E8

Topographical maps for all of Canada.

DIRECCION DE GEOGRAFÍA Y METEOROLOGÍA

Tacusaya, D.F., Mexico

Topographical maps for Mexico. Notes are in Spanish but standard symbols are used.

CHAPTER FIFTY-SEVEN

Organizations

Much has been written about that slave to mammon, the organization man, and much has been written about the "joiner," who feels so estranged from society that he joins every group that will have him. Still, the fact remains that in unity is strength and organization is necessary to accomplish many things in this world.

In this chapter, I have not only listed national organizations but a sample of regional and local groups in order to show some of the organizational structures used by them. However, problems of space and accessibility have made any attempt to create a complete listing impossible. Many of the national (and international) groups have local branches. There is no point in joining just to join except that they can generally use the money. On the other hand, they usually need good workers as much as money, so pick one in which you can really work.

When the Sierra Club used 2 per cent of its budget to fight the flooding of Grand Canyon, Internal Revenue Service declared it "primarily engaged in lobbying" and revoked its tax exemption as a non-profit, educational organization. (In spite of listing its main purpose as "securing appropriations" for the U.S. Navy, the Navy League is still tax-exempt!) The result of this action forced many of the environmental groups to split into two legally separate organizations, one for education remaining tax-exempt and the other a lobbying group without this subsidy that is given to the exploiters in the form of business tax-loopholes. While there is a legal distinction between these two organizations, there is not one in practice, so where "lobbying" is listed as a function of the organization, there still may be a separate fund for such purposes as wild land acquisition, educational activities, etc. which is tax-exempt and the term merely refers to an organized attempt to influence legislation.

CONSERVATION ORGANIZATIONS

ADIRONDACK MOUNTAIN CLUB, 172 Ridge Street, Glen Falls, New York 12801

Founded in 1922, ADK works in the New York and New England area with camping schools, community education programs, lobbying, hut and lodge operation, search and rescue teams, and organized trips to foster the care and appreciation of the Adirondack Park in New York, secondarily the Catskill and Shawangung Parks, and tertiarily all natural resources in general.

Dues are $10.00 per year with a whole family paying only $5.00 additional. Student membership is also $5.00. (There is the strong probability that these will be raised.) There are twenty-four chapters, all but one in New York state, and about a quarter of its membership is outside that area. Their publication is *Adirondac,* a bimonthly of twenty-four pages. It includes trip accounts, house-organ business, book reviews, and a couple of pages of ads.

ADIRONDACK TRAIL IMPROVEMENT SOCIETY, Saint Huberts, New York

Founded in 1897, this is one of the oldest camping organizations in the country. The group is fairly small (around 300) and makes no effort to publicize itself. However, it is responsible for an extensive network of trails in the Adirondack State Forest region of New York and adds a new trail "every few years." They are also quite active in legislative work to preserve the "forever wild" clause in the enabling legislation for the state forest system. During late summer, the Society conducts an educational-recreational program primarily for children over six.

The Society has no publication other than an occasional trail or nature guide.

There is no information on membership, although contributions are encouraged in order to help maintain the trail system.

APPALACHIAN MOUNTAIN CLUB, 5 Joy Street, Boston, Massachusetts 02108

The A.M.C. was founded in 1876, making it the oldest mountain club in the country still in existence. Their main work is in building a system of trails, backcountry campsites, and huts (the most famous being the mountain huts of the White Mountain System). In addition, they sponsor several summer camps and wilderness outings. In the off season, they have programs of slide-lectures, canoe rallies, and other activities.

Their publication is *Appalachia,* published monthly except in July and September, but twice in June and December. It is about sixty pages, generally of a house-organ nature (committee reports, notices of outings, etc.). The second issues in June and December are over 200 pages of accounts of expeditions as well as miscellaneous house-keeping notes. Ads are mostly for outfitters, resort areas, environmental schools and businesses, etc. In addition to *Appalachia,* the Club publishes a comprehensive array of trail guides for New England.

Basic membership is $15.00 per year with $5.00

initiation fee for those over 23; $7.00 and no initiation for those under.

THE APPALACHIAN TRAIL CONFERENCE, Box 236, Harper's Ferry, West Virginia 25425

The primary concern of this group is the development and maintenance of the Appalachian Trail, a foot trail extending from Mt. Katahdin in Maine to Springer Mountain in Georgia—a distance of 2,033.92 miles (3,254.27 km). While most of their effort is in the physical maintenance of the trail, they are active on the legislative scene in trying to secure laws to protect the wilderness nature of the trail (already breached in many areas).

Their publication is *Appalachian Trailway News,* a house-organ-type publication coming out quarterly. In addition, they publish a considerable volume of guide books to the trail and pamphlets on equipment, trail-building techniques, shelter plans, etc.

The basic membership is $7.00 per year and furnishes the member with all publications, other than guide books, published during the year.

BIG THICKET ASSOCIATION, Box 377, Saratoga, Texas 77585

The main work of the Association, since its founding in 1964, has been to secure the finest example of southern transitional habitat in a National Biological Reserve. Through a tortuous trail of Congressional committees and House and Senate bills that differed only in minor details but which no Joint Committees were appointed to resolve, the Association and its related Big Thicket Coordinating Committee kept plodding away, educating the public to the danger from the loggers.

As this is being written, the National Biological Reserve (the country's first) has been approved, but the exact boundaries have not yet been set. Support of this group's design is essential to ensure that the last habitat of the ivory-bill woodpecker is included in the reserve.

Membership is now over 1,000. Dues are $6.00 per year, $2.00 for students. In addition to their work for the reserve, the Association also operates a museum at Saratoga with a short hiking trail and primitive camping facilities. A quarterly newsletter (and a large number of special bulletins as the bill hit another roadblock) keep the members informed on the reserve. Guide material and other information is also provided by the Association.

CALIFORNIA ROADSIDE COUNCIL. 2636 Ocean Avenue, San Francisco, California 94132

The C.R.C. was selected as a type of roadside council existing in several states because it is both the largest and the most active. I sent all the conservation groups essentially the same letter, asking, "Why should a camper join your group?" C.R.C.'s answer was: "Insofar as a camper is concerned with (a) pleasure in driving to his take-off destination; (b) protection of the landscape from blight under the guise of "development"; (c) preservation of parks and scenic values from damage by freeways, etc.; and (d) scenic conservation generally—to that degree the California camper should belong to the California Roadside Council." The same holds true of Roadside Councils in other states where these Councils exist.

They publish a quarterly mimeographed bulletin of four to eight pages which outlines the action in the national and state legislative bodies. Their action is primarily legislative: billboard control, greenbelt preservation, keeping freeways out of wilderness areas; but some is with administrative agencies doing such as getting highway departments to mix wildflower seeds with the chemical stabilizing compounds spread on new roadway cuts. The C.R.C. has been active since 1926.

The basic membership is $6.00 per year. Your public library can find the address of a Roadside Council in your state if one exists.

CANADIAN NATURE FEDERATION, 46 Elgin Street, Ottawa, Ontario K1P 5K6

The Canadian Nature Federation traces its history back to the Canadian Audubon Society and has many similarities with the version of that organization "south of the line." The Federation is primarily a public education organization, but also co-ordinates local projects, conducts research, and produces a variety of publications.

The main publication is *Nature Canada,* a fifty-two-page publication with color photos, articles on environmental subjects, legislative information both at the federal and provincial level, house-organ material, and book reviews. While presently only in English, work is under way to begin a French version as well. In addition, booklets and monographs are published on specific subjects.

Dues are $8.00 per year for individuals, $10.00 for families. There are about 17,000 members, but no local branches.

DEFENDERS OF WILDLIFE, 809 Dupont Circle Building, Washington, D.C. 20036

This organization's main field of action is in opposing bounties and 1080 (sodium fluoroacetate) which have created serious ecological inbalances as well as the probable extinction of some species. 1080 is particularly potent, has no known antidote, and will kill through several ingestions. As a result, poisoned grain set out for rodent control is not only eaten by the rodents, but also by songbirds. In turn, the rodents are eaten by coyotes (who have a vast amount of poison set out for them directly), which are, in turn, eaten by carrion-feeding birds. Most of the losses of the California condor in recent years are directly due to their eating 1080-killed predators. The kit fox is now on the near-extinct list solely because of 1080.

Their magazine, *Defenders of Wildlife News,* is published quarterly and contains around 100 pages per issue. Their covers are first-rate color wildlife photos and the contents have many in black and white. They include excellent coverage of the legislative scene, not only giving the basics on pending legislation but complete transcripts of committee hearings of interest to conservationists.

Other concerns of the organization involve protecting national parks from flooding, encouraging the development and use of synthetic furs as a conservation device, opposing roadside "zoos," and supporting research in the development of humane traps.

The basic membership is $5.00 per year.

FLORIDA TRAIL ASSOCIATION, 33 S. W. 18th Terrace, Miami, Florida 33129

The Association was organized in 1966 and its main purpose is the development and maintenance of a hiking trail system in Florida. They now have 200 continuous miles (320 km) of trail in the north-central part of the state and about 70 (112 km) in the south and west parts. In addition to the trail, they carry out an education program to introduce people to hiking and wilderness. Both hiking and canoe trips are sponsored.

The Association has several points which make it a valuable example to other local groups trying to develop hiking facilities. It is kept fairly loose so it doesn't become "over-organized"; it takes no conservation stands (as this might generate opposition to the trail) but urges members to be active in conservation groups that are active in this area; and it restricts use of the trail to its members. While this last may seem selfish, it has often been the determining factor in getting easements through private land—the landowner is reasonably sure the easement will not be abused by tenderfoot vandalism.

A mimeographed *Newsletter* of some eight pages is published monthly and a map of the private portion of the trail is $2.00 to members only. Sixty-four miles (102 km) of the trail pass through Ocala National Forest and all public domain portions are open to the general public.

Dues are $3.00 for individuals and $5.00 for families at the time of writing, but it was probable that they would be raised to $5.00 and $10.00 in 1975 because of postage and printing cost increases. There are 6,000 members, 200 to 300 of which are out of state.

FRIENDS OF THE EARTH, 529 Commercial Street, San Francisco, California 94111

Founded in 1969, FOE has proved to be just that to pushers of the SST, fission power, extensive dams, and commercial rip-offs of public land. Their house organ, *Not Man Apart,* is a semi-monthly, sixteen-page tabloid covering up-dates on environmental issues.

Dues are $15.00 per year, twelve of which support the organization and its lobbying activities; the remainder is for the publication. There are approximately 20,000 members in fifty local branches, although I couldn't determine if this is just the U.S. group or includes all in ten nations with organizations.

GET OIL OUT!, Box 1513, 111 E. De la Guerra Street, Santa Barbara, California 93102

GOO, as it is universally known, is included in this list because it represents a purely local cause (inasmuch as any environmental problem can be "purely local") that was handled with imagination (such as the acronym) and a well-managed lobby and educational campaign that showed the world what a few irate citizens could do.

GOO was organized two days after the infamous Santa Barbara spill in 1969. Because of the publicity of this first major offshore drilling disaster, GOO was able to get to the national media and has been able to halt such operations in the Santa Barbara Channel. As a result, offshore drillers everywhere have been forced by public opinion to incorporate safety devices they otherwise would not have used.

GOO has 2,000 members, which, while large for a local action group, has outgrown this restricted geographical limit and now is a clearinghouse for information on the subject of offshore oil drilling operations and their impact on the environment.

IZAAK WALTON LEAGUE OF AMERICA, 1800 North Kent Street, Arlington, Virginia 22309

The Izaak Walton League is primarily concerned with fostering programs of conservation outside the various governmental structures—local action by individuals to stop stream pollution, to plant greenbelts, to work with landowners to reduce posting of land, etc. They are also quite active in the legislative field in working to get more wilderness areas under public ownership in the form of national forests, parks, monuments, and seashore areas.

Their magazine is the monthly, *Outdoor America.* The subjects are wide-ranging: on new parks, threatened wilderness areas, animal species, notable conservation projects by individuals, or businesses, etc. In addition, they have an action program called Save Our Stream in which the public adopts a stream and cares for it year round.

Basic national membership is $10.00 per year with state and local memberships also available. There are more than 500 chapters nationwide.

NATIONAL AUDUBON SOCIETY, 950 Third Avenue, New York, New York 10022

The Audubon Society has been identified in the public mind with ornithology, partly because of its namesake's paintings and partly because of the high percentage of birders in the organization. Yet it is by no means strictly a bird-watching society. Society activities range from maintaining almost fifty wildlife sanctuaries to an extensive program of education through films, magazines, and workshops.

Their publication is *Audubon,* a bimonthly magazine of around eighty pages, profusely illustrated, with many in color. Compared to other conservation groups' publications, it contains a high proportion of ads, mostly on items of interest to amateur naturalists, but not as many as in the average commercial publication. Articles range from history to ecology to travel, but always with a strong undercurrent of conservation.

In addition to *Audubon,* the Society publishes *American Birds,* a journal of ornithology, and a wide range of books, bulletins, posters, teaching aids, and leaflets on a wide variety of nature subjects both for adults and children.

Membership rates are $12.00 per individual or $15.00 per family per year. If designated, this includes membership in a regional organization at no extra charge. There are over 325 local chapters and over 320,000 members.

NATIONAL PARKS ASSOCIATION, 1300 New Hampshire Avenue, N.W., Washington, D.C. 20036

The National Parks Association was founded in 1919 by Stephen T. Mather, the first Director of the National Park Service. Its area of concern, of course, is with the National Park System. While it has a cooperative relationship with the National Park Service, it is independent and sometimes quite critical of Interior Department policies in this area.

Its magazine is *National Parks Magazine,* a monthly of around twenty-four pages. The articles are mainly on national parks, proposed parks, potential danger to parks and monuments (both from within the Department and outside), and similar items of interest. The magazine has a very limited number of ads for bird feeders, camping gear, etc. The covers are sometimes in color and the articles are illustrated with several black-and-white photos.

Basic membership is $6.50 per year or $12.00 for two years.

NATIONAL WILDLIFE FEDERATION, 1412 Sixteenth Street, N.W., Washington, D.C. 20036

The National Wildlife Federation was founded in 1936 and has an active program of trips, schools, publications, and a strong organization for mobilizing public pressure in the legislative field.

The NWF has an extensive array of publications. Basic are: *National Wildlife,* a 48-page, full-color bimonthly coverage of environmental concerns in the United States; *International Wildlife,* a 56-page, full-color bimonthly coverage of environmental concerns outside the United States; and *Ranger Rick,* a 48-page color monthly (except for June and September) magazine of nature aimed at the youth members. National and International members receive the appropriate publication while world members receive both and family membership brings all three. In addition to these basic publications, NWF publishes *Conservation Report,* a sixteen-page weekly report on Congressional activities, new developments in the environmental field, and short conservation articles. *Conservation Report* is free to members who request it.

Outside the periodical field, the NWF publishes a selection of books on wildlife.

Dues are $7.50 for National or International memberships, $12.50 for world, $19.50 for family, and $7.00 for youth. There are 3,500,000 members in 6,000 local clubs and fifty-three "state" affiliates (the fifty plus Guam, Puerto Rico, and Virgin Islands).

THE NATURE CONSERVANCY, 1800 N. Kent Street, Arlington, Virginia 22209

Its present structure dating from 1950, this group can trace its history back to 1917. It is unique in that its resources are solely for the preservation of ecologically and environmentally significant land. The organization has, at the production of this edition, preserved 665,000 acres (269,670 hectares) in almost 1,750 separate projects in 47 states and the Virgin Islands.

Over 60 per cent of these projects are retained by the organization; the remainder have been added to national parks. Included in this preservation are a large number of habitats of endangered species and unique areas such as the Great Dismal Swamp in Virginia.

There are 25,000 members and local chapters exist in twenty-one states, with special project committees operating in other areas. Membership is open to everyone, dues beginning with $10.00 for adults and $5.00 for youth under 18. Members receive a quarterly magazine which describes the activities of the conservancy and matters relating to land conservation. Unlike educational groups, the members of this group have a tangible "product" of their work.

SAVE-THE-REDWOODS LEAGUE, 114 Sansome Street, San Francisco, California 94104

Organized in 1918, the goal of this non-profit organization, as the name implies, is the preservation of the largest living organism, the *Sequoia sempervirens* and *S. gigantea.* Unlike most conservation organizations, which depend mostly on public-opinion education and legislative lobbying to achieve their goals, the Save-the-Redwoods League also employs direct means in buying up endangered redwood groves and giving them to the State of California for state parks. The League's current objective is to round out each of the Redwood State Parks and the Redwood National Park so that each will be a complete administrative and ecological unit.

Annual membership dues are $5.00 per year. The League has 55,000 members.

SAVE SAN FRANCISCO BAY ASSOCIATION, P.O. Box 925, Berkeley, California 94701

While obviously quite regional in its scope, the work this organization is doing could well become a pilot project for several other areas throughout the nation. The Association was organized in 1961 in reaction to unregulated filling of the bay which was destroying the natural shore habitat and was slowly turning the bay into a river. At present, out of 286 miles of shoreline in the bay, only five miles are available to the public, although only one quarter is privately owned. The Association seeks to open more areas (especially the wilder parts) to public use, to get a regional authority to avoid the problems of overlapping or competitive governmental units with only partial control of the bay, and to develop parks with camping, nature trails, etc., along the shore.

The Association publishes pamphlets from time to time, but has no periodical. Their primary work is through aroused citizens working within the state government and the press.

The membership is $1.00.

SIERRA CLUB, 1050 Mills Tower, 220 Bush Street, San Francisco, California 94104

The Sierra Club was founded in 1892 by John Muir and it has since grown to become the most influential of the militant conservationist groups. They were so effective in arousing public opinion over the flooding of Grand Canyon that the government revoked their tax exemption. Their excellent publications are banned in the national parks.

They also find time to offer a comprehensive array of wilderness outings—float trips, white-water runs, backpacking trips, mountain climbs, burro trips, etc.—and they organize trips into wilderness campgrounds to clean out debris.

Their publication is the *Sierra Club Bulletin,* a monthly magazine of forty pages with color. Content is mainly articles on current efforts to save some part of our natural heritage, notices of Club outings, brief note of major legislative and administrative action, and some strictly house-keeping matters. The *Bulletin* has a few ads, mostly for camping supplies or tours organized outside the Club organization.

In addition to the *Bulletin,* the Club publishes several pamphlets on conservation issues and a selection of books which have brought them almost as much fame as their battles for conservation. They have recently produced a selection of films, equal in quality to their books, which are available for sale or rent to interested groups. *How to Teach Wilderness Conservation* is an eight-session lesson plan for use in schools. The books are full of fantastically beautiful photographs, mostly in color. These have done much to bring the beauty of the wilderness to the vast majority of the public who have never seen it and would otherwise tend to agree with the despoilers that there is nothing in the wilderness to preserve.

The basic membership in the Sierra Club is $15.00 per year with a $5.00 admission fee. There are discounts for family memberships, students, and those under fifteen or over sixty years old.

THE WILDERNESS SOCIETY, 1901 Pennsylvania Avenue N.W., Washington, D.C. 20006

The Wilderness Society was organized in 1935. It is primarily concerned with preserving wilderness areas which it views as "critical to a healthy human culture" as well as necessary for the survival of many wildlife species.

The Society publishes a full-color, quarterly magazine *The Living Wilderness.* In articles, news, poetry, book reviews, and photography, it provides a forum for discussing a wide range of wild land and wildlife issues, natural values, and topics of immediate environmental concern. Between-issues coverage of concerns are provided in a newsletter, *Wilderness Report.*

The Society sponsors a wide range of wilderness trips on foot, canoe or raft, and horseback.

Basic membership is $10.00 per year and is tax-deductible.

CAMPING SPORTS ORGANIZATIONS

AMERICAN CANOE ASSOCIATION, 4260 East Evans Avenue, Denver, Colorado 80222

The American Canoe Association was founded in 1880 and is the governing body for canoe competition in the United States. However, in addition to flatwater and slalom competition, they are also interested in the preservation of canoeable waterways and canoe camping.

Their publication is *Canoe,* a thirty-six-page bimonthly covering techniques, products, conservation, racing, camping, beginners, and news of legislative and administrative action affecting canoeists. A small discount is offered on books bought through the Association.

Membership is $7.00 for adults, $3.00 for those under eighteen, for the first year (includes initiation), per calendar year. No information was received on the number of individual members, but there are 147 clubs in thirty-six states and D.C.

AMERICAN WHITEWATER AFFILIATION, 3115 Eton Avenue, Berkeley, California 94705

The AWA is composed of white-water canoeists and kayakers, both for competition, cruising, and wilderness exploration. There are over ninety affiliated clubs throughout the United States, Canada, and Australia. It was founded in 1960; the main purpose of the AWA is information exchange among its members which it does through its publication, *American White Water,* a bimonthly of about thirty-two pages. Contents include accounts of canoe trips, articles on paddling techniques, safety and equipment information, competition news, wild river conservation projects, etc.

Membership is $5.00 per year. There are about 2,000 members.

INTERNATIONAL BICYCLE TOURING SOCIETY, 846 Prospect Street, La Jolla, California 92037

The "Huff-and-puff society" (as they term themselves) was started with a tour in 1964 and exists primarily for bicycling tours. The tours generally cost $5.00 (for the scouting of the route) plus the daily expenses of food and shelter, which are simple and low cost. On these tours, the equipment is carried in a car—called the "sag wagon"—and car expenses are prorated.

Membership is $5.00 per calendar year for an individual or couple and is open to those over twenty-one only.

U.S. ORIENTEERING FEDERATION, Box 1081, Athens, Ohio 45701

CANADIAN ORIENTEERING FEDERATION, Box 6206, Terminal A, Toronto, Ontario

The Internationale Orientierungslauf Federation is the coordinating agency for twenty-two national orienteering organizations. National groups are responsible for the activities in that country. Orienteering combines map-reading exercise with cross-country running or skiing. While not as common because of the lack of suitable terrain, it is also applicable in canoes in areas with many islands or short portages. The national federations sponsor major orienteering meets and training programs.

Dues vary with the national group and each has an introductory publication on the sport.

SKI TOURING COUNCIL, West Hill Road, Troy, Vermont 05868

The Ski Touring Council was organized in 1962 and is interested primarily in the non-competitive form of cross-country skiing properly known as ski touring. They publish an excellent introductory book on the subject, *Ski Touring Guide,* which is available from them for $2.00. In addition to discussing techniques and equipment, they also list major ski trails in the U.S.

The Council sponsors a wide schedule of workshops, tours, orienteering meets, and an occasional race.

UNITED STATES SKI ASSOCIATION, The Broadmoor, Colorado Springs, Colorado 80906

The U.S.S.A. has a wide range to cover, cross-country, downhill, and competition skiing, jumping, ski huts, etc. I wrote them in connection with the subject of cross-country skiing for the camper who isn't interested in competition. They sent me two pamphlets, one on the Norwegian cross-country training program (which has some great exercises, even if you aren't trying out for the Olympics), and one on their current program to get ski resorts to lay out ski trails for the average skier who is tired of the same old tow-up-ski-down routine and wants to see some scenery.

In addition, the Association is building a series of A-frame ski huts in the Aspen ski area for the benefit of cross-country skiers. The huts will be available at $2.50 per night or 50¢ per day. If you don't come down and report in when your reservation is up, they will assume you are in trouble and send the rescue unit for you. Such groups take a dim view of going out when they are not needed.

Glossary

ALIDADE: A sighting device used as a portable transit in making preliminary map surveys.

ALPENSTOCK: An ice ax used for cutting steps in snow slopes, as a staff, and as a safety device in arrests.

AMMETER: A gauge for measuring the intensity of an electrical current; formerly used on cars for measuring the charge or discharge of the battery, now replaced with an "idiot light" which tells you when your battery is no longer functioning.

ANORAK: An uninsulated, water-repellent, parka-shaped windbreak with a hood.

ARRESTS: Techniques used to stop sliding falls in mountain climbing.

BACON BAR: A cooked, pressed bacon in a candy-bar shape used in cooking or as a trail snack.

BAFFLE: A partition inside a sleeping bag to keep the down insulation from shifting.

BAFFLING: A system of baffles.

BAILING OUT: In aviation or surfing, abandoning the craft to avoid crashing with it.

BANNOCK: Originally Scottish unleavened bread; now a bread made by pressing biscuit dough into a skillet and cooking it in front of a reflector fire in a nearly vertical position.

BATTS: Batting; sheets of loose textile fibers used as insulation in sleeping bags or winter clothing.

BELAYING: Anchoring a climbing rope to safely absorb the shock of stopping a falling climber.

BERM: A narrow shelf between the base of a cliff and the water; also a low, sandy reef formed at the water's edge by wave action, often with a very shallow tidal pool on the landward side; or an artificial fishing reef formed by sinking car bodies or similar junk.

BIGHT: A bend in a rope which does not cross itself.

BINDER TWINE: Unlayed hemp cordage used in hay bailers or for lashings.

BLACK GUMBO: An extremely fertile soil, high in humus, moderately high in clay, found in the South from East Texas to Alabama. It is extremely sticky after a rain.

BOTA: A Basque wineskin which squirts the contents out, often used as a water canteen because of its soft form and rationing feature.

BOYLE'S LAW: The volume of a gas is inversely proportional to the pressure.

BRACKETING: Taking exposure settings on each side of the indicated one as insurance against poorly exposed pictures.

BREADBOX: A small, buslike vehicle patterned after the Volkswagen station wagon.

BURR: A rough ridge of minute metal splinters produced when working metal with coarse tools.

CAMPER DAYS: Number of campers multiplied by number of days camped.

CAMPING MACHINE: A self-propelled vehicle, smaller than a house trailer, containing sleeping, cooking and often toilet facilities accessible without unloading, unfolding, or disassembling the rig.

CANEBRAKE, *also* CANEBREAK: River-bottom under-brush of the South—so-called because of the prevalence of cane.

CANTLE: The upward roll which forms the back of a saddle, opposite the pommel which contains the horn of a Western saddle.

CAPILLARY LEAK: The dripping that results, for example, from touching the inside of a tent in a rain; caused by destroying the capillary attraction of the canvas fibers which hold the water to the fabric.

CARABINERS: Oval or D-shaped metal rings with locking snap gates, used to attach ropes to pitons.

CARTESIAN DIVER: A scientific toy in which a barely floating tube is made to submerge by compressing the air in the top of the vessel, thereby compressing the air in the tube, making it displace less volume and therefore sink.

CHIMNEY STEMMING: The techniques used to climb a crack wide enough to get one's whole body in.

COCKPIT COAMING: A raised frame around the edge of a kayak cockpit forming a breakwater.

CORKSCREW: A spelunking term for an extremely narrow passage (generally requiring crawling to negotiate) which twists both horizontally and vertically.

CRADLE BOARD: A frame onto which a baby is strapped in Indian and related cultures.

CRAMPONS: Spikes which lace to the bottom of hiking boots for improving traction on snow or ice.

CREOSOTE BUSH: Any of several desert shrubs which give off a distinct creosote odor when broken or crushed.

DESTINATION RESORTS: A term first used by the Oklahoma State Parks to describe extensively developed areas of state parks (hotels, golf courses, etc.) which serve as the vacation destination rather than a way-stop or base of operations on a trip.

DINGLE CRANE: A stick fixed in a slanting position used to support a single pot over a fire.

DUFFEK STROKE: A hanging stroke in kayaking which resembles the forward draw stroke in a Canadian canoe. This extreme forward brace is coupled with a pronounced upstream lean, hanging from the paddle to make a very sharp turn with almost no loss of forward speed. Named for Milovan Duffek who first used the technique in the 1953 World Slalom Championships.

DULFERSITZ: The standard rappelling technique in which the rope goes between the legs toward the back, around the chest from the left, over the right shoulder and down. The left hand controls the speed of the descent.

EMU: A Polynesian pit-cooked meal, the food placed in layers in a pit lined with heated rocks, covered with leaves and dirt until done.

ESQUIMAUTAGE: Rolling techniques in a kayak, the best known and most extreme example being the Eskimo roll, in which the canoe is rolled completely around while the paddler stays in the cockpit. Useful in case of accidental upset.

FALTBOOT: The German word for the folding kayak. In this book, it refers to the folding variety where distinct from the rigid versions.

FIBRILLATING: A condition in which the various muscles of the heart contract independently without pumping blood, occurring in some types of heart attacks and traumatic or electrical shock.

FID: A tapered wooden pin used to open rope for splicing.

FIREBREAK: A wide, cleared strip in forests to aid in fighting fires.

FIRE RINGS: A metal ring set into the ground to control the ground fire from a campfire.

FLAMMING: A Canadian-canoe technique of knocking a hole in a large wave with the bow paddle to avoid shipping water amidships.

FLAT FELL: A simple lapped seam in fabric with no folding of the cloth.

FRAPPING: Taking turns of the cordage around the wrapping of a lashing to further tighten it.

FRENCH FELL: A seam folded so that the edges are hidden and the folds interlock.

FRESNEL LENS: A lens with a thick curvature, segmented concentrically to reduce thickness and therefore weight.

GAITER: A cloth tube with elastic ends used to cover

the area between the bottom of the pant leg and the top of the shoe to keep out scree, sand, or snow.

GLISSADE: A ski-like technique for descending snow fields or talus slopes using only boots and a hiking staff, or a sitting position.

GLUT: A wooden wedge used for splitting logs.

GOLDLINE: A type of nylon of extreme elasticity used in climbing ropes.

GRAPNEL: A multiple hook (much like the triple fish hook, but larger) used as an anchor or for snagging an item to be retrieved.

GREASE TRAP: A pit, covered with dry grass, used to dispose of kitchen grease in camp.

GROMMET: A metal-lined hole in a tent, pack, or poncho for attaching a rope.

GROMMET STITCHING: A round-and-round stitching used to attach a grommet ring to the fabric.

GURNEE CAN: A bullet-shaped container ten inches in diameter, with a ring on the point for dragging equipment through tight places in spelunking. From Russell H. Gurnee, its inventor.

GUY ROPE: A bracing rope to hold tent poles in position.

HAYSTACK: A large mound of water thrown up by a deep rock in a white-water stream to form a standing wave.

HEMOSTAT: A surgical clamp resembling a pair of scissors.

HINDSIGHT: The practice of looking behind you from time to time while traveling, because landmarks look different when viewed from the other side.

ICE AWL: A short pick used to grip ice for self-rescue when fallen through ice.

INBOARD OF: Toward the center of the item from a reference point rather than toward the edge or outside.

INUIT: Eskimo. Their preferred term, meaning "human" in their language rather than the Cree "eaters of raw meat" which they have never been.

JERKY: From *charqui;* air-dried meat.

KEELSTRIPS: Strips of hull material cemented to the outside of the hull over the keel and bilge stringers on a faltboot to take the abrasion of grounding.

KYAKS: Wooden boxes used as panniers in horse-packing.

LEMON SQUEEZER: An extremely narrow passage between rocks or in a cave.

LINING: A method for getting loaded canoes through mild rapids by controlling them from the bank.

LP: Liquefied petroleum. Propane and butane gas, which are typically stored in a liquid state.

MADISON AVENUE: A term originally referring to the major advertising agencies but now including the mass-communication media which are largely dominated by the advertisers.

MANTA: A tarp (traditionally six feet square) which covers a horsepack under the lashing.

MANUAL SIGNALS: An international system of ground-to-air communication for survival, using arm and body positions.

MARKER PANELS: An international system of ground-to air communication for survival, using tracks or contrasting materials laid out on the ground.

MASKING: Leaving an ax embedded in a chopping block as a safety device.

MAUL: A cylindrical wooden mallet used for hammering wedges or froes for splitting logs.

MOHS' SCALE: An irregular scale of relative hardness developed by Friedrich Mohs in 1822 and used for testing mineral hardness for identification purposes.

MONOCULAR: A prismatic telescope of a small size, so called because it is, in effect, one-half of a binocular.

ORGANIZATION MAN: From the book of the same title; a person whose first loyalty is to the business organization and its demands on his life which often have no bearing on the business at all but are designed solely to prevent him from developing other loyalties.

ORIENTEERING: A sport involving compass bearings and distances, the object of which is to cover the course in the shortest time.

OVERNIGHT PICNICKING: A form of "camping" involving extensive equipment and little encounter with nature.

PAINTER: The line normally attached to the bow of a boat to moor it.

PALO VERDE: Trees of the genus *Cercidium* which shed their leaves in late spring, but have green bark. They are often a prominent tree (despite their bushy size) in the Sonoran Desert ecology.

PANNIERS: Boxes or bags used to hold gear on a horsepack; and, by extension, similar packs for bicycles, motorcycles, and such.

PEARLING: A surfing catastrophe in which the bow catches in the water and the craft "dives for pearls," or flips end over end.

PENCELL: The AA battery, so called because the flashlights using them are the same diameter as the old bladder-type fountain pens.

PENOLE: A parched corn, coarsely ground, mixed with water for emergency rations in pioneer times. Still useful.

pH SCALE: From the negative logarithm of the hydrogen ion, a measurement, from 0 to 14, of the acidity or alkalinity, each whole number being ten times more alkaline or acidic than the adjacent whole number. The acid is low and the base is high.

PITONS: Iron wedges of various sizes and shapes for hammering into cracks in rocks in order to anchor safety ropes in mountain climbing.

PLANING HULL: A boat hull which is designed to ride on top of the water while under way rather than cutting through the water as does a displacement hull.

PLANKING: A method of cooking fish by pegging it open to a flat piece of wood and baking it before a reflector fire.

PLUG CASTER: A rod and perpendicularly mounted reel, casting relatively heavy lures, as distinguished from fly rods, spinning, or spin-casting outfits.

PLUMB LINE: A weighted string used to determine vertical in order to measure vertical angles.

POLL: The part of the head opposite the cutting edge of an ax or hatchet.

PORTAGE: The carrying of a canoe and its load overland to another body of water—almost always on foot.

PRIMUS: A small, Swedish-made camping stove burning a wide variety of fuels, a generic term for small, one-burner camping stoves.

PRUSSIK KNOT: A multiple larkshead tied around a rope to make a sliding hitch to aid in climbing.

PUGGAREE: A cloth hanging from the back of the hat to protect the neck from sunburn. Best known in the French Foreign Legion uniform, it also appears in a vestigial form as the hat band on a sun helmet.

RAPPELLING: A means of controlling the rate of descent down a mountain by rope friction.

ROCKER: The longitudinal bend in the keel of a canoe. It is most extreme on the white-water variants of the Canadian canoe, but present in all types of canoes.

SCREE: A loose slope of angular, gravel-size rocks with little stability and great ability to find their way inside of boots.

SET: A cycle of waves, typically two or three large waves followed by five or six diminishing waves, the ebb then preventing the building of more waves until it weakens and another set begins.

SETTING: The erection of a tent.

SEWING PALM: A leather strap fitting across the palm with a concave thimble in the palm to aid in pushing a heavy needle through canvas.

SHAKE: A wooden shingle made by splitting the wood rather than cutting it.

SHEARPIN: A brass pin used to anchor the propeller to the propeller shaft in a boat; designed to shear in two in case any obstruction stops the propeller so that neither the propeller nor the engine is damaged.

SHEEPSHANK: An S-bend in a rope with a half-hitch holding each bight of the S; used to shorten a rope instead of untying one end and retying it shorter.

SHIM: Thin metal, paper, or other sheet material used to increase the thickness in a mounting or other construction.

SHROUDLINES: The one-eighth-inch (3 mm) parachute cords connecting the canopy and the risers of a harness.

SKIJORING: A sport of skiing in which the skier is towed behind a horse or vehicle much in the manner of water skiing.

SLIDING GUNTER: A small boat sailing rig in which the gaff is mounted vertically, sliding up the mast when the sail is raised, essentially forming an extension of the mast. It is valuable in that it provides the advantages of the marconi rig in reefing while retaining the mast-stowage features of the lateen rig.

SLR: Single-lens reflex camera.

SNAP RIVET: A rivet made in two pieces to be joined by hammering the two pieces together, the end of the stud mushrooming inside the head.

SOLENOID: An electromagnet which produces a push-pull action to actuate various mechanical devices.

SQUAW WOOD: Dead wood still on the tree, as opposed to down wood. The name comes from its use by Plains Indian women who had no chopping tools before the introduction of iron.

STEVEDORE'S KNOT: An end knot tied as a figure-eight except that the loop is twisted a full turn instead of a half-turn. It is often used to keep a rope from coming out of a block.

STONEBRIDGE LANTERN: An obsolete, collapsible candle lantern, made of sheet metal with mica windows.

STOVE-IN: To break a hole in a hull, such as by running onto rocks.

STRIKING: Taking down an erected tent.

STRINGERS: The longitudinal framing members of a faltboot. They are typically dowels of about thumb-size diameter.

TACHOMETER: A gauge for measuring revolutions per minute.

TALUS: An alluvial slope, fairly stable, with rocks about cobblestone-size but rarely rounded. There are often small shrubs or patches of grass widely scattered throughout the slope.

TAMARACK: Several conifers which shed their needles during the winter in the manner of deciduous trees.

TARP: A tarpaulin; now almost any waterproof sheet, including polyethylene, used as a tent, ground cloth, manta, or other protective covering.

THWART: A cross-piece in a boat, especially a Canadian canoe, which keeps the sides properly spread.

TOGGLE: A pin, held at the middle by a rope, which is passed through a loop and then pivoted crosswise to the loop to prevent its withdrawal; or a pin inserted in a knot to hold it when otherwise the knot would not hold.

TOOLING COW: An easily worked, vegetable-tanned cowhide, thick enough to decorate by cutting and stamping designs in it.

TRANSIT: A telescope mounted on a vernier scale for extremely accurate measurement of angles in surveying.

TRAVERSE: Literally, cross or crossing. A mountaineering term for the basically horizontal movement across a glacier, cliff face, etc., or a climb involving the ascent of one side and the descent of the other.

TRIM: The position, in a horizontal plane, of a vessel in the water.

TUMBLEHOME: The inward curving of a hull toward the gunwales. If it continues all the way to form a deck, it is a turtle-back.

VISKLAMP: A dumbbell-shaped piece of wire and a rubber ball used to attach a rope onto a plastic or fabric tarp.

WEDELN: A downhill skiing technique in which the knees and the shoulders are twisted in opposite directions, producing a rapid change in direction. This results in a high degree of control in the speed, and a very wiggly trail behind. The word is German for "wag."

WIND-RESISTANCE: The tendency of a tent to catch the wind and blow down despite the quality of the ground or the length of the stakes; aerodynamic drag.

WIPING OUT: A surfing term for the forced separation of the surfer and the board.

WRAP: The tying of the basic pattern of a lashing.

X-C: Short for cross-country skiing.

YURT: A Mongolian portable house consisting of a round wall supporting a domed roof with a smoke-hole in the center. The frame is a geodetic construction of wood and folds for transport, while the covering is of felt.

Index

Index

Fireplaces, 3, 173–179, 186, 209, 215, 217, 219–271, 273; cast metal, 209; three-wall, 5, 209
Fireproofing, 174
Firesites, 9, 174, 208, 273, 395
Firewood, 3, 63, 65, 156, 174, 180–183, 207–208, 215, 219–271, 273–274, 446
First aid, xi, 323, 347–348, 360–384, 445
First-aid kit, 14, 65, 68, 110, 111, 112, 321, 361–364, 372, 392, 500; hiker's, 107, 109–110, 112, 361; main, 107
Fish, 93, 189–202, 207, 324, 408, 535; fresh-water, 407; fried, 199–200; salt-water, 407
Fish and Wildlife Service, 221
Fish hooks, 366, 409, 411, 433
Fish traps, 406–407
Fisherman's bend, 432
Fisherman's knot, 425
Fisherman's litter, 382, 446
Fishing, 3, 93, 197, 215, 217–271, 283, 307, 397, 409, 431, 523, 531; boats, 342; equipment, 93, 307–308; hitches, 433–434; knots, 425–426; license, 308, 409; line, 92, 399, 409, 411, 420, 425, 441, 444; magazines, 14, 523–524; photography, 529
Fishnet floats, 332
Fissures, 324
Fit (of gunstocks), 162
Flames (cooking over), 49, 56, 178, 186, 209, 276
Flamming, 475, 477, 552
Flares, 92, 323, 490
Flash bulbs, 298–299, 323
Flash floods, 207
Flash guns, 323
Flash powder, 323
Flashlight, 86–88, 306, 321, 404, 508, 554; pencell, 87–89, 107, 554
Flex-O-Fix, 42, 159
Flies (insects), 10, 275, 278–279, 386–387, 488
Flies (lures), 308–310, 433
Flies (tent), 20, 28, 106, 111, 129, 173
Flint, 88; and steel, 403–404, 411
Flintlocks, 403–404
Floats, fishing, 308, 409
Float-fishing, 7, 450
Floating, 325
Floating cushions, 471–472, 481
Flood control, 483
Flood level, 207
Flooding, 384, 403, 513
Floodplain, 513
Floors, 18–20, 23, 26, 28, 36, 119, 274, 389, 457
Floor area, 19, 22, 24, 28

Floor space, 21, 28, 122
Florida, 230–231
Florida Trail Association, 545–546
Flour, 189, 202; as a thermometer, 199
Flower drying, 345
Flowers, 296
Fluorescent rocks, 288
Fly cabinet, 275
Fly fishing, 308–309; line, 309; reels, 309; rods, 307, 309, 554
Fly whisk, 60
Flying, 8
f/ numbers, 296, 302
Foam cement, 141
Foam mattress, 64
Foam plastic, 337
Focus, 302
Focusing frame, 294
Foil, see Aluminum foil
Folding kayaks, 466, 477, 552; see also Faltboot
Folklore, 213, 388
Food, 5, 52, 64–65, 188–197, 273–274, 399, 455–456, 508
Food and Drug Administration, 508
Food bags, 47
Food containers, 14, 68
Food found in camp, 197
Food gathering, 3
Food not requiring refrigeration, 188, 190, 192
Food poisoning, 374
Food preparation, 51
Food preservation, 188
Food selection, 188
Food supply, 387, 389, 392
Football, 453; helmet, 321
Footholds, 311–314, 429
Footrests, 164, 467
Footwear, 94
Forced landings, 392, 399
Forceps, 362–363, 365–366, 378, 381
Forces of nature, 8
Ford, 167
Foreign matter in the eye, 378, 381
Forester tent, 23
Forests, 311
Forks (eating), 50–51
Forks (trail), 349
Fort Sill, 511–512
Forward draw, 473–474
Four-wheel drive, 493
Fowl, 200–201

Raisins, 190, 197
Range-finder cameras, 294–295, 301
Rangers, 211, 343, 348, 352, 385
Ranger stations, 211, 526
Rapids, 328, 468, 470, 478–481, 553
Rappel patches, 321
Rappel sling, 316
Rappelling, 318–319, 323, 552, 554
Rat, 389
Rationing water, 399
Rattlesnakes, 306, 379, 388, 407
Rawhide, 437; lacing, 156
Razor, 91
Reader's Guide, 333
Real-estate developments, 13; lobby, 519; promoters, 511, 516
Reapportionment, 519
Recipes, xi, 172, 198, 306, 523, 528
Recorders (musical instruments, 344
Records (phonograph), 534
Re-creation, 7, 516
Recreation centers, 344
Recreational Equipment, Inc., 131, 344
Recreational value, 513
Red cedar, 183
Red Cross, 325; first aid, 360; first-aid handbook, 361
Red oak, 180–181, 208
Red River of the North, 395
Reducing the weight of the gear, 112–113
Redwoods, 515
Reefs, 334
Reels, (fishing), 307
Reevair, 159, 164; seam compound, 159
Reflector fires, 18, 25, 31, 51, 125, 174, 178–201, 398, 551, 554
Reflector oven, 55, 106, 109, 154–156, 173, 178, 201–202, 344, 400, 461; making, 154–156
Reflectors (fire), 53–54, 178–179, 466, 508
Reflectors (photographic), 298
Reflex housing, 294
Reforestation, 515
Refraction, 407
Refrigeration, 5, 58–59, 189–192, 198, 374, 494, 499–500, 509–510; natural, 190, 200
Refrigerator shelf, as grill, 57
Regulations, 9
Reins, 487–488
Relative light efficiency, 286–287
Relaxation, 7
Remote areas, 361
Remote-control photography, 299, 301

Renting, 5, 45, 465, 489, 502, 541
Repair, boat engine, 484
Repair, canoe, 527
Repair kit, 71, 92–93, 107, 110, 366; aluminum-canoe, 481; bicycle, 108, 460; boat, 484; canoe, 468, 470; car, 490, 500; kayak, 482
Reptiles, 344, 407, 537
Requirements of a fire, 184–186
Rescue, 429; canoe, 527
Reservations for campsites, 215
Resilience, 40
Resort, 212–213
Resources, 7
Restaurant syndrome, 372
Rests, 455
Resuscitation tube, 362, 364, 372
Reversed half-hitches, 431
Rhode Island, 252–253
Rhododendrons, 311
Rhythm in walking, 454
Rib fractures, 376
Ribs, 163
Ridgepoles, 22–23, 37
Ridges, 18, 25, 27, 43
Riding saddle, 487–488
Rifle, 162, 304–306
Right angle in measuring, 412
Rigid kayak, 466
Rip current, 334
Rip-stop nylon, 40, 134, 139, 362
Rivers, 8
River canoes, 465–466
River-lakes, 8
Roads, 393, 395
Road maps, 352
Roarers (stoves), 53
Roasting, 199–201
Rocks, 8, 20, 33, 38–39, 42, 65, 95, 173–174, 288, 536; cooking with, 176; firebuilding, 175
Rock chutes, 457
Rock climbing, 311, 313–314, 531
Rock hunting, 246, 263
Rock slides, 457
Rocker, 465–466, 554
Rocky ground, 19, 21, 37
Rodents, 275, 305, 379–380, 409, 515, 545
Rods, fishing, 307
Roller Bandage, 361–362, 368
Roofs, 25–27
Roof rack, 167, 492
Rookeries, 516